UNCERTAIN ORDER

The World in the Twentieth Century

Blaine T. Browne

Broward Community College, Fort Lauderdale

Robert C. Cottrell

California State University, Chico

Prentice
Hall

Upper Saddle River, New Jersey 07458

Library of Congress Cataloging-in-Publication Data

BROWN, BLAINE T. (BLAINE TERRY)
  Uncertain order: the world in the twentieth century / Blaine T. Browne, Robert C. Cottrell.
      p. cm.
  Includes bibliographical references and index.
  ISBN 0-13-028703-2
    1. Twentieth century. 2. History, Modern—20th century—Chronology. 3.
  Ideology—History—20th century. 4. World War, 1939–1945. I. Cottrell, Robert C.,
  II. Title.

  D421 .B726 2003

  909.82–dc21   2002022825

Editorial director: Charlyce Jones-Owen
Senior acquisitions editor: Charles Cavaliere
Assistant editor: Emsal Hasan
Editorial assistant: Adrienne Paul
Director of production and manufacturing: Barbara Kittle
Production editor: Judy Winthrop
Project liaison: Louise Rothman
Prepress and manufacturing manager: Nick Sklitsis
Prepress and manufacturing buyer: Sherry Lewis
Marketing director: Beth Mejia
Marketing manager: Claire Bitting

© 2003 by Prentice-Hall, Inc.
A division of Pearson Education
Upper Saddle River, New Jersey 07458

This book was set in 10/12 Caslon by Compset, Inc. and was
printed and bound by Courier-Stoughton.
The cover was printed by Phoenix Color Corp.

Printed in the United States of America
10 9 8 7 6 5 4 3 2 1

ISBN 0-13-028703-2

Prentice-Hall International (UK) Limited, *London*
Prentice-Hall of Australia Pty. Limited, *Sydney*
Prentice-Hall Canada Inc., *Toronto*
Prentice-Hall Hispanoamericana, S.A., *Mexico*
Prentice Hall of India Private Limited, *New Delhi*
Prentice-Hall of Japan, Inc., *Tokyo*
Pearson Education Pte. Ltd., *Singapore*
Editora Prentice-Hall do Brasil, Ltda., *Rio de Janeiro*

To the two women who have most profoundly shaped my life for the better, my mother, Mary Etta Shockley Browne (1923–1966), and my wife, Marian.

—Blaine T. Browne

and

To my brother-in-law, Steve Marc Gerson, friend, confidante, and role model.

—Robert C. Cottrell

Contents

List of Maps   *x*

List of Photos   *xi*

Preface   *xiii*

Introduction   *1*

PART ONE   *The Decline of European Hegemony, 1900–1945*   *3*

1 The Global Order in 1900: A World of Empires   *5*

Apogee: European Civilization in 1900   *9*
The New Imperialism and Non-western World   *30*
The American Hemisphere   *43*

**2 A Burnt Path Across History:
The First World War and Its Consequences, 1914–1920**   *53*

Origins of a Catastrophe: Europe, 1900–1914   *57*
The First World War, 1914–1918   *66*
Shaping a New International Order: the Paris Peace Conference   *82*

3 The Americas between the World Wars, 1919–1939   *95*

U.S. Domestic Developments between the World Wars   *98*
The U.S. Response to World Events and America at War   *108*

Latin America between the World Wars   *111*
Central America and the Caribbean   *111*

4 *The Challenge to Western Hegemony: Asia and the Colonial World in the Interwar Years, 1920–1940*   *126*

Nationalist and Anticolonial Struggles in the Middle East and Africa   *131*
Challenges to Western Colonial Rule in Asia   *141*
China and Japan: Divergent Paths and Converging Destinies   *147*

5 *The Approaching Storm: Europe, 1919–1939*   *164*

The Postwar European Perspective: Cultural Despair and Modernism   *170*
Precarious Stability: Europe in the 1920s   *172*
Doubtful Restoration: European Democracy in the 1920s   *174*
The Totalitarian Challenge   *179*
Depression Decade: The European Crisis of the 1930s   *185*
Democratic Europe: Challenge and Response   *187*
The European Dictatorships   *192*
The Collapse of the European Order, 1935–1939   *200*

6 *Into the Maelstrom: Global War, 1939–1945*   *211*

The European War: the Years of Axis Triumph   *215*
War in the Pacific, 1941–1943   *224*
The European War, 1943–1945   *233*
War in the Pacific, 1943–1945   *240*

PART TWO   *The Age of the Superpowers, 1945–1989*   *251*

7 *Recovery and Transformation: Europe, 1945–1989*   *252*

The Postward Era: New Realities in a Transformed World   *256*
Bitter Peace: Europe in the Aftermath of War   *257*

Europe and the Cold War   *261*
Redefining Europe: the End of Empire and the Quest for a United
    Europe   *264*
Western Europe's "Golden Age": Economy, Society and Culture   *268*
Politics and Government in Western Europe   *274*
The Soviet Union and the Eastern Bloc   *286*

8 *Asia Reordered: India, Japan, and China, 1945–1989*   *298*

The People's Republic of China   *305*
Asia's Economic Powerhouse   *312*

**9 *From the Ashes of Empire: Post-Colonial Indochina,
1945–1989***   *326*

Out of Empires   *330*
Vietnam at War and Neighboring States   *332*
A Divided Vietnam and Guerrilla Insurgency   *336*
Heightened U.S. Involvement   *339*
The American War   *340*
The Fighting Widens   *343*
Postwar Developments   *346*

10 *The Challenges of Independence: Africa since 1945*   *351*

Prelude to Independence: Europe and Africa, 1945–1960   *356*
The Many Paths to Nationhood   *364*
Continuing Challenges in Independent Africa   *378*

11 *The Middle Eastern Crucible of Conflict, 1945–1989*   *387*

The State of Israel and the 1948 War   *390*
The Arab Response and Another War   *396*
Unrest in the Middle East and the Six Day War   *401*
The PLO and the Yom Kippur War   *403*
An Uneasy Peace   *406*
Lebanon and the Intifada   *408*

12 *A Superpower in War and Peace: the United States since 1945* *415*

The United States and the Early Cold War *418*
The Red Scare *421*
Ferment in Eisenhower's America *423*
America's Camelot *425*
The Presidency of Lyndon Baines Johnson *427*
A Turn to the Right *429*
Economic Doldrums and Malaise *431*
The Reagan Revolution *433*

13 *Latin America during the Cold War, 1945–1989* *440*

Postwar Latin America *443*
Latin America's Big Four during the Early Cold War *445*
The Impact of the Cuban Revolution *449*
Other Latin American Revolutions *455*
Guerrilla Warfare *466*

PART THREE   *The World Order in Transition, 1989–Present* *475*

14 *The End of the Soviet Empire, 1989–1991* *476*

From Stalin to Krushchev *479*
Bureaucratic Communism and Dissidence *482*
Soviet Foreign Policy and Postwar Eastern Europe *485*
The Reign of Mikhail Gorbachev *488*
Diplomatic Breakthroughs *491*
Eastern European Revolutions *492*
The Disintegration of the USSR *496*
The 1991 Coup and Boris Yeltsin *499*

15 *The Search for a New World Order: New Issues and Challenges,
1989–Present*   *504*

Approaching the Millennium   *507*
Western Europe in the Cold War and Beyond   *509*
A New Order in Eastern Europe and Russia   *512*
The Only Superpower   *516*
Democracy, Development and Human Rights in Latin America   *517*
The Middle East Tinderbox   *520*
Darkness and Light in Africa   *522*
Economic Development and Political Transformation in Asia   *524*
Southeast Asia at the Close of the Century   *525*

Index   *I-1*

List of Maps

1–1   Europe   *22*

1–2   Africa before the First World War   *33*

1–3   Imperialism in Asia and the Pacific   *37*

2–1   World War I   *67*

2–2   The Peace Settlement in Europe   *84*

5–1   German Expansion During the 1930s   *201*

6–1   WWII on Asia and the Pacific   *225*

6–2   The Crest of Axis Power in Europe   *235*

7–1   Divided Europe   *258*

8–1   China   *307*

8–2   Japan   *314*

9–1   Southeast Asia   *338*

10–1   Modern Africa   *380*

11–1   Middle East, 1947–1982   *397*

12–1   Blacks attending segregated schools   *424*

13–1   World of the UN and the Cold War   *464*

14–1   Contemporary Russia   *498*

15–1   Human Rights   *510*

15–2   Armed Conflict   *513*

List of Photos

1–1 Queen Victoria *7*

1–2 General Emilio Aguinaldo *50*

2–1 A deserted trench at Ypres, Belgium *70*

2–2 Vladimir Ilyich Lenin *78*

2–3 Vera Brittain *91*

3–1 Roger Nash Baldwin *97*

3–2 A bread line of the Great Depression *105*

3–3 Salvador Allende *123*

4–1 Mustafa Kemal *127*

4–2 Emperor Hirohito *161*

5–1 A stadium in Nuremberg, Germany, 1934 *165*

5–2 Benito Mussolini and Adolf Hitler, 1937 *183*

5–3 British Prime Minister Neville Chamberlain, 1938 *205*

6–1 British Prime Minister Winston Churchill, 1940 *213*

6–2 A German tank, 1941 *223*

6–3 Pearl Harbor attack, December 7, 1941 *227*

6–4 Dresden, Germany, 1945 *236*

7–1 General Charles de Gaulle and Prime Minister Winston Churchill in Paris *255*

7–2 British Prime Minister Margaret Thatcher *278*

8–1 Mahatma Ghandi and Mrs. Sarojini Naidu, 1930 *300*

8–2 General Douglas MacArthur and Emperor Hirohito *315*

8–3 Deng Xiaoping *322*

9–1 North Vietnamese President Ho Chi Minh *327*

9–2 Human skulls from mass grave, Cambodia *345*

9–3 Dith Pran *349*

10–1 Idi Amin Dada of Uganda and President Mobuto Sese Seko of Zaire *353*

10–2 Nelson Mandela in early 1990 *383*

11–1 Israel Prime Minister David Ben-Gurion *388*

11–2 Yasir Arafat, 1974 *412*

12–1 President Harry S Truman, 1945 *416*

12–2 President Ronald Reagan, 1984 *437*

13–1 Che Guevara, 1959 *441*

13–2 Eva Perón, 1952 *447*

14–1 Mikhail Gorbachev and Francois Mitterand, 1990 *478*

14–2 Brandenburg Gate, Berlin, Germany, 1989 *494*

14–3 Russian President Boris Yeltsin *501*

15–1 Wangari Maathai *505*

15–2 Parade of the Zapatista National Liberation Army, 1994 *519*

15–3 Professor Doan Viet Hoat, 1998 *529*

Preface

Anyone undertaking to write a history of the twentieth century world faces a multitude of challenges. The basic methodological decisions confronting the writer of any history text, such as organization, themes and coverage, become more intimidating still when the subject is as vast as global history and the timeframe is as broad as a century. Any such text, to be effective, must be conceived and composed to acquaint students with a wide spectrum of nations, societies, political systems, and ideologies. Thus, the writer is compelled to confront his first challenge—balancing the desire for an inclusive scope against the inevitable editorial constraints on length, and the realization that those texts that strive to be exhaustive often only prove exhausting to students. An equally daunting challenge is to accurately identify and examine the chief agencies that drive world history in the modern era. Finally, the writer faces the question of how to present the subject matter to engage the reader.

This text grew out of the authors' conviction that the history of the twentieth century world could be presented in a comprehensible, coherently organized, and intellectually engaging manner. Accordingly, readers will find that this text is organized around a clearly delineated chronological structure, within which regional historical developments are examined separately. The scope of this text is broad, reflecting an effort to balance comprehensiveness against the inevitable need for some selectivity regarding coverage according to regions, nations and events. The major nations of each region necessarily command the greatest amount of attention, but a conscientious effort was made to include significant developments elsewhere. This text focuses on three major forces as the driving engines of world history in the twentieth century: ideology, conflict and technology. Few eras have been shaped so dramatically by ideology; the "isms" of the twentieth century reordered governments, economies and societies in every region of the world. Ultimately, the more radical and aggressive ideologies provoked conflicts that ranged from localized civil wars to global conflagrations. While the former often destabilized regions, the latter destroyed existing world orders and laid the foundations for new global arrangements. Technology likewise proved an extraordinarily dynamic engine of change throughout the century, working startling and often unpredictable transformations of the human condition in both war and peace.

An important distinguishing aspect of this text stems from the authors' intent to produce a history that would not only inform but also stimulate student interest and intellectual curiosity. History, when largely detached from human agency and reduced to overly generalized socio-historical forces, loses its most compelling dimension. The nineteenth-century American essayist Ralph Waldo Emerson spoke to an important point when he asserted that "There is properly no history; only biography." This text reflects the authors' conviction that the lives and actions of individuals, famous or otherwise, must be considered as among the most significant agents driving history. While acknowledging the importance of the broad and impersonal forces that sometimes propel events, this text reflects the conviction that the richness and drama of history is most fully conveyed through the inclusion of a strong biographical component. Hence, the reader will discover that each chapter is introduced and then concluded by a biographical essay. These biographies introduce key individuals who shaped the history of the twentieth century. The essays also present one or more of the major themes addressed by that chapter. A heightened emphasis on the biographical dimension of history is also evident within the body of each chapter, through greater attention to the lives and contributions of individuals. The biographical features of this text, combined with a narrative style, aid in presenting the century's history in a manner that will both engage and inform students.

Finally, a quick glance through this text will reveal a simplified and "clean" format, with the chapters adorned by little other than photos and maps. This reflects the authors' desire to produce a history uncluttered by the array of "boxes," "spotlights," and other features that often characterize history texts. It is the authors' contention that history is best conveyed as an uninterrupted narrative. If, for example, an individual is significant enough to warrant mention, that material should be incorporated in the body of the text, rather than shorn from it and presented separately in a "box." This text eschews the use of the usual "special features," with the objective of maintaining the continuity of the historical narrative.

Acknowledgments

We would like to thank our families for their support regarding this scholarly endeavor. As always, Bob Cottrell remains deeply grateful for the encouragement received from his wife Sue and their nine-year-old daughter Jordan. Bob also thanks his sister Sharon Gerson and brother-in-law Steve, to whom this book is dedicated in part.

Blaine Browne expresses his deep appreciation for the support of his father, Teddy Jack Browne and his wife Marian. Gratitude is also extended to colleagues at Broward Community College who reviewed portions of the text and shared their expertise in a variety of disciplines: Professor Susan Oldfather, Dr. Daniel Rieger and Dr. Charles Windler. The completion of this project was greatly facilitated by the support and encouragement offered by Dr. Kevin Keating, chair of the Social and Behavioral Sciences Department. Broward Community College provided generous support for faculty travel-study abroad, which was crucial to broadening and deepening the author's comprehension of the contemporary world.

The authors wish to thank the following reviewers for their advise in preparing the manuscript: David Mock, Tallahassee Community College; Deborah Buffton, University of Wisconsin, La Crosse; Constance M. McGovern, Frostburg State University; William B. Whisenhunt, College of DuPage; Eric Nellis, Okanagan University; and Howard Graves, DeVry Institute of Technology. Any errors in the text are our own.

Introduction

The beginning of a new century inevitably provokes projections as to what the future portends and efforts to evaluate the meaning of the century just past. If the twentieth century offers a single historical lesson, it is that broad predictions as to the probable course of human events are notoriously unreliable. Most all who remarked on the advent of the twentieth century greeted it with generally optimistic forecasts. Their comments reflected what one historian described as a "profound self-confidence" throughout much of the world, born of faith in progress, science and a variety of ideologies that promised liberation or fulfillment. Now, with a new century commenced, historians have begun the task of interpreting the pattern of events that actually did mark the twentieth century, with the objective of discerning its general character. To date, many interpretive overviews of the past century have emphasized the violent nature of the era. The author of one recent study concluded that "the only constants in the 20th century have been violence, terrorism and war." Other writers, in attempting to capture the essence of the times, have variously described the twentieth century as "a century of war," a "ravaged century" and an "age of extremes."

Clearly, in the judgement of many historians, the twentieth century belied its initial promise, bringing instead massive dislocations, destruction and death. It is a difficult characterization to refute. The past century was marked by tremendous strife, born of a multitude of ideological, religious and ethnic antagonisms. The human cost of ideologically driven conflicts can only be generally estimated in the high tens of millions. Some radical ideologies proved shockingly destructive even in the absence of war. A recent study of the impact of communism in the twentieth century concludes that the ideology in practice may have cost as many as 100 million lives, victims of both state terror and disastrously incompetent policies. The century also brought wars that were often intensified and prolonged by powerful industrial economies and technological advances applied to military usage. Consequently, the century was marked by both brutal local conflicts and global wars of unprecedented magnitude. The advent of the nuclear age, which made possible weapons of almost incomprehensibly destructive capabilities, ultimately raised the specter of the complete destruction of human civilization. By the close of the twentieth century, the optimistic visions of 1900 seemed hopelessly myopic, little more than the naïve expectations of a more innocent era.

This text acknowledges the transformative impact of ideology, war and technology on the course of the twentieth century's events. However, while broad forces such as globalization often contributed to the century's major developments, the ambitions and ideals of individuals, both prominent and obscure, also undeniably shaped the contours of contemporary world history. Together, these elements brought about fundamental and unpredictable shifts in the world order over the course of the century. The European-dominated world of the nineteenth century, so seemingly secure in 1900, eroded rapidly during the first half of the twentieth century, disrupted by two world wars, a world depression and the myriad uncertainties that attended them. The same decades brought a growing challenge to Western hegemony from the East and the colonial world. As of the end of the Second World War, a new global order took shape, dominated by the United States and the Soviet Union, two superpowers forged in war. The decades-long confrontation between the two nations did much to define the postwar order, but the triumph of nationalist ambitions throughout much of the non-Western world introduced additional dimensions. The Cold War global order, which for nearly fifty years seemed destined to endure indefinitely, unraveled with startling rapidity and finality as the Soviet Empire disintegrated in the last decade of the century, leaving many unanswered questions as to the shape of the new world order. Ushered in with widespread expressions of confidence in a future of peace and progress, the twentieth century's legacy was an uncertain order in the world.

Suggested Readings

BROGAN, PATRICK. *World Conflicts: A Comprehensive Guide to World Strife since 1945.* (1998).

CONQUEST, ROBERT. *Reflections on a Ravaged Century.* (2000).

COURTOIS, STEPHEN, *et al. The Black Book of Communism: Crimes, Terror, Repression.* (1999).

GILBERT, MARTIN. *A History of the Twentieth Century, Vols. I–III.* (1997–1999).

HOBSBAWM, ERIC. *The Age of Extremes, 1914–1991.* (1996).

HOWARD, MICHAEL and ROGER LOUIS. *The Oxford History of the Twentieth Century.* (1998).

KOLKO, GABRIEL. *A Century of War: Politics, Conflict and Society since 1914.* (1994).

MAZOWER, MARK. *Dark Continent: Europe's Twentieth Century.* (1998).

REYNOLDS, DAVID. *One World Divisible: A Global History since 1945.* (2000).

ROBERTS, J. M. *The Twentieth Century: A History of the World, 1901–2000.* (1999).

PART ONE

＊ ── ＊ ── ＊ ── ＊ ── ＊ ── ＊ ── ＊ ── ＊ ── ＊

The Decline of European Hegemony, 1900–1945

Overview

＊ ── ＊ ── ＊ ── ＊ ── ＊ ── ＊ ── ＊ ── ＊ ── ＊

As the twentieth century opened, Europe dominated a world order that it had done much to define over the preceding several centuries. Having evolved into powerful national states with highly centralized government and administrative structures, the major European powers were able to wield enormous economic and military power around the world. Large portions of Africa and Asia bore the imprint of some aspect of European civilization in the form of colonization. The civilizations of the Americas were predominantly European in origin and character, further testimony to the dynamism of European civilization.

During the first half of the twentieth century, Europe's hegemonic position in the world order was rapidly eroded and finally ended in the course of events growing out of two devastating world wars, which were set apart by a catastrophic interlude of global economic depression. The First World War destroyed the last vestiges of Europe's nineteenth-century state system, obliterating four empires, creating a multitude of new and potentially unstable nations and unleashing radical ideologies that further destabilized postwar Europe. Communism, promising a "worker state" built on a socialist economy, took root in Soviet Russia and threatened to spread elsewhere. Dictatorships grounded in the concept of total state authority emerged in Italy, the Soviet Union and Germany, as similar authoritarian regimes took power across the continent.

Nationalism in Asia, Africa and the colonial world drove movements that challenged western colonialism. In China, nationalists collided with communists over the destiny of that huge nation, provoking intermittent civil warfare for decades. In Japan, a radical and militaristic nationalism was put to the service of growing imperial ambitions in Asia, which centered on Japanese control and exploitation of China. Adolf Hitler grew determined to secure German domination over Europe, a prerequisite for his genocidal policies toward those peoples he deemed "inferior." By the end of the decade, as Germany, Italy and Japan embraced diplomatically, the crises merged as one, culminating in the Second World War. The conflict proved to be the most catastrophic event of the century, devastating much of Europe and Asia. The war brought final closure to the era of Europe's world supremacy and inaugurated a bipolar world order dominated by two new "superpowers," the United States and the Soviet Union.

CHAPTER 1

·——·—·—·—·—·—·

The Global Order in 1900: A World of Empires

Despite the oppressive heat and humidity of a summer day in 1897 on England's southern coast, tens of thousands of people continued to pour into the city of Portsmouth, many arriving at the city station on the dozens of special trains commissioned for the occasion. Portsmouth had been a major naval base since the Tudor era, when England first began to establish its reputation as a seapower. Now, on Saturday, June 26, Portsmouth was the site of the climactic event celebrating the Diamond Jubilee of Queen Victoria, the assemblage of the Royal Navy for review.

Britons had long viewed their fleet as the guardian of their liberties and a major instrument of Great Britain's imperial glory. Now this same powerful manifestation of national pride assembled in the three-mile-wide protected waters between the mainland and the Isle of Wight: five lines of warships of all types, from powerful battleships with famous names such as *Renown, Inflexible* and *Alexandra* to sleek, swift torpedo boat-destroyers, 165 ships altogether. The black hulls, white superstructures and yellow funnels of the massed warships enhanced this awe-inspiring vision of British naval strength. Yet this was only the Home Fleet; vast numbers of British warships remained on station across the far-flung reaches of the empire. At Portsmouth, the offshore spectacle was made all the grander by the presence of warships from fourteen other nations, all present upon the queen's invitation. Joining the enthusiastic throngs of Englishmen to view this powerful naval review were numerous foreign dignitaries, including Victoria's grandson, the erratic German Kaiser William II.

At two in the afternoon, the reviewing procession, led by the royal yacht *Victoria and Albert,* got under way and took the fleet's salutes for the next two hours. The festivities concluded that evening with a stunning display in which the Home Fleet's vessels were outlined with electric lights, all of which were switched off simultaneously at midnight. Those who had witnessed the day's spectacles were left with an indisputable impression of British naval might.

The Queen, however, remained at Windsor. The celebrations had begun earlier in the week with myriad receptions and parties and a carriage ride of the aging queen, now often confined to a wheelchair, through the streets of London. The route from Buckingham Palace to St. Paul's Cathedral was lined with massive crowds, whose approval was manifest in their continual cheers and spontaneous renditions of "God Save the Queen." Fatigued by the events, the Queen who had ruled for sixty years, rested and found consolation in the broad public approbation expressed over the past few days.

Without question, Britain prospered and strengthened immeasurably during the first 60 years of her rule. At 78, the short, stout, often grim-faced monarch reigned as Queen of England and Ireland and Empress of India; her empire encompassed one-quarter of the world's land surface, some 11 million square miles. The Union Jack flew over 372 million people, including Asians, Africans, Pacific Islanders, and Arabs—it was no exaggeration to claim that "the sun never sets on the British Empire." In 1897, the empire was as fixed and enduring in the British imagination as was the Queen herself.

Born in 1819 to Edward, the Duke of Kent, and Princess Victoria of Saxe-Coburg, Victoria led a lonely, secluded childhood during an era in which the monarchy was in wide disrepute. Inheriting the throne in 1837 following the death of her uncle William IV, she accepted her duties as queen with solemn devotion, vowing to herself "I will behave!" A small and handsome woman in her twenties, she married her cousin Prince Albert of Saxe-Coburg in 1840, beginning a family that eventually included nine children who would later populate the thrones of Europe. Together, the two saw Great Britain through a period of growing political stability and prosperity as the nation entered the latter stages of the industrial revolution. Victoria's life was changed forever by Albert's death in 1861. Somewhat prone to self-pity and morbidity, the queen dressed in mourning black the rest of her life and developed a bizarre interest in funerals.

During the 1860s, Victoria acquired the appearance and settled into the opinions that defined her for much of the rest of her life. Described by a contemporary as "very large, ruddy and fat," the queen suffered from protuberant eyes and a red complexion that worried her physicians. Aside from excessive fondness for rich foods, it was not often that she indulged personal vanities or gave in to the burdens of her position. After the death of her husband, Victoria had adopted as her motto, "I must bear it, 'til the Lord pleases to take me." It was a credo that reflected the piety, sense of duty and self-discipline inherent in "Victorianism," the moral code that bore the Queen's name and shaped English society through the late nineteenth century. As monarch, Victoria viewed the world through a conservative lens, and was inevitably receptive to Conservative Prime Minister Benjamin Disraeli than to the Liberal William Gladstone, whom she blamed for permitting the erosion of imperial strength. When the issue of women's rights arose in the 1870s, the Queen stood solidly with those who desired to

Fig. 1-1   Queen Victoria, seated front row center, attended by her daughter, the German Empress Victoria, at an 1885 gathering of European royalty. The future British king Edward VII, Russian Emperor Alexander III and Empress Maria Fyodorovna and German Kaiser William I are among the ruling monarchs present. (Pearson Education, Corporate Digital Archive, Photo Researchers, Inc.)

uphold tradition. Women's rights, she declared, was a "mad wicked folly" and feminists "ought to get a good whipping." Efforts to achieve equality with men, she warned, would only lead women to "unsex" themselves and become "the most hateful, heathen and disgusting of beings."

Beyond women's rights, Victoria responded to a multitude of issues throughout her long reign. Economic policy, diplomacy, social issues arising out of the Industrial Revolution and "Home Rule" for Ireland were among the scores of topics that required her periodic attention. In the last quarter of the century, however, imperial issues achieved a heightened prominence. The latter decades of Victoria's reign paralleled the era of the "New Imperialism," during which a number of European powers sought to establish or significantly expand colonial holdings. With already extensive imperial holdings in Asia, the Indo-Pacific basin and the American hemispheres, the English were soon caught up in the renewed rush for empire. As Britain's imperial reach began to extend deeper into Africa and Asia, the historical justifications for empire were once again recited. Trade, commerce, markets, the need for strategic outposts and international status were all cited by enthused editorialists and politicians in defense of the expanding empire. Others argued that, as one of the "civilized" nations, Britain had an obligation to bring order and progress to "backward" peoples. Cecil Rhodes, arguably the era's most prominent advocate and practitioner of imperialism, expressed a widespread notion when he declared, "I contend that we are the first race in the world, and that the more of the world we inhabit, the better it is for the human race." Likewise, Colonial Secretary Joseph Chamberlain maintained that Britain's imperial destiny was manifest, given "that spirit . . . of adventure and enterprise distinguishing the Anglo-Saxon race [which] has made us peculiarly fit to carry out the working of colonization."

Empire did, of course, bring burdens. By 1899, a lengthy quarrel between English colonists and Dutch settlers in South Africa escalated into the Boer War, a conflict in which Great Britain prevailed by 1902, but one that proved both difficult and costly. World opinion favored the heroic struggles of the outnumbered Boers and condemned the English as inept bullies. In the latter stages of the war, British public support began to waver as disillusionment over the casualties grew and victory seemed elusive, but belief in the imperial idea remained as yet undiminished. Queen Victoria did not live to see the resolution of the conflict in South Africa. Increasingly frail, she suffered a stroke and died on January 22, 1901. The funeral ceremonies, described by a contemporary historian as "the greatest and most impressive ever known," were attended by five monarchs and nine crown princes, plus forty other princes and grand dukes. Resplendent with all the solemn pageantry that tradition required, the ceremonies were befitting of a monarch whose sixty-four-year reign had, the same historian observed, "glorified the century just ended and helped make it the most brilliant epoch in the world's history."

The world that Victoria departed in 1901 was a world of empires, some enjoying unprecedented power and influence and others showing serious signs of decay. The great empires of eastern civilization that had prospered in an earlier age were in advanced states of decline by the beginning of the twentieth century. China, which had endured for millennia, and the Ottoman Empire, a dominant power in Asia Minor for centuries, suffered from growing political disarray, territorial erosion and military impotence. Both had been largely insulated from the effects of the Scientific Revolution, the Enlightenment and the Industrial Revolution, developments that combined to give tremendous momentum to the rising power of the West between the fifteenth and nineteenth centuries. Now, as the twentieth century opened, the remarkable dynamism of western civilization was manifest in a multitude of areas. Intellectual vitality, industrial might, organizational efficiency, advanced technology and military potency all testified to Europe's unprecedented vigor. These same strengths were instrumental in the acquisition of empire, which was the ultimate manifestation of Europe's primacy. By 1900 vast expanses of the non-western world were incorporated into European empires. Even in the Americas, Europeans retained a presence in the Caribbean basin and Central America. The United States, itself an outgrowth of European civilization, had likewise established the rudiments of empire in the Pacific and Caribbean.

To all but a few in the West, empire seemed logical, just and enduring. Fewer still would have questioned the evident superiority of western civilization or the permanence of western hegemony. In the non-western and colonial world, however, there were already stirrings of dissent and restlessness. In India, Africa, Asia and elsewhere, imperial rule was being challenged and even resisted. But these voices of protest were largely dismissed by westerners, who deemed the aspirations of "natives" to be distinctly secondary to imperial considerations. As the new century opened, the outlook in Europe, as in Victorian Britain, was one of confidence in the continued dominance of western civilization. It was, as events would soon demonstrate, a deceptive vision. Only in retrospect would it become obvious that Europe had reached the apogee of its power and that, in many ways, the stately pomp of Queen Victoria's funeral marked the beginning of the end of an era in world history. Few who witnessed that occasion in 1901 could have predicted that the world represented by the attending emperors, kings and princes would disappear in a cataclysm only a few short years away. Equally few could have foreseen that the era of European supremacy and empire, this "brilliant epoch," was waning, destined to give way in the face of turbulent forces that were gathering strength even as the century began.

◆ —— ◆ —— ◆ —— ◆ —— ◆

Apogee: European Civilization in 1900

As the new century began, the world population stood at about 1.63 billion, of whom about 401 million were Europeans. Though they accounted for only 24% of the world's population, Europeans exercised remarkably disproportionate power and influence over the rest of the globe. Europe's industrial economies, coupled with the power of such financial centers as London, shaped patterns of trade and commerce in an increasingly global economy. The military and naval might of Europe's great powers was as yet unequaled and could be sent great distances to serve European ambitions. Those ambitions had, in fact, brought a huge portion of the world under direct or indirect European control; by 1914, in the aftermath of the "imperial wave" of the late nineteenth century, Europeans controlled, directly or through "spheres of influence," about 85% of the world's land surface. Even in the non-colonial world, Europe's influence was manifest; the increasingly dynamic civilizations of North and South America had been shaped largely by a European heritage. European political and social thought influenced events far beyond the boundaries of the continent, sometimes serving even those who would challenge tradition and orthodoxy in non-western societies. In the natural and physical sciences, European discoveries and insights were without parallel.

Europeans likewise viewed their cultural and artistic achievements as paramount, a standard against which the accomplishments of other civilizations might be measured. At the turn of the century, European civilization was, in the words of one historian, a "proud tower," its vitality and superiority self-evident in a multitude of achievements. As the century began, the general European outlook was one of optimism and confidence in a future in which Europe's hegemony in the world would continue undiminished. Many Europeans would have undoubtedly agreed with the historian who wrote in 1910, "In this period, the history of Europe becomes in a sense the history of the world." Without question, Europe had reached the apogee of its power and influence; few were as yet willing to acknowledge the inevitability of decline, and fewer still could have foreseen the rapidity with which Europe's supremacy would erode in the decades to come. For the moment, Europe's manifest strengths seemed evidence enough of the likely permanence of her dominant position in the world.

INDUSTRY, TECHNOLOGY AND SOCIETY

One of Europe's greatest strengths at the turn of the century was a vibrant and expanding economy, driven in large part by the continuing Industrial Revolution. Originating in Great Britain in the late eighteenth century, the initial Industrial Revolution had gradually swept across the continent during the first half of the nineteenth century, having its greatest impact in western and northern Europe. This First Industrial Revolution brought with it an "age of iron," in which the greatest growth was in basic heavy industries and transportation, both of which relied heavily on coal as a source of fuel for steam-powered machines and engines. By the 1870s, the Second Industrial Revolution was underway, ushering in an "age of steel," made possible by new technologies such as the Bessemer process, which allowed for the production of consistently high-quality steel at a much lower cost. Steel had enormous utility in both civil and military applications and the industry quickly became a driving force of the Second Industrial Revolution.

Other new technologies and manufacturing processes paved the way for the development of the chemical, electrical and petroleum industries. The burgeoning chemical industries of western Europe produced an amazing array of new goods, including pharmaceuticals, dyestuffs, synthetic fibers, fertilizers, soaps and margarine. The electrical industry was instrumental in introducing new means of power generation, illumination, transportation and communication; electric power, light, trams and telephones came into increasingly common usage, especially in western Europe.

The petroleum industry, which initially focused on producing illuminating oils and lubricants, experienced a major boom following the development of the internal combustion engine by the German engineer Karl Benz in 1885. In the following decade, the growing popularity of the automobile spurred the interest of European entrepreneurs in an industry previously dominated by the Standard Oil Company in the United States. European firms soon moved to capitalize on the productive capabilities of Russia's Baku oil fields; London's Shell Transport and Trading was soon moving Russian bulk oil through the Suez Canal for sale in

Asia. The Royal Dutch company was quick to exploit the oil-rich Netherlands East Indies, offloading its first shipload of Sumatran gasoline at the London docks in 1902. Added impetus was given to the growing petroleum industry when, early in the century, Europe's major naval powers began to move gradually away from coal, the staple naval fuel of the nineteenth century, and toward conversion to fuel-oil-powered vessels. The advent of the age of aviation, which was marked by the Wright brothers' first successful powered flight in North Carolina in 1903, not only brought with it the promise of a revolution in transportation but also the prospect of another significant new market for petroleum products.

The Second Industrial Revolution brought some significant changes in patterns of industrial development. The availability of new means of power, together with the rise of the new chemical and electrical industries, made industrialization possible in areas that had lagged in earlier years because of the absence of coal. These years also saw some major alterations in the industrial order. Britain, the early leader in industrial production, was rapidly surpassed by Germany, and by the outbreak of the First World War both were overtaken by the United States, which quickly demonstrated its industrial potential in the early twentieth century. Elsewhere, the pace and extent of industrialization varied. Though industrial growth accelerated in France, it remained far behind Germany and Britain. In the northern regions of the Austro-Hungarian Empire, both Bohemia and Moravia developed significant industrial sectors, but the southern and eastern portions of the sprawling "Dual Monarchy" remained largely agricultural. In Italy, only the northern region proved capable of supporting industrial development. On the Iberian Penin-

sula, industries emerged in northern Spain, but were little evident elsewhere. Most of Eastern Europe, with rural peasant populations and archaic social and political structures, remained industrially undeveloped. In Imperial Russia industrial growth was inhibited by shortages of capital, skilled workers and technology, and by the vastness of the country.

Agriculture also bolstered European economic growth in these years. Mechanization, more effective land use and "scientific agriculture" all contributed to greater crop yields. Agricultural specialization, especially in western Europe, led to an increasingly specific focus on dairy farming, poultry and market gardening, while cereal grains and beef were more often imported, often from Argentina. More traditional and less productive agricultural practices were prevalent in southern Italy, the Iberian Peninsula and eastern Europe. Russia, which lagged industrially, made significant strides toward improving agricultural production in the early years of the new century and by 1914 was the world leader in the export of wheat, oats, barley and rye.

All of these developments contributed to the increasingly rapid growth of a more truly global economy. The rudiments of a system of global economic relationships were first established in the sixteenth century during the initial era of significant European expansion abroad, developing gradually if not spectacularly during the following three centuries. In the late nineteenth century, this pattern of global trade expanded dynamically, driven by renewed imperial expansion, the Second Industrial Revolution, the spread of protectionist tariff policies and Europe's growing financial power. The demand for raw materials, manufactures, new markets and investment opportunities led Europeans to extend and expand their economic reach to an unprecedented degree, forging a multitude of connections with the Americas, Asia and Africa. A pattern of global economic relationships, characterized by increasingly interdependent economic regions, was taking clear shape as the new century began.

The maturation of Europe's industrial economy transformed society in numerous ways. In the most general sense, the standard of living for most Europeans, and especially those in Western Europe, improved dramatically in the last quarter of the nineteenth century and into the start of the twentieth. Rising agricultural productivity meant less expensive foodstuffs and an improved diet. This, together with advances in medicine and improvements in public sanitation, meant healthier populations and longer lifespans. Though there were exceptions, most Europeans also enjoyed better wages and housing, which did much to defuse the discontent and social unrest that had been so common in the first half of the nineteenth century. The new technologies of the era, especially electricity, improved life in immeasurable ways, perhaps most notably in transportation and communications.

Europe's cities were swollen by a general rise in population and by the movement of people out of the rural countryside and into urban industrial areas. The number of European cities with populations exceeding 200,000 nearly tripled between 1850 and 1900. The largest, Greater London, was a city of 7 million by 1914. The influx of people into urban centers exacerbated the usual social ills that attended crowding. Crime, poverty, public health and inadequate housing were all issues that increasingly demanded the attention of government, though the electrical revolution did much to improve the quality of life in Europe's large cities.

There were, of course, those who sought a better life elsewhere; emigration was a significant demographic phenomenon through the first several decades of the new century. The largest numbers of emigrants were from impoverished rural areas in southern and eastern Europe, with the greatest number being from Italy. The most common destination for the "new immigrants," as this wave was called, was the United States, though Canada, South America and South Africa attracted others.

The structure of European society was also transformed by the progress of industrialization. The major reordering of the social structure initiated by the earlier stages of industrialization had by the late nineteenth century evolved into an industrial social order comprised of workers, a middle class and an upper class. The composition and size of each class varied from country to country, and in much of eastern and southern Europe, socioeconomic relationships were still determined by a pre-industrial order in which peasant, burgher and landlord were the primary distinctions. In the industrial societies of western and central Europe, the industrial working class included artisans, skilled and unskilled workers. Most labored in factories for wages that reflected the level of their skills. Industrial labor afforded an uncertain mode of living at best, given the rapid changes in technology and production techniques that frequently eliminated existing jobs and replaced them with new ones. Though the period brought a general improvement in wages, many working-class Europeans accepted their station as permanent, assuming that their descendants would likewise be "proletarians." This outlook, together with an acute awareness of their place in the industrial order, helped foment a "class consciousness" that was crucial to the effort to organize workers in trade unions and other labor organizations.

The middle class was much more heterogeneous, traditionally composed of merchants, skilled artisans and professionals, but now expanded to include clerks, schoolteachers, bureaucrats, business managers, engineers and others considered to hold "white-collar" jobs that had come with the Second Industrial Revolution. There was, in fact, enough diversity within the middle class to permit social scientists to differentiate between a lower and upper middle class in many countries. Above all else, Europe's middle classes were dynamic, increasing in size, wealth and complexity. A crucial conduit of economic mobility, the middle classes generally desired social stability, liberal government and moral order, and saw education as a critical instrument of social and economic advancement.

At the apex of the social order was a wealthy elite, an upper class including the traditional landed aristocracy and those whose wealth was the product of the Industrial Revolution: the financiers, bankers, and industrial capitalists. Though they constituted a mere 5 percent of the population, this group controlled 40 percent of Europe's wealth. Some, like Germany's Krupp family, had built their industrial empires and personal fortunes over time; others were relative newcomers, sometimes descendants of titled families whose wealth was the product of more recent investment ventures. While the age of mass society eroded the influence of those with inherited status, it had not decreased the influence of those with wealth, and across Europe much of the old aristocracy found new status within the rising industrial elite.

Several other broad trends shaped European society in this period. In much of western and central Europe, the gradual democratization of politics brought new dynamics to the political universe, as suffrage expanded to encompass not only middle-class but also working-class Europeans. Broadened suffrage was fundamental in ushering in an age of mass politics, in which policy making was no longer the exclusive domain of the political and economic elite; public opinion, given voice and force through mass political parties, played an increasingly important role in the decision-making process. The birth of mass politics was attended by a general improvement in public education systems, which had languished during the first half of the nineteenth century. In Britain, Germany, France, the Scandinavian countries and other western European states, compulsory primary and secondary education was increasingly the norm. Varying motivations drove advocates of mass education. Liberals saw secular education as a necessary antidote to conservative religious education; politicians considered education as requisite to an informed electorate. National school systems also inculcated civic and patriotic values, considered crucial to social cohesion.

In this age of mass politics and mass education, European women still found many doors closed to them. The "woman question," which referred to the general role of women in society, generated heated debate over the issues of suffrage, education and employment. European feminism had a lengthy history, having grown out of the French Revolution, and by the last decades of the nineteenth century focused mainly on political equality. Britain's women's suffrage movement was perhaps the most dynamic in western Europe, but even there the campaign for voting rights gained little ground prior to the First World War. Educational opportunities for women did expand late in the century, but even at the elementary level, different curricula for boys and girls reflected the persistence of traditional conceptions of gender roles. The expansion of public education did increase the demand for teachers, which afforded some women the chance for higher education at women's teacher colleges. Maturing industrial economies also created new employment opportunities for women, who now found work as telephone operators, clerks and secretaries; others were still relegated to manual labor, such as doing piecework in sewing factories. Middle-class values prescribed a domestically centered life for married women, whose "leisure" was seen as a sign of their husbands' financial success and status. A new dimension of controversy, engendered partly by increasingly effective means of contraception, threatened to raise much more fundamental issues concerning marriage and family, institutions widely held to be crucial to social stability and morality. These issues would, however, not be fully addressed for some decades to come. In much of eastern and southern Europe, political democracy, mass education and women's rights advanced little if at all. In a general sense, those regions touched least by the processes of industrialization experienced these political and social changes much later and to a much lesser degree than did the heavily industrialized nations.

THE EUROPEAN INTELLECTUAL UNIVERSE

The general optimism that characterized the European outlook in 1900 stemmed from several historical sources. The Scientific Revolution of the seventeenth century, grounded in rationalism and empiricism, established that the universe was comprehensible to man. Natural laws, revealed by scientific investigation, provided the foundations for new conceptions of a mechanistic, predictable universe. Even as these advances erased the uncertainties of past ages, a growing confidence in the human capacity for intellectual growth was further cause for optimism. The Enlightenment of the eighteenth century amplified these trends, as Europeans turned to reason as the instrument of mankind's social, political and economic progress. The broad changes set in motion by the French Revolution and the Industrial Revolution confirmed many in the belief that progress was not only manifest, but also inevitable.

During the second half of the nineteenth century, new discoveries in the physical and natural sciences greatly improved the quality of life and affirmed European confidence in the utility of science in general. Louis Pasteur's germ theory of disease marked the beginnings of a revolution in medicine, as advances in the following decades in the diagnosis and treatment of disease eased the sufferings and extended the lives of millions. Perhaps the most influential scientific event of the century was, however, the publication in 1859 of Charles Darwin's *On the Origin of the Species*. In a work that was as notable for the religious controversy it generated as for its scientific content, the English naturalist presented his theory of biological evolution through the principle of natural selection, basing his conclusions on observations he had made during the scientific expedition of the HMS *Beagle* in the early 1830s. Darwin's observation of isolated animal communities in the Galapagos Islands led him to conclude that, in the struggle for existence, those organisms most capable of adapting to their environment through "variations" would be "naturally selected" for survival and propagation. The "unfit" would lose the struggle for survival and die out. In a later work, *The Descent of Man* (1871), Darwin applied the theory of natural selection to humans. Many religionists, who saw in Darwin's theories a challenge to the Biblical concept of creation and a denial of mankind's special creation, vociferously denounced the scientist, and even among scientists there were those who disputed his ideas. Nonetheless, others found Darwinian theory compelling; it posited a world that was explicable in terms of natural law discerned through scientific investigation, and one in which the processes of natural change brought biological progression, maybe even perfection. Many saw in this theory of natural evolution another affirmation of the inevitability of progress, biological and otherwise.

By the later decades of the nineteenth century, Darwinian evolutionary naturalism was appropriated by social theorists who suggested that the same natural laws were applicable to the development of human society. The Englishman Herbert Spencer was instrumental in popularizing social Darwinism, a theory that held that social evolution was driven by the struggle to survive and natural selection, both of which contributed to progress. In Spencer's view, any effort on the part of the state to aid those who failed to adapt constituted interference with natural law, thus slowing society's natural evolution, which was contingent on the "survival of the fittest." As Spencer asserted with callous frankness, "If the poor are not sufficiently complete to survive they die, and it is best that they should die." As ruthless as this outlook appeared, it gained considerable support and was adopted in modified form by nationalists and racists. Among the former, the argument was made that national greatness and progress came only through this same struggle for survival and that war was

part of the process of natural selection, bringing the superior nation to a dominant position. Darwinian principles also provided a foundation for pseudo-scientific racialist writings, such as the French count Joseph de Gobineau's *Essay on the Inequality of Human Races*, which proclaimed a distinction between "inferior" and "superior" races. Houston Stewart Chamberlain, an Englishman who sought German citizenship, argued for German racial superiority in *The Foundations of the Nineteenth Century* (1899). The Germans, Chamberlain argued, were the only pure descendants of Aryans and were thus the primary defenders of western civilization. Though relatively few Europeans subscribed wholeheartedly to social Darwinist or racialist doctrines, many did believe that the manifest material and cultural accomplishments of Europe were evidence of the superiority of western civilization and testimony to the advanced state of European peoples.

In the last quarter of the nineteenth century, the general progress of European civilization seemed irrefutable. Science and industry had markedly bettered the general conditions of life; the growing material wealth of even the lower orders of society was undeniable, and far more people enjoyed leisure activities. The advance of liberalism in western Europe portended more extensive human freedoms in the future and gave promise of making inroads into other areas of the continent. The threat of revolutions seemed at most a distant memory; there had been no serious civil eruptions in Europe since 1848. The possibility that major wars were a thing of the past was an issue of serious discussion; the Hague Conference of 1899, where delegates discussed disarmament and the need for international arbitration, seemed to demonstrate the determination of Europe's statesmen to lessen the likelihood of international conflict. The French came to refer to this hopeful era as *la belle époque*, while the British would remember it as the Edwardian Age. The writer Stefan Zweig no doubt captured the perception of many when he termed it "the Age of Golden Security." In the intellectual world, such security as existed was, however, already being called into question.

Though the European outlook was generally positive at century's end, a number of thinkers had gained growing prominence by questioning prevailing philosophic and scientific certainties. In the realm of philosophy and social theory, irrationalism was beginning to chip away at the edifice of reason. A relatively small group, the irrationalists questioned the primacy of reason, dismissed the notion of inevitable progress and extolled the virtues of the irrational. Perhaps most renowned among this group was Friedrich Nietzsche, a German philosopher who scandalized Europe with his assertion that "God is dead." A prolific author who wrote in an accessible, aphoristic style, Nietzsche sought not to formulate a philosophical system, but to force his readers to confront fundamental inconsistencies and hypocrisies in the western intellectual tradition, to "philosophize with a hammer." Disgusted with the self-conceits of Europeans, he vociferously denounced Christianity, democracy, nationalism and modern morality. Propounding a "will to power" and a "reevaluation of morals," he looked toward the evolution of a "superman," who would transcend the inadequacies of contemporary mankind. One of the century's most provocative thinkers, Nietzsche grew increasingly deranged after 1888 and died insane in 1900. Many of Nietzsche's concepts, which idealized power and struggle, were later appropriated and dis-

torted to serve totalitarian and racist ideologies after the First World War.

Nietzsche was not alone in the philosophical assault on reason. The French philosopher Henri Bergson argued that neither truth nor ultimate reality could be apprehended through rationalism. He considered consciousness to be only a "superficial psychic life;" the true source of human inspiration and progress was the "deep-seated self" or "vital spirit" which was not guided by reason. Bergson further postulated that nations as well as individuals had unique "dynamic energy" that could bring great advances if tapped. Both Bergson and Nietzsche influenced the work of the French political theorist Georges Sorel, who was likewise convinced of the limited utility of rationalism. Melding irrationalist concepts with Marxian ideas about class war, Sorel propounded the doctrine of syndicalism, which held that socialist revolution could be brought about through the general strike, a mass, violent action on the part of workers. In *Reflections on Violence* (1902), Sorel argued that the power of "mythic image" of the general strike itself would inspire workers to overturn the oppressive capitalist system through heroic action that would include riots, strikes and sabotage. A proponent of change by violent action, Sorel was no democrat; his vision was one in which a small elite would govern the liberated working classes.

Several social scientists also acknowledged the role of the irrational in social and political behavior. In his 1895 study *The Crowd*, Gustave Le Bon pondered the character of mass society, in which the individual was reduced to merely part of the crowd. The mob, he argued, was an entity unto itself, capable of violence and beyond rational discourse. A similar concern was voiced by the economist and sociologist Vilfredo Pareto, who suggested that the unchanging determinants of human conduct were fundamentally nonrational. Even as the influence of irrationalism became evident in philosophy and social theory, the work of psychologist Sigmund Freud seemed to support the notion that man was not preeminently a rational creature. Though not a proponent of irrationalism, the Austrian physician proposed in *The Interpretation of Dreams* (1899) that human behavior was determined largely by the unconscious rather than the rational faculties. The broader implications of Freud's theories were troubling, as most western political and social thought was grounded on the belief that man was essentially rational. If Freud's theories about the primacy of the irrational unconscious were accurate, the viability of liberal democracy was questionable. Though Freudian theory gained considerable attention and, by the 1920s, a certain chic fashionability, it nonetheless introduced yet another element of uncertainty into western thought.

European life was further transformed by the decline of traditional religion, which was evident in falling church attendance. The growing confidence in science and mass education together with increasing urbanization, eroded traditional religious beliefs and practices. While Protestantism moved generally away from pietism and toward an emphasis on good works in the temporal world, Catholicism faced a much more serious challenge. As late as 1864, the papal encyclical *Syllabus of Errors* refuted the notion that the Roman Catholic Church should "come to terms with progress, liberalism and modern civilization." Asserting papal infallibility in 1870, the Roman Church often supported authoritarian regimes and repressive monar-

chies, positions that undermined its popular appeal. During the papacy of Leo XIII (1878–1903), the Church made some striking accommodations with the new age. The 1891 encyclical *Rerum Novarum* committed the Church to the cause of social justice and sternly criticized the materialistic perspective of both capitalism and socialism. Nonetheless, liberals and radicals alike saw the Catholic Church as an obstacle to progress, and anticlericalism continued to be a strong political force in several nations.

Perhaps the greatest challenge to certainty came from new discoveries in physics, which forced a gradual reconceptualization of the Newtonian universe of previous centuries. New research in the field of atomic physics, most notably by the German physicist Max Planck, raised doubts about previous conceptions concerning the behavior of atoms. Planck's quantum theory asserted that heated bodies radiated energy in irregular packets or "quanta," which suggested that at the subatomic level there might be more irregularity than previously believed. The Austrian Ernst Mach introduced additional uncertainties into physics when he concluded that general laws of physics were at best only reasonable summaries of sense perceptions; because of this, such concepts as "absolute space" and "absolute time" were undependable constructions. Mach's ideas intrigued the young Albert Einstein, whose special theory of relativity asserted that time and space were not absolute, but relative to the observer. Einstein rejected the concept of three-dimensional space, proposing instead a four-dimensional time–space continuum. The greater implications of these new concepts became evident only with time; Einstein's greatest achievements and international fame came only after the First World War. Nonetheless, these advances in theoretical physics cast significant doubts on the viability of the Newtonian conception of the universe.

The intellectual challenge to rationalism, tradition and a predictably ordered universe gave rise to the outlook referred to as modernism, which acknowledged the importance of the unconscious, the symbolic, the subjectivity of perception and in general, the uncertain, disordered nature of existence in the modern world. By the turn of the century, the modernist outlook had supplanted realism in the arts, ushering in some new approaches. In literature, realism was supplanted by naturalism, which stressed man's inability to escape from deterministic forces. Symbolism, which held that true reality existed only within the mind and that the external world was an agglomeration of symbols reflecting that reality, influenced both literature and the arts. Impressionism and Expressionism transformed the art world by introducing subjective perspectives and challenging traditional concepts of reality. Impressionism also found its way into music, which was being revolutionized by a new emphasis on primitivism and unorthodox, dissonant tonal scales. These changes suggested that the civilization of nineteenth-century Europe was undergoing a fundamental transition, the ultimate scope and character of which would become evident only after the First World War.

THE MAJOR IDEOLOGIES

One of the most dynamic ideologies of the nineteenth century was liberalism, a creed which held that human progress could best be forwarded by individual liberty and free institutions. Largely the product of English political philosophers such as Jeremy Bentham and John Stuart Mill, liberalism extolled economic and political liberty, both of which could be protected by constitutional government, representative assemblies and guarantees of basic freedoms. England's expanding middle class was attracted to an ideology premised on curbing the arbitrary power of the monarchy and the special privileges of the aristocracy. Liberal thought also rejected state intervention in the economic realm, advocating instead a policy of *laissez-faire*, meaning to let people do as they chose. It was a position of obvious appeal to the rising entrepreneurial class. The major limitation in liberalism was in its unwillingness to enfranchise the working classes. Many liberals felt that the right to vote should be withheld from the uneducated toiling masses, as they were politically unsophisticated and susceptible to demagogic appeals. Liberal ideology made some inroads among the middle classes on the continent, most notably in Germany, France and Belgium, but the failed revolutions of 1848 slowed the advance of continental liberalism. In Britain, however, liberalism gradually gained force and became a major vehicle for political reform. Later in the century, liberals in England and elsewhere grew more receptive to the idea of the state as an instrument of limited social and economic reform and accepted the inevitability of working class suffrage. The progress of liberal thought across western and northern Europe was evident by 1900; constitutional government and representative assemblies were the norm, though the degree of political democracy varied from nation to nation.

Nonetheless, liberalism faced a growing crisis in the last years of the century. One major challenge came from conservatism, an ideology that gained its modern definition in response to the excesses of the French Revolution. The precise contents of conservative ideology varied nationally, but it generally stressed order, traditional institutions, a suspicion of rapid change, limited popular participation in government and significant limits to state activity in social and economic areas. Conservatism was often the ideology of landed aristocracy, industrial elites, the propertied classes and advocates of a traditional social and moral order. The latter group, it should be noted, sometimes included even the rural peasantry, which could be surprisingly tradition-bound and conservative in outlook. Europe's middle classes, shaken by rapid and unpredictable economic shifts, were not immune to the appeal of conservatism, which was heightened by the growing unpopularity of free trade, a defining position of liberalism for decades. Economic distress during the last quarter of the century converted many to the policy of tariff protection, which conservatives hailed as a bulwark of national economic strength. Conservatism manifested itself in a variety of forms. While English conservatism found voice in the broad-based Conservative Party, the conservative impulse elsewhere often took the form of relatively narrow parties that served agrarian, religious and industrial interests.

Nationalism posed a further challenge to liberalism by century's end. Modern nationalist thought took shape during the French Revolution and Napoleonic Wars, as European peoples, especially those under French occupation, developed a growing awareness of the common language, institutions and cultural traditions that distinguished them. Those distinctions could be protected and nurtured, nationalists argued, only by the creation of a strong nation-state. This basic concept drove nationalist movements throughout Europe during the first three-quarters of

the century, resulting most notably in the unification of Italy and Germany. Nationalism remained a potent force among minorities still governed by dominant national groups. In the Austro-Hungarian Empire, Czechs, Poles and Slavs were among the many minorities who resented the dominance of Germans and Hungarian Magyars. Nationalism was also at the root of the long and sometimes violent movement for Irish home rule, which was a major issue in Great Britain.

For those peoples who did not yet enjoy autonomy, nationalism was a compelling and potentially revolutionary ideology, which sometimes threatened the European order. Though not innately anti-democratic, nationalism began to assume a somewhat different aspect in the established nation-states in the latter 19th century. The tremendous expansion of the scope and authority of the nation-state and the intensification of international rivalry contributed to a significant rise in nationalist sentiment that was amplified by mass media and mass political parties. This "new" nationalism proved an unpredictable and potentially illiberal force, as it had at its core a belief in the primacy of the nation-state. Traditional liberal beliefs in the equality of men, popular sovereignty and the importance of the individual were all considered subordinate to "the national interest." In some cases, nationalism developed a symbiotic relationship with racialism and imperialism, both of which drew on beliefs of the superiority of one race or nation over others. Movements such as pan-Slavism and pan-Germanism asserted the right of those peoples to protection by and inclusion in their respective nations, a perspective that offered the potential for conflict. One of the more ominous directions that extreme nationalism took was toward anti-Semitism, as extremists in Russia, Germany and Austria denounced Jews as an alien presence, a people without a nation. Ironically, this new wave of anti-Semitism helped propel the Zionist movement, whose founder Theodor Herzl advocated the creation of a Jewish homeland. Paradoxically, nationalism could serve as an ideology of either unity or division.

Few ideas have proven as consequential as those of Karl Marx, who dedicated most of his adult life to developing the ideology that bore his name. Marxism, or "scientific socialism," presented a fundamental and comprehensive challenge to liberalism, nationalism and capitalism, bringing a new and forceful element into the political universe of nineteenth-century Europe. Born to bourgeois affluence in Trier in the German Rhineland in 1818, Marx showed no initial inclination to radicalism, idling away his early years at the University of Bonn writing poetry and brawling with fellow students. Expelled for dueling, Marx transferred to the University of Berlin, where he developed a more serious approach to his studies. Intrigued by the work of philosopher G.W.F. Hegel, Marx earned a degree in philosophy, but found his atheism precluded his employment as a teacher. Turning to journalism and political radicalism, Marx ultimately ended up in Paris, where he met Friedrich Engels, the radical son of a prosperous industrialist. In London the two developed an intellectual relationship of tremendous consequence as they sought to analyze the social and economic injustices that attended the industrial revolution. Together they authored the *Communist Manifesto*, its publication in early 1848 coinciding with a wave of revolution that swept the continent. Remaining largely unknown to all but a few for several decades,

the brief document contained both dubious assertions and memorable phrases.

Though Marx and Engels erred in asserting that "a spectre is haunting Europe—the spectre of communism," they produced a moving call to action. "Let the ruling classes tremble at the Communist revolution," the manifesto warned. "The proletarians have nothing to lose but their chains. They have a world to win. Working men of all countries, unite!" The bulk of the pamphlet was given over to an explanation of how and why this triumph of the proletariat was to occur. The foundation for Marxian analysis was the theory of historical or dialectical materialism, which held that material, or economic, relationships were the primary determinant of change. Arguing that "the history of all hitherto existing society is the history of class struggles," Marx and Engels observed that even as Roman patricians had been supplanted by feudal nobility, new productive forces had brought about the decline of this land-owning aristocracy and the rise of an industrial bourgeoisie. Industrial capitalism in turn gave birth to an industrial working class, which would be "the gravediggers" of the capitalist class, driven to revolution by their growing degradation in the course of capitalism's development. As each dominant class inevitably developed the political, social and cultural institutions to serve its needs, these too would be supplanted by new forms as a new class gained predominance. Hence, in the aftermath of the revolution, the working classes would establish a "dictatorship of the proletariat" to establish the rudiments of the new socialist society. Ultimately, this phase would be followed by a "withering away"of the state and the realization of an equitable, classless "communist" society.

Marx offered greater elaboration on these concepts and others in such works as *Capital*

(1867), by which point "scientific socialism" was already attracting enthusiastic adherents. The historical and analytical framework of Marxist socialism, together with its powerful argument for the inevitability of socialist victory, drew members to the International Working Men's Association (1864), a broad organization created to serve proletarian interests. This "First International" proved short lived, but by the time of Marx's death in 1883, socialist political parties were growing in size and influence in much of Europe, but especially in Germany and France. A frequent source of internal division was the question of how socialism was to be realized; while the purists argued for strict adherence to the concept of overthrowing the capitalist order through revolution, revisionists maintained that socialism could be brought about in an evolutionary and democratic manner by broadening the franchise and working through existing institutions. Whatever their disagreements, socialists generally disdained liberalism as a middle-class ideology dedicated to preserving the status quo and unwilling to effectively use the power of the state to rectify social and economic injustices. Indeed, the corollary to the diminishing appeal of liberalism among working-class Europeans was the growing appeal of socialism. As an ideology that acknowledged the primacy of class over national identity, socialism also encouraged internationalism over nationalism, and socialists were among the more vociferous critics of war and imperialism, both of which were seen as serving the interests of capitalism. As of 1900, socialism was established as a significant political force in Europe; by the outbreak of the First World War, Germany's Social Democratic Party was the largest party in the Reichstag, and the growth of socialist strength in France, Italy and Britain were

suggestive of the influence the ideology would have in the new century.

EUROPE'S GREAT POWERS: POLITICAL STRUCTURES

Among the western powers, constitutionalism and political democracy were most advanced in Great Britain. Britain's constitutional monarchy, in which power was shared by the crown and Parliament, had evolved over the course of centuries, during which the respective authority of each was gradually defined. By 1900, the monarchy, though venerated, was no longer the powerful political institution it had once been. In the aftermath of the Glorious Revolution of 1688 and the subsequent constitutional settlement, British monarchs exercised increasingly circumscribed authority, while the locus of power shifted to Parliament and especially the House of Commons. The gradual democratization of the political system, set in motion by the Reform Bill of 1832, accelerated in the second half of the nineteenth century with the passage of acts that further broadened suffrage in 1867 and 1884. The introduction of the secret ballot and the end of property qualifications for members of Parliament (MPs) furthered the process of democratization as the House of Commons was transformed into a more truly representative body. The increasing strength of the popular voice in British politics was affirmed in 1911 with the passage of an act that relegated the largely hereditary House of Lords to an increasingly marginal role. After 1911, the Lords could not veto money bills and retained only suspensive power over other acts passed by the Commons.

These reforms came about through a party system dominated by the Liberal and Con-

Map 1–1 Europe

servative parties, both of which contributed to the democratization of national politics between 1867 and 1911. The Conservatives, as their name implied, were more comfortable with a slower pace of change, and were generally more reluctant to grant the state a role in dealing with the social and economic problems that accompanied the Second Industrial Revolution. The Liberals were willing to concede the need for moderate state intervention in those areas and were more receptive to the advance of political democracy. Both parties faced new challenges after 1906, when socialists, trade unionists and disaffected Liberals came together to form the Labour party, which sought reforms of wider scope and at a greater pace than the other two parties. One major influence in the Labour party was Fabian socialism, which held that democratic socialism could be brought about gradually through the existing system. Though the Labour party never threatened the Liberal parliamentary majority that was established following elections in 1906, it continued to make considerable inroads among Britain's working classes.

The dominant party through 1918, the Liberals faced daunting challenges in dealing with the major issues of social and political reform, imperialism and Irish home rule. One of the most troublesome issues was women's suffrage, a movement that gained growing momentum following Emmeline Pankhurst's founding of the Women's Social and Political Union in 1903. English "suffragettes," a derisive term affixed by opponents, proved more than willing to use direct action and violence in pursuit of the right to vote, assaulting government officials, going on window-smashing sprees in shopping districts and burning railroad cars. Politicians, Liberal and otherwise, were generally dismissive of activities that

they characterized as vandalism. But the Liberals also had problems with the "Irish Question." A home rule bill was in the final stages of consideration when war broke out in the summer of 1914. After much debate, Parliament passed a bill that delayed home rule until the end of the war. Though the Liberal party had been a vital instrument of change for the previous half century, the limitations of the Liberal vision were becoming evident in the way the party handled both old and new issues. Regardless of the periodic inadequacies of its political leaders and system, Great Britain entered the new century as a stable, prosperous nation that had long before accepted the utility of gradual, peaceful change within the framework of a historical constitutional tradition.

For France, the three decades prior to 1900 proved turbulent. Defeated in the Franco-Prussia War of 1870, the Second Empire of Napoleon III collapsed, leaving in its wake a nation that was deeply divided politically. Following the capitulation and the proclamation of the Third Republic, hasty elections produced a National Assembly dominated by monarchists, who accepted Germany's severe peace terms. Popular resentment of the treaty fed into radical and republican hatred of the monarchist-dominated government, leading to the outbreak of virtual civil war in Paris by mid-March 1871. Radicals there declared the Paris Commune of 1871, an autonomous municipal government modeled on its 1792 predecessor. Following a siege, government troops entered the city and savagely suppressed the Communards, who were responsible for considerable atrocities of their own. Some 25,000 Parisians died before the fighting ended in May, and the event embittered French political life for decades. By the mid-1870s, monarchist representation in the National Assembly had eroded considerably, and in 1875, after much wrangling, a somewhat ambiguous republican constitution was approved, providing for a bicameral legislature, a cabinet and premier responsible to the legislature and a nominal presidency. One structural weakness that became apparent with time was the relative weakness of the executive, which together with a lack of party discipline and responsibility, contributed to frequent changes of government (43 between 1890 and 1914). A broad range of small political parties emerged, often representing narrowly defined economic or class interests and finely nuanced ideological distinctions. Many republicans gravitated to the Radical or Radical-Socialist parties, while the small but active Socialist party drew support from rural areas and the urban working class. These parties were often galvanized in defense of the Third Republic against those elements that were never thoroughly reconciled to secular republican government: conservatives, monarchists, Bonapartists, the officer corps of the French Army and the Catholic Church. As long as these anti-republican forces remained politically influential, the future of the Third Republic was problematic.

Two major crises had the ultimate effect of securing France's republican government by the early twentieth century. The Boulanger Affair of early 1889 grew out of the desire of anti-republican forces for a restoration of a traditional, conservative regime and a war of revenge against Germany. A former minister of war, General Georges Boulanger, gained growing popularity on the French right and following his strong showing in a Paris by-election seemed positioned to lead a coup against the Republic. Inexplicably, Boulanger lost his nerve at the last moment

and fled the country, thus ending the immediate threat.

A more serious and divisive episode began in 1894, when Captain Alfred Dreyfus, a Jewish general staff officer, was convicted of treason by a secret court-martial, largely on the basis of circumstantial evidence. The subsequent national debate over the "Dreyfus Affair" exposed the deep ideological division in France. Supporters of the Republic argued that Dreyfus, who was transported to the infamous penal colony at Devil's Island, was a victim of anti-Semitism, anti-republican sentiment and the army's determination to protect its public image without regard for justice. The "Anti-Dreyfusards" attacked Dreyfus as a traitorous Jew and denounced his defenders for undermining the prestige of the army. The naturalist writer Emil Zola leaped into the fray with his famous newspaper article *"J'accuse!"* in which he condemned the army and government for perpetuating a cover-up. Eventually, new evidence suggested that the real spy was a Catholic officer, but a second trial saw Dreyfus convicted again, though he was finally granted a presidential pardon. The Dreyfus case badly divided the French nation, but it also awakened republicans to the persistent threat from the right and strengthened anticlericalism. In consequence, the army was purged of high-ranking anti-republican officers, strengthening its political reliability and commitment to the Third Republic. The influence of the Catholic Church, long a concern of republicans, was greatly reduced by a 1905 law that formally separated church and state, thus diminishing the Church's role in education. In the decade before the First World War, with the Third Republic clearly secured, French political life moderated considerably, though the nation still faced numerous social and economic issues emanating from a growing industrial sector and the increasing challenge presented by international affairs.

Compared to Britain and France, Imperial Germany was a new nation, born in the course of the wars of unification that ended in 1871. That year, the Second Reich and the German Emperor William I were proclaimed in a ceremony in the Hall of Mirrors at Versailles. The twenty-five states of Imperial Germany spanned much of north central Europe, encompassing a large population and extensive commercial, industrial and agricultural resources. The governmental structure of the new Germany owed much to the influence of the Imperial Chancellor, Otto von Bismarck, who had played a central role in the process of unification. An East Prussian aristocrat, or *Junker*, Bismarck was an ardent opponent of liberalism and was determined to model the new German political order on that of the conservative Kingdom of Prussia. His success was evident in the structure of united Germany which, though nominally a constitutional monarchy, was fundamentally authoritarian. The new constitution established a bicameral legislature, comprised of the Bundesrat, the upper house in which the states were represented, and the Reichstag, a lower house elected through universal male suffrage. The authority of the Reichstag was, however, severely limited. Government ministers, such as the chancellor (a post that Bismarck held until 1890), were not responsible to the legislature, but rather to the emperor, in whose hands real power rested. The emperor, who was also King of Prussia, retained ultimate authority over internal administration, foreign policy and the military.

Though Imperial Germany's constitutional structure was little more than a façade, a variety of parties representing ideological, economic, regional and religious constituencies emerged. Whereas the Conservative and National Liberal parties generally represented the right, the Progressives and Social Democrats (SPD) drew support from the left. The Center party grew out of the controversy surrounding Bismarck's *Kulturkampf*, or "struggle for civilization" in the 1870s. In order to strengthen national unity within the new empire, Bismarck sought to assert the state's primary claim to the individual's loyalty, which brought him into conflict with the Catholic Church. During the early 1870s, Bismarck undertook a variety of measures aimed at weakening the authority of the Church, which was especially influential in Catholic south Germany. Ironically, one consequence of this *Kulturkampf* was the growth of the Center party, which appealed specifically to Catholics. Forsaking this failed effort, Bismarck next turned his efforts against the Social Democrats, whose growing strength threatened the conservative majority in the Reichstag. Using two attempts to assassinate the emperor as a pretext, Bismarck pressured the Reichstag to pass legislation that effectively denied socialists basic civil liberties and drove the SPD underground. When these measures failed to diminish the socialist appeal, Bismarck moved to preempt socialist proposals in the 1880s, sponsoring bills for compulsory health insurance, accident insurance and an old age and disability pension plan. A cynical and manipulative politician, Bismarck ultimately ran afoul of the brash young emperor William II, who came to the throne in 1888. The two clashed over domestic and foreign policy issues and the emperor, who dismissed Bismarck in 1890, inevitably won the war of egos.

Bismarck's departure coincided with a period in which domestic issues were increasingly overshadowed by those arising from the imperial race and international rivalry. An alliance of Conservatives, National Liberals and the Center party ensured a conservative majority in the Reichstag and even the Social Democrats were unable to resist the rising tide of nationalism that legitimized colonial expansionism and militarism. These same years also brought a new anti-Semitic undercurrent to German politics, as Conservatives equated Jews with liberalism and socialism. Even as the industrial and military strength of Imperial Germany grew, the consequences of a weak liberal tradition and a distorted constitutional structure became more evident. In an increasingly dangerous age, major policy decisions were made by a small group of men around a narcissistic emperor whose judgments could not be effectively challenged at any level of government. The inadequacies of this system would become apparent after 1914.

The Austro-Hungarian Empire, during the second half of the nineteenth century, confronted the challenge of governing a multinational, multilingual population. Comprised of what remained of the defunct Holy Roman Empire, the Habsburg domains included Austria, Hungary, Bohemia, Moravia, Galicia and Croatia. These territories boasted a few urban centers with modest industries, but also vast rural expanses with large peasant populations. Franz Joseph, emperor since 1848, experimented with a number of administrative methods until 1866, when defeat in the Austro-Prussian War forced a reexamination of the empire's governmental structure. Subsequently, the *Ausgleich,* or compromise of 1867, created the Dual Monarchy, in which Hungary and Austria maintained separate constitutions, parliaments and administrations. Franz Joseph ruled as Emperor of Austria and King of Hungary. Though autonomous in all but military and diplomatic affairs, Hungary remained resentful of Austrian dominance and the Magyars, the domi-

nant ethnic group, proved periodically troublesome. Within the Austrian realms, the most consistent problem grew out of the nationalistic sentiments of Czechs, Poles and other minorities, who were resentful of the "Germanization" of education and administration. The other major threat, as seen from the emperor's perspective, was liberalism and the democratization of politics. The conservative Austrian constitution mitigated against both, as the parliament, or Reichsrat, had limited powers and representation based in part on a national quota system, which precluded the development of broad-based parties.

In 1879, Count Edward von Taaffe, the adept new chancellor, began constructing a parliamentary coalition that would resolve both problems. Promising national concessions to the Czechs and Poles if they would support the conservatives, Taaffe created an anti-liberal alliance known as the "Iron Ring." This proved a temporary solution at best as, following Taaffe's resignation in 1893, these stubborn difficulties resurfaced. The introduction of universal male suffrage in 1907 only complicated the task of governance, as more demands for national autonomy were voiced in the Reichsrat. Having pursued no principle other than attempting to preserve the status quo and "muddling through," the imperial government increasingly resorted to the expedient of rule by decree. On the eve of the First World War, the Austro-Hungarian Empire was an unstable anachronism, uniquely vulnerable to the multiple stresses that war would bring.

Imperial Russia was a vast country spanning two continents, largely the consequence of the expansionist policies of the Romanov dynasty that had ruled for nearly 300 years. Throughout this period, tsarist autocracy remained one of the major constants of Russian life as even in the final years of the nineteenth century, Russia lacked a constitution, representative institutions and political parties. Though Alexander II (1855–1881) had initiated some reforms, most notably the abolition of serfdom, his assassination brought a return of authoritarian government and oppressive policies under his successor Alexander III (1881–1894). As Russia lacked any channels for the legitimate expression of political dissent, those opposition groups that did emerge, usually consisting of students and intellectuals, were inevitably driven to advocate radical and violent ideologies of change. In the 1870s, many reformers were drawn to populism, which held that a socialist society could be brought about by Russia's rural peasant masses, which constituted the overwhelming majority of the population. Others, driven to desperation by the brutality of the immense tsarist police apparatus and the unlikelihood of change within the system, gravitated toward anarchism and nihilism, ideologies that justified violence and terror to destroy the existing order.

The accession of Nicholas II in 1894 promised only the continuation of autocratic rule. Consistently described by modern biographers as "stupid," Nicholas was a stubborn man who was intent on preserving tsarist prerogatives and thus failed to appreciate the growing pressures for reform. When imperial issues led to war with Japan in 1905, the accumulated stresses, compounded by a series of military and naval disasters, exploded into revolution, with rioting and fighting in St. Petersburg and other major cities. Even as the government sought a negotiated end to the Russo-Japanese War, Nicholas grudgingly issued the October Manifesto, which established the rudiments of a constitutional monarchy. In addition to creating the Duma, a representative assembly to be elected by universal male suffrage, the Manifesto guaranteed basic civil freedoms. While political parties were technically legal, and the liberal Constitutional Democrats were tolerated, radical parties such as the Marxist Russian Social Democratic Labor Party were suppressed. Within a short span of time it became clear that the Duma would have little real authority and that Nicholas intended to preserve his autocratic powers as much as possible. His chief minister, Peter Stolypin, moved to destroy the revolutionary movement through arrests, jail, exile and executions. Stolypin also sought to win over the peasant masses through a series of reforms in following years, but was assassinated by a radical in 1911. Clearly, the cosmetic changes of 1905 had not reconciled either reformers or radicals to the tsarist regime. In the years to come, war and revolution would sorely test the allegiance of a broader segment of the population.

Italy, once dismissed by the Austrian chief minister Klemens von Metternich as "a geographical expression," was clearly more than that by the late nineteenth century. Unified through war and diplomatic adroitness between 1859 and 1870, modern Italy took shape as a constitutional monarchy ruled by the House of Savoy. Though victorious in their primary goal, nationalists still faced a considerable challenge in instilling a sense of national unity and common identity among a people who were divided by geography, tradition and even language. Largely rural, parochial and illiterate in 1860, the Italian populace was an unlikely foundation on which to rest an experiment in representative government. The Vatican's refusal to acknowledge the legitimacy of the newly united Italy, together with the threat of excommunication for those who participated in politics, posed an additional challenge. While Italy's growing population itself justified an arguable claim to stature as a great power, the general lack of natural resources and industrial capacity ensured that recognition as a major power would always remain more of an aspiration than a reality.

These two realities were decisive in shaping the evolution of Italian national politics. The parliamentary system rested on an exceedingly small electorate, which meant little real popular participation in politics and the development of political parties that were not particularly attentive to the general populace. To a large degree, Italy's multitude of political parties became the instruments of a class of professional politicians who were far more interested in preserving their own power and influence than in dealing effectively with the nation's social and economic problems. Self-interest rather than principle guided parties and their leaders; distinctions of right and left were often meaningless. Consequently, parliamentary politics were characterized by a process called *transformismo*, by which the same political groups, sometimes slightly reconstituted, retained office year after year through bribery and influence peddling. This pattern was altered somewhat by premier Francesco Crispi, who sought to turn the nation's attention to imperial expansion late in the century. Italy's initial bid for status as a military power proved an embarrassing failure when Italian troops were badly defeated at Adowa by Ethiopian tribesmen. The government's inattention to needed social and economic reforms provoked growing unrest and radicalism by the end of the century, as Marxism and anarchism gained adherents among urban workers. Rising political tensions culminated with the assassination of King Humbert by an anarchist in 1900. The leadership of Giovanni Giolitti, who desired to modernize Italy's economic life, restored some balance to Italian politics but his efforts too depended on the perpetuation of *transformismo*. In the last years before the war, the growing influence of radical Socialism together with the rise of aggressive nationalism brought a new volatility to Italian politics. This polarization only intensified in the aftermath of the war, when it became clear that Italian expansionist ambitions had not been fulfilled. The postwar years brought the final crisis of parliamentary government in Italy.

THE EUROPEAN PERIPHERY

On the Iberian Peninsula, Spain's decline from great power status, which had begun in the seventeenth century, went unarrested. Poor in resources and predominantly rural, Spain had few industrial centers. Though a constitutional monarchy, Spain was effectively ruled by a small group of landowners and industrialists, whose conservative perspective was shared by the business classes, the military and the Catholic Church. Against this alliance, urban workers, artisans and intellectuals could wield little influence. In the Cortes, Spain's parliament, a system similar to *transformismo* ensured that the Liberal and Conservative parties would govern alternately and avoid change. Decades of political stagnation drove the disaffected to radical ideologies such as anarchism. The breakdown of this agreement in the early twentieth century was followed by a wave of sometimes-violent political protest that exposed the deep divisions between the forces for order and those for reform. Given the tremendous obstacles in the path of peaceful reform, Spain faced a difficult future.

Similar social and economic conditions existed in Portugal, where a dictatorial monarchy had been overthrown in 1910 and re-placed by a republic. Caught between reactionary forces and radical urban workers, the liberals who supported the republic likewise looked to an uncertain future.

To the north, the Scandinavian countries provide a study in contrast. Sweden modernized and industrialized fairly rapidly during the late 1800s with a minimum of social friction. Parliamentary government evolved rapidly in this constitutional monarchy, which consented to the independence of Norway in 1905. Both Norway and Denmark were monarchies with representative institutions and few internal problems.

The Netherlands, Belgium and Switzerland had all developed as stable, prosperous nations by this time. By comparison, social, political and economic conditions in eastern and southeastern Europe, were considerably less advanced. Rumania and Bulgaria remained economically undeveloped, with largely rural peasant populations engaged in agriculture and political systems that excluded significant popular participation. Similar conditions prevailed in the small and generally impoverished nations of the Balkan peninsula.

Once among the great powers, the Ottoman Empire was derogated as "the sick man of Europe" by the late nineteenth century. Ruled by the Ottoman dynasty since the fourteenth century, this Muslim empire stretched north from Anatolia deep into the Balkans and south through the Middle East, the Arabian Peninsula and across north Africa. Bypassed by the Scientific and Industrial Revolutions, Ottoman Turkey had been increasingly unable to effectively contest the military power of the West during the 1800s. Turkish reformers, humiliated by their country's weakness, imposed a western-style constitution on the Ottoman sultan in 1876, but

within a few years it was revoked. Ottoman territorial deterioration continued, especially in the Balkans, and in 1908 members of the Committee for Union and Progress, largely civil servants and army officers, launched the "Young Turk" revolt, which demanded the restoration of the constitution as a prelude to administrative, economic and military modernization. Sultan Abdul-Hamid II conceded and the Ottoman Empire in essence bought a few more years. The First World War created the circumstances that led to the dismemberment of the Ottoman Empire and the founding of modern Turkey.

THE EUROPEAN BALANCE OF POWER

For four decades after the end of the Napoleonic Wars in 1815, the major powers, joined together as the Concert of Europe, worked to preserve the European order. This arrangement, weakened by disagreements as early as the 1820s, finally collapsed in the aftermath of the Crimean War, which sundered relations between Concert members. The dissolution of the Concert opened the path for Italian and German unification, events significantly altering the future balance of power. A new diplomatic order evolved slowly, shaped in large part by the German Chancellor Otto von Bismarck. Primarily concerned with securing the new German nation and preserving the status quo, Bismarck saw little threat from Great Britain, which was continuing a policy of "splendid isolation" that included avoiding unnecessary entanglement in continental affairs. In France, however, anti-German sentiments ran high following France's defeat and loss of Alsace-Lorraine in the 1870 war, and Bismarck concluded that Germany's security was contingent on keeping France diplomatically isolated. This led the "Iron Chancellor" to construct the "Bismarckian system," a system of informal agreements and formal treaties linking the three conservative empires: Germany, Russia and Austria-Hungary. Perhaps the most challenging aspect of Bismarck's diplomacy was maintaining amiable relations between the two eastern empires, as there was potential for conflict between Russian and Habsburg interests in the Balkans, where the continuing recession of Ottoman influence was an open invitation to meddling and intervention.

The early cornerstone of the Bismarckian system was the Three Emperors' League (1873), by which the three powers pledged to aid one another if attacked. Earlier joint talks had already led to an agreement to suppress revolutionary activity and maintain the status quo. The Russo-Turkish War (1877–1878), in which the Russian army sided with Rumanian, Bulgarian, Serb and Montenegrin rebels against the Turks, tested the viability of the League. In return for accepting Russian intervention in the Balkans, the Austrians were to be granted administrative control over the two previously Ottoman territories of Bosnia and Herzegovina. Though any Russian–Austrian disputes were thus resolved, objections from the great powers over the size of the newly independent Bulgaria resulted in the Congress of Berlin (1878), where Bismarck proclaimed his intentions of acting as an "honest broker" between interested parties. Decisions made at the conference dashed Russian hopes for influence on the Balkan Peninsula through a large Bulgaria, while stifling the aspirations of many Balkan peoples. Ultimately, Austria's effortless gain and Russia's thwarted hopes led to some enmity between the two. In response to Austrian concerns, the Dual Alliance was formalized in

1879, committing Germany and Austria to mutual defense if attacked by Russia. In an effort to again solidify the foundations of the system, Bismarck won a formal extension of the Three Emperors' League in 1881. The following year, Italian antagonism against France brought Italy into alliance with Germany and Austria, creating the Triple Alliance. Seeking to quell growing Russian suspicions, Bismarck formulated the complex Reinsurance Treaty (1887), which spelled out the specific circumstances in which two powers would remain neutral or go to war. A master diplomatist, Bismarck forged and maintained a complex alliance system that helped preserve international stability for nearly twenty years. His system unraveled rapidly following his dismissal in 1890, marking the advent of a new era of international instability, characterized by the emergence of new, antagonistic alliance systems and increasingly dangerous confrontations over colonial issues.

The New Imperialism and the Non-western World

Joseph Chamberlain, Great Britain's Secretary of State for Colonies, made an observation in 1904 that must have seemed obvious to his European contemporaries. "The age of small nations has long passed away," he asserted in a speech in Birmingham. "The day of Empires has come." Indeed, the triumph of the imperial idea seemed self-evident at the turn of the century. Four great empires dominated the European continent and Britain, an island empire, could credibly claim domination of the world's oceans. Beyond Europe, a tremendous portion of the world's land surface had come under imperial domination, directly or otherwise. At the dawning of the new century, an imperial world order promised stability, order and prosperity for colonizers and colonized alike.

THE NEW IMPERIALISM

Beginning in the 1880s, many European nations embarked on a new quest for empire. This imperial episode had greater scope and character than the initial struggle for empire that unfolded in the sixteenth century. In many cases, direct administrative rule that brought with it basic European social, political and cultural conceptions was imposed over foreign territories and populations of considerable size.

Inevitably, the transplantation of the rudiments of western civilization into non-western societies had profound, sometimes disruptive, consequences. European powers introduced western methods of production and manufacturing into colonial territories, drawing native peoples into wage labor and market economies, with a subsequent disruption of traditional economic patterns. Some historians cite these aspects of the new imperialism as contributing to the gradual "westernization" or "Europeanization" of the world in the course of the twentieth century.

A number of forces drove this imperial rush beginning in the 1880s. General economic distress beginning in the 1870s gave added weight to the argument that Europe needed new sources of raw materials and new markets for manufactured goods and capital investment. Increasing industrial competition between the major powers, which was part of a more general international rivalry that increased in intensity as the nineteenth century drew to a close, further bolstered the economic argument for empire. The quest for status was an integral part of this international competition. It was

generally accepted that empire was the ultimate testimony to national progress and development.

Imperialism was also given force by a general European tendency to see the world as divided between civilized and barbaric nations, so defined by the level of their material and cultural development. Many believed that the more advanced nations had an obligation to civilize and "lift up" backward peoples. Social Darwinism and "scientific racialism," both of which shaped the late nineteenth-century European perspective, gave this outlook further credence. More specific concepts such as Anglo-Saxonism asserted that the hegemony of northern European people was the natural consequence of their superior intelligence, morality and industry. This melange of ideas produced paradoxical impulses and the new imperialism was often inconsistent in intent and implementation, sometimes exhibiting a humanitarian face and at other times one of ruthless exploitation.

One striking aspect of the new imperialism was the scope of its reach. In the last quarter of the nineteenth century, vast expanses of the globe came under European control, including virtually all of Africa, the Pacific and much of south and Southeast Asia. During these years, the combined territorial gains of Britain, France, Germany, Italy and Belgium approached ten million square miles. Several factors help explain the relative ease and scope of these astounding imperial gains. Technological superiority played a major role, as Europeans employed new transportation and military technologies in the quest for empire. Steam power permitted the long-distance transportation of military forces by ship and their rapid deployment in colonial territories by train, thus giving imperial powers the capability of projecting their military power much farther than in past eras.

Advances in weapons technology gave Europeans a marked advantage over indigenous peoples, most notably through the development of rapid-fire rifles, machine guns (called Maxim guns at the time) and light artillery. The advantage afforded by superior military technology was dramatically demonstrated at the Battle of Omdurman in 1898, where British forces defeated a Sudanese Mahdist army. Some 11,000 Mahdists (followers of the Mahdi, an Islamic fundamentalist) fell before British machine guns; British dead numbered 28. Events such as Omdurman were undoubtedly behind the popular imperialist jingle: "Whatever happens/ we have got/ the Maxim gun, / and they have not."

European conquest was also facilitated by the distinctions between European political structures and those throughout much of the non-western world. In Europe, fully mature, stable nation-states were capable of marshalling and projecting considerable economic and military power. In Africa, where the imposition of European rule was most dramatic, weak and transient tribal governments were vulnerable to subversion and co-optation, as Europeans often successfully employed a "divide and rule" strategy. The weak and decaying monarchies of Asia, unable to mobilize effective military resources, proved incapable of resisting European demands.

Yet another development facilitating imperial expansion was the discovery of new drugs and vaccines that made it possible for Europeans to explore and settle in regions that were previously inaccessible because of disease organisms. Diseases that once served as natural biological defense mechanisms by keeping Europeans out were gradually overcome in the late nineteenth century, leaving the once-forbidding African interior and other areas more vulnerable to foreign penetration. Together, these developments greatly facilitated the realization of Europe's renewed imperial ambitions.

THE SCRAMBLE FOR AFRICA

The most spectacular example of imperial expansion took place in Africa during the last quarter of the nineteenth century. European interest in Africa went back to the fifteenth century, when explorers, usually Portuguese, began making tentative voyages down the West African coast, finally rounding the southern cape and proceeding on into the Indian and Pacific Oceans. The slave trade, which flourished until the early nineteenth century, brought continual though limited contact between European and African peoples. With few exceptions, however, Europeans remained familiar only with the coastal periphery of the huge African landmass. Though vast in size, the African continent was relatively sparsely populated, with Africans accounting for only 6.75% of the world population in 1901. Geography and climate played major roles in shaping African civilization, with the Sahara desert serving as a major barrier between the largely Arab and Islamic societies along the southern Mediterranean rim and up the Nile Valley and those of largely black sub-Saharan Africa. Social institutions, political structures and economic patterns varied greatly across the continent, determined largely by environmental factors such as topography, rainfall and soil. African peoples were thus variously hunters and gatherers, sedentary agriculturalists, herders, nomads or artisans. Along Africa's northern and eastern coasts, commerce with Europe and Asia respectively fostered societies built on trade and the skills it required. Well into the nineteenth century, however, much of

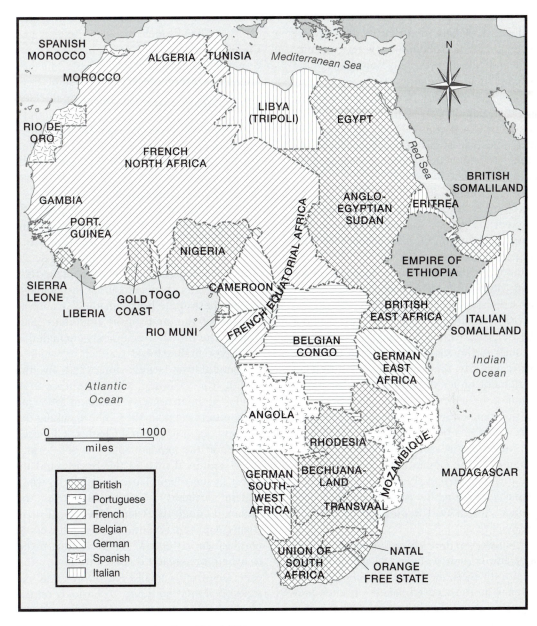

Map 1–2 Africa before the First World War

the African interior remained *terra incognito* for Europeans. Beginning in the 1860s, however, the exploratory expeditions of a few venturesome individuals awakened Europeans to the potential riches of "darkest Africa."

Henry M. Stanley became known to the world as the man who "found" the long-missing English missionary David Livingstone on the shores of Lake Tanganyika in 1871, but Stanley's greater importance grew out of his belief that the "unpeopled country" he had crossed during his search offered great opportunities for development and exploitation. A cruel man who casually murdered the Africans he encountered in the course of subsequent explorations of the Congo River, Stanley concluded that the peoples of the region could be easily subjugated because of tribal divisions and lack of effective weapons. In 1878 Stanley met with Leopold II, King of the Belgians, who had been actively seeking colonial territories, and agreed to return to Africa and lay the foundations for Belgian settlement under the auspices of Leopold's grandiosely named International Association for the Exploration and Civilization of Africa. Essentially a corporate enterprise established to profit from the ivory trade and raw rubber production, the Congo Free State, as it was eventually known, was not technically a Belgian colony during the first decades of its existence, but rather the personal property of Leopold II.

Stanley was quickly followed by others who also hoped to stake a claim to Africa's wealth. In 1880, the French naval officer Savorgnan de Brazza established a French protectorate in the Congo region. The German adventurer and entrepreneur Karl Peters was instrumental in establishing a German presence in East Africa during the same period, which led Bismarck to reevaluate his earlier opposition to African colonies. The German chancellor sponsored the Berlin Conference of 1884–1885, which resolved Belgian and French claims in the Congo and opened the Congo River to international access. The conferees also attempted to establish some basic guidelines for colonization. By 1885, the German government lent its protection to Peters' commercial venture in Tanganyika, which soon became German East Africa. In the following years, Germany's African empire expanded to include German Southwest Africa, the Cameroons and Togoland.

While the path to African empire was sometimes established by individual adventurers, broader foreign policy concerns drove European nations into Africa. Britain's declaration of a protectorate over Egypt in 1882 followed years of concern about the financial recklessness of the Egyptian khedive and the security of the strategically important Suez Canal. The British were quickly entangled in an Egyptian–Sudanese conflict in which a fundamentalist Islamic force led by the Mahdi (or "Chosen One") defeated an Anglo-Egyptian army at Khartoum following a ten-month siege in 1885. The shocking defeat and death of General Charles "Chinese" Gordon at the hands of the Mahdi's "primitive" soldiers dismayed the British, and interest in the region lapsed until 1895, when Britain declared a protectorate over the Sudan. Though the Mahdi was dead, British troops wreaked revenge on his followers at Omdurman in 1898. With the Islamic revolt smashed, the greater threat to Britain's interests came from a small French force that had trekked across the desert to Fashoda on the Upper Nile. A major international clash was barely avoided before France agreed to acknowledge British claims to the Sudan.

Though Britain established a presence on the West African coast (Sierra Leone, the Gold Coast and later Nigeria) and the east coast (Kenya), the greater British ambition in Africa was summarized as the "Cape to Cairo" vision, which foresaw a belt of British colonies extending from Egypt to Cape Colony. Though Dutch settlers known as Boers had settled south Africa in the seventeenth century, the British established themselves as the dominant presence in Capetown during the Napoleonic Wars, leading most Boers to move north in the "Great Trek" of 1835 and found the Orange Free State, the Transvaal and Natal on the southeastern coast. In the following years, Britain's annexation of Natal and Transvaal (later granted independence as the South African Republic) fueled Anglo–Boer hatred, and both groups were often in conflict with native Africans. British victory in the Zulu Wars of the late 1870s marked the advent of a new era in which English colonial ambitions expanded, driven in large part by the English diamond magnate Cecil Rhodes. An ardent imperialist, Rhodes was the guiding genius behind the "Cape to Cairo" vision, who founded Rhodesia in 1889 and became prime minister of Cape Colony in 1890. His determination to drive the Boers from the land he desired led to the ill-fated Jameson Raid of 1895 in which an English raiding party was defeated by Boers, and his resignation, which an embarrassed British government demanded. The animosity between English and Dutch settlers did not diminish, however, and in 1899 war broke out. The Boer War dragged on until 1902, when British forces prevailed through sheer force of numbers. In 1910, the disparate peoples and states were joined together as the Union of South Africa.

French influence in Africa was first established in Algeria, which French forces gradually subdued between 1830 and 1869. French imperial ambitions were driven not only by the usual desire for economic gain, but also by the need to reassert France's claim to great power status after being defeated in the Franco-Prussian War. France annexed Tunisia in 1881 and made Morocco a protectorate in 1912. France's northwestern African empire was joined to vast claims in West Africa, which stretched from Senegal on Africa's west coast to French Equatorial Africa, which abutted the British Sudan. The French Congo and Madagascar provided France with colonial holdings on both the Atlantic and Indian Ocean coasts. While the sparsely populated desert lands were of dubious value, French holdings in West Africa produced a number of exportable crops.

Italy, determined to assert a claim to great power status, joined the scramble for Africa somewhat late and laid claim to Eritrea and Italian Somaliland in the late 1880s. Efforts to compel Abyssinia to accept protectorate status led in 1894 to war, which ended disastrously for Italy. Bismarck's observation that Italy had "a big appetite and bad teeth" was confirmed by the outcome of the battle of Adowa in 1896, in which 6,000 Italian troops were killed by Abyssinian warriors armed with French weapons. Italy's imperial ambitions remained unrequited even after the annexation of Libya in 1912. Among the lesser powers, Spain and Portugal claimed African territories, with Portuguese Angola and Mozambique the most significant.

By the early years of the new century, the scramble for Africa left virtually the entire continent, save for Liberia and Abyssinia, under European control. The consequences for Africans varied, though almost everywhere native peoples were drawn into foreign-dominated market economies that severely disrupted traditional patterns of life and labor. British colonial administration was sometimes relatively benign and in West Africa remained "indirect," with British administrators leaving routine affairs to native chiefs. In Egypt, the British sought to introduce the rudiments of a modern infrastructure, including an efficient bureaucracy, educational reforms and public health measures. Nonetheless, British colonial officials were often dismissive of their colonial subjects as inferior peoples. France, invoking a "civilizing mission," sought to implant French culture and European institutions in some colonies and in general, the French were less racist in their outlook toward Africans.

The impact of European rule was also determined by the degree of European settlement; in both French Algeria and British East Africa, settlers often claimed the best lands and opportunities. In some instances, colonial rule was disastrous for native peoples. In German Southwest Africa, tens of thousands of Africans were driven out of coastal regions and into the Kalahari Desert, where they perished in great numbers.

Unquestionably the most notorious instance of colonial misrule occurred in the Belgian Congo, where King Leopold's determination to wring a profit out of his colony led to policies that created what has been described as an "African holocaust." In order to obtain the desired quantities of raw rubber, colonial authorities implemented a system of forced labor, whereby African men were compelled to search the forests while their families were held hostage; failure to meet quotas resulted in mutilation or death for the hostages. Company guards were empowered to kill Africans for the slightest infraction, real or otherwise, and did so without compunction. Native peoples were driven from their villages and into hiding in the jungle, where death by starvation or disease was common. The horrors in the Belgian Congo inspired Joseph Conrad's shocking novel *Heart of Darkness* and eventually attracted the

attention of journalists, who reported the atrocities to outraged Europeans. Though the scandal ultimately led the Belgian government to assert direct control over the colony, the consequences of decades of brutality were evident in statistics indicating a population loss in the Congo of some ten million people over forty years. A memorable passage in Conrad's *Heart of Darkness* effectively captures this dark side of the imperial impulse: "The conquest of the earth, which mostly means the taking it away from those who have a different complexion or slightly flatter noses than ourselves, is not a pretty thing when you look into it too much."

ASIA IN THE IMPERIAL AGE

Though European nations had established colonial claims in the eastern hemisphere as early as the fifteenth century, a new surge of imperial activity occurred in the last decades of the nineteenth century as Europeans sought greater economic concessions from a weakened China and imposed direct control over much of south and southeast Asia. Though pre-industrial Asian societies varied greatly in many ways, they were generally traditional, often hierarchical, largely agricultural and often ruled by monarchical regimes that did not command effective centralized authority. As in Africa, superior western industrial and military power in the service of European nationalisms allowed for the rapid and extensive imposition of European rule in Asia.

Among the European powers, Great Britain boasted an extensive Asian empire as early as the eighteenth century. Australia, which was being used as a penal colony in the 1780s, gained self-government in 1850 and became a Commonwealth ("the Commonwealth of Australia") in 1901. New

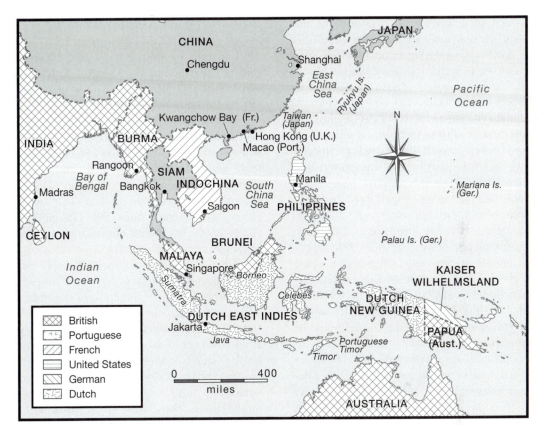

Map 1–3   Imperialism in Asia and the Pacific

Zealand came under British control in 1847 and followed a similar path, receiving dominion status in 1907. It was India, however, that was destined to become "the jewel in the crown." Following the end of the Seven Years' War in 1763, Britain asserted its dominance in India, which was administered for nearly a century by the British East India Company, complete with its own military force. In the early decades of the following century, British rule also was extended southward into Burma, Malaya and northern Borneo. British relations with their Indian subjects were always problematic, especially given the proclivity of some British officials to dismiss the Indians as "wogs," a pejorative term for inferior races from inferior cultures. British efforts to eliminate select Indian traditions that were deemed barbarous, such as *suttee* (the immolation of widows in their husband's funeral pyres) inevitably caused resentment, as did the activities of Christian missionaries. In 1857, festering antipathies sparked the "Great Mutiny," during which both Hindus and Muslims attacked their European oppressors. British forces ultimately suppressed the revolt in savage fashion and in subsequent years the British government assumed increasingly direct control of the colony. British colonial administration was not uniform, but rather evolved to fit local conditions. In India, a viceroy oversaw a system that incorporated upper-class Indians as low-level bureaucrats.

Under the British *Raj* (prince, or rule), Indians did benefit from a number of improvements and reforms. Railroads, telegraphs and postal service improved transportation and communication; an educational system was established to serve upper-class children. Public health and sanitation were also concerns of the colonial government. Ironically, the introduction of western ideas through the educational system fed Indian nationalism, which manifested itself in the Indian National Congress (1885). Open to both Hindus and Muslims, the organization demanded self-government for Indians and achieved its first major victory with the passage of the Indian Councils Act (1909), which allowed for a limited male franchise and gave Indians a political voice through elective bodies at the provincial and central government levels. A religious rift threatened Indian nationalism, as Muslims feared that self-government might condemn them to a permanent minority status. The All-India Muslim League (1906) advocated separate elections for the two religious communities, a right granted by the Indian Councils Act. Whatever their differences, Hindus and Muslims alike continued to press for self-government, convinced that British rule served British interests to the detriment of all Indians.

Already well-established on the Indian subcontinent, by the 1830s the British were inevitably attracted to the potential commercial opportunities to be had in China. An ancient civilization ruled by a succession of imperial dynasties for two thousand years,

China was clearly in decline during the final decades of the Manchu dynasty. Lacking a modern military, industrial base and effective central government, China could do little to resist the demands of western powers determined to wring economic concessions from the decaying Asian empire. British commercial interests, desiring access to Chinese silk and tea, discovered the utility of opium as a trade commodity in the 1830s and, when Chinese officials banned the narcotic, British authorities in China authorized military retaliation, which grew into the Opium War (1839–1842). Incapable of resisting western arms, Chinese officials were forced to accept the Treaty of Nanking, by which the British gained access at five new ports and annexed Hong Kong. The continuation of the opium trade under British supervision completed China's humiliation. China's obvious vulnerability led other European powers to demand similar treaty concessions and a second opium war in 1857–1858 ended in China's defeat by a joint Anglo-French force. These humiliations contributed to the outbreak in 1850 of the Taiping Rebellion, a devastating anti-government, anti-foreign uprising that lasted fourteen years and claimed as many as twenty million lives.

By the late nineteenth century, many Chinese were convinced that the Manchus had indeed lost "the Mandate of Heaven," the authority to rule. "Treaty ports" dominated by western powers dotted the Chinese coast and "extraterritoriality" ensured that foreigners charged with crimes could not be tried in Chinese courts. Europe's imperial powers, together with Japan, rushed to carve out "spheres of influence" in which they claimed exclusive commercial privileges. In 1899, the United States, alarmed at the prospect of being excluded from the much-vaunted

"China market" took steps to ensure its inclusion. Secretary of State John Hay's "Open Door" note of that year suggested that the imperial powers agree to keep the China trade open to all on an equal basis. The response was ambiguous, but the determination of the imperial powers to protect their privileged status in China was demonstrated the following year when the Boxer Rebellion broke out. Led by a secret society called the "Fists of Righteous Harmony," (referred to as "Boxers" by the imperial powers), and supported by the aging Dowager Empress Tz'u-hsi, the anti-foreign uprising swept through China. All foreigners and Christians ran the risk of being killed on sight and in Peking, Boxer-led mobs besieged the walled diplomatic compound. In response, an eight-nation international military expedition including U.S. troops was organized to relieve the siege and suppress the rebellion. Generally ill-armed, the Boxers were ultimately overcome by superior western firepower and the empress herself was forced to flee the capital disguised as a peasant woman. A subsequent treaty reaffirming the imperial status quo marked the final humiliation of the Manchu dynasty, which stumbled on for another decade before a revolution swept it away. Of significant long-term consequence was the American response to the rebellion. In 1900, John Hay issued a second Open Door note which, in addition to reaffirming the principles of the earlier note, announced that henceforth, the United States would defend China's administrative and territorial integrity. Unwittingly, Hay set the United States on a collision course with Japan, Asia's rising imperial power.

Japan's course in the nineteenth century stands in stark contrast to that of China. Sheltered by a self-imposed isolation for two centuries, Japan was untouched by the intellectual and economic revolutions that drove modernization in the west. The Japanese emperor was a figurehead of mainly religious significance in a largely feudal, peasant society. A powerful warlord or *shogun* held predominant power, with lesser warlords or *daimyo* ruling at the local level with the support of the *samurai* warrior class. Japanese complacency was dealt a serious blow in 1853 when a squadron of American warships, commanded by Commodore Matthew Perry, steamed into Tokyo Bay to negotiate a treaty establishing basic diplomatic and economic relations with Japan. Perry's "Black Ships," which exemplified the technologies of the industrial age, impressed on the Japanese the superiority of western arms and industry and their own vulnerability in the face of such advantages. The "opening" of Japan was followed by growing political unrest as reformers insisted that fundamental changes had to take place if Japan were to avoid falling victim to western imperialism.

The accession of a new emperor in 1867, followed the next year by the abdication of the shogun, marked the beginnings of the Meiji Restoration, which saw the emperor's political authority restored as a prelude to creating a modern, centralized state. Seeing "westernization" as the key to Japan's future security, the government dispatched numerous missions to Europe and the United States, where they were to take note of those institutions, concepts and technologies that would facilitate the modernization and strengthening of Japan. Consequently, French and later German advisors shaped Japan's modern army, while the British were instrumental in the construction of a modern Japanese battle fleet. Japan's new constitution, which established a parliamentary system, reflected a variety of European precedents. These political changes were imposed from above, however, and lacked a truly democratic foundation. Adeptly utilizing western technology and technicians, Japan's government launched an industrial revolution that quickly made Japan the dominant industrial power in Asia. Within a single generation, Japan was transformed from an insular medieval society to a modern, industrialized nation with significant military capabilities. Anxious to assert her new power, Japan went to war against China in 1894 and wrested some territorial concessions from the dying Manchu empire, leaving some in the West to ponder the potential challenge that the rising Pacific power might pose to western hegemony.

Rudyard Kipling, the poetic voice of imperialism, toured Japan in the course of his travels through the Far East in the late 1890s and expressed his misgivings about an already aggressive Imperial Japan. Noting the remarkably efficient manner in which the Japanese had adapted western innovations to their own purposes, Kipling warned that they were "bad little men who know too much." Within a few years, Japan demonstrated its mastery of the instruments of modern warfare in the Russo-Japanese War, in which Japan's new fleet destroyed the bulk of the Russian navy while its modern army bested inferior Russian troops on the Asian mainland. The Treaty of Portsmouth, which ended the conflict, also marked the beginning of an era in which Japan sought to establish a broad sphere of influence in the Far East. Even as Japan annexed Korea in 1910, Japanese statesmen and military officials alike were increasingly convinced that the major challenge to Japan's imperial ambitions would come from the United States.

Though continental expansion was a central theme of American development in the nineteenth century, significant interest in overseas colonies did not develop until after the Civil War in the late 1860s. In 1867, the same year that Secretary of State William Seward acquired Alaska, the United States also occupied Midway Island in the central Pacific. During the next two decades, the United States claimed several more distant, obscure Pacific outposts, including part of the Samoan Islands. While there was growing pressure from commercial interests to annex Hawaii in the late 1880s, broad enthusiasm for empire did not develop until 1898, when victory in the Spanish-American War presented Americans with the opportunity to lay claim to former Spanish colonies in the Caribbean and the Pacific. The war grew out of American outrage over the policies of Spain's military governor in Cuba, who was faced with suppressing a nationalist insurgency in the mid-1890s. Spanish brutalities against the Cuban populace, sensationalized in the U.S. press, fueled popular demands that President William McKinley compel Spain to accept the Cuban demand for self-government. Influential individuals such as Theodore Roosevelt, McKinley's Assistant Secretary of the Navy, advocated war with Spain as a means of asserting American power in the hemisphere and establishing the United States as a world power. The subsequent conflict, dubbed "a splendid little war" by the future Secretary of State John Hay, concluded with Spain utterly defeated in less than four months. The once-mighty European power was stripped of her colonies in both the Pacific and Caribbean. Though Cuba was granted provisional independence, American statesmen followed popular opinion in annexing Puerto Rico, Guam and the

Philippines. In the midst of growing public support for an overseas empire, Hawaii was likewise made a U.S. territory.

Many of the motivations that drove European imperialism likewise propelled American expansion abroad, though special emphasis was often placed on the humanitarian benefits that colonial peoples would enjoy under U.S. rule. Accordingly, the outbreak of the Philippine Insurrection in 1899, which grew out of Filipino demands for independence, shocked many Americans. At once resentful of the apparently ungrateful Filipinos and horrified by the brutality of the conflict, Americans lost some of their initial enthusiasm for empire, though U.S. forces eventually brought the rebellion to an end in 1902. Though some valued America's Pacific possessions for the economic benefits and strategic advantages they brought, their remoteness made them vulnerable, especially given the rising antagonism between the United States and Japan during the first decades of the century.

In Southeast Asia, the Dutch worked to extend their authority throughout the East Indies (later Indonesia), where they had first gained a foothold in the early seventeenth century. No longer content simply to maintain a few fortified trading posts, the Dutch imposed their administrative authority across the archipelago, claiming the larger islands of Java and Sumatra, while dividing Borneo and New Guinea with the British. Determined to exploit the considerable natural resources of the region, which included rubber and petroleum, the Dutch established a society built on racial hierarchy, with Europeans as the ruling class. Mixed-race Eurasians were accorded a middle status, while native Indonesians were consigned to an inferior position, valued largely as a labor source. The in-

equities and injustices of Dutch rule encouraged latent nationalist sentiments, which grew rapidly in the twentieth century.

French colonial interests in Southeast Asia centered on Indochina, where the French annexed Cochin (southern Vietnam) in 1862. By the 1880s, growing numbers of French traders in Indochina provoked an antiforeign movement and attacks on foreigners brought a French punitive expedition to Tonkin (northern Vietnam) in 1883. Within a few years, France extended a protectorate over all of Vietnam, Cambodia and finally Laos. Siam (later Thailand) was the only remaining independent country in Indochina, serving as a buffer with British Burma. As they had in Africa, the French pursued a policy of cultural assimilation through education, language and customs, with the objective of transforming Indochina into a virtual "Asian France." The French-style architecture in Saigon, together with the pervasive French cultural influence, led to the city being known as the "Paris of the Orient." Yet, hopes of winning the Vietnamese elite over to French rule went unmet. Rather, Vietnamese leaders and students quickly adopted both the goals and rhetoric of nationalist movements across the colonial world. Anti-French agitation was endemic in the early twentieth century, especially at French-built universities, and authorities were compelled to resort to harsh methods to suppress the activists. Though many were jailed or forced into exile, the movement for Vietnamese independence continued unabated, gaining new energy after the First World War.

While Germany's search for a "place in the sun" extended to the Pacific, German holdings were relatively small in scope, including the Caroline, Marshall and Mariana Islands, part of the Samoan group and the Bismarck Archipelago.

Elsewhere around the Asian periphery, the major powers played the "great game" of imperialism in pursuit of often-conflicting strategic goals. Most notably, Russian and British objectives collided in central Asia, where the erosion of the ancient Persian Empire opened gaps into which more vibrant modern empires were drawn. During the nineteenth century, Tsarist Russia had pushed southward into this vast, sparsely populated region at the expense of local tribes and had eventually incorporated lands totaling half the area of the United States. Having moved into the trans-Caspian region and Turkestan by the 1880s, Russia seemed poised to assert strengthened influence in Persia and potentially threaten British India through the ambiguously defined Western Frontier between Persia and Afghanistan. For decades the two nations engaged in ongoing diplomatic intrigues and intermittent military maneuvering in hopes of gaining an advantageous position in this desolate and forbidding region, before finally agreeing in 1907 to make Afghanistan a buffer state between the two empires. The problems posed for both powers by a decaying Persia were resolved through an agreement to divide that country into British and Russian spheres of influence, separated by a "neutral zone." Russian expansionist ambitions, deflected from the south by British obstruction, were next focused on Manchuria, the region of China north of the Great Wall. Russian timing proved poor, as Japan had also gained a foothold on the Asian mainland, and the conflicting ambitions of the two powers brought about war in 1904. Defeated and contained in Asia, Russia could only aspire to gain new influence in the Balkans as Ottoman power receded further in the early twentieth century.

The legacy of the imperial age was mixed. Clearly, for some peoples, imperial rule meant dispossession, oppression and, as in the Belgian Congo, cruel inhumanities. The presence of western settlers and the introduction of commercial, market economies brought radical and often disruptive changes to traditional societies. Some imperial powers, on the other hand, made concerted efforts to improve the standard of living among subject peoples, introducing health and sanitation measures and rudimentary educational systems. For better or worse, the creation of new patterns of colonial trade and commerce, together with the extension of modern means of communication and transportation into colonized areas, inevitably drew those regions more fully into a rapidly expanding global economy. In the course of this transformation, western culture and institutions left indelible imprints on those societies they touched, contributing to a general process of "westernization" that grew in scope and depth as the century progressed.

There is considerable historical debate as to whether the imperial powers "benefited" from imperialism, and no real consensus on the issue. Some nations clearly benefited economically from the raw materials and markets that colonies offered, but in general, realities did not live up to expectations. In almost all cases, colonies failed to provide the investment opportunities that imperialists promised. There were strategic benefits to be gained from well-situated colonies, which might serve as naval bases or fueling ports, but as many western powers discovered during the Second World War, such far-flung possessions could as easily become liabilities.

Britain's single greatest military humiliation came with the surrender of woefully vulnerable Singapore to the Japanese in 1941. On the other hand, colonies could provide a source of manpower reserves in wartime. During both world wars, Britain and France utilized Indian, Senegalese and Vietnamese troops in both combat and support roles. This must be balanced, of course, against the administrative cost of colonies, which could be significant.

As of 1914, however, an imperial world order seemed firmly and permanently established. In Europe, imperialism was accepted as an affirmation of the vitality of western civilization and a manifestation of advanced national development. Those nations aspiring to great power status, such as Japan and the United States, were quick to demonstrate their receptivity to a similar imperial outlook. By all appearances, imperialism seemed destined to provide the organizing principle for the world order in the coming century. As events were to prove, however, the apparent durability of imperialism was deceptive.

Almost inevitably, imperialism produced the very forces that brought its eventual collapse. Across the colonial world, nationalism emerged as one of the most potent forces opposing imperial rule. In Africa, Asia and elsewhere, indigenous peoples quickly organized to demand self-government if not independence, sometimes invoking the same concepts of individual liberty and self-determination that had driven nationalist movements in the West. Emphasizing the internal contradictions and illogic of imperialism while attacking its inherent injustices, nationalists offered their challenge even as imperialism reached high tide. However, as the course of the twentieth century would demonstrate, the viability of empire was ultimately contingent on the defensibility of the imperial idea and the ability of imperial powers to effectively assert their hegemony. The First World War, which marked the beginning of the end of Europe's world hegemony, likewise marked the beginning of an era in which the legitimacy of imperialism itself was successfully challenged.

The American Hemisphere

Since the fifteenth century, the Americas had been the site of extensive European colonial activity, generally to the detriment of Native American societies, which often faced the unpleasant alternatives of submission, retreat or destruction. By the mid-1500s, Spain controlled a vast empire extending from the Caribbean basin, southward through Central America and down the Pacific coast of South America, and from Mexico northward into the contemporary southwestern United States. During the two centuries of Spain's gradual decline as a major power, both France and England established significant colonial claims in North America east of the Mississippi River. The Seven Years' War (1756–1763) virtually eliminated France as a significant colonial power in the Americas, leaving Britain in control of Canada and the thirteen colonies to the south. Within two decades, those possessions were considerably diminished by the successful American Revolution, which brought into being a new continental power, the United States of America. The acquisition of Louisiana from Napoleonic France in 1803 and the annexation of Spanish Florida in

1819 established the United States as a major North American power. Several decades later, after having annexed Texas in 1845, the United States gained Mexico's remaining northern states during the war of 1846–1848. As the United States had already acquired Oregon in 1846 through negotiation with the British, the process of American continental expansion was largely completed and the United States was well-established as the dominant power in the hemisphere.

LATIN AMERICA

Even as the exigencies of the Napoleonic Wars brought about the transfer of Louisiana, they also provided a context for South America's wars of liberation, which began in the aftermath of Napoleon's overthrow of the Bourbon monarchy in Spain in 1808. The subsequent erosion of Spanish colonial authority in Latin America encouraged nationalist uprisings that ultimately brought independence for all of Spanish South America, Central America and Mexico by the mid-1820s. Meanwhile, Portugal recognized Brazilian independence in 1830, ending colonial rule in most of Latin America. Although the Latin American revolutionaries generally advocated republican and egalitarian ideals, establishing stable, representative government in Latin America proved difficult. Most early constitutions reflected the fear of the dominant Creole class (America-born descendants of Europeans) of the largely illiterate and poor masses, who were in most cases excluded from political participation. For decades, caste and racial distinctions mitigated against effective social integration, and large populations of Indians, mestizos (persons of mixed European and Native American ancestry) and blacks remained socially and economically isolated, never fully integrated into a viable national community. Consequently, many Latin American nations were ruled by conservative elites who preferred to maintain the status quo and feared the consequences of reform. These conservative elements often included wealthy landowners, powerful businessmen and the Catholic Church.

Political stability across the region was often threatened by competition between groups of elites who were willing to resort to extralegal means to gain power, with little regard for the sanctity of constitutional government. Consequently, dictatorship and oligarchy (rule by a small group of elites) were common. The stability of national governments was also threatened by *caudillos*, local or regional leaders supported by their own loyal armies. Though political parties emerged throughout Latin America, their leaders tended to be from the same groups, sharing a generally conservative vision with little ideological distinction between them. For all of these reasons, much of Latin America experienced frequent political turmoil during the first half-century of independence.

The last quarter of the nineteenth century was an era of greater political stability and rising economic expectations. A new generation of political leaders, inspired by American and European models of government and economic development, asserted themselves during these years, with the general objective of modernizing their nations. Like their European contemporaries, these men were convinced of the utility of science and reason in resolving society's problems, and they advocated education, free competition and secularism as instruments of progress.

Latin America's economic future was made brighter in this period by the Second

Industrial Revolution, which brought increased European demands for raw materials and agricultural products. Brazilian rubber, Chilean copper and nitrates and Peruvian guano were all lucrative exports to Europe and North America. Argentinean wheat and beef, Brazilian coffee and Honduran bananas were likewise in demand. In essence, Latin America was integrated into a global economic system in which it exchanged raw materials and foodstuffs for manufactured goods from Europe and the United States. The downside to this development was that Latin America became overly dependent on this system; the ready availability of foreign-made manufactured goods discouraged the development of domestic industry. Similarly, many Latin American nations depended heavily on single export crops and materials. Prices were often volatile and the collapse of the coffee market or the demand for guano could prove disastrous to national economies. Sometimes referred to as "neocolonialism," this economic pattern of exporting agricultural commodities in exchange for manufactured goods, also often included extensive foreign ownership of both corporate and natural resources, usually by British and American investors. These foreign corporate interests often cultivated close relationships with conservative Latin American elites, a connection benefiting both to the detriment of reformers and the lower classes, who shared in little of the new wealth. Indeed, in most countries the modernized export sector remained isolated from the rest of the economy, which was starved of the labor and capital that was drained into the export sector. One consequence was that much of Latin America remained a land of extreme contrasts. Though many nations boasted modern, urban centers supporting a growing middle class, significant

groups were excluded from the new economy and languished in urban slums or labored under oppressive conditions on the plantations of wealthy landowners, where conditions remained little improved from decades past. For most of Latin America, comprehensive modernization, economic independence and political democratization were still decades in the future.

NORTH AMERICA: CANADA AND THE UNITED STATES

The consolidation of Canada as a modern nation goes back to 1840, when the Union Act of that year united Upper and Lower Canada. It did not, however, resolve the political and cultural issues that divided French-speaking and English-speaking inhabitants. Self-government came with the British North America Act (1867), which provided for a federation of Quebec, Ontario, New Brunswick and Nova Scotia as the Dominion of Canada. Between 1870 and 1912, the western and northern provinces were gradually incorporated into the Dominion, which was governed by a bicameral parliament and a governor-general responsible to the British crown. The population, which stood at 11 million in 1900, was generally concentrated in the southeastern corner of the country within a few hundred miles of the U.S. border. A vast land with considerable natural resources, including timber, minerals and petroleum, Canada began to industrialize in the late nineteenth century, but climate, geography and a small population slowed the pace of development.

Though it wasn't until 1941 that powerful publisher Henry Luce would characterize the twentieth century as the "American Century," the remarkable potential of the United

States was evident decades before. With the long sectional division resolved by the Civil War, the United States had undergone an astounding economic transformation during the last third of the nineteenth century. Between 1865 and 1900, the industrial revolution radically altered the economic and social structure of the United States, creating an urban, industrial republic with seemingly unbounded energy, productive capacity and financial power. As early as 1870, U.S. railroad mileage was triple that of Great Britain, and by 1900, a single American company, Carnegie Steel, out-produced the entire British steel industry. A massive wave of immigration beginning in the 1870s had swollen the population to 76 million by the beginning of the new century, providing an ample labor supply for burgeoning industries. The agricultural sector also expanded as the rapid settlement of the trans-Mississippi West after the Civil War brought extensive farming and ranching to the Great Plains. The mineral and timber resources of the West were rapidly exploited as the frontier line moved westward and finally, according to the census of 1890, disappeared.

The changes that accompanied the Industrial Revolution and the development of a truly national economy were not all positive, and posed challenges for the American political system. Though agricultural production soared in the late 1800s, farmers faced growing economic difficulties, and their discontent played a major role in the emergence of the populist movement of the 1890s. Populism stressed the need for government responsive to the needs of the people rather than powerful interests and demanded government action to rectify economic inequities. As populism lost its momentum by the late 1890s, a new reform movement known as progressivism supplanted it. Progressives maintained that the many social and economic problems that attended industrialization and urbanization could be resolved through a rational, scientific approach and government action. This largely urban, middle-class movement rejected nineteenth century *laissez-faire* doctrines and social Darwinism, asserting that man could and must become an agent of his own destiny. Progressives focused on a multitude of issues, including antitrust legislation, labor rights, consumer protection laws, conservation, women's suffrage, railroad regulation and political democratization. Progressivism found a major champion in Theodore Roosevelt, who assumed the presidency in 1901 after an anarchist assassinated President William McKinley. A man of incredible energy, the Republican Roosevelt gained immense popularity by supporting progressive reforms, and was elected to a second term in 1904. His progressive legacy was continued by his successor, William Howard Taft (1909–1913) and later by the Democrat Woodrow Wilson (1913–1921).

The years known as the "Progressive Era" also saw the United States claim an expanded role in world affairs. The Spanish-American War marked the emergence of the United States as a major naval power and was followed by the establishment of an American empire in the Caribbean and Pacific. An outspoken proponent of military strength, imperialism and a permanent international role for the United States, President Roosevelt asserted that the preservation of international order and stability must be the general foreign policy objective of the United States. Two broad initiatives were implemented in pursuit of this goal. First, Roosevelt believed that the stability of the American hemisphere was contingent on U.S. hegemony. This required significant naval strength, which Roosevelt worked continually to augment, and the ability to rapidly transit naval forces from the Atlantic to the Pacific. Accordingly, Roosevelt played a central role in the acquisition of rights to a canal through the Panamanian isthmus, which were obtained in 1903. Construction of the canal began the next year and was completed within a decade, with the U.S. retaining control of the Canal Zone. Convinced that the greatest threat to hemispheric stability came from Latin American, the president announced the Roosevelt Corollary (1904), by which the U.S. claimed the authority to intervene in any Latin American nation in which there was "chronic wrongdoing or instability." This ambiguous criterion foreshadowed increasing U.S. intervention in the following decade, most often in the Caribbean basin. Through "gunboat diplomacy," Roosevelt asserted the American prerogative to maintain order in the hemisphere. William H. Taft continued this policy of intervention, though substituting the power of American capital

for gunboats. Later, Woodrow Wilson's presidency brought an unprecedented wave of U.S. intervention in the Caribbean and Central America.

Roosevelt's second foreign policy initiative was to work to maintain world peace through mediation, an approach that ended the Russo-Japanese War and headed off confrontations with Japan. Both Taft and Wilson acknowledged the importance of an active American role in world affairs and undertook initiatives aimed at ending or reducing the chance of conflict.

By 1914, the United States had taken its place among the western powers that dominated the globe. A constitutional republic with a deeply ingrained democratic tradition and a historical tradition of isolation, the United States was drawn inexorably into the wider world by the search for new markets, imperial ambitions and recognition of the responsibilities that great powers status imposed. In the immediate future, the course of events would greatly weaken Europe's world hegemony and test the depth of America's new commitment to internationalism.

* ——— * ——— * ——— * ——— * ——— * ——— * ——— * ——— * ——— * ———— *

In late March 1901, a disheveled group of some eighty-odd men trudged wearily toward the village of Palanan, some hundred miles inland from the east coast of Luzon in the Philippines. Most of the men wore the frayed clothes characteristic of the guerillas that had been fighting against American annexation of their homeland since 1898. Five, however, wore the uniform of enlisted troops of the United States Army. Some weeks before, word had been sent ahead to this jungle refuge that rebel reinforcements would be arriving, bringing with them a number of American prisoners. Waiting to take custody of the captured Americans and welcome fresh troops was the leader of the insurrection, Emilio Aguinaldo. Physically unimposing and small in stature, his face marred by childhood smallpox, the 32-year-old Aguinaldo had directed the resistance against the U.S. occupation forces for two years. He was among many Filipinos who had believed that Spain's defeat in the Spanish-American War would mean independence, only to be dismayed when the United States asserted its intention of annexing the Philippines.

Now, the struggle for independence continued in the form of guerilla warfare, in which small, lightly armed bands of insurgents sought to turn surprise, mobility and familiarity with the countryside to their advantage. Given the growing number of U.S. troops, the reinforcements heading for Palanan were sorely needed. The expected contingent arrived at the village as planned, with the Americans under escort. As the new arrivals lined up in the square facing Aguinaldo's men, their officers were escorted into a stilt home, where Aguinaldo went to meet them. After a few moments of pleasantries, one of the newly arrived officers gave a signal to a comrade below in the street. A fusillade of shooting broke out as the "reinforcements" opened fire on Aguinaldo's stunned troops, dropping many of them where they stood. It was a trap—the new troops were not rebel sympathizers, but Macabebes, an ethnic group hostile to the guerillas. They had been recruited by an American Army officer as part of an elaborate plot to seize Aguinaldo. Following the interception of information that pinpointed Aguinaldo's current headquarters, Army officers decided that the rebel leader might be captured by using pro-American Filipinos posing as guerillas. The American "prisoners" were U.S. Army officers charged with capturing Aguinaldo, and now they rushed into the stilt house. Held at gunpoint by the Macabebes who had betrayed him, Aguinaldo was confronted by an American brigadier general who informed him that he was now a prisoner of war. Stunned by the rapidity of events and the magnitude of the betrayal, Aguinaldo asked quietly, "Is this not some joke?" It was not. The Americans transported the disheartened Filipino nationalist back to Manila, soon to be the seat of the U.S. territorial government. The Army commander in the Philippines, General Arthur MacArthur, treated the rebel chief with dignity and within a few weeks Aguinaldo conceded defeat. In a public proclamation, he declared that there had been "enough of blood, enough of tears and desolation" and acknowledged U.S. sovereignty over his country. Shortly after, he returned to the family home in Kawit. For the remainder of his life, he wore a black bow tie, symbolizing his lost hopes for an independent Philippine republic.

Emilio Aguinaldo's road to Palanan began in 1869 in the town of Kawit on Luzon, where his father worked as a lawyer and served as mayor. One of eight children in a Chinese mestizo family, Emilio enjoyed the relative advantages of middle-class life in a nation whose people were overwhelmingly desperately poor. As a young man, he directed his attention to running the family's farm and sugar mill, eventually following his father as mayor of Kawit. In 1896, Aguinaldo joined the *Katipunan,* a nationalist movement that fomented a rebellion against Spanish rule in August of that year. Though only twenty-seven, Aguinaldo quickly distinguished himself in the field and by 1897 was generally acknowledged as the leader of the anticolonial resistance. Though Aguinaldo and his followers proved courageous in confronting often-superior Spanish forces, they underestimated the determination of Spanish military authorities to quell the rebellion. When the fighting proved inconclusive, rebel leaders accepted an improbable compromise. In return for a payment of 800,000 pesos, the rebels would give up the struggle and Aguinaldo would accept exile in Hong Kong. Filipino nationalist sentiment, it seemed, was at most only superficial.

Despite making public proclamations to the contrary, Aguinaldo was by no means reconciled to Spanish rule in the Philippines. As American relations with Spain deteriorated in 1898, Aguinaldo sounded out U.S. officials in Hong Kong as to the possibility of returning to the Philippines. Shortly after Commodore George Dewey's Asiatic Squadron destroyed a Spanish fleet at anchorage in Manila Bay that spring, Aquinaldo arrived aboard an American ship, where Dewey instructed him to "go ashore and start your army." Presuming that liberation from Spanish rule would be followed by independence, Aguinaldo gathered recruits and weapons and in June 1898 proclaimed the independence of his homeland. However, even as Spain acknowledged defeat, it became apparent that any assertion of Philippine independence might be premature. Indeed, by the final months of 1898, public opinion in the United States had swung strongly behind the idea of annexing the Philippines.

Following the conclusion of the Spanish-American War in August, a wave of enthusiasm for empire had swept the United States, fed by editorialists, politicians and prominent individuals such as Theodore Roosevelt, who had won national fame in the campaign in Cuba. The famed Rough Rider was among many who believed that the stunning American victories in the recent war signaled an imperial destiny for the nation. "The guns of our warships have awakened us to new duties," he proclaimed in an October speech. "We are face to face with our destiny and we must meet it with a high and resolute courage." It was a compelling argument that gave force to the new annexationist impulse pervading both the nation and Congress. President William McKinley, who was receptive to the annexation of Puerto Rico and Guam, came to accept the acquisition of the Philippines only after considerable reflection. As he later explained to a Methodist group, it finally came to him late one night that "there was nothing left for us to do but to take them all, and to educate the Filipinos, and uplift and civilize and Christianize them." Even as the Senate debate over ratifying the proposed treaty was taking place, Britain's poet laureate of imperialism, Rudyard Kipling, published a provocative poem in *McClure's* magazine. "The White Man's Burden" urged Americans to accept the responsibility of empire and the duty of civilizing "new-caught, sullen peoples, half devil and half child." The U.S. Congress proved willing, and on February 6, 1899, ratified the treaty. A resolution for Philippine independence was defeated eight days later.

The same week the treaty was ratified, hostilities between Filipinos and U.S. troops broke out. In the preceding months, Aguinaldo had begun preparing for possible American annexation, ordering his provincial commanders to stockpile weapons and food. The inevitable clash came on February 4 when a U.S. army patrol in a Manila suburb exchanged shots with Filipino troops. In the days that followed more clashes grew into widespread fighting as American forces sought to drive the insurgents out of the city.

As it evolved over the next two years, the Philippine Insurrection provided a profound lesson in the costs of empire. Some 75,000 American troops, three-quarters of the entire U.S. Army, were eventually transported to the Philippines, where they were faced with difficult tropical terrain, incapacitating heat, humidity and deadly disease. They were further burdened by the difficulties of fighting a war among a foreign population whose customs and way of life seemed primitive and disgusting, and whose allegiance was uncertain. These circumstances, combined with the racist attitudes common among American troops, produced an especially savage war, notable for callous brutality and calculated cruelty. Many American soldiers were forthright in their distaste for their Filipino opponents. "No cruelty is too severe," commented one, "for these brainless monkeys who can appreciate no sense of honor, kindness or justice." Filipino atrocities, which included the mutilation, disemboweling and decapitation of captured Americans, further strengthened these American prejudices. Consequently, U.S. forces were increasingly prone to give no quarter, even to civilians. Following an ambush of Americans near Malabon, U.S. troops retaliated against the town. "We got orders to spare no one," an artilleryman remembered. "We went in and killed every native we

Fig. 1-2   General Emilio Aguinaldo (mounted) together with troops of the rebel army he led during the Philippine Insurrection (1899–1902). After leading the rebellion for several years, Aguinaldo was captured by U.S. Army forces and soon afterwards conceded that his cause was lost. (Bettmann/Corbis)

met, men, women and children." Such tactics provoked outrage in the United States, compelling such notables as Mark Twain, Andrew Carnegie and Democratic presidential candidate William Jennings Bryan to denounce the effort to subdue the Filipinos.

It was the capture of Aguinaldo that finally defused the insurrection, though sporadic resistance by individual groups such as the Muslim Moros continued for the next decade. The Philippine Insurrection came to an official end on July 4, 1902, when President Roosevelt affirmed "the lawful sovereignty and just authority of the United States" over the islands. Suppressing the insurrection cost the United States about 7,000 dead and wounded; estimates are that some 20,000 Filipino soldiers were killed. Filipino civilian casualties ran into the hundreds of thousands. Securing a claim to this Pacific colony cost the United States about $600,000.

With colonial outposts in both the Pacific and the Caribbean, the United States entered the twentieth century as an imperial power, its statesmen echoing the same rationalizations that drove Europe's new search for empire two decades earlier. Ironically, in the decades following the end of the Philippine Insurrection, Filipino-American relations generally improved and in 1934 the U.S. Congress approved a plan for independence in 1944. The vulnerability of distant colonies was demonstrated, however, when Japanese forces easily gained control of the Philippines in late 1941 as the Pacific War began. Aguinaldo made a brief return to public life when he made propaganda broadcasts for the Japanese, who sought to present themselves as defending all Asians against a predacious West. It was a controversial move that Aguinaldo came to regret later. American forces were welcomed as liberators in 1944, and two years later the islands gained independence. The postwar era brought a rapid devolution of empire and within fifteen years most of the world's great empires were in the latter stages of dissolution. In 1960, the United States made a symbolic move toward erasing the painful memories of the imperial past when Charles Bohlen, the U.S. ambassador in Manila, hosted a ceremony in which a Spanish officer's sword was presented to the aging Aguinaldo. The weapon was a prize that Aguinaldo had seized from the Spanish during the early stages of the Philippine bid for independence in 1896; it had been confiscated upon his capture by American forces in 1901. Aguinaldo died in 1964 at the age of ninety-six, having outlived the age of empire.

◆ —— ◆ —— ◆ —— ◆ —— ◆ —— ◆ —— ◆ —— ◆ —— ◆ —— ◆

Suggested Readings

BALFOUR, MICHAEL. *The Kaiser and His Times.* (1964).

BEALE, HOWARD K. *Theodore Roosevelt and the Rise of America to World Power.* (1956).

BEASLEY. W. G. *The Meiji Restoration.* (1972).

BELOFF, MAX. *Britain's Liberal Empire, 1897–1921.* (1970).

BROOK-SHEPHERD, GORDON. *The Austrians: A Thousand-Year Odyssey.* (1996).

CECIL, LAMAR. *Wilhelm II.* Vols. I and II. (1989, 1996).

CHADWICK, OWEN. *The Secularization of the European Mind in the Nineteenth Century.* (1975).

CRAIG, GORDON. *Germany, 1866–1945.* (1978).

ERICKSON, CAROLLY. *Her Little Majesty: The Life of Queen Victoria.* (1997).

FARWELL, BYRON. *Queen Victoria's Little Wars.* (1972).

HALE, ORON J. *The Great Illusion, 1900–1914.* (1971).

HOBSBAWM, ERIC. *The Age of Empire, 1875–1914.* (1987).

HOCHSCHILD, ADAM. *King Leopold's Ghost: A Story of Greed, Terrorism and Heroism in Colonial Africa.* (1998).

HOPKIRK, PETER. *The Great Game: The Struggle for Empire in Central Asia.* (1990).

JAMES, LAWRENCE. *The Rise and Fall of the British Empire.* (1994).

KARNOW, STANLEY. *In Our Own Image: The United States and the Philippines.* (1989).

KIERNAN, V. G. *The Lords of Humankind: European Attitudes to the Outside World in the Imperial Age.* (1972).

MCCLELLAN, DAVID. *Karl Marx: His Life and Thought.* (1974).

MORGAN, H. WAYNE. *America's Road to Empire.* (1968).

MORTON, FREDERIC. *A Nervous Splendor: Vienna, 1888/89.* (1979).

MOSSE, GEORGE L. *The Culture of Western Europe.* (1988).

MOWREY, GEORGE E. *The Era of Theodore Roosevelt, 1900–1912.* (1958).

PAKENHAM, THOMAS. *The Scramble for Africa: The White Man's Conquest of the Dark Continent from 1876 to 1912.* (1991).

POLLARD, SIDNEY. *Peaceful Conquest: The Industrialization of Europe.* (1981).

RADZINSKY, EDWARD. *The Last Tsar.* (1992).

SKIDMORE, THOMAS E. and PETER H. SMITH *Modern History of Latin America.* (1989).

SMITH, DENNIS MACK. *Modern Italy: A Political History.* (1997).

SPENCE, JONATHAN. *The Search for Modern China.* (1990).

STONE, NORMAN. *Europe Transformed, 1878–1919.* (1984).

TUCHMAN, BARBARA. *The Proud Tower: A Portrait of the World before the War, 1890–1914.* (1971).

VON LAUE, THEODORE H. *The World Revolution of Westernization.* (1987).

WARNER, MARINA. *The Dowager Empress: The Life and Times of Tz'u-his, Empress-Dowager of China, 1835–1908.* (1972).

WOODRUFF, WILLIAM. *The Emergence of an International Economy.* (1970).

WRIGHT, GORDON. *France in Modern Times.* (1978).

CHAPTER 2

A Burnt Path Across History: The First World War and Its Consequences, 1914–1920

Russia's February Revolution (1917), which forced the abdication of Tsar Nicholas II and resulted in the creation of a Provisional Government, caught Marxist radical Vladimir Illyich Lenin completely by surprise. The short, balding Bolshevik leader was eating lunch with his wife Krupskaia in their Zurich flat, where they were sitting out the raging continental war, when a young friend burst in and exclaimed, "Haven't you heard anything? There's a revolution in Russia!" Lenin, who at age 46 had dedicated most of his adult life to realizing a socialist revolution in the Tsarist Empire, confided his astonishment to Krupskaia: "It's staggering! It's so incredibly unexpected!" The next days were given to desperate schemes to get back to Russia and capitalize on the political chaos. A route through Britain was deemed too uncertain; fellow Bolsheviks Leon Trotsky and Nikolai Bukharin had already been detained there. Lenin toyed briefly with an absurd ploy to transit Germany disguised as a deaf, dumb and blind Swede. Dissuaded by his wife, he considered hiring an airplane to fly him across eastern Europe, but gave up the plan as too dangerous. Ultimately, the Bolshevik exiles made contact with the German ambassador in Bern, whose government was receptive to the idea of aiding the Marxist revolutionaries in their quest to return to Russia. Though Imperial Germany had inflicted a series of defeats on the Russian army on the eastern front, the new Provisional Government continued to prosecute the war; Lenin's presence in Russia might do much to destabilize the current regime. Accordingly, the Bolsheviks were granted free transit across Germany and given a promise of non-interference by German authorities. And so, on March 27, 1917, with the world war stalemated in its third year and millions dead, a "sealed" German train pulled away from the station at the Swiss border town of Gottmadingen and proceeded into Germany toward Frankfurt. On board among the thirty political exiles, Russian Bolsheviks long prohibited from entering Tsarist Russia, were Lenin and his wife. The train was never actually "sealed," though the Bolshevik passengers were restricted to their car and were forbidden from "fraternizing" with Germans, lest they be infected with the Bolshevik "virus."

Following an uneventful journey that took the group to the Baltic coast and through Sweden, the Bolsheviks began the last leg of their journey when they arrived at the border of Russian Finland and proceeded toward St. Petersburg. Arriving at the city's Finland Station on April 3, they disembarked to find an enthusiastic crowd of thousands of workers and revolutionary sailors, eager for a glimpse of the man who promised salvation for the oppressed. Asked to address the crowd, Lenin quickly made clear that his objective was a second revolution, a worker's revolution. "Sailors, comrades, I greet you," the Bolshevik leader began. "I don't know as yet whether you all agree with the Provisional Government but I know very well that when they give you sweet speeches and make many promises, they are deceiving you, just as they deceive the whole Russian people." What the Russian people needed, Lenin asserted, was peace, bread and land. The Provisional Government, he thundered, offered only war, hunger and landlessness. "You must fight for the revolution," Lenin demanded of his cheering audience, "fight to the end, for full victory of the proletariat." He concluded with a virtual declaration of war against the existing political and social order: "All hail the world Socialist revolution!" On this early spring day in 1917, Lenin stood at the threshold of a revolution that would topple the Russian government, initiate a catastrophic civil war, provoke a foreign invasion and transform Russia into a totalitarian state. In the course of more than seven decades to come, the consequences of Lenin's revolution reshaped Russia and ultimately redefined the world order.

Born in 1870 in Simbirsk, a provincial capital on the Volga River, Vladimir Ulianov (as he was known before he adopted the name Lenin, probably in reference to the Lena River, in 1901) was raised in moderately affluent circumstances. His father, Ilya Ulianov, was a government school inspector of moderate political views; his mother, Maria Alexandrovna, was the daughter of a baptized Jew whose wealth and accomplishments entitled her husband to register as a nobleman. The Ulianov household was a comfortable, stable environment for the young Vladimir, who enjoyed games and the intellectual stimulation that the family library afforded. A good student, he seemed destined for the unremarkable life of the Russian *bourgeoisie;* there is little in Lenin's early life that would seem to provide any psychological insight into the mind of the domineering and ruthless revolutionary of 1917.

The sequence of events that changed the circumstances of Lenin's life began in the mid-1880s. The death of Ilya Ulianov in 1886 was a blow to the close-knit family, but it was the shocking activities of Lenin's elder brother Alexander that caused greater consternation. Alexander, by all accounts a serious hard-working young man, had been accepted into St. Petersburg University in 1883 to study science. In early 1887 Tsarist police arrested him for making bombs that were to be used to assassinate Alexander III. He was found guilty and hanged in May, refusing to plead with the Tsar for clemency. Lenin, recently enrolled in law at Kazan University, was stunned by the turn of events and soon came to view his brother's execution as the deed of an unjust tsarist autocracy. Shortly afterward, he was briefly arrested for participating in a student demonstration at the university. Decades later, official Soviet accounts would cite this as the point at which Lenin, driven by the desire for revenge against the unjust tsarist regime, committed himself to socialist revolution. There is little evidence for such a commitment at this juncture. He did, however, seriously reassess his chances of establishing himself as a successful lawyer in a society that deemed him a subversive. The tentative road to the Finland Station had its beginnings here, as Lenin devoted himself to several years of intense study, eagerly pouring over works of political and economic theory. Though he examined the writings of G. W. F. Hegel, Ivan Turgenev and contemporary Russian radicals, he was most taken by *What Is to Be Done?*, a utopian novel by Nikolai Chernyshevsky. From Chernyshevsky Lenin adopted his beliefs in the need for a disciplined, self-denying revolutionary vanguard, the efficacy of action, his disdain for liberal reform and the legitimacy of dictatorial methods. These concepts reemerged in later years and did much to shape the Bolshevik Revolution of 1917. In the early 1890s, however, Lenin moved to St. Petersburg, where he was attracted to the theories of Georgii Plekhanov and became an advocate of the more orthodox Marxist views of the Russian Social Democratic Labor Party (RSDLP). Here he began his career as a serious revolutionary.

Tsarist authorities rarely tolerated reformist, much less revolutionary political activities, and in 1895 Lenin and 40 fellow Marxists were arrested. They joined some 500 other party activists in jail, with Lenin ultimately exiled to Siberia, where he married Nadezhda Krupskaia. Fearful that the party, now largely leaderless, would drift into Revisionism, which held that socialism could be brought about gradually and peacefully, Lenin struggled to maintain Marxist orthodoxy. His communications spoke of the unalterable need to promote socialist ideas, encourage the political self-consciousness of the proletariat and forge a mass revolutionary party. Yet even the party leadership differed as to how these objectives were to be accomplished. In a famous 1902 pamphlet, titled, like Chernyshevsky's work, "What Is to Be Done," Lenin, now in exile in Switzerland, insisted that the workers' movement could not be allowed to diverge into mere trade unionism, but had to be wedded to social democracy and the RSDLP. For its part, the party had to be "a strong organization of professional revolutionaries." Together, party and workers would merge "into a single whole the spontaneous destructive force of the crowd and the conscious destructive power of the revolutionaries' organization." At the 1903 party congress in London, a slim majority of the delegates approved Lenin's vision of an exclusive party of disciplined revolutionaries, affording Lenin the opportunity to deem his faction the Bolsheviks (majority) and their opponents the Mensheviks (minority).

For more than a decade, Lenin's revolutionary vision remained only that. The Revolution of 1905 found the Marxists unprepared and ill-directed. Though the first Workers Soviet, or Council, was established in St. Petersburg in the midst of considerable political unrest, Lenin returned from exile only in November of that year, shortly before loyal troops crushed the uprising. Tsar Nicholas II's October Manifesto established a weak parliamentary system that little tempered tsarist autocracy in following years. Russia's Marxists remained divided over strategy and tactics, with the most prominent activists in prison or exile, the latter being Lenin's fate once again. During these frustrating years Lenin continued to lay the theoretical foundations for what would later be known as Marxism-Leninism, which reflected Lenin's interpolation of Marxist theory within the specific context of Russian economic and social development.

The First World War, though broadly denounced by socialists around the world as a capitalist war, did little to unite contentious Russian Marxists, but Lenin believed that the conflict might create conditions that would bring on the socialist world revolution. Prior to 1917, however, the prospects for a workers' revolution anywhere remained problematic. Staggered by military defeat, Imperial Russia faced growing internal unrest, but Russian Marxists could do little to direct it. Lenin and other leading Bolsheviks remained in Swiss exile; the young Joseph Dzhugashvili, later Stalin, having escaped twice from internal exile, waited uselessly in remote Arctic Russia; Leon Trotsky, together with a small group of Bolsheviks, found temporary refuge in the United States.

The unexpected February Revolution created new circumstances that afforded Lenin and the Bolsheviks the opportunity to put theory into practice and direct the unfocused unrest in Russia into channels that would lead to a socialist revolution. In the months that followed his arrival at the Finland Station, Lenin discovered that the path to his goal was not always clearly discernible, nor was the course of events predictable. The Bolshevik coup in October was followed by a costly peace with Germany, a savage civil war and armed intervention by foreign armies, all posing serious challenges to the struggling communist regime. During these years of uncertainty, the two constants that guided the course of the Bolshevik Revolution were Lenin's unswerving determination to realize his vision of a socialist society and his equally unshakable willingness to use terror to achieve his ends. By the time he died in 1924, Lenin had succeeded in securing the revolution from foreign and internal threats and establishing the fundamental political and governmental institutions of the Union of Soviet Socialist Republics (USSR). In death, Lenin continued to serve the revolution he had inspired; his successors determined that his body would be preserved and the mummified remains displayed in a glass coffin in a huge mausoleum in Moscow's Red

Square. The Cult of Lenin, which extolled the inerrant vision of the revolution's founder, and elevated him to the status of a secular messiah, ultimately attained quasi-religious status in the Soviet Union. Lenin, a convinced atheist who had once disdainfully proclaimed "Electricity is the new God," might well have appreciated the irony of the situation. In a century in which ideology was often promoted as holding the key to mankind's salvation, the new trinity acknowledged in Soviet Russia was Marx, Engels and Lenin.

♦ —— ♦ —— ♦ —— ♦ —— ♦

The Bolshevik Revolution was one of the many unexpected consequences of the First World War, which, in addition to bringing unprecedented death and destruction, undermined the foundations of four great empires, destabilized Europe politically and economically and, in a broader sense, marked the end of nineteenth-century European civilization. For Europe, the war was arguably the greatest catastrophe since the Thirty Years' War of the early seventeenth century, which had left depopulation, economic disruption and major political reorganization in its wake. The First World War, referred to as the "Great War" in its immediate aftermath, clearly deserved the distinction. The conflict brought about the mobilization of 60 million men and thrust them into seemingly unrelenting combat, often on stark, desolate battlefields that brought new and horrible dimensions to the meaning of warfare. It was the first major international conflict of the industrial age, in which the belligerents attempted to bring to bear the material power of mature industrial economies dedicated to the production of increasingly deadly instruments of destruction. These circumstances combined to bring a new intensity and scope to modern warfare, which seemed to demand a new harshness of mind and spirit. The prescription for victory in this new era was, in the words of Germany's wartime military dictator Erich Ludendorff, "total war."

The consequences are evident in the statistics: nearly nine million dead, an average of 5,600 deaths every day during slightly more than four years of war. Twenty-one million were wounded and maimed in a conflict that left untold billions of dollars in physical destruction in its wake. Historian Barbara Tuchman observed that the war left "a burnt path across history," clearly demarcating the world that was from a new, uncertain world shaped by the dynamic and often frightening forces unleashed by the war. The First World War, many historians argue, marks the real beginning of the twentieth century. Though few realized it at the time, the ultimate victim of the conflict was European civilization. The political, social, economic and intellectual foundations of European nations were seriously, and in some cases fatally, damaged by the war. *Fin-de-siecle* Europe, a proud, confident civilization that proclaimed its superiority in colonial possessions and outposts throughout the world, suffered wounds between 1914 and 1918 from which it would never fully recover.

Origins of a Catastrophe: Europe, 1900–1914

Though the late nineteenth century was an era of growing political stability, general prosperity and cultural achievement for much of Europe, the period was not without its alarmists. Friedrich Engels, colleague and collaborator of Karl Marx, in 1887 offered an apocalyptic vision of Europe's future when he predicted a "world war never before seen in extension or intensity." "Eight to ten million soldiers will slaughter each other and strip Europe bare as no swarm of locusts," he warned. The German radical envisioned "the devastations of the Thirty Years' War condensed into three or four years and spread all over the continent," resulting in "famine, epidemics, general barbarization of armies and masses." "The crowns [will] roll in the gutter by the dozens," he predicted, "and there will be nobody to pick them up." As prescient as Engels' vision may seem, it was in part the product of his desire to foresee "the creation of the circumstances for the final victory of the working classes."

No such desire inspired Helmut Moltke, chief of the Prussian general staff, when he warned the Reichstag in 1890 of a new age of "people's wars," longer in duration and more uncertain in direction that the "cabinet wars" of the recent past. "It may be a war of seven years' or thirty years' duration," the elder Moltke observed. "And woe to him who sets Europe alight, who first puts the fuse to the powder keg."

Winston Churchill, as a young Conservative member of Parliament, echoed similar fears in 1901 when he observed that he had "frequently been astonished to hear with what composure and how glibly Members, and even Ministers, talk of a European war." In this new century, he feared, "wars of peoples will be more terrible than those of kings" and would bring about "the ruin of the vanquished and the scarcely less fatal

commercial dislocation and exhaustion of the conquerors."

While concerns about rising international tensions were often voiced, they were tempered by assertions that major conflicts were a thing of the past. In 1910, a British economist published a study maintaining that there would be no major wars in the future because the great powers could not afford the cost of any conflict longer than three months. David Starr Jordan, director of the World Peace Foundation, was similarly optimistic. "What shall we say of the Great War of Europe, ever pending and which never comes?" he asked. "We shall say that it will never come. Humanly speaking, it is impossible." Among the prominent statesmen who predicted an era of international harmony were U.S. Senator Henry Cabot Lodge, President Woodrow Wilson and Britain's David Lloyd George. In the Berlin of William II, workmen proceeded with the construction of a stadium for the 1916 Olympics. Clearly, few foresaw the conflagration that would be touched off by the assassination of the Austrian Archduke Franz Ferdinand in June 1914.

The historical debate over the causes of the First World War is unabated even in the early twenty-first century as historians continue their efforts to explain the outbreak of this "impossible" conflict. Some stress general factors such as nationalism and militarism. Without question, nationalism played a role in exacerbating international tensions between the great powers, as many statesmen felt compelled to pursue potentially dangerous policies rather than risk national humiliation or the appearance of weakness. Nationalist sentiments clearly motivated crowds throughout Europe to shout for war in the summer of 1914. For the subject minorities living within the bounds of extensive empires, such as Austria-Hungary or the Ottoman Empire, nationalism was a galvanizing creed that sometimes justified violent and destabilizing acts in pursuit of autonomy.

Militarism likewise shaped diplomacy and defined policy, as military and civilian leaders alike came to advocate the threat or use of military force as a defensible, even preferable, means of attaining desired goals. The militaristic perspective of some, like Germany's Kaiser William II, was grounded in a crude social Darwinism that held that national greatness derived from struggle, which was not to be avoided but embraced as a means of national rejuvenation. It has also been pointed out that Europe's mature industrial economy was busily producing the instruments for the pursuit of such militaristic policies decades before the war broke out. Increasingly vast conscript armies, which replaced smaller professional forces in all the major powers except Britain, offered new promise of national glory by military force.

The outbreak of war has also been attributed to the structure of international diplomacy and the mistakes of those who conducted it. Alliance obligations, secret treaties, the miscalculations and even personalities of individual statesmen and national leaders have been cited as contributing to the disaster of 1914. Historians who maintain that the resort to war in 1914 was in part the product of internal political exigencies have also examined the role of domestic politics. Thus, a simultaneously accurate and simple summary of the war's origins remains elusive. One recent writer, having reevaluated the basic issues in the debate, concluded that the war "was nothing less than the greatest *error* of modern history." The origins of the war

are unquestionably complex, but reveal themselves in the course of events over a period of about two decades. It is here that the long- and short-term origins of the conflict are to be found.

PRELUDE: THE UNRAVELING OF THE BISMARCKIAN SYSTEM

As noted in the previous chapter, one source of relative international stability in the last quarter of the nineteenth century was the diplomatic system constructed by German Chancellor Otto von Bismarck. The Bismarckian system, aimed at isolating France diplomatically and assuring that Germany held the continental balance of power, was based on artfully managed alliances between the German, Austrian and Russian empires. Bismarck's genius seemed confirmed when the Dual Alliance (between Germany and the Austro-Hungarian Empire) was expanded in 1882 into the Triple Alliance to include Italy. The crucial component in the Bismarckian system was the Russian alliance, which quickly became problematic following Bismarck's dismissal in 1890 by the impetuous William II. The all-important Reinsurance Treaty with Russia was due to be renewed that same year, but the mercurial German emperor elected not to pursue it. This opened an opportunity for France that was quickly seized. Anti-German sentiment had pervaded France since defeat in the Franco-Prussian War, which had led to Imperial Germany's annexation of Alsace-Lorraine. French statesmen, long victims of Bismarck's adroit diplomacy, now acted to end France's isolation. Taking advantage of growing Russian concerns about Germany's intentions, French diplomats sought an opening to Tsarist Russia. The Franco-Russian Alliance (1893), which pledged the two nations to act if either were attacked by Germany, signaled the beginning of a major European diplomatic realignment. Bismarck's fear of a Franco-Russian alliance was realized even before the "Iron Chancellor" died in 1899. Germany now faced the potential of a future two-front war against two of Europe's most powerful nations. In the years to come, French and Russian apprehensions about Germany's ambitions grew. Those apprehensions were soon matched by similar fears in Great Britain.

ANGLO–GERMAN TENSIONS

The ultimate scope of the diplomatic realignment taking shape in the 1890s was dependent in part on the course of British foreign policy, which was undergoing a significant transformation during these same years. During the last quarter of the nineteenth century, Britain pursued a policy of "splendid isolation," avoiding continental alliances that might lead to pointless conflicts such as the Crimean War of 1854–1856. By the 1890s, circumstances seemed to point to the possibility of an Anglo-German pact, especially given Britain's concern about Russian expansionism in Asia and colonial rivalry with France. Germany's William II, faced with the loss of the Russian alliance, looked naturally toward England, not least because Queen Victoria was his grandmother. Unfortunately, within the span of a dozen years, William's diplomatic ineptness and impulsive behavior drove an increasingly apprehensive Britain into alliance with France and Russia.

Arrogant, brash, often shockingly incompetent in his judgements about crucial matters, and so erratic in his policies that he was referred to by his own ministers as "William the Sudden," the Kaiser sought to impress upon his English relations the value of having Imperial Germany as an ally. In the "Kruger Telegram" incident of 1896, William gratuitously offered encouragement to Paul Kruger, president of the Boer republic of Transvaal in south Africa, whose troops had recently fought off invading English forces from Cape Colony. The publication of the dispatch outraged British public opinion and led British statesmen to wonder if it signaled new German efforts to disrupt British colonial expansion. Ironically, William was convinced that his actions would lead Britain to see that friendship with Germany was indispensable. The chances for any rapprochement with Britain lessened rapidly during the Boer War, as German public opinion, fanned by elements of the press, was vociferous in its denunciations of British efforts to subdue the Boers in south Africa.

Relations with Britain were likewise damaged by the Kaiser's decision to expand Germany's navy in the late 1890s. The construction of this "risk fleet" (so-called because no other power would risk confronting it) seemed almost calculated to provoke alarm in London. Naval policymakers judged Britain's national security by the "two-power standard," which held that the Royal Navy should be at least as strong as the combined fleets of the next two major powers. Germany's planned naval expansion was seen as a clear challenge to British naval supremacy and quickly led to a naval race between the two nations as the British government moved to meet the apparent threat. The race grew in seriousness and cost in 1906 when an English shipyard launched HMS *Dreadnought*, the first of a new class of larger, more heavily gunned battleships. William, by now caught up in the relentless momentum of the arms race, demanded the construction of similar German warships. This feverish naval building spree, which generated dangerous apprehensions on both sides, grew out of the Kaiser's initial belief that he could both impress and coerce Britain into an alliance by striving to make Germany a major naval power. The construction of the "risk fleet" had just the opposite effect—it convinced many in England that Germany had aspirations that threatened British policies and the European balance of power. Such apprehensions were affirmed by the Kaiser's frequent advocacy of *Weltpolitik*, the idea that Germany would face decline unless a "world policy" of colonial and commercial expansion was aggressively pursued. Colonial, pan-German and naval advocacy groups, supported by numerous high government officials, loudly propounded the concept. Increasingly strident assertions of Germany's right to a "place in the sun" caused British leaders to look upon Imperial Germany with growing wariness. Consequently, when Britain and France resolved outstanding colonial issues and concluded the *Entente Cordiale* (1904), it established the basis for later military cooperation and a defensive alliance against Germany. The following year, Russia's defeat by Japan lessened the Russian threat to Britain's Asian interests and opened the path to an Anglo-Russian Accord in 1907. The diplomatic revolution was essentially complete; in the vacuum left by the dissolution of Bismarck's system, the Triple Entente of France, Britain and Russia emerged to confront the Triple Alliance of Germany, Austro-Hungary and Italy. In Berlin, the Kaiser's government viewed this development with unconcealed alarm. This perceived "encirclement of Ger-

many" had the unfortunate consequence of compelling the Kaiser to employ increasingly belligerent rhetoric and embark on risky actions that further destabilized the European order.

COLONIAL RIVALRIES

Since the sixteenth century, the contest for empire had been a source of periodic antagonism among the European powers, and the renewed drive for colonies generated by the "new" imperialism of the late nineteenth century created new potential for conflict. By the early years of the new century, the most contentious issues between Britain, France and Russia had been resolved. Germany and Italy, whose appetite for colonies and imperial influence was as yet unrequited, proved more than willing to challenge the international status quo to achieve their objectives. William's pursuit of a German "world policy" led inevitably to new attention to areas in which Germany's "rights" might be asserted. Though Asia had been of some interest to German statesmen, who succeeded in gaining special rights in China and laying claim to some Pacific island chains, Africa still offered some irresistible opportunities to challenge rival colonial powers and to realize Germany's "place in the sun."

These objectives lay behind the Moroccan Crises of 1905 and 1911, both of which involved assertions of German rights in the northwest African country, formally still part of the fraying Ottoman empire. The 1905 episode grew out of the Kaiser's ill-considered response to growing French influence in Morocco. Partly to test the strength of the Anglo-French accord, William journeyed to Tangier to announce Germany's support for Moroccan independence, a disingenuous and inflammatory act. In consequence, an international conference was hurriedly convened at Algeciras, Spain, where the delegates rebuffed Germany and affirmed French predominance. More unsettling to German statesmen, the only nation to support their position was the Austro-Hungarian Empire. Italy, increasingly viewed as an undependable member of the Triple Alliance, voted against Germany. Those who had feared Germany's isolation and encirclement saw their apprehensions affirmed at Algeciras. Such concerns were behind the formulation of the Schlieffen Plan, devised in 1905 by the chief of the German General Staff, Count Alfred von Schlieffen. This contingency plan for avoiding a two-front war against France and her ally Russia mandated a rapid German advance through neutral Belgium and into France, with the objective of forcing a French surrender before Russian forces could effectively mobilize on Germany's eastern frontier. Theoretically, the Schlieffen Plan would spare Germany the enormous challenge of fighting the two Entente powers simultaneously. The plan was fraught with enormous risks, the consequences of which would not be evident until late summer 1914; it reflected both German anxieties and fatalism about the likelihood of conflict.

The Second Moroccan Crisis was the product of more German blustering following French intervention in Morocco in the summer of 1911. France's establishment of a protectorate over the impoverished desert country led the German emperor to insist that the French Congo be turned over to Germany as compensation. The gunboat *Panther* was dispatched to Agadir to punctuate the demand, but France, diplomatically strengthened by its alliances with Britain and Russia, was not intimidated. Ultimately, Germany received a portion of the French Congo

in return for acknowledging the French protectorate in Morocco. The incident had the unfortunate effect of strengthening British and French concerns about the course and intent of Germany's seemingly unpredictable and aggressive diplomacy. In Germany, the perceived humiliations in the two Moroccan crises drove even moderate opinion to the conclusion that the Second Reich was being denied its rightful "place in the sun."

Italy's imperial activities also undercut international stability in the immediate pre-war years. Italian colonial ambitions had, since the late nineteenth century, generally exceeded Italian abilities and resources. Italy's African empire consisted only of Eritrea and Italian Somaliland; an effort to seize Abyssinia in 1896 had resulted in an embarrassing military defeat. French success in Morocco reawakened imperial desires in Rome, and Italian statesmen focused their attention on Tripoli (later Libya), a poorly defined desert region on the North African coast. Sought by no other European power and thinly garrisoned by Ottoman Turkey, Tripoli presented an opportunity for Italy to expand its African empire and keep pace with French expansion in the area with little risk of defeat. The Tripolitanian War began in September 1911 and continued through the following summer, when Turkey conceded defeat and recognized Italian claims to Tripoli and the Dodecanese Islands. The war fanned irresponsible nationalist and imperialist sentiments in Italy and, worse, helped to create the circumstances for a series of Balkan wars that led to the crisis of summer 1914.

THE "EASTERN QUESTION" AND THE BALKAN WARS

Since the nineteenth century the "Eastern Question" had periodically surfaced to challenge European diplomats. Issues arising from the continued decline of the Ottoman Empire had produced uncertainty, tensions and sometimes conflict between small and great powers. By the early years of the twentieth century, the recession of Ottoman power was of most direct interest to the two major powers whose borders were contiguous or in proximity to Ottoman territory. Both Imperial Russia and Austria-Hungary had kept careful watch over developments on the Balkan peninsula since the changes occasioned by the Russo-Turkish War of 1878 and the subsequent Congress of Berlin, which affirmed the independence of Rumania, Serbia, Montenegro and Bulgaria. The dynamics of Balkan affairs were complicated not only by the historic Austro–Russian tensions, but also by the erratic and unpredictable course of Ottoman decline and the potentially troublesome aspirations of the small Balkan nations. A tangle of often-conflicting national, ethnic and religious issues combined to make the Balkans a highly volatile region; the oft-heard description of the region as the "powderkeg of Europe" was not a simple cliche. Russian expansionist ambitions were deflected toward the troubled peninsula following its defeat in the Russo-Japanese War. Even as Russian relations with Bulgaria worsened, pan-Slavism drove Russia to adopt Serbia as a client state. Habsburg statesmen, fearful of the impact of Serbian nationalist agitation on their own minority populations, saw both Serbia and Russia as potential threats and encouraged Bulgaria to view Austria-Hungary as an ally and protector. The situation was made more precarious by Germany's determination to preserve the Ottoman Empire as a bulwark against "the Slav menace" to the east.

The potential for serious trouble in the region became evident in July 1908 when reformist officers in the Turkish army revolted against Sultan Abdul-Hamid II. These "Young Turks," outraged by the humiliations imposed on the Ottoman Empire by the great powers, demanded the restoration of the 1876 constitution as a prelude to modernization. The turmoil in Turkey led Russian diplomats to believe that this was the opportune moment to pursue a long-desired objective— free access for the Russian Black Sea fleet through the Bosporus and Dardenelles Straits to the Mediterranean. Should a rejuvenated Turkey emerge from the "Young Turk" Revolution, this Russian goal might well be rejected. Moving quickly, Russia's foreign minister sought and gained the support of Austria-Hungary, promising in return that Russia would accept the Habsburg Empire's annexation of Bosnia-Herzegovina, which had been administered by the Dual Monarchy since 1878. Though the two territories were immediately incorporated into Austria-Hungary, Russian hopes for free transit through the Straits were shattered by objections from the major powers and Russia's navy remained barred from this access to the Mediterranean. This diplomatic embarrassment did much to harden Russian attitudes toward Austria-Hungary, and inflamed Serbian opinion, given the significant south Slav populations in the annexed area. Though the crisis eventually subsided, the Russian government was hard pressed to restrain its client Serbia from declaring war on the hated Austrians. Russia, now convinced of Habsburg duplicity, began a concerted effort to strengthen its heretofore-weakened military forces.

Intense and arguably irresponsible nationalist fervor on the part of the Balkan nations did much to bring about the First and Second Balkan Wars of 1912–1913, which serve as the immediate prelude to the events of summer 1914. The Ottoman Empire, debilitated further by defeat in the Tripolitanian War, was a tempting target for dismemberment. The Balkan League, comprised of Serbia, Bulgaria, Montenegro and Greece, found the temptation too great to be resisted. In October 1912, the Balkan League nations attacked the Ottoman Empire, with the immediate objective of driving the Ottoman Turks out of the Balkans and Europe. The war was as brief (one month) as it was successful, with the armies of the Balkan League on the verge of seizing Constantinople when the major powers intervened to stave off complete dismemberment. The Turks conceded Crete and all European territory save for a small strip near the Straits.

Austria and Italy squelched Serbian ambitions for expansion to the Adriatic Sea, bringing an independent Albania into existence. This disappointment helped bring about the Second Balkan War of July 1913, in which Serbia, now desirous of a larger piece of Macedonia, joined Greece in a war against Bulgaria. Soon set upon by Romania and Turkey, Bulgaria was defeated in a month's time and forced to cede Macedonian territory to Greece and Serbia. Though these Balkan nations were impoverished, indebted and internally unstable, they pursued aggressive policies of expansion with a reckless disregard for the consequences. Less than a year later, in late June 1914, a similar lack of concern for the broader consequences of rash acts helped set in train the sequence of events that sparked the First World War.

FATEFUL DAYS:
JUNE 28–AUGUST 4, 1914

Like many Serbian nationalists, Gavrilo Princip despised the Austrian Empire. Its diplomats greedily annexed lands populated by south Slavs; its statesmen conspired to obstruct the rightful expansion of Serbia, homeland to many south Slavs. For those reasons, Princip was in Sarajevo, Bosnia on June 28, 1914. He and his accomplices, all members of the terrorist group Black Hand, intended to assassinate the heir to the Austrian throne, Archduke Franz Ferdinand, when he paid a goodwill visit to the recently annexed city. Aided by sympathizers in Serbia's intelligence service, the assassins positioned themselves along the route of the archduke's motorcade, armed with bombs and pistols. Fate intervened to thwart the trio; opportunities for a clear shot did not develop and even a bomb thrown at the imperial car only bounced into the street and exploded harmlessly. The archduke arrived at the city hall safe but thoroughly miffed, and plans were set to take a different route out of town. Here fate intervened again, bringing the archduke's misdirected car to a halt only feet away from Princip, who had been walking the streets despairing of having missed his earlier opportunity. Seizing his chance, Princip stepped up to the halted limousine, leaned in and fired twice with his revolver, inflicting fatal wounds on both Franz Ferdinand and his wife. Princip was arrested at the scene and died three years later, a prisoner in the Habsburg fortress prison at Theresienstadt.

Other than as a symbol of Austrian oppression, Ferdinand was an unlikely focus for Serb nationalist hatred. A reasonable man, he was known to advocate a new approach to imperial government called trialism, which held out the promise of limited autonomy within the empire to south Slavs. The terrorists no doubt concluded that such moderation would not have served well as a foil for extreme Serb nationalism; the murder of the Habsburg heir might do more to destabilize the Dual Monarchy and advance the Serbian cause. Whatever the immediate motivations behind it, the assassination of the archduke stunned Europe and was almost universally denounced.

For Austria-Hungary, the event's significance went far beyond the death of the heir apparent. A strong response to Serbia was imperative, lest the empire be seen as enfeebled. Because Austro-Hungarian forces required a month to be readied for action, and action against Serbia implied probable conflict with Russia as well, Habsburg statesmen sought assurance of German support for Serbia's elimination "as a power factor in the Balkans."

Germany's leaders saw no alternative to offering full support to their only remaining major ally, and in early July, the German kaiser responded to Austrian inquiries with what came to be called the "blank check"— confirmation of unlimited German support, with emphasis on the urgency of acting while Europe remained in shock from the Sarajevo murder. On July 23, nearly three weeks after the assassination, the Austrian government delivered an ultimatum to Serbia, demanding among other things the authority to investigate the crime in Serbia and the suppression of pan-Slav agitation and propaganda.

The Austrian terms almost seemed calculated to make conflict unavoidable. To make matters worse, the lengthy delay that preceded the ultimatum afforded the Serbs and Russians an opportunity to ponder their options. Nicholas II placed the Russian army on alert, a status just short of mobilization, and made clear his determination to back Serbia, hoping that a show of Russian determination would cause Austria-Hungary to back down.

The German Kaiser's initial hope for a *fait accompli* by which Austria could emphatically punish Serbia without risk of serious consequences vanished. Events began to develop a fateful momentum that rapidly accelerated in the following days.

Even as Russia hoped to deter Austria-Hungary by backing Serbia, Germany was convinced that unqualified support for her Habsburg ally would ultimately deter the Russians from intervening on Serbia's behalf. When British statesmen urged the powers to resolve the crisis peacefully, Germany incorrectly interpreted this as evidence that Britain would be hesitant to support Russia in a continental war. This strengthened German determination to press Austria-Hungary for resolute action against the Serbs. On July 28, three days after Serbia mobilized its army, Austria-Hungary declared war on the Slav kingdom. As pro-Serbian demonstrations erupted in Russia, Germany's government urged Vienna to pursue the war against Serbia regardless of Russian intervention; any other course would reveal the Dual Monarchy as an enfeebled power. Berlin also noted that if war came, every effort should be made to ensure that Russia was seen as the instigator. That opportunity arose on July 30.

By the end of July, many of Germany's leaders had come to accept the inevitability of war against the Triple Entente. On July 29, Berlin took the first quiet steps toward implementing the Schlieffen Plan, which would involve a rapid German advance into France, with the objective of encircling and capturing Paris. The success of the plan was contingent on precisely timed troop deployments and an extremely specific military timetable. Once initiated, the Schlieffen Plan would be propelled by its own inexorable logic. It would irrevocably commit

Germany to an aggressive war against France, the rapid and successful conclusion of which was crucial to next defeating the Russian enemy. Despite its enormous risks, the plan was seen by many in the government as offering the only solution to the increasingly complex challenges that had developed over the previous 20 years. The Russian Tsar's order for mobilization on July 31 provided the necessary pretext for action. Even as French and Russian diplomats frantically sought assurance of British support and Britain sought some guarantee from Germany of Belgium's neutrality, Berlin ordered the mobilization of the German army and declared war on Russia on August 1. Two days later Germany declared war on France and shortly afterward German forces invaded eastern Belgium as the early phases of the Schlieffen Plan began to unfold. Britain joined the war on August 4, following Germany's refusal to withdraw from Belgium. The most deadly European conflict in 300 years had begun.

The First World War, 1914–1918

As the conflict opened in late summer 1914, two great alliance systems took the first uncertain steps toward what would later be described as history's first "total war." The Allied Powers—Britain, France, and Russia—eventually grew to include Japan, Italy and later the United States, in addition to Rumania, Serbia and Greece. Italy's defection from the Triple Alliance in 1915 came as no great surprise to Germany and Austria-Hungary which, together with the Ottoman Empire and Bulgaria, came to be known as the Central Powers. Despite warnings in previous years about the probable nature of the next major war, none of the belligerents of

1914 had an accurate understanding of the course or character of the conflict to come; indeed, many were hard pressed to define their aims in a war that seemed to have grown out of no single, clearly discernible issue. Once the conflict was joined, the major powers simply determined to fight for victory.

Given the ill-defined nature of the conflict at its inception, the tactical and strategic blunders, disillusionments and gropings of the first years of the war do not now seem surprising. Still, there was shocking naiveté in the widespread belief that victory would be achieved before Christmas. Likewise, a broad incomprehension of the nature of modern warfare was evident in the decision of the French army to send many of its soldiers into battle outfitted in brightly colored uniforms. The nature of warfare between 1914 and 1918 brought many unexpected developments, compounding the numerous uncertainties that attended the struggle in Europe.

STALEMATE AND SLAUGHTER: THE WESTERN FRONT, 1914–1916

As the war began, there were expectations on both sides that the outcome would be rapidly determined in the west. There, German forces collided with the French army, which was soon bolstered by a small British Expeditionary Force. Both the German and French high commands were convinced of the value of aggressive offensive action. Germany's Schlieffen Plan mandated a German wheeling movement through Belgium, with the right flank extending nearly to the English Channel, with the expectation that French forces would be rolled up east of Paris and forced to a rapid capitulate. Germany's strength could then be turned to the east where, with the support of the large but less well-organized Austro-Hungarian armies, Russia could be repelled before her vast manpower reserves could be effectively mobilized. French commanders were equally devoted to the concept of the offensive, vesting great value in *elan*, the fighting spirit, as a means of willing a victory into being.

The eventual course of the war was set early on as the broad strategies of both nations failed. German forces came close to realizing Schlieffen's design, but were ultimately defeated by the calendar. Stopped at the battle of the Marne by mid-September, German forces were unable to adhere to the exacting timetable required for victory.

Map 2–1   World War I

Legend	
▨ Entente Powers, 1914	▬ Western Front, 1915–1917
▨ Post-1914 allies	•••• Furthest Russian advance in west, 1914–1915
▨ Central Powers. 1914–1918	▬•▬ Maximum extent of advance of Central Powers
▨ Neutral states	✳ Major battles

An ill-considered French offensive through Alsace-Lorraine aimed at the German heartland also collapsed that fall. Though both armies maneuvered for advantage through November in a "race for the sea," the circumstances for a stalemated war of attrition were set. The Germans held most of Belgium, but hopes for a quick defeat of France had evaporated. As 1914 came to an end, it was clear that the war would last beyond Christmas. More ominously, casualties in the first five months of fighting were staggering—France alone counted 300,000 killed and 600,000 wounded by year's end.

The stalemated situation produced in the first year of fighting on the western front continued for the rest of the war with only minor alterations. Since September 1914, efforts to dislodge German forces along the Aisne River had been repeatedly repulsed and static trench warfare took the place of the rapid war of movement that most had envisioned. A line of increasingly improved fortifications and trenchworks soon extended more than 300 miles from near Ostend, Belgium, southward through eastern France. German preoccupations with the now-threatened eastern front seemed to present French commanders with an opportunity to break through the German lines in 1915, but repeated assaults were inevitably repulsed with horrendous casualties. Few commanders on either side yet understood the inescapable impact of advances in weapons technology, which now mitigated against mass frontal assaults against an entrenched enemy. The historian who observed, "If one weapon symbolized the First World War, it was the machine gun," spoke to the essence of the issue. Newly improved automatic weapons were capable of delivering a withering fusillade of fire, 450–600 rounds per minute, and the war

brought an unprecedented expenditure of ammunition. Likewise, infantry were equipped with more powerful, accurate rifles with larger magazine capacity. Further enhancing the deadliness of the modern battlefield, all belligerents employed artillery in unprecedented numbers, and these improved field pieces were capable of accurately hurling high-explosive or shrapnel shells for great distances with appalling effect. The expanded productive capacities of modern industrial economies provided these weapons in staggering quantities.

The ultimate effect of these technological innovations combined with the circumstances on the western front was to make combat far more deadly but, ironically, less decisive. This paradox posed a major dilemma for military strategists in both camps, as armies settled into the dreariness and horror of trench warfare, which saw opposing forces huddled in filthy trenches behind barbed wire defenses, peering at one another across the empty wastes of "No Man's Land." Desperate to break the deadlock, the belligerents sought new weapons that could assure victory. Flame-throwers, tanks and poison gas were all developed and employed in the hope that they might offer the decisive advantage. All contributed to the carnage that made 1916 a year of exceptional horrors.

In early 1916, German hopes for a decisive campaign focused on the fortresses around Verdun in eastern France. The Germans believed that national honor would compel the French to attempt to hold the region at all costs. Consequently, the goal, as defined by German Army chief Erich von Falkenhayn, was "to bleed the French white" in a contest of attrition. The offensive, launched on February 21, was preceded by a nine-hour artillery barrage that dropped two million shells on the French defenders. The fighting, in which both sides used poison gas, continued for ten months and never brought the victory that Falkenhayn predicted. Attrition, he discovered, was a two-edged sword that cut both ways. More than 400,000 men died in the course of the fighting. Historian Alistaire Horne aptly described Verdun as "the worst battle in history."

Even as the latter stages of the Verdun campaign were unfolding, a joint Anglo-French offensive was opened against German lines along the Somme River on July 1. Hopes that a withering artillery barrage would obliterate the German defenses proved false, and advancing Allied troops suffered staggering losses. On the first day, British casualties amounted to 60,000, with nearly 20,000 dead, the largest single-day loss in British history. No decisive breakthrough was achieved and the struggle dragged on into November, with total casualties estimated at 1,200,000. Verdun and the Somme badly weakened all of the armies involved and demonstrated the incredibly costly character of a modern industrial war. One historian has calculated that the combined death toll from the two battles may be expressed as an average rate of 6,600 killed every day, which is more than 277 killed every minute and nearly five dead every second. At the end of 1916, a resolution to the stalemate remained elusive.

WAR IN THE EAST AND SOUTH: THE RUSSIAN AND ITALIAN FRONTS

As the Schlieffen Plan had committed the bulk of German forces to the west in 1914, the eastern regions of both Germany and Austria-Hungary were at least temporarily vulnerable to Russian offensives. German commanders were rightfully doubtful about the military capabilities of their Habsburg ally. More poorly trained, equipped and led than German forces, the Austro-Hungarian army was also hampered by a lack of internal unity, largely the product of the army's multinational, polyglot composition. Rebuffed in an initial invasion of Serbia, Austrian forces also suffered a massive defeat at the hands of the Russian army in Galicia. A Russian invasion of East Prussia, where the Tsar's armies made impressive gains, compounded the challenges facing the Central Powers in the east. As would often prove the case in the years to come, however, Russian success was short-lived. Though vast in size, the Russian army was poorly trained, led and supplied. No amount of courage on the part of individual Russian soldiers could overcome the German army's logistical advantages. As a result, German forces commanded by Paul von Hindenberg inflicted serious damage on the Russians at Tannenberg in late August and at the Masurian Lakes in early September. The Russian offensive was halted and then reversed, as German forces, later supported by Austrian troops, drove eastward and occupied all of Russian Poland by the end of 1915. The following year, Russian armies began another offensive against the northeastern frontiers of Habsburg territory with similar results—initial successes followed by a loss of momentum. By 1917 military reverses, coupled with an increasingly critical shortage of basic supplies, including weapons and munitions, were having a perceptible effect on the morale of Russian troops, many of whom were deserting. It was one of many portents of the coming political storm in Russia.

Italy's defection from the Triple Alliance in 1915, induced by the Allied promise of ter-

Fig. 2-1   A deserted trench at Ypres, Belgium, site of three major battles between British and German armies during 1914–1917. Soldiers endured long periods in such trenchworks, their lives made miserable by mud, rats, disease and the debilitating effects of alternating periods of boredom and intense terror. (Pearson Education, Corporate Digital Archive, Getty Images Inc.)

ritorial gains from Austria-Hungary, posed the most immediate threat to Austria-Hungary, though the long-term German concern was the possible need to divert resources and troops to an Austro-Italian front. As events proved, there was little justification for worry. Italy's army numbered less than a million and was ill-supplied with heavy guns, munitions and transport. Geography dictated the direction of any Italian offensive into the mountainous Isonzo River region, where in June 1915 the Italian army began the first of eleven costly battles in which they advanced only twelve miles. For the next two and a half years, Italian and Austrian forces were locked in stalemate in this harsh region, much as were their allies on the western front. This forgotten front achieved a new importance in October 1917 when the Austrians, bolstered by German reinforcements, launched a massive attack that threw the surprised Italians into a panic. The Italian rout at Caporetto brought the armies of the Central Powers to within twenty miles of Venice, where defensive lines were finally established. The Austro-Italian front, like the eastern front, was the scene of costly combat and some periodic movement, but nothing that promised to end the overall stalemate.

THE BALKANS, THE MIDDLE EAST AND PERIPHERAL AREAS

One of the war's great surprises was the fierce resistance of the Serbs, who met the initial Austrian invasion of August 1914 with unexpected vigor. Despite early successes, Serbian forces were forced into withdrawal by growing munitions shortages, and by November, the Austrians had captured Belgrade. Once resupplied through Greece by the Allies, however, the Serbs undertook a ferocious counteroffensive that drove the Austrians out of their country by December. But Serbia was confronted with a much graver threat in the fall of 1915, when Bulgaria joined with Austria and Germany in a six-week campaign that decimated the Serb army and left the entire country under foreign occupation. Slightly over 37% of the Serbian forces mobilized were killed, the highest percentage of all the belligerents. Rumania, with hopes of gaining Transylvania from the beleaguered Habsburg Empire, joined the war on the side of the Allies in August 1916, but realized no immediate gains,

given the collapse of Russian's recent offensive in the region.

The stalemate in the west led Britain to ponder striking at Turkey in early 1915. Winston Churchill, First Lord of the Admiralty, promoted the idea of using British naval strength to force the Dardenelles and seize Constantinople, thus weakening Turkey and opening the route to the Black Sea and the Russian ally. Poorly conceived in many ways, the attempt to push an Anglo-French naval expedition past the forts and minefields guarding the straits failed badly. By the time the effort was called off in late March, Allied losses were 700 dead and three battleships sunk. Political exigencies required that the campaign against the Ottoman foe be continued, but the focus shifted to an amphibious assault on the Gallipoli Peninsula, which was carried out largely by Commonwealth (Australian and New Zealand) troops. A force of 70,000 was put ashore in March on the hilly, rocky peninsula where, despite some early advances, the assault was halted by fierce and effective Turkish resistance. By May, the fighting had deteriorated into the same type of trench warfare that characterized the western front, and in December 1915 Britain's Cabinet decided to evacuate the troops.

During the same period, Turkish and Russian forces had clashed on the Caucasian front, where one of the worst mass atrocities of the war occurred. A long hostility between Turks and the Christian Armenian minority in remote eastern Turkey culminated as Turkish authorities accused Armenian partisans of aiding the Russian enemy. During the subsequent "Armenian Massacres," Turkish troops indiscriminately murdered tens of thousands of Armenian men, women and children, ultimately driving thousands more into the barren deserts of Syria. Some 1,750,000 were ordered deported into the inhospitable region, where an estimated 800,000 perished, ensuring an enduring Armenian hostility toward Turkey. Elsewhere, British troops continued to fight the Turks in Mesopotamia and Palestine. The British attempted to organize an Arab revolt within the Ottoman Empire, but the efforts of Colonel T.E. Lawrence, later renowned as "Lawrence of Arabia," brought no decisive results. Once again, Allied hopes of resolving the stalemate faded.

The war spread beyond Europe and the Middle East. Japan's entry on the Allied side in 1914 expanded the conflict into Asia and the Pacific, but in a limited manner. Japanese statesmen saw the European conflict as an opportunity to broaden Japan's imperial reach in the Far East with minimum exertion. Japanese forces easily seized German leased territory on the Shantung peninsula and the Mariana, Caroline and Marshall Island chains, all previously claimed by Germany. Japan's major military operations were concluded in early 1915. Africa was also the scene of some fighting, as British forces eventually gained control of Togoland, German Southwest Africa and the German Cameroons.

THE WAR AT SEA AND IN THE AIR

One of the war's ultimate ironies was the relative uselessness of the great battle fleets on which Britain and Germany had expended vast sums in the decades prior to the war. Though both nations utilized warships against enemy commerce, and while there were several minor engagements between British and German naval squadrons, the vast, decisive fleet engagement envisioned by prewar naval planners had not occurred as of 1916. Germany hesitated to risk her "risk" fleet; British naval chiefs were likewise wary of a major naval clash in which Britain might "lose the war in an afternoon." By early 1916, German naval leaders were under growing pressure to use their fleet, especially given the terrible sacrifices of the army on the western front. In late May, Germany's High Seas Fleet steamed into the North Sea with the intention of forcing a showdown with Britain's Grand Fleet. In the subsequent battle of Jutland off the Danish coast, the two fleets, numbering over 250 ships altogether, clashed in confused, intermittent running battles over the course of two days. The Royal Navy suffered some grievous blows, losing three battleships that exploded following German hits. (Of the HMS *Indefatigable*'s 1,000-man crew, only two men survived.) But when the results of the battle were fully assessed, it became clear that Germany's High Seas Fleet had been bested. Badly damaged, the German fleet retired to Kiel for the rest of the war, conceding control of the North Sea to the British.

Of considerably more consequence to the course of the war was the submarine, which had only recently evolved into a relatively dependable and useful weapon. Though all the major belligerents possessed submarine fleets, it was Germany that utilized the "U-boats" (*Unterseeboot*) most extensively and successfully. Cognizant that most of Germany's surface fleet was bottled up in the North Sea and encouraged by the success of *U-9*, which sank three British cruisers off the Dutch coast in one day in 1914, Germany's leaders employed unrestricted submarine warfare to enforce its blockade of the British Isles in 1915. This policy brought considerable success, with German submarines sinking some 6,000 Allied merchant and warships by 1918, but there were major risks attendant to it. Many viewed submarine warfare as inhumane, and the full repercussions of sinking neutral vessels were not fully appreciated in the early months of the war. One indication of the risks that attended submarine warfare came in May 1915, when a U-boat sank the British passenger liner *Lusitania* off the southern coast of Ireland. Among the 1,198 dead were 128 Americans, and the angry protests of U.S. President Woodrow Wilson led the German government to abandon unrestricted submarine warfare in September 1915. The military situation in Europe was not yet desperate enough to cause Germany to risk bringing the United States into the war.

The war in the air saw the widespread use of aerial balloons for reconnaissance and artillery spotting and brought a wider role for powered airships, perhaps most dramatically the German Zeppelins that bombed London. The development and use of aircraft, however, much more accurately marked the direction of twentieth-century warfare. Though aircraft were still primitive in 1914, war-driven innovations brought rapid technological advances such as sturdier airframes, more powerful engines and monocoque fuselages, in which the exterior skin of the fuselage served as the stress-bearing structure. The machine gun, so deadly in ground fighting, was quickly adapted to aerial usage, as were increasingly varied and destructive aerial bombs. By the war's end, multi-engine German bombers were terrorizing civilian populations in England. Aircraft served in a variety of roles on all fronts, as fighters, bombers, artillery spotters and for reconnaissance. The

air war between 1914 and 1918 provided a hint of the crucial roles that aircraft would play in later conflicts.

THE HOME FRONT IN A WAR WITHOUT END

In an often stalemated and closely fought conflict, all the major belligerents quickly accepted that effective mobilization of the home front might well bring the slight advantage that would bring victory. Hence, more than in any previous European war, civilian populations were mobilized, exhorted and assured that their contribution would directly affect the outcome of the struggle. The fact that this was Europe's first major industrial war made broad civilian support all the more crucial. Though the actual fighting in this war did not impact civilian populations to the degree it would in the next world war, the demands and nature of modern industrtial war unquestionably changed the lives of civilians and the shape of civilian society.

The need to mobilize rapidly both industrial resources and manpower led inevitably to an expansion of governmental authority over national economies. In Britain, the Defense of the Realm Act (1914) gave the government control of a broad range of economic activities. In Germany, wartime industrial production was directed by the High Command with the cooperation of German industrialists. An Auxiliary Labor Bill (1916) subjected all German males between the ages of 16 and 70 to war-related labor. The ultimate objective of this increased governmental oversight was industrial production, crucial to waging modern war effectively.

Even as governments sought to marshal their resources, they strove to mobilize and shape public opinion. As the war dragged on and disappointments mounted, national leaders realized that public opinion could be crucial; a populace willing to sacrifice and endure hardship might well provide the slight edge required for victory in such a close contest. Governments sometimes sought to bolster public support for the war by emphasizing ideal war aims. Tens of thousands of young Englishmen responded to the simple patriotic appeal of a famous recruiting poster announcing that the army chief, Lord Herbert Kitchener, "wants YOU." Many French undoubtedly believed that they fought in defense of their republic and its ideals, while the English saw the war as in defense of their traditional liberties. Governmental authorities found, however, that public zeal for the war was inevitably kindled most easily by negative propaganda that focused on the evil nature and deplorable acts of the enemy. Germany's destructive march through Belgium in 1914 and the murderous consequences of submarine warfare were frequent subjects of French and British propaganda efforts. Official German propaganda stressed the threat posed by the Russian menace, atrocities by British soldiers and the unjust actions of the Allied powers in obstructing Germany's legitimate expansionist objectives.

Governmental suppression of antiwar activities and restrictions on basic freedoms were common corollaries to the propaganda offensive and heightened nationalism. Many socialists opposed the war as a capitalist conflict fought by the working class and consequently were frequent targets of government action in a number of countries. Pacifists and conscientious objectors were often dealt with in callous fashion, even in supposedly liberal England, where over 1,500 pacifists were condemned to two years' forced labor; 71 died as result of ill treatment while in government custody. In another case, a military court sentenced 34 British conscientious objectors to death, although the sentences were later commuted to hard labor terms. The renowned English philosopher Bertrand Russell was prosecuted for publishing an anti-conscription pamphlet and was imprisoned in 1918 for 'insulting an ally." In Germany and Austro-Hungary, opponents of the war or the regime could expect equally harsh treatment. In Russia, where there was no tradition of civil liberties, the tsarist regime employed traditional methods of oppression in dealing with dissidents.

Although the war brought oppression and restrictions on liberties almost everywhere, it also created circumstances in which some found new opportunities. Women especially found that military manpower demands opened new areas of endeavor and employment. In Britain, some entered the military in a variety of women's auxiliary units. There, as in many other countries, women also found industrial employment that had often been closed to them in the past, though wages were usually less than those paid to males. Also, there was a general perception that such female employment was a temporary expedient that should end with the war. Nonetheless, in both the Allied and Central Powers, women found employment in a variety of nontraditional areas, such as making munitions and driving trams. As nurses and hospital attendants, those women who worked with the wounded and dying were often profoundly affected by the terrible consequences of war.

In Europe, the war inevitably brought suffering, hardship and privation, varying only in nature and degree. The terrible losses on the battlefield affected all the belligerents, creating a sense of loss in some countries that would endure for at least a generation. Those nations under foreign occupation, such as Belgium and Serbia, endured especially grueling conditions. Elsewhere, material shortages due to the interruption of continental commerce and the German and British naval blockades became more apparent with time. In Germany, with more of the nation's resources directed toward an increasingly demanding conflict and where the effects of the British blockade were clearly felt, the populace struggled through the hungry "Turnip Winter" of 1916–1917. By July 1917, public disaffection had grown to the point that the Reichstag passed a resolution asking that Germany renounce its annexationist war aims and seek a negotiated peace. Such resolutions had little consequence by this time, as the exigencies of war had brought into being a military dictatorship of Generals Erich Ludendorff and Paul von Hindenburg, whose authority over political, economic and military policy was unchallenged even by the inept Kaiser. Both were committed to seeing the war through to military victory.

1917 brought little encouragement to those on the home front. The year seemed instead to offer only war without end, as both French and British commanders believed that fresh offensives could break the stalemate. In April, some 1.2 million French soldiers attacked the German lines along the Aisne River with little significant gain. Convinced that an offensive could succeed if only the troops were fired by the necessary spirit, French generals prepared to order their men to the attack once again in May. The battered troops, many of whom had begun fatalistically bleating like sheep as they marched past their commanders, began

to resist the order to advance. The mutinies spread during June, when one French officer estimated that no more than half his troops were dependable. Before the mutinies were suppressed, 23,000 soldiers were courtmartialed and 55 were executed. The breaking point had been reached and the French offensive slowed to a halt. These events did not deter British commander Douglas Haig, who ordered an offensive around Ypres, with the hope of driving the Germans from the Belgian coast. Passchendaele, a village for which the battle was named, became a synonym for futile slaughter as 300,000 British casualties bought a mere four miles of territory. The British offensive too ground to a halt.

Morale began to collapse all across Europe in 1917. The new French premier George Clemenceau, the "Tiger of France," urged the nation to new efforts and ordered the arrest of "defeatists." Having once commented that "war is too important to be left to generals," Clemenceau sought to rally the French with his assertion that nothing mattered but the war and victory. "I wage war! I wage nothing but war!" he thundered. But the year held yet more disappointments. Beginning in late October, a combined German-Austrian offensive on the Isonzo front routed the Italian army and negated earlier minor gains. Further shaking Allied confidence in 1917, Russia, already staggered by a series of defeats that badly undermined national morale, was caught up in the throes of revolution in March.

RUSSIA: REVOLUTION AND CIVIL WAR

Like many revolutions, the February Revolution in Russia (so-called because the

Julian calendar was in use prior to June 1918) was the product of multiple causes. Most generally, significant food shortages and other privations stirred public unrest. Military defeats and the unendurable hardships of life on the frontlines caused many soldiers to desert and return to the cities, where they contributed to the growing unrest. Public loyalty to the tsarist regime eroded rapidly after 1915, due to the ineptness of Nicholas II and the misguided political machinations of the Empress Alexandra. Increasingly dependent on the advice of Grigori Rasputin, a disreputable itinerant monk, Alexandra provoked growing resentment by filling top government posts with incompetents that Rasputin favored. Both Romanovs consistently resisted suggestions that the creation of a more liberal government might restore public confidence. With the tsar away at the front, the political situation in St. Petersburg and other major cities deteriorated rapidly. In late 1916 a group of nobles who feared that Rasputin's influence and dissolute behavior would bring down the regime murdered the controversial monk. Rasputin's removal did nothing to halt growing discontent. In many Russian cities, workers' and soldiers' councils, or soviets, were springing up. These popular bodies, which had first appeared during the tumult of 1905, served as forums for dissent and centers of opposition to the regime. When massive strikes and bread riots broke out in the capital in March 1917, soldiers began joining the mobs they were expected to disperse. Seizing the moment, leading members of the Duma pressed Nicholas to abdicate. He reluctantly did so, bringing to an end 300 years of Romanov rule. The imperial family became the prisoners of the new government.

The new Provisional Government was comprised of conservative and moderate Duma members, together with the Socialist deputy Alexander Kerensky. Their commitment to constitutional government gave promise of a more popular, liberal Russia, a possibility that the western Allied powers, whose leaders had never been entirely comfortable fighting alongside autocratic tsarist Russia, welcomed. Promises of continued western aid were dependent on Russia remaining in the war, a premise that the Provisional Government accepted. Though the new government moved quickly to initiate reforms, they did not meet the expectations of vast numbers of workers, many of who supported socialist policies, or peasants, whose eternal desire for land remained paramount. More fundamentally, the government's continued prosecution of the war was cause for profound unrest among all classes.

This was the scenario Lenin found when he returned to St. Petersburg in April. In a series of pronouncements that came to be known as the "April Theses," Lenin rejected any cooperation with the Provisional Government. The "bourgeois" March revolution should be immediately followed by a socialist revolution, he insisted, which would bring about a proletarian dictatorship and vest all power in the soviets—only then could the disastrous war be ended. A premature effort to realize Lenin's vision occurred in the capital in July, when soldiers, sailors and workers rose up against the government. Though the Bolshevik leadership denounced the uprising, many were arrested or, like Lenin, forced to flee when it was suppressed. A governmental reorganization made Kerensky prime minister that same month, but he was soon confronted with the threat of a military takeover when General Lavr Kornilov prepared to turn his army toward the capital. Desperate to repulse Kornilov's troops, Kerensky sought the aid of the Bolsheviks, releasing their leaders from jail and arming their followers. The Kornilov threat soon evaporated, but by late summer the disarray within the government was increasingly evident, as was continued public disaffection. Out of these circumstances came the opportunity that Lenin and the Bolsheviks had awaited.

The strength of the Bolsheviks was not in their numbers, though they had increased steadily from 30,000 in February to 76,000 in April. Rather, Bolshevik strength stemmed from the discipline and dedication of party members to distinct objectives that could be effectively articulated in the appealing slogan "Peace, Bread and Land." Given the indirection of and confusion within the Provisional Government, these were distinct advantages. Since April, the Bolsheviks had directed their attention to infiltrating and dominating the proliferating revolutionary councils that could, if the circumstances arose, serve as a shadow government. By early November, with Lenin back in the capital, the Bolsheviks stood poised for a *coup d'etat.* Late on November 6, armed workers and sympathetic soldiers seized strategic locations in St. Petersburg. Lenin, somewhat surprised by the pace of events, disguised himself as a drunken worker to avoid loyal troops and made his way to the Winter Palace, where the Provisional Government had been arrested by Bolshevik forces. The following day, the triumphant Bolsheviks established a new government, the Council of People's Commissars, and issued decrees promising an end to the war and land for the peasantry.

It quickly became evident that Bolshevik rule was synonymous with a one-party dictatorship. Elections in late 1917 for the long-delayed Constituent Assembly, which was to devise a constitution, proved embarrassing for the Bolsheviks, as their delegates won less than a quarter of the seats. When the Assembly met in January 1918, Bolshevik delegates effectively paralyzed it by walking out. Shortly after, the Bolsheviks halted the proceedings. Clearly, there was to be no toleration of views that contradicted those of the party. In late 1917, Lenin had authorized the creation of a secret political police force known as the Cheka, which was vested with extraordinary powers of arrest and execution, in order that it might eradicate "enemies of the revolution."

With the foundations of a dictatorship established, the Bolsheviks turned to the issue of peace. Lenin was adamant in his belief that the revolution could be secured only by ending the war, even at the cost of territorial losses. When Russian and German representatives met at Brest-Litovsk to discuss Russia's withdrawal from the war, it was apparent that the price would be high. Leading the Bolshevik delegation, Leon Trotsky drew out the negotiations in hopes that worker revolts in Germany and Austria would weaken the position of the Central Powers. Ultimately, the treaty that Lenin agreed to in March 1918 cost Russia nearly half of its European territory, including Poland, Finland, the Baltic provinces, Belarus, and the Ukraine. The Bolshevik regime was also required to pay some six billion gold marks in "reparations." Russia was finally out of the war, but at a tremendous cost.

Lenin and the Communists, as the Bolsheviks were now known, soon faced new travails. Following the peace of Brest-Litovsk, the Allied powers feared that German forces might move north into Russia and seize war supplies sent earlier to aid Tsarist Russia. Accordingly, Britain, the United States and France sent some 12,000 troops into Siberia and southern Russia to secure the arms

Fig. 2-2   Vladimir Ilyich Lenin, Bolshevik leader, exhorts a crowd in Moscow's Red Square. Lenin steered the new Bolshevik regime of 1917, with dictatorial control and a willingness to use terror, through years of civil war and foreign intervention. (Pearson Education, Corporate Digital Archive, Getty Images Inc.)

warehouses, while Japan landed 60,000 soldiers on Russia's Pacific coast. This "Siberian Intervention," which finally concluded in 1922, was also aimed at influencing the direction of events within Russia. There were many in Russia who remained unreconciled to Communist rule, including tsarist officers and troops, monarchists, conservatives and even the Social Revolutionaries, a party that

had briefly made accommodations with the Bolshevik regime. By 1918 these opposition forces were engaged in an expanding civil war with the Communists. Former tsarist generals, leading "White Armies", threatened the Communists in the south, east and in Siberia. To defend the revolution, Lenin made Trotsky War Commissar and charged him with organizing the "Red Army," which became a critical instrument of the regime's power in years to come. With Bolshevik Russia under assault by both internal and external enemies, Lenin believed that the use of the harshest methods was justified. In July, a communist firing squad executed the entire imperial family at Ekaterinburg. An attempt on Lenin's life in August 1918 was followed by the "Red Terror," in which the Cheka ruthlessly eliminated anyone who fell under the broad definition of "counterrevolutionary." The success of the revolution, Lenin asserted, was contingent on "unsparing mass terror," which included arrest, forced labor and summary execution.

Severe policies were also the rule in economic matters. As conditions precluded the careful implementation of socialism, the regime introduced "war communism," a harsh policy under which workers were required to enroll in labor battalions while peasants were forced to endure forced "requisitions" of their produce. The effects on the economy were disastrous, as production collapsed, food disappeared and barter became a common means of exchange. When the civil war ended in 1920 with the Communists triumphant, there seemed little but the immediate victory to celebrate. Nonetheless, that same year the Bolshevik regime took steps to ensure its control over the direction of the "inevitable" world socialist revolution. The Third International, or Comintern, created in 1919 under Bolshevik auspices, issued its "Twenty-One Conditions" for those socialist parties that hoped to join it. Foremost, members would be required to accept the Bolshevik model of socialism, and reject reformist and democratic policies. The world socialist revolution, as Lenin's government envisioned it, would necessarily follow the same pattern as had Russia's, grounded in a party dictatorship upheld by terror and violence.

OVER THERE: THE UNITED STATES ENTERS THE WAR

Shortly after the outbreak of the European war in August 1914, President Woodrow Wilson, an idealistic and moralistic leader, announced that the United States would remain out of the conflict. In his neutrality proclamation, Wilson, aware of the potential difficulties in remaining aloof from the struggle, urged Americans "to remain neutral in thought as well as deed." Only dispassionate commitment could ensure that the United States remained clear of the spreading war. Most Americans initially viewed the war as insane, pointless and part of a historical pattern of periodic European conflicts for territory and power. Over the course of the next two and a half years, however, a number of events modified governmental and public opinion.

During the first months of the war, Wilson and his equally idealistic Secretary of State William Jennings Bryan hoped that the United States might serve in the role of mediator in the European conflict. To Wilson's consternation, it soon became evident that his invocation of neutral rights did not guarantee that U.S. merchant shipping would go unmolested. Though Britain benefited by trade with the United States, the Royal Navy, determined to enforce a continental blockade, intercepted and seized American vessels bound for Germany. The German government, irked by U.S. munitions sales to Britain, complained that American neutrality was decidedly unneutral. A major event that heightened anti-German sentiment in the United States was Germany's sinking of the

Lusitania in 1915, though Germany's reluctant abandonment of unrestricted submarine warfare temporarily defused the immediate diplomatic crisis. Though Wilson asserted the morality of neutrality and claimed that it was possible for a nation to be "too proud to fight," he was under growing pressure at home from interventionist elements, including the influential ex-president Theodore Roosevelt, who viewed neutrality as cowardly. During the 1916 presidential election campaign, Wilson stressed "preparedness" but nonetheless won reelection with the slogan "He Kept Us Out of War." At year's end, another American effort to bring the conflict to an end through negotiations failed. By the same time, anti-German sentiment was on the increase due to revelations about German involvement in the destruction of the Black Tom munitions plant in New Jersey, a disaster blamed on sabotage.

Events early in 1917 were crucial in bringing the United States into the war. First, Germany decided in February to return to unrestricted submarine warfare. German statesmen believed that American belligerency would have no immediate decisive impact on the course of the war; it would take months for the United States to mobilize, train and transport its armed forces, by which time the outcome of the war would be decided in Germany's favor. American public opinion held that U-boat warfare was both inhumane and cowardly, and the sinking of the British steamship *Laconia* in late February, in which eight Americans died, provoked an angry response and a movement away from isolationism. Second, the publication of the "Zimmermann Telegram" at about the same time resulted in an even greater public outcry. Arthur Zimmermann, German Secretary for Foreign Affairs, hoped to induce Mexico to join the Central Powers in the event of the

United States entering the war against Germany. His telegram to the German ambassador in Mexico City suggested that, if Mexico would declare war on the United States, Germany would aid Mexico in regaining the territories that had been lost in the Mexican War of 1846–1848. Given the recent antagonisms between the United States and Mexico over American intervention in the Mexican Revolution, it seemed a reasonable strategic ploy, but the telegram was intercepted by the British intelligence service, decoded and forwarded to Washington, with the implicit hope that it would push the Americans toward intervention. When the telegram's contents were revealed to the Congress and the public in late February, outrage over Germany's perfidy was universal. As tensions increased in March, Wilson ordered the arming of U.S. merchant ships, three of which were sunk by U-boats in a single week. Impelled by his own anger at Germany's duplicity and immorality as well as by public opinion, Wilson asked Congress for a declaration of war, which was approved on April 6.

German assessments were partially correct; the armed forces of the United States were nowhere near deployable in April 1917. The Army and National Guard together totaled only slightly more than 200,000 men. The officer corps was aging and uninspired and the War Department was notoriously mired in bureaucratic incompetence. Only the navy could be described as reasonably prepared, having been recently modernized and enlarged. A conscription act in May 1917 marked the beginning of serious mobilization, but training was slow and by late 1917 only four U.S. divisions had reached France. Until May 1918 there were only token U.S. forces on the western front. Most immediately, the greater contribution of the United

States to the Allied war effort came through financial support. The American military role in Germany's defeat would not be apparent until the fall of 1918.

In many ways, the war's impact on the American home front reflected the experience of the other belligerents. The national government assumed more direct control of major segments of the economy with the intent of rationalizing wartime production. The War Industries Board was one of a number of wartime agencies charged with mobilizing and directing America's industrial potential. Other government bodies oversaw food, fuel and agricultural production. As in Europe, the national government also sought to mobilize and direct public opinion, creating the Committee on Public Information to disseminate information and clarify war aims. Unfortunately, the Committee soon became an instrument of propaganda and did much to fuel wartime intolerance and hysteria. Wilson himself had presciently remarked, "Once lead this people into war and they will forget that such a thing as tolerance ever existed," and events proved him correct.

Americans were far from united in support of intervention, with opposition coming from socialists, pacifists, conscientious objectors and various religious denominations. The government's general hostility to dissent was demonstrated with the passage of the Espionage Act (1917) and the Sedition Act (1918). The former made several forms of protest illegal, while the latter literally criminalized any written or spoken criticism of the government. While some dissenters faced arrest and jail, others fell victim to mob violence. As anti-German hysteria grew, public rancor against anything remotely associated with Germany was broadly manifest. Even religious leaders contributed to the demonization of the "evil Hun;" the famous evangelist

Billy Sunday told an audience "If you were to pick Hell up and turn it upside down, you would find 'Made in Germany' inscribed on the bottom!"

Growing racial tensions augmented the general climate of intolerance, as whites often responded violently to the influx of African-Americans into the nation's industrial cities. Vicious race riots occurred both during and immediately after the war. Some black leaders had hoped that the war would provide black Americans with an opportunity to demonstrate their patriotism and gain their full civil rights, but their hopes went unmet. Altogether, American society did not bear up well under the strains of the conflict, which seemed only to reveal the many political, ethnic and racial divisions that pervaded the country. War's end brought not rejuvenation, but disillusionment and a conservative backlash.

THE FINAL CAMPAIGNS AND ARMISTICE

By 1918, a general sense of exhaustion and despair pervaded both the Allied nations and the Central Powers. The Allied offensives of the previous year had proved indecisive. Russia was out of the war, wracked by revolution and civil war, while Italy was staggered by growing economic distress and military failure. Germany's U-boat campaign continued to wreak havoc on Allied shipping. The scenario facing the Central Powers was equally grim. The Allied blockade was causing growing economic distress attended by popular disillusionment. In Austria-Hungary there were ominous signs of disintegration, especially following the death of Franz Joseph in 1916. His successor Charles was unable to stem the rising tide of nationalism amongst the Czechs, Serbs, Poles and other minorities. Both Bulgaria and Ottoman Turkey faced political disintegration. Germany's military leaders rested their last hopes on a renewed offensive in the west, where German strength could be augmented by troops now released from the eastern front. Rumania's surrender in May 1917 further lessened the threat from the east. German victory was still possible if severe blows could be inflicted on the enemy before the arrival of significant numbers of U.S. troops.

The Ludendorff Offensive in spring 1918 was based on hopes that German forces could push the British back to the Channel, isolate their armies from the French, and defeat them. France, it was believed, would then concede defeat. The initial assault, begun in late March, took German forces close enough to Paris to allow for the long-range bombardment of the French capital by giant guns, but by June the advance halted in the face of frantic Allied resistance, with newly arrived American troops engaging the Germans at Chateau-Thierry. A second German offensive was repulsed in mid-July, bringing a disastrous collapse of morale in Germany, where open criticism of the Kaiser's government was growing. An Allied counterattack the same month succeeded in pushing the Germans back to their original positions by early September. The utter failure of the Ludendorff Offensive was followed by the rapid unraveling of the Central Powers. In late September, as Bulgaria negotiated a separate peace, Ludendorff informed the Kaiser that Germany had no choice but to seek an end to the war. Even as the new German chancellor Max von Baden sought President Wilson's help in arranging an armistice, Austro-Hungarian armies were being routed on the Italian front. As Turkey left the war in October, the political disintegration of the Second

Reich accelerated. German sailors at Kiel mutinied rather than fight a last pointless engagement with the Royal Navy, while an independent socialist republic was declared in Bavaria. The end for Imperial Germany came in early November when a new government led by the Social Democratic Party declared the Kaiser's abdication and the establishment of a republic. William II fled his capital on November 9, seeking refuge across the border in neutral Holland. Two days later, on November 11, representatives of the new German republic signed an armistice with the Allies, ending the war.

Shaping a New International Order: the Paris Peace Conference

The First World War left a path of destruction that defied immediate comprehension. Four empires that had largely determined the course of European events were gone and imperial dynasties that had ruled for as long as 400 years were deposed. Economic structures and relationships that had developed over decades were disrupted. Millions of individual lives were shattered by death, wounds, disease, displacement and starvation. The fighting decimated an entire generation of young Europeans, leaving grievous physical and emotional marks on the survivors. Many of those who endured the savagery of modern warfare were psychologically brutalized, inured to the cruelties and mass death that characterized combat. Clearly, formulating a postwar settlement that effectively addressed the numerous issues left by the war would be as challenging as fighting the war. Reconciling the sometimes-contravening objectives of the major Allied participants was another formidable challenge. Not since the Congress of Vienna in 1814 had statesmen prepared to address postwar issues of such magnitude and complexity in hopes of building a stable, peaceful international order. As the delegates from 27 nations gathered in Paris in January 1919 to determine the shape of the peace settlement, most were cognizant that the terrible destructiveness of the recent war made their success all the more imperative.

THE WILSONIAN VISION AND THE VERSAILLES TREATY

When Woodrow Wilson took the United States into the war in 1917, he renounced any crass aims of material or territorial gain and instead set forth two basic idealistic objectives. It was to be "the war to end all wars" and "the war to make the world safe for democracy." The mere military defeat of Germany would be of no avail, Wilson believed, unless the broader objectives of a "lasting peace" and a democratic world were realized. As a student of history Wilson felt that the periodic wars that ravaged Europe were partly the product of faulty peace settlements. Inevitably, the victors imposed such burdensome demands on the vanquished that the roots of the next war were quickly set down. Thus came Wilson's call early in the war for "peace without victory" and his pronouncement in January 1918 of the "Fourteen Points," which he described as "the only possible program" for world peace. The "Fourteen Points" enumerated some basic policies aimed at fostering international accord and lessening the likelihood of conflict: no secret treaties, freedom of the seas, an end to economic barriers, armaments reduction, and the impartial resolution of imperial claims. The principle of national self-

determination would assure that sovereign peoples could determine their own form of government. Point 14 reflected Wilson's hopes for a new, rational world order; it called for the creation of "a general association of nations," a League of Nations, to guarantee the territory and independence of all nations. Altogether, Wilson's proposal was aimed at realizing a "just peace," a settlement lacking in retribution. For this reason, it was Wilson that the German government first approached concerning terms for ending the war in fall 1918.

Of course Wilson would not shape the peace alone. The American president was only one of the "Big Four" who would decide the broad outlines of the individual treaties. His European counterparts arrived at Versailles, just outside Paris, with perspectives that were at great variance with Wilson's idealistic scheme. As diplomatic historians note, the dominant force shaping the outlook of the European leaders was a reactive and vengeful nationalism, which made the realization of Wilson's vision unlikely from the beginning. The French premier, George Clemenceau, was cognizant that his people would not accept a lenient peace, given the huge loss of life and the amount of physical destruction in northeastern France. Not surprisingly, Clemenceau was adamant that France's future security was dependent on weakening Germany and that Germany should make reparations for war damage, regardless of the negative impact these policies might have on German public opinion. While the British, represented by Prime Minister David Lloyd George, were somewhat more flexible, they nonetheless stood behind the French position. Britain too had incurred horrendous casualties during the war and popular opinion would not support a concilia-

Map 2–2 The Peace Settlement in Europe

tory attitude toward Germany. Lloyd George's own campaign slogan in wartime elections had been "Hang the Emperor!", though his views had moderated by 1919. The Italian delegate, Count Vittorio Orlando, was primarily interested in assuring that Italy's territorial demands were met.

The likelihood of contention between the European leaders and the American presi-

dent was further heightened by Wilson's character. Moralistic, often rigidly inflexible, and perceived by some as arrogantly self-righteous, Wilson traveled to Europe convinced that his proposals alone could guarantee lasting peace. Received by cheering crowds in London, Rome and finally Paris, Wilson was confirmed in his messianic mission. He did not, however, visit any battlefield or cemetery, which might have broadened his understanding of the European perspective. Once engaged in discussions with the European leaders, Wilson was somewhat surprised to find that they were willing to challenge his presumptions about key issues. Legitimate differences of opinion played a major role, but among such monumental egos, personality clashes were also inevitable. The 70-year-old Clemenceau, an ardent French nationalist who had twice witnessed German invasions of his country, was irritated by what he saw as Wilson's naïve idealism and moralistic posturing, while Wilson was often frustrated by the apparent cynicism of the French premier. Lloyd George, frequently caught between the two, captured the dilemma of the man in the middle when he later told an English audience, "I thought I did about as well as could be expected, given that I was seated between Napoleon Bonaparte and Jesus Christ." Count Orlando, furious that Italy was denied the full range of her territorial claims, left the conference early on.

Months of deliberations produced a German settlement that reflected the triumph of European realities over American idealism. The Treaty of Versailles required that Germany endorse Article 231, soon to be infamous as the "war guilt" clause, by which Germany accepted full responsibility for the "loss and damage" resulting from a war caused by "the aggression of Germany." To add injury to insult, Germany was also required to make reparations for the damages, the final amount of which remained undetermined at the time the treaty was signed. Ultimately a figure of 132 billion Gold Marks was set. To meet French security needs, the Rhineland was to be demilitarized and Ger-

many's army reduced to a token force of 100,000 men. The German navy was reduced to insignificance and the air force was abolished. The treaty also contained humiliating territorial losses. Germany was stripped of her African and Asian possessions; Alsace-Lorraine was once again French and France gained control of the valuable Saar border region for the next fifteen years. Other German territory was lost to Belgium and the new Polish nation.

Though the new German republic had sent delegates to Paris, they were permitted no role in the discussions and were kept under virtual house arrest. Long before representatives of the Weimar Republic were compelled to sign the treaty in June, the document was being denounced by outraged Germans as a *Diktat*, a dictated peace. These deep-seated German resentments began to fester even before the conference concluded and were exacerbated by Britain's insistence on continuing the blockade until the treaty was signed. Starvation, combined with the humiliating terms of the peace, did much to undermine Germany's nascent democracy. Many Germans came to associate the leaders of the Weimar Republic with defeat and degradation. Indeed, ultranationalists like the ex-corporal Adolf Hitler strove incessantly to promulgate a "stab in the back" myth, holding that Germany's armies had not been defeated at the front, but rather betrayed by craven socialist politicians and Jews in Berlin. Many were willing to accept that these "November Criminals," not the Imperial government or military, were responsible for Germany's humiliation. In the next few years, the struggling Weimar Republic confronted monumental challenges, as extremists of both the left and the right sought to overthrow the government. Germany's path to relative stability in the 1920s was thus strewn with numerous obstacles, many devolving directly from the Versailles Treaty.

Various explanations have been offered for Wilson's acceptance of an obviously flawed treaty that was provoking dismay in Germany even as it was being drafted. Wilson was willing to concede to quite a few French and British demands in return for promises of support for a League of Nations, which he saw as critical to world peace. Wilson also fell ill during the conference, a victim of the influenza epidemic that began sweeping the world in 1918, eventually killing ten million people. One theory holds that the disease may have affected Wilson's judgment. Seriously ill for two weeks, Wilson left negotiations in the hands of his advisor, Colonel Edward House, who gave way on points that Wilson might have more stubbornly defended. Ultimately, the greatest obstacles to the realization of Wilson's vision resided in the United States, where a Republican Senate held the power to amend or block the treaty. Responding to Republican criticisms about possible League encroachments on American sovereignty, Wilson made a second trip to Paris in March to obtain the desired changes in the document. Senate opponents remained unconvinced, however, and a fundamental shift in public opinion, which was rapidly turning toward isolationism, further lessened Wilson's hopes for ratification. Despite heroic efforts, Wilson was unable to win the ratification struggle and the U.S. Senate twice voted down the treaty and League membership. The United States would not assume the international role that Wilson envisioned. Physically shattered by the long contest and debilitated by a stroke, Wilson found only repudiation during his last months as president, dying a disillusioned man in 1924.

RESHAPING EUROPE: THE MINOR TREATIES AND THE SUCCESSOR STATES

Though it may be said that Wilson failed to obtain for Germany the non-punitive peace he had originally envisioned and that he was unsuccessful in bringing the United States into his cherished League of Nations, many of his fundamental ideas for securing a new European order are evident in the treaties that dealt with the constituent components of the defunct Habsburg Empire. The postwar breakup of Austria-Hungary was determined at the Congress of Oppressed Nationalities, which met in Rome in April 1918. Several of Wilson's Fourteen Points spoke directly to the proposition that the borders of postwar Eastern Europe should be redrawn to reflect ethnicity. Adherence to the principle of "national self-determination" would not only resolve the historical problem of domestic instability caused by dissatisfied minorities, it would also establish the preconditions for democratic self-government. By thus rationalizing national boundaries, the American president believed, many of the antagonisms and conflicts of the past could be avoided.

The broadest and boldest application of this approach came in the Treaty of Saint-Germaine, which dealt with Austria, where the abdication of Emperor Charles on Armistice Day 1918 had been followed by the declaration of a republic. The treaty required that Austria recognize the independence of Czechoslovakia, Yugoslavia, Poland and Hungary, all configured so as to reflect, as accurately as possible, specific ethnic populations. In the immediate years to come, this approach brought problematic results. Czechoslovakia, brought into being in large part through the exertions of the great nationalist leader Thomas Masaryk, proved to be a durable, stable democracy in the interwar years. The Kingdom of Serbs, Croats and Slovenes, as it was known before becoming Yugoslavia in 1929, was less stable. While the non-Serb population desired a federal structure giving all nationalities and religions an equal role, Serbs advocated a "Greater Serb" vision in which Serbia would dominate. A parliamentary monarchy ruled by a Serbian dynasty in which Serbs held most high government posts, Yugoslavia was strained by growing ethnic/religious tensions during the next two decades.

The creation of an independent Poland in 1919 was the realization of nationalist aspirations that went back to 1795, when Poland disappeared from maps as a sovereign nation. Despite the best efforts of the treaty-makers, the boundaries of the new Polish state inevitably encompassed small enclaves of ethnic minorities, most notably Germans. Efforts to give Poland access to the Baltic Sea by creating a "Polish Corridor" through previously German territory separated East Prussia from the body of Germany and left Danzig, a predominantly German city, isolated and under League administration. All of these changes would later be used to inflame ultranationalist sentiment in Germany. National boundaries posed more immediate problems for Poland; a brief war with Russia and a border dispute with Czechoslovakia in 1920 grew out of the ambiguity of borders in northeastern Europe. Stable government likewise eluded the Poles. Class hatreds, an unmanageable number of political parties and persistent economic difficulties rendered the postwar parliamentary regime ineffectual. In 1926 it gave way to a military dictatorship under General Joseph Pilsudski, who declared that only time would tell if his country could be governed "without a whip."

Austria, having also been shorn of several territories that went to Italy, was reduced to a "rump" state. Formerly an empire of fifty million people, the new Austrian Republic had a population of less than eight million, two-thirds of whom were concentrated in the capital at Vienna, with the remainder living in sparsely populated rural areas. Not only was the economic viability of the country in doubt, its political stability was also questionable. Vienna, with a large working-class population with socialist inclinations, contrasted starkly with the conservative and Catholic countryside. Deprived of their imperial identity, many Austrians defined themselves by their German ethnicity, longing for union with Germany, which the treaty expressly forbad. Though Austria came out of the war as a parliamentary republic, unresolved social and political issues made its future very uncertain.

Hungary's fate was outlined in the Treaty of Trianon, which severely reduced the territory of the historic Hungarian kingdom. Territorial cessions to Rumania, Czechoslovakia and Yugoslavia cost Hungary three-quarters of its area and two-thirds of its population. Bitterness over these losses exacerbated an already unstable political situation and in March 1919 a coup, led by Communist Bela Kun, toppled the new republican government of Hungary. Kun's revolutionary regime promptly declared war on the Czechs and Rumanians, who were to receive the larger Hungarian territorial concessions. Kun's gamble failed, however, as the victorious Rumanians occupied Budapest and ousted the Communists. Political uncertainty continued into 1920, when Hungarian Admiral Nicholas Horthy proclaimed the restoration of the Habsburg monarchy with himself as temporary regent, a position that became permanent when he changed his mind about the monarchy the following year. Horthy's authoritarian rule continued into the Second World War.

The other two former Central Powers, Bulgaria and Turkey, confronted differing fates. The Treaty of Neuilly gave Bulgaria's Adriatic seacoast to Greece and lesser concessions to Yugoslavia and Rumania, leaving it the weakest of the Balkan states. Turkey faced a much more severe settlement, which was largely the consequence of secret Allied treaties negotiated during the war. The Sykes-Picot Agreement of 1916 paved the way for British and French mandates over much of the Middle East under the pretext of liberating Arab peoples from Ottoman control. Britain gained control of Iraq, Palestine and the Hejaz, a region of the western Arabian peninsula along the Red Sea, while France was granted predominance in Syria and Lebanon. For the British, Palestine posed special challenges. The 1917 Balfour Declaration pledged Britain to support a Jewish homeland in Palestine, but the complexities of realizing that promise became evident over the next twenty years. The loss of the Arab territories, acknowledged in the Treaty of Sevres, was a severe blow to Turkish pride, but efforts to reward Italy with Rhodes and Greece with portions of Anatolia proved too much to bear. Italian and Greek occupations provoked broad popular anger in Turkey and strengthened the hand of a rising nationalist movement which had strong support within the Turkish army. Led by Mustafa Kemal and other officers, the nationalists repudiated

the sultan's government and the treaty. Over the next two years, Turkish nationalists resorted to military force to secure national sovereignty and establish the foundations for a modern Turkish state.

EMPIRE AND THE NEW INTERNATIONAL ORDER

Though the principle of national self-determination was broadly applied in the postwar European settlements, it was not extended to the imperial possessions of the Allied nations. For many Europeans, empire was incontestable evidence of greatness. In the aftermath of a war that swept away a multitude of certainties, the maintenance of empire was more than a consolation; it was an affirmation of the continuity and vitality of western civilization. Those hopeful representatives of national, ethnic and religious groups who traveled to Paris seeking the realization of their aspirations were almost universally disillusioned by the response of the great powers. Ho Chi Minh, a young Vietnamese who came to ask that France recognize the civil rights of her colonial peoples, was undoubtedly among those supplicants whom Lloyd George dismissed as "wild men screaming through the keyholes." The Zionists who advocated a Jewish state alone managed to gain a hearing at the conference. Ultimately, despite Wilson's Fifth Point, which called for giving equal weight to "the interests of the population concerned" in deciding colonial issues, the desires of subject peoples were subordinated to those of the imperial powers. Great Britain, whose statesmen were determined that there be no diminution of empire, strenuously opposed Wilson's suggestion that the League of Nations or some other international body arbitrate colonial issues.

The issue of colonies was the last major item on the agenda at Versailles and it focused foremost on the disposition of former German colonies. Though Britain and Japan argued forcefully for outright annexation, Wilson succeeded in winning approval for a mandate system. Under this arrangement, colonial claims would be categorized as Class A, B or C mandates. In Class A were the Arab lands stripped from the Ottoman Empire. A gradual transition to independence was envisioned for these mandates, though it would not come for decades. Class B included most of the African colonies, with Britain gaining Tanganyika and parts of Togoland and the German Cameroons. The League was to supervise the welfare of native populations. Class C mandates, mainly Pacific islands, were virtual annexations. Nominally rational and humane, the mandate system did little more than legitimize, perpetuate and even extend imperial rule. Through this system, the British Empire gained an additional one million square miles of territory. The men at the Paris Conference also did much to meet Japan's growing imperial ambitions in the Pacific and Asia. Having succeeded in annexing Germany's former Pacific island possessions as Class C mandates, Japanese statesmen also sought recognition of claims to Kiachow and Shantung in China. Wilson, opposed to claims he believed violated China's territorial integrity, nonetheless conceded them rather than risk straining the tenuous postwar world order. Ironically, Wilson refused to support a Japanese request for a clause in the League Covenant recognizing racial equality. Deeply resented, this rebuff led Japanese statesmen to believe that Japan would never be accepted as an equal by the western powers.

As the conferees departed Paris in late June 1919, the challenge of preserving the new international order fell largely to the League of Nations, which was at best an imperfect instrument of peace. Formally established in January 1920, the League was a voluntary association of nations with few powers of coercion. Though its members were pledged to defend the independence of all, the principle of collective security meant little unless the great powers proved willing to give it force, as the League had no armed force of its own. At most, the League Council, where the major powers sat permanently, could only advise members as to possible responses to aggression. The absence of key nations further undermined the League's authority and abilities; when it first met in the fall of 1921, neither Germany, Russia, nor the United States were among the forty-one charter members. A World Court established to arbitrate disputes could act only if the aggrieved parties agreed to submit to its judgement.

More troubling, the League confronted the task of preserving a new international order that was barely established and not universally accepted. Even before the Paris Conference adjourned, civil conflict and minor border wars were igniting all over Europe. Serious disaffection with the terms of the peace was rife in Germany and Italy, while the untried governments of many of the successor states struggled with political and ethnic unrest. Soviet Russia, in the throes of civil war and propounding world revolution, posed a potential, if as yet ambiguous, threat to international stability. Throughout the colonial world, the newly kindled fires of nationalism made for further uncertainty, while in Asia, Japan's unrequited imperial ambitions posed new challenges. The Paris treaties of 1919, shaped by both idealism and sometimes-crass political realities, produced an imperfect settlement that heralded an uncertain future. Among victor and vanquished alike, there was apprehension about the consequences. The forebodings of many in Europe and elsewhere were expressed in French Marshal Ferdinand Foch's reaction to the Treaty of Versailles. "This isn't a peace," the former Supreme Allied Commander observed, "it's a twenty year truce."

◆ —— ◆ —— ◆ —— ◆ —— ◆ —— ◆ —— ◆ —— ◆ —— ◆ —— ◆

For Vera Brittain, a twenty-two-year-old Englishwoman, the full horror of the world war struck home two days after Christmas 1915. Having left Somerville College to serve as a nurse with the Voluntary Aid Detachment (VAD), she spent the last days of December 1915 tending the wounded in a convalescent ward and awaiting some word of when her fiancé, British Army Lieutenant Roland Leighton, might return from the western front on leave. Christmas Day passed with no news, and the message that finally came on December 27 transformed her mood of eager anticipation to one of uncomprehending shock. By telephone, Brittain learned that the Leighton family had received the telegram that the families of all servicemen dreaded: "Regret to inform you that Lieut. R.A. Leighton 7th Worcesters died of wounds December 23rd. Lord Kitchener sends his sympathy." Struggling to come to grips with her personal tragedy, she wrote in her diary on New Years' Eve, "All has been given me, and all has been taken away again—in one year." Now profoundly cognizant of the uncertainties of life, Brittain concluded her 1915 entries with a thought that must have crossed the minds of many as the war spilled over into yet another year. "So I wonder where we shall be," she wrote, "and what we shall all be doing—if we all *shall* be—this time next year." Like many others to whom the war had brought personal loss, Brittain could only hope to endure and maybe, someday, to understand.

Vera Brittain was born into a relatively affluent life in Newcastle-under-Lyme in 1893 and educated by a governess and at boarding school. An early interest in women's issues, an increasingly controversial topic of discussion in Edwardian England, put her at odds with her father Thomas, who held conventional views of women's proper role in society. Despite his insistence that the primary role of education was to prepare women for marriage, Thomas conceded to her desire to attend Somerville College at Oxford, where she hoped to develop her literary talents. She was introduced to the witty and thoughtful Roland Leighton in the summer of 1914 and her diary reflects the development of her affection for him. Her expectations that she would attend Oxford together with Leighton and her brother Edward were dashed by the outbreak of war. On August 5 she predicted in her diary that "the war will alter everything." Most immediately, it meant that both Roland and Edward volunteered for military service, even as Vera took on a volunteer assignment that traditionally fell to women—sewing military garments.

In the days that followed, as news of troop deployments, naval engagements and rumored German Zeppelin raids circulated, Brittain observed in a strikingly perceptive diary entry, "Truly we of this generation are born to a youth very different from anything

Fig. 2-3 Vera Brittain enlisted in England's Voluntary Aid Detachment and served as a nurse during the First World War. Overwhelmed by the horrors of war and the battlefield deaths of her brother, her fiancé and others close to her, she left the VAD and dedicated the remainder of her life to the crusade for international peace. (Hulton Archive)

we ever supposed or imagined for ourselves." Beginning her studies at Somerville in October, she often felt distracted by both the war and Roland's absence. Nonetheless, both accepted their respective obligations as they saw them. Roland saw duty on the battlefields of France and in June 1915 Vera joined the Voluntary Aid Detachment as a nurse. Disregarding wartime's uncertainties, the two were engaged that August. Roland's frequent letters from France described the horrors of warfare and reflected his disdain for those who exalted war as "a glorious golden thing." Vera sent him a personal notice clipped from a newspaper that captured the war's morbid distortion of individual hopes: "Lady, fiancé killed, will gladly marry officer totally blinded or otherwise incapacitated by the War." In her diary, Vera could only wonder at the agonized desperation of the "lady" who could not bear the thought of life alone. As the summer continued, she made note of her hope that perhaps Turkey would leave the war before her brother Edward embarked for the Dardenelles, and registered her astonishment at the mushrooming casualty count: "I saw in a paper today that the total estimate of dead in Europe in this war exceeds five million!" Her growing despair was more evident that October. "The war is like a snowball which gathers volume as it goes on rolling," she wrote. "Ever day seems to take us farther from the end."

The end was still nowhere in sight when Vera received word of her fiancé's death in late December 1915. Her diary reflects her efforts to come to terms with his death through the early months of 1916, but there was little consolation to be had in a year in which the most terrible battles were yet to come. In early March, Vera responded to a call for VAD volunteers for foreign service. "There are risks, great risks," she wrote, "but if I had refused to put down my name I should despise myself." That September, in the aftermath of the battle of the Somme, which Vera denounced as a "singularly wasteful and ineffective orgy of slaughter," she and other VAD volunteers sailed for Malta aboard the *Brittanic*. Burying her unrelenting grief in her nursing duties, Vera learned that two close friends, Victor Richardson and Geoffrey Thurlow, had been posted to the western front, where they faced all the horrors of trench warfare. In April 1917, she was informed that Victor was "dangerously wounded," and details from her brother Edward confirmed the worst: "Eyesight probably gone, may live." Only days later two more cables arrived, the first confirming Victor's permanent blindness, the second telling of the death of Geoffrey Thurlow. The last entries in Vera Brittain's wartime diary were made in the following weeks. Overwhelmed by events, she received permission to leave Malta and return to England and her family. There she had a brief opportunity to see Edward, who was home on a brief leave. She was appalled at the degree to which the experience of war had changed her brother, who had survived the nightmare of the Somme. Edward now seemed "unfamiliar, frightening," unwilling to communicate and morose.

Tragedy mounted upon tragedy as, within a week, Vera received news of Victor's death. Edward, back in France, wrote his sister that, given the loss of so many friends, "whatever was of value in life has all tumbled down like a house of cards." Vera's VAD assignment took her to France in the summer of 1917, where in the convalescent wards, both Allied and German wounded were a constant reminder of a war that seemed to have no end. Vera had returned to England and was at home when the all-too-familiar telegram brought word of the final tragedy: "Regret to inform you Captain E.H. Brittain M.C. killed in action Italy June 15th."

In a war that killed and maimed millions, wrenching personal losses like those suffered by Vera Brittain and her family were shockingly common. Such deep emotional wounds inevitably left lasting scars on individuals and nations alike, and disillusionment and embitterment contributed significantly to a dimmed postwar outlook. For some, like the German Army corporal Adolf Hitler, the war's great lesson was the unifying power of national struggle and the redemption to be found in revenge. Others, like Vera Brittain, came gradually to the conclusion that the central lesson of the catastrophe was the futility of war. Following the armistice in 1918, Brittain returned to her studies at Somerville, where she began writing poetry and established an enduring friendship with Winifred Holtby, who also had literary inclinations. After graduation, the two women moved to London, where Brittain divided her time between developing her literary talents, supporting the new League of Nations and involvement in women's issues. While her first two novels attracted little positive notice, she began to establish her credentials as a journalist and feminist theorist. Though she married an American academic, bore two children and lived briefly in the United States, she was drawn back to England by the 1930s, where she again took up residence with Winifred Holtby. Her first great literary success followed in 1933 with the publication of the bestseller *Testament of Youth,* an autobiographical account of her years as a VAD nurse and her experiences at Oxford. The death of Winifred Holtby in 1935 inspired Brittain to publish another memoir, *Testament of Friendship.*

By the mid-1930s, as aggression and rearmament threatened peace in Europe and Asia, Brittain had lost faith in the League of Nations as an instrument of peace. Increasingly, she was drawn to pacifism as the only means of maintaining peace and in 1937 she joined the Peace Pledge Union, which promoted pacifism through parades, mass demonstrations and open-air meetings. The pacifist creed, which held that war was never a legitimate means of settling disputes and could be resisted by refusing to fight, held considerable appeal for many who feared that the world was once again headed down the path to futile conflict. Even as the aggressive actions of Nazi Germany brought about a major European crisis in 1938–1939, Brittain prepared her First World War diaries, with their compelling depictions of the horrors of war, for publication as *Chronicle of Youth.*

Great Britain's entry into the Second World War in September 1939 posed enormous challenges to Brittain and other pacifists. As the war intensified, the pacifist message was increasingly unpopular with the besieged English populace. Nonetheless, Brittain continued her crusade for peace, defending her principles in her 1943 book *Humiliation with Honor.* She generated considerable controversy the following year when she published *Seeds of Chaos,* a powerful indictment of the government's policy of saturation bombing, which brought death and destruction to civilian noncombatants. The end of the war brought the opportunity for Brittain to dedicate more time to writing about women's issues, but her time was also increasingly given over to the growing campaign to abolish nuclear weapons, which made modern war an even greater threat. In 1957, Brittain helped form the Campaign for Nuclear Disarmament and remained active in the peace movement until her death in 1970. Though Brittain's pacifism was often dismissed by her critics as naïve and unrealistic, she never wavered in her lifelong commitment to the search for peace that was born, ironically, out of "the war to end all wars."

♦ —— ♦ —— ♦ —— ♦ —— ♦ —— ♦ —— ♦ —— ♦ —— ♦ —— ♦

Suggested Readings

BERRY, PAUL and MARK. *Vera Brittain: A Life* (1999).

BRITTAIN, VERA. *Chronicle of Youth: The War Diary, 1913–1917.* (1982).

CLARK, RONALD. *Lenin.* (1988).

DALLAS, GREGOR. *1918: War and Peace.* (2001).

EKSTEINS, MODRIS. *The Rites of Spring: The Great War and the Birth of the Modern Age.* (1989).

FERGUSON, NIALL. *The Pity of War.* (1999).

FIGES, ORLANDO. *A People's Tragedy: A History of the Russian Revolution.* (1997).

FISCHER, FRITZ. *Germany's Aims in the First World War.* (1967).

FUSSELL, PAUL. *The Great War and Modern Memory.* (1975).

GILBERT, MARTIN. *The First World War: A Complete History.* (1994).

GREGORY, ROSS. *The Origins of American Intervention in the First World War.* (1971).

HARRIES, MEIRION and SUSIE. *The Last Days of Innocence: America at War, 1914–1918.* (1994).

HORNE, ALISTAIRE. *The Price of Glory: Verdun, 1916.* (1962).

KEEGAN, JOHN. *The First World War.* (1998).

KENNEDY, DAVID. *Over Here: The First World War and American Society.* (1980).

LAFORE, LAURENCE. *The Long Fuse.* (1965).

MARWICK, ARTHUR. *Women at War, 1914–1918.* (1977).

MAYER, ARNO. *Politics and Diplomacy of Peacemaking: Containment and Counterrevolution at Versailles, 1918–1919.* (1967).

PIPES, RICHARD. *Russia under the Bolshevik Regime.* (1994).

REMAK, JOACHIM. *The Origins of World War I.* (1995).

SCHMITT, BERNADOTTE, and HAROLD C. VEDELER. *The World in the Crucible, 1914–1918.* (1984).

SHARP, ALAN. *The Versailles Settlement: Peacemaking in Paris.* (1991).

TUCHMAN, BARBARA. *The Guns of August.* (1962).

TUCKER, SPENCER. *The Great War, 1914–1918.* (1998).

WILLIAMS, JOHN. *The Home Front: Britain, France and Germany, 1914–1918.* (1972).

CHAPTER 3

The Americas between the World Wars, 1919–1939

Speaking before the U.S. District Court in Manhattan, Roger Nash Baldwin, fast becoming known as the nation's leading civil libertarian, explained why he had felt compelled to violate the 1917 Selective Service Act. Conscription, Baldwin asserted, violated both democratic and Christian precepts. Moreover, he affirmed, "I am opposed to this and all other wars. I do not believe in the use of physical force as a method of achieving any end, however good." Baldwin's declaration paralleled that of the American Socialist Party leader Eugene V. Debs, who had also been incarcerated because of his opposition to the wartime policies of President Woodrow Wilson. The presiding judge, Julius Mayer, complimented Baldwin's "manly" willingness to suffer the consequences of his actions. Insisting that "a republic can last only as long as its laws are obeyed," Mayer then sentenced Baldwin, an upper-class, Harvard-educated Bostonian, to a year in jail.

The case of *U.S. v. Roger Nash Baldwin* received widespread press coverage. The New York Post referred to "two strong men" looking at "each other between the eyes" and finding "no fault in the other." However, the *New York Times,* which referred to Baldwin as "the pacifist martyr," was far more critical: "Physical force must be used, as even every pacifist knows, for the achieving of about all the ends there are."

Until the United States entered World War I, Baldwin had been viewed as a major figure in the progressive movement, which was identified with the likes of President Wilson and former president Theodore Roosevelt. In St. Louis, he first taught sociology at newly founded Washington University, headed a social settlement house, and served as the Juvenile Court's chief probation officer. He later was appointed secretary of the Civic League, a good-government organization dedicated to democratic devices such as the referendum, recall, and initiative. But he also was exposed to early free speech fights involving birth control advocate Margaret Sanger and members of the anarcho-syndicalist IWW, who were known as the Wobblies. And after war broke out in Europe, Baldwin joined the American Union Against Militarism.

Shortly following his imprisonment at New York City's famous Tombs Prison, Baldwin soon received news of the Armistice ending World War I. Following a nine-month jail sentence, Baldwin briefly toiled as a day laborer in order to better understand what laborers, like those who had joined the radical Industrial Workers of the World (IWW), were experiencing. He then returned to the field of civil liberties, subsequently founding the American Civil Liberties Union (ACLU) in January 1920. This was the third in a succession of organizations he had directed that sought to protect the personal freedoms guaranteed in the U.S. Constitution's Bill of Rights. The war had ushered in repression of both a legal and an extra-legal variety, triggered by the Wilson administration's disinclination to endure opposition and the determination of businessmen and patriotic groups to crush radical forces. The Lyrical Left, among a band of intellectuals who challenged Victorian morals and heralded the need for personal liberation, which had flourished now encountered the kind of repression and divisions that afflicted organizations like Debs' Socialist Party regarding the appropriateness of the Bolshevik example for the United States.

The spigot of repression hardly slackened during the early postwar period, with the Wilson administration, led by Attorney General A. Mitchell Palmer and a young Justice Department attorney, J. Edgar Hoover, orchestrating a series of raids against left-wing groups and individuals. In late 1919 and early 1920, the infamous Palmer Raids unfolded, with several thousand radicals arrested, and more than a thousand, including anarchists Emma Goldman and Alexander Berkman, deported. The newly founded ACLU condemned the operations, intensifying the already great ire of government agents, particularly those employed by the Bureau of Intelligence (the predecessor to the FBI) and Military Intelligence. As they had during the war, those government operatives, tied to the newly emerging national security state, painstakingly followed the activities of Baldwin and his civil liberties' colleagues.

In the first decade of its existence, the ACLU, guided by Baldwin, urged an expansive reading of First Amendment freedoms involving speech, the press and assemblage. Thus, it became involved in the case of Nicola Sacco and Bartolomeo Vanzetti, two Italian immigrant anarchists accused of committing a felony murder in a small town outside of Boston. The ACLU supported labor activists who faced injunctions in Paterson, New Jersey; communists, targeted because of party membership alone; high school teacher John T. Scopes, accused of violating Tennessee's anti-evolution statute; and the Scottsboro Boys, eight African-American youngsters convicted of raping two white women in a small Southern community. Adopting Baldwin's approach, the ACLU also condemned the U.S. Postal Service's refusal to ship literature of the Ku Klux Klan (KKK) and the move by local officials to ban the sale of anti-Semitic literature, whose production had been financed by auto magnate Henry Ford.

Fig. 3-1 ACLU founder Roger Nash Baldwin, voluntarily testifying before the Special Committee to Investigate Communist Activities in the United States, Washington, D.C., December 5, 1930. (Corbis/Bettmann)

Many on both the left and right viewed Baldwin's civil libertarianism with disdain. Communists favored the censoring of both their radical adversaries, the Trotskyists, and right-wingers. Some right-of-center demanded a reining in of radical forces, particularly the communists. Baldwin, deliberately but falsely pointing to a long tradition of free speech in America, insisted that infringing on the rights of any group, no matter how unpopular or distasteful, threatened the political freedoms of all.

His absolutist civil libertarian stance ensured that controversy swirled about Baldwin and the ACLU throughout the inter-war period. So too did his identification with the American left, while it weakened immediately following World War I and as it gained more adherents during the depression-riddled 1930s. Like many political activists, Baldwin had been enthralled by the Bolshevik Revolution in 1917 and remained a critical supporter of communist Russia during the ensuing two decades. He participated in a series of United Front and Popular Front organizations that called for forces left-of-center to craft labor, civil rights and anti-fascist alliances. In 1927, Baldwin visited the Soviet Union and returned home, having completed a small book, *Liberty Under the Soviets,* which both questioned and applauded the so-called communist "experiment." At the same time, he remained friends with Goldman, who had become an embittered opponent of first Lenin's and then Stalin's regime. While defending the U.S.S.R. and welcoming communists into the ranks of the ACLU, Baldwin worked to ensure that Stalinists did not control the organizations he was involved with. On occasion, that resulted in his ouster from those same organizations.

By the late thirties, with the unfolding of the Moscow Trials—which targeted Old Bolshevik luminaries, peasants, and workers alike—Baldwin became increasingly disenchanted with events in the Soviet Union. With friends and allies prominently situated in the New Deal administration of President Franklin Delano Roosevelt, Baldwin began viewing liberal reform measures more sympathetically, as he had during the Progressive era. Fearing attacks from the newly formed House Committee on Un-American Activities and angered by the Nazi-Soviet Non-Aggression Pact, Baldwin began to move into the liberal anti-communist camp. In the spring of 1940, he led a drive to exclude communists from leadership positions in the ACLU, a highly controversial move that led some to charge that a model for repressive action had thereby been planted. Recognizing that the Roosevelt administration was mobilizing for eventual entrance into World War II, Baldwin again warned about the domestic repercussions of U.S. involvement overseas.

In 1940 and 1941, Baldwin sought to ensure that the constitutional rights of conscientious objectors were safeguarded. After the United States became a combatant, he became concerned about the plight of some 120,000 Japanese-American and Japanese aliens who were interned in relocation centers. At the same time, he argued against government prosecution of Trotskyists and native fascists, pointing to First Amendment safeguards. But during the war years, Baldwin also met repeatedly with government officials, seeking a partnership between the ACLU and the Roosevelt administration. As a consequence, both Baldwin and the ACLU acquired greater respectability, not an altogether pleasing development to all on either the right or the left.

◆ —— ◆ —— ◆ —— ◆ —— ◆

U.S. Domestic Developments between the World Wars

The interwar period was characterized by warring ideologies; at its onset, the United States experienced a red scare, while at its close, possessors of anti-fascist sentiments encouraged the country's participation in another international conflict. American engagement in World War I resulted in a waning of the previously dominant progressive movement, which had sought to ameliorate the worst aspects of industrial capitalism without altering the general socioeconomic system of the United States. The intolerance spawned by the country's nineteen-month involvement in the war worsened during the immediate postwar era. Radicals, ranging from members of two newly formed communist parties that envisioned a Soviet America to independent actors such as Roger Baldwin, remained prime targets for both state and private agents of repression. Efforts were afoot to put African-Americans, who now numbered among their ranks veterans of both the Great War and industrial plants in the Midwest and Northeast, back "in their place." Similarly, there arose a new cult of domesticity, whose message insisted that a woman's place was in the home and not in the industrial centers where so many had worked during the war.

For a brief spell, organized labor, blacks, and women fought to retain their wartime gains. Wildcat strikes appeared. A nationwide steel strike unfolded. A general strike occurred in Seattle. Policemen in Boston walked off the job. African-American soldiers proudly marched down the streets of Harlem, while a literary, cultural and political renaissance brewed. Many women, requiring the income and desirous of the greater independence it afforded them, were determined to retain their positions in the workplace. However, a backlash was triggered as the fighting terminated on the western front. A series of states passed criminal syndicalism acts, intended to be wielded against radicals. Both the Justice Department and Military Intelligence continued pinpointing those who were viewed as subversive by high government operatives. Open shop campaigns were kicked off, while company unions and relatively high wages dampened enthusiasm for labor activism. A series of race riots, in which African-Americans suffered the brunt

of the violence, also swept across the national landscape. Women were encouraged to return to the kitchen and to engage in "proper women's work."

A CLASH OF CULTURES

Once more, repression and social pressures threatened to return things to "normalcy," a vague state of affairs extolled by Senator Warren G. Harding in the midst of the 1920 presidential race. Voters appeared to agree, resoundingly electing Harding and his running mate Massachusetts Governor Calvin C. Coolidge, who had promised to get government off the backs of businessmen. During the campaign, Harding was heard to say that "America's present need is not heroics but healing; not nostrums but normalcy; not revolution but restoration; not surgery but serenity." Shortly after the Republican triumph, Coolidge insisted that "civilization and profits go hand in hand." Disillusionment over the war and a general weariness with the progressive movement's crusading fervor best explained the ease with which conservative Republicans swept into office. President Wilson's missionary zeal, along with his stroke-riddled body and mind, had withered, leaving his lofty ideals regarding U.S. involvement in international affairs to dissipate. The perception that the president had been hoodwinked at Versailles, where America's supposed allies proved ill-disposed to accept Wilsonian preachments, helped not at all. The president himself had seemingly caved in, discarding his promises of a non-punitive peace. The League of Nations, held aloft as an attainable ideal by Wilson, came into existence, but without American membership. A bitter fight in the Senate, and Wilson's refusal to compromise with American nationalists and isolationists over the question of collective security, ensured that the United States would fail to join the League.

The Harding and Coolidge administrations (1921–1929) were guided to a considerable degree by Secretary of Treasury Andrew Mellon and Secretary of Commerce Herbert Hoover. Largely discarding the progressive policies of the Roosevelt and Wilson administrations, the new Republican cabinets were characterized by a belief in a new revised business creed, associated with laissez-faire and social Darwinism. Mellon in particular argued that the federal government should ease regulatory restraints, suspend anti-trust activity, and reduce the taxes paid by wealthy individuals and corporations. Propounding the gospel of trickle-down economics, Secretary Mellon contended that the most ambitious and financially successful individuals, if allowed to retain more of their earnings, would pump money back into the private sector.

Some, including old-line progressives like Senator Robert M. LaFollette of Wisconsin, whose anti-war stance had reduced some of his luster, and Senator George Norris of Nebraska, disputed this notion. In 1922, the Conference for Progressive Political Action brought together labor, socialist, and farmers's groups to challenge administration policies and set the stage for LaFollette's third-party presidential bid two years later. Norris demanded the federal government retain control of the Muscle Shoals region in Alabama (two nitrate plants and the Wilson Dam) which private investors desired to secure. At statewide and local levels, any number of young men and women—generally, members of the new, educated, and professional middle-class—continued the progressives' fight to curb corporate dominance, protect the public interest, and involve the people in participatory democratic affairs. One of the leading state progressives at the end of this era was New York Governor Franklin Delano Roosevelt, the Democratic Party's defeated vice-presidential candidate in 1920, and a man whose political career had once appeared still-born because of polio-induced paralysis.

Throughout the decade, the political clash that continued between progressives and conservatives was paralleled by social and cultural conflicts. A highly conservative, even reactionary viewpoint was propounded by a host of different forces, including those who supported congressional legislation in 1921 and 1924 that established quotas to the disadvantage of the New Immigrants from southern and eastern Europe. Prohibitionists cheered the ratification of the Eighteenth Amendment in 1919. The Ku Klux Klan, reborn in 1915, achieved unprecedented acclaim, with a purported membership of four to five million by the middle of the twenties, and the ability to control statehouses and to elect congressmen. Both anti-immigrationists and Klansmen were driven by a professed belief in "100% Americanism," which led them to view with disfavor immigrants, non-Protestants, radicals and blacks.

Many were disturbed by the changes the nation was experiencing, as its agrarian, pastoral heritage appeared to recede, supplanted by the factory as Henry Ford's Model T rolled off the assembly line, and by teaming metropolises, with their massive skyscrapers, where America's increasingly polyglot population was most readily evident. American industry remained the world's most productive, but racial and class divisions were clearly evidenced by the blackening of inner cities such as New York and Chicago and by the greater number of affluent and fair-skinned residents moving into suburbs. The extension of American roads, highways and bridges, and the greater affordability of automobiles, provided for increased mobility, altering the very idea of community.

Pitted against those who wanted to turn the clock back to an earlier and supposedly more pristine time were the so-called cosmopolitans. As Jim Crow practices lengthened and lynchings remained a popular pastime in the Deep South, a mass migration northward began around the turn of the century. Within two decades, A. Philip Randolph, socialist head of the Brotherhood of Sleeping Car Porters and editor of *The Messenger*, heralded the appearance of the New Negro: proud, racially conscious and less willing to endure the terrors long inflicted on Americans of African ancestry. The Harlem Renaissance was one result, with blues and jazz tunes performed by the likes of Bessie Smith, Louie Armstrong and Duke Ellington wafting forth from the Savoy Ballroom, the Cotton Club and the Apollo Theater. Writers such as W. E. B. DuBois, James Johnston, Langston Hughes and Claude McKay challenged long-standing racial stereotypes. So too did the sculptor Aaron Douglas, the dancer Florence Mills and Broadway performer Paul Robeson. Randolph, DuBois and Marcus Garvey, who headed the black nationalist Back-to-Africa campaign, spurred political activism, while Harlem began electing black congressmen.

New images of women also sprang forth, associated with the realms of public service and mass entertainment alike. A host of young women, following the lead of their sisters in the social settlement and progressive movements, worked in a series of service agencies, acquired professional expertise and helped set the stage for new reform efforts. Educational, occupational and professional barriers continued to be challenged, with more women working outside the home in 1929 than at the beginning of the decade.

Social mores were in flux too, as Margaret Sanger's birth control movement and the increased appeal of Freudian ideas resulted in freer discussion of sexuality, if not quite the sexual revolution popularly associated with the period. Shaped by the purveyors of popular culture, recast images of the American woman appeared, as exemplified by both Margaret Gorman, the first Miss America in 1921, and Clara Bow, the "It Girl" in a series of popular Hollywood films. The *Ladies Home Journal*, with its ambivalent reportage of changing gender roles, and a star like Swedish-born Greta Garbo, the silver screen's most sultry temptress, also presented contrasting images for American women. The Nineteenth Amendment, which granted women the suffrage, appeared to have little direct impact on political affairs, in contrast to what its proponents had anticipated and its opponents long feared.

Chastened by their own wartime experiences and dismayed by the rightward drift of an increasingly materialistic American populace, young intellectuals displayed their displeasure by engaging in odysseys of their own. All the while, they participated in a remarkable literary renaissance, which could be compared with the outpouring of classic literature by the nineteenth-century New England transcendentalists. Some, like the poet T. S. Eliot, author of the brilliant "Hollow Men" and "The Waste Land," departed from the United States, taking up permanent residence in England. Others, most notably Ernest Hemingway, became expatriates as they hung out in Paris coffee houses and ran with the bulls in Pamplona, while crafting such masterworks as *The Sun Also Rises* and *A Farewell to Arms*. Leading members of the Lost Generation, so named by Gertrude Stein, included John Dos Passos and the poet e. e. cummings, authors of the bitter anti-war tracts, *Three Soldiers* and *The Enormous Room*, respectively. Greenwich Village was a way station for many, while F. Scott Fitzgerald both captured the spirit of the alienated young and foresaw their passage in *This Side of Paradise* and *The Great Gatsby*. In 1930, Sinclair Lewis became the first American to win the Nobel Prize for Literature; Lewis had authored *Main Street* and *Babbitt*, which castigated the infamous "boobwoisie" (or bourgeoisie) condemned by H. L. Mencken, crusty editor of *The American Mercury*.

However, most Americans, thanks to the era's apparent prosperity, were hardly displeased with the material changes that the nation was experiencing. To some extent, all were affected by the consumer culture that had been reshaping America since the late nineteenth century. Thanks to technological innovations, greater affluence and a reduction in the work week—from 66 hours in 1860 to 47 hours by 1920—the consumer culture dug deeper roots during the decade, compelling some historians to proclaim it the first modern era in U.S. history. Household appliances, improved refrigeration, suburban stores, shopping centers and the automobile transformed domestic life.

ENTERTAINMENT AND SPORTS

Entertainment too more readily entered the home, thanks to radio transmissions by the National Broadcast Corporation and the Columbia Broadcast Corporation. Phonographs spun records from Tin Pan Alley and gin joints. Americans readily devoured paperback copies of Edgar Rice Burrough's tales of Tarzan or Mars, and Zane Grey's stories of the Old West.

Mass entertainment also thrived beyond the domestic arena. American cinema, guided by Hollywood's new movie moguls,

flourished, with Douglas Fairbanks starring as Robin Hood or a swashbuckling pirate, and Rudolph Valentino appearing as the Sheik, poised to spirit women off to Middle Eastern lairs. Valentino's death in 1926 resulted in a great outpouring of grief. The following year, Al Jolson starred in *The Jazz Singer*, the first major motion picture to incorporate dialogue. Talkies were the rage, with some stars unable to make the transition, while others, like Garbo, shone as brightly as ever. Almost alone, Charlie Chaplin and his beloved Little Tramp character remained popular but mute.

During the 1920s, seemingly epochal feats were attained on the playing field, as the so-called Golden Age of Sports unfolded. Man O' War won twenty of twenty-one races, including the Preakness and the Belmont Stakes, that he entered. Free-style swimmer Johnny Weismuller set scores of world records, won a comparable number of national championships and garnered five gold medals in the 1924 and 1928 Olympic Games. Amateur golfer Bobby Jones won thirteen major championships, including an unprecedented Grand Slam—the U.S. and British Opens, along with the U.S. and British Amateur Championships—in 1930. Willie Hoppe reigned as world pool champion, while the original Celtics proved all but unbeatable on the basketball court. Helen Wills dominated the tennis court, as she took eight Wimbledons and seven U.S. Open championships. Big Bill Tilden helped the United States win seven consecutive Davis Cups, while capturing seven U.S. Open and three Wimbledon titles.

Football, boxing, and major league baseball remained the most popular spectator sports. Jim Thorpe was named president of the newly formed Professional Football League, but college football reigned supreme. In his thirteen-year tenure as head of the Notre Dame Fighting Irish, Knute Rockne amassed an unparalleled record of 105–12–5, and boasted five undefeated teams. His 1921 team featured halfback George Gipp, while the 1924 squad, highlighting the Four Horsemen—as sportswriter Grantland Rice named the backfield of Jim Crowley, Elmer Layden, Don Miller and Harry Stuhdreher—bested Ernie Nevers' Stanford Indians 27–0 in the Rose Bowl. Rockne's 1930 national championship team was arguably his finest but unfortunately his last, for a plane crash took the life of the legendary coach. The greatest collegiate player of the era was Illinois' Red Grange, the Galloping Ghost, who then barnstormed for George Halas' Chicago Bears. Thanks to promoter Tex Rickard, heavyweight title-holder Jack Dempsey, the Manussa Mauler, established attendance records in a succession of fights, capped off by two bouts with the undefeated Californian, Gene Tunney. The second contest, featuring the famous long count in which the former champ floored Tunney but inexplicably failed to head for the neutral corner, ended with Dempsey's retirement.

Baseball stood as the national pastime, notwithstanding a scandal that threatened ruin. Revelations indicated that eight Chicago White Sox players, including star pitcher Ed Cicotte and outfielder Shoeless Joe Jackson, had participated in a fix to throw the 1919 World Series to the underdog Cincinnati Reds. A jury refused to convict the Black Sox, but former federal judge Keenesaw Landis, the recently appointed commissioner of the major leagues, ruled that the players were permanently banned from organized baseball. Fortuitously, a livelier ball had resulted in an offensive explosion led by the New York Yankees's Babe Ruth, previ-

ously the American League's leading southpaw pitcher while a member of the Boston Red Sox. Ruth, who had set a World Series record for scoreless innings pitched, now began compiling batting marks that had once seemed unattainable, four times belting more than 50 home runs in a single season, topped off by 60 homers in 1927. Yankee Stadium, referred to as the House that Ruth built, witnessed seven pennants and four World Series triumphs during his tenure, with the 1927 team considered perhaps the finest of all time. Following Ruth in the lineup, Lou Gehrig batted cleanup and began compiling a string of 2,130 consecutive games played. The Detroit Tigers's Harry Heilmann and Ty Cobb each topped the .400 mark once during the 1920s, a feat the St. Louis Browns's George Sisler accomplished twice, and the St. Louis Cardinals' Rogers Hornsby did three times in a span of four years. Pitchers shone too, especially aging giants like the Washington Senators' Walter Johnson and the well-traveled Grover Cleveland Alexander, and younger fastballers such as the Brooklyn Dodgers's Dazzy Vance and the Philadelphia Athletics' Lefty Grove. Stellar managers could be found in dugouts, including the New York Giants' John McGraw, the Athletics' Connie Mack and the Yankee's Miller Huggins. But no major league participant surpassed the feats or the notoriety of the Babe, the so-called Sultan of Swat, who amassed twelve home run titles, and apparently possessed appetites as gargantuan off the playing field as on.

The legendary feats of 1920s athletes seemed to be matched by a pair of individuals outside the sporting realm. Similar to the great ballplayers, Charles Lindbergh and Henry Ford conjured up images of self-reliant, self-propelling types in the very period when such figures seemed more endangered than ever. While sports stadiums served as surrogate frontiers for an increasingly urbanized, industrialized people, travel by airplane or automobile allowed for explorations of space and rural areas, which otherwise would have been far more difficult. A young Midwesterner, Lindbergh, whose father was a former congressman, piloted his Spirit of St. Louis airplane from New York City to Paris. The Lone Eagle, as Lindy was aptly called, was the first individual to complete a solo trans-Atlantic flight. His feat suggested that even in this new, modern era, man could triumph, thanks to machinery that was transforming social and economic relationships in the United States. The motor vehicle was altering them, too, as the assembly line made Ford's Tin Lizzie available to more and more people. Thus ironically, two men who were often associated with bygone days helped to ensure that those times had passed.

THE GREAT DEPRESSION

Nevertheless, the very successes of Lindbergh and Ford, like those of the sports stars, were pointed to as examples of what individuals could accomplish in America. In reality, not all were so blessed nor as fortunate during the seemingly prosperous twenties. While the Gross National Product increased some 40%, wages went up only 9%. Indeed, maldistribution of wealth and income actually worsened during the period. Farmers endured depressed conditions, while a disproportionate number of blacks and Native Americans remained situated at the bottom of the socioeconomic ladder. Women continued to be paid considerably less than men. Most ominously, by mid-decade, California and Florida real estate, the construction industry and even the automotive trade began to slacken.

By late 1929, the bill for the era's speculative mania began to come due, thanks largely to the policies of the Republican administrations that had lessened the progressivity in the federal income tax system, gutted antitrust activity and maintained high tariff rates. In October, the stock market began to crash, while the American economy underwent a precipitous three-and-a-half year plunge. Breadlines and soup kitchens abounded, while relief agencies funded by private or state organizations proved incapable of responding adequately to the mounting crisis. Homelessness surged, as millions of forgotten men simply milled about or rode the rails. Malnutrition heightened, with some actually starving to death in what was still the world's richest land, while others were reduced to scavenging in garbage cans for morsels of food. Shanty-towns cropped up in every major city across the land; the makeshift slums were referred to as Hoovervilles, a derisive reference to the current occupant of the White House who had helped to preside over the boom of the twenties and now came across as inflexible and uncaring in a time when a soothing hand and prompt action were desperately needed.

Constantly attempting to maintain appearances and promising that prosperity loomed just around the corner, Hoover drew a line in the sand philosophically and, as it turned out, politically as well. Earlier viewed as a great humanitarian for his involvement with food relief to war-torn Europe, Hoover believed there that were certain actions the federal government could not take; if it did, he reasoned, America would head down a dangerous path. That way would lie an alien system, like those found abroad, starkly different from the enlightened capitalism Hoover celebrated. Hoover did act in his own fashion, helping in 1931 to set up the Recon-

Fig. 3-2 A breadline at the onset of the Great Depression, January 1930. (Pearson Education, Corporate Digital Archive, Library of Congress.)

struction Finance Corporation, which provided hundreds of millions of dollars in assistance to leading insurance and railroad enterprises. But he remained adamantly opposed to the granting of direct relief—the dole—to individuals, arguing that such aid would corrupt the moral fiber of its recipients. Those in dire need of some assistance for themselves and their family members failed to draw the distinctions that Hoover did. Consequently, his political stock and that of the Republican Party plummeted. A final blow might have been Hoover's disastrous decision to allow U.S. Army forces, led by Gen-

eral Douglas MacArthur, to roust a group of World War I veterans, who had encamped on the Washington Mall. Dubbed the Bonus Army, these ex-soldiers sought a one-time payment that Congress had authorized in 1921, but which was not to come due until two full decades had passed.

Anger brewed, as unemployment councils, headed by socialists or communists, demanded government action, while farmers' organizations threatened law enforcement officials attempting to carry out foreclosures. Clashes between farmers, workers and police forces sprang up across the land. While some, fearful of the growing unrest, envisioned an American equivalent of the Iron Heel favored by Italian dictator Benito Mussolini or the head of the German Nazi Party, Adolf Hitler, others viewed the Soviet Union as a model socialist state. The socialist Norman Thomas and the communist William Foster improved their respective parties' positions in the 1932 presidential election, with many intellectuals favoring Foster.

The Democratic Party candidate, Franklin Delano Roosevelt, a distant cousin of the former president, and himself a one-time vice-presidential nominee, easily won the campaign. Encouraged by his wife Eleanor, Roosevelt had twice been elected governor of New York. Operating in Albany, close to his family's manorial estate at Hyde Park, FDR acquired a reputation as a progressive chief executive. During the campaign, he hinted vaguely about some new deal, while displaying a buoyancy and optimism that contrasted markedly with Hoover's pessimistic countenance.

FDR AND THE NEW DEAL

By March 1933, the American economy plunged to its worst depths yet. Roosevelt took office and immediately proclaimed the crisis as grave as that which had beset the nation during the Great War. Having demanded congressional authority to act, FDR and his Brain-Trust advisors began crafting programs of relief, recovery, and reform during his administration's First Hundred Days. While $500 million in aid was allocated through the Federal Emergency Relief Administration to enable the states to provide direct assistance to individuals, Roosevelt favored work relief. Consequently, massive public works projects were devised, including the Civilian Conservation Corps, which targeted young men between the ages of 18 and 25, and the Public Works Administration.

The New Dealers, considering overproduction to be at the heart of the economic doldrums, also turned to planning in an effort to prop up the industrial and agricultural sectors. The National Industrial Recovery Act suspended anti-trust activity, allowed for price-fixing and encouraged labor organizing. The Agricultural Adjustment Act established subsidies to farmers who agreed to restrict crop outputs. Planning was also highlighted through the Tennessee Valley Authority, which sought to provide reforestation and public power to a depressed, seven-state area.

By 1934, the economy had improved somewhat, but discontent brewed once more. The American Liberty League, boasting support from the Duponts, among the wealthiest of all American families, and from Al Smith, the 1928 Democratic Party presidential nominee, accused FDR of leading the country down the path toward socialism. Father Charles Coughlin, the "Radio Priest," linked the Roosevelt administration with an international, Jewish-inspired conspiracy to weaken America. Louisiana Senator Huey Long, with his Share Our Wealth program, promised riches for all his supporters, while threatening a 1936 presidential run. Dr. Francis Townsend called for $200 monthly stipends to be delivered to the elderly.

Responding to critics, but particularly annoyed by those who accused him of being a traitor to his class, Roosevelt veered to the left. In 1935, his administration offered what was referred to as a "soak the rich" program, including heightened taxes on the wealthy and corporations, and new banking measures. The Wagner or National Labor Relations Act called for businesses to deal in good faith with labor representatives, while the Social Security Act established a program of old-age pensions, disability insurance, and aid to families with dependent children. Most important, the Social Security Act laid the structural foundation for the American welfare state. The Works Progress Administration contained some remarkably innovative programs for theatrical performers, artists, and historians, among other groups. Clifford Odets, John Steinbeck, Richard Wright and Langston Hughes were all part of the Federal Writers Project. Orson Welles and John Houseman participated in the Federal Theater Project, which sponsored an all-black performance of *Othello*. The socially conscious nature of certain aspects of the WPA made it controversial to some, who strove to reduce funding or terminate various projects altogether.

Following an impressive triumph in the 1936 presidential election, FDR delivered a stirring inaugural address in which he decried the continued reality that one-third of the nation remained "ill-housed, ill-clad, and ill-fed." As his administration seemingly readied for more reform efforts, a series of setbacks confronted the president. Angered by rulings of the U.S. Supreme Court declaring the NIRA and the AAA to be unconstitutional, and fearing that the centerpieces of the Second New Deal—the Wagner Act and the Social Security Act—might suffer the same fate, Roosevelt urged that the High Court be transformed. His proposal called for presidential authority to appoint a new member for each jurist who reached the age of seventy and failed to retire, with a maximum of six new appointments possible. The political fallout was considerable, as even many stalwart allies of the president decried the

"court-packing plan," which failed to garner sufficient congressional support. FDR, nevertheless, later argued that he lost the battle but won the war, for both the direction and the composition of the Supreme Court began to change. Chief Justice Charles Evan Hughes started voting more regularly with liberal members, while some of the most conservative jurists opted to retire. Consequently, the Roosevelt Court came into existence, eventually containing such justices as Hugo Black, William Douglas, Felix Frankfurter, Frank Murphy and Robert Jackson. That court gave its judicial approval to congressional legislation that placed restraints on business enterprise, an entity that previous courts had often considered inviolate.

Nevertheless, FDR's political luster dimmed somewhat due to the Supreme Court controversy, labor insurgency and a new economic downturn. Labor agitation, particularly following the passage of the Wagner Act, heightened, with a new militant confederation, the Congress of Industrial Organizations, operating in mass production industries that the American Federation of Labor had left largely untouched. The Congress of Industrial Organization's employment of sit-down strikes in factories infuriated many who viewed private property as sacred. But Roosevelt's popularity probably dipped most of all due to his decision to reduce public works spending, which was in keeping with his unfavorable reading of an imbalanced budget. Additionally, his expectation that private investors would pick up the economic slack proved wrongheaded, and within a short while, the federal government had to engage in new public works programs. A short-lived third New Deal resulted, with the passage of the Fair Labor Standards and Practices Act, which mandated a forty-hour workweek and time-and-a-half pay for over-time, and prohibited the employment of child labor in industries involved in inter-state commerce. A new AAA was adopted, but that attempt to aid sharecroppers and tenant farmers was half-hearted at best.

Still, by the mid-point of FDR's second term, it was clear that his administration had engendered a series of dramatic changes in American life. With the ushering in of the welfare state that restored faith in America's capitalistic democracy, the federal govern-ment became more intimately involved in the lives of average citizens. New groups, in-cluding workers, the elderly and, indirectly, blacks, were the beneficiaries of governmen-tal largesse. So too were giant corporations, as American capitalism rebounded from the worst depression in the nation's history, thanks largely to government intervention and support. The Democratic Party, for the first time in generations, became the major-ity political force in the land, because of the Roosevelt coalition: factory workers, farmers, immigrants, urban dwellers and various eth-nic groups. Power shifted in other ways, too, from Wall Street to Washington, D.C., as the executive branch began adopting some of the trappings of an imperial presidency.

After the 1938 congressional elections re-sulted in the defeat of several staunch New Deal proponents at both the statewide and national levels, the administration's domestic agenda proved less ambitious. FDR unhap-pily recognized that a bipartisan coalition—comprised of Republicans and conservative Southern Democrats—had appeared in Con-gress, committed to halting the passage of more reform legislation. Increasingly, too, Roosevelt's attention was drawn to interna-tional affairs, as right-wing aggressor states were on the march. That phenomenon would eventually demand redirecting of U.S. for-eign policy.

The U.S. Response to World Events and America at War

Determined to rearm the United States, Roosevelt had to contend with isolationist sentiment as well as neutrality legislation that had been passed in mid-decade. From late 1934 through early 1935, the Nye Com-mittee in the Senate charged that American banking interests and munitions makers had helped to ensnare the United States in World War I. Congress passed a series of neutrality laws designed to prevent a similar destiny from again befalling the country. Thus, an arms embargo involving belligerents was called for, loans were prohibited to such na-tions, and Americans were forbidden from traveling on the ships of warring states, sell-ing them weapons or delivering them loans. One unfortunate result was the United States' failure—which paralleled that of other leading democracies—to assist the Spanish Republicans, who faced a right-wing assault orchestrated by General Francisco Franco. Thus, while only Soviet Russia and Mexico offered any kind of assistance to the democratically elected Spanish government, its foes received considerable financial and material support, along with pilots, from Fas-cist Italy and Nazi Germany. Some 2,000 Americans, including members of the Abra-ham Lincoln battalion, joined the interna-tional brigades—comprised almost entirely of men of the left—which fought on behalf of the Republic.

Gradually, the Roosevelt administration pressured Congress to relax various restric-tions in the neutrality legislation. In 1937, a cash-and-carry component enabled the United States to sell nonmilitary supplies to beligerent nations as long as they were paid for in cash and were transported in the ships of the purchasing nation. On October 5, FDR gave a major address in Chicago, in which he talked about the need to quarantine aggressor states. He helped to defeat an attempt to pass the Ludlow Amendment, which would have required a national referendum on whether the United States could enter a war, unless the nation was attacked. Concerned about Japanese aggression in the Pacific, Roosevelt began to strengthen the U.S. naval fleet.

After initially backing the 1938 Munich Pact that allowed Germany to take over the Sudetenland in Czechoslovakia, Roosevelt sought to provide more war material to England and France. Troubled by German incursions into Latin America, the president supported American commercial enterprises in the region and strove to devise an anti-fascist front. In 1938, the Declaration of Lima called for all hemispheric countries to join together against external threats; the 1939 Declaration of Panama insisted on a "safety belt" that would prevent hostile actions from non-American states. Following the German invasion of Poland in September 1939, Roosevelt's supporters managed to amend the Neutrality acts, allowing arms to be shipped to American allies on a cash-and-carry basis.

The increased military orders and heightened defense spending helped to increase both production levels and employment in the United States. They also demonstrated the pro-Allied bent of Roosevelt, who favored "measures short of war" to aid the Allies in their battle against the Axis states of Italy and Germany. In 1940, the U.S. Congress adopted the Selective Training and Ser-

vice Act, the nation's first peacetime conscription. After the fall of France in June, the United States began shipping war supplies to Great Britain. Seeking bipartisan support in the face of the deteriorating international situation, Roosevelt named two prominent Republicans, Henry Stimson and Frank Knox, as Secretary of War and Secretary of Navy, respectively.

In his attempt to rearm the United States and to assist the Allies, Roosevelt continued to encounter considerable opposition led by the isolationist America First Committee that included General Robert E. Wood, chairman of Sears, Roebuck, and Co., and Charles Lindbergh. Pacifists, including those opposed to the draft altogether, and Trotskyists—who idolized the former Bolshevik leader Leon Trotsky—adopted an anti-war stance. Also opposing Roosevelt were various native American fascists, including members of the anti-Semitic German American Bund. By contrast, the Committee to Defend America by Aiding the Allies, led by the journalist William Allen White, warned that fascism, not war, was the greater enemy. In the 1940 presidential campaign, Roosevelt, running for an unprecedented third term, pledged that he would not order Americans to participate in "foreign wars." In early 1941, shortly after defeating the Republican nominee, Wendell Willkie, Roosevelt called for the United States to stand as the "great arsenal of democracy." The government-run National Defense Research Council and the Office of Scientific Research and Development provided federal monies for universities and institutes that assisted the war effort.

Following the United States' entrance into the war, the country's economy surged to levels of near-full employment. In fact, labor shortages once again necessitated hiring those who had often been denied job opportunities in industrial plants prior to the war: African-Americans and women, some six million of them altogether. U.S. industry poured out tanks, planes, ships, and other war material that enabled the Soviet Union and Great Britain to hold on, and armed American soldiers, sailors, and pilots. By 1945, the Gross National Product surpassed the $200 billion mark, having more than doubled in five years. Government-sponsored research and development, some British-based, resulted in tremendous breakthroughs in electronics, radar, computers, jet propulsion, synthetics, ballistic missiles, medicines such as penicillin and sulfadiazine and ultimately nuclear weapons. Government-crafted wage-and-price controls helped to spur savings and to prevent the kinds of inflationary pressures that had beset the United States during World War I. Union membership jumped from 10.5 million to nearly 15 million, while the income boasted by the wealthiest 5% of Americans actually diminished from 23.7% to 16.8%.

The attack on Pearl Harbor ensured that Americans would rally around the flag, and they did so in unprecedented fashion. Nevertheless, and notwithstanding the economic boom experienced during the war, racial problems continued to beset the United States. Determined to use the leverage caused by wartime demands, A. Philip Randolph, head of the Brotherhood of Sleeping Car Porters, threatened in January 1941 to lead a march on Washington to contest racially discriminatory practices in the U.S. military and defense plants. Worried about potential political embarrassment, President Roosevelt issued Executive Order 8802, which established the Fair Employment Practices Commission (FEPC) to examine discrimination by defense contractors. The

American military, however, remained segregated, and African-Americans were not ushered into combat until late in the war. In the meantime, racial tensions resulted in riots in the United States, the most serious occurring in Detroit in 1942 and in Harlem the following year. In June 1943, during the Zoot Suit riots in East Los Angeles, soldiers and sailors attacked Mexican-Americans, blacks and Filipinos.

A budding civil rights movement was emerging, as evidenced by the formation of the Congress of Racial Equality (CORE), which adopted the tactics of nonviolent civil disobedience employed by the Indian pacifist Mahatma Gandhi. In 1943, CORE conducted sit-ins in Detroit, Chicago and Denver. All the while, the National Association for the Advancement of Colored People (NAACP) continued a legal assault against Jim Crow, focusing on higher education and the ballot box.

The most striking example of civil rights violations involved Japanese-Americans and Japanese aliens. Fueled by racism and xenophobia, demands cropped up on the west coast that individuals of Japanese extraction be interned. Starting in early 1942, some 120,000 American citizens and immigrants of Japanese ancestry were forced from their homes, farms, businesses and schools and placed in internment centers. Heading the operation, which began on the heels of the Pearl Harbor assault, was General John De Witt, who stated that "the Japanese race is an enemy race." In February 1942, President Roosevelt issued Executive Order 9066, declaring that the internment should proceed. In December 1944, a divided Supreme Court affirmed the constitutionality of the removal of Japanese-Americans from the coast, on the grounds of military necessity. In an embittered dissent, Justice Frank Murphy refused to provide a legal stamp of approval to "this legalization of racism."

Latin America between the World Wars

During the 1930s, the United States' relationship with several of her southern neighbors was altered. The interwar era began with American marines stationed in Haiti and the Dominican Republic, American soldiers having chased "bandits" across the Rio Grande River, and U.S. investors and policymakers more determined than ever to establish dominance throughout Central America and the Caribbean. As the Mexican Revolution (1910–1920) continued to unfold, President Wilson discussed the need for the United States to "teach the South American republics to choose good men."

But the chasm between the lofty promises Wilson delivered to justify U.S. entrance into World War I and the reality of poison gas and trench warfare had engendered grave disillusionment regarding American involvement in the affairs of other countries. Though U.S. policymakers in the 1920s worked with those in other lands to curb armaments or even to outlaw war altogether, through the Kellogg-Briand Pact, isolationist sentiment prevented American statesmen from responding to the aggressive machinations of Japanese militarists in Manchuria, beginning in 1931. Similarly, the United States reacted with barely a whimper as Germany rearmed under Adolf Hitler and began to encroach on Austria, or when Italy, guided by Benito Mussolini, assaulted Haile Selaisse's Ethiopia. By the time the Spanish Civil War began in 1936 with Franco's fascist-backed forces striving to overthrow the Republic, the Roosevelt administration was saddled with the new neutrality laws. A peace movement had emerged

on college campuses, with students adopting an American version of the Oxford Pledge, taken by their English counterparts, which proclaimed an unwillingness to fight for God or country.

Central America and the Caribbean

While Americans appeared determined to avoid being ensnared in another European war or a confrontation in the Pacific, the nation adopted anything but a hands-off attitude in the Western hemisphere. U.S. dominance of Central America and the Caribbean had intensified under President William Howard Taft and then accelerated during Wilson's administration. Through the control of banks and custom houses, the running of elections, and the landing of marines, the United States acted forcefully in Nicaragua, the Dominican Republic, Haiti, Cuba and Mexico. Between 1914 and 1929, U.S. exports to Latin America tripled, encouraged by the 1919 Edge Act, which authorized American banks to establish foreign branches. In Cuba, Brazil, Chile and Venezuela, U.S. companies helped to expand infrastructures, investing heavily in electric utilities, railroads, mining and petroleum. Plantation agriculture was hardly neglected, with the United Fruit Company and the Standard Fruit Company monopolizing the so-called "banana republics" of Guatemala, Honduras, Nicaragua and Panama.

American troops occupied Nicaragua from 1912 through 1933, with only a two-month break, starting in the summer of 1925. One Nicaraguan patriot, Augusto César Sandino, and his band of supporters—largely miners, peasants, workers and Indians—engaged in guerrilla warfare against American marines and the National Guard, created and trained by the United States. Shortly following the end of the U.S. occupation, Sandino agreed to meet with newly elected President Juan Bautista Sacasa, but before he could he was assassinated by National Guardsmen on February 21, 1934. Sandino had called for the disbanding of the para-military forces, while the head of the National Guard, Anastasio "Tacho" Somoza Garcia, had demanded that the guerrilla cadre be disarmed. Within the next three years, Somoza took control of the Nicaraguan government, relying on his proto-fascist Blue Shirts.

Developments in another Central American republic proved no happier. Joined with foreign investors, an unholy trinity—landed estate holders, the military and the Catholic Church—ruled El Salvador heavy-handedly. The National Guard, patterned after Spanish forces, policed the countryside, at the bequest of the *hacendados*, who controlled large landed estates. The advent of the Great Depression devastated the monocultural, coffee-dependent El Salvadorean economy by dropping coffee prices by half. With wages and living conditions rapidly worsening, some 80,000 amassed in San Salvador on May 1, 1930, to protest their plight. Arturo Araujo, a well-intentioned landowner, who received the backing of students, peasants and workers, won the following year's presidential election. Infuriated by Araujo's proclamation that the Communist Party would be allowed to participate in upcoming municipal elections, the military staged a coup, replacing Araujo with Vice-President Maximiliano Hernandez Martinez, who proved sympathetic to fascist ideology and Franco's bid to overthrow the Spanish Republic.

A peasant revolt broke out in early 1932, spearheaded by student activists and the communist Agustín Farabundo Martí, who

had fought with Sandino's forces in Nicaragua. However, the peasants, many of whom were Indians, were armed with little more than machetes. The army responded with wholesale repression in an event known as the Slaughter of 1932, eventually killing some 30,000. General Hernandez Martinez—referred to as *El Brujo*, due to his fascination with the occult—remained in power until 1944.

BRAZIL

During the interwar period, Brazil was the Latin American republic where fascism appeared most viable. Industrialization and urbanization assisted by the United States' interests contesting English financial hegemony, resulted in the growth of an industrial proletariat and a middle-class. Inflationary pressures led to the emergence of labor campaigns, with a general strike besetting São Paulo in 1917. Other strike activity led to increased wages, but that hardly translated to improved living conditions for workers, many of whom were immigrants. Political unrest prevailed throughout the 1920s, with a pair of military revolts, spurred by monocultural realities, including demands for social and economic reform. By 1930, Brazil's foreign debt had mushroomed to $1.2 billion, with $200 million annual interest payments.

Not surprisingly, the era's economic downturn proved devastating, with coffee prices and wages plummeting, and unemployment and inflation rising. Class and regional tensions intensified, and a military coup in 1930 brought to power the wealthy rancher Getúlio Vargas, governor of Rio Grande do Sul. For the next decade and a half, Vargas reigned as something of a populist, which led his countrymen to refer to him as "the father of the poor." But his rule was leavened by a heavy dose of authoritarianism, with Brazilian federalism further weakened and power increasingly centralized. At the same time, Vargas enfranchised women, ushered in the secret ballot, established a social security system, and nationalized various companies. Illiteracy, which afflicted most adult Brazilians, remained a bar to voting.

The Constituent Assembly crafted a new constitution, which restricted foreign control of land, and elected Vargas to a four-year term as president of Brazil. Article 119 called for "the progressive nationalization of mines, mineral deposits, and waterfalls or other sources of energy, as well as of the industries considered as basic or essential to the economic and military defense of the country." The constitution also established an eight-hour workday, devised minimum wages, and constructed a social security system that included pensions and employment security. However, as historian Benjamin Keen has noted, labor unions now "became official agencies controlled by the Ministry of Labor." Unapproved strikes were harshly dealt with. Furthermore, the progressive legislation did not affect agricultural laborers, the vast majority of the workforce, as promises of agrarian reform bore no fruit.

Mobilization of various groups, with greater or lesser success, occurred during the Vargas period. Liberal military officers, intellectuals, and workers were infuriated by his refusal to challenge the landed oligarchy's preeminence. The Communist Party, guided by Luis Carlos Prestes, one of the discontented young officers who had demanded reform during the 1920s, became a force to be reckoned with. Prestes, in keeping with the Comintern's new approach regarding liberals

and socialists, sought a united front of forces on the left, an Alliance of National Liberation, which could depose Vargas. A National Security Act, passed in March 1935, handed Vargas the means to crush the left. When Prestes initiated an armed insurrection, the repression only mounted, with some 15,000 arrested and many of those tortured. Banned Communist Party members now headed underground.

Initially, Vargas seemed to view right-wing activism more favorably. Most significant, the Integralist movement, shaped by the author Plínio Salgado, looked to Portugal's Antonio de Oliveira Salazar as a model for Brazil. The Integralists condemned democracy and communists, and dismissed their proponents, along with Masons and Jews, as "enemies of the state." When impending elections seemed certain to produce a tilt to the left, Vargas called them off, grabbing dictatorial powers with the excuse of staving off a communist plot.

Declaring that a new constitution would usher in the *Estado Novo*—the New State—Vargas unsuccessfully sought to include Salgado in his cabinet. In a disastrous move, Salgado, relying on his fascist-styled Greenshirts, attempted to oust Vargas from the presidential palace. The crushing of Salgado's henchmen left Vargas with no organized opposition. Vargas turned to the techniques of indoctrination and mass propaganda characteristic of European fascist states. Press censorship, the banning of political parties, and repressive police tactics, including torture, were all relied on. As Azevedo Amaral, a government spokesperson indicated, "Docile submission to the authority of the State is not repugnant and cannot be repugnant to normal individuals, for they intuitively understand that in order for a people to transform itself into a nation, it must organize itself into a hierarchical structure."

Many Brazilians, nevertheless, appeared content with the *Estado Novo,* as the government promoted industrialization and modernization. Through planning and direct investments, the government focused on key industries such as mining, oil, steel, electricity and chemicals. It supported the development of hydroelectric power, more extensive railways and market cartels. While striving to avoid neocolonialism, the government welcomed foreign corporations, with certain restrictions.

The results of Vargas' economic program were decidedly mixed. Seemingly, market forces little affected rural Brazil. Labor organization remained restricted, with national and state unions prohibited, while corporatist-styled unions held sway in plants. A progressive labor code, passed in 1942, was inapplicable to agricultural laborers. During the first half of the 1940s, severe inflation ravaged workers nationwide.

During the Estado Novo's early life, U.S. policymakers worried about Vargas' affinity for Fascist Italy and Nazi Germany. By 1938, Germany had become a leading consumer of Brazilian cotton, coffee and cacao, while the German Bank for South America boasted 300 branches in Brazil. To assuage U.S. concerns about Germany's involvement in the Brazilian economy, Vargas leased military installations and provided quartz and natural rubber in return for American economic assistance. The United States helped to construct air and naval bases in northern coastal Brazil, and provided financial backing for the establishment of a great iron and steel mill at Volta Redonda. The German sinking of Brazilian ships resulted in a declaration of war against the Axis states in August 1942. In 1944, a

Brazilian combat division, comprised of 25,000 soldiers, joined up with the U.S. Fifth Army in Italy.

Pressured to lighten his authoritarian grip, Vargas proclaimed an amnesty for political prisoners in January 1945. He also sponsored the establishment of new political parties, including the Social Democratic Party, made up of industrialists and rural machines, and a Labour Party, which received backing from Vargas-controlled trade unions. Legal prohibitions against the Communist Party were removed, and its leader, Luis Carlos Prestes, along with other left-wing activists, was freed from prison. The Querémistas supported Vargas' hold on power, while the National Democratic Union, supported by economic liberals and elites engaged in export commerce, opposed the *Estado Novo.*

Political pressures mounted by late 1945, and in October the army demanded that Vargas resign or be removed from office. A military coup ensued, and Vargas headed for his ranch in Rio Grande do Sul. This hardly displeased U.S. policy makers, who were troubled by Vargas' populist moves to restrict foreign capital. Nor did Vargas' ouster disturb many liberal constitutionalists, military officers, and state political bosses. They opposed his apparent shift leftward, such as his recent call for the expropriation of any group considered threatening to the national interest.

ARGENTINA

Argentina's luster had dimmed considerably since the early part of the 20th century, but economic nationalism with a populist flavor still flourished. Once identified with economic progress, constitutional governance and liberal republicanism, Argentina had fallen on hard times, setting the stage for Juan Perón's ascendancy. Hipólito Yrigoyen's World War I-era efforts to curry favor with small farmers, trade unions and intellectuals resulted in a determination to crush a syndicalist general strike in early 1919. With the far rightist paramilitary Argentine Patriotic League favoring class warfare, the syndicalists and anarchists suffered accordingly. Increasingly, workers began to view socialism and communism more sympathetically. As inflation crippled the export-oriented Argentinian economy, Yrigoyen's Radical Party took another rightward turn, moving to cut state expenditures and raise tariff rates. Running in 1928 as a populist who favored nationalization of the oil industry, Yrigoyen was once again elected president of Argentina. His efforts to create jobs reignited the fires of inflation and a severe budget deficit resulted. The Great Depression increased unemployment and Yrigoyen was again compelled to battle with militant workers and university students, and the right-wing Patriotic League. In September 1930, a military coup ousted Yrigoyen. The military's greater professionalism, historians Thomas E. Skidmore and Peter H. Smith argue, led to its first successful takeover since the mid-nineteenth century.

Two wings of the military vied for power, with General José F. Uriburu heading a nationalist faction that favored a corporatist solution, such as that adopted by Mussolini, Spain's Miguel Primo de Rivera, and Portugal's Antonio de Oliveira Salazar. Another faction, led by General Agustín P. Justo, wanted to safeguard Argentina's liberal heritage. The *Concordancia*, an alliance of conservatives, anti-Yrigoyen radicals, and disaffected socialists, resulted; it dominated Argentine politics until 1943. Moves were undertaken to foster industrialization and rekindle agricultural exports. Public works were relied on to alleviate unemployment, while the building of roads and grain elevators made Argentine products more competitive. As the socialists and communists sponsored trade unions, the government received the backing of Catholic traditionalists sympathetic to fascism.

The conservative-dominated regimes of Justo and Roberto M. Ortiz, a member of the Radical Party, resorted to state intervention in economic affairs. Determined to avoid the ravages engendered by international capitalism, the Argentine governments during the so-called "Infamous Decade" strove to maintain extensive trade with Great Britain, reduce farm production and curtail imports. With foreign capital, they also sought to create import-substitution industries. Though foreign investors dominated entire industries, including meat-packing, electric power, cement, automobile, rubber and oil, the Argentine economy improved by mid-decade. Unemployment dropped sharply, thanks to public works and capital investments. While real wages diminished, consumption of consumer goods and food increased. The General Confederation of Labor in 1930 merged two trade unions, and organized labor claimed 300,000–350,000 members by 1943.

A three-year stalemate between conservative and radical forces ended at that point, when the military again moved to take over the reins of government. Throughout the 1930s, ardently nationalistic military officers championed industrialization and modernization, while viewing armed might as the means to usher in Argentine supremacy in the region. Like European fascists, the military hoped to further industrial capitalism while keeping a tight leash on organized labor. Unions were taken over by the government, which shut down newspapers and imprisoned opposition leaders.

Paradoxically, Argentina now moved to sever relations with Germany while heading down an apparent fascist path of its own. Argentina had refused to support a U.S.-sponsored Pan-American alliance opposing the Axis nations; consequently, it had been denied the American armaments that its neighbors received. However, in early 1945, President Edelmiro J. Farrell more forthrightly supported the Allies and readied for elections. A cadre of army officers, headed by Colonel Juan Domingo Perón, became more influential with the national government. Perón's star rose, thanks to his prominence as secretary of labor and welfare, minister of war and, eventually, vice-president, and his promise to restore constitutional rule. Deftly playing the labor card, Perón supported substantial wage increases, state-financed pensions and health benefits, the expansion of sympathetic unions and the creation of new ones. Between 1943 and 1946 alone, the membership of Textile Workers Union rose forty-fold to over 84,000, while the Metallurgical Workers Union's increased from 2,000 to 100,000.

Fearing Perón's influence, his opponents staged a coup in October 1945, which resulted in his imprisonment. Pro-Perón forces mobilized in the streets of Buenos Aires, demanding his release. Subsequently standing as the candidate of the recently formed Argentine Labor Party and receiving the backing of the expanded urban working class, Perón was elected president in February 1946. His candidacy had been opposed by the U.S. State Department, which, like the Communist Party, ironically enough, considered Perón a fascist. Yet Perón, astute politician that he was, recognized that fascism had been vanquished in Europe and, consequently, recast himself as a democrat ready to adhere to the people's will. He also countered the State Department's charges of his fascist leanings, while denouncing American imperialism.

CHILE

The left appeared far more potent in Chile, a Latin American republic long considered among the most stable and economically vibrant states in the region. During World War I, the Chilean Congress passed social welfare legislation, providing workmen's compensation, employer's liability and retirement benefits for railway workers. Inflationary pressures induced by World War I piqued labor unrest, and a congressional enactment allowed for the deporting of alien labor organizers; as matters turned out, however, there were few such activists. A failed general strike in Santiago in September 1919 weakened previously potent anarcho-syndicalist unions, which began to be supplanted by communist and socialist confederations. The paramilitary Patriotic Leagues, comprised of affluent right-wing recruits, attacked workers, while the government systematically repressed anarcho-syndicalists. Subsequently, in 1922, Luis Emilio Recabarren, a former member of the Workers' Federation of Chile, helped to found the Communist Party, which became the most powerful of all Latin American communist parties.

In the early postwar period, however, establishment politicians dominated Chilean public life. Some, determined to incorporate the urban masses into the political mainstream, carved out a Liberal Alliance that by 1918 held a majority of seats in the chamber of deputies. Two years later, the Liberal Alliance candidate, the attorney Arturo Alessandri, was elected president of Chile, demonstrating the electoral potency of enlightened middle-class voters and the working class. Alessandri favored redistributive policies, including social welfare and subsidized housing, which proved enormously controversial. During his first months in office, government representatives backed workers in a series of labor conflicts, but Alessandri was assailed from all sides and, by the end of the year, opted to repress workers. Nevertheless, conservatives disliked his progressive legislation and stalemated congressional action.

Finally, in September 1924, the largely middle-class Chilean armed forces carried out a coup in support of Alessandri, who refused to accept the military action. Congress obligingly passed a series of measures proposed by the armed forces, including a labor code that effectively subjected unions to government control. The January Revolution of 1925, spearheaded by Carlos Ibañez del Campo and Marmaduke Grove, led to Alessandri's return from exile abroad and the adoption of a new constitution. That document, backed by Alessandri, brought about the separation of church and state and declared government responsibility for public health and worker protection. It also augmented presidential powers and the ability of the state to intervene in economic affairs; the Constitution of 1925 remained in force until 1973.

The military government had frequently backed workers as they engaged in strikes, but Alessandri again moved against laborers.

Inflationary pressures and new labor unrest resulted in Alessandri's resignation once more. By mid-1927, Colonel Ibañez, thanks to a fraudulent election, was the next Chilean head of state. Relying on state intervention and massive American loans, Ibañez expanded the Chilean infrastructure, constructing highways, railway lines, schools, an irrigation system and port facilities. However, Chileans, who viewed themselves as relatively democratic, were taken aback by Ibañez's repressive measures, which included the jailing of foes and the suspending of civil liberties. The Great Depression led to a sharp reduction of mineral exports and reduced foreign investment. Mounting protests demonstrated the paucity of Ibañez's support, and the ensuing repression in the midst of unrest in Santiago led to his ouster. A period of government drift followed, which culminated in another military coup that led to a thirteen-day "Socialist Republic" headed by Colonel Grove in 1932. The short-lived endeavor made the Socialist Party—officially founded the following year—a force to be reckoned with in Chilean politics.

The 1932 presidential election returned Alessandri to power, but his government alienated workers by resorting to classical economic policies in curbing public expenditures and terminating state enterprises. Foreign investors controlled the mining industry, the economically regressive *latifundio* dominated rural Chile and union activities suffered brutal repression. Alessandri also shut down unfriendly newspapers, exiled political opponents and displayed little respect for Congress. More happily, Alessandri's economic policy, orchestrated by finance minister Gustavo Ross, led to unemployment dropping substantially; by contrast, inflation continued unabated, thus reducing workers' real wages. By the mid-thirties, many laborers were linking up with the Chilean left, which had adopted a united front approach. In 1935, Georgi Dimitrov, the head of the Comintern, urged the formation of left-of-center alliances that would defend democracy and repel fascism. A Chilean Popular Front, joining Communists, Socialists, and middle-class Radicals, now appeared, calling for *"pan, techo, y abrigo":* bread, clothing, and a roof. Worried about labor unrest, Alessandri ordered a state of siege, shut down Congress, sent labor leaders into exile and used troops as strike-breakers. A Nazi party, headed by Jorge Gonzales von Marees, attempted a takeover in 1938. Alessandri's forces repelled the aborted uprising and eventually killed 62 Nazis following their surrender.

As Alessandri's popularity waned dramatically, the Radical Pedro Aguirre Cerda, a university professor, landowner and candidate of the Chilean Popular Front, narrowly won the 1938 election. For the next eight years, the Popular Front seemingly remained dominant, while strengthening state capitalism with heavy reliance on the government-run Chilean Development Corporation, which emphasized planning and targeting investment in the public and private sectors. In reality, the Popular Front's record was decidedly mixed, as it never achieved congressional dominance and failed to implement structural economic and social reforms. It was also crippled by divisions involving the Communists and Socialists, which widened following the announcement in August 1939 of the Nazi-Soviet Non-Aggression Pact. Based in the urban middle class and among industrial workers, the Popular Front received little support in the countryside, which continued to be dominated by powerful land-

owners. The Popular Front suffered electoral defeat in the 1946 presidential election, provoking new sectarian splits on the left.

MEXICO

For American policymakers, developments in Brazil, Argentina, and Chile, although sometimes of mounting concern due to international events, were of secondary importance to those in neighboring Mexico. Particularly distressing were moves undertaken to nationalize American oil interests in the late thirties, which led to demands for retaliatory action. However, President Roosevelt, recognizing that the United States might soon be propelled into another world war, determined to remain in Mexico's good graces. Thus, his administration worked to smooth over relations, while attempting to placate American oil companies.

The decision of Mexican officials to protect vital national resources was in keeping with the revolutionary ferment that had rocked the southern republic during the 1910s. That tumultuous decade witnessed the vying for power by liberal reformer, Francisco Madero; a revolutionary champion of the Mexican peasants, Emiliano Zapata; a reactionary, General Victoriano Huerta; a populist fighter, Francisco Villa; the skillful General Alvaro Obregón; and a constitutionalist, General Venustiano Carranza. The period also ushered in the liberal Constitution of 1917, with Carranza's approval. Article 27 proclaimed all subsoil mineral rights to be the property of the national government, allowing for the redistribution of land; it declared national control of water and the subsoil inalienable. Article 123 called for the state to safeguard the rights of labor: it established an eight-hour workday, abolished the company store and debt peonage and guaranteed workers the right to organize and bargain collectively. Article 3 placed new constraints on the Catholic church, denying "religious corporations" or "ministers of any cult" the right to control schools. From this point forth, Mexican politicians declared their sympathies with the nation's workers and peasants.

The assassination of political leaders, initiated with the murder of Madero in 1913, continued with the killings of Zapata and Carranza, enabling Obregón to ascend to the presidency in 1920. The charismatic Obregón ruled until 1924, devising alliances with workers, peasants and the middle class. A rural education campaign, led by the intellectual José Vasconcelos, resulted in the building of schools and libraries along with the cultivating of indigenous arts and crafts. Revolutionary muralists such as Diego Rivera, David Alfaro Siqueiros and José Clemente Orozco were the recipients of government patronage. Vasconcelos, foreseeing the emergence of a "cosmic race" composed of all American ethnic groups, worked to revitalize the image of both the Indian and the mestizo, in an effort to quash racial antagonisms that had festered throughout Spanish colonialism. Obregón relied on the *Confederacion Regional Obrera Mexicana*, led by union boss Luis Morones, to keep labor in check; unions headed by communists and anarchists were repressed. Peasants were funneled into Agrarian Leagues, controlled by the state. Little land reform ensued, with only ten percent of the peasants receiving any land and no credit or technical support. The death of Pancho Villa in 1923 guaranteed that demands for structural social reform would abate, at least for a while. Obregón augmented the powers of the Mexican chief of state, while

reducing military forces by half, thus ensuring eventual civilian dominance. He also obtained U.S. recognition of his regime and arms to quash rebel forces, in return for a promise to uphold American oil concessions granted before the 1917 Constitution was devised. To his credit, Obregón allowed for the peaceful transfer of power, then an all-too-rare occurrence in Latin America.

His successor, General Plutarco Elías Calles, dominated Mexican politics for the next decade. While employing radical rhetoric, Calles supported the steady "growth of Mexican national capitalism." He ushered in the founding of the Bank of Mexico, an expanded highway system, improved irrigation and greater government involvement in electricity, oil and various industries. More agrarian reform took place, with lands of former *hacendados* collectively distributed to peasants. Much of the redistributed land, however, was pasture or forest land; some was even barren. Calles also sought to control Mexican labor, which became discontented due to low wages and the corruption of its own leaders. Like Obregón, Calles reduced the size of the military, which he professionalized.

President Calles was compelled to deal with two major crises. One concerned the *Cristeros*, militant Catholics who believed that the irreligious aspects of the Mexican Revolution had to be undone. The other involved congressional passage of legislation in 1925 to implement Article 27 of the constitution. The government compelled holders of oil leases to swap those titles for fifty-year concessions, traced back to the period of acquisition, with a thirty-year renewal allowed. American oil companies cried foul, talked of drilling despite the legislative enactment and received support from the U.S. State Department and the hard-line American ambassador to Mexico, James R. Sheffield. The possibility of intervention was aborted due to heated opposition in the United States, which forced the Coolidge administration to favor a more conciliatory approach. The new U.S. ambassador, Dwight Morrow, a partner of banker J. Pierpont Morgan, convinced Calles to adopt a new approach, and the Mexican Supreme Court ruled the time limitation for oil concessions unconstitutional. National control of the Mexican subsoil, nevertheless, remained in place.

The clash with the *Cristeros* seemingly threatened a civil war. In early 1926, church leaders proclaimed that the constitution "wounds the most sacred rights of the Catholic Church," and deemed it illegal. Calles now enforced the constitution's previously dormant anticlerical clauses. When the so-called Calles Law demanded that priests register with the government and ordered the closure of religious schools, the church responded by suspending church services nationwide. By the close of the year, armed militants, often linked with *hacendados,* formed guerrilla groups, particularly in the Jalisco mountain territory. Young government teachers and Catholic militants alike were victimized by the ongoing struggle, which finally petered out by the following summer.

Following a presidential campaign in which he ended up as the lone candidate, Obregón was assassinated. Calles filled the ensuing political vacuum by devising the multi-class National Revolutionary Party (PNR). The PNR was designed to pacify rural Mexico and institutionalize the rule by the "revolutionary family," the military figures who had held the presidency since 1920. Excluded from membership were private sector forces, required, as the historian Susan Kaufman Purcell notes, "to join semiofficial chambers of industry and commerce;" church figures; and landowners. The PNR enabled Calles, as *"jefe maximo,"* to retain control over a succession of governments, all of which adopted his top-down approach in an effort to prevent opposition.

As corruption, power and wealth increasingly characterized the revolutionary generals, they proved more antagonistic to agrarian reform, while engaging in more demagogic invectives against the church. The *Cristero* movement was briefly rekindled, resulting only in the loss of more lives. Calles' rightward shift heightened as the Great Depression demonstrated capitalism's weaknesses and produced new stirrings among the peasants and workers. Even within the ranks of the PNR, young middle-class reformers, some influenced by the apparent successes of the Soviet Five-Year Plan, demanded adherence to the promises of the Constitution of 1917. By 1933, the PNR progressives helped to bring about land distributions by the federal government and school reform, shaped by Narcisco Bassols.

With the 1934 presidential election impending, Calles designated General Lázaro Cárdenas, the well-regarded governor of Michoacan, as the PNR candidate. Cárdenas strove to cultivate his own power base; he formed alliances with regional caudillos displeased with Calles' rule, sought to improve relations with the Catholic church and strengthened the PNR's left wing. When Calles began protesting against Cárdenas' actions, the latter forced him into exile. Cárdenas then moved to distribute forty-four million acres of land, with communally owned *ejidos* supplanting the haciendas throughout central and southern Mexico. The *Banco de Credito Ejidal* provided financing for the *ejidos*, which were to contain schools and hospitals. Individual plots of lands were handed out as well. Unfortunately, many promised social and financial services were never delivered. Disorganization, low productivity and the failure to tap into broader markets often afflicted the *ejidos*. Nevertheless, the land redistribution ensured Cárdenas' standing as a hero of the Revolution.

So did his determination to improve the living standards of workers. To that end, Cárdenas helped to create the *Confederacion de Trabajadores Mexicanos,* comprised of labor unions, and the *Confederacion Nacional Campesina,* made up of peasant organizations. Along with the peasantry and the army, labor stood as the bulwark of the offical ruling body, the Party of the Mexican Revolution (PRM). The government's backing of worker demands resulted in the decision of foreign corporations to suspend drilling operations and Cárdenas' determination on March 18, 1938, to nationalize the petroleum industry. As Mexican nationalism flourished, American companies urged President Roosevelt to intervene. The Good Neighbor policy necessitated a peaceful resolution to the controversy, as did Roosevelt's recognition of international tensions that could ensnare the United States in another major conflagration. Oil companies received compensation, while the Mexican government established a state monopoly, *Petróleos Mexicanos* (PEMEX). The nationalization of the railroads soon followed.

Cárdenas' bold stances resulted in both adoration and criticism, the latter largely emanating from wealthy landowners and merchants. His welcoming of political refugees, ranging from Leon Trotsky to thousands of Spanish Republicans, displeased his foes. So too did the Cárdenas government's use of revolutionary socialist rhetoric and refusal to recognize Francisco Franco's rule in Spain; Cárdenas, during the Spanish Civil War, steadfastly supported the Loyalists. Not sur-

prisingly, right-wing opposition, supported by German agents and Franco's Falangists, increased during the final years of Cárdenas' regime. Cárdenas responded by reaching out to Mexican entrepreneurs, curbing land redistribution and downplaying the socialist aspects of his educational reform.

The 1940 election of General Manuel Ávila Camacho, Cárdenas' minister of war, ensured that the second wave of revolutionary-sponsored reform would end. The PRM allowed for the participation of lower classes in political affairs, as its corporatist makeup resulted in fuller control over different sectors of Mexican life. The state had displayed a willingness to intervene in economic affairs, both stirring national pride and providing a model for later generations. But Camacho further slackened the pace of land redistribution and supported a tougher stance regarding labor insurgency. In May 1942, Camacho's government issued a declaration of war against the fascist states. Mexico and Brazil were the only Latin American states to send soldiers to battle the Axis forces.

During the war, Roosevelt and Camacho agreed to allow Mexican agricultural workers to travel across the border to replace American laborers who had been conscripted into the armed forces. The *braceros* began acquiring non-agricultural jobs, too, angering U.S. labor unions. 300,000 Mexicans toiled in the United States, frequently under highly exploitative conditions.

CONCLUSION

Throughout the Americas, as the inter-war period unfolded, government solutions were crafted to contend with worsening economic and political conditions. Notwithstanding opposition by certain Latin American elites and the champions of *laissez-faire* in the United States, government intervention increasingly characterized national attempts to wrestle with problems engendered by rapid modernization, market forces and social transformations. The methods were as varied as the ideological forces accompanying them. Nationalization and privatization were both highlighted, as was the mixed economic approach favored by the Roosevelt New Deal and the Chilean Popular Front. Democratic ideals waxed and waned in popularity, with fascist, socialist and populist panaceas garnering more adherents before social welfare measures and concerns about right-wing aggressor states revitalized interest in liberal devices. Often genuine, that interest was, in other instances, a mere façade intended to paper over authoritarian designs of undemocratic forces and individuals.

• —— • —— • —— • —— • —— • —— • —— •

Twenty-three-year-old Salvador Allende Gossens, following the lead of family members, condemned the dictatorship of Chilean president Carlos Ibañez. To Allende's dismay, Ibañez had thrown political foes, particularly labor leaders, in jail. Ibañez had also suspended civil liberties, which angered many Chileans who took pride in their nation's tradition—albeit one not always sustained—of political democracy and personal freedoms. Already imbued with a well-developed social conscience, Allende was a medical student at the University of Chile in Santiago. Now, Allende joined in a series of demonstrations against Ibañez. The politically engaged Allende, who had read Marx's *Das Kapital,* Bakunin, Lenin and Trotsky, also participated in taking over the main building at the University of Chile. Banners sporting the word *"libertad"* could be seen flying out of the windows. The police poured onto the campus and drove out the students, resulting in some loss of life. Allende's imprisonment followed in 1931. However, in the face of mounting protest that culminated in a general strike joined by doctors, lawyers, engineers, teachers and other professionals, Ibañez soon resigned. For his part, Allende promised his dying father that same year, "From now on I shall devote my life to the struggle for the freedom of the people, for the well-being of the oppressed and for social justice." During the next four decades, Allende stood as a major figure in Chilean politics, advocating both socialism and democracy. As a consequence, he proved both highly popular among many Chileans and a controversial figure in certain circles, including some highly placed ones outside his homeland.

Born in Valparaiso on July 26, 1908, Allende, the son of a public defense attorney, was exposed early to politics as his uncles and father stood as militants within the Radical Party; his grandfather Ramon Allende Padin had served as a senator representing the party in the Chilean Congress. As a youngster, Allende proved to be an excellent athlete and a promising student. After becoming an officer in the Coraceros Cavalry Regiment, he attended medical school. At one point, his political activities resulted in his suspension from the university. Allende's final thesis for his medical studies was titled, "Mental hygiene and delinquency." In the period ahead, he took on many roles, serving as a dental school assistant, a coroner, a physician in a mental hospital and a reporter

Fig. 3-3 Socialist leader Salvador Allende delivering a speech in Santiago, Chile. (Pearson Education, Corporate Digital Archive, Getty Images Inc.)

who appeared at medical conventions, before setting up a private practice in Valparaiso. Supporting Grove's short-lived Socialist Republic, Allende was again arrested when that government fell. Two courts-martial ensued, and Allende's father died in the midst of the second one. Nevertheless, Allende eventually received his medical degree while maintaining his commitment to fight for social and economic justice.

In 1933, Allende helped to found the Chilean Socialist Party headed by Grove, basically creating the organization in Valparaiso. Adhering to a Marxist analysis of history, Allende, unlike Grove, nevertheless sought to create a party that would be "free of ties of an international nature," including communist ones. Allende viewed the Communist Party as "closed, inward looking," while the Socialist Party was nationalistic. In 1935, Allende served as editor of "Medical Newsletter" and, along with Jose Vizcarra, called for a national health system in Chile. A supporter of a Popular Front approach, Allende headed such an apparatus in Valparaiso. After serving as a coroner's assistant, Allende, in 1937, was elected to the Chamber of Deputies to represent Valparaiso and Quillota in the Senate; the Socialist Party captured 11.2% of the popular vote. Only four socialists could be found among the 45 Senators. The party drew on supporters from both the rural and urban working class and the middle class, with considerable backing from professionals, students and intellectuals. For his part, Allende subscribed to the belief that "each nation is free to choose its own way toward socialism."

Allende continued to focus on health issues related to the poor, along with public health in general, while becoming the General Subsecretary for the Socialist Party in 1939. That same year, Allende married Hortensia Bussi, who was studying geography at the University of Chile, and witnessed the publication of his book, *La Realidad Medico-Social Chilena (The Chilean Medical-Social Reality)*. He also befriended Venzuela's Rómulo Betancourt, who was living in exile in Chile. Still only thirty years old, Allende was named to the cabinet of Pedro Aguirre Cerda, whom he viewed as "the bourgeois-radical politician 'par excellence'." From 1939 to 1942, Allende served as Minister of Health, Social Security and Welfare in Aguirre's Popular Front government. In 1942, after being named secretary general of the Chilean Socialist Party, Allende resigned from his cabinet post. One scholar referred to Allende as the "dynamic Socialist Minister of Health," who had carried out painstaking studies of Chile's medical concerns.

Allende's Socialist Party was staunchly anti-imperialist and anti-fascist. Having read Lenin's *Imperialism, the Highest Stage of Capitalism,* Allende reasoned that the issue resonated in underdeveloped lands, especially in Latin America. Indeed, the socialists, as Allende later recalled, viewed imperialism as "our number one enemy." Consequently, they highlighted the need for national liberation. Socialists saw the Chilean Popular Front as "a step forward," which would not, however, usher in full sovereignty if economic dependency remained in place. Foreign capital, they contended, controlled Chile's "real wealth." Cerda's Popular Front, created in the 1930s, was even more emphatically anti-fascist. Confronted with supporting either "bourgeois democracy" or fascism, his party, like "other working-class movements," readily backed the former. In 1945, Allende—who was viewed as charming, cautious, pragmatic and gentlemanly—was again elected to the Chilean Senate and later served as president of that body. Allende's involvement in his nation's political affairs continued as the postwar era unfolded. Indeed, he later sought to carve out his own Popular Front government, much to the chagrin of Chilean aristocrats and certain American policymakers.

◆ ——— ◆ ——— ◆ ——— ◆ ——— ◆ ——— ◆ ——— ◆ ——— ◆ ——— ◆

Suggested Readings

BURNS, E. BRADFORD. *A History of Brazil.* (1993).

COTTRELL, ROBERT C. *Roger Nash Baldwin and the American Civil Liberties Union.* (2000).

DALLEK, ROBERT. *Franklin D. Roosevelt and American Foreign Policy, 1932–1945.* (1979).

DEBRAY, REGIS. *The Chilean Revolution: Conversations with Allende.* (1971).

DIGGINS, JOHN P. *The Rise and Fall of the American Left.* (1992).

GALBRAITH, JOHN KENNETH. *The Great Crash: 1929.* (1961).

HIGHAM, JOHN. *Strangers in the Land: Patterns of American Nativism, 1860–1925.* (1955).

KEEN, BENJAMIN. *A History of Latin America.* (1996).

KENNEDY, DAVID. *Over Here: The First World War and American Society.* (1980).

LANGLEY, L. D. *The Banana Wars: An Inner History of American Empire, 1900–1934.* (1983).

LEUCHTENBURG, WILLIAM E. *The Perils of Prosperity, 1914–1932.* (1958).

MCELVAINE, ROBERT. *The Great Depression: America 1929–1941.* (1984).

MEYER, MICHAEL C., and WILLIAM L. SHERMAN. *The Course of Mexican History.* (1995).

MURPHY, PAUL L. *World War I and the Origins of Civil Liberties in the United States.* (1979).

MURRAY, ROBERT K. *Red Scare: A Study in National Hysteria, 1919–1920.* (1955).

PARRISH, MICHAEL. *Anxious Decades: America in Prosperity and Depression, 1920–1941.* (1992).

SCOBIE, J. R. *Argentina: A City and a Nation.* (1971).

SKIDMORE, THOMAS E., and PETER H. SMITH. *Modern Latin America.* (1997).

SMITH, PETER H., ed. *Latin America in Comparative Perspective: New Approaches to Methods and Analysis.* (1995).

STEVENSON, JOHN REESE. *The Chilean Popular Front.* (1942).

THORP, ROSEMARY, ed. *Latin America in the 1930s: The Role of the Periphery in World Crisis.* (1984).

WILLIAMSON, EDWIN. *The Penguin History of Latin America.* (1992).

WINN, PETER. *Americas: The Changing Face of Latin America and the Caribbean.* (1992).

WOODWARD, RALPH LEE, JR. *Central America: A Nation Divided.* (1999).

CHAPTER 4

The Challenge to Western Hegemony: Asia and the Colonial World in the Interwar Years, 1920–1940

On April 25, 1915, Mustafa Kemal, an Ottoman army colonel, brought his horse to a halt on the crest of a hill on the rocky Gallipoli Peninsula. The regiment under his command, still laboring up the rise some distance behind him, had been ordered to reinforce Turkish troops holding the heights at Chunuk Bair, which overlooked the beaches of Ari Burnu, a small cape where Australia and New Zealand Corps troops (ANZAC) had come ashore that morning. The Gallipoli campaign, begun in the second year of the Great War, was the second phase of a British effort to weaken the Central Powers by capturing the Ottoman capital at Constantinople and hopefully forcing the empires's surrender. The first phase, the Dardenelles campaign, had not proceeded according to British expectations, due both to poor planning and a fateful underestimation of Turkish abilities. The failure to force the Straits resulted in severe losses and turned British planners toward an amphibious invasion of the Gallipoli

Fig. 4-1   Mustafa Kemal, first president of the Republic of Turkey, teaches the Roman alphabet at an outdoor demonstration in Istanbul, formerly known as Constantinople, the capital of the Ottoman Empire. The introduction of the Roman alphabet was part of his effort to modernize and westernize postwar Turkey. (Pearson Education, Corporate Digital Archive, Turkish Cultural office.)

Peninsula. Once control of the Straits was achieved by this means, Turkey could still be forced from the war. The untried ANZAC troops were considered adequate to fight the Turks and in fact found their initial landings unopposed. As they moved inland across steep terrain, the Australians advancing on Chunuk Bair seemed on the verge of gaining the high ground and securing their beachhead. As the Turkish soldiers defending the heights ran out of ammunition, they began to turn and flee.

  This was the scenario that Kemal observed as he sat astride his horse on the hill. As a frantic soldier raced past him, Kemal demanded to know why he was running away, and was told that the enemy was approaching. "Sure enough," Kemal wrote in his account, "an enemy line was advancing towards the hill . . . and was already nearer to me than my own troops." Determined to stop the advancing Australians, Kemal ordered the panicked men to "fix their bayonets and lie down." The result was better than he could have hoped: "As they did so, the enemy lay down too. We had won time." Soon, the arrival of Kemal's regiment emboldened the colonel, who ordered an effort to turn the Australians' flank. "I don't order you to attack," he told his men. "I order you to die. By the time we are dead, other units and commanders will have come up to take our place."

As reinforcements and artillery gradually arrived, Kemal both deployed and encouraged them, frequently exposing himself to enemy fire. The fighting continued throughout the day, which ended with the Australians stopped two-thirds of the way up the slope. Allied forces were never able to break out beyond a relatively narrow beachhead, which became a killing zone reminiscent of the trench warfare on the western front. After months of stalemate and appalling losses, British forces were withdrawn, having failed to take Constantinople or seize the straits. For his role in halting the British invasion, Colonel Kemal received the Ottoman Order of Distinguished Service and, from Turkey's German military advisors, the Iron Cross.

In the years to come, Kemal further distinguished himself on other fronts, but his successes were not matched by Ottoman forces elsewhere. After four years of war, Turkey faced defeat and humiliation, though Kemal ended the war as the only undefeated Turkish commander. This distinction, together with his national reputation as the man who saved Constantinople, left Kemal well-positioned to lead the nationalist movement that gained strength in the aftermath of Turkey's military defeat and humiliation at Sevres in 1920. His successful leadership of Turkey's national revolution won for him the honorific title by which history would know him—Mustafa Kemal Ataturk, "Father of Turks."

Born in the winter of 1880–1881 (the exact date is obscure) in Salonica, Mustafa Kemal grew up in a middle-class Muslim family, though he was never especially devout and later professed disinterest in religion. Mustafa's father, Ali Raza, a civil servant, counted himself among the proponents of modernization. His influence on his son was only slight, as he died when the boy was only about eight and the family went to live with an uncle in the countryside. Mustafa's mother, Zubeyde Hanim, was determined that her son should be educated, so he returned to Salonica in 1893 to attend military school. It was here, according to the later Ataturk legend, that Mustafa was given the name Kemal (meaning "perfection" in Turkish) by a mathematics teacher who admired the boy's abilities. An intelligent and disciplined student, Mustafa Kemal quickly advanced through a course of studies that would prepare him to serve as an army officer, ultimately graduating from the General Staff College in 1905 as a captain.

Like many young officers, Kemal was troubled by the Ottoman Empire's declining power, which he attributed to the "backwardness" of Turkish society, the ineptness of the Sultan's government and the overly-pervasive influence of traditional Islam. While posted to Damascus in 1906, Kemal and like-minded supporters founded the "Fatherland and Freedom" society, which was dedicated to reform and modernization. The following year, the group merged with the Committee of Union and Progress, an organization of army officers and bureaucrats who believed that Turkey's salvation lay in the implementation of western ideas, institutions and technology. In 1908, this "Young Turk Revolt" forced the reactionary Sultan Abdul-Hamid II to reinstate the 1876 constitution, which had been suspended for decades. Following an unsuccessful counter-revolution in 1909, the Sultan was deposed, though the Sultanate remained in place. The effort to politically modernize and strengthen Ottoman Turkey remained only partially realized.

Kemal had not played a direct role in the 1908 revolution and his military duties often kept him distant from the center of political activity in the years prior to the world war. The Tripolitanian War took him to Libya in 1912, where he led a successful offensive against the Italians at Tobruk. But as would often be the case in the future, Kemal's military successes did not translate into national victory, and the Ottoman Empire was again humiliated in war, first by the Italians and then by the Balkan League in the war of 1912. Despite the efforts of reform elements in the army and government, the military capabilities of the Ottoman Empire continued to decline even as the country joined the world war on the side of the Central Powers. Army officers like Kemal seethed at the ineptness of the Sultan's regime. Ultimately, defeat in war brought the opportunity that Kemal and the reformers sought.

The Ottoman Sultan, Mehmed VI, hoped to preserve both his power and his dynasty by cooperating with the Allies, and most specifically the British. By early 1919, it was increasingly evident that this would entail acceptance of an Allied partition of the empire, with portions going to the British, French, Italians and Greeks. Kemal, an ambitious man with a sense of destiny, saw this as the moment to assert his leadership of the nationalist movement and a rival government, which was established at Ankara. To his mind, the continuation of the sultanate meant the extinction of Turkish sovereignty, a fear that was affirmed by the terms of the Treaty of Sevres. Not only were the Allies to be given complete control of the Turkish economy, but Turkey's army was to be reduced to a mere 50,000 men. The severity of the treaty's provisions drove many Turks to the nationalist camp and brought growing support for Kemal's Turkish Grand National Assembly, which convened in Ankara in April 1920. There, Kemal recognized that the two great challenges that faced the nationalist cause were maintaining control of as much territory as possible and establishing the Ankara government as a legitimate national authority. During the following two years, he succeeded in doing both. A Greek invasion of Anatolia in 1921 ultimately ended with the expulsion of the Greeks from the Turkish mainland, a victory that further enhanced Kemal's credibility as a national leader. A friendship treaty with the new Soviet Union bolstered the legitimacy of the Ankara government and shortly afterwards, both France and Italy negotiated agreements that made the Treaty of Sevres, in Kemal's words, "merely a rag."

Granted the rank of Marshal and the title of "Gazi" (Victor) by the Assembly, Kemal proceeded to implement the first step in his nationalist revolution. In November 1922, the Grand National Assembly approved Kemal's proposal to abolish the Sultanate. Kemal knew that to compete in the modern world, Turkey would have to embrace the instruments and perspectives of modernization. He refused to disavow Islam, however, insisting that it embraced new learning: "As for Islam, it is the most natural and reasonable of all religions, and it enjoins on everyone the pursuit of knowledge." In July 1923, Kemal's determined opposition to the Allied effort to partition

Turkey was rewarded. The Treaty of Lausanne included territorial revisions that were greatly to Turkey's advantage and precluded foreign interference in Turkish economic or military affairs. Turkish cities occupied by Allied troops, such as the old Ottoman capital of Constantinople, now Istanbul, reverted to Turkish control. Alone among the defeated Central Powers, Turkey had succeeded in rejecting the harsh impositions of the Paris Peace Conference.

In the fall of 1923, the Turkish Republic was proclaimed, with Mustafa Kemal as its first elected president. Much remained to be accomplished if a new political and social order were to be successfully established, but the new president was convinced that the key to his nation's future lay in a broad program of modernization, which he equated with civilization. As Kemal was to explain to an audience in Akhisar in 1925: "The civilized world is far ahead of us. We have no choice but to catch up. . . . Uncivilized people are doomed to be trodden under the feet of civilized people."

During the 1920s, Mustafa Kemal succeeded in realizing the national, modernizing revolution that had been so long delayed. Politically, Turkey became a constitutional republic with a parliamentary government. Perhaps more importantly, Kemal Ataturk oversaw a cultural revolution that substituted the secular state for the traditional Islamic monarchy that characterized the Ottoman era. Though there was some resistance from religionists, and some criticism of his government as authoritarian, the majority of Turks supported and lauded his efforts. The republic he founded proved moderate, stable and durable, weathering the economic and political storms of the 1930s without succumbing to the appeal of dictatorship. By the time of Ataturk's death in 1938, Turkey, long stigmatized as the "sick man of Europe," had entered the ranks of the "modern" nations.

♦ —— ♦ —— ♦ —— ♦ —— ♦

Among the many consequences of the First World War, the decline of Europe's world imperium must be acknowledged as one of the most significant. The conflict left the European colonial powers weakened economically and militarily and shorn of the moral and intellectual certitude that characterized the prewar years. For many European peoples, the economic and political challenges of the interwar years were of much greater concern than ostensible benefits of maintaining an empire. Indeed, in Great Britain, arguably the only truly global power existent in 1919, the government went to considerable lengths to convince the English people of the value of em-pire, spending vast sums on the British Empire Exhibition at Wembley in 1924–1925. An advertisement for the exhibition described the British Empire as "the most powerful agency of civilization" and insisted that it "had its heart set upon the peaceful action and the good of mankind." While such exhibitions and reiterations of humanitarian mission undoubtedly convinced some Britons of the worth of empire, others were more skeptical, dismissing the nineteenth-century concept of empire as arrogant and archaic. By the 1930s, many Britons were laughing at the cartoon figure of Colonel Blimp, an archetypal representative of imperial bumbling and pretentiousness created by Australian cartoonist

David Low. Still, the British government, like most European governments, concluded that political, strategic and economic imperatives demanded the retention of some form of empire, though adjustments might have to be made.

In the non-western world, the imperial idea was severely undermined by the First World War and its aftermath. The war had destroyed any European claim to moral and intellectual superiority and its horrors had been witnessed by colonial troops conscripted from Asia and Africa. If the war had demonstrated the fallibility of westerners, the peace process revealed their duplicity. At Paris it became clear that the principles the Allied powers espoused would not be universally applied. Encouraged to revolt against their Ottoman masters by the British, the Arab peoples soon discovered that any hopes for independence would be subordinated to the territorial ambitions of Britain and France. Africans and Asians alike quickly realized that the principle of national self-determination was, evidently, applicable only in Europe. The refusal to include a statement acknowledging racial equality in the League of Nations covenant convinced many in the non-western world that the dominant western powers were determined to remain so.

Accordingly, during the interwar years, nationalism became an increasingly potent force in the colonial world, as advocates of self-government and independence struggled to develop organizations and strategies to achieve their goals. In Turkey, nationalists embraced modernization and secularism as the keys to sovereignty and strength. In British India, where the London government gradually accepted self-government, nationalists proclaimed the new goal of complete independence. In China, the revolution of 1911 opened difficult questions concerning ideology, the structure of government, society and achieving sovereignty. In Japan, already a modern power, nationalism was diverted into different channels and ultimately assumed a militaristic and imperialist character. Altogether, these developments posed a fundamental challenge to western hegemony and marked the beginning of a major transformation of the world order.

Nationalist and Anticolonial Struggles in the Middle East and Africa

Following the First World War, European colonial rule in Africa continued, the only major change being the transfer of German possessions to the Allied powers. Consequently, both the British and French empires in Africa grew enormously. African resistance to European rule took the form of political organization and rebellion during the interwar decades. In the Middle East, the dismembering of the Ottoman Empire introduced British and French rule into the Arab lands once claimed by the Sultan's government. Antagonisms between Arabs and Jews in Palestine compounded anticolonial stirrings in the Middle East. In Turkish Anatolia, however, a nationalist movement succeeded in resisting the postwar treaty terms and establishing a sovereign Turkish state.

TURKEY: THE KEMALIST REVOLUTION

Mustafa Kemal's successful leadership of Turkey's "national war for independence" brought him the credibility and authority that was required to transform Turkey fundamentally in the early 1920s. The reformers faced enormous challenges. The war left Turkey economically and fiscally weakened. In a population of some thirteen million, only ten percent were literate and the educational system was rudimentary. The country had nothing in the way of modern industry and was largely dependent on imported manufactured goods. The war had affected agriculture to the extent that Turkey was forced to import grain.

The starting point of Kemal's national revolution was political. Following the abolition of the Sultanate by the Grand National Assembly in November 1922, Kemal founded the People's Party (later the Republican People's Party), which would espouse the principle of Turkish solidarity regardless of class and serve as a vehicle for reform and modernization. The party would educate the Turkish people on their responsibilities during the era of national reconstruction. During this potentially difficult period the army, Kemal maintained, was the only "class" that could ensure the nation's safety. In late October 1923, the assembly accepted constitutional revisions that set the shape of Turkey's new government. It would be a republic with a president elected from and by the assembly; though the constitution provided for a prime minister, the president effectively headed both the executive and legislative branches of government.

Though the constitution recognized Islam as the nation's official religion, Kemal was dedicated to the idea that its influence would have to be lessened if Turkey were to become a functioning modern state. Shortly before the assembly proclaimed the republic and Kemal's election as its first president, he confided to a French writer his determination to eliminate what he saw as the irrational, superstitious elements of Islam from Turkish national life. To accomplish this, he planned to eliminate the caliphate, the highest religious office for Sunni Muslims, tradi-

tionally supported by the Ottoman dynasty. For Kemal, there was no religious or historical justification for the post, and its continued existence threatened his plans for creating a secular Turkish state. In March 1924, the People's Party put three laws before the assembly, one of which established a single, secular system of public education. The second placed Islam under direct government control, while the third abolished the caliphate.

With the basis for a secular state established, Kemal pursued a broad range of reforms and initiatives that in sum comprised a social and cultural revolution. Under Kemal's leadership, the government implemented agricultural improvement projects, created an Aviation Society to promote pilot training, promoted railway construction and abolished religious tithes. In late August 1925, Kemal launched his most symbolic assault on the "backward" customs that retarded Turkish progress in a series of speeches in which he advocated the adoption of "internationally accepted civilized dress." The most immediate target of this campaign was the fez, a soft billless cap imposed on Muslim Turks by an Ottoman edict. The fez and other traditional dress, Kemal believed, fueled western stereotypes of Turks as backward and "Asian." At one stop on his speaking tour, Kemal singled out a man in the crowd to make his point. "He has a fez on his head, and a green turban wound round the fez, a traditional waistcoat on his back, and on top of it, a jacket like mine." the President observed. "Now I ask you, would a civilized man wear such peculiar clothes and invite people's laughter?" If Turks were to be taken seriously, he believed, they would have to discard outmoded attire that made them ridiculous in the eyes of the modernized west.

Kemal also identified fundamentalist Islamic organizations as a threat to his modernizing revolution and attacked them in speeches. "In the face of knowledge, science, and of the whole extent of radiant civilization, I cannot accept the presence in the Turkish community of people primitive enough to seek material and spiritual benefits in the guidance of sheikhs," he declared. "The Turkish republic cannot be a country of sheikhs, dervishes and disciples. The best, the truest order is the order of civilization." For Kemal, civilization was synonymous with western concepts and institutions, and many of his reforms reflected that perception. In late 1925, the assembly adopted the Christian calendar and twenty-four-hour clock. Early in the following year, a new civil code based on Swiss law was enacted, granting women equal legal status. Shortly afterward, a modern penal code drawn from Italian law was enacted. In 1928, the Latin alphabet supplanted Arabic script. The scope of the reforms demonstrated Kemal's conviction that Turkey's survival was contingent on modernization. "We will become civilized . . . we will march forward," he once told an audience. "Civilization is a fearful fire which consumes those who ignore it."

Though populism was hailed as one of the guiding principles of the new Turkey, complete freedom of expression was not, and Kemal proved willing to resort to repression when he felt it was necessary to protect the stability of the new regime and secure public order. Criticism of the government by the press, opposition from Islamic clerics and an ethnic Kurd revolt in 1924 led the assembly to pass the "Maintenance of Order Law," which established tribunals to try those who challenged the regime and gave the government the authority to close down trouble-

some newspapers. The opposition Progressive Republican Party was banned later in the year. In 1926, an Independence Tribunal tried a number of individuals deemed treasonous, including former members of the parliamentary opposition and those in the Committee of Union and Progress who had split with Kemal over various issues. The court imposed numerous death sentences and lengthy prison terms on those found guilty. With his authority now firmly secured, Kemal finalized the secularization of Turkish society and removed all constitutional references to Islam in 1928.

Though he often pursued his objectives using authoritarian methods, Kemal did not set out to establish a dictatorship, and during the 1930s, when economic and social conditions might have permitted him to impose dictatorial rule, he rejected the opportunity. Instead, in 1930, he encouraged the creation of a new opposition party, the Free Republicans, though the political challenges of two-party government led him to dissolve it again within a year, restoring the one-party state. That same year, direct elections at the local level brought a democratic dimension to the political process. Kemal responded to the economic distress brought by the world depression with state intervention, building factories that would provide jobs and needed consumer goods and generally pursuing a policy of combined statist-capitalist solutions to economic problems. In 1931, as Kemal was re-elected president for a third term, a convention of the Republican People's Party defined the party's principles: republicanism, nationalism, populism, statism, secularism and defense of the reforms. Somewhat ominously, a party flag consisting of six black arrows against a red background was approved, but it did not augur a turn toward totalitarianism, as had similar symbols in Europe. Under Kemal's leadership, Turkey remained a one-party state governed by a powerful and charismatic leader, but Kemal made it clear that the party was always subordinate to the state, whereas in Nazi Germany and Soviet Russia the party, in essence, was the state. Following Ataturk's death in 1938, the constitutional and political machinery he put in place continued to function. Though the multitude of social and cultural reforms did not fully penetrate rural Turkey until after the Second World War, the modern, secular Turkish state was secured by the time of its founder's death.

THE MIDDLE EAST: A LEGACY OF BROKEN PROMISES

The First World War appeared to offer the Arab peoples of the Middle East the opportunity to gain independence from the Ottoman Turks who had dominated the region for centuries. British statesmen, hoping to destabilize their Ottoman enemy, supported and encouraged an "Arab Revolt," in part by promising to support an independent Arab state at war's end. The British offer was first tendered in 1915, when Britain's high commissioner in Egypt, Henry McMahon, began a correspondence with the titular head of the Hashemite dynasty, Hussein Ibn Ali, the Grand Sherif of Mecca, soliciting Hussein's aid in fighting the Turks in return for British support for an Arab state. Disagreements about the exact boundaries of the proposed state protracted the discussion into 1916 and ever afterward there was heated debate as to the specifics of the agreement. Rejecting Hussein's demand for all Arab lands south of Turkey, the British indicated that their strategic interests in Iraq together with French interests in Syria precluded Hus-

sein's proposed state. Arab officials later insisted that the British had agreed to an extensive Arab state encompassing not only the Arabian peninsula, but also Syria and Palestine. This ostensible Arab claim to Palestine was destined to become increasingly important in years to come. Regardless of what promises were made or broken, Hussein's hopes for an extensive Arab state were probably unrealistic. Unity in the Arab world then, as in later decades, was never more than precarious. Hussein's rule was contested and religious differences further divided the Arab peoples.

Though the majority of Arabs were Muslim, they were variously Sunni (the majority) or Shia, the division stemming from a disagreement as to the legitimate successor to the Prophet Mohammed. A smaller number were attracted to the conservative Wahabi sect. In Syria and Lebanon, Maronite Christians, Druze (a Shiite sect) and other religious minorities posed further challenges to anyone who would attempt to create a large, unified Arab state. Though the British accepted Hussein as king of Arabia in 1917, they maintained discreet contacts with Hussein's enemy, Ibn Saud, as a possible alternative. Hussein, for his part, covertly retained contacts with the Turks.

Unbeknownst to Hussein, the previous year the British had agreed with the French to partition the Arab lands between themselves once the war was over. While France would get Syria and Lebanon, Britain would be granted authority in Iraq and Palestine. The latter was of strategic interest to the British, given their concern with protecting the Suez Canal and the lifeline to India. Britain asked only for a sphere of influence in the Arabian Peninsula, as its great petroleum deposits were as yet undiscovered. As the Sykes-Picot Agreement (1916) that established these provisions was confidential, Britain's Arab "allies" remained unaware of these plans.

Further complicating the postwar disposition of Middle Eastern lands, Britain also agreed to support the creation of a Jewish homeland in Palestine. In 1917 British Foreign Secretary Arthur Balfour wrote a letter to Lord Rothschild, a prominent British Zionist, declaring Britain's support for the creation of a Jewish homeland in Palestine "without prejudice to the civil and religious rights of the non-Jewish peoples." Balfour had grown to respect and sympathize with the Zionist cause since a chance meeting in Manchester, England, with Dr. Chaim Weizmann, then a chemist and later the first president of Israel. While other Zionists had been willing to consider a Jewish homeland in places as unlikely as Uganda and South America, Weizmann had argued convincingly for Palestine. Though Zionists hailed the "Balfour Declaration," it understandably drew the ire of Arab leaders, who pointed out that the population of Palestine was ninety percent Muslim. Weizmann's oft-repeated description of Palestine as a "land without people for a people without a land." understandably offended many Arabs.

The postwar settlement essentially realized the basics of the Sykes-Picot Agreement, as the League of Nations granted France and Britain mandates over most of the Middle East. Arab hopes were realized only insofar as they coincided with British and French interests. Hussein ruled briefly over an Arab state surrounded by the British mandates in Trans-Jordan (later Jordan), Iraq, the Trucial States (now the Persian Gulf emirates), Oman and Aden. Ibn Saud, a Wahabi Muslim, ousted him in the mid-1920s and gradually gained broad support in the region, founding the kingdom of Saudi Arabia in

1932. The discovery of oil in the Persian Gulf in 1938 eventually transformed Ibn Saud's impoverished desert kingdom. The creation of Aramco, an Arab-American oil conglomerate, together with a growing influx of Westerners intent on further exploration for petroleum, were the earliest indications of the region's future economic importance. Hussein's son Feisal initially ran afoul of French ambitions, reigning only briefly as king in Syria before being ousted. Ultimately Feisal became King of Iraq with British support, and his country was granted independence in 1932, though it remained for all purposes a British satellite. Hussein's other son, Abdullah, became king in Trans-Jordan, which gained independence only in 1948.

French rule in Syria and Lebanon provoked popular unrest, as French authorities saw the mandates primarily as strategic bases for French interests in the region and demonstrated little concern for the desires of the populace. Lebanon was enlarged to the detriment of Syria, and France cultivated relations with Lebanon's Maronite Christians. Paris imposed a constitution in 1926 with little regard for Lebanese opinion. Tensions between the slim Maronite majority, Druze and Arab populations made governing Lebanon a difficult balancing act. Ultimately, the French partitioned Syria into separate autonomous districts in the belief that governance would be facilitated. During the 1920s, revolts led by both the Druze and Syrian nationalists challenged French authority. By the end of the decade the French, while still determined to rule Syria, nonetheless conceded to demands for greater self-government, introducing a constitution making Syria a republic in 1930, though France retained control over foreign affairs. A 1936 treaty providing Syrian independence was delayed because of the growing European crisis, and independence did not come until 1944.

The European powers largely determined the pace, scope and nature of Arab independence during the interwar years. Disgruntled Arabs could do little to effectively challenge the European presence or policies in the mandated territories, though there were outbreaks of violence in response to Britain's obvious disregard of wartime agreements, and rebellions against British-backed rulers. Intermittent rebellions in Iraq and Jordan continued into the 1930s, leading the British to implement a tactic known as "air control," whereby warplanes rather than ground troops would be used to suppress rebels, often by bombing villages suspected of supporting the insurgents.

Of even greater vexation to Britain during this period, however, was the issue of Palestine, where contention was inevitable because of conflicting Arab and Jewish claims and expectations. The ambiguity and inconsistency of British policy which, in aiming to please or at least mollify all parties, inevitably provoked anger all around, worsened this potentially volatile situation. Though the fundamental Arab complaint was the illegitimacy of a British-sponsored Jewish homeland in Palestine, the more immediate fear on the part of Palestinian Arabs concerned the impact that significant numbers of Jewish immigrants would have on the small territory. Fearful that Zionist settlers of predominantly European heritage would soon control the most fertile land and profitable businesses, Palestinian Arabs mounted anti-Jewish demonstrations throughout the 1920s, culminating in the riots of 1929 in which 900 Jewish settlers were killed or wounded.

The Jewish colonists were equally ardent in their belief that they were simply reclaiming a land that was theirs through God's be-

quest. While Palestinian Arabs outnumbered Jews by four to one in 1933, events in subsequent years inevitably led to an increase of Jewish settlers seeking refuge from anti-Semitism in Europe. Though Islam had historically required toleration for Jews, fears about the economic consequences of a larger Jewish population in Palestine impelled local Arab leaders to demand that the British restrict the flow of immigrants. As in the past, British officials equivocated, touching off an Arab revolt in April 1936. Though the British rushed troops to Palestine, the effort to suppress the revolt was badly organized and despite the introduction of land, air and naval forces, the British lost control of large areas of the country during the next three years. Order was restored only in summer 1939, as Europe was once again facing the possibility of war. A government "White Paper" that May proposed a continued British mandate, restricting Jewish immigration and settlement while preparing for an independent Palestine in which Arabs would be guaranteed a majority. The outbreak of war precluded any further action on the issue, though ironically, the events of the war years did much to swing world opinion in favor of a permanent Jewish homeland in Palestine.

On the eastern shores of the Persian Gulf, the course of events in Iran was determined by somewhat different dynamics than in the Arab world. Long caught between Russia and Britain in the "great game" of imperialism, Iran faced periodic intrusions by both nations. In the early 1920s, however, the British backed away from their virtual protectorate over the country; a Soviet-Iranian treaty ended the immediate threat of Russian expansionism. In the absence of the foreign presence that had often united Persian society in past years, rule by the Qajar dynasty grew more lax and capricious. Sultan Ahmed

Shah, derided as the "Grocer-Boy Shah" because he purchased the country's grain crop only to resell it to his people at exorbitant prices, came to personify corruption in the once-great empire.

As in Turkey, the army played a central role in initiating a modernizing revolution, which began in February 1921, with a coup led by Reza Khan, an officer who had served under the British during the recent war. The coup succeeded, leaving Reza's men in control of most of the capital city of Teheran. Asserting his leadership as commander-in-chief of the army, Reza consolidated his political authority during the next two years, becoming prime minister in 1923. He busied himself implementing a program of reforms, while the dissolute shah, worn out by an unending succession of parties in Paris, grew ill and finally died in an American hospital. In October 1925, the Iranian Majlis, or parliament, acting at Reza's instigation, deposed the Qajar dynasty and within a few months installed him as Reza Shah Pahlavi. Wary of the influence of the powerful Shiite mullahs, Reza did not go so far as to declare a republic, though he did seek to encourage a nationalist perspective as part of his modernizing revolution. Reza restored Iranian sovereignty in several areas, improved public education, introduced modern legal codes, abolished titles and broke up large estates. In 1933, he also succeeded in winning major concessions from the Anglo-Persian Oil Company, gaining a much larger percentage of the profits for Iran. Reza's success was twofold—the increased oil revenues could be used for modernizing projects, and the leverage that such a national resource could bring for Iran in negotiations with the Western powers was evident. As the journalist John Gunther wrote, "The Shah has done something almost unique. It isn't everybody who so successfully grabs Britain by the throat and shakes until the sterling flows." The long, contentious dispute between the two governments prefigured similar confrontations that would grow more intense in future decades, as the Western market for petroleum products expanded immensely.

AFRICA—RISING EXPECTATIONS UNDER CONTINUED COLONIAL RULE

The First World War affected European colonial rule in Africa in several ways. The postwar partition did much to rationalize political relationships on the continent, reducing a complicated tangle of prewar clans, tribes, city-states and kingdoms to around fifty states with more clearly defined boundaries. The colonial powers now assumed the responsibilities of government more seriously, in part because the League of Nations Mandate Commission deemed the mandated territories "a sacred trust of civilization." Britain's representative on the Mandate Commission, Lord Lugard, elaborated on the new approach in *The Dual Mandate in British Tropical Africa* (1922), in which he asserted that colonial powers had a responsibility to improve the moral and material status of colonial peoples, together with a broader obligation to ensure that the natural resources of colonial areas were developed and utilized in a world market.

France, the other major colonial power in Africa, was less receptive to the idea of African independence, and French colonial authorities pursued the general policy of association, which envisaged a collective economic and cultural association between France and her colonies. Accordingly, French colonial administrators had no interest in cultivating an educated African elite for eventual leadership. This was evident in French colonial educational policy, which was based on government schools with instruction in French. Secondary education was limited and the focus of study was European civilization. In general, during the interwar years the colonial powers introduced improved civil administration, European judicial codes and strove to stimulate colonial economies.

The war had also affected African peoples. For many, the European conflict brought deprivation and hardship, as locally produced commodities increasingly went to support armies fighting in Europe. Others found themselves serving in European armies, most often as labor forces. A smaller number were utilized more directly in relatively small clashes taking place between Allied and German forces in colonial Africa. To other Africans, especially the western-educated elite, it seemed only logical that the Allied nations' professed ideals would mean independence for African peoples. Much to their disappointment, they soon learned, as did other colonial peoples, that those ideals were to be applied only on a very limited basis and then only in Europe.

For educated Africans, the question then became one of how to organize an anticolonial movement. The issue of ideology was often paramount. Marxism, which the Soviet Union propounded as the salvation of all oppressed by imperialism, attracted some of Africa's new elite—Jomo Kenyatta, Kwame Nkrumah and Leopold Senghor were among a number of young Africans who had some exposure to Marxist ideology during the interwar years. While communist parties were established in some African countries, many aspiring African nationalists felt that the antinationalistic bias in Marxist theory rendered the ideology of doubtful utility, as their im-

mediate objective was the creation of a national consciousness. Others were attracted to pan-Africanism, a concept that had both political and cultural dimensions. Pan-Africanism stressed independence and unity for African peoples, while also asserting the worth and richness of African culture. The first Pan-African Conference was held in London in 1900, and in the following decades the movement was influenced by several prominent black nationalists, including the American W. E. B DuBois and the Jamaican-born Marcus Garvey. Beyond ideology, another major challenge facing African nationalists was how their struggle should be organized and how the mass of uneducated and often apolitical Africans could be mobilized to oppose colonial rule. All of these questions were compounded by the geographical immensity of the continent, the great diversity of peoples, religions and societies to be found on the African land mass, and divergent policies pursued by the various colonial powers.

In North Africa, one of the most dynamic nationalist movements as of 1919 was in Egypt, where British authority through indirect rule had been in place since the 1880s. Here as elsewhere, the British had held out the vague promise of future independence, but the adverse effects of wartime exigencies propelled a growing mass nationalist movement by war's end. The presence of a large number of Allied troops to guard the Suez Canal further goaded Egyptians, as did the imposition of martial law, forced labor and military confiscations. While a few wealthy merchants profited from the war, the Egyptian masses suffered, creating a generally hostile climate by war's end. Any hope that Wilsonian ideals would include Egyptians ended when a delegation, or *Wafd*, was prevented from traveling to Paris to present the case for self-determination. In response, violent mobs took to the streets of Cairo, so frightening British authorities that, following the bloody military suppression of the revolt, they agreed to consider Egyptian demands. The inevitable British approach to such colonial questions was to create a special commission, which marked the beginning of a lengthy period of negotiations concerning the pace and nature of Egyptian independence. Egyptian nationalists, now united under the auspices of the Wafd party, gained Britain's agreement for phased independence beginning in 1922. King Fu'ad ruled the new constitutional monarchy, but while Egypt enjoyed considerable autonomy, a continuing British military presence provided nationalists with an ongoing issue. The British occupation was formally ended in 1936, with the exception of a Suez Canal force. Neither economic nor social advances attended independence, as the Egyptian regime proved venal and self-serving. For the mass of Egyptians, improved circumstances would come only with the truly sweeping national revolution of the 1950s.

In French North Africa, where colonial policy emphasized assimilation and continued economic ties, anticolonial activity was difficult and authorities less tolerant. Throughout the 1920s, French authorities demonstrated their willingness to suppress militarily nationalist or local uprisings in Tunisia, Algeria and Morocco, where French forces squelched the Rif Rebellion with particular brutality. Morocco's French resident-general, Marshal Louis Lyautey, effectively countered nationalist activity in Moroccan cities through the skillful implementation of agricultural reforms, modernization programs and by careful respect for Islamic customs.

The advent of Benito Mussolini's Fascist regime in 1922 significantly influenced Italian colonial policy in North and Northeast Africa. In Libya, the leader of the Sanusi brotherhood, Sayyd Idris, had acknowledged Italian sovereignty in return for local autonomy; the Fascist regime rejected this agreement and subsequently found itself at war with Libyan Bedouins for the next nine years. Italian policy in Somalia and Ethiopia was even more blatantly predatory and self-serving, with no pretense of upholding the "sacred trust of civilization." By 1935, Italian intrigues culminated with the savage Ethiopian War.

Some of the same patterns of colonial rule and anticolonial activity are likewise evident in sub-Saharan Africa. British colonial policy here was professedly a type of paternalistic humanitarianism, stressing the need to create a class of educated Africans who could someday assume leadership roles in independent African states. The Governor of the Gold Coast, Sir Gordon Guggisberg, conceded in 1920 that "one of the greatest mistakes of the education in the past has been ... that it taught the African to become a European instead of remaining African. ... In [the] future, our education will aim at making an African remain an African and taking interest in his own country." The British thus pursued a policy of indirect rule, aimed at developing the administrative abilities of Africans, while simultaneously striving to improve elementary and secondary educational systems. Britain's policy of indirect rule through indigenous leaders and elites was relatively effective in colonies such as Uganda, Nigeria and the Gold Coast (later Ghana), where there were, in British eyes, clearly discernible tribal structures and leaders. Nevertheless, a number of issues fueled discontent in both East and West British Africa.

In settler colonies such as Kenya, government policies promoting white settlement and white appropriation of the most fertile lands inevitably angered Africans. Complicating matters further, the merchant class in British East Africa was largely Indian, did not assimilate with the native population and preferred British citizenship, all of which spawned resentments among black Africans. These grievances produced a nationalist movement in Kenya built around an organization created by the largest tribe. The Kikuyu Central Association, founded in 1924, drew the attention of British authorities, whose arrest of Kikuyu leaders further provoked the populace. Among its officers by the late 1920s was Jomo Kenyatta, later to become one of the greatest of Africa's postcolonial leaders. Popular opposition to British rule also grew in Nigeria in the 1920s, producing the Nigerian National Democratic Party as a vehicle for nationalist agitation.

In the Belgian and Portuguese colonies, the official response to nationalist activity was often far more severe. Not surprisingly, authorities in the Belgian Congo reacted quickly and harshly to any challenge to Belgian rule. In the Portuguese colonies of Angola and Mozambique, small white settler populations supported authoritarian efforts to suppress any nationalist protests or actions.

In the Union of South Africa, the rudiments of a system of white minority rule were firmly in place by the 1920s. Following Britain's grant of self-government to the Transvaal and Orange Free State in 1906–1907, the Boers asserted their political power and denied black Africans the franchise, a policy which was opposed by some whites, including the descendants of English settlers in the Cape. Soldier and statesman Jan Smuts had articulated the Boer rationale for white supremacy as early as 1892, when he had warned, "the race struggle is destined to

assume a magnitude on the African continent such as the world has never seen . . . and in that appalling struggle for existence, the unity of the white camp will not be the least necessary condition . . . of warding off annihilation." A National Convention in 1908–1909 determined that Africans in the Transvaal, Orange Free State and Natal would not be granted the vote. As Smuts explained, "I sympathize profoundly with the native races of South Africa, whose land it was long before we came here. . . . But I don't believe in politics for them." Accordingly, the political and economic dominance of the Afrikaners, as the Boer descendants called themselves, was established even before the war. At the same time, the Afrikaner National Party began to actively promote the policy of *apartheid*, the separation of the races that had been attempted as recently as the late nineteenth century.

An increasingly rigid system of economic exploitation compounded the political impotence and social isolation of native Africans. Though they comprised three-quarters of the population of South Africa, Africans held only eleven percent of the land as of 1913. Driven from the countryside into the cities and industrial areas, black Africans were funneled into low-paying jobs, generally earning about one-eighth of the wages that white workers were paid in mining and industrial jobs These conditions helped bring about the organization of the South African National Congress in 1912, which was dedicated to the goal of self-determination and political equality for native Africans. Renamed the African National Congress in 1923, the group faced a long struggle, as the South African government strengthened its racially exclusionary policies during the interwar years. In South Africa as elsewhere across the continent, the inherent injustices and contradictions of colonial rule would not be fully acknowledged until the aftermath of the next world war.

Challenges to Western Colonial Rule in Asia

Asian nationalists also found encouragement in developments stemming from the First World War, which loosened the grip, if not always the determination, of the western colonial powers. Though many, including the Vietnamese nationalist Ho Chi Minh, saw their hopes for national independence dismissed at the Paris Peace Conference, others, such as India's Mohandas K. Gandhi, saw reason for optimism about the future of the anticolonial struggle. The interwar years brought both challenges and opportunities for Asian nationalists as some western powers, such as France and the Netherlands, clung stubbornly to their Asia possessions. Britain and the United States acknowledged the inevitability of colonial independence and took steps, however gradual, toward facilitating the transition of power.

INDIA: BUILDING A NATIONAL MOVEMENT

Of the many anticolonial struggles of the interwar years, the most dramatic and widely observed occurred in India, where the nationalist movement founded in the nineteenth century gained considerable impetus following the world war, rapidly developing into a mass movement. Indian hopes were strengthened by the belief that, given India's loyal support during the recent war, Britain would be compelled to expand self-government or grant independence. Indeed, India's contribution to the Allied war effort had been considerable—some 500,000 Indians saw service in Europe and the Middle East, and another half million labored in European mines and factories, freeing up Europeans to serve at the front. Indians had also raised 100 million English pounds to fund Britain's war effort. In response, British authorities appointed more Indians to high administrative positions and announced Britain's commitment to policies that would bring about "responsible government" within the empire in August 1917. However, Lord Curzon, soon to be Foreign Secretary, vetoed a promise of self-government. An Indian delegation attended the Paris Conference, but failed to gain a sympathetic hearing.

The passage of the India Act of 1919 revealed that Britain was prepared at most to take very gradual steps toward Indian self-government. The act authorized popular elections at the provincial level, whereby the majority party would form a provincial government. The British intention was that Indians would first be granted responsibility for limited local matters, while the British retained police and budgetary authority. The central colonial government remained under the authority of the British viceroy and a mixed cabinet of British and Indians. As the act was to remain in force for ten years, it was evident that the transition to full self-government, not to mention independence, would be a lengthy one. Confronting the disappointing reality of ambiguous British promises and an agonizingly slow process of change, Indian nationalists now faced the challenge of how to respond most effectively to these issues.

British intransigence was only the most immediate problem that the Indian nationalist movement faced. The Indian subcontinent, with its population of 300 million people, posed daunting challenges to both the British who sought to rule it and the Indians who sought to mobilize its peoples in support of independence. Political coherence and unity, such as it was, existed largely within the structure of British colonial administration, as India was comprised of over 500 princely states and eleven British-governed provinces. India was estimated to be 89 percent rural, with life centered in some 700,000 villages and a number of great cities. Largely illiterate and poverty-stricken, the vast majority of Indians focused immediately on the daily struggle to exist. Indian society was fragmented along a number of fault lines, one being regional. As a contemporary journalist noted, "One must grasp the fact—and hold tight to it—that a Punjabi and a man from Mysore, even if they differ as much as an Englishman and a Spaniard, are both Indians, as the Englishmen and Spaniard are both Europeans." Language also divided the peoples of India; the 1931 census identified 222 different languages and dialects. The issue of an official language would later prove divisive in nationalist circles.

Historically, one of the greatest divisions was religion, which the Hindu nationalist Jawaharlal Nehru once described as "the bane of India." Though India was home to literally hundreds of minor sects, it was the division between Hindus and Muslims that most directly affected the character and course of the independence movement. The great majority of Indians were Hindus, adherents of a religion that acknowledged numerous deities but no principal god. Hinduism had no single sacred text or organized priesthood and stressed perpetual change, as souls were continually reincarnated in new bodies, carrying with them the consequences of both good and sinful deeds. Hinduism also acknowledged a hereditary system of hundreds of castes, each conferring specific social obligations and status. At the bottom of

this hierarchy were the "untouchables," a group comprising about 15 percent of the population that was relegated to the most degrading tasks and deemed "unclean" by all other castes. Muslims, who accounted for about a seventh of the population, were concentrated in the northwestern regions and Bengal, though they could be found scattered across the country. A monotheistic religion, Islam stressed submission to a single god, Allah. Mohammed was considered His prophet and the Koran acknowledged as the sacred text containing His word; Islamic law was expounded in the Shariah. Muslim customs and practices differed significantly from those of Hindus, perhaps most notably in that Islam forbade the imposition of any "caste" system on the faithful. Though Hindus and Muslims had lived in close proximity for centuries, intermittent religious conflict, or "communal violence," grew in the nineteenth century. During the interwar years, Hindu–Muslim antagonisms and communal violence posed perhaps the greatest threat to the unity and success of the Indian nationalist movement. Further complications arose from a third group, the Sikhs, constituting a significant religious minority. Settled primarily around their holy city of Amritsar in the Punjab, the Sikhs melded the Muslim belief in one god with elements of Hindu philosophy. Sikh society reflected a warrior ethic, which led many into service in the Indian army. The religious, social and cultural distinctions among these groups were among the numerous potentially divisive factors that Indian nationalists had to consider as they charted their struggle.

As was the case in many other anticolonial efforts, the men who fulfilled the crucial roles in India's movement for independence were all educated in the West, where they absorbed western concepts of freedom, liberty, equality before the law and constitutional government. Mohandas Gandhi and Jawaharlal Nehru, arguably the central figures in the Indian National Congress (INC), and Muhammed Ali Jinnah, who became the leader of the Muslim League, were all educated in England as lawyers. The great challenge that confronted them in 1919 was how to forge a mass movement dedicated to gaining India's independence. To date, the activities of the INC had been aimed primarily at educated upper-class Indians. Gandhi was among those who advocated taking the struggle for independence to the masses. British authorities did much to set the stage for just such a development in 1919 with the passage of the Rowlatt Acts. The legislation, which severely curtailed freedom of expression and assembly in order to halt "subversion," gave the INC a focus for forging a mass movement and brought Mohandas Gandhi to the forefront of the nationalist struggle.

Born in 1869 to an upper-class family, Gandhi's early years were divided among India, England and South Africa, where he worked for a Muslim law firm in Pretoria. Drawn into local controversies involving the status and treatment of colonial subjects, Gandhi developed techniques of non-violent protest that he propounded when he returned to India in 1915. Gandhi founded his program for Indian independence and renewal on three basic concepts: non-violence, home rule and attention to the welfare of all. He distinguished himself from his more westernized brethren by adopting traditional dress made of homespun cloth and identifying himself more closely with the impoverished Indian masses. Gandhi was central to organizing the response to the Rowlatt Acts, advocating non-violence, or *Satyagraha*, as a means of turning the oppressor's superior strength against him. Ultimately, Gandhi reasoned, the injustice of British rule would be revealed by the violence required to maintain it. Gandhi was convinced that Britain's national conscience would eventually be moved.

A nationwide day of protest on April 6, 1919, proved that not all Indians had yet absorbed the basic concepts of *Satyagraha*. Some demonstrations degenerated into riots, as mobs killed Europeans and attacked western-owned businesses. More disheartening, it became clear that some British officials were willing to resort to the most brutal tactics in response to the demonstrations. In the Punjabi city of Amritsar, Brigadier General Reginald Dyer ordered his force of Nepalese Ghurkas to open fire on a peaceful crowd of demonstrators. Continuous volleys of fire for ten minutes killed 379 men, women and children and left hundreds wounded. Though a British commission later dismissed Dyer, some English support for harsh measures against protestors was made evident when London's *Morning Post* opened a fund for the general and took in £26,000 from donors that included Rudyard Kipling. Though the majority opinion in Britain condemned the "Amritsar Massacre," it was clear that the nationalist movement faced a long struggle, both in winning Indian adherence to non-violence and in touching Britain's conscience. Nonetheless, Gandhi remained convinced of the rectitude of his approach and, having been granted sole executive authority by the INC in 1921, continued to build a mass movement based on the concept of non-cooperation, which held that the British could rule India only with the cooperation of Indians. By refusing to cooperate in India's administration, Indians could demonstrate both their rejection of foreign rule and the unjustness of government that could only be maintained through force.

During the 1920s, Gandhi diverted some of his time to stressing the need for social reform in Hindu society, criticizing such practices as child marriage and the treatment of the "untouchables." In reference to the latter, Gandhi observed that if Indians could not treat each other any better, perhaps they did not deserve independence. His advocacy of the need for inner spiritual strengthening and traditional Indian ways of life were not shared by many of his colleagues, who defined nationalist goals largely in political terms. Nonetheless, the Congress party, as the INC was often called, continued to mount mass demonstrations throughout the decade, often bringing about repression and the arrest of movement leaders. Gandhi regularly moved to halt violence on the part of Indian protestors by fasting, a tactic which had some success. Among the most notable protests was Gandhi's Salt March of 1930, which targeted the government monopoly on the manufacture and sale of salt, a fundamental commodity in a poor and hungry land. In protest, Gandhi and an initial group of seventy-eight followers embarked on a two-hundred-mile march to the sea, moving slowly through the countryside and building support along the way. Arriving at the coast, Gandhi challenged the British monopoly by drawing and distilling seawater for the crucial salt. In this inimitable, peaceful manner, the "Mahatma," or "Great Soul," as many had come to call him, cleverly demonstrated the injustice and absurdity of colonial rule.

The 1930s brought events that demonstrated the limitations of and conflicts within the independence movement. Despite the enormous worldwide publicity that attended the Salt March and the arrest of thousands of activists, the British government conceded only a reduction in the salt tax. While Gandhi and others were released from jail following a somewhat conciliatory conference with the British Viceroy Lord Irwin, the British government remained divided as to India's future. Some Conservatives were adamant about retaining India, maintaining that Indians were not capable of self-government. Winston Churchill responded to news of Gandhi's conference with Irwin in Delhi with a condemnation of the Mahatma as "a fakir of a type well-known in the East, striding half-naked up the steps of the Vice-Regal palace, while he is still organizing and conducting a defiant campaign of civil disobedience." Such a spectacle, the Conservative MP complained, "was alarming and also nauseating." Churchill had long been contemptuous of the Congress party, dismissing it as representing only a small group of self-seekers.

One justification for continued colonial rule that Churchill and others cited was the threat of "Hindu despotism" and the resultant communal violence that would inevitably follow the end of British rule. Indeed, Hindu–Muslim antagonism was an issue that increasingly threatened the unity of the independence movement by the 1930s. While Gandhi opposed separate Hindu and Muslim electorates because he stressed the unity of all Indians, he was willing to guarantee Muslims a percentage of positions on Congress election tickets in order to allay their fears. Some Hindus, determined to secure majority Hindu rule, opposed such a compromise. The Muslim minority, increasingly drawn to the All-India Muslim League and the leadership of Muhammed Ali Jinnah, saw separate electorates as the only means whereby Muslims might exercise any power as they sincerely feared Hindu domination. Jinnah, who had returned to India in 1935 following five years of exile in Britain, reorganized the Muslim League and built his leadership around the advocacy of a separate Muslim state. Jinnah's rationale for a Muslim state was political rather than religious. A thoroughly westernized lawyer who spoke English rather than Urdu, his vision was primarily secular.

The emergence of Jawaharlal Nehru, son of the prominent Congress leader Motilal Nehru, further altered the dynamics of the independence movement in the 1930s. Though Hindu by birth, the younger Nehru was secular in orientation and saw India's future in modernization, rather than in a return to the traditional society that Gandhi advocated. Imprisoned for long periods during the interwar years, Nehru visited Europe in the late 1920s, where he was drawn to socialism as an ideological vehicle for India's advancement. Though he and Gandhi emerged as the two leading figures in the Congress party in the 1930s, the two men had differing visions of India's future. Together with Jinnah, they held in common only a commitment to gaining independence.

That goal was not to be obtained in the 1930s. Years of negotiations between British officials and representatives of the numerous Indian interests produced the India Act of 1935, the longest single piece of legislation ever passed by the House of Commons. Opposed by Conservatives including Churchill, who dismissed it as "a gigantic split of jumbled crochet work," the act provided for an all-India federation of princely states and self-governing provinces, with Indians electing representatives to both provincial and federal legislatures. Provinces were to be essentially self-governing, as British-appointed provincial governors received only nominal authority and the majority party in each province formed the government there. At the federal level, the viceroy was to be advised by a council selected from members of the federal legislature. At the urging of the Muslim League, the act stipulated separate electorates, so as to guarantee Muslims a political voice in a predominantly Hindu society. Altogether, the act was a compromise, aimed at maintaining some degree of British rule, while granting greater self-government, if not independence, to Indians. As is the nature of compromise, the act satisfied no one and was widely viewed as a temporary expedient at best. Nonetheless, Hindus and Muslims alike strove to secure whatever political gains they could within the system and, as of the late 1930s, India's ultimate destiny remained unresolved. The one certainty was that, whatever the date and circumstances of independence, the festering religious issue, together with that of a partition of India, would not be easily resolved.

SOUTHEAST ASIA: STIRRINGS OF DISSENT IN IMPERIAL BACKWATERS

Elsewhere in colonial Asia, indigenous opposition to foreign rule continued to develop during the interwar period and the course of events in India encouraged nationalists elsewhere. Though compelled to concede changes in India, the British clung stubbornly to their other Asian outposts. The Colonial Office continued to govern Burma, separated from India by the Act of 1935, together with Ceylon. Singapore, considered to be the "Gibraltar of the East," was viewed by Britain as an indispensable naval and military base. British Malaya, consisting of the Straits Settlement, Penang and the Federated and Unfederated Malay States, remained under some form of British control as did Sarawak in north Borneo.

Both France and the Netherlands demonstrated their determination to retain their Southeast Asian possessions. The French governed all of Indochina, with the exception of Siam, combining direct and indirect rule with efforts to acculturate native elites. The greatest challenge to French rule came in Vietnam, where the nationalist movement took a more radical direction following France's refusal to consider Vietnamese independence at the Paris Conference in 1919. Ho Chi Minh, denied an audience at Versailles, became the most prominent figure in the Vietnamese nationalist movement, with fateful consequences. A founding member of the French Communist Party, Ho was expelled from that country in 1923. Traveling next to Moscow and then China, he sought recruits for a Vietnamese communist movement. The French response to growing nationalist agitation was harsh, as they arrested, tortured and executed activists. These brutalities failed to secure French authority, alienated the native populace and created converts to the nationalist cause. The vulnerability of the French position in Indochina was revealed in the early 1940s, when Japanese forces occupied the region.

Unlike the French, Dutch interest in Southeast Asia was driven less by national pride than by economics. A contemporary journalist described the East Indies as "the Big Loot of Asia," given their immense and valuable natural resources. The Indonesian archipelago, consisting of some 13,000 islands with a population of 65 million predominately Muslim people, sprawled across 3,000 miles of ocean. The only common experience the varied peoples of the region had was Dutch rule, which was uniformly despised for its racism and social and economic inequities. Organized resistance to Dutch rule emerged in 1912 with the founding of Sarekat Islam, an organization that promoted strengthening the native economy through cooperative ventures. A mass movement by 1919, it was effectively suppressed by police authorities. Those advocating a more radical response to colonial rule were attracted to the Indonesian Communist Party and, by the later 1920s, the Indonesian Nationalist Party, led by Kusno Sosro Sukarno. Sukarno's party gained a broad following as it initiated strikes and promoted non-cooperation with colonial authorities. The Dutch responded by jailing Sukarno and other activists, but nationalist sentiment grew during the 1930s and through the wartime years.

In the Philippines, where the U.S. Army had suppressed a nationalist insurrection in 1902, official American policy since the Taft administration had been "benevolent assimilation," with emphasis on cultivating and "Americanizing" the Filipino elite. The Jones Act of 1916 had promised U.S. recognition of Filipino sovereignty "as soon as a stable government can be established." Though Americans in the islands routinely countenanced social inequities such as "whites only" clubs and generally lived apart from the mass of illiterate, impoverished Filipinos, the colony had a considerable degree of political autonomy, which tended to blunt militant nationalism. Nationalist leader Manual Quezon essentially acknowledged the effectiveness of benign American paternalism when he once complained, "Damn the Americans—why don't they tyrannize us more?" In 1934, the U.S. Congress passed the Tydings-McDuffie Act, which provided for independence in ten years. American relations with Filipino leaders, who were under no pressure to implement desperately needed social and economic reforms, remained relatively cordial in the years prior to the outbreak of war in the Pacific.

China and Japan: Divergent Paths and Converging Destinies

The two largest East Asian nations faced significantly different circumstances in the aftermath of the world war. Though the collapse of the Ch'ing dynasty in 1911 had led to the proclamation of a Chinese republic, a variety of factors combined to preclude the establishment of effective, stable national government. During the interwar years, China's future remained indeterminate as two parties, the Nationalists or Kuomintang (KMT) and the Communists (CCP) engaged in an increasingly bitter struggle over which would chart China's destiny. As the conflict between the two groups approached the level of civil war in the 1930s, Japanese aggression against Chinese territory further complicated the situation. Unlike China, Japan entered the twentieth century as a modern industrial nation with an effective central government. Rapidly establishing credentials as a military and imperial power, Japan capitalized on the European war to enhance her position in the Far East, gaining new territorial and economic concessions from an internally weakened China. Though the temporary strength of parliamentary democracy helped to restrain Japan's expansionist ambitions in the 1920s, the onset of the world depression brought about circumstances in which expansionist policies propounded by Japanese nationalists and military authorities were more compelling. By the 1930s, increasingly influential Japanese nationalists, both within and outside the government, began to proclaim Japan's "manifest destiny" as the dominant imperial power

in Asia. Like the great western imperial powers, they argued, Japan was entitled to and justified in building an empire, which would bring order and prosperity to all Asians. China, mired in apparently endless internal warfare and political incoherence, was to be one of the beneficiaries of what Japanese statesmen later referred to as the "Greater East Asia Co-Prosperity Sphere." Japan's imperial ambitions, thus cloaked in terms of benevolence, ignited a conflict on the Asian mainland that grew in scope throughout the 1930s and eventually pulled both nations into the Second World War.

CHINA: REVOLUTION, REPUBLIC AND CIVIL WAR

Though the events of the Boxer Rebellion compelled the Ch'ing dynasty to undertake a feverish series of reforms in hopes of preserving the regime, the results were counterproductive. Emulating the Japanese, Manchu authorities dispatched envoys to visit the United States and Europe, with the object of discerning those ideas and institutions that might be of some value in a general program of reform. Educational reforms, including the abolition of the ancient Confucianist examination system, spurred the growth of the student population, many of whom now traveled abroad, especially to Japan and the West. Japan's example of national revival and strength through the selective absorption of Western ideas appealed to many Chinese students; others were increasingly attracted to Western concepts and ideologies as instruments for China's rejuvenation. But rather than stabilizing the government, Manchu educational reforms undermined the dynasty, creating a new generation of revolutionary students, many of whom studied at Peking University. Likewise, the dynasty's decision in 1908 to establish provincial assemblies as the first step toward a constitutional regime only created new centers of opposition. Efforts to modernize China's military and create a "New Army" also had unexpected consequences, as the new troops were often fired by revolutionary ideas and loyal to their commanders rather than to the dynasty.

Anti-dynastic forces coalesced in 1905 in the Revolutionary Alliance, which brought together a number of revolutionary groups under the leadership of Sun Yat-sen. Born in 1866 to a peasant family, Sun was educated as a Christian in Hawaii before traveling to Hong Kong to study medicine. Returning to Hawaii in 1894, he founded his first revolutionary group, drawing both financial and moral support from the extensive overseas Chinese community throughout the Pacific basin. He was among many Chinese radicals and students who devoted considerable thought to the question of an ideology for the new China. While some believed that Confucianism could be reconciled with modernizing ideologies, or perhaps should serve as an official state religion, others denounced it as fundamentally reactionary, and it never achieved broad popularity among reformers. Marxism, as a Western ideology ostensibly founded on "science," appealed to some Chinese revolutionaries. The *Communist Manifesto* appeared in Chinese translation in 1906, transforming the famous concluding exhortation to "working men of all countries" into a somewhat more lyrical expression of hope: "Then the world will be for the common people, and the sounds of happiness will reach the deepest springs. Ah! Come! People of every land, how can you not be roused." Though Marxism would play a significant role in the political events of the 1920s and after, it did not attract a broad following in earlier years.

Ultimately, it was Sun Yat-sen who formulated the ideology that drove China's 1911 revolution. The "Three Principles of the People," as Sun defined them, were Nationalism, Democracy and Socialism, a seemingly eclectic collection of concepts culled from Sun's study of Japanese, American and European ideas. Nationalism evoked opposition to Manchu rule and support for a republic, while Democracy implied an egalitarian society, contrary to Confucian precepts. Sun's Socialism was not Marxist in inspiration, but was instead derived from ideas promoted by the American reformer Henry George, who argued that economic equity could be achieved through a "single tax" on landowners who unjustly profited from rising land values. The ambiguity of Sun's "Three Principles" was both their strength and weakness. Such general and appealing principles were useful in mobilizing a mass movement; they were less useful in providing specifics about political, social and economic institutions and policies once the revolution was secured.

The final collapse of the Ch'ing dynasty followed soon after the death of the Emperor Kuang-hsu and the Empress Dowager Tzu-hsi in 1908. The boy-emperor Pu-yi acceded to the throne and government fell to an inept regent. As resentments over government incompetence and treaty and railroad concessions to foreign powers grew, members of Sun's Revolutionary Alliance, which now numbered about 10,000, worked from positions within the army and provincial assemblies to press the republican cause. The revolution of October 10, 1911, sometimes called the 10–10 Revolution, came in the aftermath of massive police arrests of revolutionaries in the Wuhan tri-city area. In the weeks that followed, most of the provinces announced their support for the rebels and renounced the dynasty. Sympathetic army troops were a major factor in the success of the uprising; by the end of the month, it was clear to Manchu officials that the situation could not be contained and the imperial government accepted demands that a parliamentary, constitutional regime be established. Ironically, the revolution occurred with only minimal involvement by the Revolutionary Alliance and while Sun was in the United States.

Upon Sun's return to Shanghai in late December, provincial delegates meeting in Nanking named him as "provisional" president of the Chinese republic. Assuming office in January 1912, Sun acknowledged a troubling reality—he did not command military power sufficient to govern alone. The direction of the new republic was largely contingent on the actions of the powerful northern army commander Yuan Shih-k'ai, who was wont to play both sides. In a letter to Yuan, Sun agreed to turn over the presidency to the powerful army leader in hopes that the republican revolution would be secured. Accordingly, in February the Manchu boy-emperor Pu-yi was forced to abdicate and Yuan assumed the presidency, given full powers by the Nanking assembly "to organize a provisional republican government." A new constitution provided for a bicameral legislative branch. Sun reorganized his Revolutionary Alliance as the Nationalist party and prepared for an election in 1912. However, the difficulties inherent in establishing republican government in the absence of any historical constitutional or parliamentary tradition quickly became evident. Political parties were as yet disorganized and were easily bullied by Yuan, who soon reverted to the authoritarian style that had characterized dynastic government. Political confusion grew when Song Jiaoren, the parliamentary leader of the Nationalist party, was assassinated in

early 1913, probably at Yuan's instigation. A few months later, Yuan ordered the army to destroy the power of pro-Nationalist governors in the south; early in 1914, he disbanded the Parliament and the provincial assemblies.

The First World War diverted world attention to Europe and created an opportunity for Imperial Japan to impose the Twenty-One Demands on Yuan's China. Japanese demands, enumerated in five groups, included Chinese recognition of new Japanese rights in Shantung, extension of their rights in Manchuria and Mongolia and acceptance of Japanese political, economic, financial and military advisers. Yuan managed to resist those demands that would have given Japan influence over China's internal affairs, but was forced to accede to others, once again highlighting China's impotence before the imperial powers. Yuan fared little better with a scheme in late 1915 to have himself proclaimed emperor. Though a rigged "representative assembly" offered Yuan the imperial throne, his accession in early 1916 was met with widespread demonstrations and he canceled the revived monarchy in March of that year. He died a few months later, leaving the presidency tarnished and the national government in Peking without authority or respect.

The Kuomintang was now little more than a group of politicians with no access to power; the nation drifted into an era of warlordism in which the ability to exercise force became a primary determinant of power. While many warlords were former army officers and proteges of Yuan Shih-k'ai, others were little more than thugs and gangsters who commanded armed troops and lived by confiscation and extortion. Some warlords were republicans, some supported the KMT and others were willing to accommodate whichever foreign powers might best serve their interests. Chang Tso-lin, the "Warlord of Manchuria," was typical of the former bandits who accrued considerable regional power and influence during this period of national disintegration. Altogether they proved a colorful if sometimes eccentric lot. Wu Pei-fu was known as the "Philosopher Marshal." Feng Yu-hsiang was widely referred to as the "Christian General" and renowned in the West through an apocryphal anecdote, which held that he subjected his troops to mass baptisms with a firehose. The warlord of Shantung, Chang Tsung-chang, was known variously as "The Monster" and "Three Don't Knows," the latter ostensibly because he didn't know how many soldiers he had, how much money he had or how many concubines he had. Chang was also known as "Old Fifty-Six," ostensibly, a contemporary journalist explained, "for reasons, alas, which as they say cannot be mentioned in a family newspaper." Through the early 1920s, much of North and Central China was in periodic turmoil as warlords contested for power and bullied or ignored the impotent Peking government.

Hopes for a united China were rejuvenated in May 1919 when students in Peking organized mass demonstrations in response to decisions made at the Paris Peace Conference. The decision to award Shantung to Japan ignited the May Fourth Movement, a nationwide protest against Japanese and Western imperialism that gave new intellectual energy to Chinese nationalism. The debate over how China's culture and society might be modernized was reinvigorated, with scholars and students at Peking University taking the lead in examining the ideas of a broad spectrum of western intellectuals. Scholars such as Chen Duxiu asserted that Confucianism had to be completely abandoned, as the independence of individuals

was at the center of modern life. He also urged the broad acceptance of "Mr. Science" and "Mr. Democracy" as paths to modernization. Other scholar-activists found appeal in the pragmatist methodology of the American John Dewey. The growing popularity of Henrik Ibsen's drama *A Doll's House*, which encouraged Chinese women, especially the younger generation, to question their status in the new China, opened up entirely new dimensions of intellectual inquiry. As thrilling as the "New Culture Movement" was to China's intellectuals, it had little immediate relevance to the more mundane and seemingly insurmountable challenges that the average rural peasant faced on a daily basis; connecting with China's immense population of some 400 million was crucial to any movement for national regeneration.

Amidst this intellectual ferment there were also new political developments. Sun Yat-sen, who had returned from exile in Japan after Yuan Shih-k'ai's death in 1916, turned to the challenge of rejuvenating the Nationalist party. Having established a political base in Canton with the support of the warlord of Kwantung province, Sun set about reexamining his "Three Principles" in the hope of more clearly defining Nationalist ideology. His stress on anti-imperialism as an element of "Nationalism" provided the ideological basis for a new relationship with the Soviet Union, which sent a Comintern agent to advise the Nationalists. A second related development concerned the creation of the Chinese Communist Party (CCP), which was organized in 1921, also with the aid of Soviet advisors. For some Chinese radicals, the appeal of Marxism went beyond its "scientific" and "Western" attributes. As Lenin had demonstrated in Russia, Marxist theory was malleable and could be interpreted so as to fit the conditions of specific countries.

China, like Russia in 1917, met few of Marx's criteria for socialist revolution, but the Russian example suggested that Marxism could also triumph in a seemingly unpropitious Chinese context. Comintern policy required that the Chinese Communists cooperate with the Kuomintang, and CCP members were joined to the KMT as a "block within" rather than standing as a separate party. From 1923 to1927, the years of KMT–CCP cooperation, both groups benefited from the alliance. The larger KMT received useful guidance and support from the Comintern connection, while members of the much smaller CCP worked their way into high positions within the Kuomintang organization while organizing the masses in both urban and rural areas. Though the ideological distinctions between the two groups were temporarily submerged, they could not be ignored indefinitely. At some point, a struggle for control of the Nationalist movement and China's destiny was inevitable.

The creation of a National Government at Canton followed Sun's death in 1925, but the contest for leadership of the KMT was not resolved until the following year, when Chiang Kai-shek emerged as the most likely successor. Born in 1887 to a poor merchant family, Chiang attended the Imperial Military Academy before traveling to Japan for military training. A disciple of Sun Yat-sen since 1911, Chiang underwent military training in the USSR in 1923 before returning to China to head the Whampoa Military Academy. In the years to come, Chiang drew much of his military and political support from Whampoa graduates. Described by an American journalist as "shrewd, suspicious, calculating and not above the use of guile," Chiang was foremost a military man rather than a politician. He was increasingly alarmed at the CCP's influence in the Nationalist party and in 1926,

acting on his own, he declared martial law, arrested Soviet advisers and moved to weaken the Chinese Communists. This accomplished, Chiang turned to the military unification of the country, launching the Northern Expedition of 1926 against warlords in North and Central China. The campaign proved successful, gaining popular support for the KMT armies, which absorbed large numbers of deserters from warlord forces. The growing power of the military within the Nationalist movement, together with the rising concern of bankers and industrialists about communist strength brought about Chiang's decision in 1927 to turn on the CCP. The suppression of the communists began in Shanghai in April 1927, where KMT troops ruthlessly executed communists and suspected sympathizers. As similar operations eradicated communist activists in other cities, the CCP was left stunned and decimated. Having expelled Soviet advisers and established a new capital at Nanking, Chiang successfully squelched a final communist uprising in late 1927 and set about convincing the major powers of the legitimacy of his government. Anti-imperialist riots in which foreigners had been attacked were successfully attributed to Chiang's left-wing opponents and Chiang's Nationalist government gained general recognition abroad, with the important exception of Japan, which did not desire a stabilized China.

Chiang now faced the tremendous challenge of realizing his nationalist revolution in political, social and economic terms. He scored some successes with the "rights recovery movement," by which he recovered much of China's sovereignty by negotiating with the powers for the end of special economic rights and concessions in China. In the domestic sphere, Chiang's successes were at best problematic. Nationalist economic policies did little to promote economic development, as the regime viewed the private sector as more a source of revenue than a national asset to be nurtured. The depression and horrendous natural disasters, together with the heavy exactions of government tax collectors, severely weakened the agricultural sector. Chiang's disinclination toward any fundamental reforms effectively precluded his government from confronting China's immense social and economic problems. Much of his political support derived from the conservative business and land-owning classes, which opposed the sweeping changes that might have won the impoverished urban and rural masses to Chiang's government. Though Chiang's regime took the initiative in pushing industrial development, the modernization of China's infrastructure and the expansion of public education, the changes effected seemed insignificant in the context of China's continued poverty and underdevelopment. Chiang himself was not a charismatic leader and never succeeded in winning the affection of either his party or his people. There remained a hollowness at the core of the Nationalist revolution, due in part to the vagueness of its founding ideology. Though something of a cult developed around the figure of the deceased Sun Yat-sen, "Sun Yat-senism" never developed into a mobilizing ideology. In hopes of providing ideological substance to his movement, Chiang inaugurated the "New Life Movement" in 1934. Less a political or social creed than a behavioral modification program, the New Life Movement encouraged the Chinese masses to observe four vaguely defined Confucian virtues and sought to delineate proper social behavior. People were exhorted to sit and stand straight, eat politely, and refrain from public spitting, smoking and urination. Chiang asserted that the New Life Move-

ment would create "a new national consciousness and mass psychology" and lead to "the social regeneration of China," but no such results were discernible. China remained, as a German observer noted in 1934, "chaotic, dark and spiritless."

Chiang's failure to inspire or win the support of China's masses encouraged the Chinese Communists, who had begun rebuilding their organization in the aftermath of the 1927 debacle. In Kiangsi province in southern China, some 10,000 communists, including the 35-year-old Mao Zedong, had found refuge from Chiang's troops. Mao, who was from a peasant family, was drawn into politics during the final years of the Ch'ing dynasty, studying political theory for years before joining the Chinese Communist Party in 1921. Though never well versed in the intricate details of Marxist theory, Mao was assigned to work with the rural peasantry. He concluded that China's peasant masses would be the vanguard of the revolution. In his report to the party, Mao also asserted his belief that China's revolution would necessarily be violent. "A revolution is not a dinner party," he wrote. "A revolution is an insurrection, an act of violence by which one class overthrows another." Now in the spring of 1928, Mao was joined in the Chinkang Mountains by Chu Teh, who was to organize the Chinese Red Army while Mao focused on political organization and indoctrination. Both agreed that the CCP should stress guerilla warfare, built on the support of the local population. During the early 1930s the communists developed a number of rural base areas.

This growth of communist strength occurred in the face of four "Annihilation Campaigns" aimed at the CCP by Chiang's armies. Having failed to defeat the communists, Chiang altered his strategy in a fifth campaign, encircling the CCP forces at their Kiangsi base. Faced with destruction, communist forces broke out in the fall of 1934 and embarked on a strategic withdrawal that is still hailed in Maoist mythology as one of the greatest events in China's long revolution. The "Long March" began in October as Mao and some 100,000 communists set out on foot from Kiangsi toward Yenan in North China, approximately 6,000 miles distant. Harried by hostile troops, the surviving marchers overcame harsh terrain and starvation, arriving at their destination after a year-long struggle. Only about 50,000 survived the ordeal, but secure in their northern redoubt, the communists began to build a popular base of support among the peasantry, promoting radical reforms such as land redistribution. During the next decade, the CCP forged an increasingly disciplined political and potent military force. More immediately, the threat that Japan's expansionist policies on the Asian mainland posed to Chiang's government superseded that of the communists.

IMPERIAL JAPAN: THE ROAD TO MILITARISM AND WAR

During the final years of the Meiji Era, Japan established itself as the dominant power in Asia, building on the territorial gains from the Russo-Japanese War by annexing Korea in 1910, even as Russian influence on the Asia mainland receded. A growing naval and industrial power, Japan nonetheless faced an internal crisis following the 1912 death of the Meiji Emperor Mutsuhito, whose guidance had assured the Japanese people during a period of rapid modernization. The succession of the Taisho Emperor Yoshihito (1912–1926) brought an era of uncertainty, in part because the new

ruler was physically weak, indecisive and unprepared to rule. A financial crisis soon brought about a major transformation of Japanese politics, as political parties asserted themselves in the Diet, supplanting the power of older political cliques. Public campaigns, demands for political democratization and party-organized cabinets characterized the era of "Taisho democracy," a period during which American political and cultural influence also began to permeate Japan. The outbreak of war in Europe offered opportunities for expanding Japan's nascent empire and strengthening both industry and trade. The Twenty-One Demands on China reflected Japan's determination to capitalize on the distraction of the Western powers and expand Japanese influence in Asia. At Paris in 1919, the Allies rewarded Japan's minimal contributions to the war with island mandates in the Pacific and China's Shantung peninsula. Japan's nominal participation in the Allied cause did much to secure her status as a major power, though the refusal of the western powers to include a racial equality clause in the League of Nations covenant convinced many Japanese that Western racism precluded acceptance of Japan as an equal. Postwar tensions between the United States and Japan, both now aspiring to influence in the Pacific basin, were somewhat defused by the Washington Conference of 1921–1922, which capped naval construction in hopes of heading off a naval arms race. Many in Japan's Imperial Navy and in right-wing political circles saw the resulting treaties as an American effort to restrict Japanese power and as part of a more general effort to deny Japan the empire that the major western powers had already acquired. In 1924, the U.S. Congress enacted the National Origins Act, which specifically excluded Japanese immigrants, further exacerbating anti-American sentiments and Japanese feelings of persecution. Otherwise, generally good Japanese–American relations in the postwar decade tempered these potentially dangerous resentments. In the aftermath of the disastrous Tokyo earthquake of 1923, Americans were quick to donate funds to aid the victims, and the Japanese continued to indulge their growing fascination with American music, film, clothes and sports, notably baseball.

As "Taisho democracy" evolved in the 1920s, Japan's stability seemed assured by a commitment to liberal government, economic expansion and continued modernization. There were, however, political and economic weaknesses that held the potential to destabilize Japanese society. Though party government appeared vibrant, it remained basically a new system of governance imposed from above and modeled on foreign examples. Japan's political heritage was essentially autocratic, while her social tradition was hierarchical. The habits of mind and practice inherited from the pre-Meiji era could not be easily or rapidly discarded. Public veneration of the imperial institution and deference to the military inhibited the development of a truly democratic political culture. Political cliques connected to influential families dominated parliamentary politics both before and after the Taisho era. Special interests such as the *zaibatsu*, huge industrial conglomerates, wielded disproportionate political power. Through the 1920s, political corruption and periodic scandals eroded public faith in the party system. "Taisho democracy" itself brought only limited liberalization, as events in 1924 demonstrated. That year the Diet passed the Universal Suffrage Act, which gave the vote to all males over the age of twenty-five. This achievement was diminished by the passage of the Peace Preser-

vation Law, which criminalized the advocacy of radical ideas, such as altering the national polity, or *kokutai*, which was seen as an affront to the imperial institution. In 1928, the law was amended to require the death penalty for any who challenged the national polity.

Japan was, of course, not the only government to enact laws restricting basic civil liberties in an era of anti-communist hysteria, but the Peace Preservation Law reflected the insecure and tenuous character of "Taisho democracy," which remained politically vulnerable in the event of crisis. Japan's economy, though outwardly strong, also concealed some internal weaknesses. Though the *zaibatsu* flourished, their growing power squeezed many smaller concerns and the future of Japan's numerous small handicraft shops was uncertain given the predominance of the giant conglomerates. Japanese farmers, many of whom eked out marginal lives in an inequitable tenancy system, suffered further as the price of rice, the main staple crop, declined. Throughout the decade, an unfavorable balance of trade plagued the Japanese economy, a problem that the Diet fully addressed only when it was too late. Events in the 1930s revealed the shallow roots of Japan's new democracy.

When the Emperor Yoshihito died in 1926 after years of declining mental and physical health, the twenty-five-year-old Crown Prince Hirohito assumed the throne and proclaimed the era of Showa, or "Enlightened Peace," an irony that would become increasingly evident in subsequent years. The new emperor became the focus of a variety of disaffected groups that advocated a "Showa Restoration," which would bring an end to party government and restore the emperor to his traditional position as the absolute and divine embodiment of Japan's national polity. Among the critics of parliamentary government were ultranationalist patriotic societies such as the Cherry Society and the Black Dragon Society, whose members considered coups and assassination as legitimate weapons in the struggle against the weak and timid liberal politicians they blamed for assenting to Japan's inferior position to the Western powers. Such groups often attracted army officers, who were increasingly wont to believe that Japan's salvation lay in expansion and conquest, which was impossible as long as Japan adhered to international treaties that served only Western interests. Officers in Japan's Kwantung Army in Manchuria demonstrated their willingness to defy their own government through provocative acts when they arranged the murder of the Chinese warlord Chang Tso-lin in 1928. Officers in the Imperial navy, though never as uniformly radical as in the army, nonetheless likewise believed that the liberal politicians who ratified naval restriction treaties had sacrificed Japan's naval strength to political expedience.

A variety of ultranationalist writers advocated a more genuinely Japanese society and denounced Western and especially American culture for its degenerative effects on Japan's unique national spirit. Influential figures in both high government and court circles sympathized with many of these objectives. In Japan as elsewhere across the globe, the world depression undermined liberal government as the economy collapsed and politicians seemed to be unable to remedy the nation's growing economic woes. By the early 1930s, it was increasingly easy to argue that Japan's shrinking economy and growing population made expansion abroad mandatory, to secure both raw materials for industry and living space for Japanese settlers. Under these pressures, parliamentary government was eclipsed by the early 1930s, supplanted

by the growing influence of the army and extreme nationalists, who propagated militarism in Japan and a policy of aggression and expansion on the Asian mainland.

The burgeoning strength of ultranationalism was manifest as early as 1930, when Japanese statesmen ratified the London Naval Treaty, which extended the restrictions imposed by the 1922 Washington treaty. The response of right-wing military officers and the patriotic societies went beyond expressions of outrage; a fanatic assassinated Prime Minister Hamaguchi Osachi, who was blamed for this surrender to Western opinion. The assassination was only the first of numerous "patriotic murders" over the next several years. In September 1931, officers in the Kwantung Army concluded that the circumstances were propitious for Japanese expansion in Manchuria, where Japanese troops were already stationed. The conspirators created a pretext for action by blowing up the tracks of the South Manchurian Railway near Mukden and blaming the explosion on Chinese saboteurs. Japanese troops then attacked nearby Chinese forces and seized strategic sites. Civilian authorities in Tokyo proved incapable of halting the offensive and the Kwantung Army moved quickly to consolidate its control over Manchuria. A puppet government headed by the deposed Manchu emperor Pu-yi was established and the new state of Manchukuo proclaimed. Fighting spread south into China by 1932, with Japanese attacks on Shanghai and Nanking. The "Manchurian Incident," as Japanese statesmen euphemistically termed the aggression, revealed both the impotence of Japan's civilian government and the League of Nations, which responded to the aggression by dispatching an investigatory committee and then voting to censure Japan. The United States, though pledged to protect China from external aggression, issued only a weak statement announcing that it would not recognize territories gained through conquest. Emboldened by the army's *fait accompli* in Manchuria, right-wing fanatics murdered two prominent civilian leaders in early 1932 and launched an attempted coup in May. Though the coup failed, the extremists succeeded in assassinating Prime Minister Inukai Ki at his residence. Arrested and tried, the assassins were generally treated with deference and permitted to use the trial as a forum for their extremist views.

By 1933, as the army extended Japanese control into China's Jehol province, much of the international furor generated by the Manchurian Incident had abated, while the influence of the military and the ultranationalist societies continued to grow in Japan. Anyone who openly opposed the policy of expansion or voiced criticisms of the imperial cult that extremists promoted ran a multitude of risks, including assassination. On February 26, 1936, a group of army officers associated with the "Imperial Way" faction attempted to seize the capital. Over a thousand radicalized troops participated, murdering several high government officials before loyal forces dispatched by the emperor crushed the coup. Even so, the military commanded even greater influence afterward, winning increases in the army and navy budgets. During these same years, right-wing elements promoted an intense propaganda and indoctrination campaign, aimed at instilling ultranationalist and militaristic ideas while stressing the threat that Communism and the West posed to Japan's unique national polity and international position. Government "thought police" targeted dissidents and leftists who advocated "dangerous thoughts". Though some political parties and individu-

als continued to oppose the military's influence, the army's determination to secure Japan's position in China led to the outbreak of a major conflict in 1937.

The Sino-Japanese War grew out of an unintentional clash between Japanese and Chinese troops near Peking's Marco Polo Bridge on July 7, 1937. Long beleaguered by Japanese political and economic pressure, Chiang Kai-shek's Nationalist regime refused to make additional concessions in the face of what was perceived to be blatant Japanese aggression. Many Japanese statesmen and military officials believed that Japan's destiny was to bring order to China and the rest of Asia, and that the major source of disorder was irresponsible Chinese nationalism. A weak disordered China, Japanese leaders feared, invited southward expansion by the Soviet Union. Japanese fears about communism in Asia had been deepened after 1936, when Chiang Kai-shek had been compelled by one of his own marshals to cease his campaign against the Chinese Communists and accept a "United Front" with the CCP against further Japanese expansion.

The intractability of both Japan and China made the rapid expansion of the conflict after July almost inevitable. Japanese forces moved quickly to press south from Peking, while other forces assaulted Shanghai and moved up the Yangtze River Valley toward the Nationalist capital at Nanking. Though Japanese commanders had long believed that China could be conquered in a matter of months, Chinese resistance, especially at Shanghai, was stiffer than expected and resulted in heavy casualties. When Shanghai fell in November and Imperial forces drove toward Nanking, Japanese troops were infused with a grim determination to punish the Chinese for their insolence. Consequently, when some 150,000 Japanese troops occupied the Chinese capital after weeks of bitter fighting, they engaged in a brutal campaign of atrocities that came to be known as the "Rape of Nanking." Having driven Nationalist troops from the city, Japanese soldiers, encouraged by their commanders, wreaked a terrible revenge on Chinese civilians and prisoners alike. Mass executions by machine gun, bayonet, flaming gasoline, beatings, beheadings, industrial acid and drowning resulted in the deaths of as many as 400,000 Chinese. Rampaging troops also raped tens of thousands of Chinese women, often killing them afterward. The atrocities were so heinous that they drew protests from a German Nazi in the city. In the aftermath of the loss of Nanking, Chiang Kai-shek, reeling under the Japanese onslaught, withdrew his government into the interior to Chunking, beyond the reach of Japan's armies.

Japan's war in China and the "Rape of Nanking" brought significant repercussions. American policymakers, previously reluctant to effectively oppose Japanese expansion in Asia, were forced to conclude that Japan's aggressive policies posed a threat to the U.S. position in the Pacific and to international peace. Japan's adherence to the Anti-Comintern Pact of 1936 had already established a perceptible link between the Asian power and Europe's fascist dictatorships. For the moment, however the Roosevelt administration was preoccupied with the depression and restrained by the strongly isolationist sentiment of the American public. The President's "Quarantine Speech" in October, as Japanese troops assaulted Shanghai, had not been followed by any indication that the public might consider a more active policy against aggression. When Japanese aircraft bombed and sank the U.S. Navy gunboat *Panay* on the Yangtze River in early December, an obvious effort to test American determination, the public was outraged but clearly unwilling to endorse more forceful policies to contain Japan. On the other hand, Japan's savage war in China catalyzed anti-Japanese sentiment in the United States. The western press widely reported the horrors of the "Rape of Nanking," and convinced many Americans that the Japanese were a cruel, fanatical people dedicated to expansion by conquest. Japan's proclamation of a "New Order" in Asia the next year did much to confirm American apprehensions. Japanese leaders, now irrevocably committed to a long and brutal war in China, were soon confronted with indications that the United States was moving gradually toward a stronger policy of opposing Japan's war in China. Moving cautiously because of obviously inferior U.S. naval and military strength in the Far East, the Roosevelt administration offered limited economic and military aid to the Chinese Nationalists and, in the summer of 1938, ended a 1911 commercial treaty with Japan and prohibited the sale of aircraft. As modest as these initiatives were, they convinced Japanese expansionists that the United States was committed to obstructing Japan's imperial destiny in Asia.

The outbreak of war in Europe seemed to bring new opportunities for the extension of Japan's Asian empire. Japanese expansionists developed the concept of a "Greater East Asia Co-Prosperity Sphere," in which Japan would liberate the colonial peoples of Asia from western imperial rule and develop "Asia for Asians." In reality, it was little more than a grandiose and thinly cloaked guise for Japanese imperialism. After Nazi Germany's defeat of France in June 1940, Japanese forces moved into northern French Indochina, an action that affirmed American fears about insatiable Japanese expansion. In September, Japan joined Germany and Italy in the Tripartite Pact, a mutual defense treaty. As much as any single event, this act confirmed many Americans in the belief that Japan was a serious threat to world peace, a partner in a militaristic, antidemocratic cabal, and not merely a regional nuisance. The Roosevelt administration responded by prohibiting the sale of aviation fuel to Japan, a largely symbolic gesture, but one that fed the apprehensions of Japan's military chiefs. Japan's ability to wage war in China was dependent on American petroleum; some ninety percent of Japan's oil needs came from the United States. A total American embargo would compel Japan to either abandon the struggle in China, where thousands of lives had already been sacrificed, or seek an alternative source of oil. Some military leaders advocated an advance southward, to seize Indochina and the resource-rich Dutch East Indies. As of 1940, few yet actually advocated war against the United States, but the preliminary planning for an attack on the U.S. naval base at Pearl Harbor, Hawaii, was already underway.

The United States had indicated its continued commitment to China by lending support to the American Volunteer Group, a volunteer group of fighter pilots known popularly as the "Flying Tigers," who flew against the Japanese in China. Both nations were caught in a dilemma, neither desirous of war, nor capable of making the concessions that would be required to avoid it; Japan could not abandon China, while the United States could not accept the Japanese presence there. Events advanced quickly after the Japanese occupied all of French Indochina in July 1941. The United States responded by freezing Japanese assets and imposing a total embargo on oil. Given the tremendous petroleum requirements of Japanese army and naval forces, the decision compelled Japan to move quickly to resolve the impasse. The appointment of Army General Hideki Tojo as prime minister that fall illustrated the growing influence of the military in the decision-making process, an ominous sign for those desiring a diplomatic solution. Pursuing a dual policy of diplomatic negotiations and preparation for war, Japan's leaders concluded that if an acceptable compromise were not reached by late November, then "things would start to happen automatically." Japan's proposal that the situation should be restored to that of June 1941 in return for an end to the oil embargo and U.S. non-involvement in China was inherently unacceptable to the Roosevelt administration. Accordingly, in late November a Japanese carrier strike force holding in the north Pacific was ordered to proceed south and attack the U.S. Pacific Fleet's Hawaiian base at Pearl Harbor, Oahu, in hopes of destroying American naval power in a single blow. The attack, which began early on December 7, marked the beginning of the Pacific War and Japan's final struggle for empire.

◆ —— ◆ —— ◆ —— ◆ —— ◆ —— ◆ —— ◆ —— ◆ —— ◆ —— ◆

In early November 1928, Hirohito Michinomiya, Crown Prince of the Empire of Japan, began the long series of formal ceremonies that would affirm him as the 124th Emperor of Japan, the head of a dynasty stretching back nearly 2,600 years. Hirohito had served as regent since November 1921, when it was no longer possible for his debilitated father, the Taisho Emperor Yoshihito, to govern. Hirohito, quiet in demeanor and small in stature, was acknowledged as the emperor following his father's death in late 1926. Not until he concluded the complex coronation ceremonies and traditional mystical rituals, however, would he be considered deified, a god-emperor descendant of the first emperor Jimmu, who according to Japanese mythology, was descended from the Sun Goddess Amaterasu Omikami. The lengthy enthronement ceremonies had begun in January, as the young ruler sent emissaries to imperial mausoleums to announce to his ancestors his pending accession. Similar historical traditions were reenacted in subsequent months and followed closely by the Japanese press, which offered lengthy commentary on the meaning and importance of the ceremonies. Parades and festivals continued into the fall, climaxing with an imperial procession from Tokyo to Kyoto, where the emperor underwent the final formal rituals, which confirmed Hirohito's divine descent and transformation into a "manifest deity," the divine embodiment of the nation and its people.

In an age in which monarchy itself was generally declining and the concept of divine-right monarchy long since discarded, Japan's emperor was an anomaly, basing the legitimacy of his rule on his personal divinity. Indeed, the young emperor, together with influential members of his court, the armed services and right-wing groups, were engaged in a concerted effort to revive the emperor cult, which had diminished in popularity in the years since the death of the Emperor Meiji. The concept of a divine emperor, a spiritually pure people and a unique Japanese mission in the world were to be the basis for a reinvigorated and aggressive Japanese nationalism, which would have as its objective the realization of Japan's rightful place in the world order. In an era in which nationalism often took the form of nation-building as in Turkey, or anticolonialism as in India, Japanese nationalism assumed an aggressive and imperialist character. As the focal point of the new nationalism, the young emperor would play a central role in charting Japan's course toward aggression and war during the following decade.

Born in 1901 in the Emperor Meiji's reign, Hirohito was raised in the isolated atmosphere of the imperial court, where from an early age he was instructed in dynastic tradition, the Meiji legacy of achievement, and military history and skills. Unlike the emperors who preceded Meiji, the adolescent Hirohito was also instructed in a broad variety of subject areas that would facilitate his ability to govern as an active, charismatic political leader. Ultimately, his education took him in two seemingly contradictory directions, instilling in him a modern, scientific perspective conjoined with a traditional, quasi-mystical conception of the emperor's nature and role. His young adult years coincided with the development of "Taisho democracy," a period of time in which the debate over the character of the national polity, or *kokutai,* became more heated. Instructors who stressed the centrality of the emperor, the case for Japanese expansion, and the threats posed by western imperialism, liberalism and individualism may have shaped Hirohito's thoughts during these years. In hopes of presenting Hirohito as a dynamic heir who could uphold the *kokutai,* court officials decided to send him on a lengthy tour of Europe in 1921. It was Hirohito's first introduction to the outside world and the attendant positive press coverage did much to revitalize public support for the monarchy and the crown prince. His wedding to Princess Nagako in 1924 was also turned into an occasion to popularize the young regent.

Those who desired to strengthen the imperial institution and elevate the emperor viewed the new political openness of Taisho democracy warily. The founding of a Japanese Communist party, an assassination attempt on the emperor, declining army morale and increasing national debate about the nature of the national policy were all seen as threats to Japan's internal strength and world position. Proponents of a "Showa Restoration" argued that national unity and strength could only be achieved through an omnipotent ruler in whose person political and military power were brought together with religious authority. Hirohito, together with court officials, supported this growing campaign to resurrect the concept of a divine emperor, stressing the glories of the Meiji past and Hirohito's dedication to recapturing them. By the early 1930s, as the problems growing out of the world depression beset Japan, the timidity and ineffectiveness of parliamentary democracy provided an opening for the advocates of the emperor cult and militaristic nationalism.

Given the hardships and frustrations the world depression brought, many Japanese saw the establishment of an Asian empire as a viable solution to economic problems and as a realization of Japan's manifest destiny in the Far East. The broad acceptance of this outlook testified to the success of an intensive campaign of propaganda and indoctrination implemented by the government and military during the years in which Japan extended its territorial claims on the Asian mainland. The Japanese were encouraged to see themselves as a divine race, possessed of unique moral and spiritual qualities lacking in Westerners and Chinese. Films, books and speakers propounded the concept of a pure people dedicated to serve the ultimate embodiment of the *kokutai,* the god-emperor Hirohito. Within the armed forces, the ideal of the *samurai* warrior was revived, together with the code of *bushido,* which allowed for no mercy toward the defeated enemy. By the end of the decade, the emperor-cult, militarism and ultranationalism had supplanted democracy as the dominant national ideology. In late 1941, in a desperate effort to secure Japan's ambitious imperial goals, Hirohito gave his assent to a war against the United States. The subsequent Pacific War transformed Japan and the imperial system in ways that would have been unimaginable a few short years before.

As Emperor Hirohito faced the issue of surrender in summer 1945, few vestiges of Japanese military strength remained. Most of the Imperial Navy had been sunk, Japanese airpower was virtually nonexistent, and major elements of the Imperial Army were either stranded on the Asian mainland or cut off in bypassed Pacific islands. His empire had shrunk to little more than the home islands, whose cities had been flattened and burned by American air raids. Yet in the face of the indescribable suffering of his people, Hirohito hesitated to accept the Allied terms for surrender, concerned lest his position as emperor or the nature of the *kokutai* be affected by the continued demand for "unconditional surrender." Only after American atomic bombs had obliterated Hiroshima and Nagasaki did the emperor accept the terms of the Potsdam Declaration,

Fig. 4-2 Japanese Emperor Hirohito in his ceremonial coronation robes at the time of his accession to the throne in 1926. Though Hirohito took the official name *Showa,* or "Enlightened Peace," for his reign, he was soon the focus of an "emperor cult" that joined belief in the divine origins of the Japanese people with ultra-nationalist and militarist sentiments. In the 1930s, Hirohito gave his tacit assent to Japan's aggressions in China. (Pearson Education, Corporate Digital Archive, Getty Images Inc.)

which had been revised to allow for the continuation of his position. Hirohito's statement of August 15th conceded defeat only obliquely and asserted that Japan's war had been one of "existence and self-defense." The carefully crafted, sometimes self-serving declaration signaled the beginning of an effort to redefine the Japanese emperor, casting him as a passive observer during the years of strife and a benevolent, apolitical figure around whom the Japanese could be united in peace. As soon as the war ended, the emperor worked actively to convince his people that responsibility for Japan's defeat belonged to incautious advisers, primarily military leaders.

The gradual rehabilitation of Japan's emperor in American eyes occurred during the U.S. occupation, beginning with a famous September 1945 meeting between Hirohito and General Douglas MacArthur, who afterward described the Emperor as "the first gentleman of Japan." MacArthur's innate political conservatism predisposed him to the idea that Hirohito could be a source of stability in a postwar Japan, and he opposed any effort to hold the emperor responsible for the recent war or war crimes. The advent of the Cold War created circumstances in which Hirohito and Japan's conservative ruling elite could use rising American fears of communism to bolster their case against any radical changes in the political structure. Thus, while Hirohito remained as emperor, it was within a redefined national polity that accorded the monarch only nominal authority. Hirohito renounced his divinity in a 1946 "Declaration of Humanity," and Shinto was disestablished as a national religion. Reduced to little more than a figure symbolic of Japanese tradition, Hirohito strove to build a public image of a reserved, dignified monarch committed to family and international peace. By the 1980s, the militant emperor-cult of the 1930s was at most a distant memory. A new generation of Japanese no longer pledged their loyalty to a god-emperor, but rather to the corporations for which they diligently worked. Since the end of the Second World War, the historical debate over Hirohito's role in the aggressions of the 1930s and the Pacific War has continued unabated in both the United States and Japan. Hirohito never gave any indication that he considered himself in any way responsible for the events of those years. He died in 1989, having lived, in the words of a recent biographer, "the unexamined life."

Suggested Readings

ANTONIUS, GEORGE. *The Arab Awakening.* (1976).

BEASLEY, W. G. *Japanese Imperialism, 1984–1945.* (1987).

BIX, HERBERT P. *Hirohito and the Making of Modern Japan.* (2000).

CHANG, IRIS. *The Rape of Nanking: The Forgotten Holocaust of World War II.* (1997).

DAVIDSON, BASIL. *Africa in Modern History: The Search for a New Society.* (1978).

DIRLIK, A. *The Origins of Chinese Communism.* (1989).

DOWER, JOHN. *Japan in War and Peace.* (1993).

EMBREE, AINSLIE. *India's Search for National Identity.* (1981).

FAGE, J. D. *A History of Africa.* (1995).

FISCHER, LOUIS. *Gandhi.* (1983).

FRANKIN, DAVID. *A Peace to End All Peace: The Fall of the Ottoman Empire and the Creation of the Modern Middle East.* (1989).

IENAGA, SABURO. *The Pacific War, 1931–1945.* (1978).

IRIYE, AKIRA. *After Imperialism: The Search for Order in the Far East.* (1965).

JAMES, LAWRENCE. *The Rise and Fall of the British Empire.* (1994).

KEAY, JOHN. *Empire's End: A History of the Far East from High Colonialism to Hong Kong.* (1997).

MANGO, ANDREW. *Ataturk: The Biography of the Founder of Modern Turkey.* (1999).

SHERIDAN, JAMES. *China in Disintegration: The Republican Era in Chinese History.* (1975).

SPENCE, JONATHAN. *The Search for Modern China.* (1990).

WILSON, DICK. *The Long March.* (1982).

———. *When Tigers Fight: The Story of the Sino-Japanese War.* (1982).

YAPP, M. C. *The Near East since the First World War.* (1996).

CHAPTER 5

The Approaching Storm: Europe, 1919–1939

An atmosphere of palpable anticipation grew as a crowd of some thirty thousand filled the Luitpold Arena just outside of Nuremberg, Germany. On this night in early September 1934, the assembled Nazi Party officials and members restlessly awaited the arrival of their *Führer,* Adolf Hitler. A wave of ecstatic noise swept the hall as a band began the "Badenweiler March"—everyone knew that the tune inevitably signaled the arrival of the German dictator. The cheering swelled as Hitler, attended by a dozen high party officials, strode purposefully down an aisle, framed by thousands of arms uplifted in the Nazi salute. The group's arrival at the stage was followed by an impressive procession of hundreds of standard bearers who carried the ornate emblems of each local party organization. The occasion was the culmination of a week of mass rallies and speeches marking the Sixth Congress of the Nazi Party. As the shouting subsided, Nazi Party Deputy *Führer* Rudolf Hess bounded to the podium. A slavish admirer of Hitler, Hess touched off yet another wave of cheering as he announced, "The *Führer* will speak!"

Having finally quieted his audience, Hitler, wearing his ubiquitous party uniform, spoke of both the history and the future of the Nazi party and the National Socialist state. "When our party consisted of only seven men," he recalled," it already had two principles. First it wanted to be a party with a true ideology. And it wanted to be the only power in Germany." The party, Hitler declared, had always sought "the racially best of the German nation" and "the nation followed and submitted itself in ever-growing numbers." As Hitler proceeded, he matched dramatic gesture and vocal intonation to his message. "Whoever feels he is the carrier of the best blood and has

Fig. 5-1 At the stadium in Nuremberg, Germany, the standard-bearers and leadership of the Nazi party parade between massed formations of storm troopers during the 1934 Nazi Party Congress. German dictator Adolf Hitler was aware of the propaganda value of such displays and persuaded director Leni Riefenstahl to film the proceedings. The resultant 1936 documentary *Triumph of the Will* stunned viewers round the world. (Pearson Education, Corporate Digital Archive, Picture Desk, Inc./Kobal Collection.)

consciously used this blood to guide the nation will keep the leadership and will not renounce it!" he thundered. "The party is the selecting ground for the German political leadership. Its doctrine will be unchangeable! Its organization will be as hard as steel! Its total image will be like a holy order!" As the audience responded with frenetic applause, Hitler affirmed the victory of his "Brown Revolution:" "It is our wish that this state shall endure for thousands of years! We are happy to know that the future rightfully belongs to us. Long live National Socialism! Long live Germany!" Pandemonium erupted as Hitler stepped aside and Hess vaulted to the podium. "The Party is Hitler!" shouted the enthusiastic Hess. "Hitler is Germany, Germany is Hitler! Hitler, *Sieg Heil!*" The climactic moment resolved as the audience broke into the Nazi party anthem, "Hold the Banners High," before departing into the night.

Hitler's "Thousand Year Reich" speech was the capstone of a week in which the dictator clearly demonstrated his mastery of the art of mass manipulation through pageantry, drama and rhetoric. Nuremberg was chosen as the site for Nazi party rallies in part because the narrow streets that wound through its picturesque medieval quarter offered a physical representation of a historical German past that Hitler sought to connect to. But Hitler also directed his architect Albert Speer to construct a suitably impressive structure for mass rallies at the Zeppelin Field, where a 1,300-foot long, 80-foot high stone structure was erected to overlook a broad parade ground. The focal point of the stadium was a massive stone podium backed by a giant Nazi eagle with a 100-foot wingspan; huge swastika banners completed the scene. At night, the Nuremberg stadium could be illuminated by over 100 searchlights, which were directed skyward to create a "cathedral of light" effect. It was in this setting that many of the week's activities occurred, as Hitler addressed 50,000 members of the Nazi Labor Service, resplendent in party uniforms and shouldering spades rather than rifles; even work, Hitler maintained, was part of the battle. A night rally brought together 200,000 Nazi party officials; the following day, Hitler reviewed 100,000 *Sturmabteilungen,* or stormtroopers, who pledged their loyalty. "Army Day" attracted 300,000 to the stadium to view a mock battle presented by soldiers of the army Hitler was secretly rebuilding.

The propaganda value of these events was not lost on Hitler. The dictator cajoled filmmaker Leni Riefenstahl into producing a documentary film of the 1934 Party Congress. Riefenstahl's crew of sixteen cameramen devised revolutionary techniques for capturing the event on film, filming from planes, cranes, roller skates and an elevator platform mounted on the tallest flagpole. There was to be no narration—the sounds of the events, together with the music and speeches comprised the soundtrack. The finished product, "Triumph of the Will," proved to be a cinematic masterpiece, albeit a controversial one. Considered by some film critics to be the greatest documentary ever made, the film ran nearly four hours in its original version. It stunned audiences around the world with its images of massed formations and oceans of flags, banners and emblems of state authority, all exemplifying the totalitarian appeal. Visual imagery, Hitler knew, could be as emotive as the rhetorical skills that had served him so well. In the years to come, he relied on both to strengthen his grip on the German people.

At the time of the 1934 Nuremberg Rally, Hitler held uncontested power in Germany. He was Reich Chancellor and the leader of Germany's single party, the Nazis. He had crushed an incipient challenge from the leadership of the S. A. and won over most of the German Army's officer corp. All major German institutions had been "coordinated" or Nazified. Rudolph Hess had barely exaggerated when he had shouted, "Hitler is Germany." The road to power had been a circuitous one, however, sometimes barred by seemingly insurmountable obstacles. Nothing in Hitler's early life even hinted at the remarkable accomplishments of the 1930s.

Hitler was born in 1889 in the Austrian town of Braunau, afterward living in Leonding near Linz, where he led an uneventful childhood, fearing his stern father and doting on his mother. Through adolescence there was little remarkable about the boy; though clearly intelligent, he was an indifferent student. He was held back more than once for poor grades, once receiving a "D-" in German. Though impressed by the rituals of the Catholic Church in which he was raised, Hitler evinced little spirituality. A recent study of Hitler's youth revealed that German nationalist sentiment, which pervaded Austria early in the century, enthused the young Adolf and his schoolmates, who often displayed the German national colors of red, black and gold in defiance of those who advocated a Habsburg allegiance. By late adolescence, Hitler's growing disregard for the monotony of "bourgeois" life and steady work was evident. He later maintained that his diffidence was the product of an artistic temperament, which led him to prefer a more bohemian lifestyle. Having moved to Linz after his father's death, Hitler took up painting, architectural drawings and even piano lessons, but excelled at none of these endeavors. He did, however, begin to show a fondness for the music of Richard Wagner, whose operas were often based on Germanic mythology and heroic themes.

The definitive period in Hitler's life began in 1907 when he moved to Vienna, the imperial capital, hoping to study at the Academy of Fine Arts. Failing the entrance exam, Hitler began a descent into a long period of indolence and indirection, doing odd jobs and living in hostels. During these stark years, the rudiments of Hitler's racist and anti-democratic ideology took shape.

Hitler was repulsed by his first encounter with an orthodox Jew, whose appearance struck him as alien, un-German and "unheroic." Anti-Semitism was rife in Vienna and was personified by the city's Christian Social mayor Karl Lueger, whom Hitler admired. Hitler's detestation of Jews was part of a broader distaste for the numerous ethnic and national minorities evident in the capital; together their presence made the young Austrian more aware of his own "Germanness" and the need to protect German culture from the erosive influence of lesser races. The Jews, Hitler ultimately concluded, posed the greatest danger, as they were a parasitic race, a "noxious bacillus" that poisoned the blood of every nation they inhabited. The political dimensions of Hitler's thought evolved from his belief that Jews promoted parliamentary democracy as a means of laying the foundations for socialism, an ideology centered on class rather than nation or race. By this nefarious means, Jews disrupted and corrupted great nations with the object of ensuring their own dominance. Having observed a session of the Austrian parliament, Hitler dismissed parliamentary government as a ludicrous farce; the ignorant and self-serving politicians he described, jabbering at each other in a multitude of incomprehensible languages, could never provide the leadership the great German people deserved. Hitler would later propound the *Führerprinzip,* or leadership principle, a critical element in his political philosophy. Finally, social Darwinism provided a general context for Hitler's outlook, positing as it did that all life was a struggle, with the strongest ultimately emerging triumphant. As Hitler would later assert, the driving force of history in the twentieth century was the struggle between races.

Hitler's drab existence continued until 1913, when he fled Vienna for Munich, hoping to avoid induction into the Austrian army. He found new purpose in life with the outbreak of the First World War, quickly volunteering to serve the German fatherland. He saw combat duty on the Western Front, where he served as a regimental messenger. The young corporal proved courageous, winning the Iron Cross and generally relishing the excitement and purpose that the war provided. Blinded in a British gas attack in November 1918, Hitler was in a hospital when word arrived of Germany's surrender. Like his comrades, Hitler was stunned, feeling that cowardly politicians had betrayed the army. These were the circumstances that set Hitler on a course that would have monumental consequences for Germany, Europe and the world. "I decided," Hitler wrote later, "to go into politics." It was at this point that Hitler began to draw together his beliefs from the Vienna period and mold them into a more coherent *Weltanschauung,* or world view.

In 1919, as a new democratic government struggled to keep Germany together, Hitler was assigned to military counterintelligence and ordered to infiltrate potentially troublesome radical groups in Munich. This brought him to a meeting of a small "folkish" group, the German Workers Party. Impressed with the nationalistic racist program of the party leader Anton Drexler, Hitler joined the group and within a short time became its most prominent spokesman. By early 1920, Hitler, having left the army, assumed leadership of what was now known as the National Socialist German Workers' Party or Nazis. The group's program was anti-Semitic, anti-capitalist, anti-socialist and anti-liberal, but it was Hitler's dramatic rhetorical assaults on the unjust Versailles Treaty and the "November Criminals" who had signed it that most attracted his listeners. In the early 1920s, the instability of the Weimar Republic and Germany's economic woes gave Hitler reason to believe that his small party, one of many such radical groups, might somehow seize power. In a fateful miscalculation, Hitler and a group of stormtroopers attempted a coup in Munich in November 1923. The "Beer Hall *Putsch*" failed miserably and Hitler landed ignominiously in Landsberg prison.

Hitler's brief time in prison proved to be another critical juncture in his life. The incarcerated *Führer* of the now-floundering Nazi party collected his thoughts in one of the century's most famous autobiographies, *Mein Kampf (My Struggle).* Though disjointed and turgidly written, the book provided a compilation of Hitler's thoughts on a variety of subjects, most importantly the menace posed by "Jewish-Bolshevism", the failure of parliamentary government and the necessity for a great national revival built around the concept of German cultural and racial superiority. Once out of prison, Hitler regained control of his divided party and sought to rebuild it with the objective of gaining power through constitutional means.

Although the message of the Nazis drew some adherents, the economic recovery of the mid-1920s and the apparent success of German democracy dimmed Hitler's prospects. As of 1928, the Nazi party had succeeded in electing only 12 deputies to the German Reichstag. It was the world depression that dramatically improved

Hitler's chances for success. By 1932, with the democratic parties incapable of dealing with the social and economic consequences of the depression, more German voters began turning to the radical solutions offered by the National Socialists. The July elections brought 230 Nazis to the Reichstag. The increasingly chaotic conditions in Germany by the winter of 1932–1933 provided the circumstances that brought Hitler to power and enabled him to justify the establishment of a Nazi dictatorship. The collapse of the Weimar Republic seemed to affirm the inability of liberal democracy to meet the pressing challenges that faced European societies in the interwar years.

The two decades following the First World War offered little respite for peoples wearied by war and deprivation. The social, political and economic reconstruction of Europe was made more difficult by the intellectual impact of the costly conflict. For many, the Great War revealed the hollowness of Europe's intellectual foundations. Belief in traditional political and religious verities, the inevitability of progress and human rationality were shattered by the worst calamity since the Thirty Years' War some three centuries earlier. Despair and cultural pessimism quickly became the intellectual touchstones of the postwar world. The response of the western democracies to the challenges of the 1920s offered little cause for optimism. Democratic government seemed enervated and uncertain, the liberal idea a relic of the previous century. The onset of the world depression brought capitalism, the dominant economic pattern in the west, into doubt and disrepute. Clearly, within a decade of the Paris Peace Conference, Europe was a civilization in distress. By the 1930s, the momentum of history seemed to be with those propounding radical solutions.

A decade earlier, Benito Mussolini had introduced the "totalitarian" state in Italy as a dynamic alternative to torpid parliamentarianism and "bourgeois" individualism. Liberalism, the Fascist dictator averred, was little more than "a deserted temple." In the Soviet Union, Joseph Stalin forged a totalitarian state that radically restructured the Soviet economy and society, promising a glorious future for the "New Soviet Man." Hitler's shockingly rapid rise to power in Germany, together with Germany's economic and military revival, seemed to affirm the vitality of the totalitarian ideal. Throughout the decade, military and authoritarian government advanced across Europe, from the Iberian Peninsula to the Carpathian Mountains. The Wilsonian vision of a democratic Europe seemed laughably naive and distant.

Likewise, the international peacekeeping structure erected in the aftermath of the Great War appeared increasingly impotent. The League of Nations, disarmament conferences and international treaties proved ineffective in deterring the expansionist ambitions of aggressive military states. Dissatisfaction with the 1919 settlements and radical nationalism were often factors that drove aggression. In Italy, where Fascist ideology propounded the innate value of militarism and conquest, Mussolini's promise of a "New Roman Empire" was an undisguised summons to conquest. Hitler's averred determination to revise the Versailles Treaty and establish a "Greater German Reich" was likewise a clear challenge to the European status quo. The cynical Soviet dictator

Stalin proved more than willing to capitalize on circumstances to gain new territories for the USSR. Consequently, the 1930s brought an accelerating pattern of aggression and conquest that led ultimately to the most destructive war in human history.

◆ —— ◆ —— ◆ —— ◆ —— ◆

The Postwar European Perspective: Cultural Despair and Modernism

Whatever exuberance Allied victory and peace brought in 1918, it proved to be short-lived in the decades that followed. The staggering cost in human lives alone was reason for somber reflection. In addition, however, a general perception grew that the war had swept away preexisting beliefs and certainties with the same finality that it had destroyed monarchies that had existed for centuries. The western intellectual tradition that had been evolving since the Enlightenment, stressing the primacy of human reason and the inevitability of progress, now seemed dubious. Now, despair and disillusionment shaped the postwar vision of European intellectuals. Shortly after the war, German author Hermann Hesse captured the widening mood of pessimism when he wrote: "For us in old Europe, everything has died that was good and unique to us. Our admirable rationality has become madness." For Hesse's countryman Oswald Spengler, the conflict also compelled some grim conclusions. In an influential 1919 work, *The Decline of Western Civilization*, Spengler asserted that Germany's defeat was a consequence of the broader phenomenon of Europe's decline as a civilization. For Spengler, traditional intellectual guideposts were of little use. "We no longer believe in the power of reason over life," he wrote, predicting that in the future "impotent democracies" would give way to powerful leaders born out of struggle and

war. German-born writer Erick Marie Remarque drew a somewhat different lesson from the conflict. His novel *All Quiet on the Western Front* stressed the futility of war and became one of the most famous antiwar works of the century.

Cultural despair and confusion were not confined to those nations defeated in the war; these outlooks were equally pervasive in the victorious Allied nations. Even as the war had begun in 1914, American expatriate author Henry James, writing from Britain, had indicated his concern that the growing conflict would give lie to the "whole long age during which we have supposed the world to be . . . gradually bettering." James' fears proved accurate as postwar western literature soon reflected the disappointments and uncertainties born of the war. Poet Ezra Pound was perhaps most cynical, bitterly mocking the civilization for which millions had died as "an old bitch gone in the teeth . . . a botched civilization." American-born poet Thomas Stearns (T.S.) Eliot offered grim visions of meaningless existence in a shattered world in such poems as "The Waste Land" and "The Hollow Men." The scenario presented in William Butler Yeats' "The Second Coming" was equally disturbing and would be cited later as frighteningly prescient. The poet wrote of a time when "Things fall apart; the center cannot hold / Mere anarchy is loosed in the land." Yeats concluded with the troubling question: "And what rough beast; its hour come round at last / Slouches toward Bethlehem to be born?" As some would later comment, the events of subsequent years quickly provided the unpleasant answer. Literary outpourings such as these reflected the erosion of both confidence and certainty in western societies in the aftermath of the war.

Pound, Eliot and others were part of a cultural and intellectual movement that gained ascendancy after the war and both reflected and emphasized the uncertainty of the times. Modernism made its debut in the years before the First World War, but not until the 1920s were its adherents clearly the dynamic force in European culture. The war provided further rationale for the modernist assault on the cultural and social conventions of bourgeois society, which was denounced for its moral hypocrisy and superficiality. Self-doubt and a growing tendency toward subjectivity also drove the modernist impulse during these years, as did the continuing influence of Freudian psychology, with its emphasis on the subconscious and symbolic meaning. In the early 1920s, several broad modernist movements that could be traced to prewar irrationalist thought emerged. German Expressionism promised to expose the brutality and perversity cloaked by conventional behavior. Dadaism, a prominent movement in France, was an absurdist response to the horrors produced by the false values of conventional society. Closely related, Surrealism offered a "logic of nonsense" and rejected humanism and reason in favor of spontaneity. Futurism, a prewar Italian movement that espoused the love of danger and the beauty of struggle, found additional followers in the 1920s.

While some of these movements were short-lived, they influenced many of the intellectuals and artists of the decade. Literary modernism had a broad impact in the 1920s, as is evident in the works of poets such as Eliot, Yeats, Paul Valery and Rainer Marie Rilke. Through innovative word usage, symbolism and cryptic meanings, they depicted a dreary world bereft of certainty and meaning. Novelists of the era were equally innovative and stressed similar themes. Czech writer Franz Kafka achieved enduring fame for his nightmarish novel *The Trial,* in which the protagonist is condemned by a faceless bureaucracy for a crime that is never specified. English novelist D. H. Lawrence challenged bourgeois sexual values with *Lady Chatterly's Lover* in 1924. Both English writer Virginia Woolf and Irish contemporary James Joyce experimented with "stream of consciousness" techniques in order to depict subjective experience and offer psychological insight into human motivation.

In painting and music, the modernist impulse had become manifest before the war, when Cubism and Expressionism had shocked conventional Europeans with abstract and nonrepresentational art. During the 1920s, artists such as Pablo Picasso, Paul Klee, Wassily Kandinsky and Salvadore Dali continued the trend toward more individualistic and abstract styles. Music, too, had experienced its great revolution on the eve of the war, most notably with the riotous 1913 premiere of Igor Stravinsky's *The Rite of Spring.* The interwar years brought further innovations from Paris as a younger generation of composers, including Darius Milhaud, Arthur Honegger and Francois Poulenc, experimented with a new music that moved beyond the influence of Claude Debussy, sometimes appropriating elements of jazz. In Vienna, Arnold Schoenberg introduced a "twelve-tone" scale that essentially redefined music by discarding the traditional diatonic scale of eight-note octaves in minor and major keys. His disciples Anton Webern and

Alban Berg carried this "atonal revolution" forward in the years to come.

Few such modernists were widely appreciated during these decades. Rather, most tradition-oriented Europeans responded with revulsion to the cultural trends of the interwar years. Modern literature was routinely denounced as shocking and immoral, while modern paintings were reviled as insane, nonsensical and decadent. Modern music found few defenders and audiences routinely hissed and laughed derisively at performances of "contemporary" works. Critics were equally vociferous in their rejection of the new music, denouncing Berg as "a musical swindler" who was "dangerous to the community." According to one reviewer, Schoenberg's *Five Orchestral Pieces* "suggested feeding time at the zoo." The most charitable comment one critic offered for Webern's unorthodox *Symphony for Chamber Orchestra* was that it had the "cardinal merit of brevity." Many Europeans, accustomed to experiencing an aesthetically pleasing reflection of their civilization in the arts interpreted the products of postwar culture as a dangerous indication of social and intellectual decay. Indeed, some governments, especially authoritarian regimes, moved to suppress these disturbing reflections of modern life. Undoubtedly, the cultural transformations impelled by the war dismayed those who hoped that the end of the war would bring a restoration of traditional culture. For most of the modernists, recognition and appreciation were decades away.

Precarious Stability: Europe in the 1920s

The first half of the 1920s was a time of considerable economic distress for much of Europe. Many nations, victor and vanquished alike, faced huge debts, disrupted economies and new international trade patterns that no longer favored them. Unemployment and inflation were endemic in these years. The war also left behind many international uncertainties and diplomatic problems, not all of which had been foreseen by the men who met in Paris in 1919. By mid-decade, however, many of these challenges had been met. Through a variety of means such as currency revaluations, austerity budgets and international loans, European economies were stabilized and moderate prosperity marked the second half of the decade. Likewise, European leaders demonstrated a new determination to resolve potentially contentious international issues through peaceful means. The League of Nations, despite the absence of the United States, was seen as a crucial foundation for a new peacekeeping structure, and enjoyed broad support. At several critical junctures, such as Germany's default on reparations in 1923, League-sponsored international committees intervened to resolve crises. On other occasions, such as at Locarno in 1924, the major powers took the initiative to win agreements to guarantee borders and lessen the likelihood of conflict.

Disarmament, or at least arms reduction, also gained favor as a means of lessening the threat of war. Modest progress toward that objective was achieved with the Washington Conference of 1921–1922. At this gathering, the U.S. Secretary of State, Charles Evans Hughes, proposed an end to battleship construction for ten years and a ratio that would determine the maximum tonnage of such ships for each of the five great naval powers, the United States, Great Britain, Japan, France and Italy. This Five-Power Treaty (1922) was viewed as a major step toward lessening international tensions and as a possible model for further future armaments reduction. Later in the decade, this idealistic approach to international peace produced the Kellogg-Briand Pact. Initially drawn up by the United States and France in 1928, the treaty pledged signatories to renounce war as an instrument of national policy. Ultimately, sixty nations signed the treaty. By the end of the decade, Europeans seemed to have reason for optimism about the future.

This same decade did bring numerous improvements in the lifestyles of many Europeans. New technologies, some advanced by the exigencies of war, made daily life less strenuous and more enjoyable. Electrification proceeded rapidly in much of western Europe in the postwar period and gas lighting was increasingly viewed as a curious relic of a distant era. Radio and motion pictures, including "talkies," offered new sources of entertainment and information. Like radio, telephones brought rural areas into closer contact with urban population centers. Affordable automobiles and modern roads shrank distances and made travel more practical. The growth of commercial aviation opened extraordinary new vistas; the first regular passenger service between London and Paris was established in 1919 and airfields proliferated throughout Europe in the following decade. Together these changes made for a Europe that was more informed, cosmopolitan and mobile. There remained, however, rural and isolated regions, where life continued much as it had in the previous century. Such areas were more common in the eastern and southern reaches of the continent.

Social trends in the interwar years confirmed that the Great War had dealt a fatal blow to the old European order. Clearly, the war significantly altered the social and political structures of Europe. Numerous monarchies had been swept away in the conflagration, and those remaining faced a very uncertain future. Aristocracies increasingly

seemed a quaint and even ludicrous vestige of a bygone age. Postwar European society proved far less subservient to tradition and custom, a trend that brought about numerous alterations in the daily patterns of life. An increasingly democratic impulse ran strong in western and parts of central Europe; even in eastern and southern Europe, previous social and political relationships were strained and sometimes broken by the stress of the war and subsequent upheavals. Demographically, Europe was increasingly a civilization in which cities, rather than rural agricultural areas, were the focal points of power and activity. There, urban working classes saw their political power grow as trade unions gained acceptance and membership. In many countries, social democratic and socialist parties successfully spoke to this growing constituency, and more often than in the past, few governments were able to ignore the desires of their working classes. These same years also brought growth in the middle or white-collar class, which tended to support a liberal political structure, while remaining conservative in temperament.

One significant change that transcended class was the emancipation of women, a trend wartime labor needs accelerated. Having gained access to many occupations that were previously restricted to men, European women pressed home the suffrage issue. In England, Parliament had granted the franchise to older, prosperous women in 1918 and within a decade removed even those qualifications. The republican constitution of Germany provided female suffrage in 1919. Women's suffrage was also granted in Czechoslovakia, Poland, Hungary, the Low Countries and the Scandinavian nations that had not accorded women the vote before the war, as had Finland and Norway. In France, Switzerland, Italy and the more conservative southern and eastern European states, women's suffrage was yet to be realized. Nonetheless, in both northern and southern Europe, more women gained access to higher education and the professions and political power that had been denied them in the past.

A fundamental demographic legacy of the recent war restrained an even more rapid liberalization and democratization of European society. Though the old political elite may have been discredited by their handling of the conflict, there was, in the postwar period, no vibrant new generation to supplant them. The war had claimed many of the most promising of Europe's youth; until a new generation that was committed to democratic ideals reached political maturity, leadership remained with the aging statesmen who had blundered into the catastrophe in 1914. Given the multitude of domestic and international challenges in the interwar period, the absence of new and innovative political leadership was sorely felt.

Doubtful Restoration: European Democracy in the 1920s

The First World War and its consequences badly strained the social, political and economic fabric of the major western European democracies. Though peace brought hopes of a restoration of stability, political leaders in many nations quickly found that both unresolved issues from the prewar era and new challenges born of the war posed difficulties that could not be easily surmounted.

GREAT BRITAIN: DIMINISHED HOPE AND FADED GLORY

Britain's wartime government had promised returning veterans "a fit country for heroes to live in," but postwar realities quickly dimmed that vision. The overwhelming reality that limited policy alternatives in the 1920s was an economy badly damaged by war. Great Britain finished the war as a creditor and debtor nation, owed nearly $18 billion by European allies and Germany, but itself owing more than $4 billion to the United States. Neither the United States nor France was receptive to suggestions to reduce or eliminate the debts. The latter was counting on German reparations to fund reconstruction. U.S. President Calvin Coolidge dismissed suggestions that war debts be forgiven with a characteristically terse rejoinder: "They hired the money, didn't they?" To make matters worse, Britain had forfeited many of its markets, as the United States became the principal trading partner of Latin America while Japan subsumed British markets in Asia. Industrial recovery was made more problematic by an aging British industrial plant and continuing difficulties in the three industries that had driven the economy in the nineteenth century: coal mining, shipbuilding and cotton manufacturing. A return to the gold standard at mid-decade had the effect of increasing the cost of British exports. Declining exports contributed to rising unemployment, which became one of the most persistent political issues of the decade, as one in seven workers went jobless. Widespread inflation, at some points driving wholesale prices to 225 percent of prewar levels, exacerbated these circumstances. Clearly, hard economic realities would shape the contours of postwar British life.

The 1920s also brought a significant shift in national politics. Though wartime Prime Minister David Lloyd George's coalition government remained intact until 1922, continuing economic difficulties and objections by some Conservatives to the 1921 Irish Treaty weakened it. The treaty followed years of strife in Ireland, accelerated by the failure to implement the 1914 Home Rule Act and by the Easter Rebellion of 1916. The treaty granted dominion status to the southern Catholic counties, while the Protestant north retained political ties with Britain. Nonetheless, some diehard Conservatives denounced it as a sellout of "Unionist" principles. These circumstances brought Andrew Bonar Law to power as prime minister with a purely Conservative ministry. Subsequent elections revealed an important trend—the Liberal Party's power was declining as the Labour Party, which was increasingly attractive to the working classes, gained growing support. Most immediately, however, the Conservatives remained in power, with Stanley Baldwin succeeding Bonar Law upon the latter's death in 1923. The continuing economic slump and the government's economic retrenchment policies, which included cutbacks in housing subsidies, set the stage for the Labour party's first government in 1923.

Coming to power in 1924 under the leadership of Ramsay MacDonald, the Labour Party propounded moderate socialist policies and a humanitarian creed. Trade unionists, socialists, intellectuals, former Liberals and working men and women comprised its main support. MacDonald, the illegitimate son of a Scotswoman, had genuine working-class credentials and was dedicated to the idea that the government had a responsibility to alleviate the social and economic ills that beset Britain. In practice this meant unemployment benefits, improved pensions for the elderly and government housing subsidies. A wave of anticommunist sentiment, fueled in part by a new trade treaty negotiated with

the Soviet Union but more immediately by the so-called "Zinoviev Letter," cut short the efforts of this first Labour government. The letter, ostensibly written by Gregory Zinoviev, secretary of the Communist International, urged Communists in Britain to prepare the groundwork for an armed uprising. Conservatives succeeded in linking the Labour Party to the letter, though it was later proven to be a forgery. The "Red Scare," together with growing public skepticism about the cost and utility of Labour policies, helped return the Conservatives to power in 1924 as support for the Liberals continued to decline.

Baldwin's second ministry coincided with a period of general diplomatic and economic stabilization and the Conservatives now hoped to restore "sane, commonsense government." That meant a rejection of "socialistic" measures and a reduction of trade union power. Rising antagonisms came to a head in the "Great Strike" of 1926, the only general strike in British history. Workers, demanding higher pay and better conditions, only aroused the ire of those that the strike inconvenienced. The Labour Party remained conspicuously aloof from the fray and the strike was broken in two weeks, which was a severe setback for the trade unions. In the years that followed, the Baldwin government did not ignore social needs, but was unwilling to pursue costly programs that went against the grain of fiscal conservatism. Though unemployment decreased in the second half of the decade, it remained an issue and Britain never enjoyed the degree of prosperity that the United States did. By 1929, overly cautious and unimaginative Conservative policies provided Labour with a second chance. Following elections, Ramsay MacDonald again became prime minister. It would fall to the Labour Party to meet the challenges of the world depression that was only months away.

FRANCE: UNEASY VICTOR

Of the major Allied powers, France was perhaps most deeply wounded by the war. Some 1.5 million Frenchmen had died; years of warfare ravaged much of northeastern France, ruining both agricultural and industrial areas. The war had revealed some shocking vulnerabilities that ate away at national pride; neither the French army nor French industry had proved capable of defeating Germany without significant external aid. The army mutinies of 1917 raised troubling questions about national *élan*. A falling birthrate suggested broader national decline. In consequence, a conservative, nationalist impulse shaped politics in the early years of the decade, built on the feeling that Germany should bear the cost of French reconstruction. Postwar elections brought to power the National Bloc, a conservative coalition led by Raymond Poincaré. The Bloc also drew strength from the intense anticommunism that pervaded postwar France. Poincaré's policy of rigid enforcement of the reparations provisions of the Versailles treaty ultimately proved disastrous. When the German government defaulted on payments in 1923, French army units occupied the industrial Ruhr Valley, provoking some deadly confrontations with uncooperative German workers. Eventually interceding to resolve the crisis, the United States, working through banker Charles G. Dawes, was instrumental in producing the Dawes Plan. Formulated by a commission, the plan included foreign loans to enable Germany to meet reparations obligations, extended the schedule for reparations and reduced Allied

war debts. The political damage was done, however, and the 1924 elections brought defeat for the National Bloc.

The new government was the *Cartel des Gauches*, a left-of-center coalition comprised of Radicals and Socialists and led by Edouard Herriot. The greatest challenge proved to be the state of national finance. Even before the war the government had failed to impose adequate taxation and control the currency supply. Now inflation set in, bringing down the Cartel in 1926. France, somewhat like Britain, now returned to conservative government after a brief leftist interlude. Poincaré, returning as premier, focused on salvaging the value of the franc, a central concern of the middle and upper classes, by raising consumption taxes. Though he succeeded in stabilizing the franc, Poincaré proved incapable of restoring political stability. The working classes were adversely affected by his financial measures and were prone to blame their situation on monied interests who were believed to control national politics. A general perception arose that self-serving politicians and entrenched government bureaucrats were standing in the way of long-needed social and economic reforms. Indeed, in France, as had been the case in Britain, the absence of innovative leadership, perhaps attributable to wartime casualties, contributed to a growing disillusionment with parliamentary government. In the following decade, the social and economic strains of the world depression pushed this political disillusionment to dangerous levels.

GERMANY: THE WEIMAR REPUBLIC

Few democratic governments have faced as many challenges at their inception as did Germany's Weimar Republic. Proclaimed at the moment of defeat in war, Germany's new republican government was faced within months by economic disarray, a starving populace, a disillusioned army in the midst of demobilization and violent political revolution in the nation's capital. In June 1919, the same struggling government was forced to accept the humiliating terms of the Treaty of Versailles. Given these formidable challenges and others that followed in the early 1920s, the stabilization of the Weimar Republic by mid-decade was a significant accomplishment. The provisional republic proclaimed in November 1918 was the first experiment in liberal government since the failed revolution of 1848; Germans had no significant experience with truly representative government and the political culture of Wilhelmine Germany had stultified the development of liberal ideas and institutions.

Social Democrats who had long sought a more liberal political order dominated the first postwar government. Their leader, Frederick Ebert, was to become the first president of the new republic. Most immediately, however, the mere existence of the new government was problematic. Radicalized sailors had mutinied at Kiel, while a socialist republic was proclaimed in Bavaria. A more direct threat came from a communist faction known as the Spartacist League, led by radical intellectuals Rosa Luxemburg and Karl Liebknecht. The Spartacists, convinced that there would be no fundamental change in a "bourgeois" regime, led an armed uprising in Berlin in early January 1919. The disorders led Ebert to turn to the army high command for support, thereby forfeiting any opportunity to end the military's disproportionate and reactionary influence on politics. *Freikorps*, volunteer units of demobilized soldiers who held little sympathy for radicals, aided the army in brutally crushing the revolt. Luxemburg and Liebknecht were both murdered while in military custody. The Spartacist Revolt left many Germans with an innate dread of communist revolution, a fear that the political right would capitalize on for years.

The Weimar Constitution of 1919 created a parliamentary government with a nominal presidency. A chancellor and ministry governed with a bicameral legislature, or *Reichstag*. Though this structure held promise, special powers granted to the president held the potential for abuse. Article 48 authorized the president to rule by executive decree in emergency situations; some years later, Adolf Hitler cynically used this feature to subvert the constitution. The most immediate problem, however, concerned continuing efforts by extremists of both the left and right to overthrow the government. Even as the "Bavarian Socialist Republic" collapsed in February, a communist uprising in Munich threatened the integrity of the new republic. A greater challenge came in 1920 when Wolfgang Kapp, a former Imperial official and *Freikorps* leader, briefly seized control of Berlin in a planned military takeover. A general strike by German workers forced Kapp to concede defeat and flee. In the next two years, as ultranationalist groups proliferated, political assassinations took the lives of Matthias Erzberger, the leader of the Centre party, and Walter Rathenau, the foreign minister.

1923 brought the low point of the Republic's fortunes. General postwar economic dislocation, coupled with the ruinous reparations imposed at Versailles, led to default and the French occupation of the Ruhr. Throughout the country, inflation ravaged savings and destroyed buying power. The German mark ceased to have any real value; by November, a single U.S. dollar bought 4.2 trillion marks. Barter became a common means of transacting business. The destructive effects of the 1923 inflation were perhaps most felt by the middle classes, especially the young, who suffered both financial ruin and a loss of social status. The crisis of 1923 damaged public faith in the efficacy of traditional authority and the Weimar regime, a development with short- and long-term consequences. The extent of extremist dissatisfaction with the republic became evident in November, when Adolf Hitler, leader of the German National Socialist Workers' Party, attempted to seize control of Munich as a prelude to a national revolution. Police and army units foiled Hitler's ill-time coup and the would-be *Führer* was jailed, but the episode seemed further evidence of a nation unraveling.

Weimar's salvation came in part through the efforts of a new chancellor, Gustav Stresemann, who stabilized the mark in November, fixing the rate at one trillion of the old marks to one of the new *Rentenmarks*. The financial impact was devastating for individuals and businesses alike, but it marked the beginning of Germany's economic recovery. By 1924, with all Europe cognizant of the importance of German economic stability, the Dawes Committee implemented policies that ended the immediate crisis.

The years 1924–1929 were an era of promise for the Weimar Republic. With the economy stabilized, political radicalism held less appeal and the German government directed its efforts toward building political democracy and reassuring neighbors that the new Germany aspired to a responsible role in international affairs. A major step in this direction came in 1925 when European leaders met in Locarno, Switzerland, to consider some postwar issues. Stresemann, now foreign secretary, signed the treaty by which

Germany guaranteed its borders with France and Belgium. Though no similar guarantee was reached for Germany's eastern frontiers, the "spirit of Locarno" seemed to point to a new age of international cooperation. Some controversy arose the same year when, following the death of President Ebert, German voters elected the former field marshal Paul von Hindenburg as his successor. Fears of resurgent German militarism were offset somewhat when Germany was admitted to the League of Nations in 1926, and the aging Hindenburg seemed no immediate threat to German democracy.

During these same years a remarkable cultural flowering occurred, in part the product of a broad perception that the war had destroyed the remaining edifices of tradition. In 1919, writer Paul Ernst had proclaimed, "Our age is over! Thank God, it is over! A new age dawns that will be different!" Weimar Germany was a veritable crucible of modernity, nurturing an amazing profusion of artistic and literary talent. The Expressionist drama of Bertolt Brecht challenged convention, while his *Three Penny Opera*, set to music by the equally innovative Kurt Weill, drew critical acclaim. Walter Gropius set new directions in architecture with his "Bauhaus" school, which sought to "break down the arrogant barrier between craftsman and artist." Paul Hindemith and Erst Krenek, who incorporated jazz into classical compositions, continued the musical revolution launched by the atonalists. Writers Thomas Mann and Hermann Hesse, among others, used their literary art as a vehicle for exploring the breakdown and transformation of European society. Though themes of despair and pessimism marked some of these works, there was nonetheless a perception that such cultural ferment indicated vitality as much as decay. By 1929, the Weimar Republic seemed to have surmounted the most critical challenges. Though parliamentary politics often seemed fractious, radical groups such as Hitler's Nazis appeared to be relegated to the margins of society. Political stability, prosperity and a newly recognized place among the responsible powers confirmed the success of the new democratic Germany. Few could have foreseen that the Weimar Republic would enjoy only four more years of existence.

The Totalitarian Challenge

The term *totalitarianism* is often used to describe a form of dictatorship that emerged in the interwar years, most notably in Italy, the Soviet Union and Germany. As a concept, it received its fullest scholarly examination in Hanna Arendt's *The Origins of Totalitarianism* (1948), which asserted that the interplay between historical anti-Semitism, imperialism and nationalism produced a new phenomenon of the total state. While there is still disagreement among historians as to the legitimacy of the concept, those who accept it define the totalitarian state as having certain discernible characteristics: a leader with near absolute power, a dogmatic and exclusivist ideology, a single mass party, a police apparatus willing to impose terror, and control over the communications media. Totalitarianism also meant the politicization of institutions such as public education, the courts, the bureaucracy and sometimes even churches. All were required to conform to the state's ideological dictates. Fundamentally, totalitarian regimes required the active support and participation of all citizens, as the barrier between public and private life all but disappeared. Contemporary advo-

cates of totalitarian rule often presented it as the inescapable culmination of historical forces, a new concept of government fitted to the demands of the twentieth century. Fascism, communism and later National Socialism were all hailed as new ideologies for a new age, destined to supplant the dying liberal creed that had shaped Europe in the previous century.

ITALY: THE TRIUMPH OF FASCISM

Liberalism had never developed deep or broad roots in Italy since unification, and in the eyes of many, parliamentary rule had done little to resolve the nation's enduring social and economic problems. The desire to achieve national greatness was one of the forces driving Italy into the war in 1915, but such hopes remained unrealized. For most, the war brought only further disappointments. The shame of the defeat at Caporetto in 1917 erased the short-lived pride engendered by Italian military victories earlier in the war. The decisions made in Paris in 1919 dashed hopes for territorial gains; Italian acquisitions from the old Habsburg lands were inconsequential. The colorful poet Gabriele D'Annunzio, leading a group of outraged nationalists, promptly seized the Adriatic port of Fiume, which had been assigned to Yugoslavia, and occupied the city in defiance of their own government. Elsewhere, disillusioned veterans returned to their towns and villages to find social unrest, a depressed economy and growing left-wing radicalism. Landowners and businessmen alike grew fearful of the expropriations that socialist revolution would bring. Trade unions agitated for working-class gains, threatening strikes and factory seizures. The shifting parliamentary coalitions that were a hallmark of

Italian government seemed powerless to address the increasingly chaotic situation.

These were the circumstances that offered an opportunity for Benito Mussolini, the son of a socialist blacksmith father and a devout Catholic mother. Born in 1883 in Predappio, Mussolini proved to be a sullen, stubborn child who quickly gained a reputation for vandalism and violent behavior, once expelled from school for stabbing a classmate. Completing his education, Mussolini found work as a substitute teacher, but indiscipline and drifting, with sporadic work at menial jobs, characterized his early adulthood. Moving to Switzerland in 1902, he established contacts with both Russian and Italian socialists and his enthusiasm for socialism grew. By 1912 he was editor of *Avanti*, the official newspaper of Italy's Socialist Party. From this position he became an outspoken advocate of antimilitarism, anticlericalism and revolutionary violence. As it had for Adolf Hitler, the First World War proved to be a defining period in Mussolini's life. Though he initially advocated the Socialist position of neutrality, Mussolini feared that Italy was once again being left behind by great events. Expelled from the Socialist party because of his interventionist views, Mussolini set up a newspaper in 1914 to agitate for belligerency on the Allied side. The following year he joined the army, serving some months at the front and evidently finding life in the trenches fairly acceptable. In 1917, he was discharged from the army after being wounded by a malfunctioning grenade launcher, having risen no higher than corporal. Mussolini returned to his newspaper, attacking the cowardice of the government and the defeatism of the military leaders. Frustrated by Italy's apparent ineptitude, Mussolini began to perceive the need for a dictator, someone who could dispense with the troublesome parliament, suppress dissenters who prevented national unity and effectively militarize the nation. Reversing many of his earlier positions by 1918, Mussolini was ready to capitalize on widespread dissatisfaction with both the war and the peace.

In March 1919 Mussolini founded the movement which, within two years, became the National Fascist Party. The initial organization, dubbed the *Fasci di Combattimento* (Combat Group) was comprised of disaffected veterans and soon took on a paramilitary appearance, replete with uniforms—these streetfighters would later be called the Blackshirts. They proved more than willing to utilize violence as a political weapon, attacking and beating socialists, trade unionists and other opponents. As the political and economic situation deteriorated, Mussolini attracted broader support from the landlord and business classes, who feared communism. By 1921, the Fascist party had won thirty-five seats in parliament and Mussolini, styling himself *Il Duce*, or leader, began to stress the need for discipline, an ordered society and a rejuvenated Italy. The disunity of the parliamentary opposition afforded Mussolini his opportunity in October 1922 when he organized his Fascist legions for a threatened "March on Rome" unless he was named as prime minister. Cowed by Mussolini's bluster and uncertain of the army's loyalty, King Victor Emmanuel III gave in to *Il Duce's* demand. Fears of communist revolution, resentment over wartime humiliations and weariness with the ineptitude of parliamentary government left many Italians willing to give Mussolini's as yet ambiguous approach a chance.

As an ideology, Fascism was an often-inconsistent amalgam of ideas. Presented as Mussolini's unique contribution to the field of political theory, it promised revolutionary change and extolled some conservative traditions. Some elements of Fascist thought were immediately evident—the emphasis on action, violence and military virtues in service to the national cause. Some of these concepts had intellectual antecedents in the writing of the irrationalists, such as Georges Sorel and Friedrich Nietzsche. Fascism was also defined in large part by what it was against: liberalism, democracy, communism, socialism, parliamentary rule and individualism. For Mussolini, the exhaltation of the state was at the core of Fascism: "The State, as conceived of and as created by fascism, is a spiritual and moral fact in itself. . . . The State is not only a living reality of the present, it is also linked with the past and above all the future, and thus transcending the brief limits of individual life, it represents the immanent spirit of the nation." Ultimately this concept would be summarized in the oft-repeated slogan, "Everything within the State, Nothing outside the State, Nothing against the State." Mussolini made clear his disdain for individualism. "The individual exists only insofar as he is subordinated to the interests of the state," he wrote, "and as civilization becomes more complex, so the liberty of the individual must be increasingly restricted." The "New Fascist Man," he believed, would realize his fullest potential when he was educated to "Believe, Obey, Fight."

To realize this vision, Mussolini moved toward creating a dictatorship. Though the monarchy remained, it posed no obstacle. Blackshirt militias, now state-funded, terrorized political opponents, precluding effective resistance. The great opportunity for the Fascist Party came in 1923 with the passage of the Acerbo Law, which provided that any party receiving a minimum of 25 percent of the vote in parliamentary elections would be granted two-thirds of the seats in the

Chamber of Deputies. This transformed the Fascists into the majority party and Mussolini proceeded to rapidly consolidate his power. Mussolini brought the army, police and civil administration under Fascist control and gradually restricted civil liberties. In 1925, Mussolini announced the abolition of all opposition parties and proceeded to establish the rudiments of a totalitarian state, expelling non-Fascists from the cabinet, suppressing trade unions and imposing media censorship. Within a year all elections ended; henceforth a Grand Fascist Council selected members of the Chamber of Deputies and the Fascist party itself was soon reduced to a mere bureaucratic appendage of Mussolini's regime. A secret police organization, OVRA (Organization to Watch and Repress Anti-Facism), was created to deal with dissidents. Fascist youth groups organized the young for indoctrination and physical culture training.

Mussolini next sought to address the country's social and economic problems through the creation of the "corporate state," which promised to resolve labor–management disputes and provide a more equitable society by restructuring the industrial economy. Under corporatism, a "corporation" committee of owners, workers and government representatives administered each branch of industry, settling such basic issues as wages and hours. The intention was to end the traditional antagonisms between the groups, but generally the policy favored industrialists, as there were no labor organizations other than Fascist unions, and they adhered to the government line. Corporatism was, to a large degree, a charade, though the generally improving economic conditions of the later 1920s tended to obscure this reality. Mussolini, accordingly, could claim credit for Italy's economic recovery.

Many aspects of Fascist social policy were conservative, stressing traditional values and an extremely restricted sphere for women, whose primary duty was motherhood. Large families were encouraged so that Italy might become a powerful and feared military nation; special prizes were awarded to mothers with more than twelve children. Likewise, Fascist law banned contraceptives and abortion, imposed a tax on bachelors and provided penalties for homosexual activities. Other discriminatory legislation aimed to discourage women from seeking higher education or pursuing professional careers. Despite Mussolini's efforts, the Italian birth rate continued to decline into the 1930s.

Greater success came in the area of church–state relations. Though privately an atheist, Mussolini recognized the importance of the Roman Catholic Church in Italy, especially as a potential source of opposition to his regime. This helps explain in part his cynical advocacy of conservative social policies that concorded with positions taken by the Catholic Church. More importantly, the Vatican had refused to recognize the unified Italian state since 1870, and Mussolini realized that his regime would gain considerable legitimacy if he could reach an accord with the Church. Thus in 1929, Mussolini signed the Lateran Pact, which recognized the Vatican as a sovereign state and restored religious instruction to classrooms. In return, Pope Pius XI acknowledged the existence and legitimacy of Mussolini's Italy, hailing the dictator as "the man sent by Providence."

By the late 1920s, Mussolini's accomplishments had won him numerous admirers, including the leader of Germany's struggling Nazi party, Adolf Hitler. In the years to come, Hitler applied many lessons learned from the Italian dictator. Extensive praise also came from more respectable figures, however. Winston Churchill, George Bernard Shaw and Sigmund Freud were among those who lauded Mussolini for restoring discipline and order in Italy. As far away as New York City's Italian quarter, prideful Italian immigrants displayed portraits of *Il Duce* in shop windows. Increasingly, however, Mussolini's growing braggadocio and self-conceit helped to shape negative and even derisory perceptions of the Fascist leader. By the late 1920s, the dictator's immense ego required that he be acknowledged as the sole source of all inspiration and genius. On village walls across Italy the painted slogan "Mussolini is Always Right" testified to his infallibility. Within a few years, Italian journalists were required to capitalize pronouns referring to Mussolini, as though he were a deity. Convinced of the importance to his rule of modern communications techniques, Mussolini was constantly before the public. His famous balcony harangues, in which he strutted, gestured wildly and adopted a variety of melodramatic poses before massive crowds, were broadcast by radio and filmed. He was the subject of innumerable newsreels, always engaged in some dramatic activity, the exemplar of Fascist energy and dynamism. Theater audiences could thrill to Mussolini swimming, skiing, harvesting wheat while shirtless, wrestling lion cubs, piloting a variety of aircraft and reviewing his Blackshirt legions. A former journalist, Mussolini was well aware of the importance of public relations. There were skeptics, however, who perceived that perhaps there was more style than substance to this regime. Detractors abroad referred to Mussolini variously as the "Carnival Caesar" and the "Sawdust Caesar." Though some depicted Mussolini as a charlatan, he was a

Fig. 5-2 Italian dictator Benito Mussolini offers the fascist salute to parading troops during a 1937 visit with German *Führer* and Chancellor Adolf Hitler in Munich, Germany. (Pearson Education, Corporate Digital Archive, Corbis)

complex individual who succeeded in creating the model for what was hailed as a revolutionary new way of social and political organization. Historians still disagree as to how truly totalitarian Fascist Italy was, with some suggesting that the regime never achieved the degree of control or brutality that Hitler's Nazi state did. Others maintain that Fascist Italy was foremost a product of Mussolini's adeptness at public relations and propaganda, an exciting backdrop that provided a worthy stage for the colorful dictator, but ultimately offering little substance. The true test of the regime's viability did not occur until the 1940s, when Europe was again plunged into war.

RUSSIA: SECURING THE BOLSHEVIK REVOLUTION

Russia entered the 1920s as a severely battered nation, ravaged by the world war, two revolutions, foreign intervention and civil war. Though the Bolsheviks had defeated the anti-communist "White Armies," it was a Pyrrhic victory. War communism, with its forced requisitions, had shattered an already badly strained economy, alienated peasant producers and contributed to an exodus from the cities, as starving Russians sought food in a desolate countryside. Demobilized soldiers roaming rural areas contributed to the chaos. Widespread famine brought suffering to new levels, as an estimated 7.5 million people perished in the "Great Famine" of 1921–1922. In March 1921, a mutiny by disaffected sailors at Kronstadt impelled the Bolshevik regime to move in a new direction. Lenin, having long since established his power, continued to stress the two principles of the party's supreme authority and centralized control; while new policy alternatives were debated within high party circles, there was to be no dissent once Lenin had decided his course.

Convinced that circumstances precluded the creation of a socialist economy, Lenin implemented the New Economic Policy. A "tax in kind" replaced the seizure of "surplus" food and peasant producers were permitted to sell what remained, the hope being that this would drastically improve food production. The *kulaks*, a marginally more prosperous group of peasants, were especially encouraged to increase production. The regime authorized free trade and free markets, as small industries were returned to private ownership. Large industries, banking, transport and communications remained under state control. The NEP was a temporary compromise, born of harsh realities, and Lenin intended that the course toward a purely socialist economy would be resumed at a propitious time. In the early 1920s, however, recovery was slow and Soviet Russia accepted such expedients as help from the American Relief Administration and encouraged foreign-financed development projects.

Political stabilization followed in 1923, as a constitution was introduced for the new Union of Soviet Socialist Republics. This document defined the USSR as a federation of independent republics, with a parliamentary system of government grounded on popular democracy, guaranteed by near-universal suffrage. The reality remained otherwise; the real power in the USSR rested in the Communist Party, the structure of which paralleled the government. The Communist Party was the only legal party and important agencies of state such as the secret political police, which had by now evolved into the NKVD, served its purposes. Control of the Communist party was virtually synonymous with control of the USSR. By 1924, this aspect of Soviet political life assumed new importance as Lenin, worn out by years of activity and stress, which had contributed to several strokes, weakened and died. There was immediately controversy over Lenin's "political testament," which presented his assessments of six potential successors. In particular, Lenin was concerned about Stalin, who as General Secretary of the party's Central Committee had "accumulated enormous power in his hands." "I am not sure," Lenin wrote, "whether he will be able to use this power with due care." The dying party leader had urged the selection of a new general secretary "more tolerant, more loyal and less capricious."

The man known as Stalin (a revolutionary alias meaning "Man of Steel") was born Joseph Dzugashvili in a Georgian village in 1879. He entered an Orthodox seminary in 1894, but was soon drawn to Marxist politics and expelled. Having cast his lot with the Bolsheviks in 1903, Stalin spent the next decade in exile or in jail, successfully escaping both several times. When the February Revolution broke out, Stalin was again in exile in Siberia, but somehow made the arduous trek to Petrograd before the Bolshevik coup in October. Though he served on the military revolutionary council, he played only a minor role in the revolution of 1917. Both Lenin and Trotsky overshadowed him during the Civil War, and by the early 1920s many in the party undoubtedly agreed with Trotsky's characterization of Stalin as a "mediocrity," a slow-witted Georgian peasant. Described by a contemporary as a "gray blur," Stalin's very innocuousness may have fed the complacency of his opponents. He had an acute comprehension of the nature of power politics and his tenure as general secretary acquainted him with the intricate workings of the party apparatus, an advantage that would become obvious within a few years.

As the struggle for the succession evolved, a major policy controversy worked ultimately to Stalin's advantage. In the years since the Bolshevik Revolution, Trotsky had advocated "permanent revolution," insisting that socialism in the Soviet Union would be secure only when world revolution had defeated capitalism. To this end, the Communist International had been established in 1919 to assist revolutionary movements abroad. By the time of Lenin's death, the failure of this policy seemed evident, given capitalist Europe's recovery. Stalin, adroitly arguing for "socialism in one country," ultimately won the party to his side. In the meantime, he deftly appointed his supporters to numerous party positions. By 1927, Stalin's maneuverings within the high echelons of the party succeeded in isolating Trotsky, whose views were now deemed subversive and antirevolutionary. Trotsky was deprived of all his party offices and expelled from the party together with a number of his followers, who were likewise denounced as "deviationists." Either unwilling or unable to call on the Red Army for support during this long struggle, Trotsky was exiled to Siberia and eventually deported in 1929. Though he found refuge in Mexico, he could not escape Stalin's reach. In 1940, a Stalinist agent murdered the exiled intellectual. By 1928, Stalin was the undisputed power in the Communist Party. He now confronted the challenge of "building socialism" in a nation only marginally recovered from the depredations of years of war and internal strife.

Depression Decade: The European Crisis of the 1930s

In 1919, British economist John Maynard Keynes published *The Economic Consequences of the Peace*, a scathing criticism of the postwar settlement. The Allied governments, he argued, had focused on national and territorial issues, virtually ignoring the economic consequences of their decisions. The burdensome reparations imposed on Germany would, he argued, have a damaging impact far beyond that country's borders—they would distort the European and hence the international economy. Similarly, Keynes cautioned that the dissolution of the Austro-Hungarian Empire would disrupt what had been an integrated central European economic entity. Later, Keynes pointed out the obvious flaw in the Dawes Plan, which was proffered as a solution to Germany's financial crisis in 1924: "The United States lends money to Germany, Germany transfers its equivalent to the allies, the allies pass it back to the United States government. Nothing real passes—no one is a penny worse."

The 1919 treaties did not in themselves bring about the depression of the 1930s. The general disregard for economic issues at Paris does suggest, however, that few Europeans understood how radically the war and the subsequent settlement had altered the world economy. In the decade before the collapse, most governments responded to new economic challenges with conventional solutions such as sound money, adherence to the gold standard and efforts to balance budgets. In the short term, Europe's economy appeared to recover. This new stability ultimately proved deceptive, merely cloaking structural weaknesses in national economies and obscuring the more fundamental challenge posed by the dislocation of international economic relationships.

The world war itself left economic scars in Europe; the cost of physical damages alone was estimated to be $150 million. Production losses and a drastic reduction of agricultural output must be added to this total. Even more significant in the years to come was the loss of foreign markets, with the United States and Japan stepping into areas once dominated by the warring European powers. Traditional European export markets in Asia and Latin America also shrank as new manufacturing sectors arose there. A further blow to European exports came in the early 1920s, when the U.S. Congress imposed high tariffs on imported manufactured goods in an effort to protect the American economy. Thus throughout the decade, European efforts to obtain cash revenues through exports met with numerous obstacles. The scarcity of export income made the repayment of war debts all the more problematic. Wartime losses in merchant fleets further retarded European postwar recovery, with Britain surrendering supremacy on the seas to the United States; Germany's merchant fleet was expropriated in partial fulfillment of reparations payments. Rising inflation in the early 1920s compounded these circumstances even as the prices of iron, steel and coal fell off.

A more general problem was the inability or unwillingness of the major powers to reconcile the interlinked issues of reparations and war debts. The United States preferred that reparations be renounced or at least kept to a minimum, but nonetheless insisted that the European powers repay their loans. The French advocated canceling war debts but demanded that reparations be paid in full. The British, never as convinced of the utility or rectitude of reparations as the French, proposed forgiving both reparations and debts, but received no encouragement from the Americans, who nevertheless continued to ask for repayment of wartime loans. Given this impasse, those efforts made to stabilize the European economy in the 1920s were mere bandaids, obscuring but not healing deep economic wounds. As the American postwar economy improved and then boomed, European economies benefited somewhat from American investments. By the late 1920s however, the surging American stock market was already drawing investments away from Europe. Following the stock market collapse of October 1929, American investors rushed to liquidate remaining European holdings, thus beginning a long and damaging flight of capital from Europe. U.S. President Herbert Hoover, who believed the causes of the widening depression to be international, approved the strengthening of the tariff wall around the United States in 1930, raising import duties to historically high levels.

As European governments struggled to come to terms with rapidly rising unemployment and declining industrial activity, the international monetary system began to collapse. The Kreditanstalt, Austria's largest bank, already weakened by the effects of the eastern European agricultural depression, stopped payments in May 1931. As the spreading shock wave toppled several of the largest German banks, President Hoover proposed a moratorium on all reparations payments and war debts. Though European powers quickly agreed, the damage was long since done. Twenty-four countries were forced to abandon the gold standard by 1932 and the United States did likewise in 1933. With the international monetary system in complete disarray and the United States reduced to a position of economic impotence, Europe faced the worst depression of the 20th century.

Democratic Europe: Challenge and Response

The 1930s brought a multitude of challenges to Europe's democracies. The world depression not only created new social and economic problems, but also exacerbated those that had gone unresolved since the end of the Great War. In some instances, existing political institutions, ideas and leaders seemed inadequate to the challenges of the decade. Some nations, such as Great Britain, stumbled uncertainly through these years,

never facing a serious danger of collapse, but never fully rising to the occasion. Just "getting by" in such times was often enough. France, however, confronted challenges that literally threatened the existence of the Third Republic. With somewhat more stable social structures and political institutions, the Scandinavian nations weathered the storm of the depression through innovative new approaches.

GREAT BRITAIN: COMING UP FOR AIR

For Britain, the most immediate consequence of the U.S. stock market collapse was the withdrawal of American investments and a rapid increase in unemployment. The Labor government of Ramsay MacDonald soon faced a terrible reality—unemployment benefits, rather than being increased, would have to be drastically reduced or Britain would face bankruptcy. The political crisis provoked by this situation climaxed in 1931 with the creation of the National Government, an inter-party coalition headed by MacDonald but dominated by Conservatives. In meeting the challenges of the Depression, the National Government generally adhered to orthodox economic counsels, implementing deflationary measures and reducing expenditures. Economist John Maynard Keynes, who argued that only energetic government intervention could bring about recovery, challenged these traditional measures. Government expenditures, even deficit spending, Keynes insisted, were crucial to increasing purchasing power and the demand for goods. The conventional wisdom, which held that governments should simply wait out depression, was inane. "In the long run we are all dead!" Keynes lamented. "Economists set themselves too useless a task if in tempestuous seasons they can only tell us that when the storm is long past the ocean will be flat again." A proponent of government-sponsored employment, Keynes found no large audience in Britain, though the New Deal in the United States reflected some of his theories. The Conservative-dominated National Government took at most cautious steps, maintaining low interest rates and promoting low-cost public housing, the latter project taking shape under the direction of Chancellor of the Exchequer Neville Chamberlain. By 1933, the years of highest unemployment were past. Propelled by a rearmament campaign after 1936, both employment and production improved steadily if unspectacularly through the later 1930s.

For Britain, the Depression did not bring the social disintegration and political crisis that occurred elsewhere in Europe. Rather, a general sense of public discouragement and apathy attended these years. The writer George Orwell successfully evoked this sense of ennui and marking time in his novel *Coming Up for Air* (1936). Orwell's middle-class, middle-age protagonist found little comfort in either the nostalgic past or the dull sameness of the present, his dilemma summarized in the words of a popular song: "He's dead, but he won't lie down." While the great majority of Englishmen likewise muddled through the Depression years, there were a few proponents of a more radical response. Sir Oswald Mosley, son of an aristocratic family and previously active in the Labour party, founded the British Union of Fascists in 1932. An admirer of both Mussolini and Hitler, Mosley sought to create a fascist movement in England, complete with squads of blackshirted thugs. Denouncing Jews, international finance capitalists and socialism, Mosley never attracted more than

20,000 adherents and achieved at best only minor notoriety.

The greatest political controversy of the 1930s did not involve radicalism, but rather the state of the monarchy. The death of George V in 1936 brought his son to the throne as Edward VIII, a monarch who was embroiled in controversy even before his coronation. A bachelor, Edward indicated his intent to marry Wallis Simpson, an American divorcee. This raised a constitutional issue and Stanley Baldwin, again prime minister, refused to authorize the coronation ceremony. Love triumphed and Edward abdicated his throne to marry Mrs. Simpson, a decision that provoked furious public controversy. In a nation still struggling out of economic depression and already confronted with the threat of a rearmed Germany, the sensation created by the "Abdication Crisis" now seems curiously disproportionate. It may have been indicative of a desire to escape the dreariness of the present and to delay confronting the uncertainties of a future in which the German threat figured prominently. For the moment, dull continuity was adequate. Baldwin retired as prime minister in 1937. His successor was Neville Chamberlain, a stubborn and unimaginative man who nonetheless had a reputation as an able administrator.

FRANCE: LAST YEARS OF THE THIRD REPUBLIC

Among the major western powers, France was the last to feel the impact of the world depression and, at least in most respects, felt it less. The French economy, with its equitable balance between agriculture and industry, remained relatively solid until 1932, when the franc was finally devalued. France did suffer rising unemployment, but it never achieved the dimensions it did in Britain or Germany. Rather, the depression seemed to exacerbate pre-existing social tensions and class divisions, which France's parliamentary system proved incapable of resolving. Some anxieties were a consequence of the recent world war; the horrendous losses cut deep into the French national psyche and produced pacifist impulses that cut across the political spectrum. Memories of the French inability to demonstrate either military or economic superiority during the world war compounded this deep-seated dread of another war. Demographic realities also fed perceptions of declining French national strength—the first postwar census indicated that the population was declining, and through the mid-1930s the birthrate continued to fall. Long before the depression affected France, a general sense of decline, together with a loss of confidence, had begun to shape the national outlook. One manifestation of these self-doubts was the Maginot Line, a complex system of fortifications along the Franco-German border. First authorized in 1929, the Maginot Line was indicative of a determination to avoid the carnage of 1914–1918. It also reflected a dangerously defensive mentality on the part of the French general staff, which was increasingly pessimistic about France's ability to win a future conflict with Germany. For the many French citizens who preferred not to even contemplate another war, the Maginot Line offered deceptive reassurance.

During the first postwar decade, French politicians had failed to address fundamental problems of government that had plagued the Third Republic since its inception. A weak presidency left disproportionate power with the national legislature, where the premier was confronted with the challenge of managing often-contentious multi-party parliamentary coalitions. The instability that was inherent in France's national government became all the more evident following the retirement of premier Raymond Poincaré, whose long career and commitment to republican principles commanded some respect. His successors lacked the experience and stature to force undisciplined deputies to focus on the emerging economic crisis. Those who preferred to dismiss the need for economic reforms were more comfortable with leaders like the cynical and self-serving Pierre Laval, whose name was to become synonymous with treason in 1940.

Given the absence of capable leadership and the inability of short-lived coalitions to address the nation's growing economic crisis, increasing political incoherence was inevitable. Between 1929 and 1934, successive governments lasted an average of three to four months. Public confidence in the government received another blow in 1934 when the Stavisky Affair drew national attention. A rather minor scandal involving Serge Stavisky, an unscrupulous promoter of fraudulent bonds, the incident assumed greater magnitude when Stavisky's suicide was followed by a bungled government investigation that had the appearance of a political cover-up. The government, it appeared, was not only inept but also corrupt, serving the objectives of powerful special interests. The burgeoning disillusionment with parliamentary government and the timid actions of the moderate parties drove a significant minority of French citizens toward the extremes of the political spectrum.

On the left, the French Communist Party attracted support from the urban working class, intellectuals and students with its promise of an end to capitalist exploitation. As the Communist International prohibited the French communists from participating in "bourgeois" governments, they contented themselves with incessant criticism of parliamentary government. The more ominous threat, however, appeared on the right, where extremists organized in paramilitary "Leagues" to advocate authoritarian solutions to the nation's crisis. Fascist organizations such as the *Croix de Feu* advocated the destruction of the republic, which was perceived as a weak form of government responsible for France's loss of vigor and grandeur. Other "Leagues" like *Action Français* and *Solidarite Français* variously promoted monarchy, ultra-Catholicism and anti-Semitism. What the groups held in common was disdain for democratic government, liberalism and the secular state. Most also professed admiration for Fascist regimes in Italy and Germany, suggesting that a French national revival might be brought about by similar means. Though membership in the Leagues was relatively small, their willingness to bring the streetfighting tactics of Hitler's stormtroopers to the streets of France threatened the precarious state of public order. In February 1934 the Stavisky Affair provided the Leagues with a pretext for an outburst of violent protest against the Third Republic. Thousands of paramilitary extremists poured into Paris streets, battling police and national guard troops, who barely prevented the rampaging mob from invading the Chamber of Deputies. After several days of bloody confrontations that left eighteen dead and hundreds wounded, the government succeeded in restoring a tenuous state of order.

The Leagues failed to produce a single charismatic leader to exploit the political chaos, as had been the case in Italy and Germany. Rather, the explosion of right-wing violence in early 1934 had the effect of uniting the French left in time for the 1936 elections. An alliance of Radicals, Socialists and Communists won an overwhelming victory and Socialist Leon Blum was named premier of the new Popular Front government. Hailed as a bulwark against antirepublican and Fascist forces, the Popular Front moved quickly to address the grievances of industrial workers through social and economic reforms. Blum won numerous concessions from employers, including a forty-hour workweek, a minimum wage, paid vacations for workers and the right to collective bargaining. The triumph proved short-lived, however, as the reforms were costly and the devaluation of the franc slowed the economy. Businessmen, always suspicious of Blum and the Socialists, were quick to blame his government for the deteriorating economic situation. The defection of the communists from the coalition further weakened the Popular Front.

For those on the extreme right, Blum was a focus of hatred from the outset. A cultured, humane Jewish Socialist, the Premier personified those aspects of the Third Republic that the far right most detested. In right-wing circles, the slogan "Better Hitler than Blum" was an increasingly frequent expression of disdain for the Socialist Premier. Foreign policy posed additional dilemmas. Though a resurgent Germany posed an obvious potential threat, the pro-fascist right and the pacifist left restrained Blum from pursuing serious rearmament policies. Any hint of efforts to seek a Franco-Soviet defensive accord to offset growing German power aroused vituperative denunciations from the French right. The defeatist attitude of the army's General Staff, which was notoriously antirepublican, restrained the government's actions further.

Prophesying disaster in the event of war with Germany, the military chiefs opposed any aggressively anti-German diplomatic initiatives. The high command also opposed efforts to modernize the French military, obtusely rejecting all proposed innovations, such as armored divisions and new types of aircraft, as unfeasible. In June 1937, Blum handed in his resignation, lamenting, "Everything that I have attempted to do has been blocked." The Popular Front staggered on into the next year, when it finally collapsed, yet another victim of the deep social and ideological divisions that left the Third Republic seriously weakened and incapable of responding effectively to the rapidly unfolding diplomatic crises of the late 1930s. The Radical-Socialist Paul Reynaud captured the frustration of many when he asked in a radio address that year, "Is it not time that we rise above ourselves, forget our party and class differences and become children of the same country, a country in danger? . . . Can it be that France has lost its instinct of self-preservation?" Within two years, Reynaud's warning proved shockingly prophetic.

THE MINOR DEMOCRACIES AND SCANDINAVIA

Although the smaller western European states of Denmark, Switzerland, Belgium and the Netherlands all felt the impact of the world depression, their political systems bore the stress relatively well. The Danes remained relatively satisfied with their constitutional monarchy. Switzerland, a multilingual nation with Protestant and Catholic cantons, grounded its system of federal democracy in a tradition of tolerance and compromise. A social welfare system established in the 1890s and a high standard of living insulated the mountainous country from the worst effects of the depression. Historically, Switzerland relied on geography and a policy of neutrality to avoid entanglement in great power confrontations. Belgium, a constitu-

tional monarchy, had also sought neutrality as a means of surviving in the midst of larger, more contentious powers, though this did not spare the Belgians from invasion in the First World War. Linguistic divisions between French- and Flemish-speaking Belgians were a source of some political antagonism and a minority of Flemings were attracted to Rexism, a Belgian version of fascism, during the 1930s. Otherwise, parliamentary government faced no serious challenge.

In the Netherlands, a conservative popular temper and a constitutional monarchy lessened radical political disruptions, and the Dutch government focused its efforts on building trade conventions with Scandinavia. It was here that some of the most unique political developments of the interwar years took place. Finland, long subject to tsarist autocracy, established a democratic government following the war. Socialist parties came to power in Norway and Sweden during the depression and implemented the policies that came to be referred to as the "Scandinavian Way." As the depression engulfed the two countries, their governments rejected balanced budgets and contraction and instead borrowed heavily to finance public works and increase purchasing power. Previously established social welfare systems were extended to provide assistance to those in need. Scandinavian socialism was not doctrinaire, but rather sought a "middle way," creating a mixed economy regulated by a coalition of government and private enterprise. The usual antagonism between labor and management was largely absent; both were willing to settle differences through compromise and arbitration. What made this possible was a Scandinavian outlook that tempered individualism with a commitment to community action. The cold climate and sparse homogeneous population of Scandinavia created circumstances in which collective action in defense of democratic ideals seemed a reasonable response to the crisis. This pragmatic approach offered hope that democracy remained viable at a time when democratic government was increasingly under assault.

The European Dictatorships

By the 1930s, Benito Mussolini's dismissal of democracy as a "deserted temple" seemed increasingly accurate. The viability of liberal, parliamentary government seemed questionable, given the inability of Europe's major democratic states to adequately address the mass social and economic distress born of the world depression. Likewise, the inherent deficiencies in capitalism were manifest in the millions of unemployed and distressed Europeans. The circumstances were advantageous for advocates of totalitarian ideologies, who promised to meet the economic crisis with radically new policies and to mobilize Europeans in dynamic, revitalized societies built on the foundation of state power.

THE SOVIET UNION: THE PATH TO STALINIST TERROR

Poised to launch the social and economic transformation of the Soviet Union in 1928, Joseph Stalin possessed few of the traits associated with powerful charismatic leaders. A physically unimpressive man, Stalin stood only 5′3″ tall and regularly wore elevator shoes to compensate for his small stature. He was an uninspiring public speaker whose addresses lacked dramatic gestures and memorable phrases, and was perhaps the least intellectual of the early Bolshevik leaders, lacking the theoretical and analytic abilities of either Lenin or Trotsky.

Shaped by the brutalities of the tsarist prison system and the incessant intrigue that was inherent in Bolshevik politics, Stalin was insecure, suspicious to the point of paranoia and capable of extraordinary ruthlessness. Though he lacked the absolute sense of personal destiny that drove Hitler, the conviction that it was he who would make socialism a reality in the Soviet Union motivated Stalin. An admirer of the uncontested power exercised by Russian tsars such as Ivan IV and Peter the Great, Stalin believed that a similarly ruthless, coercive approach would be necessary to establish the legitimacy of the new regime and realize the Marxist-Leninist vision. Even as Peter the Great had transformed backward Muscovite Russia into a formidable European empire in the early eighteenth century, Stalin intended to transform the remnants of Tsarist Russia into a modern industrial socialist society. In the course of doing so, Stalin made routine the use of extensive state terror and constructed one of the century's most comprehensive dictatorships.

By the late 1920s, the obvious failure of the NEP, which had not increased either industrial or agricultural production to desired levels, led Stalin to conclude that both sectors of the economy would have to undergo a radical transformation, guided by Five-Year Plans. In agriculture, this meant the collectivization of land, with the *kulaks* as the initial targets of squads of party activists. Deprived of their land, possessions and sometimes even clothing, those *kulaks* who were not executed outright were transported to labor camps in Siberia; they were, according to Stalin's cold decree, " to be liquidated as a class." As collectivization accelerated in 1930, military and political police units compelled the collectivization of the rest of the peasantry, many of whom were to be forced into industrial labor. Despite the fact that resistance meant either a labor camp or death, peasants often destroyed their crops and livestock rather than cooperate. A new government program of forcibly requisitioning grain, which was sold abroad to finance industrialization, compounded the growing chaos in the countryside. In 1931–1932 this brought about famine, especially severe in the Ukraine and northern Caucasus, where mass starvation became an added horror. Through compulsion and terror, Stalin succeeded in collectivizing Soviet agriculture; by the late 1930s, well over 90 percent of peasants labored on state farms. The exact cost in human lives can never be known, though some estimates put the total as high as 14 million deaths between 1930 and 1937. Though Stalin could maintain that he had gained his objective, collectivized Soviet agriculture failed to meet established production goals in the 1930s and in decades thereafter.

Stalin believed that for the Soviet Union to survive in a predominantly capitalist world, Soviet industry had to be modernized. Accordingly, the State Planning Commission implemented the first Five-Year Plan for industry, with the intent of extending government control of industry and doubling production. Stressing growth in heavy industry, the government urged industrial workers to emulate the example of "heroes of labor" like Andrei Stakhanov, a miner who was celebrated for cutting a record amount of coal on his shift. Both the incentive of better wages and the threat of punishment were used to drive production. Unmet production quotas were often blamed on "capitalist wreckers," and some unfortunate factory managers found themselves being tried as saboteurs. Ultimately, this program of "crash" industrialization produced huge mining enterprises, gigantic dams

for providing hydroelectric power and vast new industrial cities such as Magnitogorsk. Soviet industrial production rarely achieved the goals set by the first Five-Year Plan, but the growth of the economy in the early 1930s was undeniable and a foundation for a modern industrial sector was laid down. Subsequent Five-Year Plans held out the promise of more consumer goods, but the advent of war prevented their implementation.

By the mid-1930s, Stalin was the undisputed master of a nation with an indisputably socialist economy. The "New Soviet Man," committed to a collectivist vision and forsaking "bourgeois" individualism for a new social consciousness, was yet to be fully realized, but the government-controlled media constantly exhorted the public to aspire to the Marxist-Leninist ideal. Soviet women were urged to contribute to building socialism by adopting new roles, especially in industry and the professions. The Soviet people were mobilized in a vast array of Communist party auxiliaries, ranging from the Young Pioneers, a communist youth group, to the League of Militant Atheists, who advocated the eradication of religion from the new society. The dictates of "socialist realism," which held that art had the primary purpose of serving the goals of the revolution, reshaped Soviet art, literature and music. A new constitution introduced in 1936 appeared to grant Soviet citizens most of the rights guaranteed by western democracies. Abroad, a small but influential group of western intellectuals extolled the Soviet experiment as a viable alternative to discredited capitalism; British dramatist George Bernard Shaw was one of a number of westerners who were gulled by model farms and orphanages set up for just such purposes. The stark reality was that the USSR was a police state, ruled by a nearly omnipotent dictator supported by a pervasive secret police apparatus. In the mid-1930s, despite the absence of any real threat to his regime, Stalin prepared the grounds for an unprecedented campaign of state terror that spared no one, including those in the highest echelons of the party, government and military.

Historians are not agreed as to what provoked the "Great Terror" of the 1930s. The long years of purges, "show trials," and executions may have been a product of the dictator's innate suspiciousness, which created "enemies of the people" where none actually existed. Other historians suggest that Stalin saw continual terror as an efficient means of controlling a vast and populous nation, as had the tsars in previous centuries. The origins of the terror date to the Communist Party Congress of 1934, where some hint of dissatisfaction with Stalin's methods showed up in the voting for party secretary. Stalin identified Sergei Kirov, the popular Leningrad party boss, as the most likely source of this discontent, and shortly afterwards Kirov was shot to death in his office. The assassin, who most likely acted on Stalin's orders, implicated leading party members in a plot to depose the Soviet dictator and derail the socialist revolution. With feigned outrage, Stalin ordered that all "enemies of the people" be ferreted out and punished. The first victims of the subsequent terror were the "Old Bolsheviks," prominent party officials who had helped launch the revolution of 1917. In "show trials" begun in 1936, they faced absurd charges of conspiring against Stalin, the party and the revolution. Most, broken by months of physical and psychological torture at the hands of the NKVD, confessed to numerous crimes. Few were spared and those not executed immediately were sentenced to long terms in the rapidly expanding system of slave labor camps, known by the acronym

GULAG (Chief Adminstration of Corrective Labor Camps). Many, upon completing their original sentence years later, were resentenced to even lengthier terms.

Through 1938, the arrests and trials accelerated, sweeping up party members, government and industrial officials, intellectuals and cultural figures. Family members of those accused were routinely arrested and imprisoned. No one was exempt—two NKVD chiefs and the wife of the Soviet president were among the prominent victims of the terror. The regime encouraged informers and celebrated the "patriotism" of young children who turned in their own parents. The practice of permitting informers to move into desirable apartments belonging to those they accused provided additional incentive to potential informers. In 1938, Stalin unleashed the terror on the armed forces, subjecting high-ranking officers to another round of "show trials." Accused of treason, most of the Red Army high command was executed, as were all eight admirals of the Soviet Navy. The impact on Soviet military morale and readiness was staggering.

A precise accounting of victims of the terror is impossible, not least because Stalin had the chief census officials themselves shot as "enemies of the people." Soviet records have been largely inaccessible until recent years, and even then were often incomplete or unreliable. By one estimate, the "Great Terror" resulted in the arrest and trial of seven million people, with perhaps as many as one million executed, the remainder ending up in the 125 labor camps of the GULAG, where death from starvation, overwork and disease was the norm.

With his enemies, imagined or otherwise, now decimated, Stalin enjoyed virtually unrestrained power by the late 1930s. A personality cult, encouraged by Stalin some years before, now extolled the Soviet dictator as the genius behind every Soviet advance. Stalin's guidance, it was claimed, was solely responsible for the improvement in the material conditions of life. Soviet economic and military strength were the envy of the world, the official media proclaimed, all due to Stalin's inspired leadership. Unwilling to share even past glories with others, Stalin oversaw the calculated revision of the history of the Bolshevik Revolution. Official histories were rewritten so as to exclude mention of "nonpersons" such as Trotsky and to minimize the contributions of even such luminaries as Lenin. Historical photographs were skillfully doctored in order to suggest Stalin's central role in the revolution. The Soviet film industry churned out feature-length tributes to Stalin's leadership; in an instance of supreme irony, the actor who portrayed the dictator in one film had to be released from the GULAG to play the role. Judging by the images conveyed in official media, Stalin was the beloved leader of a dynamic new society that had succeeded where capitalism had failed. The grim realities of Stalinist Russia remained largely hidden from the wider world.

GERMANY: HITLER'S "BROWN REVOLUTION" AND THE NAZI DICTATORSHIP

Historian Alan Bullock once remarked, "The more I learn about Hitler, the harder I find it to explain." While Hitler's character, motivations and appeal to Germans are all topics about which historians still disagree, the circumstances that afforded the Nazi leader access to power are somewhat more explicable. First, following the failed 1923 putsch and his release from Landsberg prison, Hitler discarded any hopes of gaining power through a coup. Now committed to

gaining power legally, Hitler further asserted the centrality of the *Führerprinzip*, or leadership principle, convinced that the unquestioning acceptance of his leadership was crucial to the party's success. Through the late 1920s, Hitler focused on recruitment and propaganda, ceaselessly repeating the party's program of national revival and revenge for the humiliations of Versailles. He also built up the party's shock troops, the *Sturmabteilungen* or SA. The brownshirted stormtroopers promoted party goals on the streets, brawled with opponents such as the Communists, and as a parade group, demonstrated the disciplined determination of the NSDAP. In 1929, Hitler authorized the creation of the *Schutz Staffel* or SS, whose black-uniformed members were to serve as his bodyguard.

By this time, some segments of both the industrial and agricultural economy were already showing some weakness and the NSDAP demonstrated growing electoral strength in rural areas and in local and state elections even before the shock waves from the American economic collapse could reach Germany. Once the Depression struck, whatever tenuous stability still remained in the Weimar Republic eroded rapidly. As industrial productivity declined to disastrous levels and unemployment reached 30 percent, public faith in the centrist parties receded. The 1930 Reichstag elections brought gains for both the Communists and the Nazis, the latter winning five times as many votes as in the previous election. Though support for the Nazis came from all strata of German society, beleaguered farmers and the anxious lower middle class were most susceptible to the party's appeal. Between 1930 and 1932, a succession of chancellors and ministries proved incapable of lessening the social and economic impact of the depression, further underscoring the apparent failure of parliamentary government. The same years brought a dramatic rise in the number and intensity of street battles between rival parties, with Hitler's stormtroopers actively contributing to the growing chaos.

By 1932, Hitler was sufficiently confident of his popularity to run for the presidency. Though he lost to Hindenburg, he made a credible showing and that summer Nazi electoral strength reached new heights. In the November 1932 elections, Hitler's Nazis became the largest party in the Reichstag, though the number of Nazi voters actually declined from the high in July. Brought up short of commanding a majority in the Reichstag, Hitler's immediate political future seemed in doubt. Ultimately, the machinations of leaders on the traditional anti-parliamentary right afforded Hitler the opening he sought. Franz von Papen, leader of the right-wing Nationalist party and chancellor since summer 1932, was among a number of influential conservatives who hoped that the Weimar Republic might be supplanted by an authoritarian regime, perhaps even a monarchy. Papen, who resigned in December 1932, was succeeded briefly by General Kurt von Schleicher, another ultra-conservative who toyed with the idea of bringing the Nazis into a coalition government. Schleicher's rapid failure and resignation led Papen to actively promote the idea of naming Hitler as chancellor in a right-wing coalition government. The presumed genius of the scheme was that it would join Hitler's mass movement to the Nationalist party, while at the same time "taming" Hitler. The aging Hindenburg gave his assent, boasting "We have Hitler in a box," a sentiment that Papen and Schleicher echoed. The two opportunistic politicians, fatally blind to Hitler's radical ambitions, inadvertently opened the door to a Nazi dictatorship. Joseph Goebbels, soon to be Minis-

ter of Propaganda in the new regime, reflected the astonished glee of the party faithful when he wrote in his diary, "It is almost like a dream . . . a fairy tale . . . the new Reich has been born. Fourteen years of work have been crowned with victory. The German revolution has begun!"

Hitler began laying the foundations for his "Brown Revolution" immediately. With Nazis holding only four of the fourteen cabinet seats, Hitler announced new elections, believing that his position as chancellor and Nazi control of the police would assure a Reichstag majority. A week before the election, the Reichstag was destroyed in a fire that Hitler blamed on the Communists. Warning of the imminence of a "Red" revolution, Hitler persuaded President Hindenburg to issue a decree suspending personal liberties and political rights. Despite a campaign of SA terror and police intimidation, the Nazis fell short of an overall parliamentary majority, but the opposition parties were too cowed to oppose the Nazi assault on the constitutional state. In March, only the Socialists retained the courage to vote against the Enabling Act, which allowed Hitler to govern without the Reichstag. By June the remaining liberal parties disbanded, and in July Hitler decreed the prohibition of all parties other than the National Socialists.

Now in command of a one-party dictatorship, Hitler proceeded with the *Gleichschaltung,* or "coordination" of German society. The courts, the educational system and civil administration were all brought under Nazi direction, as were all police agencies. State governments and parliaments were dissolved and state administration turned over to Nazis. The German Labor Front organized workers after all labor unions were banned. The Hitler Youth and the League of German Girls organized youth for indoctrination and service to the regime. Though both the Catholic and Protestant churches struggled to avoid "coordination," Catholic organizations were banned and Protestants encouraged to unify under a Nazified "Reich Church." A multitude of police agencies, such as the infamous *Geheimestaatspolizei*, or Gestapo, dealt swiftly and brutally with any opposition. At Dachau, near Munich, the first concentration camp was soon populated by a variety of political opponents, dissident clergy and intellectuals.

By 1934, few obstacles remained to the complete consolidation of Hitler's power. The most immediate problem involved Ernst Röhm, head of the SA. Röhm advocated a continuing revolution, in which the SA stormtroopers would become a permanent revolutionary military force. This possibility worried the traditionally conservative army high command, which approved of Hitler's promise of a national revival, but remained uncertain as to Hitler's commitment to preserving the regular army. Hitler, aware of the indispensability of the army to the attainment of his future objectives, increasingly saw the ambitious Röhm and the SA radicals as a potential threat. Accordingly, on June 30, 1934, ever-after known as the "Night of the Long Knives," SS units acting on Hitler's orders moved to eliminate the SA leadership. In the course of the night, SS men sought out and executed some seventy SA leaders. Hitler personally arrested Röhm, who was later shot to death in a prison cell. Altogether, this "Blood Purge" claimed hundreds of victims and reduced the SA to little more than a parade force. The action also reassured the military chiefs, whose doubts about Hitler were considerably lessened. The remaining obstacle to Hitler's complete power was President Hindenburg, who conveniently died in August, whereupon Hitler

combined the powers of the presidency with his own office of chancellor. The future direction of Germany was now entirely in Hitler's hands.

National Socialist ideology offered no precise vision for transforming Germany, largely because it was comprised of an unsystematic admixture of racial, pan-German, anti-Semitic and biological concepts. Hitler himself once remarked "We have picked our ideas from all the bushes along life's path and we no longer know where they came from." Accordingly, the character of the "Brown Revolution" remained ambiguous, a product of the shifting interests of Hitler and his chief subordinates. Without question, the political revolution brought about a dictatorship, a one-party state governed according to Hitler's "leadership principle." Hitler successfully deflected the ambitions of his subordinates by a strategy of "divide and rule," whereby he tolerated and even encouraged competition among high Nazi officials for control of an ever-multiplying number of state agencies, many with unclear or overlapping authority. Heinrich Himmler, for example, capitalized on this latitude to turn the SS into a powerful "state within a state" dedicated to realizing the most radical aspects of Nazi racist thought. Thus, the Nazi emphasis on struggle as an inherent part of existence found realization even in the administration of the new Reich.

The National Socialist revolution ultimately brought little reorganization of the economy. Hitler did seek to revitalize the economy through highly publicized public works programs, but never implemented an industrial recovery program as ambitious as Mussolini's corporatism. Determined to stimulate development in those industries crucial to rearmament, Hitler authorized a Four-Year Plan in 1936, but it never achieved its intended goals. Likewise, a government campaign promoting national self-sufficiency or "autarchy" remained largely wishful thinking. Ultimately, Hitler concluded that the surest route to industrial recovery was to work with Germany's industrialists, many of whom were quite willing to cooperate with the regime in return for assured profits. Hitler's rearmament program brought Germany out of the Depression, thus engendering wide praise from the public, but fundamental economic relationships went unchanged.

The extent of the social revolution brought about by National Socialism is problematic. Hitler never envisioned a radical social restructuring for Germany; his emphasis was on the realization of a community bound by the cohesive force of a common racial or national identity. Within this "Aryan" community, all classes had their utility, and National Socialism acknowledged the "dignity" of both industrial and agricultural labor, as well as the contributions of the business classes. Nazi ideology clearly established separate though ostensibly equally valuable roles for women: *Kinder, Kirche und Küche*— children, church and kitchen. Soon after taking power, Hitler forced women out of the industrial workforce and drove them from public administration and teaching. Families with children received monetary incentives. Hitler's social revolution also included new aesthetic values, which proscribed "decadent" modern art in favor of traditional styles and subjects, such as sentimental "folk art" depicting the physical and moral wholesomeness of German life. In the sphere of public health policy, the Nazi emphasis on the "health" of society ultimately led to programs of racial eugenics, including sterilization and later euthanasia for the mentally disabled and chronically ill. Such programs were justified in Darwinian terms of "sur-

vival of the fittest" and "natural laws." Clearly, the determination to transform traditional conceptions of morality and ethics was one of the most radical aspects of the Nazi revolution.

Hitler's obsession with the creation of a racially pure German "folk community" ensured that anti-Semitism would be the least ambiguous of the regime's objectives. Legislation expelling Jews from the civil service, public office, journalism, teaching and other professions corresponded with a Nazi-directed boycott of Jewish businesses in spring 1933. The next phase of Jewish persecution was much more comprehensive. The Nuremburg Laws of 1935 deprived Jews of citizenship, required the wearing of a yellow Star of David in public, and prohibited marriage or sexual relations between Jews and non-Jewish Germans. In subsequent years, more than a dozen amendments to the Nuremburg Laws further restricted the activities of German Jews. Signs warning "Jews Not Wanted Here" proliferated in public places across Germany.

These events presaged an unprecedented wave of anti-Jewish violence that took place in November 1938. Ostensibly a spontaneous expression of public outrage following the murder of a German diplomat in Paris by a Jew, the vicious pogrom referred to as *Krystallnacht* ("The Night of Broken Glass") was cynically organized by the Hitler regime in order to force remaining Jews to emigrate. Beginning on November 9, mobs led by SS and SA men and Hitler Youth attacked Jews and Jewish businesses and burned over 11,000 synagogues in an orgy of violence across Germany. Tens of thousands of Jews were hauled off to concentration camps as the regime ordered the confiscation of Jewish businesses. The terror convinced many German and Austrian Jews to flee the country, while those who remained faced an ominously uncertain future. The "Final Solution" to what Hitler called "the Jewish problem" would not take shape until Hitler's vision of a great empire in the east was realized through aggressive war.

OTHER AUTHORITARIAN REGIMES

By the 1930s, any lingering hopes for the realization of Wilson's vision of a democratic Europe were extinguished. Eastern Europe proved especially sterile ground for democracy. Bitter party conflict in Poland led Marshal Josef Pilsudski to establish a military dictatorship in 1926. In Rumania, King Carol II deposed his infant son in 1930 and suspended the constitution in 1938. He did so in part to combat the rising power of the "Iron Guard," an anti-Semitic, fascist group that later supported the Nazi-backed wartime dictatorship of Ion Antonescu. In postwar Hungary, following the overthrow of the short-lived communist regime of Bela Kun, Admiral Nicholas Horthy established a dictatorship and appointed a fascist prime minister in 1932. The Arrow Cross, a Hungarian fascist party, organized soon afterward. Yugoslavia's brief experiment with parliamentary government ended in 1929 when King Alexander, frustrated by the ongoing hostility between the country's numerous ethnic groups, banned all political parties and assumed dictatorial powers. In 1934 a Croatian nationalist assassinated the Yugoslav monarch in Paris. In Bulgaria, modest postwar efforts at land reform by the Agrarian Party leader Alexander Stamboliski provoked his murder. Years of political chaos followed until a dictatorship under King Boris was decreed in 1935. In Greece, General Ioannis Metaxas ruled in the fascist style, even assuming the title "leader." Along the

Baltic coast, Latvia, Lithuania and Estonia all became dictatorships in the interwar years.

In central Europe, Thomas Masaryk led a newly established but resilient democracy in Czechoslovakia, but it proved the exception. In the new Austrian Republic, the future of liberal government was far more doubtful. A "rump" state left by the dissolution of the Habsburg Empire, Austria was riven by intense hatred between political left and right. German nationalism and anti-Semitism added to a volatile political climate, finding voice in the Austrian Nazi party, which sought union with Germany. Given these threats, in 1933 Chancellor Engelbert Dollfuss dissolved parliament and banned political parties, intending to govern as dictator. Viennese Socialists responded with an armed insurrection, which Dollfuss suppressed with military force. Five months later, Austrian Nazis assassinated him. Kurt Schuschnigg, his successor, temporarily stabilized the regime, vesting some power in the fascist Fatherland Front and seeking the support of the Catholic Church and the conservative middle class. The ultimate fate of this "clerico-corporate" regime was contingent on Hitler's plans to annex Austria.

Conditions on the Iberian Peninsula were similarly conducive to authoritarian government. Portugal, poor in resources, became a republic in 1911 but persistent social and political unrest led to a military coup in 1926. In 1932, Antonio Salazar became prime minister, implementing a constitution similar to Italy's and creating a dictatorship that endured until 1974. In Spain, where there was no democratic tradition, Premier Miguel Primo de Rivera ruled as dictator throughout most of the 1920s. Growing political discontent led King Alfonso XIII to oust de Rivera in 1930, but this move failed to save the monarchy. The king fled into exile in 1931 as a coalition of republicans and socialists proclaimed the Spanish Republic. Republican-sponsored anticlerical measures and land reforms provoked the ire of the clergy, landowners and other conservative elements, while leftists demanded more radical social reforms. In 1933, the Falange, a fascist movement, organized in opposition to the Republic and the political left. Fearing the threat from the far right, left-wing parties allied in a "Popular Front" in 1935, winning a slim majority in the parliament. Intense political hatreds and a willingness on the part of both left and right to utilize violence continued to undermine stability of the Republic, however, leaving open the possibility of civil war.

The Collapse of the European Order, 1935–1939

Beginning in the mid-1930s, a series of challenges and aggressions on the part of Fascist Italy and Nazi Germany strained and finally broke the European order established in Paris in 1919, ultimately bringing about the Second World War. Conflict came in part because of the aggressive designs of the two fascist powers, which could not be realized within the confines of the existing international order. The timid response of the major European democracies to acts of aggression made a major war more likely. Without doubt, this apparent weakness encouraged both Hitler and Mussolini to ever-bolder actions. Several factors constrained Britain and France from responding effectively to aggression. Memories of the Great War haunted both nations. No cause, it was believed, justified risking such horrendous loss of life again. Pacifism and antiwar sentiment were influential in both countries. The Depression weakened both nations economically and they fell far behind Germany in military spending. Britain and France also lacked bold political leadership and domestic considerations bore on foreign policy to an unhealthy degree. Furthermore, the peacekeeping structure established in the 1920s was incapable of deterring aggression. Disarmament conferences brought no international consensus, and treaties such as the Kellogg-Briand Pact were easily disavowed. In the aftermath of Japan's assault on Manchuria, the credibility of the League of Nations was an open question. The withdrawal of both Japan and Germany from the League in the early 1930s further lessened the effectiveness of that organization. The United States, burdened by economic depression and increasingly isolationist in sentiment, abrogated any major role in European or world affairs until late in the decade. These circumstances led Europe's democracies to an increasingly desperate reliance on "collective security" and when that proved unreliable, to efforts to appease the aggressors. Ultimately, appeasement foundered on the fundamental reality of Hitler's positive advocacy of war as a legitimate means to his ends. "We must clearly recognize, " he had written in *Mein Kampf*, "that the recovery of lost territories is not won through solemn appeals to the Lord or through pious hopes in a League of Nations, but only by force of arms."

THE FASCIST CHALLENGE TO THE EUROPEAN ORDER, 1935–1936

Having long boasted of having transformed Italy into a "warrior nation," Mussolini moved in 1935 to gain his "New Roman Empire." Encouraged and perhaps compelled by the growing power of Hitler's Germany, Mussolini contrived a pretext for war in Ethiopia, where Italian forces had met

Map 5–1   German Expansion During the 1930s

defeat in an earlier colonial conflict in 1896. Privately, Mussolini conceded that he de- sired "war for war's sake, since fascism needs the glory of a victory." In October, Italian forces invaded the east African nation, which was almost totally lacking in modern weaponry. Intending to impress on Britain and France the ferocity of fascist warmaking, Mussolini insisted on an absolutely ruthless campaign in which his forces used artillery, automatic weapons, indiscriminate aerial bombing, mass executions and poison gas against the essentially defenseless population. Ethiopia's Emperor Haile Selassie appeared before the League of Nations to demand action, but aside from approving voluntary economic sanctions against Italy, the body could do little to deter Mussolini's aggression. The sanctions only caused Italians to unite in support of Mussolini and pushed the dictator closer to Nazi Germany. In 1936, with the Ethiopians subjugated and mourning a half million dead, Mussolini announced the annexation of that country to the Italian empire.

The Ethiopian War was not the only challenge to the European order in 1935. Hitler, having effectively secured his authority, moved toward implementing his next goal, freeing Germany from the strictures of the Versailles Treaty. In March the German dictator announced that he was disavowing treaty limitations on the size of the army and introducing compulsory military service. An additional shock came with his announcement that the German air force, or *Luftwaffe*, had already been rebuilt in defiance of the treaty. French, British and Italian representatives met hurriedly at Stresa in Italy to confer on common action against the German threat, but several developments effectively disrupted the stillborn "Stresa Front." Mussolini's Ethiopian venture worried Britain and France. Heartened by the possibility of alliance with the USSR, France increasingly placed faith in the idea of collective security through treaties with eastern European na-

tions contiguous to Germany, thus encircling the potential foe. British leaders, many of whom felt the 1919 restrictions on Germany to be too severe, remained wary of Hitler but saw his renunciation of those provisions as perhaps justified. This perspective was the foundation for a policy of appeasement, whose advocates argued that a costly major conflict could be avoided by acceding to relatively minor German demands, thus alleviating German national resentments and, hopefully, moderating the tone of Hitler's regime.

In 1935, faced with the likelihood of German naval rearmament, Britain agreed to the Anglo-German Naval Treaty, which set a limit on the size of a new German navy. Encouraged by the temporizing and lack of unity on the part of the major democracies, Hitler offered a more dramatic challenge in March 1936, sending the German army into the demilitarized Rhineland. The decision was a tremendous gamble, as Germany's armed forces were as yet not strong enough to successfully resist a French countermove. To the amazement of Hitler's worried generals, there was no significant response from France, which was restrained by Britain's unwillingness to act jointly against Hitler's move. This evident paralysis of British and French will helped bring into being a new alignment between Germany and Italy, signaled by the proclamation of the Rome–Berlin Axis in October 1936. Later that year both nations joined in the Anti-Comintern Pact with Japan, a development that suggested that the separate crises in Asia and Europe might be assuming broader dimensions.

The stability of the European order suffered a further blow when civil war broke out in Spain. A virtual cauldron of political antagonisms since the early 1930s, the Spanish Republic was rocked by anti-republican violence in March 1936, leading the government to declare the fascist Falange illegal. The political chaos accelerated into the summer, culminating in a military insurrection in July. Rebel garrison forces in Spanish Morocco under the command of General Francisco Franco arrived on the mainland to join other army units and right-wing nationalists in an effort to overthrow the republican government. Franco, soon acknowledged as leader of the Nationalist cause, had the support of the Falangists as well as that of the traditionally conservative upper classes and many Catholics who resented the anticlerical, leftist character of the Republic. The Loyalists who fought in defense of the Republic were a disparate group including socialists, Communists, trade unionists, anarchists and Basques, together with some peasants and workers. The Spanish Civil War soon took on the dimensions of a symbolic struggle between democracy and dictatorship, polarizing Europe and inviting outside intervention. Both Italy and Germany aided the Nationalists, the former sending some 100,000 troops and some aircraft.

Hitler saw in the conflict an opportunity to test German weapons and provide military personnel with battlefield experience. Accordingly, the Nazi dictator dispatched the Condor Legion, a bomber squadron that achieved world notoriety for its attack on the small town of Guernica, which killed about one hundred civilians. Immortalized in a painting by Pablo Picasso, the raid on Guernica became a symbol of the indiscriminate savagery of modern warfare. Domestic considerations and fear of provoking a wider conflict restrained Britain and France from intervening, despite the obvious intervention of the fascist dictatorships. Nonetheless, thousands of European and American volunteers joined "International Brigades" to fight for the Loyalist cause. Driven by idealism and outrage at the inaction of the major democracies, these volunteer brigades included such notables as George Orwell, whose *Homage to Catalonia* chronicled his role in the conflict. Among the major powers, only the Soviet Union sent significant aid to the Loyalists. As the conflict intensified, atrocities and cruel inhumanities became increasingly commonplace. The French aviator Antoine de Saint-Exupery, who visited the battlefronts, effectively summarized the brutal nature of a struggle driven by ideological fervor: "You have been captured. You are shot. Reason: your ideas were not our ideas." Characterized by barbarous acts on both sides, the Spanish Civil War dragged on nearly three years, leaving some 600,000 dead and over a million in Nationalist concentration camps. Long before Franco's victory in 1939, the war undercut European stability and revealed the growing lack of resolve on the part of Britain and France.

AGGRESSION, APPEASEMENT AND WAR, 1936–1939

Following the reoccupation of the Rhineland in 1936, Hitler temporarily assumed the mask of responsible statesmen, refraining from further challenges in central Europe and presiding over the Olympic Games, which were held in Berlin that year. Hitler used the Berlin Olympics to showcase the accomplishments of National Socialism and to express his hopes for continued peace. Privately, the dictator was increasingly anxious, fearful that his age and declining health might prevent him from realizing his remaining objectives. In late November 1937, Hitler reiterated those objectives at a meeting with high military and government officials. He stressed the need for *Lebensraum*, "living room" for Germany in the east, which could be attained only through military force. This objective, the *Führer* declared, would have to be realized within six to eight years. Given the slow but inevitable rearmament of France and Britain, the timetable for conquest would have to be moved up.

Early in 1938, Hitler assumed direct control of the armed forces, replaced the army commander and purged the army of generals not sufficiently enthusiastic about Nazi goals. Thus Hitler was well positioned when events seemed propitious to proceed with the *Anschluss,* or absorption of Austria. Having promised to create a "Greater German Reich" by extending German rule to areas inhabited by ethnic Germans, Hitler was determined to annex the land of his birth regardless of the 1919 prohibitions of such a union. In February, Hitler had demanded that Austrian chancellor Schuschnigg allow a Nazi into his cabinet; Schuschnigg later determined to resist and announced a plebiscite that would indicate popular sentiment about annexation. Flying into a rage, Hitler ordered his forces to the Austrian border. Faced with invasion, Schuschnigg resigned, leaving the government in the hands of a Nazi who invited Hitler's army into the country. A subsequent plebiscite on *Anschluss* brought a 99.75 percent favorable response. Again, Britain and France voiced no significant opposition to Hitler's move. France was in the midst of another governmental crisis and feared to move without British support. British policymakers had reconciled themselves to Germany's likely union with Austria long before and Prime Minister Neville Chamberlain was committed to a policy of appeasement. Chamberlain, like many in England, believed the Versailles Treaty was unnecessarily harsh, and rationalized that many of Hitler's actions were simply a legitimate reassertion of Germany's sovereignty and equal status among nations. If a general war could be avoided by making "reasonable" concessions to the Ger-

man leader, then Chamberlain was prepared to do so.

The dangers inherent in this policy became evident almost immediately. Hitler's drive to the east made Czechoslovakia the next logical target of German expansion and Hitler cynically exploited the Wilsonian principle of national self-determination to press Germany's claim to the Sudetenland, a mountainous border region with a large German population. The region was crucial to Czech national security, given its topography and the defensive fortifications constructed there as a "mini-Maginot Line." A week after the *Anschluss,* Hitler began to set the stage for a "crisis" over the Sudetenland, informing his generals of his "unshakable will that Czechoslovakia shall be wiped off the map." This time it was not concessions that Hitler sought, but rather a pretext for war against what he considered to be a preposterous, racially mixed artificial state. Complaining of Czech "atrocities" against Sudeten Germans, Hitler secretly encouraged Konrad Henlein, the leader of a pro-Nazi organization in the Sudetenland, to provoke as much disruption as possible.

As the tensions grew throughout the summer, both Britain and France temporized. Chamberlain's overwhelming desire was to avoid war, even if that meant compelling humiliating concessions on the part of the Czechs. France, though committed to the Czechs by treaty, was unwilling to take a strong stand without a promise of British military support. Ironically, the craven timidity of the two powers deprived Hitler of the war he desired. Unwilling to risk war over "a quarrel in a faraway country between people of whom we know nothing," Chamberlain flew to Germany in September to agree to the German annexation of the Sudetenland. At a second conference the next week, Hitler tried to keep the crisis alive by threatening invasion unless the transfer was completed by October 1. A final conference took place in Munich on September 29, where Chamberlain and French Premier Edouard Daladier gained Hitler's agreement to postpone the German occupation of the contested region until October 10. Hitler grudgingly ac-

ceded to Chamberlain's request for a document stating that this was Germany's last territorial demand, a promise that the Nazi leader contemptuously disavowed in private. Arriving back in London, Chamberlain proudly waved the statement before assembled reporters, proclaiming that it meant "peace in our time." As Daladier's aircraft

Fig. 5-3 British Prime Minister Neville Chamberlain addresses a crowd at England's Heston Airport following his return from the Munich Conference in September 1938, where it was agreed that Czechoslovakia would have to surrender the Sudetenland to Germany. Holding aloft a signed pledge from Nazi dictator Adolf Hitler promising that Germany had no further territorial demands, Chamberlain announced that the agreement meant "peace in our time." Hitler had already confided to an aide that the "Munich Agreement" meant nothing to him. (Pearson Education, Corporate Digital Archive, Getty Images Inc.)

prepared to land at Paris' Le Bourget airport, the French premier, humiliated by the betrayal implicit in the "Munich Agreement," feared that the huge crowd assembled below to meet his airplane intended to kill him. Shocked to find himself hailed as a saviour of peace, Daladier muttered in astonishment, "These people must be crazy." The Czechs, abandoned by the western democracies, retreated into dull resignation. On March 16, 1939, Hitler bullied the Czech president into proclaiming a German protectorate over his country. "This is the greatest day of my life," Hitler declared to his secretaries. "I shall be known as the greatest German in history!" The following day, Hitler's army crossed the Czech border and occupied Prague. In the weeks that followed, central Europe's only remaining democracy was incorporated into the Greater German Reich.

Hitler's invasion of Czechoslovakia completed the discrediting of appeasement and stiffened determination in London and Paris to resist future German aggression. Subsequent British guarantees to both Poland and Rumania probably came too late to deter Hitler. His stunning conquests without war convinced many Germans, civilian and military, that the dictator's instincts were infallible. Hitler too was encouraged by the ease with which he accomplished his goals. In April 1939, he ordered his military chiefs to prepare for the invasion of Poland and in May strengthened the alliance with Italy through the "Pact of Steel." Again, Hitler laid the groundwork for a crisis, this time demanding that the Free City of Danzig with its predominantly German population, situated in the "Polish Corridor" that separated East Prussia from the main body of Hitler's Reich, be ceded to Germany. Alleging Polish "atrocities" against Germans living in Poland, Hitler organized a propaganda campaign that depicted his intended victim as the aggressor. Hoping to lessen the probability of British and French intervention, the dictator also began a diplomatic offensive aimed at obtaining a treaty with the Soviet Union. Despite the obvious ideological hostility between the two regimes, Stalin saw some logic in a pact with Nazi Germany. The western powers had given way before all of Hitler's demands, despite Russian offers of support for Czechoslovakia during the 1938 crisis. Furthermore, Soviet military forces had not yet recovered from the devastating effects of Stalin's purges—a German alliance might conceivably buy some much-needed time. Finally, Hitler made it clear to the Soviet dictator that he would be amenable to Soviet expansion into the Baltic States, Finland and eastern Poland. The resulting Non-Aggression Pact of August 24, 1939, stunned a disbelieving world. One week later, German forces attacked Poland, initiating the most destructive conflict of the twentieth century.

❖ —— ❖ —— ❖ —— ❖ —— ❖ —— ❖ —— ❖ —— ❖ —— ❖

In early August 1939, only weeks before Europe was plunged into war, Albert Einstein sat down to compose a letter to the President of the United States. Staying with friends on Long Island that summer, Einstein had been approached by a group of scientists who were increasingly concerned about the potential application of nuclear fission to weapons of mass destruction. Though initially skeptical about the possibility, Einstein agreed to apprise the president, with whom he had dined in 1934, of the possible threat. The scientist noted in his letter that the work of other émigré physicists such as Enrico

Fermi and Leo Szilard suggested that it might be possible to "set up nuclear chain reactions in a large mass of uranium, by which vast amounts of power . . . would be generated." Warning that it was "almost certain that this could be achieved in the immediate future," Einstein concluded that "extremely powerful bombs of a new type may thus be constructed." "A single bomb of this type," the scientist wrote, "carried by boat or exploded in a port might very well destroy the whole port together with some of the surrounding territory." Einstein thought that such weapons might be too heavy to be carried by aircraft, but stressed his concern that German physicists might well be pursuing research in this direction. The U.S. government, he advised, should begin an organized effort to do likewise. Economist Alexander Sachs presented Einstein's letter to Roosevelt in October, shortly after the European war began. Convinced of the importance of the proposed research, Roosevelt responded, "This requires action." Somewhat less than six years later, in July 1945, scientists engaged in the "Manhattan Project" succeeded in detonating an atomic bomb in the New Mexican desert. The following month, American aircraft dropped two similar bombs on Hiroshima and Nagasaki, effectively destroying both Japanese cities. Though Einstein himself had no direct role in the development of the atomic bomb, his contributions in the field of theoretical physics since the early 1900s had brought about a revolution in understanding the mechanics of the universe. Praised by a colleague as "the Copernicus of the twentieth century," Einstein had advanced theories that forced a reconsideration of the Newtonian outlook that had dominated western science for more than two centuries. Even as Einstein's theories introduced new uncertainties into twentieth-century life, the life of the great scientist was shaped by the often troubling political uncertainties of the first decades of the century.

Born to a middle-class family in Ulm, Germany, on March 14, 1879, Albert Einstein enjoyed an unremarkable childhood. His intellectual curiosity was evident by his early teen years, when he read Kant's *Critique of Pure Reason,* beginning a lifelong interest in philosophy. Driven by a growing interest in science, Einstein entered the Federal Institute of Technology in Zurich, Switzerland in 1896, where he focused on physics and mathematics. Contemporaries described the young Einstein as lively, witty, something of a nonconformist and a man who clearly enjoyed the company of women. At this time he did, in fact, meet the woman who became his first wife. Graduation from the polytechnic brought no immediate prospects of permanent employment and Einstein accepted a position as a Swiss patent officer in Bern. This required that he apply for Swiss citizenship, which he was happy to do, but the decision later damned him in the eyes of German nationalists. Einstein himself had no particular fondness for Wilhelmine Germany or strident nationalism. For that matter, he displayed little consciousness of his Jewish identity. His parents had not been religious Jews and Einstein's later support for Zionism was some years away. The years at the Patent Office proved incredibly fruitful, as Einstein produced the early scientific papers that brought recognition, including the special theory of relativity, which asserted that the concept of space and time as absolutes should be discarded, as both were always relative to the person measuring them. Awarded a Ph.D. from the University of Zurich, Einstein gained a professorship there in 1909, the same year he delivered the lecture that introduced the famous equation $E = mc^2$. By now enjoying international scientific renown, Einstein moved from one university post to another, ending up at the University of Berlin in 1913, where his refusal to reapply for German citizenship was the cause for some criticism. When war broke out in 1914, Einstein's disdain for militarism and his pacifist outlook were grounds for more controversy. Appalled that many scientists were unthinkingly offering their services to belligerent governments, Einstein signed a "Manifesto to Europeans" that denounced war and destructive nationalism. The war years proved difficult, as Einstein's physical health deteriorated and his marriage collapsed.

1919 brought peace and an opportunity to prove the general theory of relativity, by which the special theory of relativity was extended to account for the phenomenon of gravity. The crucial observations were made in the course of a solar eclipse, during which scientists on both sides of the Atlantic confirmed the bending of light rays in the sun's gravitational field. Thus confirmed, the general theory replaced three-dimensional space and one-dimensional time with a single four-dimensional space–time continuum, forever limiting the apparent certainties of Newtonian physics. Now remarried, Einstein became an instant celebrity, as relativity seemed to open promising new scientific vistas for a war-weary world. Within the distorted political universe of postwar Germany, however, Einstein was soon under attack both for what he proposed and what he symbolized. For radical German nationalists, Einstein epitomized those who were responsible for Germany's defeat. As an internationalist, a pacifist and a Jew who had rejected German citizenship, Einstein became a target for anti-Semitic and ultranationalist elements. In 1920, the "Working Committee of German Natural Philosophers" held a meeting at the Berlin Philharmonic Hall to denounce the "Einstein hoax" as a "Jewish theory" contrary to proper "German" values. Renowned for his wry sense of humor, Einstein rented a private box at the hall, applauding and laughing at the absurd assaults on his science. It was a harbinger of things to come.

One nationalist movement did receive Einstein's support. The events of the war gave the Zionist movement, which aimed at establishing a Jewish state, new impetus and the Zionist leader Chaim Weizmann enlisted Einstein to undertake a fundraising trip to the United States in 1921. Though not a practicing Jew, Einstein felt obligated to help preserve the Jewish cultural heritage and was especially interested in founding a Hebrew university in Palestine. The same year brought Einstein the Nobel Prize for Physics, after which he returned to an increasingly troubled Germany. Theoretical physics remained a major interest, but Einstein did not contribute greatly to the rapidly growing field of nuclear physics. He remained uncomfortable with the element of randomness in the quantum theories advanced by Niels Bohr and Werner Heisenberg. "God does not play at dice," he had rejoined. He did, however, apply himself to the search for an elusive "Unified Field" theory, which would explain the behavior of both light and gravity.

For the remainder of the decade, Einstein continued his political activism, supporting peace campaigns and the movement for world government. The early years of the Great Depression brought extended travel, as Einstein taught at the California Institute of Technology and then at Oxford. His presence in Germany was increasingly untenable, given the increasingly chaotic political situation. In late 1932, foreseeing the advent of a National Socialist government, Einstein left Germany together with his wife and never returned. He was one of many refugees who fled Nazi oppression and anti-Semitism in the 1930s. Returning briefly to Belgium in 1933, he publicly denounced Hitler's regime and shortly afterward resigned his positions at the Prussian and Bavarian Academies of Science; for good measure, he renounced his German citizenship for a second time. Not surprisingly, Nazi officials soon made it clear that he was *persona non grata,* including his photograph in a catalog of "state enemies" above the caption "not yet hanged." The shocking transformation of German society and the obviously aggressive designs of the Hitler regime led the scientist to reevaluate his commitment to pacifism. In a remarkably prescient letter to a young French pacifist, Einstein explained how circumstances had altered his position: "Imagine Belgium occupied by present-day Germany. Things would be far worse than in 1914 and they were bad enough even then." In this situation, military service was justified to "save European civilization."

In 1933, Einstein settled into a position at Princeton University, far removed from the threatening climate of Nazi Germany. The famous physicist enjoyed his celebrity in the United States as much as the public enjoyed hearing his equally famous eccentricities. The public was long familiar with Einstein's careless appearance and odd habits—the uncombed hair, appearing at formal occasions without socks, using uncashed checks for bookmarks in his cluttered study. An oft-repeated anecdote involved a telephone call to a Princeton dean's secretary, who was asked for Einstein's address. Explaining that she had been instructed not to give it out, the secretary heard the caller lament, "Oh dear! This *is* Professor Einstein. I've forgotten where I live!" The death of Einstein's second wife did not significantly interrupt his pursuit of the unified field theory, but not until 1939 was he sought out by the physicists who were alarmed by the potential military application of nuclear physics. Einstein refused any role in the American project to develop an atomic bomb and likely would have had difficulty gaining security clearance. Einstein's previous political activism was enough to cause the FBI, which compiled a 1500-page file on the German émigré, to view him as a potential security risk. In 1943, Einstein did go to work for the Navy's Bureau of Ordnance, reviewing plans for new weapons systems. When the atomic destruction of Hiroshima was announced by radio in 1945, his reported reaction was a horrified "O Weh!"

Einstein retired from the Princeton faculty the same year, pursuing research that took him into increasingly rarified realms of physics, far beyond the comprehension of all but a few. Although he never considered himself a true Zionist, the founding of Israel brought some satisfaction, perhaps more so in 1952 when he was proposed as president of the Jewish state. David Ben-Gurion supported the idea, hailing Einstein as "the most illustrious Jew in the world, and possibly the greatest man alive." In the last decade of his life, however, Einstein dedicated himself to the campaign to abolish nuclear weapons. The potential the Cold War held for nuclear annihilation alarmed him and he never saw the Soviet Union as the threat that American policymakers did. Accordingly, he accepted a leading role in the Emergency Committee of Atomic Scientists, which sought to educate the public as to the nature and danger of nuclear weapons. After several years of declining health, he died in 1955. Einstein's life spanned some of the most tumultuous decades of the twentieth century and, as absorbed with the complexities of theoretical physics as he often seemed to be, he found it impossible to ignore the political dimensions of the world. He would always be most remembered, however, as the gentle, humane and somewhat enigmatic professor whose theories helped lay the foundations for a twentieth-century scientific revolution that redefined the nature of the universe.

◆ —— ◆ —— ◆ —— ◆ —— ◆ —— ◆ —— ◆ —— ◆ —— ◆ —— ◆

Selected Readings

ARENDT, HANNAH. *The Origins of Totalitarianism.* (1948).

BRENDON, PIERS. *The Dark Valley: A Panorama of the 1930s.* (2000).

BULLOCK, ALAN. *Hitler: A Study in Tyranny.* (1964).

BURLEIGH, MICHAEL. *The Third Reich: A New History.* (2000).

CHILDS, MARQUIS. *Sweden: The Middle Way on Trial.* (1984).

CONQUEST, ROBERT. *The Great Terror: A Reassessment.* (1990).

———. *Stalin: Breaker of Nations.* (1991).

FEST, JOACHIM. *Hitler.* (1973).

FISCHER, KLAUS. *Nazi Germany: A New History.* (1996).

FRIEDRICH, OTTO. *Before the Deluge: Berlin in the 1920s.* (1972).

GRAVE, ROBERT and ALAN HODGES. *The Long Weekend: A Social History of Great Britain, 1919–1939.* (1963).

JACKSON, JULIAN. *The Popular Front in France: Defending Democracy, 1934–1938.* (1988).

KERSHAW, IAN. *Hitler: Hubris, 1889–1936.* (1999).

KINDLEBERGER, CHARLES. *The World in Depression.* (1986).

LAFORE, LAURENCE. *The End of Glory: An Interpretation of the Origins of World War II.* (1970).

LARGE, DAVID CLAY. *Between Two Fires: Europe's Path in the 1930s.* (1990).

LUKACS, JOHN. *The Hitler of History.* (1997).

MACHTAN, LOTHAR. *The Hidden Hitler.* (2001).

MARKS, SALLY. *The Illusion of Peace.* (1976).

NICHOLLS, A. J. *Weimar and the Rise of Hitler.* (1979).

NOLTE, ERNST. *Three Faces of Fascism.* (1963).

ROSENBAUM, RON. *Explaining Hitler.* (1998).

RIDLEY, JASPER. *Mussolini.* (1997).

SCHOENBAUM, DAVID. *Hitler's Social Revolution.* (1980).

SMITH, DENNIS MACK. *Mussolini.* (1982).

———. *Mussolini's Roman Empire.* (1976).

SONTAG, R. J. *A Broken World, 1919–1939.* (1971).

THOMAS, HUGH. *The Spanish Civil War.* (1997).

TUCKER, ROBERT. *Stalin in Power.* (1990).

WEBER, EUGENE. *France: The Hollow Years.* (1994).

CHAPTER 6

Into the Maelstrom: Global War, 1939–1945

On June 4, 1940, Winston Churchill stood before the British House of Commons to address the latest developments in the war, now in its ninth month. The circumstances were not auspicious. Named as prime minister less than a month before, Churchill now faced the difficult task of announcing another Allied reversal. The German *Blitzkrieg* that had blown through Poland in the fall of 1939 had swept across Denmark, Holland, Belgium, Luxembourg, Norway and France in the spring of 1940. With the last of the British Expeditionary Force evacuated from France at Dunkirk, the collapse of the Third Republic seemed inevitable; Britain would soon stand alone. With an eloquently defiant tone that was to be characteristic of his wartime rhetoric, Churchill acknowledged Britain's plight but made clear its determination: "We shall go on to the end, we shall fight in France, we shall fight in the seas and oceans, we shall fight with growing confidence and growing strength in the air, we shall defend our island, whatever the cost may be." In carefully measured phrases, the prime minister articulated the creed that would undergird Britain's resolve in the difficult months to come: "We shall fight on the beaches, we shall fight on the landing-grounds, we shall fight in the fields and in the streets, we shall fight in the hills; we shall never surrender." Given the situation, it was a daring declaration.

A few weeks later, in the aftermath of France's collapse, Churchill again addressed Parliament, this time to steel Britons to the coming trials and to give a broader perspective to the conflict. The battle of France was over, he announced; the battle of Britain was about to begin. The stakes were high. "Upon this battle depends the survival of Christian civilization," he asserted, together with "our own British life, and the long continuity of our institutions and Empire." Britain would play a key role in the titanic struggle only barely commenced. "Hitler knows he must break us in this island or lose the war," Churchill asserted. The cost of failure would be unimaginable. "If we fail," he warned, "then the whole world, including the United States, including all that we know and care for, will sink into the abyss of a new Dark Age, made more sinister, and perhaps more protracted, by the lights of perverted science." Britain's duty was clear. "Let us therefore brace ourselves to our duties," Churchill urged, "and so bear ourselves that, if the British Empire and its Commonwealth last for a thousand years, men will say, 'This was their finest hour'." In the Second World War, Winston Churchill clearly found his finest hour.

It is ironic that Churchill's greatness was defined by a war that unleashed forces that ended forever the world he sought to preserve. Though a commanding figure in the twentieth century, Churchill clearly belonged to an earlier era of western supremacy and imperial certitude. Born in 1874 to an English lord and an American mother, Churchill grew up in the late Victorian Age, shaped by its moral imperatives and certainties. Restless, young Winston found excitement with the British Army in India and Africa, and later in the Boer War. Churchill's keen sense of history and destiny emerged early, as he published accounts of the events that carried him along. A reputation for duplicity attended his political career, as he abandoned the Conservative party for the Liberals in 1904, eventually serving as First Lord of the Admiralty in Lloyd George's wartime government. His tenure here was not without criticism; many blamed him for the disastrous Gallipoli campaign. His history of the Great War brought some fame, but occasioned snide comments from those who saw in it more evidence of the immense Churchill ego. "I hear that Winston has written a big book about himself and called it *The World Crisis,*" sneered Conservative Arthur Balfour.

The interwar years brought little satisfaction to the man whose outlook was more fitted to the previous century. "What a disappointment the twentieth century has been," Churchill complained as revolution and social dislocation reshaped postwar Europe. Churchill returned to the Conservative party in the early 1920s, serving as Chancellor of the Exchequer in Stanley Baldwin's second ministry, but he was unable to regain the trust of his colleagues. His intransigence on self-government for India was an embarrassment even to many Conservatives. His egotism and self-righteousness offended many, though these characteristics were tempered by an acerbic wit. At a dinner party, Churchill was confronted by Lady Nancy Astor, a political opponent of long standing. "Winston," she told him, "if I were your wife, I'd poison your soup." Unruffled, Churchill rejoined, "Nancy, if I were your husband, I'd drink it." After 1929, Churchill was without political office for a decade. During this period in the political wilderness, he sought consolation in painting and struggled with bouts of melancholy, which he referred to as his "black dog."

The opportunity for political rehabilitation came with the growing crisis of the late 1930s. Quicker than most to perceive the potential danger of Hitler's Germany, Churchill became a persistent opponent of Neville Chamberlain's policy of

Fig. 6-1 British Prime Minister Winston Churchill (center), accompanied by aide Brendan Bracken (right), inspects bomb damage at the Houses of Parliament in London during the German "Blitz" of 1940. Churchill's resolute defiance of Hitler's Germany, together with his skill at bolstering public morale, made him a superior wartime leader. (Pearson Education, Corporate Digital Archive, Getty Images Inc.)

appeasement. Denounced by many as an alarmist or even a warmonger prior to the Munich Conference, Churchill seemed almost prescient in light of the events that followed. With the resignation of the Chamberlain government and the German invasion of France on May 10, 1940, Churchill was called to Buckingham Palace and asked to form a new government. The sixty-five-year-old prime minister spoke before the House of Commons three days later. "I have nothing to offer but blood, toil, tears and sweat," Churchill proclaimed. But, unlike his predecessor, he offered a determined policy: "Victory, victory at all costs, victory in spite of all terror; victory, however long and hard the road may be."

Critical to that victory, as Churchill saw it, was an alliance with the other great English-speaking power, the United States. He quickly developed a close relationship with President Franklin Roosevelt by which, he hoped, the New World might come to the aid of the Old. Having gained increasing American commitments for material aid during the period when Britain stood alone, Churchill traveled to Washington, D.C., in late 1941, shortly after U.S. entry into the war. He made a great impression at the White House, not least for his personal habits, which included conversations until 3 o'clock in the morning and an incredible capacity for liquor. Among his requests to the butler was a standing order for "a tumbler of sherry in my room before breakfast, a couple of glasses of scotch and soda before lunch and French champagne and 90-year-old brandy before I go to sleep at night." Roosevelt, apparently unfamiliar with Churchill's habit of dictating to his secretary in various states of undress, once arrived in the prime minister's room early in the morning. Having just emerged from the bath, Churchill had been striding back and forth cloaked in a towel, but it had fallen away; noting the president's apparent embarrassment, Churchill gamely remarked that he had "nothing to conceal from the President of the United States." In the course of his activities in following days, including a speech before the Congress, Churchill came to be seen by many Americans as the embodiment of British courage and determination. Without question, Churchill's ability to inspire and lead helped to define him as a great war leader in the difficult years to come.

Winston Churchill's years of fame coincided almost exactly with the duration of the war. Following Germany's defeat in May 1945, Churchill was ousted from office in a July election that gave power to Clement Attlee and the Labour party. Outside the context of wartime, Churchill seemed an anachronism. His social and economic vision was clearly at odds with that of the majority of the British electorate, which demanded government activity in both areas. Though he regained the prime ministership briefly in the 1950s, his later tenure in office did little credit to his reputation. The Second World War transformed the world and Great Britain's place in it. The ideals that had shaped and inspired Churchill and which had served him in his efforts to inspire his countrymen now seemed vestiges of a distant past. The idea of empire was archaic and onerous; the meaning of glory was increasingly elusive in a complex world. Nonetheless, the Churchill of the Second World War years remained an imposing figure in the minds of many Britons, perhaps because he was emblematic of what Great Britain had been. Sir Winston Churchill died in January 1965, departing a world that was far removed from the romantic age of which he was a product. The *London Times* marked his passing with the headline "The Greatest Englishman of His Time."

◆ —— ◆ —— ◆ —— ◆ —— ◆

The Second World War was the greatest calamity of the twentieth century, easily eclipsing the Great War in the havoc it wrought. Truly global in scope, the conflict left entire nations and even continents ravaged; the American hemisphere alone escaped significant destruction. The war brought the mobilization of whole popula-tions and economies behind opposing ideologies. The very nature of some ideologies, such as National Socialism and Japanese militarism, sanctioned a new level of savagery in the conduct of the war. New technologies adapted to military usage likewise assured unprecedented destructive capabilities on the part of all belligerents. These forces combined to produce a titanic struggle that gave new meaning to the concept of total war. With entire nations mobilized for war, the ability or desire to distinguish between military and civilian targets diminished. Total war brought comprehensive vulnerability, with grievous consequences. The war produced unprecedented devastation and ultimately cost more than 55 million lives.

The European War: the Years of Axis Triumph

For the first three years of the European war, the momentum was clearly with the Axis powers. Hitler's armies dominated most of Europe from the Pyrenees Mountains deep into western Russia and extended German control even into north Africa. German military capabilities were such that Italy's failed campaigns around the Mediterranean rim were ultimately salvaged by German intervention. Though Britain successfully staved off invasion in 1940, the United States remained neutral until late 1941, and most Allied military efforts to that point were minor or ineffectual.

THE CONQUEST OF POLAND AND THE "PHONY WAR"

Historian John Keegan has described Adolf Hitler as "the most dangerous war leader ever to have afflicted civilization." This stemmed from three of Hitler's beliefs which, Keegan notes, "were often found separately but never before combined in a single mind." First, Hitler was obsessed with the technology of war and strove to ensure that Nazi Germany possessed superior weapons. Second, Hitler was convinced of the racial

superiority of a warrior nation such as the German people. Last, he was a firm believer in military strategist Carl von Clausewitz's dictum that war was merely a continuation of politics. An examination of the German campaign against Poland in the fall of 1939 seems to confirm Keegan's insight. The conquest and eradication of the Polish nation was clearly fundamental to Hitler's broader political objectives in Europe and Hitler was not averse to employing the most cynical deceits to justify his aggression. For months prior to the assault on Poland, German theater audiences were barraged with propaganda "newsreels" about the mistreatment of ethnic Germans in Poland and the injustices perpetrated on the German citizens of Danzig. Even as Hitler announced the beginning of the Polish campaign to a somewhat uncertain Germany, he maintained the fiction that the German invasion was a response to a Polish attack on a German radio station on the border. The "enemy soldiers" found dead at the scene were actually murdered concentration camp inmates, supplied by the S.S. In Danzig, a predominantly German city in the Polish Corridor, the German battleship *Schleswig-Holstein*, ostensibly in the harbor on a goodwill visit, instead opened fire on nearby Polish installations, marking the beginning of a massive German invasion. Even as Hitler had provided a thin pretext for his demands on the Sudetenland in 1938, he once again portrayed Germany as the wronged party before launching his forces against his victim.

The German forces that attacked Poland on September 1 reflected the technological superiority in which Hitler placed so much faith. The German *Luftwaffe* destroyed much of the Polish air force in short order. The often-obsolete Polish aircraft that opposed the Germans in the air proved no match for the modern Messerschmitt fighters flown by *Luftwaffe* pilots. With air superiority achieved, the terrifying *Stuka* dive bombers wreaked havoc on Polish forces, which rapidly discovered the necessity for air cover in modern warfare. Poland's military leaders, who had a romantic but misplaced faith in the utility of cavalry charges, soon found such tactics were suicidal against well-equipped infantry. Moreover, there were few anti-tank weapons to slow the advance of German armor. The four German armies that invaded Poland introduced the world to what quickly came to be called *Blitzkrieg*, or "lightning war." It was a tactic combining speed and mobility, made possible by technological advances in armor and aircraft, permitting rapid penetration of enemy territory and disruption of the enemy's supply and reinforcement capabilities. In Poland, German forces were aided by the terrain, which offered no major geographical barriers to invasion. The backwardness and unpreparedness of Polish forces also facilitated German success, as did the inability of the British or French to aid Poland rapidly enough. As Poland's forward defenses crumbled, German forces poured into the interior. Chaos intensified as German bombers attacked Warsaw and other cities. The final blow came as the Soviets, now taking advantage of the secret protocols of the Nazi-Soviet Pact, invaded Poland from the east. Completely demoralized, Polish forces, which had previously fought courageously, began giving up en masse. German and Soviet officials formalized their joint conquest at Brest-Litovsk, site of Russia's humiliation in 1918.

The ultimate meaning of Nazi conquest and the radically different nature of the un-folding conflict quickly became evident in Poland. Hitler had no intention of treating the Poles as merely a defeated foe and imposing relatively mundane conditions such as the transfer of territory. In Hitler's eyes, the Poles and especially Polish Jews were *Untermenschen*, subhumans vanquished by a superior race. The price Poland was to pay was national extinction; those Poles permitted to survive would lead the degraded lives of slave laborers. The arrests, executions and deportations to concentration camps began almost immediately. It would be several years yet before the systematic destruction of undesirable races would be perfected; the Poles were only the first of many peoples to experience the horrifying consequences of Hitler's racial policies.

The German *Blitzkrieg* against Poland cowed some western leaders. Both Britain and France were reluctant to attack Germany from the west during the Polish campaign. Together the two Allied nations were capable of fielding numerically superior forces along Germany's western border and might well have altered Hitler's plans had they taken offensive action during September. That they failed to do so is testimony to Allied misconceptions about Germany's warmaking abilities and a general reluctance to enlarge the conflict on the continent. It was not known at the time that Hitler's generals had expressed doubts about Germany's readiness for war, or that at best, Germany was at this stage prepared to fight only wars of limited duration.

What evolved from this situation came to be known as the "Phony War" or more cynically, the *Sitzkrieg* or "Sit-down War." After Poland's defeat and until the opening of new German offensives in April 1940, the Allies made no overt moves on the continent. British discussions of air raids on Germany foundered on fears of retaliation. Prewar German propaganda had been quite successful in spreading rumors of invincible German airpower; the 1936 film *Things to Come* had horrified English audiences with its realistic depiction of an air raid on London. Thus, as Hitler continued to assert his desire for peace with the western powers, British bombers restricted their activities to dropping propaganda leaflets, and the French hunkered down behind the Maginot Line, with far too much time for gloomy reflection.

The "Phony War" in the west provided Joseph Stalin with an opportunity to seek additional territorial gains for the Soviet Union. In the fall of 1939 the Soviet government demanded that the Baltic republics permit Soviet troops to be garrisoned there. The following year, the USSR annexed Latvia, Lithuania and Estonia. Stalin was not as fortunate in dealing with Finland. Insistent on Finnish land cessions that would safeguard the security of Leningrad, Stalin was not satisfied with the Finnish response and on November 30 the dictator ordered Soviet armies to attack. The Soviet offensive was badly bungled as massive Russian formations were mangled by smaller but better-prepared Finnish units. The "Winter War" was fought in conditions in which temperatures reached $-70°F$, circumstances that greatly hindered the overconfident Soviets. Despite fierce resistance, Russian numbers ultimately prevailed. Stalin eventually overcame his opponents with an army that was larger than the entire male population of Finland and achieved his goals by early March 1940.

One champion of the Finnish cause in the "Winter War" was the United States, where the Finns were held in special regard because they alone continued to pay the interest on their First World War debt despite the depression. Of at least equal importance was a general American disregard for Stalin as Hitler's current cohort and a perception of a Finnish David battling a Soviet Goliath. Aside from general public sympathy, no aid was forthcoming. The American public had reacted to the outbreak of war in Europe with sympathy for the Allies but a determination to avoid involvement. President Franklin Roosevelt, though increasingly cognizant of the potential danger posed by Nazi victory, was unable to provide significant U.S. aid to any of the Allied powers. The Neutrality Acts, which had kept the United States aloof from the crises and conflicts of the late 1930s, severely limited the president's response to aggression abroad.

One major demonstration of solidarity with the Allied cause came shortly after the war began; the U.S. Congress amended the Neutrality Acts to include a "cash and carry" provision. This permitted the sale of American arms to belligerents as long as the transaction was in cash and the buyer nation provided transport. The amendment clearly benefited the western Allies, and it was hoped that America might fulfill its role by providing material support. The isolationist tone of public opinion precluded any more direct involvement in the war. The general impression was that this was "just another European war." Few Americans in 1939 could have comprehended the magnitude of Hitler's designs or how radically the current conflict differed from the last war. These realities would become evident only with time. The decision to provide material support to the Allies did, however, plant the seed for a relationship that ultimately proved crucial to Allied victory. As American officials journeyed to London to confer with British officials, Churchill, again at the Admiralty, recognized the importance of the tenuous connection with the United States. "Time is on our side," he commented, foreseeing a closer alliance with the primary New World power that might eventually help tip the balance against Hitler's Germany.

GERMANY ON THE OFFENSIVE: FROM THE NORWEGIAN CAMPAIGN TO THE BATTLE OF BRITAIN

Despite the success of his armed forces, Hitler faced a major dilemma as the campaign in Poland drew to a close. Germany was engaged in a war he had not desired; the French and British declarations of war on September 3 had surprised and depressed the Nazi leader. Although Hitler believed that war with both France and Britain was inevitable, he had thought war against the two western powers was still several years in the future. In 1939, his immediate objectives lay eastward. Any long-term continuation of the standoff in the west promised to work against Germany; already British forces were arriving in France. The Russo-Finnish conflict had attracted the attention of the British to the strategic importance of Scandinavia, and German dependence on crucial mineral ores from neutral Sweden.

Additionally, Admiral Erich Raeder, head of the German navy, was pressing Hitler to occupy Denmark or Norway to gain bases for Germany's U-boat fleet. Faced with these developments, Hitler proceeded with plans for a new offensive against Scandinavia and the western Allies. In early April 1940, German forces marched into Denmark and landed in Norway. The former was not a military power and capitulated immediately when Hitler threatened to bomb Copenhagen. Norwegians, though surprised, resisted the German sea and air assault against

Oslo with some success. Ultimately, as German troops seized most strategic points, the government fled, though resistance continued across the country. Two Allied expeditions mounted against German strongholds in northern Norway failed to oust the invaders; Hitler's western offensive derailed further efforts.

On May 10, 1940, the *Blitzkrieg* was again unleashed, catching the western powers unprepared. Holland, with an army comprised of only ten divisions and a minimal air force, fell victim to Nazi paratroops, who rapidly seized strategic sites. After only five days, the Dutch government sought terms. The bombing of Rotterdam by the *Luftwaffe* (possibly due to faulty communications) hastened matters and enhanced the growing German reputation for ruthlessness. Neutral Belgium's ability to resist was fatally weakened when German paratroops seized key fortifications; a decisive German thrust came through the Ardennes forest, long considered impenetrable by French military planners. This event greatly compromised the utility of the vaunted Maginot Line, as German tanks and infantry were now pouring around the fortified line through Belgium and Luxembourg. The rapidity of the assault and growing German air superiority stunned French and British forces, who proved unable to stem the German tide. In one week, German columns drove from the Meuse River to the Channel coast, cutting Allied forces in half.

By late May, the bulk of Allied forces in the north established a perimeter around Dunkirk, the last channel port from which an evacuation could be made. Hitler's decision to halt German armored units advancing up the coast aided frenzied efforts to evacuate the British Expeditionary Force and remnant French forces. The controversial order was evidently the product of concern among German generals over the status of their depleted armored forces; it was thought that they should be held back for the final blow against France. This decision, together with Hitler's willingness to believe Herman Goering's boast that his *Luftwaffe* alone could finish the Allied force, provided the beleaguered Allied troops with the necessary respite.

Britain initiated Operation "Dynamo," the extraction of Allied troops from the Dunkirk pocket by the Royal Navy and literally any other English vessels that could cross the channel. Though pounded by Goering's planes, the ragtag fleet succeeded in rescuing some 340,000 Allied soldiers by June 3. It was a heart-lifting feat, but it signaled the final phase of the catastrophe in France. Reoriented, German armies smashed the remaining French forces as defeatism in the higher ranks spread to soldiers in the field. On June 10, as the French government unraveled, Benito Mussolini cynically declared war on a nearly prostrate France. "I need a few thousand dead to sit at the peace conference," the dictator confided to an associate. This "stab in the back," as President Roosevelt termed it, preceded the German occupation of Paris by only four days. On June 16, representatives of the new government headed by the aging Marshal Philippe Petain signed an armistice in a humiliating ceremony that Hitler personally arranged and witnessed. The Third Republic, born out of France's defeat by Germany in 1870, now died in the midst of yet another German victory.

The rapid collapse of France, which left Britain facing Nazi Germany alone, stunned the world. Though Hitler still hoped that Britain would consider compromise, Churchill was steadfastly defiant: "We shall seek no terms, we shall tolerate no parley; we may show mercy—we shall ask for none." An indication of British resolve came with the

Royal Navy's attack on the French fleet at Mers-el-Kebir in French North Africa in early July. Churchill was determined that Germany be denied the use of this potentially dangerous naval force. Hence, when French naval commanders refused to accede to demands to sail to British ports, the French West Indies or demobilize, a Royal Navy force blasted the French fleet at its moorings. By mid-July Hitler was formalizing plans for Operation "Sea Lion," an invasion of England. Prior to the amphibious assault, the *Luftwaffe* was to crush the Royal Air Force. Hence the genesis of the Battle of Britain, an unprecedented struggle in which air power almost exclusively determined the outcome. The balance of forces appeared to favor Germany—the *Luftwaffe* could bring to bear about 3,000 aircraft, while RAF strength stood at 1,200 planes. Following efforts in late July to drive British shipping from the channel, the Germans initiated their primary strategy, which aimed at the destruction of British Fighter Command.

The crucial events began on August 13 as German raiders struck at British radar stations and fighter bases. The contest raged for three weeks, during which both sides absorbed punishing losses. Even as Fighter Command's losses came to seem insurmountable, German strategy changed. On September 7, German bombers attacked London, signaling the beginning of an effort to destroy British morale. The change was based in part on faulty German intelligence, which held that the RAF had been effectively destroyed. Though the attacks on London wreaked considerable havoc, they provided Fighter Command with a respite during which fighter aircraft and pilots could be marshaled. Subsequently, German bomber losses were soon unacceptable. On September 17, Hitler called off Operation

"Sea Lion." Churchill's summation of the Battle of Britain was perhaps the most succinct: "Never in the field of human conflict was so much owed by so many to so few." The Nazi *Blitz* against London and other English cities would continue for some months, but Britain never again faced the serious threat of invasion.

The Battle of Britain had the effect of mobilizing American public opinion in support of the beleaguered island, encouraging Roosevelt to provide further aid. In September, the president arranged for the transfer of fifty World War I destroyers to the Royal Navy in exchange for ninety-nine-year leases to eight British bases along the western Atlantic rim. The intent was to aid Britain in combating the growing German U-boat menace, which threatened to disrupt Britain's transatlantic supply lines. It was a stop-gap measure at best, but Roosevelt was still greatly restrained by isolationist opinion. Churchill tested his rapidly developing friendship with the American president in late 1940, when he wrote Roosevelt and made clear Britain's increasingly dire straits. There was no money for "cash and carry;" if Britain were to survive, U.S. policy would have to be altered. Roosevelt, convinced of the danger to U.S. security that would be presented by a triumphant Nazi Germany, succeeded in urging Congress to pass the Lend-Lease Act of 1941. The United States, he announced, could serve as the great "Arsenal of Democracy" by "forgetting the silly old dollar sign" and lending Britain needed war materials. The United States, Roosevelt argued, could best stay out of the war by keeping Britain in the war. It was a disingenuous claim, but the policy circumvented the Neutrality Act's restrictions on loans and bought time, a precious commodity at this juncture.

With American material aid now readily available, the British still faced the problem of transporting the badly needed supplies and equipment across the Atlantic. 1941 brought the opening phases of the battle of the Atlantic, in which Germany's submarine fleet sought to sever the Atlantic lifeline with North America. The Royal Navy, hardpressed elsewhere, lacked adequate escort vessels and the Roosevelt administration faced growing pressure to permit the U.S. Navy to assume some convoy escort duties. Roosevelt, still constrained by public opinion, finally issued ambiguous orders to U.S. naval commanders in late summer, granting them the latitude to aid the Royal Navy whenever possible. This policy was bound to lead to confrontations between American warships and U-boats; by fall these had escalated to an undeclared naval war between the U-boats and American escort vessels, which were now escorting Allied convoys halfway across the Atlantic. The Anglo-American alliance was strengthened in August when Roosevelt and Churchill met on the British battleship *Prince of Wales* at Placentia Bay, Newfoundland. There they formulated the Atlantic Charter, a statement of joint principles and war aims. It was part of Roosevelt's general effort to prepare the American people for the task ahead. American public opinion still rejected direct intervention, though concerns about the consequences of Nazi victory were growing. Something more than German submarine attacks would be required to bring the United States into the war.

WAR IN THE MEDITERRANEAN, 1940–1943

Of the major Axis powers, Italy was the least prepared for war. Prior to Hitler's invasion of Poland, Mussolini sent an envoy to suggest to the German dictator that it might be well to delay hostilities for four, seven or even eight years. When Hitler insisted on an Italian commitment, Mussolini responded with a request for massive German material aid for Italian rearmament. Nonetheless, when war broke out, Mussolini was unwilling to sit on the sidelines. His fascist creed preached war; several years before Mussolini had boasted of his ability to summon "eight million bayonets" at a moment's notice, to launch an air force that would darken the skies and to send forth a fleet that would make the Mediterranean *mare nostrum* (our sea). Thus the initial Italian status of "non-belligerence" (neutrality, Mussolini insisted, was a concept alien to the fascist mind) gave way to war against France and even broader commitments with adherence to the Tripartite Pact of September 1940, which bound Germany, Italy and Japan to mutual aid if attacked. Mussolini's Italy was clearly unprepared. There were arms and supplies for an army of less than one million; most of the arms were obsolete and the armored divisions of which Mussolini bragged were the products of his fertile imagination. Morale was problematic, especially after the United States entered the war. The air force, which was depicted in fascist propaganda as an invincible armada of over 8,500 planes, actually consisted of slightly more than 3,200 aircraft, most of which were obsolete or outmatched by their Allied counterparts. The Italian navy was an imposing force, but the larger warships had sacrificed armor plating for speed, a deficiency that was to prove fatal. Italy's supposed military might was a product of years of government propaganda and Mussolini's willingness to delude himself. Not surprisingly, beginning with the last-minute attack

on France in June 1940, Italian forces endured continual defeat on the battlefield.

Resentful of Hitler's serial conquests by 1940, Mussolini began to speak of a "parallel war" in which Italy would gain glory. The defeat of Ethiopia was years in the past and the conquest of Albania in April 1939 paled in comparison to Germany's feats. North Africa and Greece, Mussolini hoped, would provide the arena for a demonstration of fascist valor. Instead, both provided only humiliating defeat. A foretaste of events to come occurred in early July 1940 when Italian battleships escorting a convoy to Italian Libya ran into a British naval force. A brief skirmish saw the Italian warships withdraw in haste, suffering the added indignity of being bombed by their own air force in the confusion of battle. An Italian move into British Egypt in September brought no better results. A British attack in December routed the numerically superior Italian army and, by early 1941, the British had captured most of Italy's Libyan strongholds and over 100,000 prisoners. During this same period, British forces pushed the Italians out of British Somaliland, Eritrea and liberated Ethiopia. These blows came on top of a major Italian naval disaster; in early November 1940 British-carrier-borne aircraft had attacked the naval base at Taranto, sinking half the Italian battlefleet. It was around this same time that Mussolini, driven largely by his desire to outdo Hitler, launched a highly misguided attack on Greece. Eager to repay Hitler for never informing him prior to a German invasion, Mussolini, with virtually no preparation, ordered his forces into Greece. His hopes of carving out a Balkan empire for Italy were quickly dispelled; the Greek army routed the Italians, driving them back into Albania. As British troops arrived to reinforce the Greeks, Mussolini, much to his chagrin, was compelled to request the support of German forces.

To this point, Hitler had pursued a Balkan policy of granting Italy primacy in the coastal states of the region—Albania, Greece and Yugoslavia—while Germany drew Hungary, Bulgaria and Romania in under its wing with varying degrees of coercion. Now Hitler faced the necessity of rescuing his ally. Hitler's attention was drawn to Greece in early 1941 when the British deployed troops there. Yugoslavia, which was to be the German springboard, was bullied into signing the Tripartite Pact, but an unexpected military coup deposed the government and rallied popular opinion against an Axis alliance, thus interrupting Hitler's plans. Characteristically, the German dictator ordered his armies into Yugoslavia as the *Luftwaffe* pounded Belgrade with bombs. Even as Serb resistance collapsed in early April, German armies were invading Greece, where British forces were forced to endure a "second Dunkirk" and withdraw. In late May, the Germans further secured their position in the eastern Mediterranean when they quickly overcame a British force defending the island of Crete.

There was also the Italian debacle in North Africa to be rectified. This time German intervention came in the form of the *Afrika Korps*, commanded by Erwin Rommel. Arriving with a small armored force in Tripoli in February 1941, Rommel launched an offensive that drove British forces back almost to the Egyptian frontier, leaving an Australian garrison besieged at Tobruk. For the next two years the struggle swept back and forth across the North African desert. A British offensive in November 1941 drove the *Afrika Korps* westward; a German drive in January 1942 pushed the British back into Egypt, where they made a stand at El-Alamein. By October

1942, British forces attacked the Germans and forced Rommel to retreat toward Tunisia. The last stage of the desert war began that November, when an Anglo-American invasion force landed in French North Africa and pushed eastward. The *Afrika Korp's* position deteriorated in the following months and remaining German and Italian forces surrendered in Tunisia in May 1943.

OPERATION "BARBAROSSA": HITLER STRIKES EAST

"The world will hold its breath!" Hitler had boasted to his generals as he finalized preparations for his ultimate goal, the invasion and destruction of the Soviet Union. Hitler had few doubts about the outcome. The USSR, governed in Hitler's view by Jews and Bolsheviks, would be incapable of resistance. "One need only kick in the front door," he asserted," and the whole rotten edifice will come crashing down!" All of Hitler's moves in eastern Europe to this point had been calculated toward this end. The occupation of Czechoslovakia and Poland, together with the coercion of the Balkan nations had left Hitler's armies perfectly positioned to step off into the Soviet Union. The war in the west and Mussolini's ill-fated ventures unexpectedly delayed Operation "Barbarossa," but by the summer of 1941 Hitler had resolved these problems, save for the continuing British role in the war. His intended victim was shockingly vulnerable. Stalin was disposed to discount warnings of an impending Nazi invasion. The armed forces of the Soviet Union were woefully unprepared; Stalin's murderous purges in the 1930s had devastated the upper ranks in all branches. Centralized operational directions from Moscow, far distant from the borders, precluded field commanders from exercising individual initiative in crisis situations. Much Soviet equipment was inferior or in short supply. The USSR was thus ill-prepared to stop the massive forces gathering on its western flank. Nearly four million German troops supported by some 3,500 tanks and 2,000 aircraft took their positions along a thousand-mile frontier in late June. It was the largest military force ever assembled.

Operation "Barbarossa" began in the early hours of June 22, 1941, as three German army groups crossed the frontier along historical invasion routes that led toward Leningrad, Moscow and Kiev. Surprised Russian defend-

ers suffered immediate and devastating losses in troops, tanks and aircraft; the Soviet Air Force lost 1,200 planes on the first day of the invasion alone. Incurring massive casualties, Red Army troops had little choice other than to exchange ground for time during the first several months of the Russo-German war. In much of the western world, the common assumption was that the USSR would be defeated by the fall. Terrible destruction marked the path of German armies, made worse by the ideological nature of the conflict. Hitler had warned his generals in March that the war against Russia would be con-

Fig. 6-2 A German tank provides transportation for infantry as Nazi forces advance into Soviet territory during Operation "Barbarossa," launched in June 1941. German dictator Adolf Hitler was confident that his *Blitzkrieg* strategy, which involved a coordinated assault by armored forces, infantry and tactical air support, would bring about the collapse of the Soviet Union within months. (Corbis)

ducted with "unprecedented, unmerciful and unrelenting harshness." German soldiers who broke international law need not fear punishment, Hitler had declared. In fact, invading troops were followed by "special groups" of SS troops, whose duty was to implement Hitler's racial policies on an immense scale. This included the extermination of Jews, Soviet commissars and intellectuals. Ultimately, the remaining population was to be reduced to a subclass of slaves, uneducated, stateless and existing only to serve their Nazi masters.

By the fall, a German triumph seemed inevitable. Three million Red Army soldiers were dead while additional millions were in captivity, where death was a certainty for the majority. German forces held vast expanses of Soviet territory including several major cities; Leningrad would soon face a siege that lasted nearly three years. Yet the situation was deceptive. The Red Army had been mauled, but hardly destroyed; it was also far larger than the Germans had estimated. The Soviet Air Force, nearly eliminated in the first days, recovered rapidly, supplied with new and effective aircraft produced in plants east of the Ural Mountains, beyond the reach of German bombers. Perhaps most disquieting from the German perspective was the Russian refusal to bend before the German onslaught. "The Russian civilian was tough," wrote one German general, "and the Russian soldier still tougher. He seemed to have an unlimited capacity for obedience and endurance." Compounding this problem was the weather. Rain and mud in October slowed the German advance, and a few weeks later the advent of a traditional Russian ally, "General Winter," halted it altogether. Temperatures that immobilized machinery and froze weapons debilitated ill-clothed German troops. Consequently, in early Decem-

ber, with the spires of the Kremlin within eyesight of advance units, the German drive on Moscow collapsed. For the first time, the concept of the *Blitzkrieg* had failed; Germany now faced a long war in the east. On December 11, four days after Japan's attack on the American naval base at Pearl Harbor, Hawaii, Hitler made German victory problematic when he declared war on the United States. An enthusiastic Mussolini committed Italy to an enlarged war on the same day.

War in the Pacific, 1941–1943

The first months of the Pacific War brought almost continual defeat for the Allied powers. British, Dutch and French forces in the region were too small or too poorly prepared to offer much resistance to Japan's rapid advance southward. While American military and naval strength in the Pacific was more significant, U.S. forces were also caught unprepared by the Japanese onslaught and were initially incapable of effectively opposing Japan's superior forces. Nonetheless, key American victories in the late spring of 1942 determined the limits of Japanese expansion and portended future triumphs.

JAPAN TRIUMPHANT, DECEMBER 1941–JUNE 1942

The Japanese decision to go to war against the United States was the product of several decades of growing antagonism and, as of late 1941, increasing desperation. The stalemate in negotiations begun in the fall led many in the Japanese military to believe that compromise was impossible and that with every passing week Japan's strategic position in the far Pacific was deteriorating. No more propitious moment would occur; the only question

Map 6–1 WWII on Asia and the Pacific

concerned what strategy would permit Japan to gain her objectives. In general, these included American acceptance of Japan as the dominant Asian power, allowing exploitation of the material riches of south and southeast Asia under the umbrella of the "Greater East Asia Co-Prosperity Sphere." Many of Japan's military leaders saw this as a legitimate goal; a few were aware of the likely difficulty of defeating a major industrial power.

One such individual was Admiral Isoroku Yamamoto, commander of the Combined Imperial Fleet. Having studied at Harvard University, Yamamoto was more familiar with the United States and American behavior than were some of his more impetuous colleagues. He warned of the industrial and agricultural potential of the traditionally isolationist United States. He was skeptical of Japanese beliefs about Americans being a materialistic and indolent people, lacking spirit and discipline. Nonetheless, it was Yamamoto who proposed the bold plan by which Japan could conceivably strike a decisive blow against American forces in the Pacific. Inspired by the successful British air attack on the Italian fleet at Taranto, Yamamoto designed a plan by which Japanese aircraft carriers would launch a massive aerial assault on the major units of the U.S. Pacific Fleet at Pearl Harbor. If the endeavor were successful, the American naval presence in the Pacific would be largely eliminated and amphibious forces could seize U.S. Pacific possessions. Once a Japanese defensive perimeter was established running the length of the Pacific from the Aleutian Islands to the Solomon Islands, the United States would hopefully perceive the futility of a protracted war and concede Japanese supremacy in the Far East. The scheme offered the possibility of unprecedented triumphs and a reorganization of the colonial world. Japanese forces would oust not only the Americans, but also the European imperial powers from Asia. Ulitmately, however, the strategy rested on a tremendous gamble; if the war were not won quickly, the consequences could be disastrous. Yamamoto was remarkably prescient in his assessment of such a war. "In the first six to twelve months of a war with the United States," he had observed, "I will run wild and win vic-

tory after victory. After that . . . I have no expectation of success."

For the first six months of the war, Imperial Japan did in fact enjoy an almost unbroken string of victories. The attack on Pearl Harbor was carried out with almost textbook precision, with few exceptions. As American servicemen slept in on the morning of Sunday, December 7, an aerial armada of fighters, dive bombers and torpedo bombers launched from Japanese aircraft carriers some 200 miles to the north of Oahu roared in over the island, catching the defenders completely unprepared. The results, at first glance, seemed catastrophic for the Americans. Battleship Row, where the capital ships were moored two abreast, was left a shambles; *Arizona* was destroyed in a terrible explosion that tore the ship in two and killed more than 1,000 of her crew, while *Oklahoma* capsized. Six other battleships were left sinking or badly damaged and eleven smaller ships were sunk or badly hit. Japanese aviators strafed and bombed airfields and barracks, destroying 188 aircraft on the ground. By the time the last of two waves of attackers had headed back out to sea, American casualties amounted to slightly more than 3,400. Yamamoto had accomplished his mission with the loss of only 29 aircraft and five midget submarines. There were a few consolations for the Americans. None of the American aircraft carriers, so crucial to the coming conflict in the Pacific, had been in port that morning; the Japanese had failed to destroy the fuel depots, the repair yards and the submarine docks. In the months to come, these omissions would prove critical. Yamamoto, while aware of his triumph, had doubts about the future. "I fear that all we have done," he remarked, "is to waken a sleeping giant and fill him with a terrible resolve."

Fig. 6-3 American battleships USS *West Virginia* and USS *Tennessee* were among the capital ships struck during the Japanese air attack on I the U.S. naval base at Pearl Harbor, Hawaii, on December 7, 1941. The U.S. Pacific Fleet, though badly mauled, recovered rapidly, with all but two of the battleships sunk in the attack refloated and returned to service. More significantly, the attack united Americans in their determination to wreak vengeance on Japan. (Pearson Education, Corporate Digital Archive, National Archives and Records Administration)

Most immediately, however, even as President Roosevelt asked for a declaration of war on December 8, the Japanese juggernaut drove through Southeast Asia. Japanese forces attacked American bases in the Philippines only hours after Pearl Harbor, with similar success. Only days later, Japanese aircraft sank the British battleship *Prince of Wales*, together with the battlecruiser *Repulse*, off Malaya. British Hong Kong fell on December 19. Japanese troops captured both Guam and Wake Island from the Americans the same month. Britain suffered a humiliating defeat at Singapore in February 1942, where some 130,000 Commonwealth troops were led into captivity. In the East Indies, the Imperial Navy annihilated the combined naval forces of the United States, Britain, Australia and Holland by March. The Japanese occupation of the Dutch East Indies followed. American and Filipino forces surrendered Corregidor in May, marking Japanese control of the archipelago. The tide of Japanese conquest appeared unstoppable.

Japanese triumphs were the product of several factors. Japan could easily bring to bear superior military and naval forces, especially air power. Japanese aircraft, such as the nimble Mitsubishi A6M "Zero" fighter, were superior to most western types at this stage and Japanese aviators were experienced. The demands of the war in Europe, unpreparedness, overconfidence and the realities of geography all hampered the western powers. These disadvantages could be overcome with time, which worked against the Japanese, especially if the United States refused to quit the war. It was here that Japanese strategy began to unravel. The attack on Pearl Harbor not only united a divided American public, but also imbued Americans with a fierce determination to fight the war through to absolute victory. Additionally, Japanese overconfidence, or "victory disease," led Japanese strategists to make some fateful miscalculations early in the war. Shortly after the Pearl Harbor attack, Yamamoto had written to his sister that "this war will give us much trouble in the future." Once again, the admiral proved remarkably perceptive.

STEMMING THE JAPANESE ADVANCE, SPRING–SUMMER 1942

The sequence of events that decisively changed the course of the Pacific war began in early April 1942 as the USS *Hornet* steamed out of San Francisco Bay. On board the aircraft carrier were sixteen B-25 bombers and their crews, commanded by Army Air Force Colonel James Doolittle. Their objective was to steam within range of Japan and launch the small force of normally land-based bombers against Tokyo and other cities, where an attack of this nature would be unexpected. It was understood that little real damage would result; the objective was to boost American morale by striking the heart of the Japanese Empire. Doolittle's bombers

succeeded in their surprise attack, though all the planes save one crashed in China. The effect went much beyond what the Americans could have expected. Japanese military leaders were enraged and humiliated by the raid and the decision was soon made to destroy the remaining units of the U.S. Pacific Fleet by luring them into a trap. The plan was to draw the American Navy into battle through an invasion of Midway Island; a simultaneous feint would be made toward the Aleutians.

Even as these plans proceeded, the Japanese moved south, dispatching a fleet to secure Port Moresby on New Guinea's southern shore. The United States dispatched a small force including two aircraft carriers to intercept the Japanese. The resulting Battle of the Coral Sea in early May 1942 was not decisive; both sides lost one aircraft carrier. But the American countermove stopped the Japanese advance toward Australia and disproved Japanese invincibility. Equally important, the value of American intelligence efforts was made clear. Decrypted Japanese signals had tipped off the Americans to the Port Moresby operation. The decryptions soon revealed Japan's planned strike at Midway, and two U.S. task forces sailed to meet the threat. The battle of Midway, which unfolded June 4–6, broke Japan's offensive and marked the turning point in the Pacific conflict. While part of the struggle centered around Japanese assaults on the small installations on Midway, the greater battle took place miles away at sea as two great naval forces struggled to locate and destroy one another. In this battle the opposing vessels never came within sight of one another; air power and the events comprising what one historian termed "the fatal five minutes" determined the outcome. Even as Japanese carriers, their decks jammed with fully fueled and armed aircraft, prepared to launch an attack against the U.S. fleet, American dive bombers, having finally located the enemy fleet, attacked with devastating accuracy. Massive fires and detonating munitions quickly sank three Japanese carriers; U.S. aircraft sank a fourth carrier later that day. Japanese aviators succeeded in sinking the U.S. carrier *Yorktown*, but the clash at Midway was a decisive American victory, sweetened by the fact that the enemy carriers destroyed had all participated in the Pearl Harbor attack. Japanese naval aviation was dealt a staggering blow as neither the carriers nor the pilots were replaceable. Following the battle of Midway, Japanese energies were directed largely to defending the sprawling empire gained in the first six months of the war.

The remaining months of 1942 brought the first Allied offensives in the south Pacific, undertaken to maintain open sea lanes to Australia and in response to public demands for aggressive action against the enemy. A major test of American capabilities and endurance grew out of the struggle for Guadalcanal in the Solomon Islands. An amphibious invasion put Marines ashore in August 1942, but a disastrous naval engagement soon jeopardized the landing. The Battle of Savo Island took place when a Japanese cruiser strike force surprised the Allied warships guarding the troopships off the contested island. In a short but devastating night battle, Japanese warships sank four Allied cruisers. The Allied support ships withdrew, leaving the Marines on their own as both sides sought to get more troops to the island. The next several months brought further naval battles that were costly but indecisive as bitter fighting raged between the Marines and Japanese ashore. By December, Allied air and naval forces foiled the final Japanese efforts to send in reinforcements. The Japanese finally abandoned Guadalcanal in February 1943.

The other major struggle occurred in New Guinea, where new Japanese troops had arrived in July 1942. The threat to Australia led the Allied commander, General Douglas MacArthur, to send U.S. and Australian troops to halt this new Japanese move against Port Moresby. The two armies clashed in Papua, where some of the most difficult fighting of the Pacific war took place around "Bloody Buna." By the end of 1942, the Allies had gained the initiative and Australia faced no further threat. As of early 1943, the greatest challenge for the Allies was mapping out a general offensive strategy for the defeat of Japan.

TOTAL WAR AND MODERN SOCIETY

The war reshaped societies around the world in ways both subtle and profound. Those nations directly involved experienced the most dramatic transformations, but as warfare spread to even the most distant colonial peripheries, few peoples remained unaffected. The war's magnitude was such that the North African Berber was at times as much in the war's path as was the French farmer or the Indonesian peasant. Arctic regions, mountains, tropical jungles and deserts were all scenes of conflict. The war's impact was most immediate and far-reaching in Europe and Asia, though many peripheral areas were affected.

Among the Axis powers, Germany had been most prepared for war in 1939, but proved surprisingly inefficient in early mobilization for a sustained war effort. Though the German people were immediately subjected to air raids, rationing, requisitions and restrictions, the government did not seriously compel an atmosphere of urgency until after the defeat at Stalingrad in early 1943. Only then did Minister of Propaganda Joseph

Goebbels deliver his famous address at Berlin's *Sportpalast* exhorting the German people to "Total War." Likewise, Germany's industrial output until 1943 was laggard, despite the resources and labor available from Nazi-occupied Europe. This was due in part to the Byzantine structure of the Nazi government; a contentious bureaucracy often distorted or obstructed Hitler's order. The military's domination of production also worked against the successful implementation of mass production. Minister of Armaments Albert Speer eventually organized a more rational system of production, but this was offset by the increasingly disruptive impact of Allied bombing, which affected transportation and oil supplies as well. By war's end, the German industrial economy was buckling under the weight of lost opportunities and Allied pressure, though faith in victory remained high until the final weeks.

Both Italy and Japan confronted far graver problems. Italy faced critical shortages of strategic materials when Mussolini entered the war and the country's industrial capabilities declined rapidly. Deprivations of all kinds brought growing unrest among Italians that culminated with Mussolini's ouster in 1943. Japanese social cohesion was more successfully retained during the war, as Japanese dutifully sacrificed in the face of growing food and housing shortages. Such sacrifice could not compensate for Japan's industrial deficiencies, however. With limited industrial facilities and dependent on imports for almost all strategic materials, Japan was extremely vulnerable. As Allied advances deprived Japan of the resources of Southeast Asia and American submarines destroyed her merchant shipping, eventual industrial collapse was inevitable. By summer 1945, only the intransigence of Japan's military leaders

and the resigned obedience of her people sustained the nation's war effort.

In perilous proximity to Nazi Europe and alone by 1940, Great Britain undertook extensive mobilization. Defense industries absorbed a huge proportion of the labor force as men and women alike worked long hours. Civil defense and Home Guard duties further occupied a people who lived routinely with blackouts, bombings and evacuations. Altogether, Britons endured a long, dreary war striving valiantly to meet the conflict's material needs, but never overcoming the obstacles of a small industrial base and outdated plant facilities. The very precariousness of Britain's position, however, did much to strengthen the public determination to endure, and American Lend-Lease aid provided crucial material support.

The Soviet Union faced a much more serious crisis by fall 1941; with the main industrial and agricultural regions in German hands, the Soviet economy appeared on the verge of collapse as entire populations fled eastward. Military reversals, in part the consequence of Stalin's murderous purges, seemed to prefigure complete defeat. Yet in the next two years, industrial and military recovery bordering on the miraculous occurred, as industrial output soared and the Red Army and Soviet Air Force were rebuilt. The Soviet military effort was also greatly aided by Lend-Lease materials from the United States. Soviet society remained cohesive despite repeated hammer blows for several reasons. One was the general realization that, whatever the deficiencies of Stalinist rule, it was preferable to the degradation and likely national extinction that Nazi victory would bring. This led many Russians to see the war in a fundamentally nationalistic context; hence the references to the conflict as the

"Great Patriotic War." Concessions by the regime, such as easing the restraints on religious practices, bought further popular support. The fierce determination to resist German aggression helped bolster wartime production in the industrial refuge east of the Ural Mountains. Here Soviet factories worked nonstop to produce equipment that was simple in design, extremely rugged and easily repairable, such as the T-34 tank. The need was such that many were driven straight off the assembly line into battle. The Soviet industrial recovery provided one foundation for a reborn Soviet military machine, which by 1943 reversed the course of the war on the eastern front. Years of war and Nazi occupation took an unimaginable toll, however, and Russians could rightly claim that it was they who bore the brunt of the war in Europe. Ultimately, the war cost the USSR an estimated 26 million dead.

One of the ironies of the Second World War is that the major power most thoroughly reshaped by the conflict was a nation that remained immune from the devastation suffered by most of the belligerents. The United States, insulated by the same geography that nurtured a historic isolationism, was radically transformed by the exigencies of the conflict. At war's onset, the United States was distinctly unimpressive as a military power, with an army that was only the 18th largest in the world and an air arm of 1,700 outdated aircraft; only the navy was of any consequence. By war's end, the United States Army alone boasted over eight million personnel, while the Army Air Force and Navy were the largest and most modern forces in the world; clearly, the United States was the first superpower.

The other great transformative effect was economic. American industrial mobilization began in 1939 as federal agencies were set up to oversee conversion and coordinate materials. After Pearl Harbor, more comprehensive governmental supervision determined priorities, the allocation of materials and the mobilization of the labor force. Roosevelt's "Arsenal of Democracy" became a reality as a skilled workforce, an abundance of most strategic materials (save raw rubber) and mass-production facilities combined to supply not only American needs but also those of allied powers. By 1944, Ford's Willow Run aircraft plant was producing one bomber every 63 minutes; a shipyard constructing cargo vessels produced one such "Liberty" ship in just eight days. This astounding industrial capacity did much to turn the course of the war by 1943. It also did much to reshape American society. Labor shortages provided new opportunities for women and blacks. Despite shortages and rationing, American workers enjoyed unprecedented prosperity. Wartime did produce some injustices; nearly 120,000 Japanese-Americans, victims of racial prejudice and exaggerated fears of sabotage, were relocated from the West Coast to "internment camps" in the interior. Black Americans and Mexican Americans fell victim as racial tensions exacerbated by war generated several vicious riots. Overall, however, the wartime experience united Americans and infused them with a renewed faith in their political, social and economic institutions. When the war ended, most Americans were enjoying a level of prosperity that would have seemed unimaginable only a few years earlier. Only in the United States would World War II be commonly referred to as "the Good War."

The war also served as an engine driving scientific research and technological advance, most often in the service of military necessity. The British need for defenses against German bombing spurred advances in radar technology, while the American search for more effective antisubmarine techniques led to more advanced sonar capabilities. The development of heavily armored tanks compelled the need for explosive projectiles capable of stopping them, which was part of a more general search for more powerful explosives of all types. The air war alone brought about uncountable changes in aircraft technology, culminating with the development of rocket and jet-propelled aircraft. The German search for the ultimate "victory weapon" produced robot flying bombs and the V-2 rocket, forerunner to the modern intercontinental ballistic missile. It was in fact fears about the direction that German research was taking that led the United States to establish an atomic weapons program in late 1941. The Manhattan Project employed thousands of research personnel at three "secret cities" in a top-secret effort to develop an atomic bomb. While German and Japanese programs stalled, scientists at Los Alamos, New Mexico, successfully detonated a plutonium bomb at a desert test site in July 1945. The United States became the world's first nuclear power as the Pacific War entered its final phase.

OCCUPATION, REPRESSION AND THE HOLOCAUST

For many peoples the war years meant occupation and hardship. In Asia, Japanese boasts of reclaiming "Asia for Asians" proved a cynical cloak for exploitation. In areas under Japanese occupation, native peoples were treated at best as inferior subjects and at worst with calculated brutality. Some of the worst depredations occurred in China, where a sin-

gle "vengeance offensive" by Japanese troops in the aftermath of the Doolittle Raid in 1942 left an estimated 250,000 Chinese civilians dead. In northeastern China, Japan's Kwantung Army set up the infamous "Unit 731," where scientists subjected Chinese, American and Russian prisoners to tests of biological warfare agents and vivisection. Resistance movements sprang up in the Philippines, Indonesia and Vietnam, where anti-Japanese guerillas operated at great personal risk.

In Europe, those peoples under German occupation faced years of police terror, arrests, deportations and summary executions. By late 1942, German forces occupied fourteen European countries; their role in Hitler's "New Order" was that of providing materials and labor for the Greater German Reich. Successful exploitation required order, and German military and police forces were aggressive in imposing it. In occupied France, the collaborationist Vichy regime of Marshal Petain aided the Nazis in deporting French workers to toil in German factories and in rounding up political dissidents and Jews to be sent off to concentration camps. In Norway, the name of the leader of the collaborationist regime, Vidkun Quisling, became a synonym for traitor. Notable resistance movements were organized in Norway, Denmark, the Netherlands and France among others, but the willingness of Nazi authorities to employ savage policies of retribution undercut their effectiveness. The death of a single German sometimes brought the execution of a hundred arbitrarily chosen civilian hostages. Such policies faced resistance movements with cruelly paradoxical choices.

In Eastern Europe, Nazi authorities demonstrated even less regard for the consequences of policies of exploitation and repression. SS chief Heinrich Himmler once commented that the fate of Russians or Czechs concerned him "only to the extent that we need them as slaves for our culture." Acts of barbarous repression confirmed his sentiment in policy. The assassination of SS official Reinhard Heydrich by Czech partisans in 1941 brought about an orgy of retribution in which approximately 5,000 people were murdered and the entire village of Lidice was razed to the ground. In the Soviet Union, whose population Hitler deemed to be both racially and politically suspect, inhumanities were commonplace. For Jews especially, the war's course by late 1941 had fateful consequences. By that year, Nazi Germany was in a position to determine the fate of not only western and central European Jews, but also that of the nine million Jews of eastern Europe and western Russia. As noted previously, "special commandos" had accompanied the German armies into Poland and the USSR, with instructions to murder Jews and some other categories of civilians. By June 1941, Himmler had organized a more systematic campaign of extermination in the eastern area of occupation, his killing squads murdering one million Jews by November. The usual means of execution, mass shooting, was deemed inefficient, however. In January 1942 at the Wannsee Conference in suburban Berlin, Himmler authorized his subordinates to implement a comprehensive plan for the destruction of European Jewry. This "Final Solution" envisaged the assembly and transportation of Jews to supposed "resettlement" in the east; in reality, they were to be delivered to a growing network of SS-run camps in both the occupied areas and in Germany. At camps such as Auschwitz in Poland, inmates were worked to the point of exhaustion and then gassed. At extermination camps such as Treblinka, inmates were

gassed on arrival. By war's end, Himmler's empire of death camps had done much to realize Hitler's plan for a Jew-free Europe; ultimately some six million Jews, about 40 percent of the world's Jewish population, were exterminated in the course of the Holocaust.

Jews were not the only victims of Hitler's concentration camps. Gypsies, Slavs and others considered racially inferior also disappeared through camp gates bearing the deceptive ironwork slogan "Work Brings Freedom." The camps also served as repositories for political dissidents, outspoken clergy, homosexuals and even deposed foreign heads of state. Some camps, such as Auschwitz, were the sites of ghastly "medical experiments" performed on both inmates and prisoners-of-war. Altogether these horrors comprised, as historian Gordon Craig wrote, "a holocaust unequalled in European history." The question of culpability is a controversial one to the present day. Many Germans denied any knowledge of the events, while others maintained that they only carried out orders issued by a superior. A recent study by Daniel Goldhagen asserts that significant numbers of Germans willingly participated in the Holocaust, often with a shocking degree of enthusiasm. Hitler's "Final Solution" was without question an unprecedented manifestation of the darkest of human impulses.

The European War, 1943–1945

1943 brought the first significant Axis defeats in the European war, as German armies faced major reverses on the Russian front and in North Africa. Allied armies drove Italian forces from North Africa and invaded Italy in 1943, bringing the end of Mussolini's dictatorship. Increasingly under pressure at sea and in the air, Germany's fortunes waned as the Red

Army pushed Nazi armies back across Eastern Europe. The invasion of France by the western Allies in 1944 signaled the final phase of Germany's defeat as Allied armies drove toward Berlin from east and west.

WAR AT SEA AND IN THE AIR

In 1943 the European war began to turn in favor of the Allies on several fronts, perhaps most importantly in the Battle of the Atlantic. This struggle, which pitted German naval and air forces against Allied merchant shipping usually bound for British or Siberian ports, was the one campaign that Winston Churchill later admitted to having grave doubts about winning. Indeed, from the onset of the U-boat campaign in spring 1940, the Royal Navy was hard-pressed to protect the Atlantic lifeline. As shipping losses mounted in spring 1941, the challenge was compounded by the appearance of German surface raiders, such as the battleship *Bismarck*. Though *Bismarck* was sunk by British naval and air forces in May 1941, similar warships remained a threat. Intelligence successes such as the capture of a German "Enigma" encrypting device bought a brief respite, but American entry into the war in late 1941 offered Germany the opportunity to expand the U-boat campaign beyond previous constraints. 1942 proved disastrous for Allied shipping as German submarines ranged along the U.S. east coast, the Gulf of Mexico and the Caribbean basin with little effective opposition. Not until 1943 did new technologies, weapons and tactics combine to give Allied navies the advantage. Improved sonar and better depth charges were joined to escort groups that included aircraft carriers to provide trans-Atlantic convoys with adequate protection and to make duty in Germany's U-

boat service increasingly dangerous. Ultimately, of the 830 U-boats engaged in operations 696 were destroyed, making for the highest proportional losses suffered by any service of any country.

By 1943 the Allied air offensive against Germany had assumed both definition and growing intensity after several years of experimentation. As of summer 1941, British Bomber Command pursued a policy of "area bombing" at night, in hopes of "dehousing" German workers and interrupting war production. By spring 1942 the British, in hopes of overwhelming German defenses, mounted the first "thousand-bomber raid" on Cologne. The bomber offensive reached new heights in July 1943 when four nights of raids on Hamburg, Germany, created a "firestorm" that produced winds of up to 400 miles per hour, temperatures of nearly 1,000 degrees F and killed nearly 40,000 people. U.S. Army Air Force units began arriving in England in summer 1942 and by late that year would become part of a "combined bomber offensive" in which the Americans would bomb pinpointed targets by day while the RAF continued nighttime raids. The cost to both the British and the Americans was high, especially prior to the introduction of long-range fighter escorts in late 1943. By war's end 21,000 bombers together with 140,000 British and American aircrew were lost.

The air offensive did not destroy German industry completely, nor did it shatter civilian morale. It did, however, force the Germans to disperse production facilities and divert badly needed resources to air defense, impeding the war effort in innumerable ways. By early 1945, Allied bombing had badly disrupted German production schedules, leaving the enemy with far fewer tanks, trucks and aircraft than would have been available otherwise. The destruction of fuel

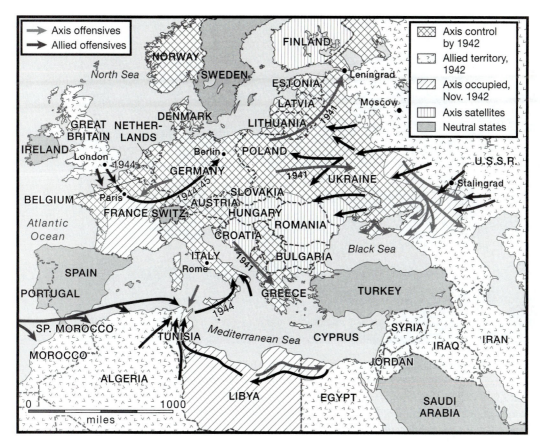

Map 6–2 The Crest of Axis Power in Europe

supplies as far away as Romania effectively grounded much of the *Luftwaffe* in the last year of the war. Without question, the bombing campaign had a direct and crucial impact on Germany's ability to wage war.

RED ARMY RESURGENT: THE ROAD TO STALINGRAD AND BEYOND

Many historians consider the struggle on the Eastern front as the hinge on which the outcome of the entire war swung; Hitler too was aware of its importance as Operation

"Barbarossa" stalled on the doorstep of the Soviet capital in late 1941. Though Hitler confided to a general that "victory can no longer be ours" he nonetheless prepared for a summer campaign in 1942. Overall the plan aimed at the destruction of Leningrad, a defensive stand in front of Moscow and an offensive thrust aimed south at the Caucasus and its petroleum resources. Soviet forces were once again caught off guard and by late summer suffered several major defeats. In August, Hitler was emboldened to order his forces against Stalingrad, an error of major

Fig. 6-4   Ruined buildings were all that remained of the center of Dresden, Germany, following Allied air raids on February 13–14, 1945. Over 2,000 British and American bombers dropped incendiary bombs that turned the city into an inferno in which an estimated 135,000 people died. (Pearson Education, Corporate Digital Archive, Index Stock Imagery, Inc.)

proportions. The city itself had little strategic importance; as Hitler's generals argued, the capture of Moscow would have been of greater value. Further, German forces were spread thin throughout southern Russia and supply lines were stretched. An assault on Stalingrad would require the use of less dependable Italian, Romanian and Hungarian troops. Most importantly, the Soviet Union was not, as Hitler believed, exhausted by earlier battles, but was in fact marshaling new material resources and troops.

Thus, as German forces fought their way into the city in late August, they initiated what was to become the first major German defeat of the war. A furious Soviet counteroffensive in November sparked weeks of savage house-to-house fighting during which Soviet armies encircled the German Sixth Army. Hitler refused to permit a breakout and retreat, opting to believe that an airlift could keep his troops fighting. Meanwhile, additional Russian armies drove north from the Caucasus and tore through German lines along the Don River north of Stalingrad. By late December, German forces in Stalingrad, deprived of any hope of resupply by air or reinforcements, were clearly trapped. To the end, Hitler was adamant that there should be no surrender, even promoting German General Friedrich Paulus to field marshal, as no German officer of that rank had ever surrendered. The final Soviet offensive began on January 10, 1943, and on February 2 what remained of Paulus' Sixth Army surrendered. A quarter of a million German troops were lost at Stalingrad with 90,000, including 23 generals, taken into captivity. A mere 5,000 survived as prisoners-of-war.

Journalist Alexander Werth, who spent the war years in the Soviet Union, recalled after the battle of Stalingrad that "no-one doubted that this was *the* turning point in World War II." German military losses since November had been tremendous and with the destruction of the Sixth Army, a pervasive atmosphere of gloom settled over Germany. Propaganda Minister Goebbels attempted to capitalize on the disaster by exhorting Germans to embrace "total war," but the slogan seemed to connote only future hardships and uncertainty. Hitler responded by accusing Paulus of cowardice, then refusing to speak of the debacle again. Observers agree that from this point, Hitler became withdrawn, prone to bouts of unreality and increasing ill health.

On the Eastern front, one final scene remained to be played in this act of a long and costly drama. As of July 1943, Soviet advances and German counterattacks had created a "bulge" in the front line, with the city of Kursk at its center. German hopes were to cut off Soviet forces in this salient and destroy them. These plans led to the month-long battle of Kursk, which began on July 4

and turned into the largest pitched battle of the war, pitting almost one million German troops against one and a half million Russians. Prior to the Gulf War of 1990–1991, Kursk was considered to be the greatest tank battle in history, with a total of some 3,500 armored vehicles involved. Though the Germans inflicted heavy losses on the Soviet side, they were so badly weakened that the German position in the USSR was now untenable. Following this last significant German offensive in Russia, an increasingly powerful and motivated Red Army began the arduous task of driving the enemy armies from Russian soil. At the Teheran Conference in November 1943, Stalin agreed to mount a major offensive westward in conjunction with an Anglo-American invasion of France. Beginning in late June 1944, the Red Army began pushing the Germans back along a front that ran from the Baltic to the Carpathian Mountains; by late July, Soviet forces were on the outskirts of Warsaw.

Even as Hitler confronted the specter of defeat on the eastern front, he narrowly escaped assassination. On July 20, a bomb planted by anti-Nazi army officers detonated in a conference room at Hitler's East Prussian headquarters. The explosion left the *Führer* wounded but all the more convinced of the need to fulfill his destiny. The plotters were quickly arrested, given a farcical trial and then cruelly executed, ending any likelihood of military revolt. But Hitler still faced other difficulties. Germany's unreliable Balkan allies were growing restive as Soviet forces approached. In late August, Romania abandoned Hitler for the Allies. Bulgaria followed with a declaration of war against Germany in September, and by October Hungary had quit the war. Three years before, as the Nazi *Blitzkrieg* blew through western Russia, many observers had predicted the imminent collapse of the Soviet state. Now, after years of almost inconceivable hardship and endurance, the men and women of the Red Army stood poised for the advance into Eastern Europe and Germany itself. Through their sacrifice, the Soviet Union was delivered from annihilation. The Russians' stubborn determination to resist in the face of overwhelming odds was, according to historian Richard Overy, the key element in achieving the critical victories on the Eastern Front. "The Soviet people," he wrote, "were the instrument of their own redemption from the depths of war."

THE ITALIAN CAMPAIGN AND THE COLLAPSE OF FASCIST ITALY

By 1943, Mussolini's promise of a "New Roman Empire" seemed laughably implausible. Half of the Italian army had been sacrificed on the Russian front and the air force was reduced to a paltry few hundred planes. What remained of a once fine navy was immobilized for lack of fuel, and continual defeats left Italians demoralized. It was, Winston Churchill believed, a propitious time to attack the "soft underbelly" of the Axis, a course of action he proposed at the Casablanca Conference in January. Operations began that July as British and American forces invaded Sicily. The political fallout was immediate; the Italian king dismissed Mussolini as prime minister and *il Duce* was whisked away to a mountaintop prison. A German commando team liberated the despondent dictator in September and eventually installed him as ruler of the "Salo Republic," a truncated fascist state in northern Italy. In Mussolini's absence, his fascist regime unraveled rapidly. Marshal Pietro Badoglio formed a new government which,

unfortunately, dithered too long in considering Italy's future direction. The delay confirmed Hitler's concern about Italy's trustworthiness. American landings on the mainland in September preceded a prematurely announced armistice, which led to the royal government's flight to allied lines and the rapid German disarmament of now leaderless Italian forces.

Italy's desertion to the Allied side in October did not alter Allied prospects. The German occupation of the peninsula as far south as Naples set the stage of a long grueling campaign in which geography favored defense. Additional Allied landings in early 1944 brought no great breakthroughs, as German forces established successive defensive lines over the next year, making the northward drive costly. In April 1945, Allied armies began a final drive against German forces in northern Italy, aided by popular uprisings in the cities. Late that month, Mussolini, disguised as a German soldier, was captured by partisans as he attempted to cross into Switzerland. The former dictator and his mistress were executed together and the bodies taken to Milan. There, in a final act of degradation, angry Italians defiled and mutilated the body of the man whose New Roman Empire had brought only hardship and defeat.

FROM NORMANDY TO BERLIN: THE END OF THE EUROPEAN WAR

The long-awaited Allied invasion of western France on June 6, 1944, was, in the minds of many, the final prelude to German defeat. Allied planners were well aware of the formidable obstacles to success. Hitler had long bragged of the invulnerability of the "west wall" of his "Fortress Europe." Vigilant troops manned huge coastal defense guns shielded by tons of steel-reinforced concrete. The beaches were a nightmare of mines and obstacles both above and below the low-tide line and could be swept by well-sited machine gun emplacements. Rapidly changeable weather and shifting tides compounded the difficulties. Yet by late spring 1944, the joint Anglo-American Operation "Overlord" was near implementation. Some nine million tons of supplies and about 800,000 troops had arrived in England since January. Artificial harbors had been built to be towed across the English Channel to the Normandy coast. Elaborate deceptions aimed at misleading the enemy as to the site of the invasion had been ongoing for months. Reports on June 5 of several days of favorable weather led General Dwight Eisenhower to order the invasion to proceed, and a massive amphibious armada headed for the French coast.

On "D-Day," June 6, a fleet of over 5000 vessels supported by a force of 12,000 aircraft was given the task of getting an initial 90,000 troops ashore. Though caught by surprise, German defenders resisted strongly and the difficulties encountered on the five invasion beaches varied. By the next day, however, nearly 180,000 American, British and Canadian troops were ashore, aided by clear Allied air superiority. Rapid German recovery and the nature of the Normandy countryside slowed progress, however. Air photo-reconnaissance had not shown the hedgerows, earthen mounds covered with brush, that surrounded most fields. This terrain proved perfectly suited to defense. Grinding progress was made through June, but not until late July was a definite Allied breakout achieved. The area under Allied control expanded rapidly in the following month. Scenes of wild celebration marked the liberation of Paris on August 25, and the presumption

grew that the steady German retreat signaled the nearness of war's end. By mid-September, most of Belgium, Luxembourg and France had been cleared of German forces. However, Allied logistical needs brought a deceleration of the eastward advance. This delay in the autumn of 1944 provided the respite required for Hitler to organize the last major German offensive of the war.

The Battle of the Bulge began on December 16 as newly strengthened German forces launched a surprise assault against American lines in Luxembourg and Belgium. Aided by inclement weather that negated Allied air superiority, German infantry and armor smashed through unprepared U.S. positions with the intention of recapturing Antwerp, disrupting Allied supply lines and encircling the British army in Belgium. Surprise, speed and creative commando operations combined to ensure initial successes. However, some U.S. units, such as those holding Bastogne, stubbornly refused to give way, slowing an offensive dependent in part on speed for success. The German effort was ultimately dependent on the capture of large stocks of fuel from the Allies, a hope not realized. Meanwhile, reoriented Allied units attacked the German "bulge" in the front from both north and south. The final blow to German chances came on December 23 when the weather cleared. Allied fighter-bombers immediately filled the skies to pound and harass German forces. Hitler's last gamble had failed at the cost of 100,000 men and irreplaceable equipment. Anglo-American armies stood on the German frontier, poised for the final assault on Hitler's "Thousand-Year Reich."

The final phase of the war against Germany began with a Soviet offensive in January 1945. Hardened by years of conflict, strengthened in numbers, equipment and material support, the Red Army was arguably now the single most powerful military force in Europe. With confidence strengthened by the successful liberation of Eastern Europe, Soviet forces drove into Germany with a determination born of the desire for vengeance. By early February Soviet units were on the Oder River, only 40 miles east of Berlin. On the western front, Anglo-American forces had pushed to the Rhine River, a geographic and psychological barrier that was surmounted in early March. Hitler's growing desperation was evident in his order that the defense of Germany should include the destruction of its industrial infrastructure, so as to create a "desert" before the advancing armies. By now, however, the outcome was largely predetermined. Beginning with the Teheran Conference of 1943, the final defeat and disposition of Germany had been an ongoing consideration for Allied leaders. At the Yalta Conference in February 1945, plans for the final campaign and the division of Germany were formalized. As the proposed Soviet zone included about 40 percent of eastern Germany, there was no compelling reason for the western Allies to advance beyond the Elbe River, where U.S. and Soviet forces linked up at Torgau on April 27. By then the final Soviet assault on Berlin was in its last stage. An army of 2.5 million under Marshal Zhukov fought its way into the Nazi capital against stiff resistance. With Soviet tanks and troops only several hundred yards from his underground bunker, Hitler shot himself on April 29. To the end he blamed others for the catastrophe he had brought upon Germany and bitterly denounced the German people as unworthy of the mission he had set before them. On May 7 German General Alfred Jodl signed a general surrender of all German forces. Hitler's war cost 4.5 million German lives; 8 million were made

refugees and another 10 million were prisoners of war. Germany lay prostrate, a nation in ruins, occupied by four foreign armies and burdened by the responsibility for horrors unprecedented in history.

War in the Pacific, 1943–1945

With the failure of Japan's Pacific strategy, which was based on perceived American irresoluteness and hopes for a correspondingly short war, Japanese forces were increasingly fighting defensive actions after 1942. The perimeter of Japanese control in the Pacific shrank as the American "island-hopping" campaign slowly but relentlessly pushed Japanese armies out of conquered territories and back toward their homeland. The struggle to position American forces within bombing range of Japan was long and costly, and by the summer months of 1945 there was doubt among U.S. policymakers that Japan would ever surrender. Those fears led to the decision to use nuclear weapons to compel a Japanese surrender.

THE ISLAND-HOPPING CAMPAIGN

Though Japan's drive across the Pacific had been clearly blunted by late 1942, a comprehensive Allied strategy for victory had yet to evolve. What was evident was that Nationalist China would not play a major role in Allied war plans. Japan's armies controlled the most productive regions of China with little effective resistance from either Chiang Kai-shek's ill-used troops or Mao Tse-tung's communist forces in the northwest. Any hopes that the U.S. might mount an air campaign against Japan from China foundered on the Nationalists' inability to secure air bases from Japanese attack. The China-Burma-India Theater remained a backwater, though British Commonwealth forces fought a long and costly campaign against the Japanese in Burma, one of Britain's south Asian colonies. In May, 1943, U.S. forces launched an essentially symbolic offensive in the Aleutian Islands that hinted at what was to come in the course of the final Pacific offensive. A year before, Japanese troops had occupied several of the small, rocky islands, the only portion of the continental United States to come under Japanese control. In part to demonstrate the changed dynamics of the war, U.S. forces landed on Attu in early May. The Japanese garrison, outnumbered 4 to 1, fought to the death, making suicidal assaults on U.S. positions; only 26 of 2,500 Japanese troops were taken alive. It was an ominous portent.

Early in 1943, the model for a campaign of "island-hopping" grew out of discussions as to how the important Japanese base at Rabaul on New Britain might be captured. While the Joint Chiefs of Staff felt that there were not adequate material resources available for the capture of the base, they did eventually agree to General Douglas MacArthur's proposal to begin a two-pronged offensive toward Rabaul, attacking Japanese weak spots in the Solomon Islands and New Guinea, capturing existing air and port facilities and then leaping forward to the next conquest. Operation "Cartwheel" profited from growing American air superiority and naval strength. Increasing numbers of deadly attack bombers were being brought to bear against Japanese troop transports; a new fighter aircraft, the F6F "Hellcat," specifically designed to counter the dread Japanese "Zero," began to arrive in large numbers. Fleet carriers were joining the Pacific Fleet at the rate of one a month; small escort carriers were proliferating in numbers that the Japanese could never counter. An increasingly effective U.S. submarine campaign destroyed both enemy warships and merchant vessels, leaving Japanese garrisons

starved and ill-supplied. Growing numbers of specially designed landing craft and broadened experience in amphibious campaigns also facilitated the Allied task.

A comprehensive Allied strategy was formulated in May 1943, proposing a twin drive by U.S. forces across the central and southwest Pacific, with the objectives of liberating the Philippines (MacArthur's great concern) and bringing American forces within bombing range of Japan's home islands. The campaign of island warfare that followed produced a series of exotic placenames that became synonymous with savage fighting and death in the heat of tropical jungles. Tarawa, Kwajalein, Eniwetok, Saipan and Tinian were all battles that involved fighting an enemy who was well-entrenched and willing to fight to the death. Americans and Japanese alike rarely gave quarter in a conflict that historian John Dower described as "war without mercy." The American advance into the Marianas provoked the Japanese into dispatching a massive fleet including nine carriers to force a decisive battle in the central Pacific. The subsequent battle of the Philippine Sea began in June 1944 with Japanese carrier-borne aircraft attacking U.S. carrier groups. In the resulting debacle, known as the "Great Marianas Turkey Shoot," U.S. fighters downed hundreds of Japanese planes. Subsequent American attacks on the Japanese fleet destroyed three aircraft carriers. Remaining Japanese forces retreated and it soon became clear that Japanese naval air power in the Pacific had been dealt a staggering blow.

FROM THE PHILIPPINES TO OKINAWA

General MacArthur, who believed that the United States could not morally bypass the bulk of the Philippines and leave the Filipinos at the mercy of the Japanese, ultimately won the debate over strategic priorities in the south Pacific. Preparations for the invasion got a boost when U.S. naval forces off Formosa succeeded in destroying the greater part of Japanese air power in the area. American forces went ashore on Leyte on October 20 and began to push inland against moderate opposition. This precipitated the naval battle of Leyte Gulf as the main Japanese fleet moved eastward from north of Borneo to oppose the U.S. invasion. Beginning on October 24, a series of running battles saw Japanese naval forces initially set back by the sinking of the superbattleship *Musashi* and then staggered by another costly encounter with U.S. battleships in Surigao Strait. Subsequent encounters in Leyte Gulf cost the U.S. Navy a number of vessels, but ultimately the Japanese fleet withdrew, leaving the American invasion fleet intact. The battle of Leyte Gulf, described by Gerhard Weinberg as "the greatest naval battle in history," was a disaster for the Imperial Navy. Massive ship losses left Japan with only three carriers; Japanese naval aviation barely existed in the aftermath. Japan's only chance to slow the U.S. advance now rested on the *kamikaze,* suicide pilots willing to fly their aircraft into enemy vessels. The first such efforts had come in the final phase of the Leyte Gulf struggle and had resulted in the loss of the escort carrier *St. Lo.* It was a frightening example of greater horrors that awaited.

With Japan's navy checked, the American liberation of the Philippines proceeded; the island of Mindoro was invaded in mid-December. Mass *kamikaze* attacks and a horrendous typhoon pummeled the invasion fleet, but the preparations for an invasion of Luzon proceeded. U.S. Army troops went ashore on that island on January 8, 1945, with the ultimate objective of retaking Manila,

which was reached in early February. The ensuing battle of Manila was unique in that it involved the first fighting in a major urban setting in the Pacific War. It proved to be a bloody experience. Rather than abandon the city, the Japanese commander chose to engage in a pointless month-long, street-by-street defense of the capital. The fighting, together with the intentional Japanese destruction of the city and the massacre of its citizens, left 100,000 Filipinos dead. As the fighting ended in Manila's streets, Bataan, the site of American defeat and degradation in 1942, was regained. The fortress island of Corregidor was in U.S. hands by early March, and some forty amphibious landings brought about the liberation of the remaining islands to the south. Japanese resistance in the northern mountains of Luzon continued until the end of the war.

The island-hopping campaign culminated in the spring of 1945 with the invasion of Iwo Jima in the Bonin Islands and Okinawa in the Ryukus. The islands were crucial to the U.S. bombing campaign against the Japanese home islands. Though American bombers had been flying from the Marianas since fall 1944, the distance was great and Japanese radar on Iwo Jima was able to provide advance warning of raids. U.S. air bases on the two targeted islands would greatly facilitate the strategic bombing campaign and, hopefully, lead to Japan's surrender. The Japanese recognized the importance of the islands and heavily fortified them, the consequences becoming evident as marines landed on Iwo Jima on February 19. Savage fighting killed nearly 7000 marines and most of the 21,000-strong Japanese garrison. The Japanese defense of Okinawa proved as stubborn, and the invasion fleet was subjected to the most punishing *kamikaze* attacks of the war shortly after it arrived in early April. In the course of several weeks, over 1,000 suicide planes hurled themselves at the massive invasion fleet, with horrific results. The number and ferocity of the attacks overwhelmed even the best anti-aircraft defense; 30 vessels were sunk and over 350 were damaged, with some 5,000 sailors perishing. Such losses bordered on being unsupportable, but the fleet remained and the island eventually fell to the invaders. Victory cost nearly 7,000 American lives. Most of the Japanese garrison chose to adhere to the samurai code of *bushido* and die fighting rather than surrender; some 70,000 Japanese troops were killed on Okinawa, along with 80,000 Japanese civilians.

THE DEFEAT OF JAPAN AND THE END OF THE WAR

With Iwo Jima and Okinawa secured, the strategic bombing campaign against Japan accelerated. Key to the effort to pound Japan into submission was a new long-range bomber, the B-29 "Superfortress." A perfect example of war-driven innovations in aviation technology, the huge bomber had a range of 7,000 miles, a 2,000-pound bomb-load, pressurized crew spaces and remotely controlled gun turrets with computer-assisted targeting. The B-29s had been flying missions out of China since June 1944, but U.S. control of the Marianas provided a more secure base for larger raids on Japan by early 1945. Those raids assumed a new intensity under the direction of Army Air Force General Curtis LeMay, who devised the tactic of low-altitude nighttime raids using incendiary bombs. On March 8, over 300 B-29s conducted such an attack on Tokyo. The consequences were devastating; huge fires burned out 16 square miles of the city, killing over 80,000 Japanese. The pattern was repeated through June with major industrial cities as

the targets. As Japan's air power was already nearly nonexistent, there was virtually no defense against the attacks. By July, Japan's cities lay in ruins, her industries destroyed, her people homeless and hungry. U.S. fighter-bombers roamed the skies unopposed, attacking the few remaining targets. One question remained—given the hopeless situation, would Japan surrender?

There was no clear answer to this question by mid-summer. To some American policy-makers, Japanese conduct during the island-hopping campaign seemed to suggest that Japan might in fact commit "national suicide" rather than surrender. Indeed, even as Japanese aviators commonly resorted to suicide attacks, attempting to ram the B-29s over their country, Japanese civilians were being instructed how to repel American invaders with bamboo spears. The prospect of an invasion of the home islands chilled American planners; casualties would likely be horrendous, possibly doubling the U.S. casualty rate to that point in the war. There was some division among Japanese leaders as to the direction of the war, but the Army remained a strong voice for continued resistance and threatened retaliation against those counseling peace.

For President Harry Truman, Japan's rejection of the Potsdam Declaration in July clarified the options. The document came out of a conference between the American president, Stalin and Churchill (who was replaced nine days into the conference by the new Labour prime minister, Clement Attlee) during which both European and Asian issues were discussed. Gathering in Potsdam, just south of the ruined German capital, the Allied leaders looked toward bringing the war in the Pacific to a conclusion. Stalin reiterated an earlier Soviet pledge of belligerency against Japan in early August. Truman received news of a development that might preclude the need for significant Soviet involvement—the successful test of an atomic bomb in the New Mexican desert. The Potsdam Declaration, which spelled out the term for Japan's surrender, made no mention of nuclear weapons. It did, however, warn that rejection of the terms would lead to "the utter devastation of the Japanese homeland."

The American decision to use nuclear weapons against Japan stirs considerable controversy to this day; some argue that Japan was on the verge of surrender, or that a crucial misinterpretation marred the chances for ending the war without the bomb. However salient these points, Japan's apparent rejection of the Allied ultimatum led Truman to authorize history's first nuclear strike. On August 6, the *Enola Gay,* a B-29 flying out of Tinian in the Marianas, dropped the first atomic bomb on the city of Hiroshima, most of which was obliterated in a cataclysmic blast accompanied by blinding light and searing heat. Estimates vary, but probably close to 100,000 died in the explosion. On the morning of August 7, as Japanese authorities attempted to discern what had occurred, the Vice Chief of the Imperial Army General Staff received a terse and shocking report on the attack from officials on the scene: "The whole city of Hiroshima was destroyed instantly by a single bomb." Even so, Japan's government refused to bend; Army officers insisted that there were no more bombs. A second strike on Nagasaki on August 9, killing about 35,000, discredited that argument. That same evening the USSR declared war on Japan. But the imperial cabinet remained deadlocked, unable to find a context for the unthinkable possibility of surrender. Ultimately, Emperor Hirohito provided that context, noting in the Imperial Rescript read over the radio to his people that, given

the use of the "new and most cruel bomb," the only alternative to national obliteration and the "total extinction of human civilization" was surrender. To save their nation and mankind, he counseled, the Japanese people "must bear the unbearable." Two weeks later, on September 2, Japanese delegates boarded the battleship *Missouri*, anchored in Tokyo Bay at the center of an awe-inspiring fleet of Allied warships. There, as directed by General MacArthur, they affixed their signatures to the surrender document. MacArthur signaled the end of the ceremony and the end of the most destructive war in history with the simple phrase, "These proceedings are closed."

Allied victory was the product of a variety of factors. Without question, the Allies benefited from the incredible productive capacity of the United States, which provided Allied fighting forces with an ever-increasing supply of the equipment and machines that the conflict required. The logistical capabilities of the major Allied powers were also remarkable, often drawing comments reflecting amazement and envy on the part of German, Italian and Japanese participants. Superior production and distribution ensured that as the war progressed Allied soldiers were almost always better armed and supplied than their opponents. For every U.S. soldier in the Pacific, for example, there were four tons of supplies; for his Japanese counterpart, there were only two pounds. Added to this was the fact that as the war proceeded, Allied forces simply fought better. Early defeats taught harsh object lessons, but they were generally well-applied in subsequent operations.

While it could be argued that the Allied cause was in several famous instances aided by sheer fortuitous circumstances, Allied governments also strove to shape circumstances through intelligence operations and analysis. Most notably, American and British efforts to break Japanese and German codes produced some striking successes, apparent in the battle of Midway and the anti-submarine war in the Atlantic. Successful efforts at disinformation likewise befuddled German forces prior to the Normandy landings.

Historians cite a myriad of other reasons for Allied success. The role of air power and the gaining of air supremacy are sometimes accorded great importance. Some note that Nazi Germany and Imperial Japan drastically underestimated their opponents. Hitler contemptuously dismissed the United States as a land of "Hollywood, beauty queens and stupid records," whose people were "half-Negrified and half-Judaized." Initial Japanese strategy in the Pacific was based in part on the belief that Americans were materialistic and self-indulgent, incapable of sustaining the will to win. Civilian and military leadership was also important and here the Allies were generally well served. Last, the role of ideology and morality should not be overlooked. Totalitarian systems could often compel obedience, but not necessarily will, as Stalin discovered. Soviet triumph was built on the foundations of historical nationalism, which combined elements of patriotism for "Mother Russia" and Orthodox devotion. The peoples of the western democracies easily defined the nature of the struggle by comparing their beliefs with those propounded by their Axis opponents. Fascism, Nazism and militarism were perceived as antithetical to democratic ideals and Judeo-Christian morality. Churchill's warning in 1940 that the outcome of the conflict would determine "the survival of Christian civilization" was not dismissed as hyperbolic rhetoric; to many in the democratic world, totalitarian and racist ideologies posed an obvious threat to fundamental western po-

litical values and moral ideals. This may have imbued Allied peoples with the determination to persevere in what was seen as a "just" war. Such factors are unquantifiable, but no less crucial in consequence.

The Second World War did much to shape the events of the second half of the twentieth century. Most immediately, it signaled the end of an era of European dominance of world affairs. Most of the traditionally "great" powers of Europe, Allied and Axis alike, were reduced to secondary status by the war's effects. Once-powerful states such as Great Britain and France could no longer expect to exercise the diplomatic, military and economic power that they had enjoyed at the century's beginning. Neither could they afford to maintain the extensive empires that they had acquired by the late nineteenth century. Even if the cost of empire had not been a question, the war set in motion other forces that worked against a continuation of colonialism. Across the colonial world, subject peoples had been witness to wartime defeats and humiliations that demonstrated the vulnerabilities of their European masters. Japan's armies had clearly demonstrated that Asians could defeat the greatest of the European powers. The oft-professed war aims of the Allies added further fuel to the already smoldering fires of nationalism in the colonial world. The Atlantic Charter's call for the self-determination of all peoples was clearly subversive of the imperial concept. In the two decades following the end of the war, Europe's imperial claims would shrink to the point of insignificance. The war also brought an end to Japan's imperial ambitions, leaving that nation economically shattered and under U.S. military occupation. Contrary to American hopes, China failed to replace Japan as the predominant Asian power, but instead staggered out of the conflict broken by years of wartime depredations and weakened by political uncertainties. The final phase of China's long revolution, a clash between Nationalist and Communist forces, hovered on the horizon.

Historian Stephen Ambrose characterized the Second World War as a European civil war in which no European power was victorious. Clearly, the war did much to establish a new bipolar world order, in which the United States and the Soviet Union emerged as superpowers. Both nations had remained isolated in the 1930s and neither had demonstrated any consistent military strength. The war created new circumstances that led each to build permanent, large military establishments and seek worldwide influence in the course of a decades-long ideological struggle. Much of Europe fell hostage to the emerging Cold War. Germany and Austria were partitioned and occupied, and the growing confrontation between the two superpowers soon brought about the creation of two ideologically antithetical German states. Most of Eastern Europe was incorporated into a new Soviet empire. But if the war created new rivalries and tensions, it also compelled a wider appreciation for the need to prevent future conflicts. The League of Nations, defunct in 1939, had not enjoyed the support of the United States or the Soviet Union. Both nations led the effort to establish the United Nations, a new international body founded at the San Francisco Conference in April 1945. Some fifty nations, whose delegates were to be represented in the General Assembly, joined as charter members. The other major charter agency, the Security Council, was empowered to investigate disputes, recommend settlements or make referral to the new International Court. The Security Council, whose five permanent members included the United States and the Soviet Union, was also granted the authority to use military force, a power that the League had lacked. One of the primary responsibilities accorded to the Security Council was "the maintenance of international peace and security." In a world shattered by war, the challenge of restoring the fragile balance was resumed.

◆ ▬▬ ◆ ▬▬ ◆ ▬▬ ◆ ▬▬ ◆ ▬▬ ◆ ▬▬ ◆ ▬▬ ◆ ▬▬ ◆ ▬▬ ◆

In the early months of 1945, as Allied armies advanced deeper into the collapsing Third Reich from both east and west, they began to encounter the physical remnants of Hitler's "Final Solution." From southern Germany to western Poland, dozens of Nazi concentration camps, ranging in purpose from transit camps like Theresienstadt to extermination camps like Auschwitz, were discovered by horrified Allied troops. In some cases, as at Auschwitz, the Nazis had destroyed much of the physical evidence of the camp's design before forcing the enfeebled survivors to march westward and away from the approaching Red Army. Upon liberating the soon-to-be infamous camp in January 1945, Soviet troops found only 5,000 debilitated inmates left. At Dachau, Germany's first concentration camp just outside Munich, U.S. troops were so enraged at the inhumanities that met their eyes when they entered the compound that they summarily shot over 300 remaining S.S. guards. In April, U.S. commanders Dwight Eisenhower, Omar Bradley and George Patton inspected the camp at Ohrdruf, near Gotha. Though thoroughly familiar with the horrors of war, the generals were stunned beyond speech at what they saw; the normally unflinching Patton was literally sickened. Eisenhower was determined that extensive proof of the camp's existence be established; the U.S. Signal Corps was ordered to film the nightmare scenario of piles of uncounted corpses and groups of living human skeletons, and German civilians from the nearby town were compelled to view the horrors themselves. Eisenhower was among a growing number of Allied officials who were determined that, in the future, evidence of the Nazi atrocities would be well documented and incontrovertible. Throughout the early spring, other camps whose names would soon be synonymous with suffering and death were liberated: Nordhausen, Bergen-Belsen and Buchenwald all testified to the terrible efficiency and inconceivable cruelty of the Nazi system of mass murder.

Mauthausen, in Austria, was the last of the extermination camps to be liberated. Though Mauthausen provided slave laborers to a nearby Messerchmitt arms factory and men to quarry granite for Nazi monuments, it was preeminently an extermination camp, as was indicated by its "Category Three" classification within the camp system. Over the years, Mauthausen inmates had been murdered by gunfire, in mobile gas vans and gas chambers, through beatings, starvation, overwork, or sometimes by being flung over the rock quarry's "parachutists' wall" by sadistic guards. The killing continued until the last feasible moment; some 30,000 died between January and May 1945. As the German military situation deteriorated, SS guards developed plans to rid themselves of some 30,000 prisoners at the nearby Ebensee satellite camp by forcing them into underground tunnels and then collapsing the structures with explosives. Though the inmates successfully resisted the scheme, Mauthausen abounded with evidence of the SS's homicidal activities when the U.S. Army's 11th Armored Division arrived in early May and discovered some 18,000 survivors. Among them was Simon Wiesenthal, a 37-year-old Polish Jew. Weighing only 99 pounds on the day of his liberation, Wiesenthal had survived wartime ordeals that few could imagine. Only months before, in February, Wiesenthal had arrived at Mauthausen together with other prisoners evacuated from the Buchenwald camp when the Red Army neared. Wiesenthal, who was put to work removing dead inmates from the barracks, labored under huge clouds of smoke from the crematorium, which operated ceaselessly in a vain effort to keep up with the number of dead. Now, in the unreal days following the arrival of the Americans, Wiesenthal gave some thought to seeing the world beyond the compound; to do so, he was told, would require obtaining a pass from another prisoner, a former camp auxiliary. Unaccountably, when Wiesenthal visited the man in his office, he was beaten and thrown out. Stunned by the injustice, Wiesenthal sought out U.S. commander Colonel Richard Seibel, to request that his tormentor be punished. The events that followed forever changed Wiesenthal's already remarkable life. Directed to wait in the previous camp commandant's office, Wiesenthal arrived there to find men from the U.S. War Crimes unit interrogating SS guards. Having feared that he would never survive to see those responsible for the Nazi horrors arraigned, Wiesenthal watched the proceedings for hours. In following days, he persistently pleaded with the Americans to permit him to join the War Crimes Unit and was told to jot down all the relevant information he could provide. Wiesenthal returned with a comprehensive account of his years in the "Empire of Death," providing the names of numerous Nazi officials whose crimes he had personal knowledge of. Shortly afterward, he was accepted into the War Crimes Unit. Simon Wiesenthal had discovered his calling. He would dedicate the remainder of his life to seeking not vengeance, but justice for those responsible for the horrors of the Holocaust.

Geography was in part responsible for the many travails that Simon Wiesenthal faced in the years following his birth in 1908. His family lived in Buczacz, a small town in Austro-Hungarian Galicia, a region where the conflicting ambitions of the great powers often met. During the First World War, the town changed hands six times and the Wiesenthal family, minus the father Asher, who was killed serving in the Austrian Army, eventually fled to the relative safety of Vienna rather than suffer the constant harassment of Russian Cossacks. At the end of the war, the Wiesenthals returned to Buczacz, which had since become part of the newly independent Poland. As a young adult, Simon studied architecture in Prague, hoping to establish a career prior to his marriage to Cyla Mueller. The couple took up residence in Lvov, Poland, which was destined to fall under the control of the Soviets after Poland's defeat in the fall of 1939. Wiesenthal's stepfather and stepbrother were both murdered by the NKVD, as were other "bourgeois" Jewish merchants. The terror worsened when the German army occupied the area following Hitler's invasion of the USSR in 1941. Local Jews were again terrorized, but this time by Nazi "Special Groups" and anti-Semitic Ukrainians supporting the Germans. Wiesenthal and his wife were assigned forced labor, while his mother cared for their home. On August 23 of that year, while Simon was away from the house, his mother Rosa was caught in an SS roundup of Jews and deported by train to the extermination camp at Belzec. He never saw her again and most of Wiesenthal's relatives were swept away in the Holocaust. Soon separated from Cyla, Wiesenthal endured years of privation, beatings and starvation as a victim of Nazi concentration camps. On more than one occasion, he found himself in a line of inmates singled out for immediate execution, only to be reprieved at the last moment for seemingly trivial reasons. He came to see his close escapes as evidence that he was destined to survive for some as-yet-unknown reason. Following his liberation in the spring of 1945, Wiesenthal began to see more clearly the purpose to which his life would be dedicated.

There was no question of Wiesenthal returning to Lvov that summer after liberation. "Poland was a cemetery," he later wrote. "If I wanted to make a new life, I was not going to make it in a cemetery, where every tree, every stone reminded me of the tragedy which I had barely survived." Thus he remained in Austria, attached to the U.S. War Crimes Unit and then the Office of Strategic Services (OSS). He soon realized, however, that the Americans' perseverance in ferreting out war criminals was doubtful, in part because of growing U.S.–Soviet tensions. Reunited with his wife, who gave birth to a daughter in 1946, Wiesenthal began to give consideration as to how the search for the guilty might be continued. In order to pursue an independent course and collect relevant information, he established a Documentation Center in Linz, Austria, with the help of the Jewish Survivors Committee. The center opened in 1947 and functioned as the institutional base for Wiesenthal's ongoing efforts to bring the perpetrators of the Holocaust to justice. Though Wiesenthal's desire for justice extended to include the least Nazi functionary, he was especially determined that those who played a major role in administering the "Final Solution" be discovered and held to account.

Chief among these was Adolf Eichmann, an SS official, who was on the Jewish Agency for Palestine's "most wanted" list of "instigators and perpetrators of crimes against Jews." Since the late 1930s, Eichmann had played a central role in the persecution and then mass extermination of European Jews. With cold efficiency, Eichmann had helped implement the "Final Solution," once reprimanding an associate who expressed dismay at Hitler's order to exterminate the Jews. "Don't be sentimental," Eichmann had rejoined. "It's a 'Führer Order'." The subsequent lengthy quest for the fugitive Nazi was chronicled in Wiesenthal's most famous book, *I Hunted Eichmann.*

Through the 1950s, Wiesenthal was instrumental in keeping the search alive and preventing efforts to have Eichmann declared legally dead. By the mid-1950s, Wiesenthal, working with the World Jewish Congress, accumulated significant evidence that Eichmann was in fact alive and living in Argentina, which became a postwar refuge for former Nazis. Finally, in May 1960, agents of the Israeli intelligence agency Mossad succeeded in tracking Eichmann down in Buenos Aires, where he was kidnapped and returned to Israel for trial. The trial, during which the full extent of Eichmann's role in the Nazi terror was established, did much to rejuvenate interest in the Holocaust and justice for its many victims. Eichmann's conviction and execution suggested that while justice might be delayed, the passage of time itself was no guarantee that it could be evaded. The Eichmann trial also compelled a reconsideration of the recent past in both Germany and Austria, where there was a general reluctance to revisit the crimes of the Nazi era. In the years to come, Wiesenthal was instrumental in the search for other "missing" Nazis, perhaps most notably Dr. Josef Mengele, the infamous "Angel of Death" who conducted sadistic "medical experiments" on unfortunate inmates at Auschwitz. After many years, it was determined that the Nazi doctor had died in Brazil in 1979. A similar search for Hitler's deputy Martin Bormann concluded with the authentication of Bormann's death.

Wiesenthal's activities were not limited to the quest for former Nazi officials. In the late 1950s, Wiesenthal became aware of the phenomenon known as "Holocaust revisionism," which holds that Nazi crimes were either greatly exaggerated or nonexistent. In 1958 in Linz, a play based on the diary of Anne Frank, a Jewish Dutch girl who died at the hands of the Nazis, was disrupted by anti-Semitic demonstrators who claimed the diary was a fraud, calculated to win sympathy for Jews and Israel. Determined to reveal the lies and distortions inherent in Holocaust denial, Wiesenthal set out to locate the SS officer who had sent Frank and her family to the Bergen-Belsen camp. Though the man was eventually located serving on the Vienna police force, the Austrian government refused to prosecute him. Nonetheless, Wiesenthal, who described his efforts in his 1967 book *The Murderers Amongst Us,* had established the authenticity of Frank's diary, winning praise from the Dutch government.

There were other noteworthy controversies. In the late 1980s Wiesenthal was among those who called for the resignation of Austrian president and former U.N. general secretary Kurt Waldheim when evidence of his wartime role in the "Final

Solution" was made public. An international commission only concluded that the Austrian president should have been more forthcoming about his past, but Waldheim, subsequently shunned at home and abroad, chose not to seek reelection.

Having moved his Documentation Center to Vienna in 1961, Wiesenthal gradually gained a worldwide reputation for his endeavors. In 1980, a speaking tour in the United States climaxed when he was awarded the Congressional Gold Medal and fêted by Jewish war veterans. In 1986, he was nominated for the Nobel Peace Prize, his name put forth by several individuals including German Chancellor Helmut Kohl. Though the prize ultimately went to fellow Nazi-hunter Elie Wiesel, Wiesenthal was lauded by Kohl as "far more than a Nazi-hunter." "He is a visionary," Kohl asserted, "who has understood that neither the individual nor a people can live without a system of moral coordination." A more permanent tribute to Wiesenthal's efforts was established in Los Angeles, California, where the Simon Wiesenthal Center and Museum for Tolerance were constructed. Dedicated to continuing Holocaust research, monitoring anti-Semitism and the continuing search for Nazi criminals, the Center is complemented by the Museum, which offers visitors a look at the origins and consequences of the Holocaust. As visitors complete a tour of a replicated concentration camp and all its attendant horrors, they are left to contemplate a placard bearing a final thought from Simon Wiesenthal: "Hope lives when people remember."

◆ ——— ◆ ——— ◆ ——— ◆ ——— ◆ ——— ◆ ——— ◆ ——— ◆ ——— ◆

Suggested Readings

ALLEN, THOMAS B. and NORMAN POLMAR. *Code-Name Downfall: The Secret Plan to Invade Japan and Why Truman Dropped the Bomb.* (1995).

BERGERUD, ERIC. *Touched with Fire: The Land War in the South Pacific.* (1996).

CALVOCORESSI, PETER and GUY WINT. *Total War: Causes and Courses of the Second World War.* (1979).

COSTELLO, JOHN. *The Pacific War.* (1981).

DAVIDOWICZ, LUCY S. *The War Against the Jews, 1933–1945.* (1975).

DOWER, JOHN S. *War without Mercy: Race and Power in the Pacific War.* (1986).

FRANK, RICHARD B. *Downfall: The End of the Imperial Japanese Empire.* (1999).

FUGATE, BRYAN. *Operation Barbarossa.* (1984).

HASTINGS, MAX. *Overlord: D-Day and the Battle for Normandy.* (1984).

KEEGAN, JOHN. *The Second World War.* (1989).

KERSHAW, IAN. *Hitler: Nemesis, 1936–1945.* (2000).

KNOX, MACGREGOR. *Mussolini Unleashed, 1939–1941: Politics and Strategy in Fascist Italy's Last War.* (1982).

LAMB, RICHARD. *Churchill as War Leader.* (1991).

MEE, CHARLES L., JR. *Meeting at Potsdam.* (1975).

MORRISON, SAMUEL ELIOT. *The Two-Ocean War: A Short History of the United States Navy in the Second World War.* (1963).

OVERY, RICHARD. *Why the Allies Won.* (1995).

PICK, HELLA. *Simon Wiesenthal: A Life In Search of Justice.* (1996).

SPECTOR, RONALD H. *Eagle Against the Sun: The American War with Japan.* (1985).

WEINBERG, GERHARD. *A World at Arms: A Global History of World War II.* (1994).

WILLIAMSON, MURRAY and ALLAN R. MILLETT. *A War to Be Won: Fighting the Second World War.* (2000).

PART TWO

The Age of the Superpowers, 1945–1989

Overview

World War II, the greatest military conflagration in human history, dramatically altered the international landscape. European hegemony continued its decline, thanks to the ravages of war and the loss of imperial possessions, before the continent experienced an economic and cultural rebirth. The United States, its own territory virtually unmarred by the events of 1939–1945, became the most powerful nation on the face of the globe, but was unable to prevail in a distant war in Southeast Asia. The chief rival of the U.S. was the Soviet Union, the communist behemoth that for a time seemingly threatened American preeminence before fatal flaws became apparent.

World War II helped to usher in sweeping, even revolutionary changes throughout Asia, the Middle East, Africa and Latin America. War-torn Japan experienced economic revitalization by the 1950s, thanks to support from former enemies. China underwent its own communist revolution, which proved enormously destructive in human terms; nevertheless, economic reforms eventually enabled that massive nation to become a world powerhouse. India discarded the yoke of British imperialism and adopted democratic trappings, but was afflicted with political and religious sectarianism. Israel emerged as the Middle East's lone democracy, but many of its Arab neighbors floundered despite possessing great natural resources, particularly oil.

African nationalism also flourished in the postwar period and more new nation-states appeared on that continent than anywhere else. Countries like Nigeria struggled to succeed economically and to sustain human rights, but South Africa remained an apartheid state and tribal wars proliferated elsewhere. In Latin America proponents of democratic rights and social democracy battled against conservative, even reactionary elements. Following the Cuban Revolution of 1959, revolutionary forces appeared in greater numbers, frightening and infuriating right-wing groups and governments.

CHAPTER 7

Recovery and Transformation: Europe, 1945–1989

One of the defining moments of Charles de Gaulle's adult life unfolded on June 18, 1940, when he strode into the London studios of the British Broadcasting Corporation. BBC employees and announcers had maintained a frantic pace in recent weeks as they attempted to keep up with the grim news from France, where German armies had overrun both French and British forces with astonishing speed. Now it appeared that the battle of France was lost; two days earlier, a new French government, headed by the aging Marshal Phillipe Petain, had accepted humiliating Nazi terms for an armistice. France, like much of the rest of continental Europe, seemed fated to be a subservient satellite in Hitler's empire. De Gaulle, a junior French general who had flown into England only the day before, was determined that both hope and resistance in France should be kept alive. Described by a BBC newsman as "a huge man with highly-polished boots, who walked with long strides, talking in a very deep voice," de Gaulle seated himself before the radio microphone at 8:15 p.m. and began a broadcast that laid the foundations for a political career that would span three decades. In a sonorous voice, the general spoke to his countrymen about the new government that had conceded defeat. "Must hope vanish?" he asked. "Is the defeat final?" His answer was an emphatic "No!" France was not alone, de Gaulle asserted; there remained the French Empire, together with Great Britain's naval strength and the industrial might of the United States. "The war has not been decided by the Battle of France," he observed. "This war is a worldwide war." De Gaulle closed with a summons to all French nationals who had fled into exile to contact him. "Whatever happens," he declared, "the flame of French resistance must not and shall not go out." De Gaulle's dramatic broadcast, of which no recording was made, received little attention at the time, largely swallowed up by more momentous events. In subsequent days, the collaborationist regime in France denounced the renegade general and ultimately issued orders for his court-martial. The June 18 broadcast signaled de Gaulle's break with the Petain regime and all it stood for. It also marked the beginning of the general's lengthy struggle to gain recognition from Allied governments as the leader of a French government-in-exile and as the personification of "Free France." Ultimately, de Gaulle's famous radio appeal laid the foundations for a remarkable political career during which he was instrumental in defining the modern French republic.

There was little in de Gaulle's family background or early years that hinted of his postwar reputation as the saviour of republican France. Born in Lille in 1890, de Gaulle grew up in a family shaped by an aristocratic heritage, Catholicism and monarchist sentiment. His childhood coincided with some of the most divisive years of the Third Republic, as conservative elements engaged anticlerical republicans in the political struggles that the Dreyfus Affair generated. A student of only modest ability, Charles demonstrated an early affinity for military affairs and his father Henri sent him to the military academy at Saint-Cyr as a preliminary step toward a military career. By then an astounding 6'4" in height, Charles was often the object of taunts by fellow cadets, who dubbed him "the huge asparagus" and the "double yardstick." Nonetheless, he dedicated himself to his studies with a fervor that was to that point uncharacteristic. He left Saint-Cyr in 1912 as a second lieutenant, his commanding officer noting in a final evaluation: "Cannot fail to make an excellent officer." De Gaulle was serving in the infantry when the First World War broke out and was soon at the front in Belgium, where he was wounded in combat. Following his recovery, de Gaulle fought at Verdun in 1916, where he was again wounded before being captured. Humiliated at his fate, he made numerous unsuccessful attempts to escape from various German prisoner-of-war camps.

Returned to France following the 1918 armistice, de Gaulle dedicated his energies to building a career in the army, but his willingness to challenge the shortsightedness of his superiors in strategic matters earned him a reputation as a troublemaker and slowed his advance through the ranks during the interwar years. His 1934 book *The Army of the Future* emphasized the geographical vulnerability of France and the need to acknowledge the growing importance of mobile armored units and aircraft. De Gaulle's superiors generally dismissed his contentions as absurd. The shortsightedness of the French high command was dramatically revealed in early May 1940 when hundreds of German tanks roared through the Ardennes Forest into France, supported by fleets of German aircraft. De Gaulle worked frantically to organize and deploy the armored division he commanded, but the rapidity of the enemy advance and the chaos disrupting both military and governmental activities overwhelmed him. In June, he was belatedly named as Undersecretary of National Defense as a morale-boosting measure, but was unable to overcome the despair and defeatism that pervaded Premier Paul Reynaud's government. Only when Reynaud turned the government over to Petain, whose defeatism and disdain for the Third Republic predisposed him to seek terms with Hitler, did de Gaulle make the decision to carry on the struggle from overseas.

De Gaulle's years in exile were difficult. He was relatively unknown and even among those French who desired to carry on the struggle against Nazi Germany, de Gaulle's leadership of a "Free French" movement was contested. A stubborn, sometimes arrogant man with an authoritarian temperament, de Gaulle often provoked irritation and anger from the Allied leaders whose support he desperately needed. De Gaulle's abrasive manner and aggressive quest for support grew out of a deep sense of personal destiny. His mission, he sincerely believed, was to redeem the honor of France by continuing the struggle against Germany from abroad, and to one day bring about liberation and redemption of his homeland. De Gaulle, who established the French National Committee as his instrument, eventually was acknowledged by the Allied leadership and the Free French of the Interior, the main resistance organization, as the *de facto* leader of the French government-in-exile. In the aftermath of the Allied occupation of French North Africa in late 1942, de Gaulle adroitly gained control of the French Committee of National Liberation in Algiers, which provided him with a governmental base. In May 1944, he moved his headquarters to London in anticipation of the coming Allied invasion of western France.

Yet another memorable radio broadcast signaled the climactic phase of de Gaulle's long struggle to return in triumph to a liberated France. Speaking on the afternoon of June 6, 1944, as Allied invasion forces fought on the beaches of Normandy, the long-exiled general informed his countrymen of their duties: "The supreme battle has begun. It is the battle of France. France is going to fight this battle furiously. She is going to conduct it in due order. The clear, sacred duty of the sons of France, wherever they are and whoever they are, is to fight the enemy with all the means at their disposal." His broadcast did much to fire the Resistance in France. In the following months, as Allied armies pushed the Germans into the interior and back toward the Rhine, de Gaulle lobbied ceaselessly for an early liberation of Paris led by French forces. As insurrection against the German garrison occupying the city broke out in August, the situation became more urgent. Eisenhower finally acceded to de Gaulle's pleas and gave General Jacques Leclerc's French 2nd Division the honor of being the first Allied unit into the French capital. De Gaulle arrived in the city on August 25, even as sporadic fighting between French and German forces continued. The following day, despite the very real threat of snipers, de Gaulle headed up a massive procession down the Champs-Elysees, cheered by tens of thousands of ecstatic Parisians. With the liberation of France, his triumph seemed complete.

For the next eighteen months, de Gaulle headed the French provisional government as his countrymen came to grips with the consequences of the war and the German occupation. De Gaulle's consistent and principled resistance to the German enemy and Marshal Petain's Vichy regime mitigated the stain of collaboration, which tormented the French national psyche after liberation. To many, he was the embodiment of the eternal conscience of France, a seemingly invincible symbol of France's national strength and republican ideals. Despite the tremendous moral authority de Gaulle

Fig. 7-1   French General Charles de Gaulle meets with British Prime Minister Winston Churchill in Paris in the last months of the Second World War. (Pearson Education, Corporate Digital Archive, Getty Images Inc.)

commanded, events soon proved that his destined moment had not yet arrived. His insistence on a strong presidency in a reconstituted republic met with broad opposition and De Gaulle resigned in November 1945 rather than serve in a Fourth Republic dominated by an overly powerful legislative branch. Though he organized a new political movement, the Rally of the French People, it failed to gain broad popular support and the famous general retired from public life in 1953.

Within a decade of the war's end, it was evident that the leaders, political institutions and governmental mechanisms of the Fourth Republic were fundamentally inadequate to the task of resolving the numerous challenges that postwar France faced.

A major political and constitutional crisis in 1958, growing out of a divisive colonial war in Algeria, offered an unexpected opportunity for de Gaulle to reemerge and capitalize on his reputation as the nation's redeemer and liberator. Seizing the moment, de Gaulle agreed to return to public life if a new constitution providing for a strengthened executive was ratified. A desperate nation once again turned to the man who had upheld France's honor nearly two decades earlier, and de Gaulle was made premier and given the authority to supervise the drafting of a new constitution, which established the Fifth Republic. During his lengthy tenure as President, de Gaulle finally realized the destiny he had first perceived in 1940. Given the authority of a strong presidency, de Gaulle restored political stability, resolved critical colonial issues and made clear his intention of restoring French grandeur. Charting an independent foreign policy, he established France as a nuclear power and frequently challenged U.S. leadership in the North Atlantic Treaty Organization and U.S. Cold War policies. To the general acclaim of his people, de Gaulle continued to assert French greatness and uniqueness in an increasingly homogenized Europe.

A remarkably adept political leader, de Gaulle was nonetheless baffled by the growing political and social unrest of the 1960s, unable to comprehend the disaffections of a younger generation that culminated in violent protests in Paris in 1968. Though de Gaulle survived the immediate crisis, he seemed to realize that his imperious style of leadership, and perhaps even his vision for France, were increasingly out of place in a society once again undergoing a significant transformation. He resigned the presidency in 1969. At the time of his death in November 1970, de Gaulle remained a controversial figure, revered by many as the saviour of France at the nation's darkest moment and denounced by others as an egotistical reactionary who sought to preserve an outdated nationalism. Most would agree, however, that Charles de Gaulle played a crucial role in preserving the essence of republican France in wartime and in shaping the political institutions that established a stable, modern France in the postwar era.

◆ ——— ◆ ——— ◆ ——— ◆ ——— ◆

The Postwar Era: New Realities in a Transformed World

As the Second World War came to an end in Europe in May 1945, Europeans faced a multitude of sobering realities. Among the most incontestable was that Europe's world preeminence, seemingly so permanent at the beginning of the century, was clearly over. The war ruined economies, shattered societies, disrupted and destroyed governments and left in its wake shock, despair and profound uncertainties about even the immedi- ate future. Clearly, a civilization so thoroughly ravaged could no longer aspire to maintain a dominant position in the world order. Indeed, even as the war ended European supremacy, it created the circumstances for a bipolar world dominated by two non-European powers, the United States and the Soviet Union. The evolving Cold War between the two superpowers inevitably shaped Europe's destiny, bringing about a division of the continent and international tensions that lasted for half a century. Another consequence of the war was to give new energy to nationalist movements in the colonial world, compelling the European imperial powers to address the issue of empire and the necessity of decolonization. Together, these circumstances suggested a comprehensive reevaluation of Europe's place and role in the world.

Within Europe, division and unity were prominent issues throughout the postwar decades. The Soviet occupation of much of Eastern Europe and the subsequent imposition of Communist government in those nations created a semi-permanent division on the continent. Such unity as existed in Eastern Europe was the product of coerced ideological conformity. In the western European states, the debate over unity arose out of the realization that strident and irresponsible nationalism had played a central role in the destruction of Europe's primacy in the world. Many postwar leaders argued that nationalism would have to be redefined and subordinated to the need for a more stable unified Europe. In a superpower-dominated world, only a united Europe would be capable of wielding significant economic and political power.

Another new reality that demanded attention in the western European states was the obvious inability of many prewar governments to effectively resolve basic economic and social problems. Europe's postwar situation demanded innovative policies, moderation and a turn away from the overly dogmatic ideologies and obstructive political tactics of the past. The times required not only self-examination on the part of existing political parties, but also new political movements that could hopefully surmount stubborn obstacles to more responsive and effective government.

With astonishing rapidity, Europeans successfully met most of the immediate postwar challenges. By the early 1950s, the world was remarking on the "European Economic Miracle," which was achieved not only through massive American economic aid but also through the industry of Europe's peoples. For the next quarter century, western Europeans enjoyed a "Golden Age" of growing prosperity and material abundance, which contributed significantly to the marked stability of postwar society. Though the political currents in Western Europe shifted between liberal and conservative approaches throughout the four decades following the end of the war, political moderation and governmental stability were increasingly characteristic of the region. The radical ideologies that had so disrupted European politics in the prewar decades receded into insignificance as governments responded more effectively to social and economic problems. New intellectual and cultural trends that challenged conventional perspectives and values further transformed western European society during this period. In Eastern Europe, economic progress and social change came more slowly due to the ideological rigidity and oppressive character of communist governments, but even there a persistent if subdued popular impulse for change was discernible, sometimes erupting into popular revolts that were forcibly suppressed. The ideological division of the continent, the most enduring consequence of the Second World War, continued to shape European life for nearly forty-five years, postponing any conclusive definition of a "New Europe."

Bitter Peace: Europe in the Aftermath of War

The most immediate challenge that Europeans faced in the spring of 1945 was coming to grips with the consequences of the war. The extent of physical destruction almost defied description, though Winston Churchill provided a fair approximation with his observation that Europe had been reduced to "a rubble heap, a charnel house, a breeding ground of pestilence and hate." In Berlin, the American journalist William Shirer, who had chronicled Hitler's rise to power, described the German capital as an "utter wasteland" and concluded "I don't think there has ever been such destruction on such a scale." Much more than in 1914–1918, the destructive power of modern war impacted Europe's civilian population in the Second World War. Six years of increasingly intense warfare, during which immense armies swept back and forth across the continent both in advance and retreat, and huge fleets of bombers pounded urban areas, left unprecedented devastation. In the Soviet Union alone, some 1,700 cities and towns were destroyed, to-

Map 7-1   Divided Europe

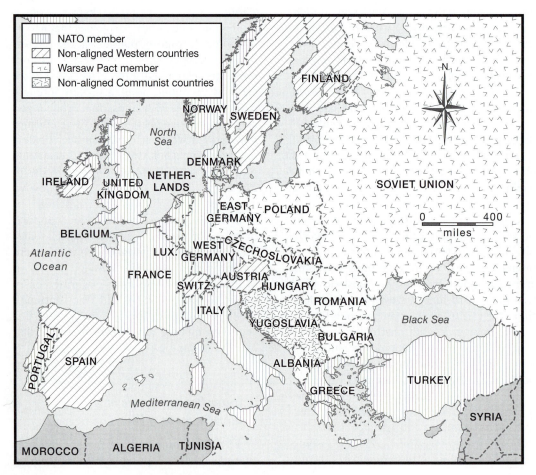

gether with an estimated 70,000 villages. Few cities of significant size or strategic value escaped aerial attack and some, such as Hamburg and Dresden, were virtually obliterated. Long sieges ruined other cities, including Stalingrad and Leningrad, while Warsaw was leveled at Hitler's order by retreating German forces. Paris escaped a similar fate only because the German commander in the "City of Light" refused to carry out Hitler's demand that the entire city, together with its innumerable cultural treasures, should be destroyed. Elsewhere, countless irreplaceable artistic and architectural masterpieces disappeared in the whirlwind of destruction. Mass homelessness was another consequence of the war; in the USSR alone, the destruction of 6.5 million buildings left 25 million homeless. For much of the continent, the destruction of the economic infrastructure compounded these realities. Those portions of Europe's transportation network and industrial base not destroyed by Allied bombing had, in many cases, been wrecked by retreating German forces. At war's end, the reconstruction of a continent so thoroughly ravaged seemed an impossible task.

The demographic impact of the war reflected the conflict's ferocity and scope. Some thirty-seven million Europeans were dead, perhaps as many as twenty-six million of those in the Soviet Union. Losses among specific national and ethnic groups often followed the direction of the conflict and the focus of Nazi policies. Poland was especially hard-hit, with twenty percent of its population killed, among those ninety percent of Poland's Jews. They comprised a significant portion of the six million Jews, that the Nazis murdered. Likewise, the staggering losses in the USSR were a direct consequence of Nazi racial and political policies that required the extermination of Jews, Communists and partisans, and countenanced the indiscriminate slaughter of "subhuman" Slavs.

In addition to the incomprehensible cost in human life, the war brought about the greatest mass population transfer in European history. With the war's end, an estimated fifty million refugees, including former prisoners, forced laborers, concentration camp inmates and demobilized soldiers filled European roads, struggling to return home or, if that were impossible, to find some place of refuge. Ironically, Germans comprised one of the largest groups of DPs, or "displaced persons." In the final stages of the war, as the Red Army pushed down the Baltic Coast and into East Prussia, hundreds of thousands of Germans had fled west in desperation. Some families had lived in these eastern regions for generations; others were more recent "settlers," beneficiaries of Germany's conquest of eastern "living space." The Allied conferees at the Potsdam Conference agreed that the Germans would have to be ejected, as Poland's postwar boundaries were shifted 200 miles to the west. German minorities in Czechoslovakia, Romania, Hungary and Yugoslavia also faced expulsion after the war. Eventually, between twelve and thirteen million Germans faced resettlement in the immediate postwar period.

Beyond displacing millions, the war shattered innumerable families through death and separation. Across the continent, the new United Nations Relief and Rehabilitation Administration (UNRRA) struggled to cope with hundreds of thousands of orphaned or unaccompanied children. For children and adults alike, the most immediate concern was often survival. The first peacetime winter was one of the most bitter in history and the lack of shelter and food (many Europeans were subsisting on 1,500 calories or less a day) threatened to increase the mortality rate. In the most ravaged regions, such as in much of urban Germany, the near total destruction of the public infrastructure worsened these privations. In some instances, all vestiges of prewar social order disintegrated in the absence of government, and daily life became a grim Darwinian struggle to survive, with little concern for the indefinite future.

If the future was only a distant concern for many, seeking justice and retribution for the misdeeds of the recent past was an immediate objective for others. With the end of the war, the settling of accounts was inevitable and many chose not to await the lengthy and cumbersome processes of legal justice. Reprisals against those who had collaborated with fascist authorities swiftly followed liberation in France and Italy. French resistance forces executed about 10,000 "traitors" during the first weeks after liberation. Later trials of Vichy officials condemned both Marshal Petain and Premier Pierre Laval to death for treason. Although the former was spared due to his age, some 2,000 lesser Vichy officials were not. In Italy, Italian partisans executed about 15,000 Fascists, not the least of whom was Mussolini, but few postwar trials followed. Elsewhere across former German-occupied Europe, collaborationists fell victim to both vigilante justice and tribunals. Norway's hated Vidkun Quisling was among the more notable collaborators sentenced to death.

The most ambitious postwar tribunal convened at Nuremberg, Germany, where the surviving Nazi leaders were tried for their role in the recent catastrophe. As the trial of the twenty-four "Major War Criminals" opened in November 1945, four Allied judges read out the charges, which included conspiracy against peace, crimes against peace, war crimes and crimes against human-

ity. In proceedings that lasted nearly a year, prosecutors presented evidence that included thousands of Nazi documents, films of concentration camps and the testimony of victims of Nazi crimes. Most of the defendants were unwilling to acknowledge responsibility for their actions, maintaining that they were "only following orders." Only Albert Speer, the Nazi Minister of Armaments, conceded that the Nazi leadership had to accept the burden of guilt. Ultimately, the tribunal sentenced ten of Germany's political and military leaders to death by hanging. One of the condemned, the former *Luftwaffe* chief Herman Goering, committed suicide in his cell. Other top Nazis, including the clearly insane Rudolf Hess, received lengthy prison sentences, and a few were acquitted. The Nuremberg Tribunal generated considerable controversy, with critics questioning its legality and denouncing it as nothing more than "victor's justice." Given the scope and nature of Nazi crimes, however, there was widespread agreement that some effort had to be made to render justice, if only to establish some general standard of international conduct. As the U.S. prosecutor Robert H. Jackson observed, "Civilization asks whether law is so laggard as to be utterly helpless to deal with crimes of this magnitude." In subsequent years, there were similar trials of lesser Nazi authorities, including the "Nazi doctors" responsible for sadistic "medical experiments" on camp inmates and prisoners. Many Nazis, including Hitler's deputy Martin Bormann, were never found or otherwise escaped prosecution. The search for fugitive Nazis continued through the rest of the century.

For many in Europe, however, the most compelling immediate problem was reconstruction and recovery. Given the vast scope of physical destruction, some experts predicted that the most heavily devastated areas could not be fully rebuilt in less than twenty years. In the early postwar years, the sheer magnitude of the task hindered government initiatives to begin the reconstruction process. The broad destruction of economic assets, the general disruption of state administrative machinery and political uncertainties combined to make recovery a slow and inconsistent process across the continent. Most states lacked the ability to deal adequately with ruinous currency inflation or black market economies. In many areas, barter became a common means of exchange. Military and occupation governments provided some emergency aid and food supplies, but U.S. Army forces in France and Italy pulled out as early as late 1945. Both the United States and the UNRRA provided aid in the immediate postwar period, but it was entirely inadequate to the staggering task at hand. Not until the advent of the Cold War did American policymakers accord Europe's recovery a high priority, and only then did significant recovery take place.

Europe and the Cold War

No general peace conference, such as that which occurred in Paris in 1919, followed the Second World War. Rather, the disposition of postwar Europe was largely determined in the last year of the war, as disagreements among the leaders of the "Grand Alliance" became manifest at the Yalta and Potsdam Conferences. Though Winston Churchill, Franklin Roosevelt and later Harry Truman objected to Joseph Stalin's increasingly obvious design for a broad sphere of Soviet influence and Communist domination in Eastern Europe, military realities in the winter of 1944–1945 precluded any effective opposi-

tion. At the time of Germany's surrender, the Red Army, by then an awesome military machine, had pushed deep into central Europe, having joined up with U.S. troops on the Elbe River in Germany. Stalin was quick to perceive the long-term political consequences of the military situation. "This war is not as in the past," he observed. "Whoever occupies a territory also imposes on it his own social system. Everyone imposes his system as far as his army can reach. It cannot be otherwise." The Soviet dictator's axiom confirmed what British and American policymakers had increasingly feared in the last months of the war—that the Soviet liberation and occupation of Poland, Romania, Bulgaria, Hungary, Yugoslavia and parts of Czechoslovakia, Austria and Germany portended an effort to establish a permanent sphere of Soviet influence throughout the region.

Stalin's argument that the USSR required a buffer zone of friendly states between itself and Germany seemed disingenuous at best to Western statesmen. More ominously, Stalin's Yalta promise to include non-Communists in the Polish government and permit free elections remained unfulfilled by summer 1945. British and Americans viewed these developments as another indication that the Soviet premier had no intentions of honoring the terms of Yalta's "Declaration of Liberated Europe," which acknowledged the principle of national self-determination. Capitalizing on the presence of the Red Army and the postwar stature of Eastern European Communists, many of whom had actively resisted the Nazi occupation, Stalin strengthened his hand across the region. At the Potsdam Conference in July, Stalin succeeded in winning Anglo-American acceptance of substantial Soviet territorial gains, including the three Baltic republics (incorporated into the USSR in 1940 as a result of the

Nazi-Soviet Pact of 1939) along with portions of East Prussia, Finland, Czechoslovakia, Poland and Romania. The conference brought no resolution of the issue of the disposition of Eastern Europe, but only further revealed the fundamental differences in the postwar visions of western Allied leaders and the Soviet leadership. By summer's end, the final rupture of the wartime Grand Alliance was evident and a permanent division of Europe seemed increasingly likely.

With the Red Army securely holding Poland and most of Eastern Europe, the future of Germany became the most immediate issue between the Western powers and the Soviet Union. By the time of the Potsdam Conference, American advisers had abandoned the "Morgenthau Plan," which proposed that Germany should be de-industrialized and transformed into a harmless "pastoral" nation. Suggestions that Germany be broken up into a half dozen smaller states, so as to prevent a future resurrection of German power were also dropped. With each passing month, Anglo-American fears of a resurgent Germany receded as concern about Soviet intentions grew.

As had been agreed at Yalta, the four major Allied powers had established occupation zones as they advanced into Germany in the last months of the war and as of July 1945, these zones demarcated a more definitive four-way partition of the country. Berlin, situated in the heart of the Soviet zone, was itself divided into four sectors, a decision that ensured that the city would later be at the center of several Cold War confrontations. An Allied Control Council was established for the administration of the divided nation. Germany's fate was further delineated at the Potsdam Conference, where German reparations to the USSR were set at ten billion dollars. British and American conferees reluctantly agreed to Soviet demands to move

Germany's eastern border westward to a boundary along the Oder and Niesse Rivers, thus compensating Poland for territories incorporated into the USSR. The western powers refused Stalin's request that the Soviet Union be granted a role in the administration of Germany's industrial Ruhr region.

Though the four Allied powers generally agreed on the common policies of democratization, demilitarization and de-Nazification in Germany, it soon became clear that the Soviet zone was to be exploited for political and economic purposes. Interpreting democratization to mean the unchallenged dominance of Communist and pro-Soviet elements, the Russians compelled a merger of Communists and Social Democrats into the Socialist Unity Party, which was intended to be the ideological vehicle for communist rule in the Soviet zone. In addition to stripping the Russian zone of its remaining industrial assets, which was permitted under the Potsdam Agreement, the Soviets also began drawing from current German production, which was in direct violation of another joint provision. In response, British and American authorities began to administer and develop the economy of their zones jointly as the Bizone, later expanded to the Trizone with French participation.

As the political and economic foundations of two separate German states began to take shape, rising tensions between East and West disrupted the process of de-Nazification. The urgent need for local intelligence led authorities in both zones to seek out and utilize former Nazis as sources and operatives, thus derailing comprehensive de-Nazification. Moves by the western Allied powers to stabilize the Trizone's economy through currency reform in 1947 caused a further rift with the Soviets, who in early 1948 walked out of the Allied Control Council.

Stalin's suspicions about western motives led him to impose a blockade of West Berlin in June 1948, closing the western zones of the city to ground access and shutting off utilities. The Berlin Blockade was in part a test of western resolve, and the Allied response caught Stalin by surprise. The Berlin Airlift, a massive Anglo-American effort to supply West Berlin by air, brought food, fuel, medical supplies and other necessities to the beleaguered population for more than a year. Though Stalin called off the blockade in 1949, a permanent partition of Germany was inevitable. The same year, a Communist East German state was formalized as the German Democratic Republic, while the German Federal Republic was established in the former western Trizone. As the Cold War expanded in subsequent years, both the Soviet Union and the United States facilitated the rearming of the two Germanies.

Postwar Germany was only the focal point of a broader confrontation between the western democracies and the Soviet Union. As early as 1946, Churchill observed that "an iron curtain has descended across Europe," isolating the Soviet-dominated eastern nations. Though serious concern about Soviet intentions developed only gradually in the West, events in 1947 led the United States to formalize a Cold War policy and shoulder the burden of the confrontation with the USSR. Early that year, the Truman Doctrine was announced in response to the threat of Soviet aggression against Turkey and Communist subversion in Greece, which was in the midst of a civil war. In a speech to the U.S. Congress, President Truman offered American aid to those nations threatened by external aggression or domestic insurrection by "armed minorities" as part of a general effort to "contain" Communism.

Events in 1948 seemed to affirm the reality of the Communist menace. Only months before the Berlin Blockade, a Communist coup in Czechoslovakia overthrew central Europe's last democratic government. While "containment" sometimes meant direct action, as in the Berlin Airlift, it also took the form of broad, long-term policies such as the Marshall Plan. With the objective of restoring Europe's political and social stability by rapidly rebuilding the economy, the United States offered both economic aid and technical assistance to the war-torn continent. Ultimately, in the years between 1948 and 1952, 16 European nations received $13.2 billion in assistance. Given Western Europe's remarkable recovery by the early 1950s, the plan was among the most successful U.S. Cold War policies. The eastern bloc nations rejected Marshall Plan aid, turning instead to the Council for Mutual Economic Assistance (COMECON), which the USSR established in 1949 as a counter to the American program.

The emergence of two opposing military alliances marked the final stage of Europe's division. In 1948, five western European states signed the Brussels Pact, which committed them to collective self-defense for fifty years. The concept was expanded in 1949 with the establishment of the North Atlantic Treaty Organization (NATO), which brought the United States into a more extensive mutual defense pact with thirteen initial signatories in western Europe. In 1955, the USSR countered with the formation of the Warsaw Pact, a military alliance of the Communist bloc nations. Austria, partitioned since 1945, regained independence by agreeing to remain neutral. The basic parameters of the European Cold War were firmly set, providing the context for intermittent confrontations and crises throughout the next four decades.

The European Cold War was in the most general sense a lengthy, ideological struggle in which the major antagonists, the United States and the USSR, never directly attacked one another, but rather maneuvered for strategic advantage while attempting to maintain the strength and solidarity of their respective European allies. Given the military standoff in Europe, both sides sought to gain advantage through espionage and covert activities, though the introduction of new weapons systems, such as ballistic missiles, sometimes promised to alter the balance of power. Within the Communist bloc, popular discontent periodically erupted into rebellion, inevitably provoking Soviet intervention. Such was the case in East Berlin in 1953, Hungary in 1956 and Czechoslovakia in 1968, with revolt suppressed by Soviet intervention in each case. The Brezhnev Doctrine, proclaimed in the aftermath of the Czech crisis of 1968, reaffirmed the authority of the USSR to intervene in Warsaw Pact states to "protect socialism" and reflected Soviet determination to maintain orthodoxy within the Communist bloc. While there was no serious discord within the nations of western alliance, popular campaigns against nuclear weapons, Cold War policies and specific weapons systems sometimes had political repercussions in NATO states from the 1950s onward.

The most dangerous confrontations occurred in Berlin, where U.S., British and French forces coexisted in uncomfortable proximity to the Russians in the divided city. In an effort to stem the flow of East German refugees to West Berlin in 1961, Soviet Premier Nikita Khrushchev threatened to restore the city to East German control, a clear threat to the status of West Berlin. The resulting superpower crisis continued for months as U.S. President John Kennedy struggled to formulate a response that would spare the world a nuclear confrontation but maintain West Berlin's freedom. Not until August was a resolution reached—East German security forces began construction of a wall around the western portions of Berlin, a move that largely resolved the refugee problem without threatening West Berlin's special status. In 1963, a defiant Kennedy delivered a speech at the Berlin Wall, deriding it as a monument to the failure of socialism and affirming U.S. support for the encircled city.

Cold War confrontations generally lessened in intensity by the later 1960s as the United States pursued a policy of *détente*. In 1975, agreements at the Helsinki Conference in Finland did much to defuse East–West tensions. Delegates from both the western and Communist bloc nations agreed on means to avoid accidental confrontations, improve economic and technological cooperation and accept international conventions on human rights. Tensions in Europe increased somewhat by the later 1970s and into the 1980s as popular unrest in Poland threatened to provoke Soviet military intervention and as American President Ronald Reagan renewed the U.S. challenge to the USSR. Ultimately, the duration of Europe's Cold War proved contingent on the durability of the Soviet Union. After 1989, the disintegration of the USSR and the Communist bloc brought an astonishingly rapid and final end to the decades-long struggle.

Redefining Europe: the End of Empire and the Quest for a United Europe

In the aftermath of the Second World War, Europe's imperial powers were compelled to reevaluate the viability of colonial empire. Already undermined by the effects of the First World War, colonial rule was increasingly difficult to justify after 1945. Europe's imperial powers no longer commanded either the economic resources or the military capabilities to maintain overseas colonies. Earlier rationales for western colonial rule rapidly lost their intellectual force in the postwar era, especially in light of the proclaimed wartime principles of the Allies. Throughout the colonial world, subject peoples were quick to take note of the Allies' advocacy of self-determination, freedom and liberty as universal concepts. Many of these same peoples had seen their European overlords defeated and humiliated in battle, which punctured any Western pretensions of superiority. Before his death in April 1945, U.S. President Franklin Roosevelt had made clear his desire that the European allies should divest themselves of their colonies at war's end. Americans, Roosevelt observed, would not fight to preserve European empires. As a body, the United Nations was similarly unsupportive of colonial rule. All of these circumstances fueled nationalism and rising hopes for independence in the colonial world.

The five major European imperial powers approached the issue and process of decolonization with varying degrees of promptness and success. Debilitated by a war-ravaged economy, Britain moved relatively quickly to address the issue of decolonization. Though Winston Churchill had once huffed that he had not "become the king's first minister to supervise the dissolution of the British Empire," his electoral defeat in July 1945 and the advent of a Labour government accelerated the process of imperial liquidation, which was already well underway in India before the war. A long tradition of preparing subject peoples for self-government and the opportunity to become part of the British Commonwealth, a voluntary association which brought economic benefits, facilitated decolonization in India and elsewhere. Like India,

most former British colonies opted for Commonwealth status. Indian, Pakistan, Ceylon and Burma all gained independence by 1948, followed by Malaysia (1957) and Singapore (1965). British rule in Hong Kong continued until 1997.

British statesmen proved equally eager to pull out of the Middle East, granting Jordan independence in 1946 and relinquishing the mandate over Palestine in 1948. Britain's African empire was gradually dissolved between 1957 and 1963 with relatively ease. The soul exception was Kenya, where the presence of a significant number of white landholders provoked resentments leading to the Mau-Mau Rebellion of the early 1950s. Most of British Africa made the transition to independence with a minimum of disruption, adopting British parliamentary institutions and seeking Commonwealth status. The white-governed colonies of Rhodesia and South Africa proved more troublesome, leaving the Commonwealth to preserve policies of white rule and racial segregation.

In France, a reluctance to part with some colonial possessions brought considerable tribulation, including costly wars and the collapse of the first postwar French government. Though France abandoned both Syria and Lebanon, the desire to recapture national grandeur following the humiliations of the Second World War led France into a disastrous war in French Indochina. Rejecting Vietnam's 1945 declaration of independence, France entered into a lengthy struggle with Vietnamese nationalists led by Ho Chi Minh. This First Indochina War came to an end in May 1954 when French forces suffered a staggering defeat at the hands of Viet Minh troops at Dien Bien Phu in Vietnam's northern highlands. As French Indochina unraveled, Vietnam, Laos and Cambodia subsequently emerged as independent nations.

Forced to abandon Indochina, French political and military leaders were all the more determined to retain Algeria, where 1.2 million French settlers faced a nationalist uprising in 1954. The struggle between the Algerian National Liberation Front and the French Army degenerated into a savage conflict with horrendous atrocities on both sides, and aroused growing opposition in France. Ultimately, the conflict provoked a political crisis, the threat of a military coup and the collapse of the Fourth Republic in 1958. The 8-year struggle finally ended in 1962 when President Charles de Gaulle conceded Algeria's independence. As Tunisia and Morocco had achieved independence in the mid-1950s, French North Africa ceased to exist.

In sub-Saharan Africa and West Africa, French policy was more conciliatory and legislation in 1956 introduced representative institutions into France's twelve West Africa colonies and Madagascar. Two years later, the colonies were given the option of independence or autonomous status within a "French Community," somewhat akin to the British Commonwealth. Only Guinea initially chose independence, but within several years the others followed. Most continued to require economic and administrative support from France and retained close ties through the 1960s.

The other remaining major colonial powers resisted decolonization as long as possible. The Netherlands, economically debilitated by the wartime German occupation, desperately sought to retain the resource-rich Dutch East Indies, which the Japanese had seized during the war. Though British forces attempted to hold the region pending the return of Dutch authorities, Indonesian nationalists declared independence in August 1945. Consequently, Dutch military forces waged a savage war against the nationalists through the late 1940s, reimposing Dutch rule throughout much of the archipelago. Dutch control remained tenuous and dependent on brutal repression, however, and when the United States threatened to withdraw Marshall Plan aid to the Netherlands, Dutch officials conceded Indonesia's independence in late 1949. Belgium intended to retain the Congo for similar economic reasons and sought to stave off independence during the 1950s by offering concessions to Congolese nationalists. Having made no effort to prepare the Congo for self-government, the Belgian government hastily abandoned the colony in 1960 following continued popular unrest and rioting. Subsequently, the Congo's transition to independence was chaotic, as civil war between competing political and tribal factions kept the new nation in turmoil for years.

Portugal, one of the few remaining western European dictatorships, struggled to maintain its hold on Angola and Mozambique for decades. A nationalist uprising brought conflict to Angola from 1961 to 1975 and the two Portuguese colonies did not gain independence until 1975, the year after the Salazar dictatorship was overthrown. Civil war wracked both countries in subsequent years. Though some minor vestiges of European empire could be found even late in the century, European decolonization was substantially accomplished within two decades of the war's end.

The dissolution of empire occurred partly as a result of a broad recognition of Europe's diminished position in the postwar world. The loss of empire in return had significant economic repercussions for the former colonial powers. Now deprived of lucrative resources and markets, these nations confronted the issue of restructuring their postwar economies. These realities were among the many factors that drove a postwar movement for European unity, seen as increasingly vital given the fundamental transformation of the world order after 1945. The idea of a united Europe went back centuries, but the concept was charged with a new urgency in the aftermath of what was essentially a six-year European civil war of unprecedented destructiveness. Among the many prominent Europeans who recognized the terrible consequences of unbridled nationalism was Winston Churchill, who spoke of the need for a united Europe only months after he acknowledged Europe's division in his 1946 "Iron Curtain" speech. Speaking in Zurich, Switzerland, the ex-prime minister advocated the formation of "a kind of United States of Europe," and warned, "we must begin now."

In 1948, Churchill was among some 800 attendees at the Congress of Europe, where the issue of unity was the topic of discussion. Churchill urged the creation "of a United Europe whose moral conception will win the respect and gratitude of mankind, and whose physical strength will be such that none will dare molest her tranquil sway." He looked forward to the evolution of a Europe "where men and women of every country will think of being European as of belonging to their native land." The general "European Movement" which grew out of the Congress took shape even as efforts to achieve European economic unity were underway. The Marshall Plan presented the first opportunity to establish a common plan for economic recovery and a framework was provided by the Organization of European Economic Cooperation (OEEC), which sought to liberalize European trade during the years of massive U.S. aid. A more permanent organization, the European Coal and Steel Community (ECSC) was formed in 1950. The ECSC, a

product of collaboration between French Foreign Minister Robert Schuman and economist Jean Monnet, sought to pool heavy industrial resources and eliminate tariffs in Western Europe's industrial core: France, West Germany, Italy and the Low Countries.

The movement toward unity advanced in the mid-1950s with the establishment of Euratom, which oversaw common atomic energy research and resources, and the creation of the European Economic Community (EEC). Founded in 1957, the EEC established a common agricultural and industrial market with the intent of harmonizing member economies. National assemblies selected delegates to a new European Parliament, which functioned in an advisory capacity. The three organizations were merged in the European Community (EC) in 1967. One of the lengthiest controversies faced by the EEC concerned the status of Great Britain, which initially forsook membership in the Common Market. Changing circumstances led Britain to apply for membership in 1961 and again in 1967, only to be vetoed both times by de Gaulle's France. Not until 1973 did the EEC admit Britain. Though controversy over membership and policy occurred intermittently during the postwar decades, the European Community was broadly accepted as an effective vehicle for European unity.

Military and diplomatic exigencies also furthered European integration. In the bipolar postwar world, individual European nations could not hope to command either the diplomatic or military strength to ensure national security. Western Europe's obvious vulnerability in the growing Cold War had brought into being the Atlantic Alliance (NATO) in 1949, which offered the promise of collective security and U.S. support in the event of Soviet aggression. As the Cold War intensified in 1950 with the outbreak of the Korean War, there was growing pressure from the United States for the creation of an integrated European military force. The limits of European unity were revealed in subsequent discussions over the composition of a proposed European Defense Community (EDC). Understandably reluctant to accept a rearmed West Germany as part of an integrated European defense force, French leaders balked at the scheme. Though six European governments signed the treaty by 1953, the French parliament effectively killed the EDC by refusing to ratify the treaty. The following year, France acceded to a subsequent proposal for West German membership in NATO. In the years to come, disagreements as to how Europe might best be defended eroded unity within NATO. British and French statesmen were increasingly doubtful of the utility of relying on the American nuclear umbrella, and moved to develop their own nuclear capabilities. European fears that U.S. policies would turn Europe into a nuclear battlefield in the event of a superpower confrontation sparked further divisions through the 1980s. NATO brought a semblance of unity to Europe in the postwar decades, but like the efforts to achieve economic unity, fell short of bringing full integration.

Western Europe's "Golden Age:" Economy, Society and Culture

At the end of the Second World War, Europe's future looked bleak. Devastation of unprecedented scope, together with the near-complete disintegration of society and government in some regions, indicated a lengthy, painful period of recovery and an extraordinarily uncertain future. The division of Europe and the hardening of ideological lines in the early years of the Cold War loomed as additional obstacles to the rebuilding of the continent. Yet within less than a decade, recovery and restoration were well underway, especially in Western Europe. One of the most surprising developments of the postwar era was the European "Economic Miracle" of the 1950s and the subsequent quarter century of unprecedented prosperity. Few who surveyed Europe at war's end could have forecast the "Golden Age" that was to come. Given the billions of tons of rubble that filled the streets of bomb-shattered cities and the vast damage to transportation, communications and utility networks, the physical reconstruction of Europe alone promised to be a decades-long endeavor. Yet with remarkable swiftness, the cities were cleared and rebuilt, the new structures often reflecting modern architectural concepts that altered the look of Europe's urban centers and emphasized the disappearance of the old Europe. The restoration of motorways, railroads and telephone systems, made more urgent by the emerging Cold War, proceeded apace. The rapid reconstruction of Europe's infrastructure was a prerequisite to general economic recovery.

With Fascist and collaborationist regimes destroyed and discredited, legitimate national governments reemerged to grapple with a multitude of problems. Across Western Europe, even in those states in which government had not been displaced or disrupted, there was a broad perception that the postwar situation demanded new and innovative institutions, parties and policies. Some nations made the necessary adjustments with alacrity, ensuring both political and social stability in an era of expanding prosperity. For those nations less receptive to fundamental institutional changes, political reconstruction was often incomplete or delayed, resulting in continued social and political discord. Throughout Western Europe, however, there was a general realization that the lessons of the 1920s had to be taken to heart. In the aftermath of a war that came close to destroying European civilization, Europe could not afford to repeat the mistakes of the past.

Western Europe's economic recovery was one of the great success stories of the postwar period. The accomplishments of the wartime Bretton Woods Conference did much to facilitate Europe's reconstruction. Meeting in New Hampshire in July 1944, representatives from forty-four nations established some of the mechanisms for international economic management, including the International Bank for Reconstruction and Development (World Bank) and the International Monetary Fund. The Conference was evidence of a determination not to leave the direction of the world economy to "natural forces," as had been the case prior to the 1930s.

Bolstered by Marshall Plan aid, the economies in the West expanded with unprecedented speed after 1950. A liberal political climate, which fostered mixed economies in which moderate state intervention and planning were tempered by a general receptiveness to free market capitalism, further aided recovery. New industrial and agricultural technologies, together with advances in transportation and power all contributed to an increasingly dynamic economy in which employment levels reached new highs. A trend toward industrial concentration may have contributed to the increasing organizational and productive efficiency of industry. As early as 1952, as the Marshall Plan ran its course, the Gross National Product (GNP) of the Western states had increased by 25 per-

cent. Steel production soared an astounding 70 percent. The expansion of the chemical, automaking, electronics and later computer industries also drove growth in the industrial sector. Rates of improvement in industrial productivity varied nationally, and some nations, such as Britain, lagged in the early postwar years even while experiencing general recovery. Elsewhere, as in Italy and West Germany, growth in industrial productivity was nothing short of spectacular. West Germany's *Wirtschaftwunder,* or "economic miracle," established the German Federal Republic as a potential economic giant as early as 1960, by which time industrial production had quadrupled from 1948 levels. The West German GNP tripled between 1950 and 1964, and a labor shortage led to policies promoting the immigration of foreign "guest workers," often Italians or Turks. Though the European industrial sector remained strong into the 1960s, it gradually lost its preeminence due to growing competition from Asia (especially Japan) and as employment in white-collar and service jobs increased.

The agricultural economy of Western Europe was similarly transformed in the two decades following the war as a result of the "Green Revolution," during which productivity rose 30 percent. The rapid modernization and large-scale commercialization of agriculture permitted far fewer farmers to produce larger quantities of foodstuffs. Government programs promoting mechanization, land reform and education also contributed to an agricultural revolution that ultimately resulted in Western Europe easily meeting its food requirements.

The apparently boundless prosperity of the "Golden Age" came to an abrupt end in the early 1970s. Finance markets were already registering the impact of growing U.S. borrowing to fund the American war in Vietnam, which was driving up credit rates and inflation. The international economic order received a more serious shock in the aftermath of the Yom Kippur War of October 1973 when the Arab members of OPEC, the Organization of Petroleum-Exporting Countries, retaliated against western nations supporting Israel by imposing an embargo on oil sales. The short-term impact was on the price and availability of petroleum products, most importantly fuel. In the longer term, inflated fuel prices rippled through most western economies, driving up prices of both durable and consumer goods, generating unemployment, disrupting industrial relations and generally dislocating already vulnerable economies. Though Western Europe did not face the dire circumstances of the 1930s, there was a general lowering of expectations during more than a decade of recession and retrenchment. Stiff competition from Asian industry, which often had the advantage of newer plant facilities and much cheaper labor, further eroded the industrial base of the European economy, as Japanese auto manufacturers made significant inroads in the European and American markets.

The post-industrial age was clearly upon Western Europe by the 1970s, marked by a shift away from heavy industry and manufacturing and toward an economy built on more service-sector and information technology jobs. The transition was gradual but discernible, bringing with it all of the social and political stresses inherent in a major economic transformation. Europe weathered the most difficult challenges by the mid-1980s, however, when a lengthy period of U.S. economic growth was attended by a similar revival in Western Europe.

The social contours of Western Europe were shaped in large part by the phenomenal economic growth of the region, which vastly improved standards of living and reduced the socioeconomic tensions that had been so disruptive in the prewar years. One dimension of the "economic miracle" in Italy, for example, was a huge increase in real wages, which by 1954 were more than fifty percent higher than in prewar years. The new prosperity transformed Western Europe's social structure. Though perceptions of class identity persisted, they were not as marked as in previous decades and eroded further as economic mobility grew in the postwar period. Employment in the industrial sector remained steady or grew only slightly in most countries throughout the 1950s and 1960s, but began to decline in following decades as the service sector became more important. Accordingly, traditional "class loyalties" were increasingly less relevant or even definable. Though the trade-union movement remained generally vibrant, emphasis on "class consciousness" and political activity receded in favor of a new pragmatism focusing on improving wages and working conditions. The new economic mobility saw many move into Europe's increasingly amorphous and diverse middle-class, enlarged in the postwar period by new groups of white-collar workers, including managers, technicians and administrative personnel staffing expanding government agencies. Women played a much larger role in postwar Europe's economy, gaining admittance into jobs that had once been predominantly male, and finding new opportunities in the service sector and later high-technology industries.

Low unemployment and rising wages combined with growing productivity to fuel a new consumerism that greatly reshaped European life by the 1960s, with many more families able to afford such modern conveniences as washing machines, refrigerators, telephones, automobiles and televisions.

These years saw a tremendous increase in automobile ownership; whereas there were only 3.6 million cars in Europe in 1939, the number had ballooned to nearly 10.5 million in 1970. Not only was Europe's urban landscape altered to accommodate the new automobile culture, but Europeans themselves enjoyed a new mobility. Recreational travel across Western Europe, where there were now virtually open borders, was increasingly practicable.

Television affected European society and culture as fundamentally as it did their American counterparts, further fostering consumerism and serving as the primary vehicle for a radically altered mass culture. Cultural conservatives condemned the new visual medium for undermining tradition and morality, while others who feared the "Americanization" of Europe likewise assailed television. A pronounced European affinity for select aspects of American culture had become evident in the 1950s, and by the following decade some traditionalists voiced concerns that American economic dominance, conjoined with the influence of U.S. films, television and popular culture, might eventually subsume Europe's own unique character. France proved most sensitive to this issue, its government attempting as early as the 1950s to restrict the American export of Coca-Cola, which was seen as a threat to the French wine industry and traditional French culture. In later decades, the French Academy strove to ensure that popular "Americanisms" did not subvert the purity of the French language. On the other hand, Americans became increasingly receptive to European cultural exports, embracing the "British Invasion" of the 1960s, which brought "Beatlemania," and demonstrating a growing if still relatively limited interest in European film.

This cultural exchange was partly the consequence of the postwar European "baby boom," which, like its counterpart in the United States, resulted in an unexpected rise in population. Though Europeans accounted for a smaller percentage of the world population than they had in 1900 (about 16 percent by 1990), the population grew from 264 million in 1940 to 320 million in the early 1970s. The rise in birthrates may be explained by improved economic circumstances, better diets and improved health care, the latter often now a service provided by the welfare states that became the norm across the continent after 1945. Entering adulthood by the 1960s, the first wave of "baby boomers" were at the forefront of the cultural revolution of that decade, challenging social conventions, traditional morality and political orthodoxy. They were the beneficiaries not only of affluence but also of improved educational systems, which not only nearly erased illiteracy but also made higher education more widely available. The number of university students tripled between 1938 and 1960, as many public universities required little or no tuition. This generation was instrumental in the broad movement for political democratization and social egalitarianism that swept Europe by the late 1960s.

Western Europe's intellectual course in the postwar period broadly parallels economic recovery. Unsurprisingly, the war left considerable intellectual wreckage in its wake. The absolute truths that had been the pillars of European optimism and certainty at the onset of the century were among the many casualties of the terrible conflict. British novelist George Orwell captured the despair and pessimism of many when he observed that "since about 1930 the world has given no reason for optimism whatsoever. Nothing in sight except a welter of lies, cruelty, hatred and ignorance." Orwell's 1948 novel *1984*, which depicted the grim brutality of life in a totalitarian England, offered a frightening portrait of a potential future. The same year, Hannah Arendt's *The Origins of Totalitarianism* sought to uncover the historical roots of the phenomenon that had so tragically shaped recent events.

Those not paralyzed by the catastrophe attempted to come to grips with its meaning. Experiences in the wartime resistance influenced some, such as French novelist Albert Camus, who sought to discern new lessons from the inhumanities, betrayals and small triumphs that the war had brought. Camus' *The Plague* (1947), an allegory of man's struggle against disease and death, was something of a reflection of Camus' fight against the new barbarism of the Nazis. Germans writers also sought to understand their wartime experiences and to draw from them some broader understanding of the human condition. Eugen Kogon's *The Theory and Practice of Hell* (1946) was among a number of works that sought to make sense of the concentration camp experience, which led men to both admirable self-sacrifice and questionable moral compromises in order to survive.

Perhaps the most influential postwar intellectual development was the growing appeal of existentialism. An anti-intellectualist philosophy with roots in the nineteenth century irrationalist tradition, existentialism rejected philosophical systems in an effort to get to the heart of the human experience. In the 1920s, German existentialist Martin Heidegger focused on addressing dread, despair and death, which he saw as fundamental to human existence. Although Hedigger's accommodation with the Nazi regime somewhat discredited him, existentialism gained new prominence in the postwar era through French intellectual Jean-Paul Sartre, whose

1943 treatise *Being and Nothingness* did much to define postwar existentialism. Sartre's existentialism held that the world was by itself unintelligible, bereft of both God and reason, and that it remained with man to choose a meaning for his life. Sartre's Marxist outlook, which led him to advocate commitment to the ideological battle, somewhat tempered his conception of the absurdity of life. Some meaning, it seemed, was to be found in making the choice to commit oneself to a cause, regardless of the greater meaninglessness of existence. Existentialism's immediate postwar prominence was very much a product of specific circumstances born of the war. With the passage of time and the general stabilization of European society, the influence of existentialism, which never extended far beyond the intellectual and student community, receded.

A broader debate that shaped Western Europe's intellectual life was the "Great Confrontation" of the 1950s, which saw intellectuals divided over the support or rejection of Marxism. Defenders of Marxism cited the tradition of Communist wartime resistance and the failure of "bourgeois" parliamentary democracy. Many were also cognizant of and highly critical of the injustices of Western society, such as racism and imperialism. Opponents of Marxism were appalled by the brutalities of Stalinism and the willingness of Marxist intellectuals to suspend their critical faculties in support of a dogmatic ideology. By the late 1950s, revelations concerning Stalinist crimes and Communist oppression in the eastern bloc badly undermined the position of Marxist intellectuals. Nonetheless, Marxism underwent a revival in the politically charged climate of the late 1960s as intellectuals, students and sometimes workers attacked the failures of "capitalist" democracy. Denouncing poverty, racism, war and the threat of nuclear annihilation, some radicals promoted a neo-Marxism that rejected both the Soviet example and liberal democracy. Though these movements were short-lived, some spawned terrorist groups such as Italy's Red Brigade. Marxist variants receded by the 1980s, as European intellectuals turned away from political concerns and toward more abstract philosophical realms. One of the most noteworthy developments was deconstructionism, a methodology formulated by Jacques Derrida that maintained that all evidently rationalist thought could be "deconstructed" and shown to have no absolute meaning. In the increasingly complex and sometimes fragmented world of the late twentieth century, the primacy of reason and the existence of certainty remained in doubt.

Similar uncertainties shaped postwar European literature and art. The "theater of the absurd" produced existentialist dramas including Irish-born playwright Samuel Beckett's *Waiting for Godot*, which baffled audiences in the 1950s with its disconnected, seemingly directionless plot. The novel remained a major vehicle for literary expression and in Germany, the long-exiled Thomas Mann sought to address the rise of Nazism in *Dr. Faustus* (1948), an allegory centering on an increasingly insane composer who has bargained his soul in return for his compositional powers. In later decades, the novels of Heinrich Böll and Gunter Grass dealt with the consequences of the war and the perplexities of postwar society. Italian literature also blossomed after the war, as neo-realist writers strove for a more popular, poetic and political art form. Film assumed an increasingly central role in Western European culture, as Italy, France and Germany all produced a new generation of directors who grappled with postwar social and political issues in innovative and sometimes shocking ways. In painting and sculpture, the triumph of the abstract was manifest in the postwar decades. Likewise, in music, modernism asserted its dominance. Atonality, unorthodox harmonies and jarring rhythms seemed perfectly suited to expressing the anguish of the wartime experience and the disconnections of modern life. Polish composer Kryszstof Penderecki's compositions exemplified the bold directions that postwar music often took. His *Auschwitz Oratorio* sought to capture the horror of the Holocaust in sound, while his *Polymorphia for 48 Strings* hinted at more abstract terrors. Postwar literature and art alike reflected both the pain of recent experience and the disconcerting uncertainties of the contemporary world.

The postwar period also brought a reevaluation of women's issues and the emergence of the modern feminist movement. As suffrage was not an issue across most of Europe, the focus in these years was often on social rather than political issues. One of the most influential thinkers to address the subject was French intellectual Simone de Beauvoir, whose *The Second Sex* (1949) established much of the framework for postwar discussion of women's issues. The book addressed the subject of how being female had distinctly shaped de Beauvoir's life to her disadvantage. Being the "second sex," she argued, compelled women to develop specific psychological strategies to compensate for their inferior status in a male-dominated society. She asserted that economic freedom and advancement were crucial to individual fulfillment, themes that were subsequently amplified as the debate over women's status in European society unfolded in following decades. Postwar European feminists grappled with a wide range of issues, including legal equality (especially concerning divorce law), birth control rights and workplace issues.

Europe's Christian churches confronted the need for both self-reflection and adaptation in the years after the war. Though many clerics and laymen alike had resisted Fascist tyranny and oppression, it was equally clear that there were those who had not acted or had even supported totalitarian regimes. One moral and spiritual question of undeniable urgency and fundamental concern was the meaning of the extermination of a great portion of European Jewry. Christian and Jewish scholars alike struggled with the Holocaust's meaning for Christianity for decades to come. More immediately, Germany's Protestant churches confronted the task of reconstruction following the spiritual debacle of the Nazi era. Chief among the reformers was Martin Niemoeller, founder of the anti-Nazi Confessing Church in 1934. Released from eight years in a concentration camp in 1945, Nielmoeller was instrumental in the rebuilding of the German Protestant Church, whose pastors continued their efforts to compel Germans to confront the Nazi past.

The Roman Catholic Church was also faced with coming to terms with its wartime behavior. Though there were numerous Catholics among the anti-Nazi Resistance, the Church itself, and specifically Pope Pius XII, were intermittently the focus of controversy concerning concordats with both Fascist Italy and Nazi Germany and the Vatican's lack of response to Nazi crimes. While those controversies continued for decades, Catholic political influence grew in Western Europe with the emergence of Christian Democratic parties. The Roman church's uncompromising opposition to Communist regimes further defined it in the postwar period. The papacy of John XXIII brought both a new tone and direction to the Roman Church in the years after 1959, as.the new pontiff believed that the church had to be brought up to date by confronting the problems of the modern world. The encyclical *Mater et Magistra* (1961) stressed the responsibility of the developed world to the impoverished people of undeveloped countries, while *Pacem in Terris* (1963) was an appeal for international peace and a condemnation of nuclear war. The Second Vatican Council, which met between 1962 and 1965, brought all Catholic bishops together to begin a systematic revision and definition of church policies and practices.

Though such efforts undoubtedly improved the stature of the Roman Catholic Church, the growing secularization of western society posed a challenge that could not be entirely overcome. Catholic and Protestant churches alike strove to assert the timeless value of spirituality in a world that was increasingly secular and material in orientation.

Politics and Government in Western Europe

The course and consequences of the war also shaped the process of political reconstruction in Western Europe. The reconstitution of free government followed closely in the path of the Allied armies that advanced eastward across the continent beginning in the summer of 1944. In those nations liberated from Nazi rule, the issue of collaboration and resistance was often a major factor in postwar politics. Those groups that had actively opposed German occupation and Fascism, most notably Communists, enjoyed new moral stature and political strength in both France and Italy. The newfound legitimacy of the Communists began to erode by the late 1940s, however, as the Cold War reshaped Europe's political universe. Antagonisms stemming from the occupation years embittered politics in a number of nations, especially in France and Belgium. In the latter, Walloons decried Flemings as collaborators and in 1951 King Leopold III was compelled to abdicate because of similar allegations. Across the rest of northern Europe, the restoration of sovereignty brought few major political problems. The Netherlands, Denmark and Norway recovered rapidly in the postwar era, retaining nominal monarchies and reinstating parliamentary systems. Across much of the rest of Western Europe, the turmoil and dislocations of the immediate postwar years were followed by a lengthy era of political moderation and general stability. This came in consequence of a general realization on the part of postwar leaders that radical, dogmatic ideologies had tremendous disruptive and destructive potential. If Europe were to recover, liberal democracy would have to be reaffirmed and rejuvenated; radical solutions would have to be forsaken in favor of moderate though innovative policies.

One general characteristic of postwar Western European politics was the broad rejection of radical ideologies. Fascism, for all practical purposes, died with its inceptors in 1945. Though neo-Fascist revivals occurred in West Germany, Italy and elsewhere by the 1970s, they were marginal movements of no real political consequence. Ultranationalism resurfaced in both Britain and France around the same time, driven largely by nativist reactions against immigrant populations, but again, these movements never attained the broad popular appeal that drove nationalist movements in the prewar years. On the radical left, Marxism, badly tainted by Stalin's excesses and repression in eastern bloc regimes, was widely repudiated, with the Communists retaining only marginal influence in Western Europe. Beginning in the late 1950s, Europe's social democratic parties began to move away from orthodox Marxist doctrine and to adopt a more pragmatic approach to politics and governance. While clear ideological and policy differences continued to distinguish the parties of the left and right, bringing contentious politics to some nations, the stark polarization and combat mentality of the 1930s were largely relegated to the past.

One of the more consequential political developments in Western Europe was the emergence of mass parties committed to Christian principles, democratic government and moderately conservative policies. "Christian Democracy" manifested itself in new political parties in West Germany, Italy, France and a number of the lesser powers and quickly became a dominant force in the early postwar decades. With some notable exceptions, once the nations of Western Europe surmounted the difficulties of the immediate postwar period, stable, democratic government became the political norm.

GREAT BRITAIN: FROM SOCIALISM TO CONSERVATISM

One of the greatest shocks of 1945, at least outside Britain, was the rejection of Winston Churchill and the Conservative party in the July elections. Many in the Western world viewed Churchill as the backbone and conscience of a nation that had stood alone against Nazi aggression in 1940. The Conservatives had held power since 1931, however, and considerable public grievances had built up both before and during the war. With the Nazi threat removed, the British electorate indicated its desire for both economic and social reform, bringing to power a Labour government headed by Clement Attlee. Thoroughly lacking in charisma, Attlee had once been lampooned as "a sheep in sheep's clothing," and was the object of more than one jibe by Churchill, who claimed to have watched as "an empty cab pulled up at 10 Downing Street (the Prime Minister's residence) and Attlee got out." As the leader of the first Socialist party to win power in a major European state, Attlee faced the difficult tasks of supervising the dissolution of the empire, rebuilding the nation's economy and finances and laying the foundations for a modern welfare state, a proposition to which Britons were increasingly receptive. The latter task was rapidly undertaken as Parliament passed legislation providing for social benefits such as national health insurance, retirement pensions and unemployment benefits. Accepting the concept of a "mixed economy" comprised of both public and private enterprises, the Labour government nationalized most major transportation industries, including airlines, railways and buses, coal and steel industries and even the Bank of England.

Britain's industrial economy continued to stagnate, however, due to aging factories and overseas competition. Overall British economic growth fell behind other European countries. These economic woes, together with an increasingly heavy tax burden that the new social welfare measures mandated, brought public disillusionment. In 1951, elections returned the Conservatives to power with Churchill as prime minister until 1955. Despite the urgings of diehard Conservatives, the new government did not dismantle Labour's welfare state. Responsible Conservatives acknowledged the popularity of the programs and, in line with the new moderation of the postwar period, sought instead to limit their excesses and costs. Anthony Eden, who succeeded Churchill, fell victim to public backlash over the Suez Crisis in

1956, when Britain joined France and Israel in a short-lived war against Egypt, which had recently nationalized the Suez Canal. The United States pressured the three nations to back away from the conflict so as not to invite Soviet intervention on Egypt's behalf, and Britain's international position was weakened. Eden's successor, Harold Macmillan, regained the public's confidence and the Conservatives retained office until 1964.

The Labour party, weakened by internal squabbles and its opposition to nuclear arms during the 1950s, was in an improved position by the early 1960s, as public opposition to Conservative reductions in social welfare benefits cut into the party's popularity. The 1964 "Profumo Scandal," which concerned Defense Minister John Profumo's questionable relationships with a call girl who was carrying on a simultaneous affair with a Soviet military attaché, together with a stagnating economy, helped bring about a Labour victory at the polls that year. The new prime minister, Harold Wilson, typified a younger generation of Labourites who were concerned more with the practical results of policy than with ideology. Though his government moved to introduce economic and social reforms, such as the Equal Pay Act, which prohibited gender-based wage differentials, it advanced no broad socialist designs. Since the war's end, the recurring challenge had been strengthening Britain's economy. In 1967, in order to resolve the ongoing balance of payments problem, the Wilson government devalued the British pound and implemented an austerity program. Efforts to restrain wage increases, which contributed to inflation, provoked strikes and general disillusionment.

Growing unrest in Northern Ireland, where the Catholic minority resented Protestant dominance in the six British-controlled provinces sometimes referred to as Ulster, compounded Wilson's problems. Protestant fears of absorption into the Catholic Irish Republic further inflamed tensions. In the aftermath of violent clashes in 1969, sectarians on both sides organized paramilitary groups such as the Irish Republican Army (IRA) and the Ulster Defense Association. British Army troops sent to restore order were caught in a literal crossfire as hostilities accelerated—by the end of 1993 over 3,000 had been killed in the fighting.

Though these troubles brought about a Conservative government under Edward Heath in 1970, its tenure was brief. The Arab oil boycott imposed more strains on an already weakened economy, and efforts to hold down inflation by imposing wage limits on coal miners provoked a strike in 1973. Conservative party failures in the economic realm resulted in a restoration of Labour's power in 1974 when Wilson returned to office, but the complex economic difficulties of the 1970s confounded his Labour government. Unable to appease trade union demands for higher wages, Wilson's successor James Callaghan faced multiplying strikes and uncontrolled inflation, the annual rate of which peaked at eleven percent. Politically incapable of either placating or repudiating the trade unions, Labour lost the 1979 elections.

In May 1979, Margaret Thatcher, the first woman to serve as British prime minister, took office. Thatcher's rise to a leadership position in the Conservative party was not uncontested, but she had demonstrated her consummate political skills in a number of government posts throughout the 1970s. Thatcher was representative of a new conservative wave that swept Western Europe and the United States during the 1980s, rejecting government intervention in economic affairs, opposing the extension of the welfare state,

and extolling free market capitalism as the engine of prosperity. Thatcher and fellow conservatives in the western world also supported a strong national defense policy and aggressive measures to combat Communism.

As a first step toward recovery, Thatcher's government introduced strong austerity measures, including a reduction in public spending, caps on wages in nationalized industries and reductions in inheritance and capital gains taxes. Most immediately, these policies produced severe unemployment levels, reaching 12.2 percent by 1982. Thatcher's opponents, including Labour, denounced her policies as callous, aimed at balancing the budget on the backs of the least prosperous citizens. As conditions worsened, riots broke out in a number of industrial cities, including London and Liverpool. Thatcher braved the political storm, however, and her position was considerably strengthened by her conduct of the Falklands War of 1982, as the government dispatched forces to liberate the isolated South Atlantic islands from an Argentine military occupation. Her popularity bolstered by the eventual British victory, Thatcher won reelection in a 1983 electoral landslide. Her unshakable determination to pursue her chosen course, growing national prosperity after 1981 and internal divisions within the Labour Party ensured Conservative dominance throughout the decade. Not until 1990, when Conservative party leaders feared a revival of Labour's popularity, did they oust Thatcher from the party's leadership, replacing her with the colorless and generally ineffective John Major.

FRANCE: THE FOURTH AND FIFTH REPUBLICS

Having established his authority as the head of the French government-in-exile dur-

Fig. 7-2   British Prime Minister Margaret Thatcher leaves 10 Downing Street, her official residence, following news that British troops had landed in the Falkland Islands, which had been seized by Argentina. The 1982 war, in which Britain triumphed, provided Thatcher, the first woman to hold the prime ministership, with an opportunity to demonstrate her steadfastness and infuse a somewhat listless nation with a newfound patriotic spirit. (Pearson Education, Corporate Digital Archive, Getty Images Inc.)

ing the war, Charles de Gaulle was well positioned to dominate the provisional government established in 1944. His first priority as premier was constitutional reconstruction, as he believed that structural weaknesses in the Third Republic were largely responsible for its abrupt collapse in 1940. The majority of his countrymen agreed and overwhelmingly supported a referendum for a Constituent Assembly in October 1945. Any semblance of national unity over the shape of the new republic soon dissipated, however, as Communists and Socialists won the greatest number of seats in the Assembly. Strongly opposed to de Gaulle's design for a greatly strengthened executive branch, the left parties supported legislative supremacy in the new government. Disgusted by the turn of events, de Gaulle resigned in January 1946. The constitution of the Fourth Republic, approved by a narrow majority in October, recapitulated most of the defects of its predecessor, providing only for a weak president and premier. It virtually guaranteed the political instability and gridlock that had immobilized the Third Republic. Indeed, during the next twelve years, the Fourth Republic had twenty-four different governments. De Gaulle, who had returned to his home village in eastern France, busied himself founding a Gaullist political party, the Rally of the French People, thoroughly convinced that in time, France would once again call upon him.

For postwar governments, economic recovery and restructuring was a high priority. Even before the European war was over, France's provisional government moved to implement reforms that had been discussed before the war. The state assumed a larger role in the postwar economy, taking over the larger banks, the airlines and the Renault automobile plant, along with coal, steel and electricity. The government played a major role in economic planning with an eye to the general modernization of the business and agricultural sectors. While inflation and deficits were persistent problems, French economic recovery was surprisingly swift, with the GNP doubling in ten years. Political reconstruction remained incomplete, however, due largely to the constitutional structure of the Fourth Republic, which fostered legislative irresponsibility and frequent

deadlock. The war had altered the political order, leaving the Socialists without dynamic leadership or unity, while the Radical Socialists had all but disappeared and the Communists remained on the margins of political life after 1947. A new Christian Democratic party, the Popular Republican Movement (MRP) offered some promise, but lacked the electoral support to govern alone. Subsequently, most Fourth Republic governments were built around coalitions including the MRP, Socialists and ambiguous left-liberal groupings. Changes in government most often meant only rearrangements of ministerial posts, and by the 1950s the absence of enthusiasm and clear direction characterized national political life.

Ultimately, the challenges of decolonization revealed the political inadequacies of the Fourth Republic. The First Indochina War, begun in 1946 in order to maintain France's claim to great power status, had grown increasingly divisive by the time of the fall of Dien Bien Phu in May 1954. Premier Pierre Mendes-France acknowledged the end of French empire in Southeast Asia, only to be excoriated by opponents and ousted after only seven months in office. The new premier, Socialist Guy Mollet, hoped to resolve the growing crisis in French Algeria, but his plan of conciliating Algerian nationalists collapsed as violence spread to the capital of Algiers. Under pressure from French settlers, the military and right-wing opinion in France to suppress the rebellion, Mollet complied, thus accelerating a conflict he had hoped to end. As the war intensified, France grew more divided and Mollet was ousted in 1957. In May of the following year, right-wing groups, supported by the local army command, seized the civil administration in Algeria. This "Committee of Public Safety" sought a reassertion of French authority abroad and the creation of an authoritarian regime in France. The crisis provided Charles de Gaulle with the opportunity that he had awaited for twelve years.

Though de Gaulle's Rally of the French People had been disbanded five years earlier, an ardent corps of devotees quickly floated his name as the crisis of 1958 mounted. With the insurrection spreading to Corsica and rumors of an army parachute assault on the capital circulating, the National Assembly moved quickly to head off an expected military coup d'etat, naming de Gaulle as prime minister on June 1 and giving him emergency powers for six months, pending approval of a new constitution. The document, which established the framework of the Fifth Republic, won 80 percent approval in a popular referendum that September. It clearly reflected the former general's desire for a presidential government in which the locus of power was shifted from the National Assembly to the presidency; the president, elected by popular vote, served a seven-year term and was given the authority to appoint the premier.

De Gaulle's resolution to the pressing Algerian question disappointed the military and political right, who had been among his greatest advocates. In 1959 de Gaulle proclaimed that France must accept Algerian self-determination and in 1961 the public approved a national referendum to that effect. Disaffected army officers in Algeria attempted a second insurrection, but in the face of de Gaulle's considerable national stature, it collapsed and Algeria gained independence in 1962.

As president, de Gaulle affected a semi-authoritarian style and exuded a degree of self-assuredness that detractors at home and abroad decried as conceit, but his vision for a modern France clearly resonated with the majority of his countrymen. An unabashed advocate of national grandeur, de Gaulle once declared "To my mind, France cannot be France without greatness." In the realm of foreign policy this meant distancing France from the United States as part of a general effort to diminish postwar Anglo-American influence. His periodic refusals to permit Britain into the Common Market stemmed in part from this desire to lessen English influence on the continent. His moves to detach France from NATO as early as 1959 also demonstrated his determination to establish French military power as an independent entity. In 1966, France ended all participation in NATO. He also set about strengthening the French armed forces, a policy that reconciled many previously aggrieved military officers with his regime. His decision to provide France with a nuclear weapons capability may have annoyed U.S. policymakers, but it met with approval from those who shared his vision of restored grandeur. De Gaulle further irritated American statesmen by his diplomatic overtures to the USSR and surprised many with his warm support for West Germany, which he no longer viewed as a threat but rather as a barrier to Soviet expansion into central Europe.

De Gaulle's adeptness in foreign policy did not extend to domestic affairs. Though the French economy expanded through the 1960s, bolstered by the automobile and armaments industries, government deficits and a rising cost of living contributed to moderate but growing discontent. The tensions that culminated in the spring of 1968 were the product not only of economic unease but also of political discontent and intellectual ferment. The turmoil began in May in Paris, where students protesting the archaic university system battled police for days, during which the issues driving the protest ballooned far beyond academic discontent. The omnipresent threat of nuclear destruction, the American war in Vietnam, broad social and economic inequities and general distaste for the de Gaulle government's imperious style combined to drive tens of thousands of students and workers into the streets. A general strike on May 13 was the largest the country had seen since 1936. Stunned by the scope and intensity of the unrest and with memories of 1958 still vivid in his mind, de Gaulle dissolved the National Assembly only after receiving assurance of the loyalty of French Army units stationed in Germany. Though de Gaulle survived the subsequent elections, he seemed increasingly weary and cognizant that perhaps his era had passed. Following the defeat of a minor referendum on local reforms in 1969, he resigned the presidency and returned to his home, where he died in late 1970.

De Gaulle's passage from the scene heralded an era of uncertainty presided over by leaders of considerably less charisma. His immediate successor, Georges Pompidou, abandoned the extreme nationalism of de Gaulle's foreign policy and acceded to Britain's admission to the European Community. Before his death in 1974, he emphasized prosperity and sought to resolve the grievances of trade unions and students, whose disaffection had fueled the uprising of 1968. Pompidou's successor was the moderate Valery d'Estaing, who had scant opportunity to apply his technocratic approach to economic modernization before the oil embargo and scandals undermined his presidency. A pragmatic Socialist, Francois Mitterand, assumed the presidency in 1981 and initiated a program of nationalization aimed at banks and large corporations, together with extensive social reforms. Mitterand's government never overcame the suspicions of the business community and the continuing transfer of assets abroad further weakened the franc. After only a year in office, Mitterand was compelled to devalue the franc and impose a freeze on prices and wages.

The Socialist failure to revive the economy worked to the advantage of the right, which succeeded in electing the Gaullist Jacques Chirac as mayor of Paris. Elections in 1986 strengthened the right in the National Assembly and forced Mitterand to accept Chirac as premier. This unusual era of "cohabitation" brought a partial reversal of Socialist policies, as the government sold off nationalized banks and businesses and ended wage and price controls. At the end of the 1980s, the French electorate appeared divided as to what direction to take, but the political uncertainty was no longer attended by the crisis atmosphere and disillusionment with government that were so common in prewar decades. Unlike its predecessors, the Fifth Republic enjoyed broad public confidence and the structural integrity requisite to stable government. As France faced the century's final decade, the apparent durability of the Fifth Republic stood as testimony to the accomplishments of the postwar era.

WEST GERMANY: THE TRIUMPH OF DEMOCRACY

In the immediate aftermath of the war, there was little to suggest that the Western zones of partitioned Germany would coalesce as a viable democracy within four years. The cataclysmic final months of the conflict left most Germans stunned and uncomprehending in the face of homelessness, starvation and the near total collapse of civil society. Of the forty-seven million Germans in the West, one in five was a refugee. The Allied High Commission, which oversaw the occupation, found the populace sullen and resentful; their ultimate rehabilitation seemed problematic. A 1945 U.S. government information film, "Your Job in Germany," informed American servicemen slated for occupation duty that Germany's national history was one of deceit and war and warned that the defeated Reich swarmed with ex-Nazis and fanatical Hitler Youth. GIs were cautioned to remain alert and aloof from the German population; "You are not their friend," the narrator warned. The suspicions of the early postwar period diminished gradually as Germans and occupiers alike focused on reconstruction. By summer 1947, Germany achieved a modicum of stabilty, as de-Nazification ended and the Supreme Economic Council provided the foundation for a central German government. The three Western Allied powers allowed the German political parties a growing role in administration, a development no doubt hastened by growing tensions with the USSR.

As Allied policymakers pondered the reconstitution of West Germany's government, their primary concern was to ensure that Germany's new political leaders possessed unimpeachable anti-Nazi credentials. Kurt Schumacher, leader of the Social Democratic party, spent almost the entire Nazi era imprisoned because of his opposition to Hitler. The SPD emerged as a major party in the postwar period, but leadership of the new German Federal Republic (GFR) established in 1949 fell to Konrad Adenauer, also an opponent of the Hitler regime who was jailed following the 1944 plot on Hitler's life. Now in his early seventies, Adenauer headed the Christian Democratic Union (CDU), a new party committed to democracy, social responsibility and free-market capitalism. In coming decades, the CDU was destined to become a mass party and the primary competition of the

SPD. In some ways a German version of de Gaulle, Adenauer had a semi-authoritarian style tempered by a paternalistic outlook. Shrewd, resolute and persistent, Adenauer feared that unfettered democracy would destabilize the GFR as it had the Weimar Republic. As the first Chancellor of West Germany, he believed that a firm guiding hand from the new capital at Bonn was requisite to the success of German democracy.

The West German constitution created a federal republic with a bicameral parliament and an executive branch consisting of a president and chancellor. The document was clearly drawn up with the inadequacies of the Weimar constitution in mind. Executive power was restricted, with the parliament electing the president, who held only nominal power, and appointing the chancellor. Small parties, which had contributed greatly to the parliamentary chaos of the late Weimar period, were kept out of parliament by a requirement that they receive a minimum of five percent of the vote in elections. Political stability, economic growth and support for U.S. Cold War policies characterized Adenauer's Germany, which was admitted to NATO in 1954. The following year, the dissolution of the Allied High Commission marked the end of the occupation of West Germany. When he retired in 1963, "Der Alte" (the Old Man), as Germans affectionately called him, could be justly proud of his role in establishing West Germany as a responsible, peaceful democratic nation.

The CDU retained its political predominance throughout the 1960s, a decade during which West Germany was often at the forefront of Cold War confrontations. The Berlin Crisis of 1961, which culminated with the construction of the Berlin Wall, seemed to signal the more or less permanent division of Germany and pushed the West German government closer to the United States. Though West Germany's economic expansion continued, the electorate was increasingly desirous of change and in 1969 Social Democrat Willy Brandt, former mayor of West Berlin, was named chancellor. His party had evolved considerably since the prewar period. In keeping with the ideological moderation of the postwar years, the SPD had repudiated the remaining vestiges of Marxist orthodoxy in 1959, renouncing the idea of class warfare and advocating only modest nationalization. The party had also dropped its opposition to remilitarization, thus generally increasing its appeal to middle-class Germans. As chancellor, Brandt was a proponent of expanding social welfare benefits and access to education, but his greater accomplishments came in the area of foreign policy. Brandt's primary concern was improving relations with the German Democratic Republic, or East Germany. Between 1970 and 1972, Brandt's *Ostpolitik* (Eastern Policy) produced treaties that eased tensions with the USSR, gained Soviet acceptance of the Allied presence in West Berlin and culminated with the two Germanies acknowledging each other's existence.

Though Brandt was hailed for establishing a framework for cooperation between the two nations, his inattention to domestic matters proved his undoing. Growing economic problems stemming from the 1973 oil crisis weakened his popularity and the revelation that one of his aides was an East German spy brought his resignation in 1974. His successor, Helmut Schmidt, grappled with rising unemployment and recession through the remainder of the decade. His request in 1979 that the United States deploy medium-range ballistic missiles in West Germany provoked outrage on the part of environmentalists and anti-nuclear groups, core constituents of the Green party formed that year.

In 1982, a conservative resurgence throughout much of Western Europe also swept the GFR and the Christian Democratic Union returned to power under the leadership of Helmut Kohl. Like his conservative counterparts elsewhere, Kohl addressed the economic situation by cutting taxes and reducing government spending, making cuts in social welfare programs and the defense budget. In the early 1980s, his government confronted growing demonstrations by anti-nuclear forces that feared a superpower confrontation would inevitably make Western Europe a nuclear battlefield. By the end of the decade, the Kohl government faced growing opposition from the left, which objected to the institution of cost-cutting social welfare reforms. Somewhat more ominously, a new challenge also arose on the extreme right as animosity against foreign "guest workers" and refugees from the East took political form. The Republican party, organized in 1983 by a former SS officer, was a register of economic resentments and extreme nationalist sentiment. Though small in numbers and electoral strength, the Republican party was seen by some as the political edge of a neo-Nazi revival. As of 1989, whatever mandate the CDU once had seemed to have diminished considerably and a general weariness with the Kohl government set in. That same year, however, the political situation was transformed by the previously inconceivable possibility of German reunification.

ITALY AND THE MINOR POWERS

Italy's political reconstruction began in the midst of the war, following Mussolini's ouster in 1943. When the subsequent Badoglio government sought an armistice with invading Allied forces, German troops occupied much of the northern portion of the country and bitter conventional and partisan warfare continued until the spring of 1945. By the end of the war, the great majority of Italians had repudiated Fascism, which they held responsible for their country's sufferings. The prominence of Communists and Socialists in the anti-Fascist resistance assured their influence in the postwar government, which underwent a major reconstruction in 1946. A popular referendum in June dissolved the Italian monarchy, which King Victor Emmanuel III's passive acceptance of the Fascist dictatorship had discredited. The existing constitution was nearly a century old and had been in suspension for twenty years, so Italian voters, now including women, elected representatives to a Constituent Assembly, charged with framing a new government. The constitution of the First Republic, ratified in 1948, established a bicameral parliamentary system, in which the two popularly elected chambers elected a nominal president. Effective political power, such as it was, rested with a premier.

As was the case in West Germany, a moderately conservative party dedicated to democracy quickly gained ascendancy. The Christian Democratic party, led by Alcide de Gasperi until 1953, dominated national politics as the strongest party, but never attained the electoral strength to govern on its own. Many of the fundamental political trends of the pre-Fascist era surfaced again during the First Republic, most notably those related to political fragmentation and a multiplicity of parties. This contributed to ministerial instability and frequent changes of government; in the first four decades of its existence, the Italian Republic went through over fifty ministries.

This apparently chronic political instability had fewer detrimental consequences than might be surmised. The predominance of the Christian Democrats through most of the postwar era guaranteed some basic continuity of policy, and the astounding expansion of Italy's economy beginning in the 1950s did much to counterbalance governmental transience. Christian Democratic governments were generally amenable to the establishment of modest social welfare programs, which further diminished popular disaffection. The Italian Communist party, though a significant minor party, remained outside the government. The need for economic reforms by the early 1960s produced governments in which Italian Socialists cooperated with the Christian Democrats, but the alliance unraveled by the end of the decade in the face of disagreements over policy and growing Communist electoral strength. A succession of undistinguished Christian Democrat premiers led the nation into the 1970s, by which time a growing number of Italians were voicing complaints about government ineptitude, immobility and corruption. A 1970 survey showed 72 percent of Italians either "highly" or "completely" dissatisfied with their government. As Italy struggled with the consequences of inflation, industrial downturn and the Arab oil embargo, never-ending financial scandals that further discredited politicians compounded the economic distress. Terrorism by extreme left factions such as the Red Brigade, whose members kidnapped and murdered the former premier Aldo Moro in 1978, further complicated Italian political life.

The 1980s, which brought dynamic if controversial conservative governments to power elsewhere in Europe, proved a period of drift for Italy. The Christian Democrats, who had done much to provide a stable political context for Italy's postwar economic recovery, seemed increasingly directionless and uninspiring. Bettino Craxi, premier between 1983 and 1986, was emblematic of Italy's political enervation, able to govern only with Socialist coalition partners and ultimately convicted of corruption himself. Italy's widespread political corruption, fed by the growing weakness of the Christian Democrats, left the populace deeply cynical about politics. Though few of the disaffected embraced radical solutions of either the left or right, public pressures for a major political housecleaning finally climaxed in 1992, when the era of the First Republic came to an end.

The Iberian nations had avoided the destructive consequences of the Second World War by remaining neutral. In a 1940 meeting at Hendaye, Spanish dictator Francisco Franco had so stubbornly resisted Hitler's entreaties to join the Axis that the Nazi leader later confided to Mussolini that rather than meet with Spain's *Caudillo* again, he would prefer to have two or three teeth extracted. Between 1939 and his death in 1975, Franco maintained an oppressive, authoritarian regime in which political parties and trade unions were banned. Deftly manipulating right-wing forces such as monarchists, the army, reactionary Catholics and the Falange, Spain's Fascist party, Franco molded a personal dictatorship that was avowedly anti-secular and anti-Communist. For the latter reason, the United States often courted Franco's Spain, which prevented the United Nations from imposing sanctions on the regime after the war. Presuming that the dictatorship would be continued after his death, Franco took steps to ensure that Juan Carlos, the heir to the deposed Bourbon monarchy, would be his successor.

Though Franco's police were fairly successful in suppressing the political left, separatist movements in Catalonia and the Basque country began to challenge the regime openly in the 1960s, most often through terrorist acts of sabotage and assassination aimed at government officials. The personal aspect of the dictatorship became evident upon Franco's death in 1975. Though Juan Carlos succeeded as king, he did not maintain the dictatorship, which was constructed largely around Franco's person. In a surprisingly short time, Spain became a constitutional monarchy, in which the new premier, former Falangist Adolfo Suarez, energetically undertook the democratization of Spanish political life. The Spanish economy expanded rapidly in the post-Franco period as Spaniards enjoyed new economic and cultural freedoms. An attempted military coup in 1981 tested the strength of the new democratic government, but the army plotters failed ingloriously. The extent of the public's repudiation of right-wing dictatorship became evident the following year when elections brought Spain's Socialist party to power, marking the advent of a lengthy period of social democratic government. Long isolated as an international pariah, Spain had fully rejoined the community of democratic states.

Portugal followed a somewhat similar course in the postwar years. Ruled by authoritarian dictator Antonio Salazar since the early 1930s, Portugal remained politically isolated after 1945, seeking to bolster its struggling economy by retaining its African colonies. Salazar's death in 1970 brought a period of uncertainty during which his successors dealt ineptly with the country's economic problems and continued a costly, unwinnable war against Angolan nationalists. The dictatorship was overthrown in a 1974 coup that liberal army officers organized, and in subsequent elections the Socialists came to power, overseeing a relatively tranquil transition to democracy.

In general, the postwar trend in the minor states of Western Europe favored democratic government. Austria, formerly incorporated in the German Reich, regained its independence in 1955 as a stable, non-aligned republic. Parliamentary government was quickly reestablished in the nations previously under Nazi occupation: Luxembourg, Belgium, the Netherlands, Denmark and Norway. Both Sweden and Switzerland, neutrals in wartime, entered the postwar era with little political dislocation. On the Mediterranean rim, Greece encountered far greater difficulties, enduring a three-year civil war beginning in 1946. The threat of Communist subversion, tensions with Turkey and disagreements over the role of the monarchy contributed to political instability until 1967, when a military coup overthrew the civilian government. Strongly anti-Communist, the military regime violently suppressed dissent in the years before its collapse in 1974. A popular referendum that year abolished the monarchy and an era of stable democratic government followed.

Turkey, a neutral until January 1945, when it joined the Allied camp, was a key component of NATO in the Cold War era and thus enjoyed considerable American support. Kemal Ataturk's successors governed along lines that he had established, often exercising near-authoritarian power when dealing with the Turkish parliament. The Turkish army remained an important element in national politics, intervening periodically to oust weak presidents or to assure public order. The major challenges in the postwar era included the ongoing dispute with Greece over Cyprus and the growth of radical ideologies, such as Marxism and Islamic fundamentalism. The latter in particular threatened the very nature of the secular state that Ataturk had designed. By the late 1980s,

after a period of martial law, a more open democratic political culture was restored.

The Soviet Union and the Eastern Bloc

The end of the Second World War left the Soviet Union in far different circumstances than it had faced in 1918. Though severely battered by the conflict, which cost millions of lives and left much of western Russia devastated, the Soviet Union commanded enormous military power and occupied territory that extended deep into central Europe. Soviet dictator Joseph Stalin, once a proponent of "socialism in one country," was quick to perceive the opportunities presented him in 1945. The Soviet Union was clearly in a position to influence, if not to dominate, almost all of Eastern Europe, and the foundations for a bloc of pro-Soviet Communist states were laid down quickly in the postwar period. For more than forty years, the Soviet Union was instrumental in setting the political, social and economic direction of the "Eastern Bloc" nations, which were subject to military intervention if they deviated from the approved course. Stalin was convinced that his unquestioned authority was crucial to the success of this endeavor and set about strengthening the grip of his already fearsome dictatorship. While his death in 1953 brought a moderate relaxation of police terror in the USSR, his successors were determined to prove the viability of the Soviet experiment and maintain Soviet dominance over Eastern Europe.

Though clearly a nuclear superpower by the 1950s, the Soviet Union, like its Eastern European satellites, never realized the economic advances that Soviet Communism promised. By the 1970s, a stagnating economy and uninspiring leadership by an ossified Communist party bureaucracy left the Soviet experiment stalled, the promise of Soviet greatness manifest only in a still-powerful military. The future of Eastern Europe, where communist governments still retained power by virtue of police oppression and the threat of Soviet intervention, hinged on the durability of Soviet Russia, which was increasingly in question by the 1980s.

THE USSR: FROM STALIN TO BREZHNEV

Having endured inconceivable hardships and having made unprecedented sacrifices in their struggle against national extinction, many Russians looked forward to a brighter future in the summer of 1945. With the Fascist threat destroyed, hopes for a relaxation of state political and economic controls blossomed. During the war, the Communist regime had moderated its ideological rigidity, stressing nationalism, ceasing its persecution of the Orthodox Church and limiting the authority of party commissars over the military. It soon became evident, however, that these wartime exigencies were to be discontinued. Stalin's personal authority had grown immensely in the war years and he was determined to preserve his dictatorship, encouraging the further development of the grotesque personality cult of the late 1930s and making loyalty to his person the primary criterion for advancement in the Communist party.

Fearful lest any vestige of Western "bourgeois" culture and thought contaminate the Soviet people, Stalin took steps to isolate any Soviet citizens who had been in contact with the West. He callously ordered that repatriated Soviet prisoners of war should be shipped to slave labor camps or executed, as they might have been tainted by their exposure to Western society. The regime made it clear to intellectuals that no dissidence would be tolerated and the NKVD, under the direction of the much-feared Lavrentia Beria, regained its previous prominence as arrests of alleged conspirators accelerated. The regime imposed new ideological rigidity on the nation, affecting virtually every field of endeavor from biology, where the dubious genetic theories of Trofim Lysenko were deemed incontrovertible, to the arts where "socialist realism" was enforced with new rigor. The return to Stalinist political orthodoxy continued state control of the economy through five-year plans and brought government decrees that Soviet citizens, most of whom lived in circumstances far worse than in the prewar years, would now have to work even harder and longer to bring about recovery. Stalin's periodic declarations that war between capitalism and socialism was inevitable crushed any hopes for a future unblemished by the threat of war.

By 1953, a new wave of purges was in the offing as a consequence of the alleged "Doctors' Plot." A concatenation of Stalin's increasing paranoia and cynical anti-Semitism, the conspiracy ostensibly involved schemes by Kremlin physicians, many of whom were Jewish, to murder top Communist leaders. Fortunately, Stalin died before the contrived "plot" could be used to justify a renewed police terror. The dictator's death in March 1953 provoked a public response in the USSR that baffled much of the rest of the world. A massive, emotional outpouring of grief swept the huge country, the hysteria climaxing with the death of hundreds of mourners who were crushed in the mob waiting in Red Square to view Stalin's body. His corpse was embalmed and placed beside Lenin's in the great mausoleum in Red Square.

Stalin's death brought a period of uncertainty in which an informal group of five

Communist party leaders ruled the USSR. The group was gradually reduced in size by political intrigue and most notably by the arrest of Beria only months after Stalin's funeral. The brutal NKVD chief, who was responsible for the murder of millions who had been deemed traitors, was himself denounced as a capitalist agent and executed along with six subordinates. During the next three years, Nikita Khrushchev emerged as Stalin's successor as general secretary of the party and later premier. A longtime Communist of peasant origin, Khrushchev was a proponent of agricultural reforms and supported a new international policy of "peaceful coexistence" with the capitalist West, which he hoped would bring reductions in the military budget, the savings turned to improving the lagging standard of living. Khrushchev positioned himself as the defender of Leninist purity and in 1956 delivered a speech at the Twentieth Party Congress in which he denounced Stalin's purges and the cult of personality. The subsequent process of "de-Stalinization" meant a turn away from the most egregious excesses of the police state and a moderate relaxation of censorship and of curbs on intellectual and artistic expression. Khrushchev intervened personally to ensure the publication of Alexander Solzhenitsyn's *A Day in the Life of Ivan Denisovich* (1962), a fictional account of the horrors of the slave labor camps. On the other hand, the regime banned Boris Pasternak's *Dr. Zhivago* (1958), a novel that depicted the disruptive impact of the Bolshevik Revolution on individuals and families. Among the political consequences of de-Stalinization, Khrushchev's assertion that there were different paths to socialism seemed to signal somewhat greater autonomy within the Soviet republics and for the Eastern European satellite states. That there were limits to the latter became evident when So-

viet forces intervened in Hungary and threatened Poland in 1956.

The new direction in the Soviet Union also provoked a growing rift with Maoist China, where the Soviets were denounced as "revisionists" for abandoning Stalinist precepts. Despite de-Stalinzation and a modest "thaw" in the Cold War in the early 1950s, Khrushchev's tenure also coincided with a reintensification of the confrontation between the USSR and United States. Khrushchev was committed to demonstrating socialism's superiority to capitalism in all areas of endeavor and in the growing "space race," the USSR took a quantum leap forward in 1957. That year, Soviet scientists successfully launched *Sputnik*, the first satellite to orbit the earth. This event and rapid advances in the Soviet thermonuclear weapons program provoked considerable alarm in the United States. Crises over the Suez Canal, American reconnaissance flights over the USSR and the status of West Berlin all heightened tensions between the two superpowers.

Nonetheless, Khrushchev continued to press his program for internal reforms. Though Soviet industry was still incapable of producing the consumer goods so long promised, it had otherwise recovered rapidly after 1945. Collectivized agriculture, however, had consistently failed to meet either quotas or basic food needs, and Khrushchev was an ardent advocate of designs to increase the amount of land under cultivation and remove the bureaucratic obstacles to increased agricultural production. Whatever the merit of his schemes, the proposed changes alarmed bureaucrats and party functionaries, while party leaders resented his constant tinkering with the economy. Khrushchev also alienated many in the military, which saw his foreign policy as unnecessarily risky and misguided.

Ultimately, in the aftermath of the Cuban Missile Crisis (1962), in which the USSR agreed to remove ballistic missiles from Communist Cuba, the opposition to Khrushchev's leadership congealed. Although Khrushchev was ousted in 1964, it was perhaps indicative of the change wrought by de-Stalinization that, rather than being liquidated, the ex-premier was merely deemed a "non-person" and permitted to return quietly to private life.

Khrushchev's fall brought Leonid Brezhnev to power. Colorless in comparison with the sometimes-bumptious Khrushchev, Brezhnev was uninspiring and vain; among the many state honors he arranged for himself was the Lenin Prize for Literature, which he received for his autobiography, aptly described by one historian as "a work of monumental insignificance." Brezhnev was the archetypal *apparatchik* who never challenged the party line and sought preeminently to preserve the status quo. Under his leadership, the power of the secret police, now the KGB, was reaffirmed, party bureaucrats were assured of their authority and massive spending on armaments pacified the military. Previously tolerated dissident intellectuals such as Solzhenitsyn, who asserted in *The Gulag Archipeligo* (1973) that Communist crimes originated with Lenin, were now silenced. Brezhnev sought to meet the long-delayed demand for consumer goods and televisions, refrigerators and other greatly desired appliances began to appear more commonly in Soviet households. However, his commitment to the continuation of centralized economic planning and agricultural collectivization ensured that the USSR would remain economically stagnant and technologically backward. Likewise committed to maintaining Soviet dominance in Eastern Europe, he gave his name to the 1968 doctrine that justified Soviet military intervention to preserve political orthodoxy in the satellite states. He nonetheless accepted the need to pursue a policy of détente with the United States and gave his support to the Non-Nuclear Proliferation Treaty (1968) and the Strategic Arms Limitation agreement of 1972. "SALT" froze the number of intercontinental ballistic missiles (ICBMs) and limited anti-ballistic missile deployments by the two superpowers.

Brezhnev was far less successful in domestic affairs. By the late 1970s, most Soviet citizens could no longer accept the official fiction regarding the success and future of the Communist experiment. A growing pessimism pervaded the nation, fueling a general popular numbness in the face of the grim and apparently endless deprivations of daily life in a failed system. The eventual collapse of détente with the United States and the 1979 Soviet invasion of Afghanistan in support of a Marxist regime pointed to an indefinite continuation of the Cold War, which meant that public needs would remain subordinate to growing military expenditures. The geriatric state of the Soviet system was confirmed in the aftermath of Brezhnev's death in 1982, when he was succeeded briefly by the infirm Yuri Andropov, who died only months later. The aging Konstantin Chernyenko, who became general secretary and president in February 1984 at 73, seemed the personification of Soviet debility. Absolutely bereft of charisma, energy and ideas, Chernyenko barely clung to life. Even before his death in March 1985, Chernyenko was increasingly overshadowed by a younger member of the Politburo, who was positioning himself for the succession. It fell to Mikhail Gorbachev to attempt to remedy the vast inadequacies of the Soviet system and salvage the legacy of 1917. For the next half-dozen years, Gorbachev confronted the daunting task of saving the Soviet system by reforming it.

EASTERN EUROPE— VARIATIONS ON A THEME

The military course of the Second World War largely determined Eastern Europe's postwar destiny. The resurgent Red Army, which after 1943 drove Nazi armies out of western Russia and eastern Europe, overran almost all of the nations either allied to or occupied by German forces. Having "liberated" Eastern Europe, Soviet forces were well positioned to assist in implementing the gradually evolving political goals of Stalin's regime, which most immediately involved establishing provisional governments in which native Communists were heavily represented. Though European Communists did in fact enjoy some popularity because of their wartime record of resisting the Nazis, their political strength in many cases rested on Soviet support and the presence of the Red Army. Throughout most of Eastern Europe, these postwar coalition governments were gradually taken over by Communists committed to the creation of "People's Democracies," transitional regimes that would pave the way for true communism by effecting radical social and economic changes. Inevitably, one of the most immediate changes was the creation of one-party states in which competing political parties were prohibited, giving the Communists an assured monopoly on power.

The most dramatic enactment of this process occurred in Poland, where a Communist government established by the Soviets at Lublin contended with the Polish government-in-exile in London over the direction of postwar Poland. The transparent Soviet effort to install a communist regime was a major point of contention at the Yalta Conference, where Stalin had agreed to permit free elections and grant the non-communist London Poles a role in a coalition government. While elections were held, they were far from free and in a short span of time the Polish Communists ousted their coalition "partners."

An even more blatant Communist coup took place in Czechoslovakia, only recently liberated from Nazi rule. A coalition government including Communists was formed following elections in 1946, with two famous Czech leaders, Eduard Benes and Jan Masaryk (son of the Czech founder Thomas Masaryk) taking office as president and foreign minister respectively. When the Czech government moved to seek U.S. economic aid in 1948, the Communists overthrew the coalition government and banned other political parties. During the coup, Masaryk was either pushed or jumped to his death from a high window in a government building.

In East Germany, the installation of a Communist government took a similar course, as German Communists who had fled into exile in the USSR during the war created the Soviet-backed Socialist Unity Party (SED). In 1947, the Communist Information Bureau (Cominform) succeeded the disbanded International as an instrument for asserting Soviet control over the Communist parties of Eastern Europe. The creation of COMECON two years later provided the framework for joint economic development of the region, again under the auspices of the Soviet Union.

During these same years, Soviet-inspired purges swept across the Eastern Bloc nations, utilizing Stalinist methods intended to crush any incipient political opposition. Show trials reminiscent of the 1930s were held throughout the region in a search for "bourgeois-nationalist traitors" who in all likelihood did not exist. In heavily Catholic nations such as Hungary, clerics who were openly hostile to communism ran the risk of arrest and imprisonment. The construction of a vast system of political prison camps, some seventy in Bulgaria alone, completed the recapitulation of the Stalinist Terror in Eastern Europe. Vague estimates suggest that the victims of the purges may have numbered in the hundreds of thousands.

Clearly, Stalin's design was that the new Eastern Europe should emulate the Soviet Union in every respect. To that end, the Soviet economic model was also applied in the Eastern bloc nations. Five-year plans for rapid industrialization and agricultural collectivization were to be implemented, with the objective of transforming Eastern European society. Consequently, the region's economy eventually reflected the defects of the Soviet model. Industry generally recovered and grew, but remained technologically backward and inefficient; the agricultural sector was almost retrograde in some aspects, barely attaining prewar production levels and never capable of meeting the demand for foodstuffs. Stalin's death, the advent of Khrushchev and de-Stalinization portended a somewhat better era, with greater latitude for national economic policies, but Eastern bloc economies, always subject to the dictates of centralized planning, lagged behind Western economies into the latter decades of the century.

Despite the ideological uniformity of Eastern Europe, some variations in national direction and government became evident, perhaps most immediately in Yugoslavia. There postwar leadership fell to Josip Broz Tito, a longtime Communist who had forged a wartime anti-Nazi military force that incorporated most of the nation's often contentious ethnic groups. Stressing national unity on the basis of ethnic equality, Tito led his partisans in a determined struggle against the German occupation army, driving it from the country before the arrival of the Red Army. He emerged as head of a Communist government in November 1945, but in subsequent years proved unwilling to accept the policy dictates of the Soviet Union. The Cominform ejected Yugoslavia in 1948, when Tito refused to grant the USSR control over the Yugoslav army and political police. Tito pursued a nationalistic variation of communism that differed from Soviet orthodoxy. He rejected total central planning and experimented with a mixed economy; he was especially committed to the concept of workers exercising control in their own factories. Yugoslavia rejected membership in the Warsaw Pact and remained an anomaly among the European communist states. Though he headed an authoritarian regime, Tito effectively managed the conflicting ethnic interests that had proven so disruptive in the past. Following his death in 1980, the country began a long and agonizing slide into fragmentation and civil war.

Other national variations within the Eastern Bloc became evident by the mid-1950s in response to Khrushchev's recognition of "several paths to socialism." In the German Democratic Republic, Communist party boss Walter Ulbricht headed a Stalinist regime that requested Soviet support in suppressing a workers' revolt in 1953, but he gradually recognized that the regime would have to meet the material needs of East Germans as a first step toward gaining their political allegiance. State planners gave relative priority to the production of consumer goods and ultimately East Germans enjoyed a better standard of living than most of the Eastern Bloc. Material shortages and political oppression nonetheless fueled an ongoing exodus from the country, especially through West Berlin, where the contrast between the affluent West and the struggling East was most apparent. Ulbricht eventually antagonized Soviet leader Brezhnev in 1970 with his assertion that "we are not a Soviet Republic" and was ousted in a coup the next year. His successor, Erick Honecker, struggled to strengthen the GDR through modest reforms, but ultimately opposed Mikahil Gorbachev's proposed reforms in the mid-1980s and came to rely heavily on the army and the hated *Stasi*, the state security police. Subsequently, popular pressure for change in East Germany continued to build until 1989, by which point it was irresistible.

In Poland, Khrushchev's "New Course" sparked demands for reform that quickly transgressed the limits of Soviet tolerance. Wladyslaw Gomulka, forced from Communist party leadership in 1951, returned to power in 1956, tasked with quelling growing industrial and political unrest and preventing a Soviet military intervention. Though the Soviets distrusted Gomulka, he assured them of Poland's loyalty to the Warsaw Pact. Over the next several years, he introduced a number of reforms, reducing the power of the secret police, limiting the repression of the Catholic Church and reversing the collectivization of agriculture. His failure to improve living standards led to growing popular disillusionment by the late 1960s, and succeeding governments faced rising discontent into the 1980s, which threatened to provoke Soviet military intervention on several different occasions.

Events in Hungary, where the reforming prime minister Imre Nagy had been ousted because of his rejection of the Soviet model for heavy industry and collectivization, partly determined the Soviet decision not to invade Poland in 1956. Nagy's removal provoked massive demonstrations and demands for the liberalization of the Communist regime. When riots broke out in Budapest in October, Hungary's Communist party leaders requested Soviet military support, but also reappointed Nagy, hoping for a restoration of order. Nagy, however, announced that he intended to end the Communist monopoly on political power and called for Hungary's withdrawal from the Warsaw Pact. These declarations, which threatened the basis of the USSR's control of the Eastern Bloc, brought a swift response. In early November, over 150,000 Warsaw Pact troops invaded Hungary supported by 2,000 tanks. The "Hungarian Revolt" died in the streets of Budapest as Nagy was arrested and later executed. His successor, Janos Kadar, led an initially repressive regime, but in later years began a process of moderate liberalization aimed primarily at improving the economy. Kadar's "Goulash Communism" introduced market-oriented reforms and conceded to a modest degree of free enterprise, changes that eventually gave Hungarians the highest standard of living in the Eastern Bloc.

In Czechoslovakia, Stalinism long outlived its namesake, and political oppression and disastrous economic mismanagement persisted into the late 1960s, when growing popular pressure for change brought Alexander Dubcek to power. Dubcek hoped to reinvigorate Communism by reforming it and supported open discussions as to how "socialism with a human face" might be created. The unprecedented free exchange of ideas blossomed into the "Prague Spring" of 1968, as hopes for change rose dramatically, especially among students and intellectuals. In April the Czech Communist party introduced its "Action Programme," which included basic civil rights and economic decentralization. Though Dubcek met with Soviet leaders in late July to reassure them of his nation's fidelity to Communist rule and the Warsaw Pact, they remained unconvinced. On August 20, Warsaw Pact forces invaded Czechoslovakia and occupied Prague. Dubcek and his close associates were arrested as Soviet tanks dispersed furious but impotent protestors in the capital. Communist orthodoxy was restored, though dissident groups such as Charter '77 kept alive the flame of opposition during the two decades prior to the end of Communist rule in 1989.

In other parts of the Eastern bloc, hard-line Stalinist regimes ruled virtually unchallenged for decades. In Bulgaria, Todor Zhivkov held power as Secretary-General for thirty-five years, ensuring that his isolated and economically backward nation was among the most loyal of the Soviet satellites. In tiny, mountainous Albania, previously an Italian protectorate, Enver Hoxha headed a fiercely Stalinist regime from 1946 until his death in 1985. Albania broke with the USSR following Khrushchev's denunciation of Stalin and moved into the orbit of Communist China, remaining strictly isolated and impoverished until late in the century. In Romania, Communists forced the abdication of King Michael in 1947 and established a rigid Stalinist regime that eagerly supported the suppression of the Hungarian rebels in 1956. In 1965, Nicolae Ceausescu began twenty-three years of oppressive rule during which the Romanian economy was badly hobbled by his inept and capricious policies. A vicious megalomaniac who encouraged a grotesque personality cult, Ceausescu styled himself "the Genius of the Carpathians" and ensured his authority by establishing a massive secret police apparatus. Though popular discontent grew through the 1980s, Ceausescu successfully retained his iron grip until 1989.

Communist rule in Romania, as in the rest of Eastern Europe, relied on the exclusive authority of national Communist parties, none of which could retain power in the event of free elections. The Communist monopoly of power was maintained by oppression on the part of secret police agencies and the threat of armed military force. As had been made clear in Hungary in 1956 and Czechoslovakia in 1968, Eastern European Communists were ultimately dependent on the ability and willingness of the Soviet Union to intervene on their part. The Soviet Union remained the linchpin of the Eastern Bloc; a radical change of leadership or direction there would destabilize Communist Europe. It was a reality that was acknowledged long before it happened. In the aftermath of the Prague Spring in 1969, the historian Francois Fetjo had written, "One may hope that the next Dubcek will appear in the nerve center of the system: Moscow."

◆ —— ◆ —— ◆ —— ◆ —— ◆ —— ◆ —— ◆ —— ◆ —— ◆

Her admirers referred to her as the "Iron Lady." With equal fervor, her detractors denounced her as the "Iron Bitch." Clearly, Margaret Thatcher, the first woman to hold the post of Prime Minister of Great Britain, was a leader who engendered and thrived on controversy. Thatcher and the Conservatives came to power in 1979 as a result of public concern over economic issues and disaffection with the apparent ineffectualness of the Labour party. "Unless we change our ways and our direction," she warned during the campaign, "our greatness as a nation will soon be a footnote in the history books."

As prime minister, Thatcher introduced a broad program of austerity measures aimed at curbing government spending. Though her supporters argued that harsh medicine was necessary to cure Britain's economic ills, it appeared to many that the cure was worse than the disease. Unemployment rose to 11 percent, while industrial production fell 18 percent. The inflation rate soared to 20 percent. By early 1982, with Britain suffering through the worst recession in 40 years, the "Thatcherite Revolution" appeared doomed. The dismal scenario was transformed, however, by events in early April. On Friday, April 2, Argentinean troops, acting on orders from the military *junta* that ruled in Buenos Aires, landed in the Falkland Islands and occupied the capital at Port Stanley. A desolate island group some 400 miles off the Argentine coast, the Falklands were among a number of obscure South Atlantic Islands that Britain had claimed as early as the seventeenth century and had occupied in 1833. As of 1982, the Falklands, populated by 1,800 inhabitants and 400,000 sheep, were one of the few remaining vestiges of the once-extensive British Empire. The Argentinean invasion, a blatant act of aggression against British territory and citizens, presented Prime Minister Thatcher with an unexpected challenge, but also an opportunity to reassert Britain's traditional ideals and role in the world. "Since the Suez fiasco in 1956," she wrote in her memoirs, "British foreign policy had been one long retreat. The tacit assumption made by British and foreign governments alike was that our world role was doomed steadily to diminish."

Thatcher had no doubts as to what Britain's response to the Argentine invasion should be. The question, as she phrased it in postwar memoirs, was whether it was acceptable "that a common or garden variety dictator should rule over the Queen's subjects and prevail by fraud and violence." Her terse response reflected the "iron will" that won her so many admirers: "Not while I was Prime Minister." On April 5, only four days after the Argentine invasion, a British naval task force steamed out of Portsmouth and toward the Falklands, some 8,250 miles away in the South Atlantic. Great Britain, the Prime Minister had determined, would defend her own.

The Falklands War, though a short conflict lasting only from April through June 1982, provided Margaret Thatcher's government with an opportunity to remind the British people who they were and what they stood for. The diminution of Britain's international power and economic strength since 1945 had been attended by an erosion of national confidence, which was at least partially restored by the war to liberate the Falklands. Unlike many late twentieth century conflicts, the war seemed, at least to the British, morally unambiguous. Most agreed with Thatcher's depiction of the conflict as a just struggle to repel a foreign aggressor from British soil, and displays of newfound patriotism were common. Large crowds assembled at Portsmouth to cheer the troops as they boarded the transports, serenaded in one instance by a military band that played the popular Broadway tune "Don't Cry for Me, Argentina." The Royal Navy, though much reduced in strength and circumstances, performed admirably, pulling together an improvised fleet that still boasted names redolent of history and fame; the warship names *Invincible, Fearless, Ardent* and *Resolute* all evoked the unrivaled glory of eras past. It fell to a British submarine, HMS *Conqueror,* to achieve the war's most notable naval victory by sinking the Argentine cruiser *General Belgrano,* thus depriving the Argentines of one of their most powerful vessels. But if the war promised glory, it also required sacrifice. The task force of more than 20 warships carrying some 6,000 troops struggled through heavy seas for three weeks before arriving at their destination. Though British troops easily routed Argentine soldiers at Stanley and elsewhere and the Argentine Navy offered little challenge, the Argentine Air Force proved a determined and deadly foe. In a conflict that offered a unique opportunity to combat-test new and generally untried weapons systems, Argentine aircraft demonstrated the fatal accuracy of French-built "Exocet" anti-ship missiles. HMS *Ardent* was among the ships that fell victim to the technologically sophisticated weaponry of the late twentieth century, reduced to a smoking hulk following a single missile strike that ignited uncontrollable fires that swept the length of the ship. Britain's ultimate victory in June came at the cost of six warships sunk and 250 lives lost. The Falklands War did not resolve Britain's myriad problems, but it did remind the nation of the principles for which it had traditionally stood and infused many with a new pride. Speaking at Cheltenham in July, Thatcher offered her perspective on the meaning of the war. "We have ceased to be a nation in retreat," she declared. "We have instead a newfound confidence. . . . Britain found herself again in the South Atlantic and will not look back from the victory she has won."

The feisty and resolute Margaret Roberts Thatcher was born into relative affluence in 1925, daughter of a Midlands grocer who also served as mayor of Grantham. She studied chemistry at Oxford, where she became president of the university's Conservative Association. Hoping to pursue a political career, she shifted her studies to the law and married the influential Denis Thatcher. She won her first seat in the House of Commons in 1959 and gradually worked her way up in the Conservative party, gaining appointment as Minister of Education in Edward Heath's government in 1970. Heath's irresolution brought down the Conservatives in 1974 and in the subsequent party reorganization, Thatcher became Conservative leader in 1975. It was at this juncture that she began to develop a much more strongly conservative perspective, disdaining governmental solutions to social and economic problems, promoting the utility of free-market capitalism and taking a strong anti-Communist stance. Her outlook placed her on the right margin of her party, but she carried the Conservatives to victory in 1979 with her indictment of Labour as the party of big government and a hostage to the trade unions.

Determined to reduce the role of government and cut expenses, Prime Minister Thatcher relaxed government regulations, privatized nationalized industries, increased sales taxes while decreasing capital gains and inheritance taxes, eliminated some health and education programs and steadfastly resisted trade-union demands for higher wages. She was also an advocate and practitioner of monetarism, a theory that holds that an economy can be managed by controlling the money supply. Though praised by supporters for her innovative and determined approach to reform, her numerous detractors inevitably pointed to the distress her policies were causing; by the early 1980s, millions were unemployed and dependent on reduced government compensation. Critics denounced Thatcher's remedies as ill conceived and callous. Her close association with and support of U.S. President Ronald Reagan was an additional cause for criticism from those who disapproved of Reagan's belligerently anti-Communist policies and escalation of the Cold War. Echoing the sentiments of many who felt that Thatcher was tying Britain too closely to American policies, one opposition MP derided her before the House of Commons as "Ronald Reagan's poodle." Such barbs stung Thatcher, but she refused to back away from either her policies or her commitments. However, the level of economic distress rose to such heights by 1982 that her party's prospects in future elections seemed questionable. The decision of Argentina's military government to divert popular discontent by seizing the Malvinas Islands, as the Argentines called the Falklands, gave Thatcher's government a new lease on life.

As events proved, the worst of Britain's economic woes receded after 1982. The wave of oil price increases that disrupted the economy in the early Thatcher years were soon weathered and afterward, Thatcher's policies produced a gradual but discernible recovery. Her refusal to give in to a year-long coal miner's strike in 1983 amplified her public standing, as many now conceded that trade-union power had become excessive. Continuing weak leadership and disarray in the Labour Party contributed to Thatcher's reelection in a Conservative landslide the same year. By the mid-1980s, interest and mortgage rates were declining along with inflation, while Britain's now-reduced industrial sector was increasingly internationally competitive. Thatcher continued to reduce government expenditures by cutting social services as unemployment began to decline. Increased revenue from taxes and North Sea oil production helped to strengthen the economy. By 1989, however, when Thatcher celebrated her tenth year in power, there were growing indications that Conservative policies were not infallible. Inflation began to rise once more, carrying interest rates with it as economic growth slowed. Thatcher was increasingly under fire for the excesses of her privatization policy, most notably for water and electricity, while revisions in health care policy provoked further grumbling. A major public relations disaster resulted from her proposal to implement a poll tax; deep public indignation over the measure found expression in violent riots. There was also a palpable sentiment that her time was past; her ideas had served their purpose for a given period, but it was now time to move on. Elections in June confirmed that Conservative strength was giving way in the face of Labour's revival. Challenged for leadership of the party in 1990, Thatcher resigned. Her successor was John Major, who fended off Labour's challenges until 1997.

Thatcher was part of a general conservative wave that swept a number of Western nations in the 1980s and like her counterparts in the United States and Germany, she left a mixed record. Though her principled leadership during the Falklands War undoubtedly restored a degree of national pride among Britons, Thatcher's economic policies have provoked disagreements among those who have assessed her years as prime minister. Some argue the worth of her perspective of reduced government and her policies favoring private initiative. Others counter that her dogmatic commitment to monetarism was short-sighted, that her austerity programs were callously implemented with little concern for those adversely affected and that such economic recovery as did occur was the consequence of more general world developments. Today a Baroness and still committed to the cause of conservative ideology, Thatcher remains a controversial figure in Britain, where the debate over her legacy continues.

◆ —— ◆ —— ◆ —— ◆ —— ◆ —— ◆ —— ◆ —— ◆ —— ◆ —— ◆

Suggested Readings

ASH, TIMOTHY GARTEN. *In Europe's Name: Germany and the Divided Continent.* (1993).

BARNETT, CORELLI. *The Pride and the Fall: The Dream and Illusion of Britain as a Great Nation.* (1987).

CHAMBERLAIN, MURIEL E. *Decolonization: The Fall of the European Empires.* (1985).

CRAIG, GORDON A. *The Germans.* (1991).

DEPORTE, A. W. *Europe between the Superpowers.* (1979).

FETJO, FRANCOIS. *A History of the People's Democracies.* (1974).

GINSBORG, PAUL. *A History of Contemporary Italy: Society and Politics, 1943–1988.* (1990).

LACOUTURE, JEAN. *De Gaulle: The Rebel 1890–1944.* (1990).

———. *De Gaulle: The Ruler, 1945–1970.* (1991).

LAQUER, WALTER. *Europe in Our Time, 1945–1992.* (1992).

———. *Stalin.* (1990).

MAZOWER, MARK. *Dark Continent: Europe's Twentieth Century.* (1999).

MCCAULEY, MARTIN. *The Khrushchev Era, 1953–1964.* (1995).

MILWARD, ALAN S. *The Reconstruction of Western Europe, 1945–1951.* (1984).

PATERSON, THOMAS G. *On Every Front: The Making and Unmaking of the Cold War.* (1992).

PELLS, RICHARD. *Not Like Us: How Europeans Have Loved, Hated and Transformed American Culture since World War II.* (1997).

POSTAN, M. *An Economic History of Western Europe, 1945–1964.* (1967).

PRESTON, PAUL. *Franco: A Biography.* (1993).

RIDDELL, PAUL. *The Thatcher Era and Its Legacy.* (1991).

ROTHSCHILD, JOSEPH. *Return to Diversity: A Political History of East Central Europe since World War II.* (1993).

SMITH, BRADLEY F. *Reaching Judgement at Nuremburg.* (1979).

TURNER, HENRY A., JR. *Germany from Partition to Reunification.* (1992).

THATCHER, MARGARET. *The Downing Street Years.* (1993).

ZUBOK, VLADISLAV and CONSTANTINE PLESHAKOV. *Inside the Kremlin's Cold War: From Stalin to Khrushchev.* (1996).

CHAPTER 8

Asia Reordered: India, Japan, and China, 1945–1989

On April 13, 1919, a group of 10,000 Sikhs, Hindus and Moslems gathered in the Jallianwalla Bagh, a public gathering place, to condemn the repression then unfolding in the Punjab. Indians, who had provided loyal troops and economic support in backing the British war effort against the Central Powers, hardly anticipated such treatment. Expecting self-government, India had only been promised "a gradual development of self-governing institutions." As violence broke out at the close of the war, the British issued the Rowlatt Act, which established martial law across India and restricted personal liberties. Mohandas Karamchand Gandhi, an increasingly important figure in the nationalist movement, urged that a *hartal* take place, which would result in a cessation of activities throughout the country. Gandhi was disappointed when violence occurred, with a handful of Englishmen killed and a missionary woman brutalized in Amritsar. He attempted to travel to Amritsar to urge that the bloodletting cease, but he was arrested.

In Amritsar, as William L. Shirer later reported, Brigadier General Reginald E. Dyer determined to deliver a message to the local populace. Without warning, some fifty soldiers, firing machine guns, rained death on the gathered throng. Dyer also presented his "Crawling Order," which compelled Indians passing through the area where the missionary woman resided to crawl on the street. Gandhi wrote that "before this outrage, the Jalianwala (sic) Bagh tragedy paled into insignificance in my eyes." Nevertheless, the slaughter proved to be a turning point for Gandhi. "I had faith in them—until 1919," he later declared, referring to British officials. "But the Amritsar Massacre and the other atrocities in the Punjab changed my heart. And nothing has happened since to make me regain my faith."

Through repeated prayers, fasts and meditation, Gandhi—attired in a loincloth and shawl—personally exemplified the spiritual and ascetic quest for an independent India. Equally important, he helped to reshape modern political discourse and tactics through the successful application of nonviolent civil disobedience. The Mahatma or "great soul," as Gandhi came to be known, provided a model for future social activists, including America's Martin Luther King Jr., Poland's Lech Walesa, and Burma's Aung Sun Suu Kyi. They in turn helped to challenge racial barriers, communist tyranny and repression meted out by a right-wing military regime, respectively. Their legacy was large, although both Gandhi and King, the victims of assassination, paid with their lives for their ideals.

Born in Porbandar on October 2, 1869, Gandhi received legal training at University College in London. In 1891, the young attorney returned to India to set up a law practice in Bombay. Within two years, Gandhi was hired to represent a company that did business in British-controlled South Africa. For over two full decades, he resided in that racially segregated land where, to his dismay, Indian immigrants were treated as inferiors. Influenced by Jesus Christ, the great Russian author Leo Tolstoy and the American transcendentalist Henry David Thoreau, Gandhi urged nonviolent resistance to South African policies. Gandhi called for reliance on Satyagraha—truth and firmness—as exemplified by civil disobedience campaigns and a strike by Indian miners. Although beatings and numerous arrests came his way, Gandhi maintained his belief in the good intentions of Great Britain and headed a Red Cross unit during both the Boer War (1899–1902) and the Zulu Rebellion (1906). At the close of the conflict, he again agitated for Indian rights and established a cooperative colony, Tolstoy Farm, outside Johannesburg, for his native Indians. In 1914, the Union of South Africa, in recognizing Indian marriages and abolishing the poll tax as it applied to Indians, finally acceded to many of Gandhi's demands.

The following year, Gandhi returned to India, where he soon headed the nationalist movement. When the British government in 1919 attempted to make it illegal to organize opposition to the imperial regime in India, Gandhi resorted to Satyagraha once more, triggering massive resistance. Gandhi halted the campaign when riots unfolded, hoping to underscore the importance of adhering to nonviolence. The Amritsar Massacre belied Gandhi's belief in the basic beneficence of British policy, but he became only more determined to employ Satyagraha in government halls, courtrooms, schoolhouses and city streets to support the cause of Indian independence. In championing homespun garb through village industries and a corresponding economic boycott, Gandhi sought to promote Indian autonomy, the dignity of labor and self-government.

In the early 1920s, Gandhi led the pro-independence Indian National Congress, but again halted a nationalist campaign following an outbreak of riots. Imprisoned by British authorities in 1922, he was released two years later. In 1930, after a period of seeming calm, Gandhi and several thousand followers undertook a 200-mile walk to the sea to demonstrate displeasure with the Salt Acts that criminalized the

Fig. 8-1   Indian pacifist Mahatma Gandhi and Mrs. Sarojini Naidu, in
the midst of a 200 mile march to the sea to condemn the Salt Acts,
promulgated by the British imperial government, 1930.
(Corbis/Bettmann)

purchase of salt from any entity other than the imperial government. In 1931, Gandhi
was arrested once again but was released after the granting of concessions by British
officials. The next year witnessed additional civil disobedience drives, arrests of Gandhi
and ensuing fasts. One such fast involved the Mahatma's challenge to the treatment of
Hindu Untouchables. Relinquishing control of the Congress Party to Jawaharlal Nehru in

1934, Gandhi sought to terminate the Hindu caste system that discriminated against different social classes.

During World War II, Great Britain refused to grant Indian independence, and Gandhi maintained his nonviolent civil disobedience crusade. Arrested in 1942, he remained in jail for two years—his time in prison now added up to seven years—until his faltering health compelled British officials to release him. With the Muslim League and the Congress Party vying for supremacy, Britain agreed to liberate India in 1947, provided that a partition would follow. Gandhi had long opposed partition but eventually agreed to it in a fruitless effort to avert sectarian conflict. The deeply saddened Mahatma witnessed the separation of Pakistan from India and the resulting violence pitting Hindus against Muslims. On January 13, 1948, Gandhi undertook yet another fast to protest the bloodletting. Within five days, an agreement to halt the fighting was announced and Gandhi's last fast ended. Still troubled by indications of corruption involving some of his supporters, Gandhi asked, "How can we look the world in the face if this goes on? The honor of the whole nation hinges on those who have participated in the freedom struggle. If they too abuse their power, we are sure to lose our footing." While heading for a prayer gathering, Gandhi was shot three times on January 30 by a Hindu fanatic distressed about the Mahatma's insistence on religious tolerance.

Mourning unfolded worldwide regarding the assassination of Mahatma Gandhi. Albert Einstein referred to him in the following manner: "Generations to come will scarcely believe that such a one as this walked the earth in flesh and blood." Less than a decade following Gandhi's death, the American Martin Luther King Jr. preached the gospel of nonviolent civil disobedience in an effort to challenge racial segregation on the other side of the globe. Tragically, like his mentor Gandhi, King too gave his life in service to the ideals of pacifism, along with the quest for social, racial and economic justice.

◆ —— ◆ —— ◆ —— ◆ —— ◆

Following Great Britain's lead, India declared war on Nazi Germany on September 3, 1939. Although the Indian National Congress initially refused to back the British war effort, India proved supportive after the collapse of France the following spring. Notwithstanding his pacifism, Gandhi backed the fight against the Axis Powers; so too did the socialist Nehru. India provided troops, industrial goods and raw materials to the Allied side, which also built air bases on Indian territory. In 1943, the Allies began constructing a road—eventually called the Stilwell Road—to link northeastern India and China. British and Indian soldiers pushed back a Japanese invasion that ensued in March 1944.

During the war, Britain offered to include India as an independent dominion within its Commonwealth of Nations, but such efforts proved unavailing. The Indian National Congress demanded full autonomy, while the Muslim League called for the establishment of two religiously drawn nations. In 1945, riots broke out, with the protestors continuing to demand Indian independence. The following year, Great Britain promised to grant independence, provided Indian leaders agreed on the type of government they intended to set up. They proved unable to do so and the Muslim League, on August 16, 1946, urged "direct action" to create a Muslim state, Pakistan. The following day witnessed a bloody riot between Hindus and Muslims in Calcutta; others soon followed.

Fearing the outbreak of civil war, the British government announced in February 1947 that British rule would terminate shortly. The well-regarded new viceroy, Lord Louis Mountbatten, expedited the process. In June 1947, Mountbatten revealed that the country would be split into two sovereign states, India and Pakistan, with most of the princely states taken over by India. Mohammed Ali Jinnah, who headed the Muslim League, spoke from Karachi to proclaim Pakistan's independence on August 14. That evening, in Delhi, Nehru eloquently asserted that at midnight,

> India will awake to life and freedom. A moment comes, which comes but rarely in history, when we step out from the old to the new, when an age ends, and when the soul of a nation, long suppressed, finds utterance. It is fitting that at this solemn moment we take the pledge of dedication to the service of India and her people and to the still larger cause of humanity. . . . The service of India means the service of the millions who suffer. It means the ending of poverty and ignorance and disease and inequality of opportunity.

But more sectarian strife followed, while as many as twelve million refugees emerged, with Muslims heading for Pakistan and Hindus moving to India. Bengal was now quiet, but in the Punjab, Muslims, Hindus and Sikhs battled one another. Hundreds of thousands were slaughtered in the first few months of independence. As the tragedies in the Punjab began to recede in October 1947, India and Pakistan clashed over Jammu and Kashmir. A Hindu maharaja headed that largely non-Hindu state, but great mountain areas and the Kashmir valley were heavily Muslim. Consequently, Jinnah anticipated that Jammu and Kashmir would become part of Pakistan. But both Nehru and the Congress Party possessed strong links to Kashmir. Fighting broke out between Pakistani Muslims and the supporters of Maharaja Hari Singh and Sheikh Abdullah—the so-called "Lion of Kashmir"—that led to the introduction of Indian troops. In 1949, the United Nations helped to bring about a cease-fire that resulted in another partition, which placed Kashmir's northwestern sector under Pakistani control.

Ironically, several of the most significant opponents of British rule died shortly following the granting of independence and the carving out of partitions. Jinnah died of cancer in 1948, while his successor Liaqat Ali Khan was assassinated three years later. Indian deputy prime minister Vallabhai Patel, a prominent leader of the Congress Party, died in 1950. And a Hindu brahman enraged by the Indian leader's ecumenical approach killed Gandhi in late January 1948. Anointed by Gandhi, Nehru became the dominant figure in Indian political life. The head of Congress, Nehru saw his party retain its preeminence throughout his tenure as Indian prime minister (1948–1964). Under his leadership, the world's most populous democratic nation devised five-year plans to foster industrialization, increase agricultural production and improve living standards. However, the several states that comprised India often stymied efforts to bring about educational reform or land redistribution. Moreover, central and state governments shared responsibility for many economic matters, such as planning, while the states retained authority over public health, agriculture and the police. Due to Congress's overwhelming control of the national parliament in Delhi, critics of the national government concentrated their energies in the states. There, ethnic conflicts emerged, often swirling around native languages. The number of states mounted, while the dilemma of the caste system continued to afflict India as a whole.

All the while, Nehru sought to meld democracy and socialism. The Constitution of the Republic of India, which became effective in January 1950, spoke of "We, The People of India" who "resolved to constitute India into a Sovereign, Democratic Republic and to secure to all its citizens: Justice, social, economic, and political; Liberty of thought, expression, belief, faith and worship; Equality of status and opportunity; and to promote among them Fraternity assuring the dignity of the individual and the unity of the Nation." India's prime minister envisioned "freedom of the masses of India from want." To achieve that end, Nehru believed, required the adoption of socialism.

> We have accepted socialism as our goal not only because it seems to us right and beneficial but because there is no other way for the solution of our economic problems. It is sometimes said that rapid progress cannot take place by peaceful and democratic methods. I do not accept this proposition. Indeed, in India today any attempt to discard democratic methods would lead to disruption and

would thus put an end to any immediate prospect of progress.

Equally significant, Nehru spearheaded India's effort to serve as a leader of nonaligned nations in the Third World. India refused to take sides in the Cold War conflict between East and West, and would not join the Southeast Asia Treaty Organization, sponsored by the United States in 1954. Additionally, India, despite an earlier promise to safeguard Tibet's autonomy, declined to protest against China's invasion of that Asian state in 1950. India did welcome the Dalai Lama, the Buddhist leader, who along with some 100,000 Tibetans, fled into exile in 1959. Tensions mounted between India and China, which shared a lengthy border. Armed conflict unfolded, with Chinese troops entering India in 1962. A shaken Nehru successfully sought arms from the United States, Canada and Great Britain. Speaking to the nation, Nehru declared, "We are men and women of peace in this country. We are unused to the necessities of war." Now, however, "everything else is secondary to the freedom of our people and our Motherland." By the close of 1962, China withdrew its forces from Indian territory. Nehru, nevertheless, determined to strengthen India's military. He died in 1964 and was succeeded by Shri Lal Bahadur Shastri.

Another threat soon emerged as Pakistan, allied with China, sought a reexamination of the question of Kashmir. In 1965, the short-lived Indo-Pak war broke out. Thanks to Soviet diplomacy, the fighting terminated, resulting in a return to the status quo, the rejection of force and promises of non-interference and improved relations between India and Pakistan. The issue of Kashmir continued to simmer, as Pakistan strengthened its ties with Beijing.

The death in 1966 of Shastri—who had just signed a peace agreement terminating another Indo-Pak conflict—enabled the Congress Party to select a new head of state. Considering her manageable but popular, the party leaders selected Indira Gandhi, the late prime minister's daughter. Determined to acquire her own base of support, Mrs. Gandhi moved to bolster the Congress Party and adopted a more conciliatory attitude toward the Sikh Akali Dal. She allowed for the establishment of a new state where Punjabi was spoken and Sikhs would dominate. This displeased many party leaders, as did Mrs. Gandhi's nationalization of banks, termination of special privileges afforded princes who had become part of the Indian union and stances on the issues of land ownership, commercial profits and maldistribution of income. Such moves, however, coupled with the campaign slogan, "Out with Poverty," enabled the prime minister to receive backing from the Indian left and to prevail easily in the 1971 national elections.

Mrs. Gandhi antagonized many with her heavy-handed tactics, including the repeated dismissal of state governments through the President's Rule. Nevertheless, her popularity soared as India, so recently afflicted with famine, became self-sufficient in food production, thanks to improved irrigation and grain yields. This Green Revolution, with United States and UN backing, enabled the most prosperous of India's farmers to thrive. Revolutionary ideals, however, appealed to many landless and unemployed Indians and to the mounting number of university graduates who were unable to find jobs. The chasms between the rich and the poor continued to grow, a social phenomenon that the Congress Party and its major opponents failed to address adequately. Indira Gandhi resorted to emergency decrees to reduce in-

flation and rein in corruption, and attempted to bring about some redistribution of wealth through her Twenty Point Program. At the same time, she insisted, "There is only one magic which can remove poverty, and that is hard work sustained by clear vision, iron will and the strictest discipline."

In the meantime, Pakistan endured civil war, with millions of refugees pouring into India. With assistance from the Indian government, East Pakistan prevailed, resulting in the creation of the independent republic of Bangladesh. Before that occurrence, the West Pakistani army, which relied on American military hardware, slaughtered hundreds of thousands. As a consequence, India signed a twenty-year Treaty of Peace, Friendship and Cooperation with the Soviet Union in August 1971. Russian equipment, including planes, tanks and artillery, poured into India, only to end up in Bangladesh.

The liberation of Bangladesh boosted Indira Gandhi's reputation both at home and abroad. By 1971, India was the dominant power in South Asia, although Pakistan experienced a revival under the leadership of Zulfikar Ali Bhutto. Pakistan also began to assemble an atomic bomb, something that India, notwithstanding protestations to the contrary, developed in 1974.

India was beset during this period by mounting inflation, which resulted largely from the oil embargo engineered by the Organization of Petroleum Exporting Countries (OPEC). Then, in June 1975, the high court in Allahabad ordered Mrs. Gandhi to be removed from office owing to illegal campaign practices. Refusing to resign, she proclaimed a state of emergency, suspended the constitution, censored the press, clamped down on the courts and jailed over 100,000 political opponents. Mrs. Gandhi's supposed experiment in "Disciplined Democracy" proved highly unpopular and led to her resounding defeat in the 1977 parliamentary elections. The Janata Party won the greatest number of seats, with Morarji Desai selected as the new prime minister. The coalition that made up Janata, however, soon fell apart and Mrs. Gandhi's new Congress-I Party, which campaigned under the slogan "government that works," swept to victory in 1980, enabling her to take power once more.

Religious strife continued to afflict India. In early 1983, the most ferocious fighting involving Hindus and Muslims since independence took place in the state of Assam. The largely Hindu Assamese condemned the central government's decision to allow Bengal-speaking Muslims from Bangladesh to cast ballots in state elections. In an attempt to achieve political revenge, Mrs. Gandhi sought to create divisions among the Sikhs, particularly the Akali Dal. To that end, she backed Sant Jarnail Singh Bhindranwale, who engaged in terrorist practices in Punjab. Once more, the President's Rule was resorted to, enabling paramilitary forces from the central government to move into Punjab. In June 1984, Indian soldiers, conducting "Operation Bluestar," attacked the Golden Temple, the holiest shrine of the Sikhs, where Bhindranwale now was stationed. The temple was battered, with both sides suffering many casualties. The soon-to-be-martyred Bhindranwale died and more bloodletting followed. On October 31, Mrs. Gandhi was herself murdered by a pair of her bodyguards, both Sikhs. In Delhi, Hindus targeted Sikhs as the killing continued.

A reluctant Rajiv Gandhi, the late prime minister's son and an airline pilot, replaced his mother as head of state. Considered incorruptible, Rajiv Gandhi triumphed in new elections in late 1984 and managed to restore calm in both the Punjab and Assam. Adopt-

ing a lighter hand and relying less frequently on the President's Rule, Rajiv Gandhi enabled the states to regain various powers. He also discarded many of the state-directed programs of Jawaharlal Nehru. Market developments and private investments increased, while taxes and quotas diminished. High technology, ranging from computers to satellites, was featured. Resorting to trickle-down economics, Rajiv Gandhi appeared less concerned than either his mother or grandfather about tackling the problem of mass poverty. Unfortunately, capital flight occurred, with currency illegally stored in Swiss banks.

Inflation resulted in large price increases for foodstuffs, leading to Rajiv Gandhi's defeat in the 1989 election. Vishwanath Pratap Singh, Rajiv Gandhi's former finance minister, whose calls for several investigations had led to his removal from the cabinet, became India's latest prime minister. Viewed as a man of the left, Singh attempted to curb inflation but also promised the "right to work" to all adults desirous of employment. Singh was also concerned about environmental issues, including India's diminished forest land and air and water pollution.

The People's Republic of China

With the end of World War II, different dramatic transformations were in store for China. The precarious and contentious nature of the Chinese Republic, established under Sun Yat-sen's leadership in 1911 as a result of civil war and experiencing internal strife throughout its short-lived existence, provided an opening for communist forces. Sun Yat-sen and other former revolutionaries formed the Kuomintang or Nationalist Party. The Soviet Union convinced the Chinese Communists to join the party in the early

1920s. But following Sun's death in 1925, the military commander Chiang Kai-shek became head of the Nationalist Party. After battling with warlords in northern China, Chiang forced communist leaders, who had adopted the strategy of armed revolt, to head for the mountains in the south. The Green Gang, a mafia-type secret society, aided Chiang. The communists contested his dictatorial hold on power, formed rural bases, established a rival regime in southern and central China and conducted the celebrated Long March from the Chinese Communist Party's central base in Jiangxi to Shaanxi in 1934 and 1935. About 100,000 comrades began the 5,000-mile odyssey, led by Mao Zedong, but fewer than 20,000 completed the entire journey.

At its close, Mao's preeminence within the Communist Party was greater than ever. Born in Hunan Province in 1893, Mao was the son of wealthy peasants. After supporting the efforts of republican revolutionaries to oust the Manchu dynasty, Mao completed his education, attaining a teaching degree and becoming a member of the University of Beijing's library staff. In contrast to most traditional Marxists, Mao championed a revolution in his homeland that would revolve around the peasantry. This seemed logical to him as most Chinese resided in rural areas and the Kuomintang or warlords controlled urban centers. Marxist ideology, with its call for collective ownership of wealth and the sharp lessening of income maldistribution, Mao reasoned, could appeal to the peasants.

Along with his "Sinification of Marxism," Mao propounded the gospel of the "people's war." A revolutionary struggle, he insisted, required the support of the general populace. It also demanded politically driven military forces that would exemplify the ideals of the revolution. Such fighters, Mao contended, would willingly battle against oppressive land-

lords, greedy capitalists and puppet armies. The revolutionary soldiers and party leaders would serve as models for the Chinese people. As a consequence, they would win the allegiance of vast numbers of their countrymen. This was essential for, as Mao put it, "The people are the water, the army are the fish; without the water, the fish will die."

The Nationalist government faced not only a potent communist movement, but also Japanese encroachments, including the occupation of Manchuria in 1931 and a further drive into northern China. With Japanese support, both Hebei and Inner Magnolia boasted autonomous governments by 1936. The threat the Japanese posed led to another united front involving the Kuomintang and the CCP. The Sino-Japanese war began in 1937 and resulted in considerable portions of eastern China being taken over by the invading army. Soldiers and civilians alike suffered atrocities of all kinds. The communists, who established roots in the area, spearheaded resistance in the north. Despite wartime exigencies and the supposed alliance, the communists continued to battle with the Kuomintang.

In many regards, World War II proved equally trying for the Nationalists, who confronted the Japanese occupation, substantial inflation and the growing appeal of the CCP; the communists expanded their operations in the northwest while party membership soared, reaching 1.2 million by 1945. The Kuomintang mandated rising prices, taxes and conscription, all of which alienated peasants. The communists, with the number of their soldiers swelling, took control over parts of northern China, where some 100 million inhabitants resided. Temporarily downplaying demands for social revolution, the communists redistributed land to peasants, which helped to weaken the hold of the Nationalists. The growing perception of Chiang's

Map 8-1 China

regime as undemocratic, corrupt and ineffective further afflicted the Kuomintang. Many came to identify the communists, not the Nationalists, with opposition to the Japanese. The U.S. Ambassador to China, General Patrick Hurley, sought to maintain the Nationalist–communist alliance.

With the end of the war, the Kuomintang and the communists vied for power. Both oc-cupied land that the Japanese previously controlled, while the Soviet Union took over Manchuria. The Nationalists obtained international backing and seemed to have the advantage militarily. Following the Japanese surrender in mid-1945, their military forces controlled key coastal cities. The communists, on the other hand, held no coastal regions, boasted little industrial backing and even lacked much Soviet support. In January 1946, the new U.S. Ambassador to China, General George C. Marshall, again attempted to bring about a cease-fire between the warring factions; the United States considered a strong, unified China to be necessary for peace in the region. Although Chiang agreed to demobilize a quarter of his troops, he, like the communists, geared up for a civil war. Chinese communist soldiers replaced the Russian forces, who confiscated industrial machinery before departing from Manchuria in March.

Initially, the Kuomintang appeared to possess marked advantages, holding the upper hand in large cities and boasting control over much of China's industry. Moreover, the Nationalist army was twice as large as its foe, while Chiang, unlike Mao Zedong, also possessed an air force and a navy. America rescinded its embargo on arms to China in 1947, enabling the Kuomintang to obtain sufficient military hardware. U.S. economic assistance, amounting to $2 billion, poured into China from August 1945 through early 1948. At the behest of the American government, a new constitution supposedly provided the formal basis for a democratic state.

However, severe problems continued to afflict China. With the communists refusing to compete politically, the Kuomintang monopolized governmental offices. Inflation crippled the economy, while corruption and preferential treatment for a few privileged families characterized Chiang's regime. Battlefield developments proved no more pleasing to Chiang, as the communists took control of Manchuria in late 1948. Communists victories mounted, with the capture of Beijing and a great military victory at Xuzhou. As Western aid dried up, the Nationalists were pushed back toward southern China. The People's Republic of China was proclaimed on October 1, 1949. In December, Chiang fled to Taiwan. There, the Kuomintang declared that the Chinese government in exile was being set up; eventually, two million of Chiang's supporters joined him in Taiwan or the Republic of China. As had occurred repeatedly throughout Chinese history, "dynasties" again fell and rose without much consultation involving the people as a whole.

THE COMMUNISTS IN POWER

While dominated by revolutionaries, the initial government of the People's Republic of China contained non-communist elements, including Madame Soong Ching-ling, Sun Yatsen's widow. Chairman Mao Zedong and Premier Zhou Enlai led the Chinese communists who increasingly strengthened their hold on their nation, treating supposed counterrevolutionary forces harshly. Such repression heightened following the introduction of Chinese troops in the Korean War. In the first six months of 1951, over 100,000 individuals were executed, with many others incarcerated or compelled to toil in labor camps.

The revolutionary government initiated sweeping changes, including a massive land reform. At least one million people, many targeted as large landlords, died as the communization of China proceeded apace. Beginning in 1953, China undertook its initial Five-Year Plan to foster economic development; during that period, the government established large-scale agricultural cooperatives and took control of industrial production, too. Eventually, Chinese farmers experienced collectivization, while the government set up state farms. Adopting the Soviet model, the Chinese also relied on potent bureaucracies and centralized planning to foster industrial growth. Those dismissed as Kuomintang, counterrevolutionaries or foreigners lost control of factories. Government operatives secured control of trade and commerce. Great public works projects began, with civilians and soldiers comprising the necessary labor force. China built up its armed forces, including the People's Liberation Army, soon boasting the third largest military in the world. Determined to establish firm control over the Chinese people, the Communist Party relied on the secret police and extensive propaganda campaigns.

Under communist rule, formal religion suffered, while the party controlled education. Intellectual activity was severely restricted, although a short-lived period of greater tolerance occurred in 1957. Party leaders spoke of the need to "let the hundred flowers bloom," but soon adopted a more rigid approach. The following year, China initiated the Great Leap Forward or the second five-year plan. Intended to speed up Chinese economic development while purportedly ensuring greater worker and peasant involvement, this campaign relied on Mao's proclamation that human will could surmount any impediments. The Great Leap Forward anticipated that heavy industry, light industry and agriculture would all be emphasized. Distinctions between rural and urban areas were to be lessened, with factories placed in the countryside and urban laborers engaging in some agricultural work. Women and the unemployed were considered new sources of labor.

Despite certain advances, the Great Leap Forward proved disastrous overall. Many unemployed Chinese became more productive and women were said to be empowered by their inclusion in the workforce. Dams and irrigation systems were constructed along with industrial plants in rural areas. But with CCP architects refusing to allow basic maintenance of industrial equipment, the Chinese economy suffered grievously, experiencing depression, famine and diminished industrial production. The cutoff of economic and technical assistance from the Soviet Union hardly helped matters, resulting in the closing of a number of power and industrial plants. While supposedly "higher-stage" or "fully socialist" giant agricultural communes were formed, workers toiled long hours in factories. Rural factories produced poor-quality goods, but more serious still, agricultural productivity plummeted. Coupled with three successive years of bad weather from 1959 to 1961, food shortages unfolded, resulting in an estimated 20–25 million deaths.

During this same period, the Chinese encountered other difficulties, including confrontations with both the Soviet Union and India. The first involved ideological conflict; the second resulted in actual hostilities. Initially, Sino-Soviet relations had been cordial. Soviet recognition had been forthcoming on the very day that the People's Republic of China was proclaimed. The following year, Mao, on a visit to Moscow, agreed to a thirty-year treaty of friendship with the Soviet state. Also resulting from that trip were a loan package of $300 million from the USSR, a promise to evacuate Manchurian railroad stations and ports after a peace treaty was carved out with the Japanese, recognition of the independence of the Mongolian People's Republic and the setting up of jointly run companies to exploit natural resources in Xinjiang. Following the Korean War, the Soviets provided more assistance for additional projects. In late 1957, the Soviets agreed to aid China in developing nuclear weapons.

Within two years, that promise was jettisoned as tensions between the two great communist states were already deteriorating.

Mao had grown steadily critical of Nikita Khruschev's de-Stalinization efforts and the Soviet leader's call for improved relations with western powers. By 1960, the Soviet Union refused to provide technical aid for China. Clashes began along the Manchurian territory. Then, in 1962, the Soviet Union failed to back China when it warred with India over mutual borders. The signing of a nuclear test ban treaty by the United States, Great Britain and the USSR angered the Chinese, who soon severed diplomatic relations with the Soviets. In mid-October 1964, China became a nuclear power, which hardly pleased Soviet officials.

China had also rebounded economically to a certain extent following the disastrous Great Leap Forward. Paradoxically, as centralized economic planning was reemphasized, the size of communes was capped at around 160 households. Peasants, although still required to work on collective farms, were permitted to cultivate private plots. Worker participation in factories was abridged, as factory managers again held more power.

The latest changes proved troubling to Mao and other radical leaders. Increasingly concerned about the lessening of revolutionary zeal, Mao blamed the development on the spread of "bourgeois culture." New revolutions or mass movements, he contended, were required to ward off the emergence of new elite classes. Mao was arguing, in effect, that "permanent revolution" was necessary. Such a revolution, he believed, would help usher in a new culture that would enable a new "consciousness" to flower; that in turn would allow greater movement toward a communist society. Mao envisioned a new socialist man springing forth from a political and cultural revolution. Beginning in 1966, he spearheaded the Great Proletarian Cultural Revolution, through which radicals in the Chinese Communist Party hoped to bolster communist principles. The proponents of the Cultural Revolution insisted that power must be redistributed among the Chinese people. Many top party leaders, along with some 700,000–800,000 government officials, lost their posts, while young people, often led by student radicals, joined the Red Guards who carried out major demonstrations and attacked supposed counterrevolutionaries. Numerous schools, including many universities, were shut down altogether, with students compelled to toil at manual labor in rural areas. In the quest to destroy supposedly decadent, anti-Maoist practices, many buildings and historical artifacts were obliterated. Several hundred thousand individuals, accused of "elitist" or "antidemocratic" ways, were jailed.

By late 1966, Red Guard members began squabbling over the direction of the Cultural Revolution. Subsequently, the pace of the Cultural Revolution intensified, as supporters and opponents clashed in armed conflicts. At that point, Mao directed the People's Liberation Army to reestablish order. Nevertheless, tens of thousands perished in the confrontations involving Red Guard units, their foes and the military. While the tumult of 1966–1968 dissipated, the impact of the Cultural Revolution proved profound. The CCP reasserted its primacy in Chinese society, but the battle between radical and moderate forces hardly disappeared altogether.

THE "OPENING" OF CHINA

With revolutionary fervor lessening, Chinese diplomatic relations underwent striking changes, although Mao's regime continued to support Middle Eastern and African national liberation movements. While China continued to provide military assistance to North Vietnam, it also participated in negotiations to scale back or end the war in Indochina. Trade agreements were carved out with Western European nations, Canada, Australia, New Zealand and Japan. Attempts were made to establish diplomatic and commercial ties to Middle Eastern states. The United States now called for UN membership for both the Nationalist government in Taiwan and the People's Republic of China. In late 1971, the UN opted to recognize the People's Republic and not Taiwan as the representative of China. The United States under President Richard M. Nixon began allowing some trade with China. In a 1972 visit to China, Nixon met Premier Zhou Enlai and Mao. The American and Chinese leaders inked the Shanghai Communique, which envisioned the normalization of diplomatic relations.

As the Bamboo Curtain began lifting, new power struggles evolved inside China. The deaths of Zhou Enlai and Mao Zedong in 1976 resulted in clashes that pitted radicals, headed by Mao's widow Jiang Quing, against moderates, led by Prime Minister Hua Guofeng. On October 6, Hua, now the party chairman, ordered the arrest of Jiang and other top leftists who comprised the so-called Gang of Four; they were accused of seeking to "foment civil war by allegedly arming the Shanghai militia and planning an attack on the organs of state." Hua proved unable to bring about a compromise between Maoist and more conservative elements in the CCP, while the national economy endured inflation and budgetary deficits.

That set the stage for Deng Xiaophing, who in 1977 was named vice premier and vice chairman of the CCP. Earlier twice deposed from power, Deng favored a pragmatic, moderate governing style. Under his leadership, China established normal diplomatic relations with the United States on January 1, 1979. The next year, Deng's preeminence within the Chinese government was solidified with the resignation of Hua as premier; the following year, Hua relinquished his post as head of the CCP. Deng also presided over the removal of leading Maoists from top positions and the rehabilitation of those like himself who had been victimized during the Cultural Revolution. Even Mao was criticized, along with his designs for both the Great Leap Forward and the Cultural Revolution. At the same time, the party was careful to refer to Mao as a "great Marxist and a great proletarian revolutionary." The Cultural Revolution, on the other hand, was condemned thoroughly for failing to usher in greater democracy, producing economic stagnation, wreaking havoc in Chinese education and favoring incompetent bureaucrats.

Downplaying ideology, Deng and his allies, including Premier Zhao Ziyang and general secretary Hu Yaobang, strove to bring about marked economic changes to foster greater productivity. Rather than extolling the Maoist idea of the New Man, the new Chinese government discarded centralized planning, while encouraging material incentives and small business operations. Along the same lines, farmers were allowed to sell surplus crops in the open market. State-run enterprises also came to rely on supply and demand considerations, while foreign investment was encouraged. Economic zones were established along the coast in an effort to attract foreign capital; money poured onto the mainland from Hong Kong. China strove to acquire technical and scientific expertise from advanced industrial states and allowed an ever-lengthening number of graduate students to study abroad.

The Communist Party under Deng's leadership remained the dominant political entity in China, although changes beckoned. In Beijing during the winter of 1978–1979, a Democracy Wall appeared that featured broadsheets, long used by the Chinese to register disapproval with government policy. Although out of favor throughout the period of communist dominance, broadsheets, including one that praised democracy, now pointed to CCP and government failings.

Calls for more than economic change were soon forthcoming. The 1982 constitution encouraged greater participation by the Chinese masses in political affairs. Throughout the decade of the 1980s, Chinese intellectuals proved increasingly restive. Charges of government corruption were heard, while a model of greater political freedom inside a communist state had emerged in the Soviet Union under President Mikhail Gorbachev. Beginning in late 1986, university students, who conducted a series of demonstrations in urban centers, began insisting on greater political freedom and expanded democratic opportunities.

Conservatives within the CCP reacted by removing Hu Yaobang, viewed as too supportive of political reform, from his position as general secretary. Another Deng protégé, Zhao Ziyang, replaced Hu. Eventually, hardliners Li Peng and Jiang Zemin became prime minister and party chairman, respectively. The new Chinese leaders supported Deng's Four Modernizations, involving agriculture, industry, defense and science and technology. Political reforms, on the other hand, generally were avoided.

Hu's death in April 1989 led to student demonstrations in Bejing. The students had viewed Hu as a champion of democracy and also were concerned about government corruption and limited employment opportunities. Great parades took place on May 4, a date long associated with modern Chinese nationalism. Students began amassing in Tiananmen Square with some initiating a hunger strike, confounding CCP leaders about how to respond. Matters were complicated further by the state visit of Soviet premier Gorbachev. At one point, a purportedly sympathetic Zhao spoke with some of the protestors. Li Peng, on the other hand, demanded that the demonstrations cease and empowered the People's Liberation Army to act. The student demonstrators produced a statute of the Goddess of Democracy in the central square. While soldiers initially appeared reluctant to attack the protestors, army units, beginning on the evening of June 3, fired on the gathered throng, killing hundreds, including many non-students.

The Chinese government insisted that counter-revolutionaries, backed by foreigners, had been plotting to overthrown the communist regime. Another shakeup of the party leadership ensued, with Zhao, blamed for his purported leniency, removed from his post. Deng also targeted Li Peng, replacing him as secretary-general with Jiang Zemin, the mayor of Shanghai. Deng, while still championing economic liberalism, continued to oppose the possibility of political pluralism.

Asia's Economic Powerhouse

While a revolutionary state had emerged in China shortly after World War II, that conflagration had left Japan humiliated and economically prostrate. Within a relatively short period of time, however, observers referred to "the Japanese miracle" as the former Axis state became an economic powerhouse and boasted a representative system of government. Japan recovered rapidly from the loss of the empire, including the Philippines, Singapore, the Dutch East Indies, Burma, the Solomons, the Gilberts and other important South Pacific islands, acquired during the early stages of the war.

For a brief spell, wartime successes threatened to make real Japan's "Greater East Asia Co-Prosperity Sphere." The Japanese advance had been viewed in varying perspectives by Asians. Some, including those who collaborated with the Asian power, applauded Japan for supposedly liberating colonial lands. Others, such as the Chinese and communist-led guerrillas in both Vietnam and the Philippines, warred with the Japanese or their surrogates. But after a series of victories in the Pacific, Japan suffered defeats at the hands of the U.S. Navy; as early as May and June of 1942, the Americans triumphed at the Coral Sea and Midway, which resulted in the smashing of many Japanese aircraft carriers. More setbacks led to General Tojo's resignation in July 1944, although succeeding Japanese governments sought to continue the fight with greater determination.

Following the American takeover of Okinawa in 1945, the United States conducted massive fire raids against leading Japanese cities. As the wartime situation continued to worsen, Japanese generals called for the employment of kamikaze pilots to conduct suicide runs. By July, however, Emperor Hirohito sought an end to the war. The United States still demanded the unconditional surrender of Japan and dropped atomic bombs on the Japanese cities of Hiroshima and Nagasaki on August 6 and August 9, respectively. The emperor beseeched the Japanese people on August 15 to "endure the unendurable" and accept defeat. Possibly thousands of military officers, distraught by events, committed suicide. On September 2, Japanese officials surrendered on the American battleship Missouri in Tokyo Bay.

THE OCCUPATION

Japan, which suffered almost three million fatalities during the war, confronted a period of demilitarization and occupation. The Supreme Commander of Allied Powers (SCAP), U.S. General Douglas MacArthur, headed the Occupation, which lasted seven years. The Japanese received MacArthur as a new shogun; he intended to create a democratic state. As MacArthur later recalled,

> I had to rebuild a nation that had been almost completed destroyed by the war. . . . Japan had become the world's great laboratory for an experiment in the liberation of a people from totalitarian military rule and for the liberalization of government from within. It was clear that the experiment must go far beyond the primary purpose of the Allies—the destruction of Japan's ability to wage another war and the punishment of war criminals.

Yet those very goals were sought, resulting in over 200,000 officials—proclaimed "active exponents of militant nationalism and aggression"—losing their posts. War crimes trials were held throughout Southeast Asia, involving 6,000 individuals; over 900 received capital sentences. The Tokyo Trials involved twenty-five top Japanese figures; seven, including Tojo Hideki and one-time prime minister Hirota Koki, were hanged; several attempted suicide.

In a highly controversial move, MacArthur argued against a trial of the emperor; Hiro-

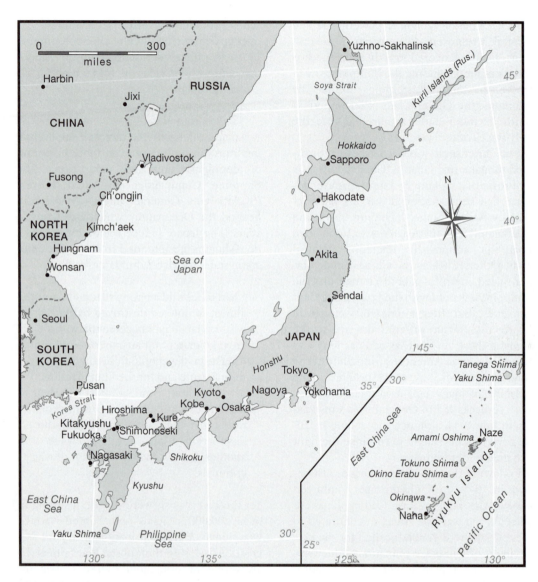

Map 8-2 Japan

hito, in fact, was allowed to retain his throne. At the same time, Hirohito was compelled to broadcast the Declaration of Humanity on January 1, 1946, in which he decried "the false conception that the Emperor is divine and that the Japanese people are superior to other races and fated to rule the world." Increasingly, Hirohito presented the image of

Fig. 8-2 General Douglas MacArthur and Emperor Hirohito, Tokyo, Japan. (Pearson Education, Corporate Digital Archive, Getty Images Inc.)

an all-too-human emperor who possessed paternal concerns for his people.

The Occupation forces, headed by General MacArthur, soon placed in power his preferred candidate, Prime Minister Yoshida Shigeru. More important, the Civil Liberties Directive of October 1945 and a new constitution, termed the MacArthur Peace Constitution, were devised. The civil liberties measure demanded that all political prisoners be released and supported freedom of assembly,

which resulted in a bounty of political parties. Patterned after the U.S. model, the Japanese constitution vested sovereignty in the Japanese people, renounced war as a national instrument and called for separation of church and state. The document also created an independent judiciary, and guaranteed equality of the sexes, the right of workers to organize and to bargain collectively, human rights for all, freedom of assembly, thought, belief and expression and suffrage for adults over twenty years of age. It also supported land reform, rent control and tenant rights.

In an effort to ensure demilitarization and democratization would take place, the Occupation insisted that the *zaibatsu* (financial clique) holding companies be disbanded. In early 1947, MacArthur invited Roger Baldwin, longtime director of the American Civil Liberties Union, to help form comparable organizations in Japan. That same year, the Anti-Monopoly Law became effective, placing several hundred corporations at risk. While union membership was encouraged, leading to the organization of 56 percent of the labor force by the decade's end, a general strike slated for February 1, 1947, and backed by communists was banned. MacArthur, on the other hand, allowed for a new general election in April 1947; the results saw a coalition guided by Katayma Tetsu, a Christian and a member of the Socialist Party, replace Yoshida's cabinet.

The advent of the Cold War increasingly influenced the course of postwar Japanese political life. This benefited Yoshida, who earlier had warned that Japan threatened to become "submerged in a sea of red flags" and now talked about an "excess of democracy." MacArthur and the occupation forces began distancing themselves from the socialists and softening their demands for democratic reforms. In October 1948, Yoshida was returned to power; he continued as premier until 1954. At the same time, the *zaibatsu* began establishing industrial cooperatives. Conservative fiscal policies were resorted to, union drives blunted and strikes smashed and communists pushed out of the government, while former proponents of Japanese militarism reentered the public arena. One individual convicted of war crimes, Kishi

Nobusuke, a cabinet official in Tojo's government, eventually became premier.

Following the outbreak of the Korean War in June 1950, U.S. policy regarding the Occupation shifted once more. The invasion by North Korean forces, Yoshida claimed, was a "gift of the gods." American dollars poured into Japan as war matériel was produced, allowing for an economic boom to take place. Japan was referred to as the "bastion of democracy in Asia." As demanded by SCAP, Yoshida created the National Police Reserve, made up of 75,000 men; this unit's members later were referred to as Self-Defence Forces. At the same time, the premier attacked communist "sympathizers," including the socialists.

In early 1951, President Harry S Truman dismissed the head of the Occupation, General MacArthur, from his posts in both Japan and Korea, where he had commanded American troops. Truman believed that MacArthur had violated the U.S. Constitution's directive that the military be under the command of the chief executive. Consequently, on April 11, he ordered the general to return home; the departure of the American Shogun proved startling to the Japanese.

In the meantime, Yoshida increasingly discarded SCAP edicts that he disliked. His so-called Yoshida Doctrine called for Japan to avoid confrontations and to concentrate instead on economic development. Along those lines, Yoshida capped military spending at one percent of the government budget. While his New Partnership carved out transformed relationships with the United States, Japan was welcomed back into the community of nations. In September 1951, a Peace Conference in San Francisco saw some forty-nine nations, including Japan, sign a peace pact.

Japan accepted the loss of its empire, including control over both Korea and Taiwan. The Soviet Union received Southern Sakhalin and the Kurile Islands. An American trusteeship was established for the Ryukyu and Bonin islands.

The treaty became effective on April 28, 1952, allowing the Occupation to officially end; the United States, however, retained a considerable presence in Japan. A joint security pact was signed that enabled the Americans to retain military bases in Japan, particularly in Okinawa; U.S. military forces and their dependents secured extra-territorial status in Japan. Not all Japanese were pleased with such an arrangement. In fact, riots erupted shortly following the announcement that independence was at hand. Concerns intensified after the explosion of a U.S. hydrogen bomb near the Pacific island of Bikini in 1954; the crew of a Japanese fishing boat returned home, gravely affected by the nuclear fallout.

POLITICAL AND ECONOMIC CHANGE

While its relationship with the United States remained complex, Japan experienced considerable political and economic changes during these Cold War years. Hatoyama Ichiro, pushed aside by Yoshida for the premiership, experienced a political rebirth. Crafting a coalition with Kishi Nobusuke, Hatoyama helped to lead the highly conservative Democratic Party to power in 1954. Hatoyama's government curtailed opportunities for women to enter the political arena and sponsored anti-radical measures. Large corporations and rural agricultural cooperatives benefited from the regime's pro-business

policies, which trade with the United States, Taiwan and South Korea sustained. In 1955, Hatoyama and his allies formed a new Liberal-Democratic Party, in an effort to keep the Socialist Party from power.

With strong backing by the Hatoyama government and the U.S. military "subsidy," the Japanese economy thrived. The Ministry of International Trade and Industry, established in 1949, brought together business moguls, bureaucrats and government officials. Controlled planning measures were devised; these involved investments, the strengthening of various industries and the decision to allow other enterprises to fail. Initially, the government favored heavy industry, especially in the iron and steel trades. During the 1960s, however, electrical products and cameras were highlighted, although shipbuilding remained one of the preferred heavy industries. More and more workers became employed in manufacturing and construction, fewer in agriculture. Similarly, service industries increasingly occupied an important role in the national economy. Additionally, Japan's bullet train or *Shinkansen* was viewed as a model of its kind.

The holding of special events in Japan demonstrated more clearly how fully the Asian state had been welcomed back into the community of nations. In 1964, athletes from across the globe gathered in Tokyo to participate in that summer's Olympic Games. Six years later, Osaka hosted the World Exposition, enabling Japan to display its economic prowess.

Both the average Japanese family and the nation as a whole appeared to benefit from the economic boom that lasted until the early 1970s. Real wages reportedly tripled from the mid-1950s until oil prices skyrocketed in

1973. During that period, the Japanese economy, now the world's third richest, grew more than 10 percent annually. Many considered Japan an economic superpower and referred to its economic miracle, which benefited from the industriousness of the Japanese workers, a favorable balance of trade, high savings rates and considerable capital accumulation. Helpful too was the stable nature of Japanese political life, with the Liberal Democratic Party retaining its hold on power. The alliance of government, bureaucratic and business entities likewise remained intact.

This period witnessed the continued rehabilitation of previously disgraced individuals such as Kishi, who became prime minister in 1957. Five other individuals similarly involved in the Japanese bureaucracy prior to the war came to head the Japanese government. While in power, they acted to reassert earlier practices, including centralized government control over education. The Ministry of Education became increasingly powerful, possessing great authority to select and censor textbooks.

All were not pleased with the conservative direction of Japanese politics, the continued reliance on the United States, or the economic growth that obviously was being inequitably shared. Sometimes-violent labor clashes ensued, including one in 1953 at Nissan that resulted in a crushing defeat for the All-Japan Automobile Industry Union. The shattered union was converted into company-run associations. Another contentious affair involved Mitsui-operated Miike coal mines in Kyushu, where workers protested the switch to oil to fuel Japan's economy. Strike-breakers and national policemen helped to defeat the union drive.

Increasingly, businesses featured "enterprise unions," largely impotent company-run affairs. However, as the economy continued to surge, wages increased, conditions improved and worker unrest was reined in. Furthermore, white-collar workers at the giant corporations received "lifetime employment," along with higher salaries.

CONTINUING RELATIONS WITH THE UNITED STATES

The relationship with the United States and fears of revitalized militarism proved troubling as well. In 1959, Premier Kishi revealed that the security pact with the United States had been revised. American President Dwight David Eisenhower planned a trip to Japan. U.S. forces remained in Japan but for the first time, Japanese officials would be consulted about their possible deployment elsewhere. American soldiers and their dependents lost the extra-territorial protection previously accorded them.

While the provisions of the treaty, intended to last ten years, appeared more favorable to Japan than previous agreements, protests erupted. Left-of-center groups, labor unions, students, politicians ill-disposed to the Liberal-Democratic Party and many right-wing organizations opposed the agreement. Government foes agreed that American soldiers should depart from Japan. The leftists were also dismayed by how the treaty seemed to join Japanese and American foreign policies; in this period of the Cold War, the United States remained determinedly anti-communist and supportive of authoritarian governments throughout Southeast Asia. Large-scale demonstrations unfolded, while the police responded with beatings, arrests and the killing of one student. Tensions rose so mightily that Kishi, in May 1960, felt compelled to order the police into the national assembly. With the socialists boycotting, the treaty was passed. Eisenhower's planned trip was called off and Kishi himself soon resigned.

Nevertheless, protest continued against the renewal of the Mutual Security Treaty and other government policies, leading one right-wing extremist to assassinate Asanuma Inejiro, the head of the Japanese Socialist Party; millions of horrified television viewers witnessed Inejiro stabbed to death. Student demonstrations, some triggered by the radical student federation, Zengakuren, unfolded, as firebombs were hurled and campuses shut down. Later protest against the Vietnam War led to the emergence of the Red Army, which called for the use of terror to overturn the government.

In general, however, Japan experienced a period of political and economic stability throughout the 1960s. The new Japanese premier, Ikeda Hayato, concentrated on economic growth, promising to double wages by the end of the decade. Hayato's promise actually was fulfilled in less than four years. This delighted many urban workers, along with members of the economic elite, who benefited from the government's pro-business policies. Still, the economic bounty was shared unequally, producing greater ferment as both taxes and inflation rose.

Troubled by the rising discontent, the Liberal-Democratic Party retired Ikeda, replacing him with Sato Eisaku, Kishi's younger half-brother. It was Sato who presided over the Tokyo Games, got the United States to agree to relinquish control of Okinawa and revised the security pact once again. An opponent of the spread of both nuclear weapons and nuclear technology, Sato later received the Nobel Peace Prize.

The tenure of his successor, the wealthy industrialist Tanaka Kakuei, proved less happy. Tanaka, who became prime minister in mid-1972, envisioned "Rebuilding the Japanese Archipelago." Before two years had passed, however, Tanaka resigned in disgrace. An economic downturn and his conviction for influence peddling involving the U.S. industrial giant Lockheed brought down Tanaka. In the same period, U.S. President Richard Nixon, concerned about an unfavorable balance of trade, placed a ten percent surcharge on a number of Japanese exports, before resorting to an embargo on soybeans. Sorely dependent on Middle Eastern oil, Japan suffered negative growth in 1974 as inflation soared.

Japan quickly rebounded from its temporary economic difficulties and political scandals, rekindling talk that it was Asia's financial powerhouse and the most stable country in the region. As a succession of Liberal-Democratic figures served as prime minister, they worked mightily to ensure that Japanese companies thrived in the world marketplace. Both the Finance Ministry and the Ministry of International Trade and Industry provided government backing, giving subsidies and restricting markets. Charges rang out, particularly in the United States, that Japan was "dumping" goods abroad. This practice involved undercutting the prices of domestic goods in America to the point that companies were forced into bankruptcy.

As Japan's economy became the world's second most potent, many Japanese proved discontented with the relationship involving the United States. Controversies brewed when Premier Suzuki Zenko guided cabinet officials to the Yasukuni Shrine on August 15, 1980, the thirty-fifth anniversary of Japan's surrender during World War II. Japanese leftists, along with the governments of both

China and Taiwan, worried about rekindled militarism. Another furor was triggered the following year when the author of a textbook refused to rewrite passages regarding past Japanese imperialism.

The next premier, Nakasone Yasuhiro, was a highly conservative figure who befriended the American president Ronald Reagan, beefed up the Self-Defense Forces and purchased advanced military hardware from the United States. To the chagrin of many, Nakasone, a one-time military officer, permitted U.S. ships, in Japanese waters, to carry nuclear weapons. Nakasone, in his official capacity as the nation's top elected official, also visited the shrine for Japanese war dead at Yasukuni. He even allowed for joint naval exercises involving the American navy. Nakasone's cabinet, which included a series of hard-line nationalists, was decidedly conservative. The Nakasone government championed supply-side economics, sliced social welfare programs, boosted military spending and privatized a number of publicly owned utilities and railroads. Some, such as the politician and writer Ishirara Shintaro, criticized Nakasone, who had demeaned the United States because of its multi-racial makeup, for continuing to defer to the United States.

During Nakasone's two-term reign, additional charges were heard regarding Japanese trade practices. Fearing the possibility of Western protectionism, Nakasone warned in 1985, "If we do not solve the existing trade frictions today, there is a possibility that there will arise a very serious situation affecting the life and death of our country." Due to a scarcity of natural resources, Japan was compelled to rely on trade, as Nakasone recognized. That same year, Japanese companies were said to have invested $14 billion in the United States. An anti-Japanese backlash threatened to break out, thanks to a $44.4 billion trade surplus during the fiscal year 1984–1985.

Notwithstanding the criticisms coming its way, Japan, as the 1980s neared a close, appeared ready to become a larger player on the world stage. Changes were unfolding at home, as Takeshita Noboru, Nakasone's appointed heir, became premier in 1987; tax revisions worked to benefit Takeshita's strongest backers. In January 1989, Hirohito, the Emperor Showa, died, bringing an end to an era. During Hirohito's final days, the mayor of Nagasaki, among others, leveled charges that the emperor had prolonged the war needlessly, resulting in many additional Japanese casualties. Although this assertion resulted in an attempt by right-wing forces to assassinate the mayor, other Japanese, especially in Okinawa, highlighted atrocities Japanese soldiers had committed during World War II. Concerns were expressed about the violent treatment of prisoners of war and civilians, many of whom who were subjected to horrific "scientific experiments." Some called for war reparations to be paid the victims of Japanese practices; discussion occurred about the "Comfort Women" from Korea, China, the Philippines, the Dutch East Indies and Indonesia, who had been treated as sexual slaves by Japanese soldiers throughout the war. Initially, the Japanese government sought to dismiss these concerns as involving women who were "probably already prostitutes." Eventually, as a public furor took hold in South Korea and elsewhere, the government established a fund for reparations that allowed for private contributions only. Another issue that rose to the public forefront involved Okinawa, with claims of wartime atrocities, mass rapes and coerced mass suicides aired.

As the decade neared an end, questions were posed about the coronation of Akihito as the Emperor Heisei; that affair suggested the mythical, god-like aura that had been discarded following the war. Another controversy involved the so-called Recruit Scandal, which involved over 150 politicians and other prominent figures, who had received individual contributions, other moneys and shares of stock whose value soon increased five-fold. This "stock-for-favors" scandal eventually compelled about 20 Diet Members to resign, along with several cabinet officials. Among those forced to leave office were both Prime Minister Takeshita Noboru and Nakasone. Elections to the Upper House of the Diet in 1989 saw the Japan Socialist Party achieve majority status for the first time; the Liberal-Democratic Party still controlled the Lower House.

As they watched the democracy movement unfold, Chinese Communist Party officials headed by Deng Xiaoping (1904–1997) worried about their very fate. Aware of the events that were unfolding in the Soviet Union and Eastern Europe, they saw cracks in the communist wall appearing. On June 4, 1989, tens of thousands, convinced that "The People's army won't attack the people," remained gathered at Tiananmen Square in Beijing, with many situated around the Monument to the Heroes of the People. Early that morning, soldiers attired in camouflage, steel helmets and gas masks, and wielding machine guns, poured out of the Great Hall of the People. Flopping down on their stomachs, the soldiers aimed their weapons in the direction of the Monument. Other soldiers and armed police soon appeared, sporting electric prods and rubber clubs. The latter forces began attacking the demonstrators, forcing a retreat. As that occurred, machine gun fire rang out. A number of students were killed, but most of the victims were workers, small business people and professionals. Many were shot down as they attempted to escape the onrushing troops. Among the casualties were women, children, soldiers and police.

The orchestrator of these events at Tiananmen Square was Chinese Communist Party leader Deng, who feared that the system he had dedicated his life to was at stake. He also believed that his fortune and that of his compatriots could well be determined by how they responded to the crescendo of events that had culminated in the massacre at Tiananmen Square. Deng and many other communist bosses had determined that "a planned and organized anti-party and anti-socialist drive to produce chaos" was unfolding. On June 9, Deng appeared on television speaking to army commanders who could be found throughout Beijing. Deng saluted the soldiers and police who, he declared, had perished "as heroes" at Tiananmen. The developments, he indicated, were "inevitable and independent of all human will." He lashed out at the demonstrators, stating, "We must never forget the cruelties of our enemy for whom we must show no mercy or even an iota of forgiveness."

A survivor of two purges, Chinese Communist Party leader Deng was determined to usher in the kind of economic modernization that Japan had experienced. Born in the Sichuan province, Deng received an early classical Confucian education before studying in France, along with Zhou Enlai, in the early 1920s. Raised in a landlord family, Deng

(Xixian) toiled as a factory worker in France before joining the Chinese Communist Party in 1924. Following the time he spent in Moscow at the Communist University for Toilers of the East and Sun Yat-sen University, Deng returned to China in 1926; he became a party organizer in southwestern China. Deng also guided several largely unsuccessful military assaults against Kuomintang forces and warlords in Guangxi Province. In 1931, he linked up with Mao Zedong in Jianxi, an area in southeastern China the communists dominated. Having joined the Long March, Deng was named a political commissar in the Chinese army during the Sino-Japanese War. In 1945, he became a member of the CCP Central Committee. Deng was a significant figure during the Chinese civil war, as his participation in the Huai-Hai campaign exemplified.

After the establishment of the People's Republic of China in 1949, Deng was selected as the first secretary of the CCP's southwest bureau. By 1954, he was serving as the

Fig. 8-3   Deng Xiaoping, in the midst of a parade celebrating Chinese Communist Party leaders. (Pearson Education, Corporate Digital Archive, Getty Images Inc.)

party's secretary-general, while occupying a seat on the Politburo, a position he held for the next dozen years. In 1957, Deng, during the midst of Mao's Hundred Flowers Campaign, supported the repression of intellectuals. However, along with Liu Shaoqi and Zhou Enlai, Deng attempted to usher in more moderate policies following the disastrous Great Leap Forward. That resulted in Deng's vilification during the Cultural Revolution, when he was compelled to relinquish all his government posts, experienced house arrest and was denounced as a "capitalist roader." Thanks to Zhou Enlai, Deng was rehabilitated by 1973 and chosen as vice premier of the State Council. In the midst of Zhou's illness, Deng became a still more important figure and emerged as vice chairman in 1975. The death of Zhou led to Deng's ouster by the Gang of Four, who drove him into exile in Guandong Province.

After the arrest of the Maoist purists, Deng became an even more powerful party leader than before. Although readmitted to the Politburo thanks to Premier Hua Guofeng, Deng helped to remove Hua from office in 1980, replacing him with Zhao Ziyang. Deng now stood as the preeminent CCP leader and called for a more pragmatic approach to governance that would replace the ideologically charged nature of Mao's rule. Downplaying Mao's edicts, Deng highlighted the need for modernization, calling for economic growth and individual enterprise. He championed "Four Modernizations," involving agriculture, industry, technology and the military. Deng also carved out closer relationships with both Japan and Western states. At the same time, he sought to reestablish Chinese hegemony over both British Hong Kong and Portugese Macau.

In a letter to Prime Minister Margaret Thatcher, Deng attempted to lessen concerns about the impending fate of Hong Kong, scheduled to return to China after over a century-and-a-half of British rule. "The concept of 'one country, two systems'," Deng declared, was applicable to socialism as well as to capitalism.

> There are one billion people on the mainland, approximately 20 million on Taiwan and 5.5 million in Hong Kong. A problem arises of how to handle relations between such widely divergent numbers. Since one billion people, the overwhelming majority, live under socialism in a vast area, we can afford to allow capitalism in these small, limited areas at our side. If this were not the case, capitalism might swallow up socialism.

Holding the positions of chairman of both the Central Military Commission and the party's Central Advisory Commission, Deng supported the CCP's continued monopoly of political power. He supported the rewriting of the history of the CCP, lauding Mao but condemning him for both the Great Leap Forward and the Cultural Revolution. Deng helped to rehabilitate a number of Chinese luminaries who had been denounced, as he had, during the Cultural Revolution. In the mid-80s, he compelled a number of old guard leaders to retire, replacing them with younger, more professional figures who supported his programs.

The economic revitalization of China ushered in social and political ferment that proved less pleasing to both Deng and the CCP. At the end of the 1970s, a pro-democracy movement briefly unfolded; a decade later, student activists and workers, disturbed by government corruption and inflation, began conducting mass demonstrations in Tiananmen Square. Although party leaders were divided about how to respond to the growing unrest, Deng determined to quash it. The result was the Tiananmen Square massacre of June 4, 1989, as troops fired on demonstrators, killing hundreds at a minimum. Thousands more were arrested, while many dissidents were forced into exile. Deng had opted for this course, fearing the loss of political power for the CCP. A purge was conducted within government ranks, resulting in the dismissal of general secretary Zhao Ziyang, who was considered sympathetic to the protestors.

As these events unfolded in the very period when communist hegemony in the Soviet bloc was unraveling, the Chinese communist leaders chose to maintain a two-fold path of economic liberalization and continued political strangulation. Deng soon departed from his government posts, while retaining control of the party apparatus and the military. He continued to propound the need for economic liberalization, while professing steadfast belief in socialism:

> The fundamental difference between socialism and capitalism does not lie in the question whether the planning mechanism or the market mechanism plays a larger role. (The) planned economy does not equal socialism, because planning also exists in capitalism; neither does (the) market economy equal capitalism, because the market also exists in socialism. Both planning and market are just economic means. The nature of socialism is to emancipate and develop the productive forces, to eliminate exploitation and polarization, and finally to achieve the goal of common affluence.

◆ —— ◆ —— ◆ —— ◆ —— ◆ —— ◆ —— ◆ —— ◆ —— ◆ —— ◆

Suggested Readings

AKBAR, M. J. *Nehru: The Making of India.* (1988).

ALLINSON, GARY D. *The Columbia Guide to Modern Japanese History.* (1999).

BAUM, RICHARD. *Burying Mao: Chinese Politics in the Age of Deng Xiaoping.* (1994).

BECKER, JASPER. *Hungry Ghosts: Mao's Secret Famine.* (1996).

BOUTON, MARSHALL and PHILIP OLDENBURG. *India Briefing: A Transformative Fifty Years.* (1999).

BRASS, PAUL B. *The Politics of India since Independence.* (1994).

BROWN, JUDITH M. *Gandhi: Prisoner of Hope.* (1989).

CRUMP, THOMAS. *The Death of an Emperor: Japan at the Crossroads.* (1991).

DOWER, JOHN. *Embracing Death: Japan in the Wake of World War II.* (1999).

EVANS, RICHARD. *Deng Xiaoping and the Making of Modern China.* (1993).

FAIRBANKS, JOHN K., EDWIN O. REISCHAUER, and ALBERT M. CRAIG. *East Asia: Tradition and Transformation.* (1989).

FRENCH, PATRICK. *Liberty or Death: India's Journey to Independence and Division.* (1997).

GUPTA, PRANAY. *Mother India: A Political Biography of Indira Gandhi.* (1992).

HENSHALL, KENNETH G. *A History of Japan: From Stone Age to Superpower.* (1999).

KARNOW, STANLEY. *Mao and China: Inside China's Cultural Revolution.* (1985).

KEAY, JOHN. *India: A History.* (2000).

MEYER, MILTON W. *China: A Concise History.* (1994).

NOMAN, OMAR. *Pakistan: Political and Economic History since 1947.* (1988).

PEREZ, LOUIS G. *The History of Japan.* (1998).

PHILLIPS, RICHARD T. *China since 1911.* (1996).

ROBERTS, J. A. G. *A Concise History of China.* (1999).

SALISBURY, HARRISON E. *The New Emperors: China in the Era of Mao and Deng.* (1992).

SCHALLER, MICHAEL. *The American Occupation of Japan: The Origins of the Cold War in Asia.* (1986).

SHIRER, WILLIAM L. *Gandhi: A Memoir.* (1979).

SIMMIE, SCOTT and BOB NIXON. *Tiananmen Square.* (1989).

SMITH, DENNIS B. *Japan since 1945: The Rise of an Economic Superpower.* (1995).

SPENCE, JONATHAN. *The Search for Modern China.* (1990).

TABB, WILLIAM K. *The Postwar Japanese System: Cultural Economy and Economic Transformation.* (1995).

THOMAS, J. E. *Modern Japan: A Social History since 1868.* (1996).

THURSTON, ANN. *The Ordeal of the Intellectuals in China's Great Cultural Revolution.* (1988).

WARSAW, STEVEN. *Japan Emerges: A Concise History of Japan from Its Origins to the Present.* (1988).

WOLPERT, STANLEY. *A New History of India.* (1993).

CHAPTER 9

From the Ashes of Empire: Post-Colonial Indochina, 1945–1989

On September 2, 1945, with American officials present and U.S. planes flying overhead, Ho Chi Minh, speaking from an elevated podium in downtown Hanoi, proclaimed the establishment of the Democratic Republic of Vietnam. In an effort to attain American support, Ho deliberately drew on the "immortal" words penned by Thomas Jefferson in crafting the Declaration of Independence, "All men are created equal . . . they are endowed by their Creator with certain unalienable rights." Ho also hearkened back to the French Revolution, proclaiming "Freedom, equality and fraternity," while indicating that French imperialists had violated such a lofty vision. All political rights had been denied the people of Indochina, who had been saddled with "inhuman laws." The French, Ho asserted, had acted "counter to the ideals of humanity and justice," and "built more prisons than schools. They have callously ill-treated our fellow-compatriots. They have drowned our revolutions in blood." Ho maintained that the French forced alcohol and opium on the people of Vietnam in an effort to weaken their race. The French were no better masters economically, as Ho accused them of having "shamelessly exploited our people, driven them into the worst misery and mercilessly plundered our country. . . ." The French "have ruthlessly appropriated our rice fields, mines, forests, and raw materials. . . . They have imposed hundreds of unjustifiable taxes, and reduced our countrymen, especially the peasants and petty tradesmen, to extreme

326

poverty." The French, according to Ho, had quashed native economic endeavors and exploited native laborers "in the most barbarous manner."

Ho proclaimed that the Vietnamese people stood "determined to fight to the death against all attempts at aggression by the French imperialists." His countrymen believed that the Allies—the capitalist, democratic United States; parliamentary, imperialist Great Britain; and the communist Soviet Union—could not fail but recognize Vietnamese independence. Ho insisted that a people who had contested French dominion for eight decades and fought against fascists possessed the right to be free and "must be independent."

Ho Chi Minh—born Nguyen Sing Cung in French Indochina in 1890, but called Nguyen Tat Thanh by the age of 10—appeared frail physically but possessed an inner strength capable of overcoming a lengthy period of exile outside his home country of Vietnam, imprisonment, a death sentence, malaria, and a pair of extended wars with

Fig. 9-1   North Vietnamese President Ho Chi Minh and members of the Political Bureau of the Vietnamese Workers Party. (Pearson Education, Corporate Digital Archive, Black Star)

two major Western powers. A combination of passion and ingenuity long characterized the thin, ascetic-looking individual, who was raised in the village of Kim-lien in Annam, the son of a minor imperial official who was strongly opposed to French colonialism. As a youth, Ho carried messages back and forth between rebel forces. Ho's father eventually lost his government post because of his criticism of French policies. Though formally educated at a French-Annamite institution in Hue, Ho was also dismissed because of his own anti-colonial activities. After briefly serving as a teacher, Ho also participated in tax revolts before determining to head overseas. In 1911, he left for Marseilles, covering his passage as a kitchen boy aboard a French ocean linger. At this point, a French police file was already being kept on the Vietnamese nationalist. For a time, Ho served as a apprentice to Auguste Escoffer, the celebrated chef at the Carlton Hotel in London. Moving to Paris, Ho dabbled in photography and was influenced by the left-wing ideas coursing through the continent shortly after the Bolshevik Revolution. He adopted the name Nguyen Al Quoc, Nguyen the Patriot. During the Versailles Peace Conference in 1919, Ho unsuccessfully presented a manifesto documenting French abuses and championing Vietnamese self-determination to President Woodrow Wilson of the United States.

Having joined the Socialist Party, Ho, like many political activists of the era, was soon drawn to a new political organization, the French Communist Party, which he helped to found in 1920. "Patriotism . . . not communism . . . inspired me," he subsequently reported. In 1923, Ho attended Moscow's East University. The following year, now serving as a translator for Soviet diplomats, Ho went to Canton in southern China where he helped a number of other Vietnamese nationalists to establish a revolutionary movement. Working for the Comintern, Ho traveled incognito throughout Asia, adopting various aliases ranging from a businessman to a journalist to a Buddhist monk; he appeared in Burma and India at various points. In 1927, as Chiang Kai-shek's troops and those of the Chinese communists bloodied one another, Ho left for Moscow.

Ho was soon back in the Far East; operating out of Hong Kong, he helped to establish the Indochinese Communist Party (ICP). Rumors of his death repeatedly surfaced, while French authorities placed a death sentence on his head. In February 1930, Ho drafted a manifesto for fellow Vietnamese communists who were gathered in the British colony. Referring to their organization, he proclaimed, "It will help the proletarian class lead the revolution in order to struggle for all the oppressed and exploited people." Ho maintained that the ICP would help overthrow French imperialism and the reactionary Vietnamese capitalist class while making Indochina completely independent and establishing a worker-peasant and soldier government. It would "confiscate all of the plantations and property belonging to the imperialists and the Vietnamese reactionary capitalist class and distribute them to poor peasants," he claimed. The ICP sought to usher in an eight-hour work day, discard unjust taxes that burdened the indigent, bring about freedom to the masses, support universal education and ensure equality between man and woman.

Still serving as a Comintern agent, Ho worked to set up communist parties throughout the region. In June 1931, British officials, seeking to rein in political revolutionaries, arrested Ho in Hong Kong. He escaped from prison the following year and headed back to the Soviet Union, where he remained for the next few years, wrestling with tuberculosis. During that period, Joseph Stalin conducted bloody purges of party members and many others, but Ho escaped the fate of numerous nationalist communists despite his somewhat unorthodox Marxist views. Like Mao Zedong in China, Ho considered the peasantry, not the industrial proletariat, to be the dominant revolutionary force in Asia. For Ho, national liberation appeared at least equally important to social revolution, although he remained a dedicated believer in communist ideology. In 1938, Ho returned once again to China to serve as an adviser to the communist army, then in the midst of the Sino-Japanese War.

In 1940, Japanese troops moved into Indochina, where they linked up with Vichy French forces. Many Indochinese viewed the Japanese as liberators, but Ho Chi Minh did not. Indeed, he allied with Chiang Kai-shek's Nationalists in an effort to expel the Japanese. In 1941, Ho reunited with Indochinese Communist Party leaders and joined with Vo Nguyen Giap, a former history teacher, in southern China to create the League for the Independence of Vietnam, comprised of nationalists and communists. The members of this organization were called the Vietminh. Late that year, Ho returned to his homeland for the first time in three decades to lead the nationalist revolt against the now Japanese-guided French occupation. Operating out of a rural base in northern Vietnam, the long-time exile first became known as Ho Chi Minh, the Bearer of Light. During the war, Ho's fighters partnered with agents of the U.S. intelligence apparatus, the Office of Strategic Services; the Vietminh provided the Americans with information about downed pilots and enemy troop movements in return for war matériel and an apparent stamp of approval. At one point, Ho again warded off death, thanks to aid from an OSS medic.

After helping to engineer the Japanese surrender in Indochina in August 1945, the Vietminh moved to take control of their nation-state. The following month, however, French soldiers, who had been sent back to southern Vietnam, drove the Vietminh and other nationalists forces out of Saigon. Compelled to move into the countryside, Giap's military units soon battled regular French soldiers and Legionnaires who had been ordered to reassert France's colonial hegemony. Following the collapse of negotiations, the French-Indochina War began in December 1946. A battle of over seven years' duration ensued, with Vietminh guerrillas fighting in jungles, rice paddies and mountainous areas, culminating with the capture of over 10,000 French forces at Dien Bien Phu by May 1954. Ho, Giap, and the Vietminh had prevailed, notwithstanding ever-increasing U.S. assistance that included the establishment of a major military mission, $2.6 billion in aid, and, by war's end, American funding of 80 percent of the French effort. The Geneva Accords of 1954 acknowledged the defeat of the French.

Ho's death in 1969 denied him the opportunity to experience what he had long envisioned: the reunification of Vietnam. Yet he, more than any other individual, had helped to bring that about, in the process defeating the greatest military to be found, the armed forces of the United States.

❖ —— ❖ —— ❖ —— ❖ —— ❖

Out of Empires

Like the earlier successful conclusion of the Russo-Japanese War, the Japanese victories during the initial stages of World War II helped to destroy the aura of European invincibility and thus to weaken colonial rule throughout Asia. In the period ahead, nationalist movements unfolded in countries as diverse as India and Vietnam. Different means were used to expel white-skinned rulers, ranging from the pacifism of Mahatma Gandhi to the nationalistic-driven communism of Ho Chi Minh. The imperial powers responded differently, too, with the Americans granting the Philippines independence in 1946, and the British doing the same to India the next year and to Burma in 1948, while the French fought a bloody and protracted war to hold onto Vietnam, the crown jewel of their Southeast Asian empire. The Netherlands, in turn, relinquished the territory its officials referred to as the Dutch East Indies—Indonesia—after another brutal conflict. Rebellion also unfolded in British-controlled Malaysia, eventually resulting in the granting of independence. Hong Kong, by contrast, long remained a part of the dwindling British Empire. Thailand, the former Siam, was the lone Southeast Asian state to avoid the yoke of European colonialism.

The granting of independence to the Philippines didn't prevent the outbreak of guerrilla warfare there as communist forces, the Huks, demanded land reform from the American-sponsored government. With the aid of British and American counterinsur-

gency experts the uprising was quelled by 1954. The selection of a charismatic figure, Raymond Magsaysay, to head the Philippine state helped greatly. The later choice of Ferdinand Marcos to preside over the Philippines proved far unhappier; at various points during his two-decade reign (1965–1986), democratic governance and civil liberties were discarded. The government-sponsored assassination of Marcos' chief foe, Senator Beningo Aquino Jr., and fraudulent election results that had Marcos defeat Corazon "Cory" Aquino, Beningo's widow, produced an uprising and ultimately led to a restoration of Philippine democracy. Unrest remained, however, fed by economic difficulties, the continued U.S. military presence and government corruption.

Military rule often proved the norm in Thailand, with Marshal Sarit Thanarat and Marshal Thanom Kittikachorn maintaining martial law from the mid-fifties into the early seventies. A citizen uprising in 1973, spurred on by charges of corruption and mismanagement, compelled King Phumiphol Adunyadej to name the lone civilian government since the early postwar era. Democratic governance was short-lived and marked by a period of economic troubles, with the military taking power again in 1976. Fears of the new communist states in Laos, Cambodia and Vietnam also played into the hands of those who claimed that authoritarian rule was necessary. For another dozen years, the military remained dominant, although beginning in 1980, General Prem Tinsulanond in his role as prime minister began supporting more representative government. In 1988, Prem allowed Chatichai Choonhavan to become head of state after the Thai people demonstrated such a preference in a parliamentary election. Although Chatichai proved a popular leader, Thai politics remained beset by both personal intrigue and factionalism. By 1990, the seventy-year-old Chatichai was expressing doubts that he could rule much longer and the military carried out a coup the following February.

Political intrigue and military coups also afflicted other Southeast Asian countries during the postwar period. In Burma, independence was followed by a decade-long period referred to as the "Time of Troubles." Ethnic groups demanded autonomous states and a civil war threatened. By 1958, the Burmese government of U Nu was in such disarray that General Ne Win was handed the reins of power. Although U Nu was returned to the presidency by Burmese voters in 1960, the dissatisfied military carried out a nonviolent coup within two years. Once again, Ne Win was in control and he now called for the carving out of the "Burmese Way to Socialism," which featured the nationalization of many industries. Relying on his newly formed Burmese Socialist Program Party, Ne Win restricted personal liberties and condemned westernization. In 1974, Burma was renamed the Socialist Republic of the Union of Burma. Ne Win remained the Burma strongman until 1988, but that year witnessed the unfolding of massive demonstrations, which followed on the heels of the demonetization of most Burmese currency. Troops under General Saw Maung thwarted the uprising and returned the military to power. In 1989, the country took on the name of Myanmar. A leading spokesperson for democracy and human rights, Aung San Suu Kyi, was placed under house arrest; she would later be awarded the Nobel Prize for Peace. In May 1990, Myanmar undertook the first multiparty elections in three decades, producing a victory by the leading opposition party; the military refused to accept the results.

Developments were, if anything, still more eventful in Indonesia and Malaysia. The leader of the Indonesian independence movement, Sukarno, became the first president of the new republic that was proclaimed on August 17, 1950. While parliamentary democracy prevailed in the first several years of Sukarno's rule, a transition to so-called "guided democracy" began in 1957. Sukarno emphasized consensus, rather than Western-style democratic practices. Eventually, Sukarno banned several political organizations, curbed parliamentary powers and restricted personal freedoms; in 1963, Sukarno became president for life. Corruption flourished, while inflation and unemployment soared, producing great discontent. In 1965, the government quashed a coup blamed on the communists, who were growing in strength. Over 300,000 supposed communists—most Sino-Indonesians—were murdered as the military asserted control. Increasingly, General Suharto assumed power, with Sukarno placed under house arrest. Suharto, who ruled in an authoritarian manner for the next three decades, declared a New Order for Indonesia.

Malaya gained its independence in 1957, after the defeat of communist guerrillas. A British-spearheaded "Bargain" led to an agreement that various constitutional privileges would be afforded Malays. Six years later, the Federation of Malaysia was formed, comprised of Singapore, Borneo and Northwest Borneo. In 1965, however, Prime Minister Tunku Abdul Rahman expelled Singapore from the federation, because of ethnic tensions involving the majority Chinese in Singapore and Malays. As riots broke out in Malaysia in 1969, the government dissolved Parliament and restricted civil liberties. By 1972, parliamentary democracy had been restored. In the 1980s, led by Prime Minister Datuk Seri Mahathir bin Mohamad, Malaysia sought to replicate the economic successes of Japan, South Korea and Taiwan. When challenges to his rule unfolded late in the decade, Mahathir relied on the Internal Securities Act to silence his political opponents. The booming economy enabled Mahathir and his National Front to easily prevail in national elections in 1990.

Singapore gained its independence in 1959, although it remained an autonomous state within the British Commonwealth. In 1963, it become part of the Federation of Malaysia; two years later, Singapore had to go it alone. Throughout this period and indeed for over three decades, beginning in 1957, Lee Kuan Yew guided Singapore as a one-party state. To safeguard its sovereignty, Singapore undertook a program of economic development. By the 1990s, Singapore, despite a few off-years, had experienced considerable economic growth, becoming the region's banking center. Another of the "little tigers" of South Asia, Hong Kong, also thrived economically.

Vietnam at War and Neighboring States

Perhaps the most complicated scenarios were in post-World War II Southeast Asia. French rule of Indochina began in the mid-19th century. In 1862, the Vietnamese emperor ceded the southern section of his country, Cochin-China, to France. Just over two decades later, France took over the provinces of Annam and Tonkin. In 1887, Vietnam and Cambodia merged, creating the Indochinese Union, with Laos added half a dozen years afterward. French sovereignty, as crafted by Governor-General Paul Doumer, proved extremely brutal. While the French constructed various schools, hospitals and roads, their subjugation of Indochinese labor was markedly exploitative and often strikingly shortsighted. The building of the Trans-Indochinese Railroad, for example, relied on near slave labor, which was conscripted, and resulted in thousands of casualties due to overwork and malaria; moreover, the railroad duplicated earlier pathways laid by the Vietnamese, who often refused to use it. Confiscatory taxation policies, which included the taking of foodstuffs, led to sharp reductions in rice production and corresponding dietary deficiences that, in the early 1940s, culminated in a catastrophic famine. Some Vietnamese, of course, benefited from French colonialism, further compromising a collaborationist class that was deeply resented; a sizable portion of that group, in turn, became addicted to the opium in which the Westerners readily trafficked. The emperor himself generally bowed to French dominion; the boy-sovereign who refused to do so, Ham Nghi, suffered exile and imprisonment.

Deeply distressed by the takeover of their country, bands of Vietnamese nationalists battled against French rule. The French responded to their efforts with heavy-handed repression designed to forewarn other Vietnamese against following the lead of the rebels. The colonizers meted out lengthy prison sentences, exiled various political prisoners onto offshore islands and beheaded others. The French government was determined to maintain the colony that enabled French colonialists to live lavish lifestyles featuring palatial estates, luxurious restaurants and opera houses and an overwhelming sense of racial superiority. Those very realities, coupled with the conditions besetting so many Vietnamese, led the likes of Pham Boi Chau and Pham Chu Trinh to contest French authority. By the 1920s, a new group of anti-colonial nationalists could be found throughout the region. They included social revolutionaries who were drawn to Marxist ideas and looked to communism as a means of transforming their society. By the end of World War II, the Vietnamese Communist Party and the Vietminh fighters considered themselves destined to rule over their country.

However, the French quickly displayed a determination to reestablish control over Indochina. As General Jean Lelerc asserted in late September 1945, "I did not come back to Indochina to give it back to the Indochinese." Over the course of the ensuing fourteen months, Ho Chi Minh's Democratic Republic of Vietnam had to contend with the presence of 200,000 Chinese troops in the north, while striving to avoid war with France. The Chinese soldiers eventually departed but the French proceeded to attack Haiphong. There, on November 23, 1946, bombardment by the French warship *Suffren* killed over 6,000 civilians. The following month, the French also targeted Hanoi, at the time still under the control of Ho's forces. Ho and the other DRV leaders, along with 40,000 troops, headed for the countryside of Tongking.

During the initial stages of the First Indochina War, the communists, who had dissolved their party, emphasized Vietnamese nationalism. General Vo Nguyen Giap led the Vietminh, who relied on guerrilla tactics to confront the French. At the same time, the Vietminh established provisional authority over both the territory they moved into and the land that was under French dominion.

The Vietminh were strongest in the northern sector of the country, where most of the fighting took place. There, major battles eventually occurred, while in the south guerrilla warfare continued to be relied on. The readiness of the Vietminh to wage a protracted war worked against the interests of the French, who had to contend with mounting domestic opposition. The French strove to pacify occupied territory and to conduct "mopping-up operations" in the countryside, particularly in southern Vietnam. The Vietminh, however, increasingly controlled the pace of military operations. French stations suffered constant attack, while the Vietminh struck at the major Vietnamese cities.

Concerns about Ho Chi Minh and the French position in Vietnam led the U.S. State Department to push for the establishment of a puppet government that featured Bao Dai, who had resigned from his throne in 1945. On May 20, 1949, Secretary of State Dean Acheson fired off a telegram to the American consulate in Hanoi, underscoring "Ho's known background." As Acheson noted, Ho could only be viewed as an "outright Commie so long as 1) he fails unequivocally repudiate Moscow connection and Commie doctrine and 2) remains personally singled out for praise by internatl Commie press and receives its press." In Acheson's estimation, the question of whether Ho was a Vietnamese nationalist was "irrelevant." "All Stalinists in colonial areas are nationalists," he claimed. "With achievement natl aims (i.e., independence) their objective necessarily becomes subordination state to Commie purposes and ruthless extermination not only opposition groups but all elements suspected even slightest deviation."

In mid-1949, the United States backed Bao Dai's "new unified States of Vietnam," which purportedly would result in Vietnam taking its rightful place in the family of nations. The United States government applauded Bao Dai for seeking to link "all truly nationalistic elements" that would further "the legitimate aspirations of the Vietnamese people." The following February, France agreed to support Bao Dai's government. But the former emperor's rule proved to be in name only. The ferocity of the war actually heightened, with over 10,000 colonial forces killed and a great amount of territory lost to the Vietminh from 1949 through 1950. In the fall of 1950, the Vietminh attacked French garrisons along the Chinese borders. The great French journalist-historian Bernard Fall reported: "When the smoke cleared, the French had suffered their greatest colonial defeat since Montcalm had died at Quebec. They had lost 6,000 troops, 13 artillery pieces and 125 mortars, 450 trucks and three armored platoons, 940 machine guns and more than 8,000 rifles." The discarded materials could outfit an entire Vietminh division. The French debacle led to the declaration of martial law in Hanoi. French political parties were sorely divided about how to respond, as some urged a pullout while others called for additional troops and greater U.S. involvement.

General Jean de Lattre de Tassigny assumed command of French forces in December 1950. He emboldened French soldiers by insisting that "a decisive victory" would be carved out within fifteen months. De Lattre determined to "yellow" the war by having more Vietnamese engage in the fighting, as expanded pacification campaigns involving "sweep-and-clean" operations were carried out. With increased American assistance, French air raids intensified, with some designed to create famine conditions. A U.S. State Department memo in October 1951 attempted to justified the greater level of American support for the French war effort.

On the one hand, it acknowledged the long-standing force of Indochinese nationalism. At the same time, the document dismissed Ho as a Moscow-trained Communist, but admitted that some of his advisers had been battling French colonialism for three decades. Nevertheless, the U.S. governmental paper concluded, "It is important to the security of the United States that Indochina remain among the free nations of the world." The fall of the six Indochinese countries, it was declared, "would complete Communist domination of Asia east of India."

However, de Lattre's promises of a quick victory ended as civilian casualties mounted. His replacement, General Raoul Salan, promised a "total war" that would crush the Vietminh. He too, however, suffered defeat at the hands of Giap's army, which was buttressed by considerable aid flowing forth from the communist powers. With more territory controlled by the Vietminh, General Henri Navarre took over for Salan in May 1953. The "Navarre Plan" relied on quickly subduing the Vietminh but proved unsuccessful. In the spring of 1954, the French station at Dien Bien Phu threatened to fall to Giap's fighters. The Eisenhower administration briefly considered the use of nuclear weapons and the landing of troops to ward off a seemingly inevitable French defeat, but proved unwilling to undertake those steps without support from its European allies. On May 7, 1954, the French commander surrendered his fort and more than 16,000 soldiers. On July 20, the Geneva Accords temporarily divided the country at the 17th parallel, with Ho's forces in control of the north and the French soldiers allowed to remain in the south. Reunification elections were planned within the next two years. The accords assured the termination of French colonialism in the Far East.

Left to be determined was the fate of the nation-states that had previously been under French dominion. Those countries included Cambodia and Laos, which had experienced liberation movements of their own. From 1941 to 1945, Japanese and Thai forces occupied Cambodia. Goaded by the Japanese in an effort to weaken recently liberated France, Norodom Sihanouk, earlier named king by the Vichy French, asserted Cambodia's independence on March 11, 1945. Within a month, Laotian King Sisavang Vong did the same for his country. With the Japanese takeover, Paris-educated Son Ngoc Thanh, who had been born in Vietnam, headed the Khmer Issarak or Free Khmer movement that contained some 2,000 fighters, and joined the Vietminh in opposing French rule. General Leclerc, who had briefly served as foreign minister and premier, arrested Son and placed him under house arrest. Son escaped to Thailand, where he headed a government-in-exile and strengthened the Free Khmer movement.

To the chagrin of many Cambodian nationalists, France in January 1946 incorporated Cambodia into the French Union as an autonomous state. Elections were held for a Constitutional Convention in 1946 and a National Assembly in 1948; both were won by the Democratic Party, associated with anti-French and anti-Sihanouk nationalists who were tied to Son and more radical organizations. In late 1949, Cambodia secured still greater internal autonomy, while France controlled diplomatic relations, staffed the police and ran the military and the courts. In early 1950, a Unified Issarak Front was established, while in mid-1951, a Khmer Revolutionary Party (KPRP) was set up; both moved to take control of large portions of the countryside. In October 1951, Son came back to Cambodia, still determined to fight French

control. Attempts at repression, spearheaded by Sihanouk, proved unpopular, as did his dissolving of the National Assembly and proclamation of a national emergency that restricted political freedom. Then in 1953, the king began seeking international support for Cambodia's independence. Later that year, France agreed to his wishes, as confirmed in the Geneva Accords. Required to lay down their arms, some 5,000 KPRP forces or "Hanoi Khmers," led by Son Ngoc Minh, headed into North Vietnam.

In Laos, when the Japanese supplanted the French in March 1945, Prime Minister and Prince Savang Vatthana, who sought to maintain formal ties to France, had declined to assert his nation's independence. Following the defeat of Japan, Chinese and British forces occupied Laos. Another member of the royal family, Prince Phetsarath, was named as the new head-of-state but was removed from power at year's end. King Sisavang Vong fired Phetsarath and announced that Laos remained a French protectorate. At that point, the Lao Issarak or Free Lao movement emerged, calling for the establishment of a provisional government, headed by the half-brother princes Souvanna Phouma and Souphannouvong; a provisional assembly demanded the king's ouster and an end to French colonialism. French troops returned in early 1946; they defeated Souphanouvong and a group of Vietnamese soldiers at Thakhek in late March. The Lao Issarak leaders moved into Thailand, where they established a government-in-exile that Phetsarath headed, while the French restored the king to his throne. Divisions among Laotian nationalists led to Souphanouvong's resignation from the Lao Issarak; the Vietminh backed another resistance campaign.

In 1949, France allowed Laos, like the other Indochinese states, a degree of autonomy. It disbanded the Lao Issarak, whose top figures, other than Prince Phetsarath, returned to Laos. The Vietminh picked up the pace of their operations in Laos, supporting Laotian communists in the north and northeast. Once again, Laotian nationalists splintered, with Souphannouvong, referred to as the Red Prince, heading into northeastern Laos, where he established communications with the Vietminh. During the summer of 1950, Souphannouvong, speaking from Hanoi, declared that a band of Laotian guerrillas, the Pathet Lao (Lao Country), had been formed. He also set up a resistance government, which included a series of leading Laotian communists. The following year, Souvanna Phouma took over the reins of power in Laos; Souvanna struggled to ensure Laotian self-rule free from foreign domination. Two years later, the Laotian Communist Party was established; General Giap's cadre tutored the Laotian communists or Khmer Rouge, who grabbed control of both Phong Saly and Sam Neua, provinces in the northeast. The Vietminh temporarily held Thakhek, a central Meking town. Laos's formal independence was granted through the 1954 Geneva Accords. Those agreements called for the merger of Royalist and Pathet Lao forces and the sharing of cabinet ministries.

A Divided Vietnam and Guerrilla Insurgency

With pressure brought to bear by Western and communist powers alike during the negotiations leading to the Geneva accords, Ho and the Communist Party leadership based in Hanoi agreed to a temporary partition at the 17th parallel. Reunification elections within two years were called for, which Ho

appeared certain to win as even President Dwight David Eisenhower readily acknowledged in his memoirs. Those elections were never held. Instead, the United States proceeded to construct the Republic of Vietnam. Its head was another Vietnamese exile and nationalist, Ngo Dinh Diem, who acted to construct a neo-Confucian dictatorship that sought to annihilate the stay-behinds, the Vietminh fighters who had been urged by Ho to put down their weapons. An election held in late October 1955 resulted in Diem garnering over 600,000 votes, although a mere 400,000 were eligible to cast ballots. Diem subsequently proclaimed the establishment of the Republic of South Vietnam, to be headed by its newly "elected" president who reputedly polled over 98 percent of the votes that had supposedly been cast. In late April 1956, the last French troops departed from Vietnam. The Diem regime proceeded to alienate the peasantry by taking back land that had been distributed by the Vietminh and returning it to landlords. Little helping matters were the blatant favoritism afforded the Catholic minority by Diem, an ardent Catholic himself, and the nepotism that characterized his regime.

Communist rule in the north proved troubled in its own fashion but benefited from its identification with Ho Chi Minh, a far more esteemed nationalist than his counterpart in the south. While some 100,000 Vietminh cadre and their families headed north after the Geneva Accords were announced, approximately one million Vietnamese, many Catholic, moved south; several of those who did so had responded to CIA leaflets warning of an impending bloodbath. In the north, the heavily populated Red River Delta region stymied the promised land redistribution. With trade embargoes in place, famine loomed likely. The expansion of infrastructure through forced labor heightened discontent. The resumption of a land reform effort in 1956, which resulted in tens of thousands of casualties as old scores were settled, only exacerbated that unhappiness. Despite its many troubles, however, the North Vietnamese regime retained considerable support, because of the respect accorded Ho and his communist compatriots.

In South Vietnam, the level of repression greatly intensified, eventually resulting in the unfolding of a new guerrilla campaign. Thousands were imprisoned, sent off to "re-education camps" or executed. By 1957, on the verge of being obliterated altogether, the Vietminh remnants in the south, along with other nationalists distressed by the repressive ways of Diem and his brother Ngo Dinh Nhu, who headed a vast array of police and para-military units, began fighting back. Shortly thereafter, Ho and other leading Vietnamese communists began supporting their campaign. Diem derisively referred to the latest guerrillas in the south as the Viet Cong, intended to besmirch them as communists, but their numbers mounted. This occurred despite the increasing number of U.S. military "advisers," who totaled more than 800 by the end of the Eisenhower administration. Despite such backing for Diem and notwithstanding the praise he received in the American press and from U.S. political leaders, the insurgency threatened to topple the American client-state. While largely indigenous in nature, the guerrilla movement increasingly received backing and guidance from communist leaders in the north, including Ho Chi Minh, who would soon battle another western power in his determination to ensure national autonomy.

The level of repression in the south only mounted, as exemplified by the promulgation of Law 10/59 in May 1959. Under that measure, military tribunals ordered capital sentences, generally by guillotine. Those were to occur within days of charges being brought involving the commission or attempted commission of "crimes of sabotage, or of infringing upon the security of the State" or of belonging "to an organization designed to help or perpetuate (such) crimes." Also receiving the death penalty was anyone "who intentionally proclaims or spreads by any means unauthorized news about prices, or rumors contrary to truths, or distorts the truth concerning the present or future situation of markets in the country or abroad, susceptible of provoking economic or financial perturbations in the country." Similarly, those who opposed the government's land or tax policies could receive death sentences.

Perhaps in response to the passage of Law 10/59, the central committee of the Communist Party in May 1959 called for reunifying Vietnam through all appropriate means. As guerrilla warfare heightened, the rebels established the National Liberation Front (NLF) in December 1960. The following year, they proclaimed a Provisional Revolutionary Government, comprised of communist and non-communist nationalists.

Cambodia, under Norodom Sihanouk, appeared more stable through the end of the 1950s. In March 1955, Sihanouk abdicated his throne but named his father as king and established the Sangkum Ryaster Niym or Popular Socialist Community, comprised of right-of-center parties. The now Prince Sihanouk and the Sangkum dominated Cambodian political life, holding a monopoly in the National Assembly. As leading leftists headed underground, Sihanouk enjoyed considerable popularity with peace and prosperity characterizing his nation-state. Sihanouk's determination to carve out a neutralist foreign policy angered U.S. officials.

His domestic policies were no more pleasing to many Cambodian leftists, particularly the communists who had moved underground or headed for Vietnam. Many who had remained in Cambodia suffered repression at Sihanouk's hand but a new band of young activists, many western-educated, appeared. Among these were Ieng Sary, Khieu Samphan, Hou Yuon and Saloth Sar, who had studied in Paris and was later referred to as Pol Pot; all were intensely nationalistic and hence anti-Hanoi. They damned the Vietminh for selling out Cambodia through the Geneva Agreement. By 1960, they helped to reestablish the Cambodian Communist Party, which they took over.

Following the Geneva conference, Laos, in contrast to both Vietnam and Cambodia, appeared both independent and undivided. Pathet Lao forces either disbanded or entered the Laotian National Army, while former guerrillas participated in the political arena. Good relations prevailed between Prime Minister Souvanna Phouma and Souphannouvong, head of the Pathet Lao. In late 1957, the National Union government featured Souvanna Phouma as premier with Souphannouvong joining in the cabinet.

Map 9-1   Southeast Asia

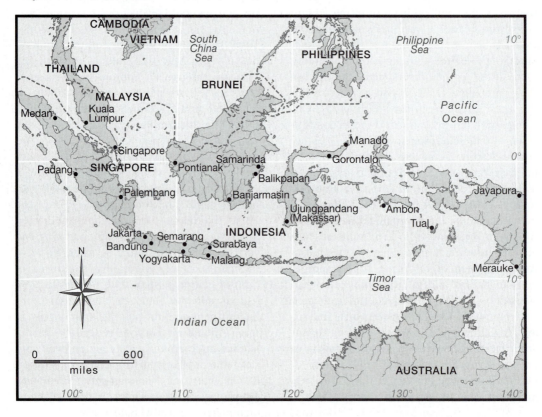

Both seemed determined to maintain Laos's non-aligned neutrality.

The election results in May 1958 proved displeasing to the United States, rightists, and even Souvanna Phouma, however. With CIA backing, a right-wing group, the Committee for the Defense of National Interests, pushed for Souvanna Phouma's resignation and for a government headed by Phoui Sananikone. While Souvanna Phouma became ambassador to France, the Laotian government arrested Pathet Lao deputies, along with Souphannouvong. Another effort was undertaken to incorporate Pathet Lao forces into the national military, but one battalion moved into North Vietnam while another soon deserted. Guerrilla action heightened in Laos. Then on May 24, 1960, Souphannouvong and several other Pathet Lao leaders escaped from prison and joined their compatriots in the field. Captain Kong Le led a coup in early August that sought Souvanna Phouma's return as premier of a neutralist government. Fighting broke out, compelling Souvanna's backers to leave Vientiane and link up with the Pathet Lao. The cut-off of American military aid compelled Souvanna to seek an accommodation with rightists. Denounced as pro-communist, Kong Le journeyed to Xieng Khouang to band with the Pathet Lao.

Heightened U.S. Involvement

Opposition to the Diem regime continued to grow throughout 1961 and 1962, which proved troubling to the new administration in Washington, D.C. In his inaugural address, John F. Kennedy insisted that the United States must support "free" institutions or "the whole world . . . would inevitably begin to move toward the Communist bloc." The American people, he declared, had to stand as the "watchmen on the walls of freedom." During his short-lived tenure, Kennedy magnified U.S. involvement in Vietnam, increasing the number of military advisers from 800 to over 16,000. While initially more concerned about developments in Laos, Kennedy and his advisers believed that the fate of Vietnam would determine that of its fellow Southeast Asian nations; thus, it was considered an integral part of the intensifying Cold War.

The Kennedy administration's relations with Ngo Dinh Diem were difficult throughout. While denounced by his foes as an American puppet, Diem actually proved troublesome to Kennedy because of his own nationalistic bent. American officials sought to induce Diem to reform his regime in return for new aid packages, but the South Vietnamese leaders told Ambassador Frederick Nolting that the Republic of South Vietnam "did not want to be a protectorate." Increasingly, Diem's government relied on the strategic hamlet program employed by the Englishman, Sir Robert Thompson, in dealing with guerrillas in Malaya and the Philippines. With American support, Diem sought to separate the guerrillas from the peasants by placing the latter in encampments. Unlike Diem, American officials also envisioned the carrying out of land reform, the holding of village elections and the providing of educational and medical services to attract support from the peasants.

However, all-too-often, U.S. military planners supported large-scale operations by the Army of South Vietnam (ARVN) forces that the Vietcong frequently were able to avoid. The NLF, for its part, resorted to political indoctrination, the selective use of assassinations and land reform to garner support among South Vietnamese peasants. In the field, matters went no better for the ARVN troops and their American advisers, as evidenced by a startling defeat suffered near the village of Ap Bac on January 2, 1963, although the ARVN outnumbered the Viet Cong 10 to 1. At the same time, the strategic hamlet program was faltering badly. Diem continued to ignore American warnings that political reform was essential, becoming ever-more reliant on his brother Nhu and his beautiful sister-in-law, Madame Nhu, who was referred to as the "Dragon Lady." By the close of 1962, young journalists such as David Halberstam and Neil Sheehan were condemning the corruption, repression and nepotism that characterized Diem's regime; they argued that the war could not be won if the United States continued to back Diem.

Even more disturbing to American policymakers were reports that Nhu was discussing the possibility of a negotiated settlement with both the Viet Cong and the North Vietnamese government. Protests against Diem received widespread news coverage that also bothered the Americans. In early May, Archbishop Ngo Dinh Thuc, another of Diem's brothers, refused to allow Buddhist flags to be displayed in Hue or festivities to be held. As Buddhists contested the orders, tear gas and shots rang out, resulting in nine fatalities. Demonstrating their dismay over the government's actions, a number of monks, including Thich Quang Duc, engaged in public self-immolations. Madame Nhu dismissed such developments as merely involving a "barbecue of bonzes" or Buddhist monks. Ngo Dinh Nhu ordered a raid on Buddhist pagodas.

ARVN generals began plotting Diem's overthrow, the possibility of which already seemed pleasing to the new U.S. Ambassador, Henry Cabot Lodge Jr. On November 1, Diem was ousted and he and his brother Nhu were subsequently murdered. Informed of the killings, President Kennedy exhibited "a look of shock and dismay." Three weeks later, JFK himself was slain while riding in a presidential motorcade in Dallas, Texas.

During Kennedy's administration, developments proved relatively uneventful in Cambodia but not so in Laos. His predecessor, Dwight D. Eisenhower, had forewarned Kennedy that Laos was the stickiest spot in Southeast Asia. Yet for a time, Kennedy's handling of events there seemed to promise the possibility of a peaceful resolution of the ongoing strife. With guerrilla forces having taken control of much of eastern Laos, a second Geneva Conference began in mid-May 1961. An agreement was finally crafted in June 1962, which allowed for the construction of a coalition government involving Souphanouvong, Souvanna Phouma, and the rightist Prince Boun Oum. It also guaranteed Laos's neutrality under an International Control Commission's supervision. All foreign troops had to leave the Southeast Asian state. However, the following year, Souphanouvong departed from the government and fighting involving Pathet Lao and governmental units resumed.

The American War

To the chagrin of U.S. policymakers, the termination of the Diem regime only resulted in greater instability in South Vietnam. A succession of military-dominated regimes came and went, all proclaiming themselves pro-American and all requiring U.S. assistance to maintain a semblance of government and continue the fight against the Vietcong. Worrying about the potential collapse of the South Vietnamese regime, the United States intensified its involvement. The new American president, Lyndon Baines Johnson, remained determined to maintain an independent non-communist government in the south. At the same time, he made a conscious decision to take the war to the north, through covert operations, commando raids carried out along the North Vietnamese coast and retaliatory air strikes. A series of reported attacks on the American ships in the Gulf of Tonkin, including some that may not have actually occurred, led to congressional passage of a resolution that effectively gave President Johnson, at least as he saw matters, a blank check to wage the war in Vietnam. By the close of 1964, the number of American military advisers in Vietnam had increased to 23,000.

The following year, 1965, saw the greatest escalation of American involvement in Indochina. In February, the United States began an orchestrated bombing campaign against the north, entitled Operation Rolling Thunder. Within a month, the U.S. government sent land troops to Vietnam to defend air bases, planes and pilots. Shortly thereafter, those same forces began offensive operations as the Americanization of the war unfolded. The U.S. troop deployment figures continued to soar, reaching 185,000 that December. The following year saw 365,000 American troops in Vietnam; by 1967, there were 475,000 forces; in mid-1968, 550,000 U.S. soldiers were there.

The scale of fighting continued to mount, too. The air war focused not just on the north, but on supposed guerrilla territory in South Vietnam too, with more tonnage of bombs eventually dropped there than over the north. Pilots were frequently given free-strike zones in which they could strafe anything—including vegetation, huts, livestock or people—within sight. Chemical agents poured forth from U.S. planes, including herbicides intended to remove vegetation coverage for guerrillas—Agent Orange eventually wiped away half of South Vietnam's forest lands—and napalm, a jellified gasoline that stuck to its target as it burned. The range of potential targets increasingly was broadened, eventually including areas surrounding the larger North Vietnamese cities. The fighting on the ground also covered a wide swath, as American soldiers with their ARVN allies sought to ferret out the Vietcong through search-and-destroy missions or to engage NVA troops in battle. The aim was to produce a favorable kill-ratio, which resulted in a fixation on body counts. That in turn, coupled with the massive bombardment conducted by U.S. planes, resulted in a high level of civilian casualties and the destruction of huts, religious sites, gardens and even entire villages. Increasingly relying on counterinsurgent tactics, the United States by 1967 sought to decimate the Vietcong through a systematic campaign that involved the CIA: Operation Phoenix. Once again, the body count of slain Vietnamese was the criteria used to indicate the success of this undertaking.

Such military practices often proved to be counter-productive, given that the war in Vietnam, even more than most, revolved around the winning of hearts and minds. The Communist Party leadership in the north and the NLF cadre in the south appeared more fully appreciative of this fact than did U.S. policymakers or the succession of governments that reigned in South Vietnam. Ho Chi Minh's government often seized the diplomatic offensive. While the Democratic Republic of Vietnam through Prime Minister Pham Van Dong offered to revisit the Geneva Agreements, the Johnson administration appeared determined to carve out a military victory by crushing the resistance in the south and pummeling the north. To maintain morale, the Politburo in North Vietnam evacuated civilians from cities and sent them into the countryside. Similarly, industrial facilities were often moved, sometimes to caves or underground. A massive underground network of tunnels was constructed, enabling many to escape the fierce bombing. On a seemingly ongoing basis, bridges, railroads and roads damaged by American aerial bombardment were repaired. To overcome the loss of equipment and supplies, greatly increased levels of aid poured forth from both the USSR and China. Chinese troops, moreover, helped to extend the northern infrastructure. Through it all, the Vietnamese refused to share decision making with their allies, whom they often played off against one another. At the same time, the Communist Party leaders in Hanoi became more involved in the war in the south, with 8,000 NVA forces a month heading down the Ho Chi Minh trail (a network of roads throughout much of Vietnam and eastern Laos that the North Vietnamese relied on to transport soldiers and supplies). Thus, as the United States increased its troop deployment levels in South Vietnam, so too did Ho Chi Minh and General Giap.

With some notable exceptions, the North Vietnamese soldiers, like their southern allies, performed best when they adopted hit-and-run tactics. At times, however, they waged more standard battles, which generally played to American strengths, including superior firepower. Nevertheless, even apparent setbacks could prove advantageous for the forces seeking to reunify the country and induce the United States to withdraw altogether. One such epochal occurrence involved the Tet Offensive of early 1968, in

which an estimated 84,000 NVA troops and VC fighters engaged in wholesale assaults on provincial capitals, district towns and several major South Vietnamese cities. The scale of the offensive surprised American policymakers. Then, as *The Pentagon Papers*—which explored the origins of U.S. involvement in Vietnam—acknowledged, "its strength, length and intensity prolonged this shock." And despite public disclaimers to the contrary, General Earle Wheeler, the chairman of the Joint Chiefs of Staff, acknowledged to President Johnson that Tet was "a very near thing."

In Saigon, guerrillas fought on the U.S. embassy grounds. In Hue, the NVA forces held control for twenty-five days. Throughout the South Vietnamese countryside, battles raged. Eventually, both the NVA and particularly the VC suffered terrible losses, while winning the propaganda war. This offensive, as many in the West saw it, refuted the notion propounded by U.S. military commander William Westmoreland and the Johnson administration that "light could be seen at the end of the tunnel." As the Tet Offensive diminished, disillusionment over the war, already growing in the United States, heightened further. President Johnson soon announced that peace negotiations would be held in Paris and that he would not seek re-election.

On March 16, 1968, one of the greatest tragedies of the Vietnam War occurred. In the rural hamlet of My Lai, soldiers from Company C of the 23d Infantry (Americal) Division of the U.S. military engaged in a rampage that left hundreds dead, including many women, children and elderly men. A cover-up hid the enormity of the crimes from the American public for nearly a year and a half. The My Lai massacre demonstrated the depths to which frightened and angry young men, having suffered losses among their compatriots, could sink.

As the war dragged on, Cambodia and Laos increasingly were caught up in it. The relatively placid nature of Cambodian life under Norodom Sihanouk began to end following a 1963 student riot that sparked government repression and corruption. This occurred despite the fact that Sihanouk had come to adopt a pro-Vietnamese, pro-Chinese foreign policy displeasing to the United States. A clash ensued with leftists but U.S.–Cambodian relations deteriorated nevertheless. Cambodia rejected American economic assistance because of the United States' apparent support for Sihanouk's foes. Moves to nationalize businesses aided only those few who took advantage of the state control, as the government pressured the rural population to increase rice production for export purposes. Per capita rice consumption in Cambodia itself, however, actually began to decline in 1965. To stifle illegal trade with Thailand and Vietnam, the government effectively compelled peasants to sell their product at lower-than-market value to the state.

During this same period, not surprisingly, opposition to Sihanouk's government grew. By 1963, militant communists including Saloth Sar, Leng Sary and Son Sen sought to mount a rural insurgency; they did so despite disapproval from North Vietnamese leaders. In April 1967, peasants in the southwestern Cambodian village of Samlaut directed their ire at a state farm. A clash between peasants and government troops ensued, which lasted for months. Additional confrontations broke out at the same time.

The continued reliance by Vietcong guerrillas on sanctuaries in both Cambodia and Laos also troubled the U.S. government. As early as 1964, the United States had considered military action involving "border control" operations to prevent its foe from making use of such safe havens. At the close of the 1968 Tet Offensive, General William Westmoreland again urged that the U.S. military cross the borders to attack enemy units. Aerial retaliatory strikes were also called for; they had been resorted to in Laos as early as 1963. Initially, American pilots joined in strikes with the Royal Lao Air Force, but soon went on their own to pound the Ho Chi Minh Trail and other targets in the northern sector of Laos. The bombing often proved ferocious, disrupting food production and resulting in untold numbers of refugees.

The attempt to establish a coalition government in Laos had collapsed in 1963, when Souphanouvong headed for the countryside and set up his own government structure in Sam Neua. The government in Vientiane continued to receive considerable aid from the United State and a number of Western European countries, while North Vietnam, China and the Soviet Union backed the Pathet Lao; eventually, thousands of North Vietnamese troops joined the fight. The CIA continued to train a clandestine army comprised largely of Hmong, Mien and Meo tribesmen; the funding of that operation drew on opium-trafficking that the CIA encouraged. South Vietnamese and Thai troops, along with American military advisers, also backed the Laotian government.

The Fighting Widens

The dynamics of the Vietnam War both changed and remained the same at the start of the administration of Richard Nixon in Washington, D.C. Along with Henry Kissinger, his top foreign policy adviser, President Nixon appeared torn about what to do concerning the Vietnam quagmire, as many had long referred to it. On the one hand, they hoped for a military victory, fueled by American air power. At the same time, the U.S. policymakers had to contend with a potent anti-war movement, a weakened economy and heightened criticism from allies and foes alike. Consequently, Nixon opted for a Vietnamization policy that would allow for fewer American forces, a stronger ARVN military and an intensified air war. Such an approach led to U.S.-sponsored incursions into Cambodia in 1970 and Laos in 1971, but the American-backed regime of General Nguyen Van Thieu and Air Marshall Nguyen Cao Ky failed to garner an adequate level of support.

The expansion of the war resulted in the wreaking of tremendous havoc throughout Vietnam, Cambodia and Laos. The United States released more than five million tons of bombs over Indochina, the greatest percentage over the very territory that the United States claimed to be defending—South Vietnam. The CIA-sponsored Phoenix Program, which targeted Vietcong leaders and sympathizers, produced over 20,000 casualties, further crippling the guerrillas but resulting in greater North Vietnamese involvement in the war in the south. The war produced millions of refugees in the region, while the death count steadily mounted. As the war wound on, the social order in South Vietnam, Cambodia and Laos crumbled. Soaring inflation, black marketeering and mounting drug usage and prostitution ravaged the region.

By the end of the 1960s, communist infiltration into Cambodia had increased, with NVA troops seeking to escape the devastating impact of U.S. bombing runs. Angered by Vietnamese efforts to take control of the province of Ratanakiri, Sihanouk attempted to improve relations with the United States. To that end, he appointed General Lon Nol,

a staunch anti-communist, as prime minister. However, in the midst of an overseas trip, Sihanouk in March 1970 suffered a coup led by Lon Nol and Sirik Matak. For a brief period, the repression initiated by Sihanouk abated, with even various moderate leftists hoping that more modern, democratic governance might be possible. Sihanouk, for his part, headed for Beijing, where he established a government-in-exile. A massive U.S. air strike, which saw the introduction of B-52 bombers, took place in Cambodia. In April 1970, over 50,000 American and ARVN forces headed into Cambodia in an effort to root out enemy sanctuaries and destroy the Vietcong headquarters. The Cambodian incursion actually enabled VC fighters to rebuild their strength to a certain extent.

The following year, the United States backed an ARVN drive into Laos, which was intended to display the might of the now one-million-man strong South Vietnamese army and attack enemy supply routes. Confronting 36,000 NVA forces and Soviet tanks, the ARVN, despite U.S. air support, suffered heavy losses and proved unable to cut the Ho Chi Minh Trail. The Laotian invasion indicated the failure of Vietnamization.

A Spring Offensive was attempted by the NVA in 1972, resulting in the heaviest bombing of the north to date. Negotiations to end the war soon were undertaken in earnest. After the collapse of an earlier effort, the United States conducted the so-called Christmas bombings that saw B-52s systematically bomb Hanoi and Haiphong. Nevertheless, on January 27, 1973, the United States accepted terms that could have been agreed to four years earlier.

The Paris Peace Accords, which led to the withdrawal of the last American troops but allowed NVA forces to remain in place, hardly brought an end to the turmoil in Indochina.

The Provisional Revolutionary Government, the Democratic Republic of Vietnam and the Republic of South Vietnam all quickly violated the peace terms. A sharp increase in the number of NVA troops and supplies soon occurred, along with augmented aid to the Khmer Rouge in Cambodia and the Pathet Lao in Laos. In 1973 and 1974, the Thieu regime carried out an economic blockade against areas the PRG controlled, producing widespread hunger and starvation. It resulted in a depression that left three to four million unemployed in Saigon and surrounding environs. Crime and demonstrations, on the other hand, surged. These developments, coupled with the conduct of military operations against VC-dominated areas, led the PRG to begin battling back.

Once again, the heightened tensions in Vietnam spread into Cambodia and Laos. The short-lived hopes that the Lon Nol regime might provide rational administration were discarded as inflation exploded, corruption abounded and the army treated peasants brutally. For a period, the Khmer Rouge, VC and NVA troops appeared more sympathetic to the interests of the Cambodian peasantry. Sihanouk, still in Beijing, announced support for

Fig. 9-2 Human skulls from a mass grave of victims at the Change Ek torture camp, operated by the Khmer Rouge, Phnom Penh, Cambodia. (Pearson Education, Corporate Digital Archive, AP/World Photos)

the revolutionary movement opposing the Laotian government. Some 5,000 Hanoi Khmers returned home, only to do battle with the Khmer Rouge, who murdered many of them. Refusing to heed the admonitions of the North Vietnamese, the Khmer Rouge continued fighting after the announcement of the Paris Peace Accords. Between February and August 1973 alone, over a quarter of a million tons of American bombs fell on Cambodia. The bombing struck hard against the nation's heavily populated agricultural mid-section; it also fed a hatred of urban areas such as Phnom Penh, where the Lon Nol government still ruled. However, by 1974, hunger confronted many residents of Phnom Penh.

By the time of the Paris Accords, the Pathet Lao controlled some three-fourths of the Laotian countryside. The U.S. bombing of Laos continued unabated, amounting to some 2.1 million tons altogether, leveling a series of towns controlled by the guerrillas; survivors relocated to caves or forests. Carpet bombing of the Ho Chi Minh Trail was maintained. Nevertheless, the Royal Laotian Government proved incapable of subduing the Pathet Lao. Still, the pace of life in Laotian villages was strikingly altered. The onslaught produced hordes of refugees, nearly one-third of the Laotian populace by 1973. In April 1974, Souvanna Phouma again became prime minister of a government whose cabinet included both Royalists and Pathet Lao.

At the close of 1974, the Communist Party leadership in North Vietnam determined to begin the final offensive. The expected two-year-long struggle took just over four months, concluding with the capture on April 29, 1975, of Saigon, soon renamed Ho Chi Minh City. Chaos reigned as the last American civilian and military personnel departed, while some 70,000 South Vietnamese boarded U.S. ships.

Events unfolded just as rapidly in both Cambodia and Laos. As the Lon Nol government crumbled, the Khmer Rouge marched toward Phnom Penh, where they herded together some 2.7 million people. On April 17, the Khmer Rouge guerrillas took control of the Cambodian capital. Following their triumph in South Vietnam, NVA troops joined with the Pathet Lao in Laos. In early December, the king abdicated his throne and the Lao People's Democratic Republic was proclaimed.

Postwar Developments

Postwar Vietnam experienced more difficulties, ranging from political repression to economic woes engendered by decades of war, an international economic boycott and communist policies. Tens of thousands, including former VC and RPG forces, endured "reeducation" camps, as the Communist Party leadership in Hanoi spearheaded the process of reconstruction. Hundreds of thousands of physically disabled Vietnamese and orphans lacked basic economic resources. Millions, ranging from ARVN soldiers to prostitutes, were now without work. Some ten million refugees could be found in the former South Vietnam alone. Eventually, as many as one million Vietnamese left their country altogether, which was officially reunified in 1976. Favoring the slogan "All for the brotherly South; all for the building of socialism," the regime sent vast quantities of foodstuffs and other supplies to the war-ravaged territory that had previously comprised the Republic of South Vietnam.

Barely two years after the war had ended, Vietnam still confronted an economic embargo orchestrated by the United States, and now faced an increasingly hostile China, which was funneling military aid and advisers to the Khmer Rouge. After enduring relentless attacks from Pol Pot's cadre, the Vietnamese invaded Kampuchea—the renamed Cambodia—in December 1978, which only further strained relations with China. Within weeks, the Khmer Rouge had been forced to leave Phnom Penh for the Thai-Kampuchean border. In mid-February, China attacked Vietnam. Chinese troops departed after a month, but border clashes continued intermittently. Vietnamese forces underwent a gradual pullout from Kampuchea, beginning in 1982.

The Vietnamese economy, still wracked by war, experienced growing budgetary deficits, massive inflation, decreased food production, an ever-expanding population, and increased dependence on the Soviet Union. Economic reforms instituted in 1988 provided greater incentives for farmers, curbed inflation and produced economic growth. Helpful too was the pullout of Vietnamese troops from Kampuchea.

In Kampuchea, the Khmer Rouge left a legacy of vast misery, deprivation and terror. Most urban dwellers crowded into rural areas, where government officials, professionals, and religious leaders were forced to till the soil; many perished because of overwork, food shortages, and illnesses. All were instructed to dress alike and to discard religious rituals. Commercial enterprises were taken over by the government and currency was destroyed. Massive repression was meted out in the ferocious campaign to create a perfect agrarian state far removed from any western ideals. As many as one to two million people became part of the infamous Killing Fields that characterized the soon-to-be-renamed Cambodia.

Some of the worst of the horrors lessened following the Vietnamese invasion, which resulted in the proclamation of the People's Republic of Kampuchea. Headed by President Heng Samrin, the new government removed the repressive grip of the Khmer Rouge and sought to craft socialism on top of a private sector. However, the PRK had to confront both continued hostilities from the Khmer Rouge and diplomatic pressure. Vying for power was the Coalition Government of Democratic Kampuchea, established in 1982; it was comprised of Pol Pot's forces, the Khmer People's National Liberation Front under Son Sann and a group headed by Norodom Sihanouk.

In Laos, where some 50,000 Vietnamese troops were stationed, Souphanouvong served as president until 1986. Like Cambodia, Laos faced both economic uncertainties and a resistance movement; Hmong and Mien guerrillas continued to fight for two years after the takeover. Collectivized agriculture failed and the government halted the practice in mid-1979. Some 350,000 Laotians, a full 10 percent of the populace, left the country, among them the great bulk of educated citizens. Those remaining had to contend with untold numbers of land mines, which resulted in hundreds of casualties annually. Laos also clashed repeatedly with Thailand, with military conflicts breaking out in 1984 and again in 1987.

Thus as the decade of the 1980s neared a close, Vietnam, Laos and Cambodia continued to suffer from the aftermath of years of warfare, revolution and economic trauma. Changes in the broader world community would soon impact those now sovereign, but still troubled, lands. The Cold War had dramatically affected all three nations; its termination would leave in its wake new uncertainties, of both a political and economic nature.

◆ —— ◆ —— ◆ —— ◆ —— ◆ —— ◆ —— ◆ —— ◆ —— ◆ —— ◆

As Khmer Rouge guerrillas approached in April 1975, Americans and those Cambodians associated with the government fled from Phnom Penh. Like a small number of other Western journalists, Sydney Schanberg of the *New York Times* remained in Phnom Penh as Khmer Rouge soldiers swept into the capital city on April 12, 1975, though several journalists had already been murdered by the Khmer Rouge. The guerrilla forces rounded up Schanberg along with his photographer who also served as an interpreter and guide, the Cambodian Dith Pran, and two other journalists, Jon Swain and Al Rockoff. Schanberg and Rockoff were Americans, perhaps the most dangerous nationality to be at that point, while Swain was British but had served in the French Foreign Legion. Swain's equipment was strewn about and a gun was placed to his head, but Pran convinced the Khmer to put the weapon down.

At gunpoint, the Khmer Rouge forced Schanberg, Swain and Rockoff into an automobile, while Pran was told that he could depart. After all, the Khmer Rouge informed him, they sought only the "rich and the bourgeoisie." Pran and the driver, however, refused to leave, and Pran somehow managed to edge his way into the vehicle before it took off. In the midst of the twenty-five minute ride, Pran spoke in Khmer: "They are French journalists. They are here to write about your great victory." As Pran later recalled, "Something inside me told me I had to lie. I told them we were French because the French were considered neutral and were respected." As Pran continued to talk, the Khmer Rouge decided to release the two. Pran's quick thinking undoubtedly saved their lives.

The extraordinarily courageous photojournalist Dith Pran was born on September 27, 1942, in Angkor Wat, site of the fabled temples, relatively close to the Thai border. Previously involved in the tourism trade, Pran became a war correspondent when the Vietnam conflagration spilled over into his homeland. Along with the American journalist Sydney Schanberg, Pran helped to cover the war between the Lon Nol regime and the Khmer Rouge that unfolded between 1972 and 1975. After their capture and release by the Khmer Rouge, Schanberg, Pran, Swain and Rockoff eventually headed for the French embassy, where they encountered other Westerners and Cambodians seeking sanctuary against the cataclysm that was enveloping Cambodia. They remained there, but Cambodians like Pran were soon arrested; those who were not executed toiled in the countryside. Later, the Khmer Rouge allowed the foreigners in the embassy compound to depart, but Pran had already begun a torturous odyssey that would last four years; during that period, as he later recorded, Pran would be "an eyewitness to torture, murder and forced starvation." At one point, Pran was compelled to reside in a labor camp where he served as a cook but starved for food himself. He took a handful of grain from a rice field but was captured and beaten with bamboo sticks by guards, several of whom were teenage girls. After a night in which his arms and legs were tied, Pran was released.

In the meantime, Schanberg received a Pulitzer Prize in journalism for his reportage on Cambodia; the award, he insisted, was for Pran too. Pran continued to endure,

Fig. 9-3 Dith Pran (on right) at the annual awards ceremony of the British Academy of Film and Television Arts, London. (Pearson Education, Corporate Digital Archive, Getty Images Inc.)

returning to Angkor Watt after the Vietnamese invasion pushed the Khmer Rouge back. He discovered that the Khmer Rouge had killed his three brothers, sister, brother-in-law, and their two children. Fleeing through jungle territory filled with land mines, Pran reached a refugee camp in Thailand. By this point, Pran and a sister were the only members of their family to avoid the fate of so many Cambodians, including their father and their four murdered siblings. On hearing of Pran's arrival in Thailand, Schanberg immediately flew to greet him.

Reaching the United States, Pran obtained a job with the *Times*. While working for *The New York Times Magazine,* his account of the Cambodia holocaust appeared: "The Death and Life of Dith Pran: A Story of Cambodia." In 1984, an Oscar-nominated film, *The Killing Fields* appeared; it related the tale of Schanberg and Pran, tracing the horrors that Cambodia endured. The following year, the United Nations High Commissioner for Refugees named Pran Goodwill Ambassador. He tirelessly spoke on behalf of refugees and other victims of military conflicts. Eloquently and simply, Pran affirmed, "As a survivor, I must speak out."

Pran also insisted that the full story of Cambodia be told. As he declared,

> I'm a one-person crusade. I must speak for those who did not survive and for those who still suffer. Since coming to America, I have visited Cambodia three times to evaluate the ongoing Cambodian crisis. The problems Cambodia faces are not only political but also economical and social. The Khmer Rouge have brought Cambodia back to year zero and that's why I'm trying to bring the Khmer Rouge leaders to the World Court. Like one of my heroes, Elie Wiesel, who alerts the world to the horrors of the Jewish holocaust, I try to awaken the world to the holocaust of Cambodia, for all tragedies have universal implications. . . . Part of my life is saving life. I don't consider myself a politician or a hero. I'm a messenger. If Cambodia is to survive, she needs many voices.

Suggested Readings

CHANDLER, DAVID. *A History of Cambodia.* (2000).

DUIKER, WILLIAM J. *Ho Chi Minh.* (2000).

———. *Vietnam: Revolution in Transition.* (1995).

EVANS, GRANT. *The Politics of Ritual and Remembrance: Laos since 1975.* (1998).

GETLIN, JOSH and KARI RENE HALL. *Beyond the Killing Fields.* (1992).

HERRING, GEORGE C. *America's Longest War: The United States and Vietnam, 1950–1975.* (1995).

LANGGUTH, A. J. *Our Vietnam/Nuoc Viet Ta: A History of the War 1954–1975.* (2000).

NEHER, CLARK D. *Southeast Asia in the New International Era.* (1999).

OSBORNE, MILTON. *Southeast Asia: An Introductory History.* (1997).

PRAN, DITH, compiler. *Children of Cambodia's Killing Fields: Memoirs by Survivors.* (1994).

SARDESAI, D. R. *Southeast Asia: Past & Present.* (1997).

STEINBERG, D. J., ed. *In Search of Southeast Asia.* (1985).

SWAIN, JON. *River of Time.* (1995).

TARLING, NICHOLAS. *Nations and States in Southeast Asia.* (1998).

TEMPLAR, ROBERT. *Shadows and Wind: A View of Modern Vietnam.* (1998).

CHAPTER 10

The Challenges of Independence: Africa since 1945

On April 11, 1979, cheering crowds thronged the streets of Kampala, capital city of the East African nation of Uganda. The celebration marked the overthrow of Field Marshal and President-for-Life Idi Amin Dada, whose eight-year dictatorship had been brought to an inglorious end by invading forces from neighboring Tanzania. Amin's reign, which began in 1971 when the former army officer ousted then-President Milton Obote, had been characterized by increasingly savage and capricious brutality. As many as 300,000 Ugandans had fallen victim to Amin's murderous soldiers and the innocently named State Research Bureau, which was in reality a secret police organization that meted out torture and death to suspected dissidents. Tanzanian soldiers securing the Bureau's headquarters found offices full of files on citizens and a basement full of bodies. Even as educator Yusufu Lule was proclaimed as the leader of a new National Liberation Front government, curious Ugandans wandered through the modest hillside house that the dictator had abandoned when he fled the country. The odd assortment of items scattered around the interior testified to a mercurial, perhaps disordered, mind: boxes of hand grenades under a bed, photos of military aircraft taped to the walls, a closet filled with reels of "Tom and Jerry" cartoons and a file cabinet containing hundreds of photographs of tortured Ugandans.

One of the most enigmatic of contemporary dictators, Amin left behind little that offered any clear insight into his motivations. He was arguably the most extreme example of a recurrent problem in post-independence Africa. Since the early 1960s, constitutional and democratic government in Africa had often proven fragile, susceptible to political instability and corruption. In many instances, unsteady or inept civilian government opened the door to military men who proclaimed themselves better suited to maintaining order than bickering politicians. Sometimes civilian leaders themselves unwittingly paved the way for military strongmen by distorting or subverting the constitutional institutions to which they were ostensibly committed. As Ugandan

Prime Minister, Obote abandoned any pretense of democratic government in 1966 when he proclaimed a one-party state, suppressed all opposition and arranged his election as president-for-life. The overthrow of his dictatorship in January 1971 had brought Ugandans into the streets to cheer their new liberator, Idi Amin.

Born in northwest Uganda in 1925, Idi Amin belonged to the small Kakwa tribe, renowned largely for its tradition of soldiering. Receiving little in the way of formal education, Amin was virtually illiterate and aspired to a military career, which he began in 1946 as a kitchen helper in Britain's 4th King's African Rifles. Like many of his tribe, he was both courageous and physically imposing, at six feet four inches in height. At nearly 240 pounds, he became the heavyweight boxing champion of his regiment. The British Army acknowledged his soldierly skills, promoting him to the rank of lieutenant, despite one officer's description of Amin as "a bit short on the gray matter." He was thus well positioned to secure an influential position when Uganda gained independence in 1962.

Initial prospects seemed good for the nation of 19 million, which was approximately the same size in area as Great Britain. Many Englishmen had remarked on Uganda's natural beauty; Churchill had once described it as "the pearl of East Africa." The largely agricultural economy was sound, tourism was growing and the University of Makerere was acclaimed as "the Harvard of Africa." At independence, Uganda adopted a parliamentary system, in which three political parties vied for representation. As events were to prove, however, both national unity and political stability were at best tenuous, undermined by the presence of four major tribal kingdoms and forty different ethnic groups within Ugandan borders. Milton Obote, Uganda's first prime minister, proved more than willing to manipulate tribal loyalties to serve his own political purposes. His suspension of Uganda's constitution in 1966 was the prelude to years of oppression and misrule, which were seemingly ended by Amin's 1971 coup.

Initially greeted with popular enthusiasm, Amin played the role of the conciliator, ending the state of emergency and releasing political prisoners. Touring Uganda, Amin appeared jovial and gregarious, clearly relishing his newfound prominence. Abroad, he was perceived as colorful if not eccentric. An outrageous and larger-than-life figure, Amin declared himself the boxing champion of Uganda and the chancellor of Makerere University; he wore so many self-awarded medals that a specially designed uniform coat was necessary to accommodate them all. His buffoonish public persona concealed a more sinister side, however. Innately suspicious, Amin purged his own army of those outside his tribe; by summer 1971 some 5,000 had been killed. Rebuffed in his efforts to purchase military hardware from Britain, Amin began a personal crusade to humiliate the few remaining British subjects in Uganda, on one occasion compelling a number of English expatriates to carry him into a meeting on a shoulder-borne litter. He lashed out at Britain indirectly by ordering the expulsion of all Asians, many of whom were British citizens. As the Asian community of about 30,000 comprised most of the professional, merchant and business classes, their forced emigration within 90 days had a devastating impact on the Ugandan economy. Amin had hoped to curry popular favor by simply turning over Asian enterprises to Ugandans, but few had the expertise to manage

Fig. 10-1 "President-for-Life" Idi Amin Dada of Uganda greets President Mobutu Sese Seko of Zaire as the latter arrives in Kampala, Uganda, for a state visit. While Mobutu retained power for 32 years, Amin governed with such capricious brutality that he was ousted after only eight years. (Pearson Education, Corporate Digital Archive, Getty Images Inc.)

them, and economic chaos followed. Nonetheless, Amin publicly proclaimed himself "Conqueror of the British Empire."

Amin believed that his increasingly aggressive posturing against the British would secure his reputation among African nationalists who longed to see their former colonial overlords humiliated and discredited. In a further bid for prominence, Amin undertook to reorient Uganda's foreign policy. Denouncing Britain, Israel and the United States for thwarting his military ambitions by denying him arms, Amin requested assistance from the Soviet Union. Though he had never been devout, Amin conveniently rediscovered his Moslem heritage as part of a bid to promote the Islamic cause in Africa and the Middle East. He established close ties with the revolutionary regime of Libya's Muammar Gaddafi and declared his support for Yasir Arafat and the Palestinian guerillas.

The tenor of Amin's anti-Israeli crusade became more inflammatory as he announced his intentions of erecting a monument to Adolf Hitler, whom he praised for exterminating Europe's Jews.

Ultimately, Amin's reckless utterances and behavior brought humiliation for his regime. In June 1976, pro-Palestinian terrorists hijacked an Air France flight from Tel Aviv and forced the pilot to land at Entebbe airport in Uganda. Sensing an opportunity to gain the world stage, Amin began a dangerous double game of sheltering the hijackers, who were demanding the release of Palestinian prisoners in Israel, while publicly assuring the terrified passengers of his goodwill. The Israeli government, distrustful of the erratic Amin and unwilling to await a denouement, organized an airborne commando rescue operation. Deep in the night, two Israeli military transport planes carrying the commandos touched down at Entebbe, where the Israelis deceived Ugandan security forces through an elaborate ruse. Having brought with them a Mercedes limousine identical to Amin's, the commando team disguised one of their men as the Ugandan dictator and easily penetrated the security checkpoints at the terminal. In the subsequent firefight, Israeli commandos killed all of the hijackers, some twenty Ugandan troops and, for good measure, destroyed most of the Ugandan Air Force on the ground before departing with almost all of the passengers alive. An elderly British woman who had earlier been transported to a hospital in Kampala and was left behind was the only remaining target for Amin's vengeance. State Research Bureau thugs dragged her from her hospital bed and murdered her, dumping her body in the countryside outside the capital. An international furor followed Amin's coddling of terrorists and the very public murder of a British citizen; the Ugandan leader was no longer seen as a clownish eccentric, but as a dangerously erratic and cold-blooded tyrant. His stature among Africans began to fall and the presidents of Tanzania and Zambia both denounced his cruel regime.

Condemnation from abroad was not Amin's only problem; by the late 1970s, Uganda was slipping further into economic and administrative chaos. In the aftermath of the expulsion of the Asians, Amin's general disregard of the economy had contributed to an inflation rate of 1,000 percent over eight years. Production dropped by 50 percent during the same period. Administrative agencies, purged of competent civil servants in favor of Amin's cronies, virtually ceased to function. Rising domestic dissent led Amin to lash out with a new wave of comprehensive police terror, which was all the more frightening because of its capriciousness. Ugandans from all walks of life simply disappeared for no apparent reason and many were never seen again. Terrible stories circulated about Amin's operatives throwing victims into the crocodile-infested Nile River; more darkly, it was rumored that the dictator practiced cannibalism. As Ugandan and world opinion turned against him, Amin resorted to a cynical diversion. In September 1978, he ordered his army to invade neighboring Tanzania. It proved a fatal miscalculation. Tanzanian President Julius Nyerere, who despised Amin, assembled a force of 45,000 troops, which pushed deep into Ugandan territory by early 1979. Amin's troops, more comfortable with shooting unarmed civilians, fled before the Tanzanian offensive. Amin departed in haste, but his removal did not resolve Uganda's extensive problems. Continuing political instability precluded any significant efforts to rebuild the shattered economy or restore the nearly nonexistent public infrastructure. As late as 1989, one observer concluded that "Uganda no longer exists today as a viable nation." Amin, who never faced justice for his crimes, currently resides in a well-appointed estate in Saudi Arabia, accompanied by several of his wives and some 40 children.

Uganda's travails illustrate some of the fundamental difficulties that many African nations faced in the post-independence era. At best an artificial nation-state, Uganda was riven with tribal and regional divisions that precluded immediate national unity. Governmental institutions were based on European models that had no tradition or proven efficacy in an African context; their smooth functioning presumed political habits of mind and practice that were often absent in Africa. A fundamentally unstable political system easily gave way before the ambitions of dictators who found it convenient to ignore irksome constitutions and difficult parliaments. It is not an exclusively African pattern, just a more recent one; similar developments swept Europe in the 1930s. Uganda's misfortunes, while partly the product of the absence of any historical tradition of constitutional or democratic government, were amplified by other factors.

As in other newly independent African nations, the army was the only national institution capable of imposing order and unity, and under Amin's leadership it was reconstituted so as to serve specific personal and tribal ambitions. Uganda's national tragedy offers some insight into the challenges that faced independent Africa, but it is not necessarily a model for universal generalizations. While Africa produced Idi Amin, it also produced Nelson Mandela and scores of others who struggled courageously to build a more stable, free and prosperous future for their nations.

◆ —— ◆ —— ◆ —— ◆ —— ◆

In the late nineteenth century, European nations began the process of colonizing Africa and within 20 years most of the continent had been incorporated into European empires. In 1945, following the end of the Second World War, the colonizers gradually came to accept the inevitability of African independence. Within another 20 years, most of the European powers had withdrawn, ending their domination of the continent as rapidly as they had achieved it. The scope of the transformation was immense, if for no other reason than the continent's geographic and demographic scale. The African landmass covers over 11,650,000 square miles, occupying 20 percent of the earth's land surface. The population, which stood at about 93 million at the beginning of the century, approached 385 million by 1975. The fundamental reorganization of such a huge portion of humanity was one of the century's most notable developments. The change in Africa's political landscape alone was staggering; in the 20 years following Ghana's independence in 1957, 51 independent states came into being. The transition to nationhood, a process of vast scale and complexity affecting peoples of diverse ethnic, religious and cultural backgrounds, posed innumerable and sometimes bewildering challenges. The subsequent course of modern African history is marked by both remarkable achievements and troubling failures.

Prelude to Independence: Europe and Africa, 1945–1960

Even as the Second World War heightened nationalist sentiments throughout colonial Asia, it also encouraged advocates of African independence. Colonial Africa's contributions to the Allied war effort were indisputable. More than 160,000 troops from French Northwest Africa together with 374,000 recruits from British Africa served the Allied cause in both combat and support units. Africa also supplied crucial raw materials; the Belgian Congo was an indispensable source of uranium for the American atomic bomb project. The need for iron, tin, copper and zinc drove a rapid expansion of those industries in several African colonies. For the French government-in-exile under General de Gaulle's leadership, colonial Africa provided a base of governmental operations during the German occupation of France. In French Equatorial Africa, Brazzaville served as a temporary capital for the Free French government; de Gaulle later observed that it was in Africa that France found "her refuge and the starting point for her liberation." Between 1940 and 1943, North Africa was the scene of extensive fighting between Allied and Axis armies; the final defeat of Germany's Afrika Corps in 1943 opened the way for an Anglo-American invasion of Italy. In many ways, Africa was more directly involved in the Second World War than in the first, with significant consequences for both Europeans and Africans.

While newly cognizant of the importance of Africa's material and manpower resources, Europeans faced the postwar years with the realization that their mastery over the continent must inevitably give way to some new arrangement, though the idea of complete or immediate independence seemed as yet inconceivable. For many Africans, the significance of the war was less ambiguous. Any lingering illusions about the invincibility or superiority of Europeans died with the war. Zimbabwean writer Ndabaningi Sithole observed how the wartime experience transformed the perspective of African soldiers, who "found themselves at the front line of war with one purpose in view; to kill every white enemy soldier they could get hold of." The effect was fundamental: "After spending four years hunting white enemy soldiers, the African never again regarded them as gods."

Others who looked toward independence found encouragement in the professed aims of the Allies. Clause Three of the Atlantic Charter indisputably proclaimed that the United States and Great Britain "respect the right of all peoples to choose the form of government under which they live; and they wish to see sovereign rights and self-government restored to those who have been forcibly deprived of them." At the October 1945 meeting of the Sixth Pan-African Congress in Manchester, England, delegates made clear their determination to see the promise realized. In a final resolution, the Congress warned that Africans would no longer accept second-class status under colonial rule: "We are unwilling to starve any longer while doing the world's drudgery, in order to support by our poverty and igno-rance a false aristocracy and a discarded im-perialism. . . . We will fight every way we can for freedom, democracy and social better-ment."

Despite apparently unambiguous state-ments of principle and Europe's obviously reduced capacity to continue to govern colo-nial Africa at the end of the war, the major imperial powers temporized about the de-gree of and timeframe for African indepen-dence. When the issue arose during the war, there was general agreement that Africa was unsuited to self-government for the foresee-able future. British Colonial Office authori-ties estimated that their African territories would require sixty to eighty years of prepa-ration before independence was feasible. An American official guessed that Belgian colonies would require more than one hun-dred years of preparation for self-government; Portugal's more benighted possessions, he opined, might not be capable of self-rule in less than a thousand years. French au-thorities, who considered the issue at the French Africa Conference in Brazzaville in 1944, concluded that there was no possibil-ity of colonial self-government outside the French Empire "even in the distant future." British Prime Minister Winston Churchill argued vehemently that the principles of the Atlantic Charter were meant only to apply to European nations that Nazi Ger-many conquered. Among the major Allied leaders, only Franklin Roosevelt pressed ardently for rapid decolonization; the Phil-ippine Islands, the only remaining U.S. colony, was scheduled for independence in 1946.

Stubbornly resistant to granting immedi-ate independence to territories that repre-sented international status and material wealth, Britain and France set about formu-lating policies that held out the vague promise of some form of self-government in the indeterminate future. Conceding that African nationalism would grow rapidly in coming years, British policymakers devised a program in 1947 for the gradual transfer of power in their African colonies. The new pol-icy marked the end of the historical practice of indirect rule. British colonial administra-tors would no longer work through tribal chiefs, but would prepare the native edu-cated elite to assume authority. Local govern-ment was to be democratized, with elected assemblies naming government ministries.

The process accelerated much more rapidly than expected in the Gold Coast, where riots drove British authorities to speed up the intended timetable. In 1951, the elec-toral triumph of Kwame Nkrumah raised ex-pectations across much of British Africa, and colonial officials were compelled to accept a more rapid transition toward independence than had been initially anticipated. The Gold Coast gained independence as Ghana in 1957 and the process of devolution accelerated in subsequent years as Africans voiced their growing impatience. At the 1959 meeting of the All-African People's Conference, Kenyan delegate Tom Mboya effectively captured the African mood in a concluding speech in which he admonished the colonial powers. "Your time is past," he declared. "Africa must be free. Scram from Africa!" Not until 1960, however, did the British government appear to fully acknowledge the depth of African nationalist sentiment. That year Prime Minister Harold Macmillan observed that "the wind of change is blowing through this continent" and conceded that "we must accept it as a fact and our national policies must take account of it."

Postwar French governments were initially less receptive than the British to the idea of African independence. Determined to preserve national grandeur and the economic benefits of close ties with French Africa, French policymakers sought to offer Africans a limited degree of self-determination by allowing for the election of colonial representatives to the French Legislative Assembly. In 1945, twenty-nine African deputies took their elected seats in Paris. The government of the Fourth Republic ended the much-resented colonial practice of forced labor and granted French citizenship to the people of French Africa. French officials encouraged Africans to think of themselves as Frenchmen and of their countries as part of a worldwide "French Union."

Though the French government moved to create local assemblies in each African territory and federal assemblies for French West Africa and French Equatorial Africa, the general scheme for retaining central French control of the colonies began to unravel in the mid-1950s under the pressure of nationalist sentiment. In North Africa, France conceded to independence for Morocco and Tunisia in 1956, in large part because the army was already bogged down in a vicious war against Algerian nationalists that had begun two years earlier. Following the collapse of the Fourth Republic as a result of the Algerian War and the spreading nationalist enthusiasm that followed Ghanaian independence, French President Charles de Gaulle sought to salvage the situation by offering French Africa the choice of independence or autonomy within a "French Community." Guinea became the first French African colony to gain independence when its president Sekou Toure told de Gaulle "We prefer poverty in liberty to riches in slavery." Ivory Coast followed shortly and in 1960, fourteen French colonies declared independence. Large numbers of French settlers and the intransigence of the French army complicated the situation in Algeria, but in 1962 the country gained independence.

Neither Belgium nor Portugal, the remaining major African colonial powers, demonstrated any intention of preparing their possessions for eventual self-government. Under Belgian rule, Congolese received virtually no role in government or administration. The concept of African self-rule was considered so subversive in Belgium that, in 1956, a Belgian lecturer who proposed a thirty-year program for Congolese independence was denounced as a dangerous radical. Belgium's refusal to make even minimal preparations for African self-rule proved disastrous to the future of the Congo.

Portugal's similar unwillingness to consider self-government for Angola and Mozambique stemmed from several sources. A very poor country, Portugal was heavily dependent on the economic benefits reaped from her African colonies. The Salazar dictatorship was unreceptive to the demands of African nationalists, viewing Portuguese colonies as symbols of national pride and strength. Throughout the postwar period, the Portuguese government stressed its role as a civilizing force in Africa and encouraged the emigration of settlers to the colonies. Beginning in the early 1960s, Portugal responded to intermittent nationalist uprisings in both colonies with armed force. Clearly, in the postwar years, African nationalists faced European powers that were at best reluctant and slow to accept the inevitable, and at worst determined to resist independence with oppression and brute power.

IMPEDIMENTS TO NATIONAL DEVELOPMENT

In the thirty years following the end of the Second World War, forty-five African nations gained independence. However, the path to stable nationhood in postcolonial Africa was strewn with enormous obstacles and problems that often seemed to defy resolution. Geography and climate often played a fundamental role in determining and in some cases limiting national development. The Sahara Desert, which covers one quarter of the continent, an area as large as the lower forty-eight American states, inevitably shaped national life in a belt of countries extending from Mauritania on the Atlantic coast to Sudan, which borders the Red Sea. The Sahara, which is expanding at the rate of 250,000 acres a year, imposed myriad hardships on the peoples of nations such as Chad, where as late as 1986, the per capita annual income was $78. Drought and desertification produced periodic famines across the Saharan regions and into the Horn of Africa. To the south, the Kalahari Desert, the world's seventh largest, shaped the development of Namibia, a sparsely populated nation with rich but as yet incompletely exploited mineral resources. The African coastal strip is narrow, giving way to inland belts of often-dense tropical rain forest that defy easy penetration or, south of the equatorial regions, grassy plains and wooded savanna. For some new nations, geography and climate proved to be obstacles to transportation, communications, administration and economic development.

Not surprisingly on such an immense continent, linguistic, religious and tribal divisions posed additional obstacles to national development. There are some 750 African tribal languages, 50 of which are spoken by 1 million or more people. Linguistic diversity often proved to be a hindrance to national unity, as in Zaire (formerly the Belgian Congo), where 75 different languages are spoken. The multiplicity of indigenous languages led some new African nations to adopt European languages as the official tongue for government, administration and education. A number of African states adopted the language of the former colonial power as a matter of necessity as much as convenience. In Ghana, formerly the Gold Coast, English became the national language, while Niger retained the official language of French West Africa.

While religion has sometimes been a unifying and stabilizing factor, as in those nations like Mali that are predominantly Moslem, it has as frequently been a source of division. Ethiopia, for example, is divided almost evenly between Moslems and Ethiopian Orthodox Christians, though as much as twenty percent of the population subscribes to animist beliefs. In some nations, religious divisions also assumed regional dimensions; in Sudan, the government at Khartoum in the overwhelmingly Islamic north engaged in periodic armed struggle with rebel groups in the predominantly Christian southern region of the country.

Racial divisions also affected African development. While sub-Saharan Africa is overwhelmingly black, minority white populations in Rhodesia, South-West Africa (Namibia after 1968) and the Republic of South Africa retained political and economic control of those nations for decades after the end of the Second World War. The ongoing struggle for majority rule and racial equality in these white-ruled states produced continual tensions and periodic violence over the years.

While these factors brought division to some African nations, tribalism proved to be an almost universal obstacle to unity and stability. This was in part because of the colonial legacy of "divide and rule," which pitted Africans against one another for the purpose of facilitating European control. European colonial authorities further heightened tribal antagonisms by recruiting members from specific tribes for specialized duties; while some tribes were cultivated to provide "native elites," others were exploited as sources of military recruits. The boundaries of most African states, drawn to serve European colonial requirements, often included only portions of tribes or encompassed tribes that were historically antagonistic. At the point of independence, most African states were fundamentally European creations, which rarely reflected African realities or traditions; the concept of nationhood itself was relatively new and arguably alien throughout much of the continent, except among a relatively small group of largely western-educated African nationalists. As tribalism historically provided the basis for political organization and social and cultural identity throughout much of Africa, its stubborn persistence in the postcolonial era is not surprising, but its impact was nonetheless troublesome. Very few African countries have the advantage of some semblance of ethnic uniformity; Somalia, Lesotho and Swaziland are among the exceptions. Most African states faced a multiplicity of tribal allegiances—in Zaire there are some two hundred tribes. Still very much

an operative factor in the years after independence, tribalism too often subsumed any national identity, as by its very nature it required granting primary consideration to tribal members, be it in the quest for jobs, education, economic gain or access to military and political office.

Numerous African leaders acknowledged the disruptive effect of tribalism. Kenyan President Daniel arap Moi described tribalism as "the cancer that threatens to eat out the very fabric of our nation." Many African leaders discovered that creating a viable alternative to tribalism was one of their most daunting challenges, as tribal loyalty contributed significantly to the political instability that seemed endemic in post-independence Africa. The persistence of tribalism often prevented broad popular acceptance of any national ideology or identity and frequently subverted efforts to establish viable national political parties.

Tribalism was only one of many obstacles to stable national government in newly independent Africa. Though many African nations adopted political institutions and systems inherited from the colonial powers, they often proved unworkable in the African context. In undeveloped or underdeveloped states with largely illiterate and politically unsophisticated populations and no significant tradition of constitutional or representative government, efforts to establish functioning parliamentary systems based on democratic precepts often faced insurmountable obstacles. Prior to independence, many Africans were united primarily in opposition to their colonial rulers. Whatever unity existed frequently dissipated following independence, as tribal, religious and regional differences reemerged to destabilize newly established governments. In the early years of independence, charismatic nationalist leaders who had distinguished themselves during the era of anti-colonial struggle strengthened national unity. Both Kwame Nkrumah of Ghana and Jomo Kenyatta of Kenya capitalized on their stature as anti-colonial activists to establish enduring and relatively stable governments when their countries achieved independence.

This first generation of African leadership sought to realize nationhood through a variety of approaches and with varying degrees of success. Tanzania's Julius Nyerere was an advocate of "African Socialism," a developmental ideology critical of both capitalism and orthodox Marxism. Though Kenya's Kenyatta propounded a nominally socialist creed, his economic policies were pragmatic, as was his approach to government. Elsewhere, the perceived need for unity often took precedence over open and democratic government. Guinea's President Sekou Toure typified this approach, maintaining that domestic stability and economic development could be achieved only through the creation of a one-party state. Though Guinea's political system was theoretically democratic, Toure ruthlessly suppressed political opposition and emulated the Soviet economic model by nationalizing much of the economy. Toure typified those African leaders who rejected Western political and economic models, which were deemed responsible for Africa's exploitation under colonialism. President from 1958 to 1984, Toure provided Guinea with a lengthy period of political stability, though it came at the cost of economic decline and domestic repression.

During the early years of national development, the first generation of African leaders faced a multitude of problems, any one of which would have strained the capabilities of even well-established governments. In addition to creating coherent national political systems, African leaders faced the challenges presented by growing populations, illiteracy and rapid urbanization. Economic development was imperative and in the early 1960s generally favorable world economic trends held out the promise of advancement in new African states. However, a number of factors combined to render these hopes futile. The economies of many African states were overwhelmingly agricultural and shaped by old colonial policies, which had encouraged the production of single staple crops that were highly vulnerable to external market and price trends. African agriculture also tended to be inefficient by Western standards. Some African leaders sought to avoid dependence on agricultural staples by implementing programs for rapid industrialization, but most such efforts foundered due to poor planning, managerial inefficiency, corruption and governmental instability. In many instances, those nations with significant and potentially lucrative natural resources proved incapable of successfully exploiting them for similar reasons. By the mid-1960s, accumulating economic, social and political problems brought new instability across the continent. Lingering hopes for the emergence of popular, democratic governments dissipated as military leaders and authoritarian presidents stepped into the breach with promises of renewed order and national revival.

POLITICAL INSTABILITY

The innate political instability of much of independent Africa was manifest in the growing number of *coups d'etat* that plagued the continent, especially the sub-Saharan regions, beginning in the 1960s. During a twenty-five-year period, more than seventy leaders were overthrown in twenty-nine African countries; thirteen nations experienced two or more *coups* after independence. In West Africa, Benin (formerly Dahomey) suffered five military *coups d'etat,* ten attempted *coups,* twelve different governments and six different constitutions between 1963 and 1972. Military leaders, often junior officers, who were disgusted by the ineptness and inefficiency of civilian rule, or offended by the specific actions of national leaders, engineered most of the revolts. One of the first victims, President Sylvanus Olympio of Togo, was gunned down in 1963 on the steps of the U.S. embassy in Lomê while seeking asylum. Though generally considered an able leader, Olympio had opposed increasing military salaries. His murder demonstrated the seductive power of the gun, even if wielded by a relatively small military establishment; the Togolese Army numbered only 250 men.

Across Africa, military men driven by personal ambition or genuine concern for their nation proved both willing and capable of seizing power by force. In the absence of firmly established constitutional traditions and viable political institutions, African armies, however small, were often the only coherent national institution and military leaders saw them as the obvious instrument of national salvation during periods of growing domestic instability. While many military leaders proclaimed their intentions of restoring power to a civilian government when circumstances improved, few honored their promises. Even in those cases where they did, civilian leaders were always cognizant that their tenure in office was only at the sufferance of the military. In some cases, as in Ghana in the 1980s, military leaders proved

moderately successful in restoring order, though efforts by military governments to improve economic conditions have often faltered. In other instances, as in Uganda under Amin, the consequences of military coups were disastrous, ushering in arbitrary rule, police terror and economic collapse.

Idi Amin, like several other military leaders, established an authoritarian presidential regime and promoted "presidential cultism," another phenomenon that developed in those African states where representative government proved weak or unstable. In nations with no historical tradition of central government, the strong presidential figure sometimes supplanted the tribal chieftain as a symbol of authority and some African leaders capitalized on this circumstance to strengthen their authority and extend their rule. Some, like Kenyatta, the "Old Man" of Kenya, were generally benevolent and genuinely revered by their people, as was Julius Nyerere, Tanzania's "Teacher." In other instances, however, "presidential cultism" became a sinister instrument for misrule and terror in the hands of egomaniacal despots. Life-President Macias Nguema Biyogo of Equatorial Guinea, who designated himself "the National Miracle," conducted a reign of terror that took 50,000 lives. In a bizarre 1975 incident, he arranged the Christmas Eve execution of 150 political prisoners, who met their deaths at the national soccer stadium as the public-address system played the song "Those were the Days." Perhaps even more notorious was the Central African Republic's President Jean-Bedel Bokassa, who in 1977 crowned himself "Emperor of the Central African Empire" in a $25 million ceremony that his impoverished nation could ill afford. His regime collapsed only after he personally participated in the murder of 80 schoolchildren who refused to buy uniforms from a family-owned company. In independent Africa, military dictatorships and authoritarian presidential regimes alike sometimes deteriorated into "kleptocracies," in which governmental officials took advantage of their positions to enrich themselves, fellow tribesman and their families through graft, bribery and corruption.

Perhaps the most extreme manifestation of the political instability that plagued much of postcolonial Africa was civil war. In the aftermath of independence, religious, tribal, political and regional antagonisms sparked civil wars in a number of nations. Ethiopia, Somalia, Nigeria, Sudan, Angola, Morocco, Rwanda, Burundi and Zaire are but a few of the nations that suffered the sometimes-catastrophic impact of civil war. In some cases, these internal conflicts were given an international dimension by the Cold War, which drew the United States and the Soviet Union into African wars in support of competing factions. Offering financial and military aid together with modern weaponry, the superpowers inevitably complicated and sometimes lengthened internal struggles in Africa. In Angola, 50,000 combat troops from Communist Cuba intervened to support the socialist Popular Movement for the Liberation of Angola in a complex struggle for political dominance of the newly independent nation. In the 1980s, civil war in Chad led to limited military intervention by Libya's Muammar Gaddafi in support of the rebels. In response, both France and the United States provided support to the government of Hissene Habre, rather than permit the extension of Libyan influence into the largely desert nation. African leaders, cognizant of the political and economic benefits to be gained, willingly accepted aid from either or

sometimes both of the two superpowers. The flow of arms and military advisors into Africa during the Cold War era extended the life of authoritarian regimes and provided rebel factions with the means of conducting extended and violent insurgencies.

THE QUEST FOR UNITY

In view of the multitude of difficulties that African nations faced after independence, many African leaders perceived the need for ideologies and institutions that could serve as a framework for African unity and hopefully facilitate the transition to mature nationhood. Many feared that Africans were as yet captive to a "psychology of inferiority," a lingering mental vestige of slavery and colonialism that hindered Africans from realizing their full capacities. Some, like Senegal's Leopold Senghor, propounded the liberating energy of *negritude*, a philosophy of black consciousness which held that Africa's future was contingent upon acknowledging and utilizing the unique aspects of "Africanness." Others, like Nkrumah and Kenyatta, continued to invoke the power of some form of traditional pan-Africanism as the key to Africa's successful development. Ultimately, these impulses and others found institutional expression in the Organization of African Unity (OAU), established at the Ethiopian capital of Addis Ababa in May 1963. Julius Nyerere captured the idealism and perhaps naïve expectations of that year when he asserted, "For the sake of all African states, large or small, our goal must be a United States of Africa. Only this can really give Africa the future her people deserve after centuries of economic uncertainty and social oppression." Though Nyerere's vision of a united Africa failed to materialize, the original thirty member nations of the OAU drafted a Charter of African Unity, by which they agreed to respect "the territorial integrity of every state and the inalienable right to an independent existence," a laudable and ambitious goal in a century that had witnessed unparalleled aggression elsewhere in the world.

For a variety of reasons, the Charter was widely respected. With only a few notable exceptions, African states abstained from war against one another. Broader OAU goals included fostering African cooperation and solidarity, resisting colonialism and racism and defending human rights. The OAU's eventual record in these areas was problematic, as the sheer diversity among African states precluded any comprehensive or enduring cooperation, and human rights violations by black African governments were rarely addressed, whereas the transgressions of white-dominated states were consistently denounced. Likewise, the record of achievement in independent Africa is at best mixed. While many new states began the era of independence with idealistic aims and high hopes for both economic development and political liberty, expectations frequently fell victim to intractable problems and ambitious individuals.

The Many Paths to Nationhood

Even as the path to economic progress remained elusive for much of independent Africa, so too did the quest for stable and democratic government. As of the late 1980s, only seven states in sub-Saharan Africa boasted governments that were to some degree democratic. The sheer number and diversity of African states precludes any definitive generalization, but an examination of the course of several representative national histories affords some greater insight.

GHANA: AFRICA'S HOPE AND DESPAIR

Though Ghana was not the first colony in black Africa to gain independence (Sudan achieved that status in 1956), it was the focus of considerable attention because of its perceived potential as a model for steady development and stable government. At independence in 1957, the former Gold Coast possessed the natural resources requisite to economic growth; cocoa, hardwoods, valuable mineral ores, diamonds and gold promised a diverse, dynamic economy. The West African country also boasted a high literacy rate and an educated elite experienced in administration and government. In the eyes of many, however, Ghana's greatest asset was the charismatic and energetic nationalist leader Kwame Nkrumah (1909–1972), who by the late 1950s was widely considered a model for leadership in independent Africa. As a young man, Nkrumah worked and studied in Britain and the United States. The sight of the Statue of Liberty inspired Nkrumah as he was leaving the United States in 1945; as he later wrote, he swore that he "would never rest until I have carried your message to Africa." He returned to the Gold Coast in 1947, where he became active in the growing nationalist movement. Convinced that the movement for self-government had to rest on a mass base, rather than just on the educated elite, he founded the Convention People's Party (CPP) in 1949 and adopted the slogan "Self-Government NOW." Nkrumah's growing prominence in nationalist circles landed him in jail on charges of sedition, but it soon became clear to Colonial Office officials that the demand for self-government in the Gold Coast could not be ignored. As a system of internal self-government was established in the early 1950s, Nkrumah's influence and popularity grew and in 1952 he was elected Prime Minister. His Convention People's Party maintained its electoral majority and Nkrumah became Prime Minister of independent Ghana in 1957.

Much of the African and world community acknowledged the dynamic and intelligent Nkrumah as a symbol of and spokesman for the new Africa. Numerous world dignitaries, including U.S. Vice President Richard Nixon, attended Ghana's independence ceremony, and the cover of *Life* magazine featured Nkrumah. A dedicated pan-Africanist, Nkrumah advocated African unity and the creation of uniquely African governmental systems. Speaking before the All-African People's Conference in 1959, Nkrumah asserted that Africans should "develop our own community and an African personality. . . . Others may feel that they have evolved the very best way of life, but we are not bound, like slavish imitators, to accept it as our mold." Regrettably, Nkrumah's broad ambitions for Africa and his nation led him down the path to dictatorship and the course of events in Ghana in subsequent years followed a pattern that became distressingly commonplace throughout independent Africa. Describing himself as "a nondenominational Christian and a Marxist socialist," Nkrumah soon resorted to repressive measures to ensure the creation of the model socialist society he envisioned. Within a year of independence, Nkrumah implemented laws allowing the lengthy detention of government critics and restricting freedom of the press. Elected president in 1960, Nkrumah worked through the CPP to gain control of most of the country's associations, such as trade unions and the civil service. To secure his objectives, he also encouraged the growth of a presidential cult, one manifestation of which was omnipresent pictures of the dictator on stamps, banknotes, coins and shop walls. Assuming grandiose titles such as "Man of Destiny" and "Star of Africa," Nkrumah encouraged accolades from a subservient press. One compliant newspaper editor asserted in a 1961 article that "Kwame Nkrumah will be written of as the liberator, the Messiah, the Christ of our day."

Nkrumah's abuse of political power was both distressing and disappointing, but his disastrous economic policies were of much greater consequence. Impatient for economic progress, Nkrumah embarked on a reckless program of rapid industrialization with little attention to cost or feasibility. Vast construction projects of dubious profitability were undertaken, often funded by the generous foreign developmental aid that flowed into the country after independence. Even as Ghana's export earnings fell because of a decline in cocoa prices, Nkrumah initiated additional projects by borrowing against future revenues. Growing economic distress and political unrest sparked conspiracies and assassination attempts, bringing only further repression from Nkrumah, who announced a one-party state in 1964. Nkrumah also sought closer ties with the USSR, despite his own earlier advocacy of an African policy of "nonalignment." Despite the objections of his army chiefs, he accepted a Soviet proposal to train some of Ghana's soldiers. Such decisions inevitably deepened the suspicions of American policymakers, who were increasingly sensitive to Communist influence in Africa. Increasingly isolated in his presidential compound, where he was protected by Soviet-trained presidential guards, Nkrumah clung tenuously to power. In 1966, while Nkrumah was abroad visiting North Vietnam and the People's Republic of China, resentful army officers ousted him. He spent the rest of his life in exile, ascribing his failures to insufficient "Marxian analysis." He died in Romania in 1972.

Nkrumah's failure to live up to the expectations established in 1957 set Ghana on a course of intermittent and generally ineffectual civilian rule interspersed with military coups. A 1979 coup brought to power Jerry Rawlings, an air force fighter pilot. Though Rawlings restored civilian rule, continuing economic decline weakened the authority of the new government. The 1970s had been bad years, with export revenues declining fifty percent, while average real income fell by a ruinous eighty percent. Within a year of the return of civilian government, the annual inflation rate exceeded one hundred percent and the national debt approached two billion dollars. These circumstances led Rawlings to initiate a second coup in late 1981. An intelligent and charismatic man, Rawlings was sincerely committed to national recovery and successfully appealed to the World Bank for assistance. Economic reforms introduced in the early 1980s produced a high rate of economic growth, but unemployment and poverty remained major social problems. By the late 1980s, Ghana had achieved only a tenuous state of economic and political stability. After a quarter of a century of independence Ghana, proclaimed as a symbol of

Africa's hope in 1957, seemed more a disturbing omen of Africa's possible fate.

KENYA: OASIS OF STABILITY

Kenya, in East Africa, entered the era of independence in 1963 under the steady hand of Jomo Kenyatta, whose broadly accepted authority was a great stabilizing force through the fifteen years prior to his death in 1978. Born around 1892 in the highlands north of the capital of Nairobi, Kamua wa Ngengi, as he was known prior to adopting his more familiar name, was educated at a mission school, much as were many others of the first generation of African leaders. His consciousness of the inequities of colonial rule developed while he was working as an interpreter in Nairobi in the 1920s. In 1928, he joined the Kikuyu Central Association, which was initially concerned primarily with addressing the grievances of that tribe. After 1931, he left Kenya for fifteen years, traveling and studying in a number of European nations, including the Soviet Union. Unlike some other Third World nationalists, he rejected Marxist socialism as a solution to Africa's problems, later cautioning, "Don't be fooled into looking to Communism for food." His dedication to the cause of African independence grew during his long exile, during which he adopted the name Jomo, which means "burning spear." (It remains unclear whether his last name derived from his country or from the word for a type of beaded belt). Upon his return to Kenya in 1946, he was widely acknowledged as a leader of the African nationalist cause, which explains in part why British authorities arrested him in 1952 during the "Mau Mau Emergency" despite the absence of any evidence of his involvement in the rebellion. Imprisoned in 1952, Kenyatta spent the next seven years behind bars, isolated from the swelling impulse for African independence.

Accepting the inevitability of Kenyan self-government, British colonial authorities permitted the establishment of two political organization, the Kenyan African National Union (KANU), which was the vehicle for the larger Kikuyu, Luo and Kamba tribes, and the Kenyan African Democratic Union (KADU), which represented the smaller ethnic groups. Following an electoral victory by KANU candidates, Kenyatta was released from prison in 1961. Despite the injustices visited upon him, Kenyatta voiced no resentment of white authorities and urged conciliation and restraint. "Where there has been racial hatred," he declared, "it must be ended. Where there has been tribal animosity, it will be finished. Let us not dwell on the bitterness of the past. I would rather look to the future, to the good new Kenya." It proved to be an auspicious statement. Following his swearing in as Prime Minister in December 1963, Jomo Kenyatta pursued a generally moderate course with the twin goals of economic progress and political stability.

Kenya's generally good economic health during the 1960s stemmed in part from Kenyatta's realistic appraisal of Kenya's resources and potential. With few exportable natural resources other than coffee and tea, Kenya was necessarily dependent on agriculture and tourism. Kenyatta had moderate success in promoting both, and resisted the impulse to pursue costly and questionable industrial development programs. Acknowledging the economic importance of the remaining white settlers and the Europeans and Asians who provided managerial and technical expertise,

Kenyatta refrained from expelling non-Africans or confiscating their properties, as occurred elsewhere in Africa. He also refused to squander national revenue on military expenditures, devoting less than seven percent of the national budget to an area that absorbed fifty percent of Uganda's budget under Amin.

Unlike proponents of African Socialism, Kenyatta embraced capitalism, though he did promote the "Africanization", or nationalizing, of large foreign-owned businesses. His land reform programs and stress on agricultural development ensured that Kenya could meet its own food needs. His generally pro-Western foreign policy stance assured amiable relations with the United States, which also brought economic benefits. Politically, Kenya eventually became a one-party state with dissolution of KADU and the absorption of many of its members into Kenyatta's KANU. The focus of a burgeoning presidential cult, Kenyatta judiciously exercised strong presidential powers to forge the national unity he espoused. Nonetheless, parliamentary debates remained energetic, political prisoners were few, the press was given broad license and the judiciary remained independent. A competent civil service, an anomaly in much of Africa, assured administrative efficiency. There were justifiable complaints that Kenyatta consistently favored his own Kikuyu tribe and family in governmental appointments and economic favors, but his immense personal authority assured that dissent remained minimal. There were exceptions; unknown parties murdered at least two outspoken critics of the regime. Kenya was, however, spared the systematic and open repression that was characteristic of many other African states.

Upon Kenyatta's death in 1978, vice-president Daniel arap Moi pledged to follow in the "Old Man's" footsteps while reducing the corruption that proliferated behind the scenes during Kenyatta's presidency. The peaceful transition of power was in itself an accomplishment, but in the absence of the widely respected Kenyatta, the nation's political stability eroded rapidly. Moi soon demonstrated his determination to inherit the presidential cult that had surrounded his revered predecessor. He demanded uncritical loyalty from government officials, proclaiming in a 1984 speech, "I would like all ministers, assistant ministers and others to sing like a parrot after me. That is how we can progress." As he decidedly lacked Kenyatta's authority, his hectoring caused resentment, as did his efforts to lessen Kikuyu representation in the government. As criticism of his regime grew, Moi adopted ever more authoritarian methods of repression. Undercurrents of popular dissatisfaction grew by the early 1980s as the economy soured due to a decline in commodity prices. In 1982 Moi suppressed an attempted air force *coup* only with difficulty and some loss of life. Though Moi preserved his position with the army's support, internal opposition grew in the latter part of the decade as the nation faced a new economic crisis that foreign indebtedness caused. Kenyatta's legacy of national stability and modest prosperity, so much the product of his own popularity, proved difficult to maintain in the years following his death.

TANZANIA: THE AMBIGUITIES OF "AFRICAN SOCIALISM"

Counted among the most respected and enduring leaders of independent Africa, Julius Nyerere guided his country from 1961 to 1985, leaving an indelible imprint and a problematic legacy. Born in 1920 in what was then the newly British colony of Tanganyika (before the First World War it was German East Africa), Nyerere was a studious youngster who went on to earn an education degree at Uganda's Makerere University prior to attending the University of Edinburg on a scholarship. His political consciousness was further awakened through his studies of history, economics and political science, and he returned to Tanganyika in 1952 with a master's degree. Nyerere was central in founding the Tanganyika African National Union (TANU), which served as the organizational vehicle for Tanganyikan nationalism, uniting the country's diverse ethnic groups behind the campaign for independence. TANU electoral victories prior to independence assured that Nyerere would lead the new nation as prime minister in 1961.

Nyerere faced major challenges in forging a viable nation. Since 1919, the British had ruled Tanganyika as a protectorate rather than as a colony and, accordingly, expended little effort or money on internal improvements. The country had few natural resources, almost no industry and inadequate infrastructure at independence, and the scattered population depended largely on subsistence farming These circumstances did not dim Nyerere's idealistic vision for Tanzania, as the country was known after its merger with the coastal island of Zanzibar in 1964. Nyerere believed that Tanzania's future lay in constructing a society based on the values of pre-colonial Africa. There, he argued, self-sacrifice and self-reliance had been the basis of a broad sense of communal responsibility that made for a stable and moral society. "African Socialism," as Nyerere defined it, had little to do with Karl Marx. Rather, it was an indigenous ideology that would spare Africans from the exploitative effects of capitalism and the dogmatic strictures of doctrinaire socialism. *Ujamaa,* or "familyhood," as Nyerere described his conception of African socialism, was to be founded on principles of mutual respect, shared property and a national commitment to the common good. The fundamentals of Nyerere's program were articulated in the 1967 Arusha Declaration, which established principles for political leadership and a broad outline for economic and social organization.

An advocate of strong presidential government, Nyerere was nonetheless aware of the pitfalls that one-party states such as Tanzania faced. Even by the late 1960s, many African regimes had deteriorated into malevolent dictatorships or self-serving kleptocracies. The Arusha Declaration required that government and party leaders receive no more than one salary. Nor could they own rental properties or stock in private companies, or hold directorships in private firms. Nyerere himself set an example of public probity by accepting only a very modest salary and forgoing expensive cars, villas and the other privileges of high office that were so common among other African leaders. Government office, he believed, should be synonymous with public service, not self-aggrandizement. Nyerere had significantly reduced governmental salaries the previous year as part of a general effort to reduce the gap between rich and poor, which was growing across much of the continent. The national government was to manage economic development, with an emphasis on agriculture. Nyerere's program envisioned regrouping the nation's scattered rural population into self-sufficient villages, where land ownership and utilization would be communal in nature. Governmental services, aimed at improving health, education and agricultural productivity, would be administered and paid for at the village level. What Nyerere sought through the Arusha Declaration was the creation of an egalitarian society based on traditional African village life.

Julius Nyerere's idealistic vision, together with his charisma and personal affability, brought considerable world acclaim and massive foreign aid during the first decade of his presidency. Few African leaders have enjoyed the prominence or influence that Nyerere did. Former U.S. ambassador to the United Nations Andrew Young described Nyerere's dominance of African affairs as "nothing short of miraculous" and "something you would expect from the leader of a nation of great wealth or military strength." Nyerere's world reputation was in part the product of his ability to articulate and implement a coherent design for national development. There were more specific successes; Nyerere successfully promoted Swahili as the national language, supplanting the multitude of Tanzanian dialects. Universal primary education and adult learning programs greatly enhanced national literacy, bringing it to upward of ninety percent by the early 1980s. Tanzanian social services helped extend life expectancy by fifty percent by the same date.

Tanzania's achievements under Nyerere, however, must be measured against some troubling realities and undeniable failures. Nyerere's presidency, however popular, ultimately rested on a one-party system in which dissent was not tolerated. Presidential elections were conducted Soviet-style; voters cast "yes" or "no" votes for the single candidate, Nyerere, who ostensibly won the approval of ninety-nine percent of the electorate in 1970. Prior to 1979, Nyerere's regime incarcerated more political prisoners than South Africa. Unlike other African leaders, Nyerere also demonstrated his willingness to intervene in the affairs of his neighbors, most famously in 1979 when Tanzanian troops invaded Uganda. In the aftermath of Amin's ouster, Nyerere contrived to remove two successive Ugandan leaders of whom he disapproved.

Perhaps the greater disappointment was the failure of Nyerere's much-heralded African socialism, which foundered on the persistent individualism of the Tanzanian people. Few of the cooperative villages functioned as planned, as many peasants preferred individual farming. Popular reluctance to relocate to *ujamaa* villages led Nyerere to compel resettlement in 1973. Much of the population was eventually compulsorily resettled in some 7,500 cooperative villages, with the army rounding up those who continued to resist. The economic consequences were disastrous, as falling food production compounded by drought produced the threat of serious famine by the late 1970s. Forced to import food from abroad, Nyerere's government faced growing budget deficits and increased reliance on foreign aid and food donations. His program of state control over the rest of the economy produced equally poor results. Numerous state-owned farms, banks and industries were poorly run, their budgets drained by vast numbers of superfluous employees. Indeed, as initiative and investment in the private sector were discouraged through fiscal policies aimed at reducing distinctions in wealth, the government sector alone continued to offer opportunities for employment.

Much to Nyerere's disappointment, the public corruption so commonplace across Africa also made inroads in Tanzania. On the tenth anniversary of the Arusha Declaration,

Nyerere reviewed the nation's progress, candidly acknowledging economic shortcomings but refusing to concede that they might have resulted from his socialist policies. Rather, Nyerere insisted that his approach had spared the nation the much worse ravages of unbridled capitalism and explained Tanzania's economic woes as an inevitable but temporary consequence of implementing his innovative programs. He reasserted his belief that African socialism remained the correct path. By the early 1980s, however, the deteriorating economy forced Nyerere to make some modest concessions to free enterprise, such as allowing large-scale farming on a public or private basis and inviting foreign investment in such ventures. The government's pressing need for international loans compelled a reduction in the number and cost of government agencies. Much of the initial foreign enthusiasm for Nyerere's African socialism had dissipated by the time he resigned the presidency in 1985. Nyerere provided Tanzania with over two decades of relative stability and a unique creed that offered direction and a significant degree of hope for his people. However, Nyerere's inability to realize the economic progress that African socialism promised must also be accounted as part of his ambiguous legacy.

NIGERIA: DEMOCRACY ON TRIAL

British colonial authorities considered Nigeria, on Africa's West Coast, as having tremendous potential for development. Now the most populous nation in Africa, Nigeria's pre-independence population of 32 million produced a small but energetic class of businessmen, professionals and intellectuals, and the British believed them especially fitted for self-government. As early as the 1920s, colonial policy allowed for the participation of Nigerians (who were referred to as such by the British) in regional councils, and by the end of the Second World War complete self-government was the ultimate objective of British administrators. Exportable commodities such as cocoa, palm oil and rubber gave promise of a stable economic base, but it was petroleum that most raised expectations for economic growth. Nigeria was blessed with considerable oil reserves and by the 1980s the country was the world's sixth largest exporter of crude oil. Still, in the 1950s the country remained overwhelmingly agricultural and foreign firms and businessmen dominated much of the economy.

On the eve of independence, the greatest potential obstacle to a stable independent Nigeria was the country's ethnic and linguistic diversity; there are at least 250 different tribes speaking nearly 400 languages. The largest tribal groupings also reflected a North–South division. Nigeria's northern regions were overwhelmingly Moslem and dominated by the Hausa and Fulani tribes, whereas the primarily Christian South was home to the Ibo and Yoruba. Aware of these fundamental divisions, both the British and Nigerian leaders perceived the advantages of a federal scheme of national organization, which would hopefully give all the major groups adequate voice in government.

Upon independence in October 1960, Nigeria was a federal state with a parliamentary form of government modeled on the British example. Three major parties emerged, each controlling a regional government, while Abubakar Balewa, a moderate Northerner, served as Prime Minister through 1966. Unfortunately, tribal and regional loyalties quickly destabilized the political system as officeholders competed to obtain appointments, funds and favors for their constituencies. In the absence of any

strong and nationally respected leader, Nigeria was increasingly pulled apart by the centrifugal forces generated by these antagonisms. The political situation deteriorated as parties and politicians resorted to deceit, illegalities and violence to win elections. Chaotic civilian rule, the curse of much of independent Africa by the mid-1960s, provoked a military coup in January 1966. Rebel troops murdered Balewa, but loyal troops under the moderate General Ironsi, who proclaimed his intent of restoring order and ending the destructive effects of regionalism, crushed the intended radical revolution. In May, Ironsi, whose appointments favored the Ibos, proclaimed the end of federated Nigeria and banned all political and tribal organizations. Major civil disturbances preceded another military coup in July, when disaffected northern officers executed the hapless Ironsi.

The man who emerged as head of the reconstituted military government was Yakubu Gowon, a Northern Christian who hoped to reorganize the federal state so as to achieve better minority representation. The proclamation of the separatist state of Biafra in the Ibo-dominated east cut short Gowon's efforts in May 1967. The subsequent 3-year Biafran War demonstrated not only the dire consequences of unbridled tribalism and regionalism, but also the impact of foreign partisanship on African civil wars. Desirous of gaining influence with the likely winner, numerous foreign governments offered moral and military support to the federal government at Lagos. Arms from Britain and aircraft from the Soviet Union (often flown by Egyptians or East Germans) heightened the violence and destructiveness of the conflict. Increasingly isolated, the Ibos gained some sympathy from the outside world when photographs of starving Biafran children were widely publicized, but ultimately only Haiti recognized the struggling Republic of Biafra. By the end of the war in January 1970, approximately 600,000 Nigerians, Biafran and otherwise, had been killed.

While many civil wars generate enduring hatreds, the Biafran War produced only a widespread desire among Nigerians to move on. As head of government, Gowon pursued a policy of conciliation and the former rebels were generally reabsorbed into the military and federal government. Ibos were not excluded from high positions in the public or private sectors in the postwar years. Growing national revenues from the sale of crude oil, the price of which was escalating enormously in the early 1970s, aided recovery from the war. Even so, the agricultural sector languished due to government inattention and a decline in commodity prices. As occurred in similar circumstances throughout Africa, the stagnation of the rural economy drove peasants into increasingly crowded urban centers such as Lagos. Inadequate public infrastructure contributed to persistent popular frustrations, which were rarely resolved by inefficient and sometimes corrupt regional administrations.

Gowon's temporizing about a return to civilian rule brought about his ouster in 1975, when reformist army officers seized control of the government while he was abroad. What distinguished this military coup from others across Africa was that the soldiers genuinely intended to restore civilian government. Trained at Britain's Sandhurst Academy, Nigeria's senior military officials accepted that the military's role was to serve rather than to govern and were acutely aware of the need to restore Nigeria's international reputation as an island of democratic government in Africa. Among the many tasks the

military undertook was to reduce the army's size by roughly half. Murtala Muhammed, head of the new regime, also announced a four-year schedule for the restoration of civilian government. Though disgruntled officers soon assassinated Muhammed, his successor proclaimed his commitment to Muhammed's goals and a new constitution, designed with the objective of reducing the impact of tribalism, was eventually adopted. Nigeria discarded its parliamentary government in favor of a system that was closely modeled on that of the United States, with a presidential executive, an independent judiciary and a bicameral legislature.

The nation's latent political vitality was demonstrated as soon as the military's ban on party activity was lifted in 1978; fifty-two political parties were founded, though only five were eventually certified as "truly national." Prior to the 1979 election, the National Party of Nigeria emerged as a dominant political force and nominated a Northern Fulani, Shehu Shagari, as its presidential candidate. Shagari's running mate was an Ibo, as the new constitution required that presidential and vice-presidential candidates could not be from the same tribe. Shagari's presidency ushered in five years of democratic government, though problems such as sectarian violence, political intrigue and corruption were not resolved. Though Shagari won reelection in 1983, he served barely three months before falling victim to another military coup in early 1984. The new military regime suspended the constitution and began an earnest effort to investigate and punish corruption, but the greater damage to Nigerian democracy was already done.

A recurring pattern in Nigerian political life seemed well established by the early 1980s, as periods of democratic but disorderly government gave way to orderly but moderately authoritarian military rule. Neither seemed capable of resolving the nation's fundamental divisions or its lingering economic ills. Though military rule in Nigeria was relatively benign compared to elsewhere on the continent, the intermittent resort to military government in a nation with Nigeria's advantages and promise demonstrated the inherent difficulties of establishing viable democratic government in Africa.

ZAIRE: THE HERITAGE OF CHAOS

Few African colonies were as ill prepared for independence as was the Belgian Congo. Brutally exploited in the late nineteenth century, the people of the huge central African colony were permitted virtually no experience in self-government or administration even during the last decade of Belgian rule. Political parties and freedom of the press were banned; many among the small group of African elites in the colony concerned themselves primarily with greater privileges for themselves. No broad nationalist movement existed, nor did Belgian authorities cultivate any cadre of potential leaders. Not until 1958 did colonial officials give any serious consideration to a transitional scheme, and even then only agreed to implement a gradual program of self-government that would take years.

Violent rioting in Leopoldville and Stanleyville in 1959 ultimately compelled the Belgian government to ponder the inevitability of Congolese independence, but not until the Round Table Conference of January 1960 in Brussels were the Congolese themselves actually consulted as to their country's future. By then, developments in the vast colony did not bode well for the future. In

the face of Belgian intransigence, political activity in the Congo finally exploded in 1959, producing over 120 officially registered political groups. Ominously, these political groupings reflected the ethnic diversity of the Congo, which has 200 tribes. Only one party, the Congolese National Movement led by Patrice Lumumba, propounded a nationalist creed. Panicked by the growing unrest in their colony, Belgian authorities at the Round Table Conference agreed to independence for the Congo on June 30, 1960. The potential for a stable transition of power was virtually nonexistent, as the colony was almost entirely administered by Belgians. Only three Congolese held posts in the colonial civil service; there were only 16 university graduates in the country. There were no Congolese doctors, secondary school teachers or military officers. As events soon proved, such ill preparation for self-government was an invitation to chaos.

The first independent government reflected the troubling divisions in the Congo. Though Lumumba's party won the largest number of seats in the National Assembly, it could govern only as part of a complex coalition of twelve parties. The articulate and charismatic Lumumba, now prime minister, desired a unified national state. The president, Joseph Kasavubu, hoped to rebuild the ancient kingdom of Kongo by reuniting the Bakongo people. The president of the Katanga provincial government, Moise Tshombe, sought autonomy for the mineral-rich province under his own tribal party. The fragmented national government was immediately faced with a mutiny among Congolese soldiers, who demanded the Africanization of the officer corps. When Lumumba gave in, military authority collapsed and ill-disciplined troops went on a rampage, assaulting whites and provoking the panicked exodus of some 25,000 remaining Belgians. Belgium responded to the chaos by flying in 10,000 troops, leading Lumumba to fear that Brussels intended to renege on independence. Further complicating matters, Tshombe declared Katanga's independence in July and invited Belgian troops into the province to expel the Congolese army. Lumumba saw no alternative other than to request military assistance from the United Nations, which ultimately deployed a 19,000-man 26-nation force in the Congo.

The continued presence of Belgian troops led Lumumba to an intemperate decision that fundamentally altered the nature of the confrontation; he requested military aid from the Soviet Union. The arrival of Soviet arms, aircraft and advisors in August transformed the struggle over Katanga into a Cold War confrontation as American policymakers concluded that Lumumba was now an aspiring Soviet client. U.S. President Dwight Eisenhower's expressions of concern about Lumumba's intentions were interpreted by the Central Intelligence Agency as implicit authorization to assassinate the Congolese leader, and an operative was sent to Leopoldville for that purpose. Before the plot was realized, Kasavubu, who was under pressure from American and Belgian officials, dismissed Lumumba. In response, Lumumba announced in a radio address that he had removed Kasavubu, and the nation plunged deeper into chaos. The situation was resolved in mid-September when army colonel Joseph Mobutu seized power and declared that he was "neutralizing" the squabbling politicians. Mobutu ejected the Soviets, repaired relations with the UN and the United States and restored Kasavubu as president in late 1960. Lumumba was arrested in November and imprisoned, but his continued presence proved troubling. In January 1961, Lumumba was transferred to Elizabethville in Katanga, where he was arrested at the airport and later murdered by Tshombe's soldiers or Belgian mercenaries. In death he became a political martyr, praised as an exemplar of pan-African socialism even by those who engineered his downfall. Katangan rebels abandoned their struggle in 1963.

The restoration of the Congo's constitutional government brought several years of relative stability, during which Mobutu strengthened the army and his own authority. He was thus well positioned to lead a second military coup in 1965 when a political power struggle destabilized the Kasavubu government. Mobutu laid the foundations for a thirty-two year dictatorship by reducing parliamentary power, suspending provincial assemblies, assuming control of the police and executing potentially troublesome rivals. Like most military leaders, Mobutu's promise was order and prosperity, which he believed could only be achieved through his unchallenged authority. A new constitution in 1967 gave Mobutu, as president, effective control of political affairs and a new party, the Popular Movement of the Revolution (MRP), served as a vehicle for his ambitions. Significantly, the MRP's official ideology was "Mobutuism," one of a growing number of indications that Mobutu intended to promote presidential cultism Though never clearly defined, "Mobutuism" came to include a campaign for "African authenticity," which began with the renaming of the nation as "Zaire." Mobutu insisted that cities, villages and people adopt African names. For himself, the Zairean president took the name Mobutu Sese Seko Kuku Ngbendu Wa Za

Banga, which translates as "the all-powerful warrior who, because of his endurance and inflexible will to win, sweeps from conquest to conquest leaving fire in his wake." He forbid western-style clothing and designed a national uniform called the "Mobutu suit." Mobutu's immodesty and egomania were further evident in his rapid accumulation of expensive properties abroad and his extravagant lifestyle, which included eleven presidential palaces. This was made possible by rapid economic growth in the early 1970s, when record copper prices portended a bright future for Zaire. Massive amounts of U.S. foreign aid, which came as a reward for Mobutu's outspoken anti-communism, also boosted Zaire's economy.

The good times were destined to be temporary, however. Like many other president-dictators, Mobutu was seduced by the appeal of prestigious but costly construction projects and squandered much of the nation's wealth. In 1974, Mobutu spent $15 million dollars to sponsor a prizefight between Muhammed Ali and George Forman, largely for the prestige it brought his regime. The effects of uncontrolled spending were compounded by ill-considered expropriations of foreign-owned businesses and the expulsion of Asian businessmen and Belgian technicians. Consequently, Zaire's economy unraveled in the 1980s, bringing widespread misery and even hunger, as food had to be imported. Desperate, Mobutu requested that foreign specialists assume the direction of Zaire's financial institutions and businesses. Not surprisingly, he promoted this program of economic recovery as "the Mobutu Plan." By the late 1980s, Zaire suffered from all of the problems of a stagnant economy, an eroding public infrastructure and stifling one-party presidential rule. Mobutu's most noteworthy legacy was

the dubious stability provided by his enduring hold on power.

RHODESIA AND SOUTH AFRICA: BLACK MAJORITIES AND WHITE RULE

Some of the greatest challenges to African nationalism came in the south-central and southern regions of the continent, where white minorities retained exclusive political authority and economic predominance in states with black majorities. Rhodesia's fundamental inequities were established with the colony in 1894, when the fertile half of the territory was granted to white settlers, who comprised only five percent of the population. Black Rhodesians, relegated to "Tribal Trust Lands," were rarely able to survive as subsistence farmers and most were destined to seek work as poorly paid laborers in the racially segregated colony. A separate Northern Rhodesia was created in 1899, becoming a British protectorate with considerable autonomy in 1924. Indirect rule allowed some political participation on the part of the black population, which was not the case in Southern Rhodesia. In 1953, as decolonization accelerated, Northern and Southern Rhodesia were joined with Nyasaland to create the Central African Federation, largely for administrative convenience. Growing demands in Northern Rhodesia for an end to white minority rule led to the colony's independence as Zambia in 1964.

In Southern Rhodesia, whites determined to preserve their monopoly on political power were drawn to the racist Rhodesian Front led by Ian Smith, who won election as Prime Minister in 1965. As Britain refused to grant independence unless blacks were accorded political equality, the fiery Smith issued a

Unilateral Declaration of Independence announcing Rhodesia's secession from the Commonwealth. Five years later in 1970, Smith, by now a worldwide symbol of white resistance to black rule in Africa, proclaimed Rhodesia's independence. Though both Britain and the UN imposed economic sanctions, they proved ineffective due to South Africa's support of Smith's government and the willingness of numerous western oil companies to ignore them. The end of Portuguese rule in Mozambique in 1975 gave encouragement to nationalist guerillas in Rhodesia and through the late 1970s, Smith's regime struggled to suppress the increasingly determined Patriotic Front, as the various insurgent groups were jointly called. Unable to sustain the costly war, the Rhodesian government accepted a British-sponsored agreement, by which Rhodesia would revert to colonial status for a short period, during which free elections would be held. A majority of voters supported Robert Mugabe's Zimbabwe African National Union and Rhodesia became independent Zimbabwe in April 1980. As lengthy and intense as the struggle for majority rule in Rhodesia was, the greater drama took place to the south in the Republic of South Africa, the last bastion of white minority rule in black Africa.

Between the creation of the Union of South African in 1910 and the outbreak of the Second World War, a preeminent concern of the colony's government was the unity of the white minority, which was deemed necessary to securing broad autonomy within the British Empire and preserving white rule. Accordingly, the Dutch or Afrikaner majority was encouraged to put aside their historical antagonisms against the English-speaking minority. Nonetheless, in 1914 Afrikaners formed the Nationalist Party to promote their

language (Afrikaans), culture, lessened ties with Great Britain and the necessity of maintaining white supremacy. Already undermined by growing Afrikaner nationalism, the white consensus eroded badly during the Second World War when Afrikaner extremists revealed their lingering resentments about the past by opposing entering the war on Britain's behalf. Though the declaration of war passed narrowly, expressions of pro-Hitler and pro-Nazi sentiments by some Afrikaners testified to the depth of their anti-British and racist beliefs; among the Nazi sympathizers was John Vorster, a future prime minister.

Energized by this surge of Afrikaner nationalism, the National Party won a surprise electoral victory in 1948, initiating nearly fifty years of Nationalist government. Strengthened by the support of the Dutch Reformed Church, which provided a theological justification for "separate development," the government set about institutionalizing *apartheid*, or racial separation, as an instrument for assuring continued white dominance in a predominantly black nation. The *apartheid* laws governed almost all areas of human activity, from intimate relations to employment and residence. The Prohibition of Mixed Marriages Act (1949) and the Immorality Acts (1950,1957) criminalized interracial marriage and sexual relations, making either punishable by prison terms. The Population Registration Act (1950), which established a system of "racial classification" so complex as to delineate seven subcategories of "Coloreds," addressed the ambiguities of race. The absurdities of the system, which classified Chinese as a "white" subgroup and visiting Japanese as "honorary whites," were obvious but nonetheless degrading for all those affected. The Population Registration

Board was charged with the task of reclassifying those who believed they were wrongly categorized.

The Group Areas Act (1959) authorized the designation of all South African territory to specific racial groups. Urban areas were almost universally restricted to whites and excluded races faced "removal" to approved areas. As many as 3.5 million black Africans were forcibly removed to rural "homelands" over a twenty-year period. Only in these "Bantustans," the South African government argued, could blacks enjoy some form of citizenship and separate development under the direction of tribal chiefs. Blacks who worked in urban "white only" areas were deemed temporary inhabitants and relegated to inferior rental housing. The Group Areas Act required a system of control to regulate transit to and from racially exclusive areas, so pass and travel permits were instituted to restrict the movement of non-whites. The Bantu Education Act (1953) provided separate and inferior education for black Africans, while the misnamed Industrial Conciliation Act (1956) assured that blacks would be channeled into menial, low-paying jobs through a system of "job reservation" which assigned employment opportunities according to racial classification. In its entirety, the *apartheid* system was aimed at assuring white supremacy in every area of life while relegating "lesser" races to circumscribed lives of hardship, privation and humiliation.

Though *apartheid* was aggressively enforced by an extensive state police apparatus, its blatant injustices inevitably provoked opposition. Though there was some dissent on the part of South African whites, most notably through the United Party and the Liberal Party, it was insufficient to break the National Party's stranglehold on power. Ultimately, opposition on the part of the non-white majority proved of far greater consequence. The preeminent opposition organization was the African National Congress (ANC), which had challenged government policies since its inception in 1912. A largely middle-class group that traditionally relied on modest means of protests, such as petitions and public rallies, the ANC adopted more aggressive, though still nonviolent, tactics in the aftermath of the Nationalist victory in 1948. In the early 1950s, Oliver Tambo, Albert Luthuli, Nelson Mandela and Walter Sisulu led the ANC in the Defiance Campaign, a multiracial effort that emphasized civil disobedience in protesting the pass laws and other injustices.

The government at Cape Town quickly demonstrated its intolerance of dissent and its willingness to disregard basic civil liberties. As early as 1950, the Suppression of Communism Act established the basis for banning individuals and organizations deemed communist, a designation easily stretched to include any dissident group. An act in 1953 enabled the government to arrest those who supported even passive resistance. Later acts in the 1960s and 1970s authorized the government to detain individuals without trial and to conduct virtually unrestricted surveillance activities. Refusing to be intimidated, ANC leaders organized a Congress of the People in 1953 and adopted the "Freedom Charter," a statement of political philosophy that asserted that "South Africa belongs to all who live in it, black and white." The charter endorsed universal suffrage, racial equality and individual freedoms, all concepts sufficiently subversive in the government's estimation to justify the arrest of 156 of the Congress leaders. The subsequent "Treason Trial" lasted four years and brought no convictions.

The level of government violence against protestors reached unprecedented heights in 1960 when a campaign organized by the Pan-Africanist Congress (PAC) against the pass laws culminated in the Sharpeville Massacre. On March 21, police fired on a group of peaceful demonstrators in the southern Transvaal town. The resultant seventy-two deaths provoked a massive demonstration in Cape Town and more deaths. The Sharpeville Massacre generated worldwide condemnation of the South African regime, which only drove the government to further repression. The government banned both the ANC and PAC and most of the leadership was sentenced to life prison terms in a 1963 trial. The burden of continued opposition fell to other groups such as the South African Students Organization, led by the "Black Consciousness" advocate Steve Biko, who argued that blacks should assume primary responsibility for leading the struggle against the regime and depend less on liberal whites.

In the face of the near-complete intransigence of the Vorster government, disaffection grew in the late 1970s and finally exploded in the 1976 Soweto uprising. Soweto, or Southwest Townships, was a large black residential area southwest of Johannesburg whose inhabitants lived isolated, impoverished lives in substandard housing as a consequence of *apartheid*. On June 16, schoolchildren marched in a mass protest against the inferior education imposed on them and police responded by firing on the crowd. Outraged blacks rioted in a number of townships and the government stepped up repressive measures.

Among the opposition leaders arrested in a massive government roundup was Steve Biko, who was subsequently beaten to death while in custody. A court absolved the police of any responsibility for the murder, but widespread outrage brought new recruits to the ANC, which was the target of increasingly aggressive government repression by the early 1980s. Driven to desperation by government intransigence and increasingly despondent of bringing about change peacefully, the ANC resorted to a campaign of sabotage and armed resistance. The highly respected Anglican Bishop Desmond Tutu, a 1984 Nobel Peace Prize winner, was among a number of prominent South Africans who warned that continued government oppression and resistance to change might well make violent revolution inevitable. Though Prime Minister P.W. Botha made some minor concessions in the 1980s, such as abolishing the pass laws and granting "Coloreds" and Indians limited representation in parliament, he was determined to preserve the fundamentals of the *apartheid* system, which allowed South Africa's 4.5 million whites to dominate over 25 million non-whites. Condemnation by the United Nations, the Vatican and numerous secular and religious organizations around the world, together with a multitude of boycotts, failed to shake the resolve of the Cape Town government, which clung to its course despite South Africa's growing isolation. Though rich in natural resources that drove the most productive economy on the continent, South Africa's greater potential remained unfulfilled at the end of the decade. As long as *apartheid* persisted, the vision of an equitable multiracial society remained a dream unrealized.

Continuing Challenges in Independent Africa

In the thirty years since Africa's "Year of Freedom" in 1960, the diverse peoples of the continent have experienced both the exhilaration and the myriad challenges of independence. The achievement of self-government, many discovered, only marked the beginning of the long and often difficult path to mature nationhood. For many of the new African nations, political liberty and stability seemed mutually exclusive and the struggle to achieve a balance between the two persisted well beyond the early years of independence, with no easy resolution in sight. The search for a single unifying ideology that might chart the course for independent Africa produced nothing that was universally applicable. The hopes of the Pan-Africanists ultimately foundered on competing national aspirations and the sheer diversity of Africa's peoples. Pan-Islam proved unworkable in the many religiously diverse sub-Saharan nations. African variants of socialism brought only problematic results, while revolutionary Marxist ideology only brought dictatorship or disruption, as Ethiopians and Angolans discovered in the 1970s. For the majority of African nations, governmental stability and democracy remained elusive. It has been observed that the development of the European nation-state occurred over the span of several centuries, during which national identities and loyalties were only gradually constructed. To expect the immediate establishment of fully functional national polities in Africa might be unrealistic, given the vastly different political and social traditions of the continent. All considered, the process of national development in much of Africa was still in its formative stages by the late 1980s.

Political instability, misrule, administrative incompetence and corruption contributed greatly to widespread economic malaise and growing social problems. The extent and magnitude of these socioeconomic ills led one writer to conclude that much of Africa could no longer be categorized as part of the developing Third World, but rather as a retrograde "Fourth World." Despite some notable advances, mostly in oil- and mineral-exporting nations, much of Africa experienced serious economic problems even after the first quarter-century of independence. In 30 of the 46 sub-Saharan nations, economies not only failed to develop, but actually regressed. Many industries limped along at much less than capacity, and agricultural production languished badly. While Africa produced 95 percent of its food needs in 1960, by the 1980s every nation except South Africa was importing food. As of the same date, according to the United Nations Council on Africa, 60 percent of sub-Saharan Africans were malnourished and severe food shortages and famines continued to plague parts of the continent. The declining African standard of living was reflected in the world's lowest annual per capita income of $365. Social problems were equally serious. The infant mortality rate in black Africa, 137 deaths per 1,000 births, was the highest in the world. Even so, the population expanded enormously, growing from 220 million in 1950 to 642 million in 1990. The press of a burgeoning population contributed to other problems. Only a small percentage of Africa's increasingly young population received the benefit of an education; a mere 11 percent of age-eligible African children attended school and the overall illiteracy rate approached 75 percent.

This growing, often illiterate population gravitated toward urban centers, driven by rural decline and the lure of employment in the cities, where the process of modernization was most evident. Consequently, the social and economic ills that inevitably attend rapid urbanization were greatly exacerbated in many African cities. Inadequate housing,

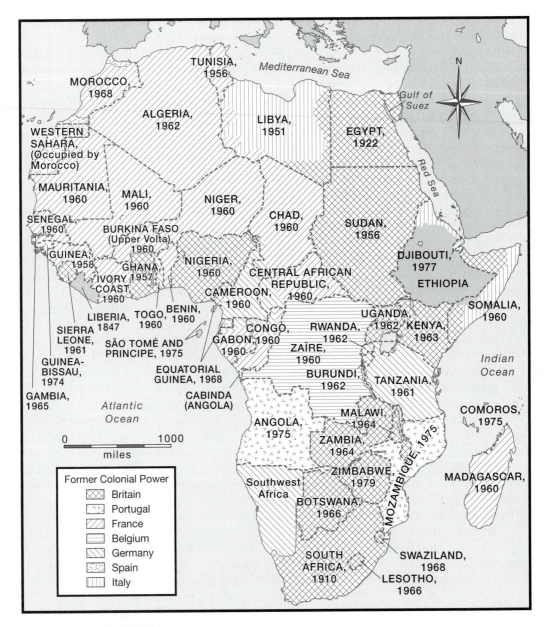

Map 10-1   Modern Africa

shantytown slums bordering urban centers, unemployment, the absence of adequate health care and crime became commonplace in cities across the continent. Governments, hard-pressed to maintain their own stability and lacking in financial resources, were rarely able to even begin addressing the multitude of urban problems. Public infrastructure, often minimal to begin with, eroded further under these conditions, making the everyday life of many Africans all the more difficult and uncertain. Given these challenges, few African governments had the resources or will to respond effectively, if at all, to the continent's growing environmental problems. Soil erosion, accelerated by the often reckless harvesting of hardwood forests, threatened agricultural production and water quality. The rapid deforestation of some nations drastically affected plant and animal populations, some of which faced extinction. Some endangered species, such as elephants, were given protection in state game preserves, but even there they often fell victim to ivory poachers who pursued their quarry with automatic weapons.

In the 1980s, the spread of Human Immunodeficiency Virus (HIV) and the Acquired Immune Deficiency Syndrome (AIDS) deepened the African crisis. The diseases, of uncertain origin, spread rapidly through urban areas in Central and East Africa. By the late 1980s, some estimates held that 8–10 percent of the population of some major cities in those regions were infected. There were troubling indications that endemic social problems contributed to the spread of the disease; in Nairobi, Kenya, more than 80 percent of the city's prostitutes tested positive for HIV. In the aftermath of the virtual destruction of Ugandan society during the Amin regime, the viruses gained a deadly foothold; one grim projection forecast that as of the year 2000, half of all Ugandan adults might have AIDS. Though that prediction proved inaccurate, AIDS had a devastating impact on populations where social controls were lacking and adequate medical care was almost nonexistent. In Kenya, one of Africa's most developed nations, there was only 1 doctor for every 25,600 people (the rate in Europe was 1 : 580).

Africa's continuing problems long after independence must be viewed in context. During the long colonial era, traditional African society, culture and political institutions were subjected to tremendous stress and in many cases fundamentally disrupted. In the years following the Second World War, the rapid and uneven pace of decolonization brought additional dislocations. Few civilizations have been subjected to the degree of change that has swept Africa in the second half of the twentieth century. The various processes of modernization, which produced significant political, social and economic dislocations in Europe in the eighteenth and nineteenth centuries, proved even more jarring when introduced in a much shorter timespan in Africa.

Despite Africa's persistent and often disheartening political and economic ills, African culture attained a new vibrancy during the post-independence era. African intellectuals enthusiastically addressed the multitude of issues the continent faced and often spoke to them with eloquence and even humor. Fiction, poetry and drama all served as vehicles for African writers who explored the social, political and cultural contours of a civilization in flux. Nigerian Chinua Achebe, the first major African writer in English, strove to forge a new African identity in his novels. Senegal, Guinea and Kenya were among the many other African nations that produced writers of note who dealt not only with the injustices of the colonial era, but were also willing to criticize the failings of Africa's new political elite. The struggles in South Africa inspired white African writers Nadine Gordimer and Alan Paton. The latter's *Cry, the Beloved Country* (1948) won worldwide acclaim. By the later 1980s, African women writers such as Nigerian Buchi Emecheta became more prominent, often using their art to explore the changing role of women in traditionally male-dominated African societies. In the 1960s, film emerged as a major vehicle of social, political and cultural discourse and African cinema attained a small but growing world audience. African music, traditional and contemporary, gained broader popularity worldwide. Some in Africa turned their attention to the resurrection and preservation of traditional African art forms, sometimes gaining government support for these efforts. Overall, African culture demonstrated its continuing vitality even in the face of the tremendous challenges independence presented. Near the end of the twentieth century, however, the myriad problems confronting Africa remained largely unresolved.

◆ —— ◆ —— ◆ —— ◆ —— ◆ —— ◆ —— ◆ —— ◆ —— ◆ —— ◆

On December 3, 1963, Nelson Mandela stood before a court in Pretoria, South Africa, as the court registrar requested that he plead to the charges laid against him. The forty-five-year-old Mandela, long an influential leader of the African National Congress, stood accused with several compatriots, black and white, of more than two hundred acts of sabotage aimed at fostering guerilla warfare, violent revolution and armed invasion of the South African state. Mandela, maintaining his customary reserve and defiance of the white-minority government, responded tersely: "The government should be in the dock, not me. I plead not guilty." Technically speaking, Mandela and his compatriots were arguably guilty of the charges. Most had been recently apprehended in a police raid on a rural ANC hideout in nearby Rivonia, where authorities confiscated plans detailing "Operation Mayibuye," an ambitious scheme for armed struggle against the state. Other recovered evidence included large numbers of maps of intended targets. At another ANC gathering place, police found bomb-making equipment. These damning materials reflected the recent preparations of *Umkhonto we Sizwe,* an organization formed in 1961 to carry out the struggle against the South African government's oppressive and racist policies. The resort to armed struggle was a reflection of the rising despair over bringing about change by peaceful means. Mandela, the group's commander-in-chief, had defied the law to travel to Ethiopia to address a Pan-African Freedom Movement conference and was arrested shortly after his return. Sentenced to five years in jail, Mandela was serving time on South Africa's notorious Robben Island when the raid on the Rivonia camp took place. Now he stood before another court to answer the more serious charges stemming from that incident.

Over the next several months, the prosecution produced hundreds of witnesses and documents in order to demonstrate that the accused were in fact dangerous communist-inspired revolutionaries who threatened the order and peace of the state. The defendants were determined to use the trial as a podium, to ensure that the world fully understood why they were driven to such extremes in their opposition to the

Fig. 10-2 African National Congress activist Nelson Mandela, accompanied by his wife Winnie, raises his fist in triumph following his release from prison in early 1990. For his opposition to South Africa's *apartheid* regime, Mandela spent more than two decades incarcerated, but remained the symbolic leader of the campaign for racial and political equality. (Pearson Education, Corporate Digital Archive, AP/Wide World Photos)

apartheid regime. Consequently, Mandela's courtroom statement, some four hours in length, presented a comprehensive history of the freedom struggle in South Africa, with particular attention to the objectives and means of the ANC. He reviewed the events that led to acceptance of armed struggle; he renounced Marxism as undemocratic and embraced the fundamentals of liberal democracy, as revealed in documents such as the English and American Bill of Rights. Africans, he asserted, "want a just share in the whole of South Africa," which could come only with racial and political equality. Mandela summed up by declaring his commitment to "the ideal of a democratic and free society in which all persons live together in harmony and with equal opportunities." "It is an ideal which I hope to live for and to achieve," he concluded. "But if needs be, it is an ideal for which I am prepared to die." In early June 1964, a judge found all the accused but one guilty. Those convicted were spared the death penalty and sentenced instead to life imprisonment. The sentence was, the judge acknowledged, "the only leniency I can show." Shortly afterward, police officials returned Nelson Mandela to Robben Island to begin twenty-six years of imprisonment.

Nelson Mandela was born in a village in the Transkei on July 18, 1918, even as Europe experienced the last paroxysms of the First World War. The son of a village headman, Mandela was given the Xhosa name "Rolihlahla," which translates literally as "pulling on the branch of a tree," but was colloquially interpreted as "troublemaker," an ironic omen of his future role. Though Nelson was in line for high tribal office, he demonstrated an early affinity for the law and, after his primary education at a mission school and secondary work at a Wesleyan school, he enrolled at University College of Fort Hare. His studies for a bachelor's degree were interrupted when he was expelled for participating in a student boycott. After moving to Johannesburg he completed his undergraduate degree by correspondence. In the early 1940s, he earned a law degree at the University of Witwatersrand, but was increasingly drawn into political activism, joining the African National Congress in 1942. During the years of the Second World War, Mandela joined with Walter Sisulu, Oliver Tambo and others to transform the ANC into a mass movement that could draw strength from the largely illiterate workers and peasants as well as the educated elite. Mandela and the younger activists contended that the tactics of the ANC's "Old Guard" were increasingly unsuited to the task of gaining national self-determination, as petitions and polite objections to the inequities of South African society had brought no discernible advances. In the fall of 1944, the group was instrumental in founding the African National Congress Youth League for the express purpose of mobilizing the younger generation for the struggle ahead.

The nature of the struggle became clearer in 1948 when the Nationalist Party, proclaiming white supremacy, won control of the government. Even as the new regime set about constructing the institutions of *apartheid,* the ANC responded, adopting a "Programme of Action" that advocated new tactics and strategies in the fight against racial inequality and oppression. Boycotts, strikes, civil disobedience and non-cooperation were all accepted as weapons in the ANC's arsenal. ANC goals soon included full citizenship and direct parliamentary representation for non-whites as well as trade union rights, land redistribution and free compulsory education. The South African government reacted to the ANC's expanding activities with increasingly repressive laws, but they only provoked the Campaign for the Defiance of Unjust Laws in 1952, of which Mandela was the National Volunteer-in-Chief. Mandela traveled across the country to organize the mass civil disobedience campaign and was soon arrested and tried for his activities. Prosecuted under the Suppression of Communism Act, Mandela was convicted and given a suspended sentence, but was shortly banned from public gatherings and confined to Johannesburg for six months. Somewhat ironically, it was during this period that he gained admission to the bar and, together with Oliver Tambo, established the nation's first black law firm. The multitude of injustices reported by their largely poor and illiterate clients testified to the fundamental inequities of the *apartheid* state. Authorities soon challenged the law firm for having violated the Group Areas Act and insisted that the office be moved far from the city and its black clientele.

When Mandela and Tambo fought the order, the government tried unsuccessfully to disbar Mandela on the basis of his previous conviction. The remainder of the decade brought continued challenges, as Mandela played a major role in organizing opposition to the Bantustan policy and separate education for blacks. His growing prominence in the ANC brought increased government scrutiny and through much of the latter part of the decade, the burden of defending himself in the "Treason Trial" of 1956–1961 distracted Mandela.

Though the government failed to secure convictions in the "Treason Trial," the banning of the ANC in 1960 imposed new burdens on Mandela and the rest of the leadership as they were forced underground. Nonetheless, Mandela was a prominent critic of the new republican constitution of 1961 as an instrument of continued *apartheid,* and challenged the government to call for a new and racially inclusive convention to adopt a truly democratic constitution. He also urged a mass general strike to coincide with the inaugural of the new South African Republic. Now a wanted man, Mandela was forced to live apart from his family, often in disguise, to avoid arrest. It was during these desperate times that he helped found *Umkhonto we Sizwe* as the instrument of a new policy of armed struggle. As committed as the group's members were to direct confrontation with the South African state, they were amateurs at revolution and made careless mistakes that led to the police raid on the farmstead in Rivonia. Unfortunately for Mandela, who was already serving time for having illegally left the country, the evidence gathered in the raid was sufficient to implicate him in a far more serious activity. Hence his return to Robben Island in the winter of 1964 as "Prisoner 466/64."

A small, desolate island separated from the African mainland by cold, strong currents, Robben Island had first been used as a prison colony in the 1840s. In the early 1960s, South African authorities restored it to that purpose. Mandela and his fellow political prisoners shared the meager facilities there with often-violent common criminals, who were encouraged by prison authorities to terrorize the "politicals." The daily regimen on the island was harsh, as the poorly fed prisoners labored in a lime quarry or sometimes harvested seaweed from the cold Atlantic waters. Mandela's efforts to maintain his personal dignity in the face of constant torments and humiliations brought frequent punishment, including solitary confinement and denial of "privileges" such as reading and writing. His first marriage had collapsed some years earlier under the pressures of his activist commitments and police harassment, and now his second marriage to Winnie faced similar stresses. Prohibited from any personal contact with his family for years, Mandela feared for the future of his children in the absence of their father's guidance. Increasingly active in ANC activities, Winnie experienced arrest, jail and banning as she sought to continue the struggle against *apartheid* and to keep her husband's name and legacy alive.

The opposition movement was badly weakened in the aftermath of the Rivonia Trial, which left much of the ANC leadership in jail. During the 1970s, the South African government continued to implement its programs of "separate development" for the races. The Soweto Uprising in 1976 demonstrated the continuing depth of disaffection among black South Africans, but the government was unwilling to concede anything more than cosmetic reforms while maintaining its commitment to *apartheid*. Throughout this lengthy period of continued oppression, Mandela confronted all the frustrations of one who could do little more than observe from a distance the struggle to which he had dedicated his life. He did, however, serve his cause even from prison. By the early 1980s, Mandela's lengthy and unjust imprisonment was an increasingly prominent cause, not only in Africa but around the world. A vocal "Free Mandela" campaign begun in South Africa attracted broad support around the globe, focusing international attention on the inequities of the South African regime. In part because of the growing international clamor, Mandela was transferred in 1984 to Pollsmoor Prison in Cape Town, where prison life was considerably more amenable than on Robben Island. In hopes of defusing rapidly rising tensions, President P.W. Botha offered to release Mandela if he agreed to renounce violence. Mandela, who declared that "only free men can negotiate," rejected the offer, noting that the ANC was still prohibited and his wife was living in banishment. Mandela's statement, which was read at a mass rally in Soweto, was his first public pronouncement since his trial twenty years before. Mandela remained a prisoner for the rest of the decade, a living symbol of self-sacrifice in service to an ideal, a people and a nation. The final leg of his long journey would come in 1990, when the new South African president F.W. de Klerk bowed to the inevitable and decreed the dismantling of the *apartheid* state.

◆ —— ◆ —— ◆ —— ◆ —— ◆ —— ◆ —— ◆ —— ◆ —— ◆

Suggested Readings

BAYART, FRANCOIS. *The State in Africa: The Politics of the Belly.* (1993).

CARTER, GWENDOLEN and PATRICK O'MEARA. *African Independence: The First Twenty-five Years.* (1985).

DAVIDSON, BASIL. *Modern Africa: A Social and Political History.* (1989).

FIRST, RUTH. *Power in Africa: Political Power in Africa and the Coup d'etat.* (1972).

GUNTHER, JOHN. *Inside Africa.* (1953).

HARGREAVES, J. D. *Decolonization in Africa.* (1988).

KYEMBA, HENRY. *A State of Blood: The Inside Story of Idi Amin.* (1977).

LAMB, DAVID. *The Africans.* (1987).

LEONARD, RICHARD. *South Africa at War: White Power and the Crisis in Southern Africa.* (1983).

MEREDITH, MARTIN. *The First Dance of Freedom: Black Africa in the Postwar Era.* (1984).

———. *Nelson Mandela: A Biography.* (1997).

OLIVER, ROLAND and ANTHONY ATMORE. *Africa since 1800.* (1981).

READER, JOHN. *Africa: The Biography of a Continent.* (1997).

RUBIN, BARRY. *Modern Dictators: Third World Coup Makers, Strongmen and Populist Tyrants.* (1987).

UNGAR, SANFORD J. *Africa: The People and Politics of an Emerging Continent.* (1989).

CHAPTER 11

The Middle Eastern Crucible of Conflict, 1945–1989

Cadets studying at the Jewish Officers' School joined with military police from the Jewish security force, the Haganah, to ring the nondescript Museum Hall in the heart of Tel-Aviv. This security force, checking out all who desired to enter the building, included men from throughout Europe, Africa, and the Middle East, including former inmates of Hitler's concentration camps. Inside the Hall, members of the National Administration and the National Council were surrounded by representatives of the Zionist Council, Haganah commanders, advisors, and financial backers. At four o'clock in the afternoon of May 14, 1948, David Ben-Gurion gaveled the meeting to order. All rose, singing the *"Hatikvah"* ("The Hope"), long the unofficial Zionist anthem.

Ben-Gurion, in response to the refusal of the Arab nations to accept a UN mandate that divided Palestine into a Jewish state and an Arab state, declared the establishment of the Republic of Israel. From the Tel Aviv Museum, he proclaimed: "The land of Israel was the birthplace of the Jewish people. Here their spiritual, religious and national identity was formed. In their exile from the land of Israel the Jews remained faithful to it in all the countries of their dispersal, never ceasing to hope and pray for the restoration of their national freedom." Ben-Gurion continued: "Therefore by virtue of the natural and historic right of the Jewish people to be a nation as other nations, and of the Resolution of the General Assembly of the United Nations, we hereby proclaim the

387

establishment of the Jewish nation in Palestine, to be called the Medinat Yisrael: the State of Israel." The following day, the Arab League, comprised of Lebanon, Syria, Jordan, Egypt, and Iraq, along with Palestinian militias, attacked the new state. A year-and-a-half long battle, the first Arab-Israeli War, ensued, with the Jewish nation ultimately prevailing. The costs were high, with thousands killed and over half a million Palestinians made refugees. Once again, as had been the case earlier in the century and throughout ancient times, the Middle East stood as the crucible of conflict.

The fiery, tempestuous Ben-Gurion became the founding father and first prime minister of Israel. A Zionist who sought to carve out socialism in Palestine, Ben-Gurion desired that Israel serve as a "Light unto the Nations." Born in Plonsk, Poland, a depressed Jewish village outside of Warsaw, Ben-Gurion—first known as David Grun—

Fig. 11-1   Israel Prime Minister David Ben-Gurion, c. 1965. (Pearson Education, Corporate Digital Archive, Getty Images Inc.)

was tutored in Zionism and Hebrew by his grandfather and father, an unlicensed lawyer. Appalled by anti-Semitic pogroms unfolding in Eastern Europe, Ben-Gurion, who had become a confirmed Marxist, headed for Palestine, which was then part of the Turkish Empire. A leader of the socialist *Po'alei Zion* (Workers of Zion), Ben-Gurion wrote for a Zionist publication, *Achdut* (Unity), and studied law in Salonika and Constantinopole.

In the early stages of World War I, Ben-Gurion, along with thousands of other Zionists, was expelled from Palestine, owing to his support for Zionism and socialism. After a stop in Egypt, Ben-Gurion went to New York City, where he learned English and married a nurse, Paula Munweis, with whom he had three sons. Following the war, Ben-Gurion returned to Palestine to fight against the Turks with the Jewish Battalion of the Royal Fusiliers, under the leadership of General Edmund Allenby.

The collapse of the Ottoman Empire resulted in the League of Nations awarding Palestine to Great Britain as a legal mandate. The League declared Palestine a "National Home" for Jews. For the next two decades, Ben-Gurion, who had discarded his belief in Marxism, was an important figure in the socialist-Zionist movement. He served as the long-time secretary of Histadrut, a potent labor federation, and was selected to lead the largely socialist Mapai (Labor) Party in 1930. In 1935, Ben-Gurion became chairman of the Jewish Agency, the governing body of the World Zionist Organization. To the chagrin of British officialdom, Ben-Gurion supported Jewish immigration and the emergence of an underground Zionist militia.

Seeking to dampen the flow of immigration from Europe, Great Britain in 1939 crafted the MacDonald White Paper, which urged construction of a bi-national Arab–Jewish state, devised immigration quotas for Palestine, and restricted the right of Jews to purchase property. Ben-Gurion urged young Palestinian Jews to enter the British army to participate in the fight against Nazi Germany, but he also strove to evade the British regulations by helping to set up an underground agency that transported refugees into the Middle East.

Following the close of World War II and the revelation of Hitler's attempted "Final Solution," international sentiment led to the 1947 United Nations resolution calling for Palestine to be divided into a Jewish state and an Arab State. The declaration of the state of Israel followed, and war broke out. Guiding Israel into the war and beyond was Ben-Gurion. From 1948 to 1953, he served as Israel's first prime minister, determinedly helping to establish a democratic nation, while encouraging the immigration of over one million Jews. In 1952, when West Germany agreed to make reparations for the Holocaust, Ben-Gurion expressed Israel's readiness to help resettle the survivors from the Nazi terror. In late 1953, Ben-Gurion retired to Sed Boqer, a kibbutz in the Negev Desert. Returning to government service as Minister of Defense in 1955, Ben-Gurion again became prime minister later that year. As the second Arab–Israeli conflict unfolded in 1956, Ben-Gurion believed that the taking of the Sinai Peninsula and the Golan Heights afforded a buffer for the Jewish nation. After resigning as prime minister in 1963, Ben-Gurion headed the opposition Labour (Rafi) Party and opposed the taking of additional properties other than Jerusalem following the 1967 Six

Day War. Ben-Gurion left the Knesset, the Israeli parliament, in 1970, and he unhappily observed the October War of 1973. He died on December 1, 1973.

Ben-Gurion had helped to create something of an oasis in a Middle Eastern desert: the lone democratic state and one that was long devoted to the socialist principles its founder favored. By the end of his life, however, Ben-Gurion, like a growing number of Israelis and Jews across the globe, was concerned about the future course of the nation he had helped to birth.

◆ ——— ◆ ——— ◆ ——— ◆ ——— ◆

The State of Israel and the 1948 War

As the postwar period unfolded, the remnants of colonialism continued to haunt the seemingly changeless Middle East, while revolutionary alterations influenced by fundamentalist, Marxist, and late twentieth-century thought swept through the region. Seemingly intractable conflicts arose between the newly created state of Israel and its neighbors.

IMMIGRATION TO PALESTINE

At the midpoint of the 19th century, approximately 10,000 Jews resided in Palestine, with most of them congregated in Jerusalem. The vast bulk of those Jews, or their families, had emigrated from Poland and Lithuania. Jews suffering from poverty, religious persecution and violence, heightened by pogroms in Russia in the latter stages of the century, increasingly dreamed of dwelling in Palestine. Another 25,000 Jews headed there from 1882 to 1903.

The journalist Theodor Herzl, a Hungarian Jew by birth who resided in Austria but was working in Paris, became an ardent Zionist after the infamous Dreyfus case in 1891 that reeked of blatant anti-Semitism. French courts convicted a Jewish military officer, Albert Dreyfus, of treason. The 1893 election of Karl Lueger, an anti-Semite, as mayor of

Vienna also influenced Herzl. From this point forth, Herzl insisted that a Jewish homeland must be established. In his book, *The Jewish State* (1896), Herzl declared, "Palestine is our ever-memorable historic home. The very name of Palestine would attract our people with a force of marvelous (sic) potency."

The state Herzl envisioned would be a modern one, secular in nature and rooted in scientific, commercial and industrial developments. Once secure in their own land, Herzl wrote, "The Diaspora cannot take place again unless the civilization of the whole earth shall collapse." There, "The Maccabeans will rise again. We shall live at last as free men on our own soil, and die peacefully in our own homes." Herzl helped to establish the World Zionist Organization, while remaining flexible about the creation of Jewish settlements, even welcoming the British government's offer of land in Uganda where a million Jews would be allowed to reside. Herzl's death in 1904 foreclosed such a possibility, as Jews both in and outside of Palestine were part of a divided Zionist movement.

The young David Ben-Gurion was one of the growing number of Jewish immigrants—many influenced by radical ideals—who now headed for the Middle East. The Jewish National Fund purchased land that was converted into collective farms (kibbutzes), which, along with the increased number of settlers, resulted in conflict with Arab villages. By the outbreak of World War I, 90,000 Jews, the vast bulk of whom were immigrants from Russia or Romania, were in Palestine. In the summer of 1914, the Turkish government clamped down on Jewish immigration, while expelling nearly 20,000.

In an effort to curry favor with Russian Jews, the British government, spurred on by the chemist Chaim Weizmann, issued the Balfour Declaration on November 2, 1917. The pronouncement stated that "His Majesty's Government views with favour the establishment in Palestine of a national home for the Jewish People." The British capture of Jerusalem in early December seemed to afford that very possibility.

Greatly complicating matters, of course, was the presence of some 600,000 Arabs in Palestine. Significant, too, were British attempts to appease various Arab leaders. The British, who had secretly agreed to divide up the Middle East with the French, had also sought to obtain Arab support against the Ottoman Empire by promising to back the creation of an Arab kingdom. Prince Faisal, who headed the Arab revolt against the disintegrating empire, became the short-lived king of Syria. Following his ouster by the French, Faisal became the Iraqi head of state. His older brother, Abdullah, guided Transjordan, established by Britain in 1921. That same year, the British high commissioner, Sir Herbert Samuel, who was himself a Jew, had anointed the strongly anti-Zionist Hajj Amin al-Husseini the grand mufti of Jersulem. The grand mufti and his family had bitterly opposed the British mandate and Jewish immigration to Palestine. The Nashashibis, somewhat uniquely among elite Palestinian

Arab families in Jerusalem, had also condemned that immigration but had demonstrated a greater willingness to work with the British to champion the Arab position.

Weizmann, for his part, signed a pact with the Hashemite Faisal and Abdullah, who supported the Balfour Declaration. Many Arabs in the region bitterly opposed the new pact and its call for cordial relations between Arabs and Jews. In an obvious effort to placate Arabs, the British government issued a white paper in 1922 that restricted Jewish immigration on economic grounds and denied Jews the right to settle in Transjordan. At the same time, Winston Churchill affirmed that Jews were situated in Palestine "as of right, and not on sufferance."

Jewish immigration continued to mount, with some 65,000 Poles entering Palestine from 1924 to 1927. Arab riots in 1929 failed to stem the tide of immigration but resulted in the greater appeal of groups such as the Betar youth movement, whose militant Zionists engaged in both self-defense training and street-fighting. With the Nazi takeover in Germany in early 1933, immigration from that central European state intensified. In 1934 alone, 42,000 Jews came to Palestine, with the approval of the British government. As anti-Semitism spread, Jews from Poland and Romania followed suit. Distrustful of British officials, Zionists funneled illegal immigrants into Palestine, with 61,000 Jews entering in 1935. Notwithstanding an Arab general strike in mid-April 1936 that the Higher Arab Committee backed, and ensuing violence, the number of Jews in Palestine approached 400,000 by year's end. Recognizing the dilemma, Ben-Gurion acknowledged on May 19: "We and they want the same thing: We both want Palestine. And that is the fundamental conflict." In 1936, Hajj Amin al-

Husseini was elected president of the Arab Higher Committee. The following year, he fled first to Lebanon and then to Iraq to avoid capture by British officials angered by his opposition to partition. While in exile, Hajj Amin al-Husseini lost support from many members of the Arab Higher Committee.

PAPERS AND PROTOCOLS DON'T RESOLVE PROBLEMS

The British cabinet received the Peel Commission Report on Palestine on June 25, 1937. It forthrightly declared:

> An irrepressible conflict has arisen between two national communities within the narrow bounds of one small country. About 1,000,000 Arabs are in strife, open or latent, with some 400,000 Jews. There is no common ground between them. The Arab community is predominantly Asiatic in character, the Jewish community predominantly European. They differ in religion and in language. Their cultural and social life, their ways of thought and conduct, are as incompatible as their national aspirations. These last are the greatest bar to peace. . . . National assimilation between Arabs and Jews is . . . ruled out. In the Arab picture the Jews could only occupy the place they occupied in Arab Egypt or Arab Spain. The Arabs would be as much outside the Jewish picture as the Canaanites in the old land of Israel.

A subsequent white paper, issued on May 17, 1939, called for "the establishment within ten years of an independent Palestine State." Such an independent state would purportedly enable "Arabs and Jews (to) share in government in such as way as to en-sure that the essential interests of each community are safeguarded." The document also called for capping Jewish immigration at 75,000 over the ensuing five years "unless the Arabs of Palestine are prepared to acquiesce in it." The illegal immigration was to end. Furthermore, the white paper declared that the British government was in no way obligated to support the establishment of "the Jewish National Home." Ben-Gurion responded in the following fashion: "We will fight with the British against Hitler as if there were no white paper; we will fight the white paper as if there were no war."

The heightening of the Nazi terror in Europe led to an attempted "Final Solution" in which the mass extermination of all Jews was envisioned. By the time World War II ended, approximately six million Jews had perished, many in death camps designed for that very purpose. The sheer enormity of the Holocaust spurred the determination of many Jewish leaders, including Ben-Gurion, to establish a Jewish state in the Middle East. This decision was inevitable, notwithstanding the disinclination of the democracies to open their doors to Jewish immigrants. Recognizing that harsh reality, Zionists such as Weismann proclaimed that "Palestine alone could absorb and provide for the homeless and the stateless Jews uprooted by the war." The Irgun and the Stern Gang, two Jewish terrorist groups, championed Jewish rule on either side of the Jordan River.

During World War II, the mufti, unlike most Arab leaders, supported the Axis powers and resided in Germany; his nephew Jamal al-Husseini was interned in Southern Rhodesia. At the close of the war, the Palestine Arab party and the Istiqlal were among the most prominent Arab organizations. The former insisted on Arab control over the whole of Palestine, while the Istiqlal accepted the idea of a Jewish National Home, but opposed further immigration. Political factionalism weakened the Arab cause, although in October 1944 Arab rulers had issued the Alexandria Protocol, affirming the importance of Palestine to the Arab community, while regretting the Nazi horrors inflicted on European Jews. The report, however, then condemned the Zionist position: "But the question of these Jews should not be confused with Zionism, for there can be no greater injustice and aggression than solving the problem of the Jews of Europe by another injustice, that is, by inflicting injustice on the Palestine Arabs of various religions and denominations." Following the lead of the Alexandria Protocol, a League of Arab states was established in March 1945.

Arab spokesmen informed the Anglo-American Committee that continued Jewish immigration would produce greater Arab resistance. Albert Hourani of the Arab Agency warned that "no room can be made in Palestine for a second nation except by dislodging or exterminating the first." Arab representatives contended that a Palestinian state should feature an Arab majority but safeguard Jewish rights. In February 1946, Jamal al-Husseini had been allowed to return to Palestine, but the British refused to let the mufti do the same. Hajj Amin al-Husseini ended up in Egypt, where he called for all Jews to be expelled from Palestine.

Political and humanitarian considerations guided U.S. President Harry S Truman's support for Jewish immigration. In August 1945, he asked the new British prime minister, Clement Attlee of the Labour Party, to permit 100,000 Jewish immigrants into Palestine; Truman's suggestion angered both King Ibn Suad of Saudi Arabia and the Arab League. That November, Attlee's foreign secretary Ernest Bevin encouraged an Anglo-American Committee of Inquiry to examine the refugee dilemma. The report, issued on May 1, 1946, called for the immediate admission of 100,000 Jews, a possibility that Bevin refused to accept. Opposing both a Jewish state and an Arab state, the report urged the creation of a country that would welcome Jews but not enable them to acquire majority status.

The attempted compromise and others that followed placated neither Arabs nor Zionists. Underground passage to Palestine resulted in some 40,000 Jews arriving between August 1945 and May 1948. Infuriated by the British policy, the Irgun and the Stern Gang also determined to spearhead a military revolt against imperial rule. They assassinated British officials, while the Haganah similarly engaged in guerrilla action. All three groups demanded unrestricted immigration, which now focused on the displaced persons who had been released from concentration camps. From November 1945 to July 1946, 18 British military personnel died, while more than 100 were wounded. In July 1946, Irgun guerrillas, operating under the direction of Menachem Begin, bombed the King David Hotel in Jerusalem. Some 90 fatalities resulted, including both Jews and Arabs.

Both Jews and Arabs resorted to additional terrorism, as British officials moved closer to allowing the United Nations to resolve the dilemma of Palestine. The granting of independence to India in 1947 undoubtedly induced British officials to seek a means to retain a foothold in the Middle East. Zionist leaders like Ben-Gurion demanded partition, while the Arabs continued to insist on a unitary state and a halting of Jewish immigration. In late November, the UN General Assembly voted 33–13, with 10 abstentions, to support partition, with the Soviet Union supporting the Zionist position. The UN vote effectively terminated the British mandate.

PRELUDE TO WAR

Once again, the turn of events displeased any number of groups. The Irgun and the Stern Gang expressed their displeasure, with Menachem Begin proclaiming that the partition was "illegal" and would "never be recognized." Furthermore, Begin asserted, "Jerusalem was and will for ever be our capital. Eretz Israel will be restored to the people of Israel. All of it. And for ever." The leaders of the Jewish Agency opposed the idea of an independent Arab state in Palestine and opposed Jerusalem's placement under international control. Palestinian Arabs were deeply distressed, with the Arab Higher Committee insisting that the UN design was "absurd, impracticable, and unjust." Proclaiming that it was illegal too, the committee urged a three-day strike, while Arab terrorists attacked Jewish civilians.

Seemingly inevitable movement toward war unfolded, notwithstanding efforts by various moderate Palestinians to ward off such a development. Wartime events had divided Arab leaders, with the mufti's pro-Axis stance inevitably weakening his position. Yet by the end of 1947, the Husseinis were again the dominant figures in the Palestinian Arab camp. Like the Zionists, Abdullah, who had been annointed king of Transjordan when Britian recognized its independence, feared that the UN-sponsored partition would produce a Palestinian state guided by the mufti. Abdullah envisioned instead an Arab Palestine becoming part of a Greater Syria. To that end, Abdullah had spoken with Jewish Agency representatives, who agreed that he could annex Arab Palestine. Abdullah, for his part, agreed not to fight with the Jews or to

oppose the creation of a Jewish state. But as tensions mounted, Abdullah was unable to ward off pressures to support the Arabs who wanted war.

In December 1947, Syria established the Arab Liberation Army for the Arab League states. The following month, its members traveled to Palestine. By the close of March, some 5,000 Arabs, largely from Syria, Iraq and Lebanon, had entered Palestinian territory. However, few Palestinians joined them, worrying about their intentions; many, moreover, backed partition and appeared ready to accept a Jewish state. The Husseini and al-Nashashibi factions remained divided, while the Arabs generally lacked training in modern military practices.

By contrast, the Zionists possessed superior leadership and organization, along with many World War II veterans. However, military communication was often difficult, due to widely dispersed settlements and a scarcity of armaments. Ben-Gurion and the Haganah commanders, who favored strong reprisal strikes, guided them. Meanwhile, both the Irgun and the Stern Gang intensified their actions, continuing to resort to terrorism and frequently viewing the Haganah responses as too limited. As the Arab attacks mounted, the Haganah determined to respond in kind.

Initially, the Arab Liberation Army advanced, placing the Haganah on the defensive. By March, the Arabs had effectively taken control of Jerusalem. Nevertheless, on March 1, 1948, David Remez, the long-time Secretary-General of the Histadrut, successfully called for the establishment of a Provisional Council of State. On March 19, the United States representative to the UN, Warren Austin, declared that because of the chaos in Palestine, partition no longer appeared to be a viable option. American policymakers, particularly Secretary of State George C. Marshall, feared that the Soviet Union would soon take advantage of the tumultuous Middle Eastern situation by backing one of the combatants. Marshall warned the Zionists against declaring their own state, while the U.S. called for a UN Trusteeship over Palestine. Almost immediately, a defiant Ben-Gurion responded: "It is we will decide the fate of Palestine. We cannot agree to any sort of Trusteeship, permanent or temporary. The Jewish State exists because we defend it." It was clear, however, that U.S. backing for a Jewish state was essential.

In April, the fortunes of war improved for the Haganah, bolstered by an arms shipment from Czechoslovakia. Terror tactics played a part, including fear induced by the April 9 massacre of 250 men, women, and children at the hands of the Irgun and the Stern Gang in Dayr Yasin. Four days later, the Arabs struck back, murdering 77 Jewish personnel from a medical convoy outside Jerusalem. Concerns about additional terrorist tactics, however, undoubtedly played a part in the departure of Arab leaders from Haifa on April 21 and 22; within three days, 50,000 Arabs had followed suit. By mid-May, an estimated 300,000 Arabs had fled.

As the British readied to pull out, Ben-Gurion, on May 14, proclaimed the establishment of the state of Israel. Ben-Gurion spoke of Israel as "the birthplace of the Jewish people," where "their spiritual, religious and national identity was formed." Jews throughout the diaspora, he declared, hoped to return to "the land of their fathers and regain their statehood." Now, Ben-Gurion asserted, "It is the natural right of the Jewish people to lead, as do all other nations, an independent existence in its sovereign State." The Jewish state, Ben-Gurion insisted, would open its door to Jews from all other lands and "will be based on the principles of liberty, justice and peace as conceived by the Prophets of Israel." Thus, "full social and political equality of all its citizens, without distinction of religion, race, or sex" would be afforded. So too would "freedom of religion, conscience, education and culture."

The following day, armies from Egypt, Transjordan, Syria, Lebanon and Iraq entered Palestine, joining with the Arab Liberation Army and Palestinian irregulars. The Haganah was now called the Israel Defense Force, while moves were afoot to disband the Irgun and the Stern Gang. The first Arab–Israeli war was hard fought and prolonged, with some 6,000 Jews losing their lives in the conflagration, which ended only in January 1949. The Israelis had incorporated the Negev and had acquired passage to the Red Sea. By that point, the UN estimated that 726,000 Arab refugees existed. Approximately 150,000 resided within the Jewish state. Some 470,000 now could be found in camps located in Arab Palestine that were run by Jordan and in others in the Egyptian-controlled Gaza Strip. The rest were situated in Lebanon, Syria, Iraq and other parts of Jordan and Egypt. Abdullah opposed the mufti's attempt to construct an Arab government for Palestine; he feared the loss of control over eastern Palestine.

AN UNEASY TRUCE

Elections in January resulted in Labour parties prevailing, with Ben-Gurion asked to form Israel's first elected government. Begin, the head of the now-disbanded Irgun, and former leaders of the Stern Gang, along with three Arabs, joined the new parliament. The Knesset was comprised of 120 members, chosen on the basis of proportional representation. For nearly three full decades, Ben-

Gurion's Labour Party dominated Israeli politics.

The Israeli population grew rapidly, with over 100,000 displaced persons arriving by the end of 1948; at that point, European or Ashkenazi Jews comprised nearly 75 percent of the populace. With more Jews arriving from central and eastern Europe, the population approached 1,200,000 by 1950. Increasingly, more Sephardic and Oriental Jews, many expelled by Muslim states, also began emigrating from North Africa and the Middle East; by 1952, over 300,000 Jews had migrated from the Arab lands. Many of these individuals were impoverished and undereducated. While life was trying for many settlers, it was particularly so for those who were housed in transit camps. Economic woes in the early 1950s slowed the pace of immigration.

It was scarcely easier for Israelis in general. An economic boycott by Arab states proved crippling, taxes to further infrastructural developments and to provide defense remained high and Israel required external assistance, particularly from the United States. In 1953, the Federal Republic of Germany agreed to pay Israel over $700 million in reparations for economic losses Jews suffered at the hands of the Nazis. All the while, the democratic state emphasized education and required military service.

With the establishment of the Israeli nation, Palestine effectively ceased to exist. Israel took over much of the western portion, along with several hundred towns and villages; Transjordan claimed the rest. Over half the Palestinians of the region became refugees. Many Palestinian intellectuals and businessmen were able to make their way in large Arab cities, but the great bulk of Palestinians, the *fellahin*, ended up in refugee camps. The greatest opportunities were available in Jordan, where citizenship could

be attained, and in Lebanon, where commercial possibilities and political freedom allowed many to thrive. The lot of the 150,000 Arabs who resided in Israel was mixed. Ben-Gurion and many Israel leaders viewed them with distrust and disdain; many Jews, in fact, saw the Arabs as potential fifth columnists with many dwelling in military zones. While the franchise was available for Arab men and women alike and equal rights were theoretically available, Arabs could not serve in the Israeli military, which presided over them, and they could not establish political organizations. Until the mid-1960s, military governors could exile, arrest or detain Arabs if they saw fit to do so; furthermore, Arab villages and lands could be confiscated for security purposes.

The Arab Response and Another War

To many younger Arabs, defeat at the hands of the Jews discredited the established Arab leadership. The humiliating Israeli triumph appeared to be the by-product of western technology, lacking in the Arab states. Consequently, the younger generation sought revenge, feared the Israeli military and reasoned that their lands had to be modernized. To that end, a series of revolts unfolded in the Arab world, encompassing Syria, Jordan and Egypt by the early 1950s. A Palestinian refugee's assassination of King Abdullah, who favored the negotiating of a peace agreement with Israel, brought Abdullah's eighteen-year-old grandson, Hussein, to power by 1953. A year after Abdullah's murder, a group of army officers, headed by Muhammed Naguib, overthrew King Farouk of Egypt. Within two years, Gamal Abdul Nasser, a proponent of Pan-Arabism and an implacable foe of the Israelis, had become

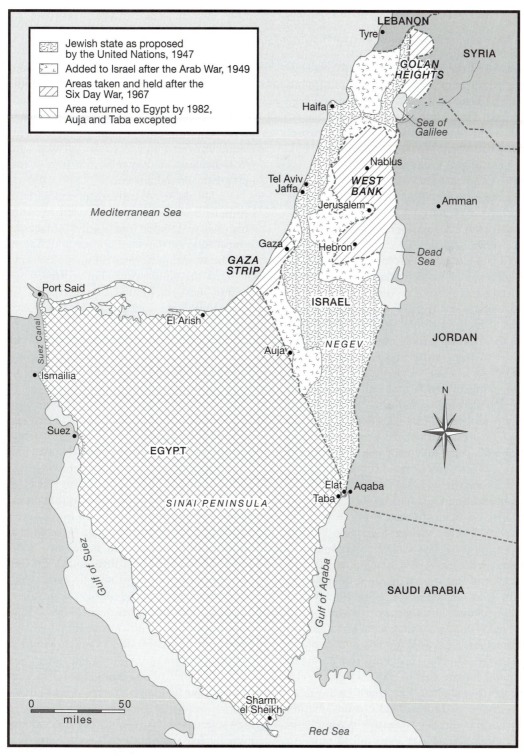

Map 11-1 The Middle East, 1947–1982

Legend:

- Jewish state as proposed by the United Nations, 1947
- Added to Israel after the Arab War, 1949
- Areas taken and held after the Six Day War, 1967
- Area returned to Egypt by 1982, Auja and Taba excepted

LEBANON
Tyre
SYRIA
GOLAN HEIGHTS
Haifa
Sea of Galilee
Nablus
Tel Aviv
Jaffa
WEST BANK
Amman
Jerusalem
Mediterranean Sea
Gaza
Hebron
Dead Sea
GAZA STRIP
ISRAEL
JORDAN
Port Said
El Arish
NEGEV
Suez Canal
Auja
Ismailia
Suez
EGYPT
SINAI PENINSULA
Elat
Aqaba
Taba
Gulf of Suez
Gulf of Aqaba
SAUDI ARABIA
N
0   50
miles
Sharm el Sheikh
Red Sea

the head of the Egyptian state. Egypt's continued refusal to allow Israel access through the Suez Canal helped to bring about a second Arab–Israeli war.

The unwillingness of the Arab states to acknowledge Israel's existence, coupled with the determined stance of Jewish leaders, all but ensured that such a conflict would take place. The matter of the Palestinian refugees remained a sticking point, as did the insistence by some Arab leaders that the 1947 partition plan, which they had previously rejected, should now be accepted. Israel, with its borders expanded by the 1948–1949 war, refused to accept such a possibility. Along the Jordan border, in particular, tensions remained high, with Palestinians infiltrating and the Israelis responding with retaliatory strikes of their own. The issue of security proved paramount in the minds of Israeli prime minister Ben-Gurion and his followers, and they insisted on military superiority and heightened Jewish immigration. Other top Israeli figures, particularly Foreign Minister Moshe Sharrett, called for more conciliatory moves, which demonstrated that divisions existed among the new nation's leaders. Moshe Dayan and Ben-Gurion often viewed Sharrett dismissively, with the Israeli prime minister declaring that he was "cultivating a generation of cowards." But while Ben-Gurion envisioned peace talks, Begin urged the Israeli takeover of the West Bank and the ouster of Arabs who resided there. Both Ben-Gurion and Begin foresaw an expanded Israel.

The Arab states, which were experiencing considerable flux, adopted no uniform policy toward Israel. The Hashemite kingdoms of Iraq and Jordan, tied to Sharif Hussein's descendants, sought to link those lands, along with Syria, and perhaps Lebanon. Earlier plans to include Palestine now became stillborn. Arab nationalism appeared strongest in Syria, while both Iraq and Jordan attempted to shape Syrian politics. Egypt and Saudia Arabia, fearing any kind of union, backed Syrian figures who were adverse to such a possibility. Foreign influences remained considerable, with Iraq and Jordan aligned with Great Britain and Egypt hostile to that former great colonial power.

In 1949 alone, colonels spearheaded three coups in Syria. The final one, led by Adib Shishakli, resulted in him playing off factions sympathetic to the Hashemites and Egypt, until he was himself overthrow in 1954. Iraq financed the coup, which Great Britain apparently backed; France, in turn, had supported Shishakli in order to reestablish French influence in the region. Elections results in October 1954 benefited both independents and the socialist Ba'ath Party, which championed Arab unity and a neutral stance regarding big power squabbles.

Beginning in the late 1940s, Egypt also endured considerable domestic unrest. While nationalists insisted on full independence, including control over the Suez Canal, the Muslim Brotherhood demanded wholesale transformations rooted in Islamic ideals to overcome deep-seated economic inequities. Defeat at the hands of Israel led to the assassination of the prime minister by agents of the Muslim Brotherhood. Policemen murdered the leader of that organization, Hassan al-Banna, in February 1949. In early 1952, much of Cairo—viewed as too Westernized by many Egyptians—was burned down. That July, young military officers, headed by Colonel Gamal Abd al-Nasser, expelled King Farouk from his throne.

On the staff of the Army Staff War College, Nasser had been dismayed by the corruption besetting Egypt's national army, a view shared by many of the young military men he had befriended. Nasser helped to shape the Free Officers Movement, comprised of cadets and junior officers. After leading the revolt against King Farouk, Nasser became minister of the interior deputy under President Mohammed Najuib. Disturbed by Najuib's support for civilian-dominated parliamentary governance, Nasser took on the title on prime minister in 1954.

The charismatic Nasser quickly became the key proponent of Pan-Arabism, social revolution and anti-colonialism; and a figure much feared by Israeli leaders. Distrusted by the western powers, including the United States, Nasser was well-loved throughout the Arab world. He desired to improve the condition of the *fellahin*, the Arab peasant, and the *shaab*, "the forgotten ones;" to unite all Arabs under Egyptian control; and to cultivate a sense of nationalism among his people.

To the delight of a younger generation of Arabs, Nasser in July 1954 induced the British to agree to withdraw their forces from the Suez Canal Zone within two years. The U.S. Secretary of State John Foster Dulles believed that British desires to maintain Egyptian bases only fed anti-western nationalism. The Baghdad Pact between Iraq and Turkey on February 24, 1955, which Great Britain soon joined, and a deadly Israeli assault in the Gaza Strip against an Egyptian post, dramatically affected Egypt's relations with the West. An attempted assassination of Nasser by a member of the Muslim Brotherhood afforded him the opportunity to repress its leadership. In 1956, the immensely popular Nasser, who had replaced Najuib as president, declared political parties illegal and shut down the Egyptian parliament.

Nasser's stance toward Israel hardened, as he now backed Palestinian assaults on the Jewish state and sought arms to beef up his military forces. Dismayed by the American refusal to supply arms unless accompanied by supervision, Nasser reached out to the Soviet Union. The communist power agreed to provide an unlimited amount of arms, including the most modern tanks and planes in return for "deferred payment of Egyptian cotton and rice." Nasser declared his leadership of a united Arab world committed to throwing off the yoke of colonialism. While the American leaders urged caution, French, British and Israeli officials determined that Egypt should be attacked, which they hoped might lead to Nasser's overthrow. France had recently suffered a disastrous defeat in Indochina; now, it was confronting a revolution in Algeria reportedly ignited by Nasser's impassioned call for the dissolution of colonial ties. French leaders also mistakenly reasoned that Nasser was funneling military and economic aid to the Algerian rebels.

Israel, in turn, began to be perceived as a staunchly pro-western ally. Shimon Peres' dealings with the French resulted in a secret agreement, evidently discovered by Egypt, in August 1954, to send jets, tanks and other military equipment to Israel. France's displeasure regarding the Baghdad Pact strengthened the French–Israeli ties. In November 1955, France and Israel carved out a major arms pact including advanced jets and tanks, with the United States' approval. All the while, tensions heightened along the Egyptian–Israeli border, particularly in the Gaza Strip. Palestinian raids increased and proved more deadly, while Israel conducted retaliatory assaults against both Egyptians and Palestinians. In December, Ben-Gurion ordered an Israeli strike against Syria, which had recently formed a military alliance with Egypt; the move angered American officials, who now refused to consider the possibility of a military alliance.

Middle Eastern dynamics changed dramatically after the western powers declined to back the construction of the Aswan Dam and Nasser nationalized the Suez Canal. In late 1955, both Great Britain and the United States, concerned about the growing Soviet influence with Egypt, had tentatively agreed to help finance the Aswan Dam. At the same time, American and British officials were becoming still more distrustful of Nasser. Egypt's recognition of Communist China in May appalled U.S. Secretary of State John Foster Dulles, and the United States subsequently withdrew support for the project. An angered Nasser took control of the Suez Canal, an action that proved enormously popular in Egypt. Nasser condemned "imperialist methods . . . the habits of blood-sucking and . . . usurping rights, and . . . interference in the affairs of other countries." Egypt, he insisted, "shall maintain our independence and sovereignty." Now, Anthony Eden, who compared Nasser to Hitler, warned that "the megalomaniacal dictator" had to be reined in soon. The grabbing of the canal, Eden felt certain, was merely "the opening gambit in a planned campaign designed by Nasser to expel all Western influence and interests from Arab countries." That way, Eden feared, would lead to revolution and the cutting off of Middle Eastern oil to the West.

The nationalization of the canal served as a justification for an attack on Egypt by France, England and Israel in late October and early November 1956. Angered by the allied action, the United States convinced the financially troubled British in particular to cease operations, while the Soviets delivered threats of their own. Censured by the United Nations, the British and French halted their offensive. Israel, for its part, had taken control of the Sinai up to the Canal, as well as Egyptian territory at Sharm al-Sheikh adjacent to the Strait of Tiran. Pressure from the United States led Ben-Gurion to agree to

a withdrawal of Israeli forces provided that UN peacekeepers would patrol Sharm al-Skeikh and the Gaza Strip to ward off Palestianian incursions.

The Suez invasion was a debacle for both Britain and France, whose standing in the Arab world fell dramatically. Israel, on the other hand, considered its military action to have been successful. It had pulled off another military triumph, this time with a small number of casualties. The Straits of Tiran had been opened up to Israeli shipping. For an extended period, more tranquil relations were to be found along the Israeli–Egyptian border, with UN forces in place; the threat the *fedayeen*, the Arab commandos, posed was lessened. Of equal importance, the bond between Israel and the United States appeared strengthened. Both Eisenhower and Dulles proved more determined to isolate Nasser. In early 1957, the American president proposed the Eisenhower Doctrine, which supported military and economic aid to countries desirous of the same. Furthermore, Congress authorized the president to use American military personnel "to secure and protect the territorial integrity and political independence of such nations, requesting such aid, against overt armed aggression from any nation controlled by International Communism." This was designed to curb Nasser's growing influence in the Middle East, particularly as he increasingly turned to the Soviet Union for foodstuffs and other products the United States embargoed.

Yet despite the military debacle, Nasser benefited in his own fashion from the Suez crisis. More than ever, he stood as a hero to many Arabs, representing the pan-Arabist who confronted colonialism and Zionism. By contrast, more conservative, pro-western regimes, like those in Iraq and Jordan, suffered from their alliance with Great Britain.

Nasser's own radical stance only hardened, resulting in a still more strident position regarding Israel and support for what he viewed as the liberation of Palestine.

Unrest in the Middle East and the Six Day War

Israel and the leading western states viewed Nasser's heightened stature and the greater appeal of pan-Arabism with concern. Moreover, the Sinai campaign planted additional seeds for future conflicts. In 1958, a civil war—induced in part by Nasser's allure—unfolded in Lebanon, resulting in the landing of 14,000 American marines along the shorelines. Jordan also experienced turmoil; King Hussein dissolved parliament and asked for British forces. The following year, a military regime replaced the Iraqi monarchy and pulled out of the Baghdad Pact.

Most ominous of all to western observers and the Israelis, Egypt linked up with Syria to form the United Arab Republic; Yemen was a federated member. Leaders of the Baath party, which propounded the gospel of "Arab freedom, Arab socialism, and Arab unity," pushed for the union. Fearing the growing strength of Syrian communists, a reluctant Nasser agreed to the confederation. It proved to be an unhappy marriage, with Egypt the dominant partner, as Nasser's issuance of sweeping nationalization decrees in 1961 exemplified. That September, Syria departed from the United Arab Republic. After civilian control briefly held sway in Syria, Baathist military coups occurred in 1963 and 1966. The later development ushered in the reign of General Salah Jadid, who condemned other Arab leaders for their supposed timidity, supported guerrilla insurrection by Palestinians and damned Israel outright. Syria established greatly improved relations with both the Soviet Union and China and supported liberation movements worldwide.

Nasser suffered additional setbacks as the Egyptian economy foundered, in part due to his country's intervention in a civil war in Yemen. Inflation and unemployment lengthened, as the Egyptian population grew. Egypt, in contrast to some of the Arab nations, continued to be afflicted by a dearth of natural resources. Thus, his country's economic state might have prevented Nasser from adopting a more militant posture toward Israel for a full decade following the Suez war.

In Israel, the political preeminence of David Ben-Gurion grew after the Suez crisis. Believing that greater territory could not be obtained, Ben-Gurion was determined to maintain Israeli security by acquiring sophisticated military hardware. Worried about the Soviet Union's greater antagonism toward Israel, he sought support from the United States and Western Europe and began cultivating good relationships with newly independent African states. Fearing a concerted assault by Arab forces, Ben-Gurion determined to develop nuclear arms for the Jewish nation, something that President John F. Kennedy opposed. The Kennedy administration, on the other hand, did not demand that Israel halt production of a nuclear reactor and allowed the sale of both tanks and Hawk surface-to-air missiles to the Jewish state.

Israel prospered economically. Trade abounded with African and Asian nations, with oil from Iran transported through the Gulf of Aqaba. Irrigation allowed the exploitation of the Negev Desert, enabling the region to become self-sufficient in the production of many foodstuffs. Additional immigrants arrived in Israel and established new communities. New immigrants came from the Soviet bloc countries, following the crushing of the Hungarian revolution in 1956; from Egypt after the Suez conflict; and from Northern Africa.

A sea-change in Israeli politics likewise unfolded during this period. Always authoritarian and temperamental, Ben-Gurion became even more so as he aged. He was particularly distressed by an announcement on April 17, 1963, that Egypt, Syria and Iraq had established an Arab federation. Significantly, the measure referred to "the question of Palestine and the national duty to liberate it." Deeply troubled, Ben-Gurion urged the full demilitarization of the West Bank and the carving out of a security arrangement with the United States, which President Kennedy rejected. To the amazement of his countrymen, Ben-Gurion in mid-June relinquished his post as Israeli prime minister. Another Labor Party member, Levi Eshkol, replaced Ben-Gurion.

The new Israeli leader had to contend with the decision that the Palestine National Council made in May 1964 to establish the Palestine Liberation Organization and a Palestine Liberation Army. The initial head of the PLO was an attorney, Ahmad al-Shuqayri, long Saudi Arabia's representative to the UN; Shuqayri was viewed as a Nasser lieutenant. Shuqayri denied any intentions of conducting raids against Israel. As for the Palestinian refugees, the PLO leaders appeared no more concerned about their plight than did the Arab governments.

In reality, the most important Palestinian organization during this period was *al-Fatah*. In 1959, young Palestinians who had resided in Gaza following the establishment of Israel created Fatah. Among its most important figures were Salah Khalaf, Khalil al-Wazzir and Yasser Arafat, who was related to Haji Amin al-Husseini. All had studied at Cairo University but departed following the Suez conflict, ending up in Kuwait. In contrast to many Arab leaders, these young men, influenced by the Algerian rebels and the African psychiatrist Franz Franon, who extolled revolutionary violence as necessary, believed that militant guerrilla action was necessary to bring about Palestine's liberation. In early 1965, Fatah commandos, operating with Syrian support, conducted strikes across the Israeli border. After General Jadid took power, Syrian assistance increased markedly. In late 1966, Shuqayri linked up more directly with Fatah; Jordan's King Hussein, who feared the possible creation of "a state within a state," repressed the PLO.

During the first several months of 1967, tensions rose in the Middle East. Fatah intensified its incursions into Israel, while clashes occurred involving Syrian and Israeli planes. On May 16, Nasser insisted on the removal of UN forces from the Sinai. UN Secretary General U Thant accepted Nasser's demand. Saudia Arabia and Jordan goaded Nasser, who closed the Straits of Tiran to Israeli ships. Resorting to increasingly harsh rhetoric, the Egyptian president asserted on May 26, "The battle will be a general one and our basic objective will be to destroy Israel." Nasser predicted a military triumph that would terminate the state of Israel. Speaking in Amman, Shuqayri stated that Israel would soon be wiped out, with few Jews surviving. In a speech before the Egyptian National Assembly on May 29, Nasser insisted that "the issue now at hand is . . . the rights of the Palestine people." Talking before the United Nations Security Council, Israeli Foreign Minister Abba Eban claimed that Nasser had earlier declared, "We intend to open a general assault against Israel. This will be total war. Our basic aim is the destruction of Israel."

The Six Day War began on the morning of June 5 with an Israeli strike virtually obliterating the Egyptian air force while the planes were still on the ground. Later that day, the Israelis also smashed Syrian and Jordanian air forces, along with an Iraqi airbase. After midnight, Yitzhak Rubin, the Israeli Chief of Staff, reported that over 400 enemy aircraft had been destroyed; Israel controlled the air from the Sinai to the Golan Heights. The war continued for another five days but the Israelis won resoundingly. When King Hussein refused to halt Jordanian shelling, Israel took control of Jerusalem. Israeli units headed into the West Bank toward the river Jordan. Israel pushed Syrian forces out of the Golan Heights and approached Damascus.

The results of the Six Day War and the unanticipated scope of the Israeli victory were profound. Israel now held the Sinai, the Golan Heights, the West Bank, the Gaza Strip and East Jerusalem; Israeli territory, now including 28,000 additional square miles, was three times the size it had been following the 1948–1949 war. The broadened Israeli borders seemingly afforded greater protection from Arab armies. Nasser's resignation from office acknowledged the stunning Arab defeat. A public outcry resulted in Nasser's return to power but his stature in the Arab world was clearly diminished. Ahmad Shuqayri's leadership of the PLO was thoroughly discredited. There now existed a greater determination to resort to guerrilla warfare.

The PLO and the Yom Kippur War

Two significant unresolved dilemmas remaining after the Six Day War were Israeli occupation of land captured during the war and the plight of the ever-increasing number of Palestinian refugees. Israeli leaders, who had formed a national unity government as war approached, were divided about the status of the occupied territories. Menachem Begin, like the Greater Land of Israel movement, supported Jewish settlements in those lands. Moshe Dayan, who contended that security demanded this, also supported settlements on the West Bank. Labor minister Yigael Allon called for Israel security forces to be stationed by the Jordan river valley to ward off Arab invasions. At the same time, he appeared willing to recognize Jordan's sovereignty over Arabs in the West Bank.

Arab responses were diverse as well. King Hussein wanted the United States to guarantee that the West Bank would be returned to Jordan and that his military would be rebuilt. Syria, with Iraqi and Algerian support, opposed any diplomatic resolution. Nasser continued to threaten to retaliate but he also employed diplomatic channels. Hoping to reconstruct his decimated army, Nasser became friendly to both Jordan and Saudia Arabia, seeking thereby to improve relations with the United States. Simultaneously, Nasser strove to retain his preeminence in the Arab community, something that Syria contested. Nasser, like Hussein, desired financial support from the oil-rich Saudis, Kuwaitis and Libyans. In addition, he sought to end the Yemen quagmire and to better relations with the Saudis.

At a conference in Khartoum, Sudan, which Syria boycotted, Arab leaders "affirmed the unity of Arab ranks" to bring about "the withdrawal of aggressive Israeli forces from Arab territories that had been occupied since the aggression of 5 June." This would be accomplished, the manifesto declared, based on "the main principles by which the Arab States abide, namely, no peace with Israel, no recognition of Israel, no negotiations with it, and insistence on the rights of the Palestinian people in their own country." A halt to oil production, the conference indicated, could "be used as a weapon in the battle."

The document, analysts have contended, was a compromise. Nasser—and King Hussein with the Egyptian president's encouragement—appeared willing to negotiate with Israel through UN representatives if the recently captured lands were returned. The Israelis, for their part, refused such a ploy, insisting on direct negotiations with the various Arab states. Indeed, Israeli leaders sought not only to retain some of the occupied territory but to receive Arab acknowledgment of the Jewish state's right to do so. A stalemate ensued, induced in part by Arab support for military action to recapture the lost land and by Israeli desires to maintain larger borders.

With American and Soviet backing, the UN General Assembly on November 22 adopted Security Council Resolution 242, which called for Israeli withdrawal from territory occupied since the end of the Six Day War. The measure also insisted, however, on "termination of all claims or states of belligerency and respect for and acknowledgement of the sovereignty, territorial integrity and political independence of every State in the area." The resolution affirmed the need to guarantee freedom of navigation through Middle Eastern waterways and a "just" resolution regarding the plight of the refugees.

Fatah and Israeli leaders remained implacable foes. Arafat's call for a war of liberation due to Israel's occupation of the West Bank produced little support among Palestinians living there. Sharing Arafat's concern that Israeli annexation of the region might be forthcoming, Hussein refused to condemn Fatah's incursions into the Jewish state

through the West Bank. Israeli reprisals produced considerable Palestinian resistance, resulting in favorable publicity for Fatah. Increasingly, Fatah and other Palestinian groups sought control over the refugees. Among Fatah's leading rivals was the newly formed Popular Front for the Liberation of Palestine, which Dr. George Habash headed.

In July 1968, the Palestine National Council again affirmed that Palestine was "the homeland of the Palestinian Arab people." Armed struggle was "the only way to liberate Palestine and is therefore a strategy and not tactics." *Fedayeen* fighters, the covenant declared, comprised "the nucleus of the popular Palestinian war of liberation." To achieve that goal compelled Arabs "to repulse the Zionist, Imperialist invasion from the great Arab homeland and to purge the Zionist presence from Palestine." The PLO moved to incorporate commando groups and to select Arafat as chairman.

Throughout 1969, Palestinian groups continued establishing bases in Lebanon to attack Israel and to plan hijacking operations. That December, the PFLP attacked an El Al plane in Athens. Israeli forces responded by destroying 13 aircraft at the Beirut airport. One unforeseen result was the collapse of the Lebanese government, whose military forces had, at various points, attempted to restrict Palestinian groups.

During this same period, a series of clashes took place involving Israel and Egypt. The Israeli cabinet that Golda Meir led sought to oust Nasser through a series of bombing strikes. Seeking to conduct a war of attrition, Israel hardly attained the results it had anticipated. Large numbers of civilian casualties were forthcoming and Nasser soon received greater assistance from the Soviet Union; Egypt acquired sophisticated SAM missiles while Soviet pilots conducted missions.

All the while, the Palestinian situation remained a tinderbox. King Hussein's apparent support for diplomatic dealings led Palestinian splinter groups, including that headed by Habash, to seek his ouster. The PLO demanded "a place where the revolutionaries (possessed) complete control and authority." That place was the West Bank, which Hussein himself desired to rule. After a series of humiliating events, which included the landing of a series of hijacked aircraft close to the king's palace, a bitter battle was waged between Jordanian forces and Palestinians. Some 3,000 Palestinians died before Hussein prevailed. That victory proved possible after Israel prevented Syrian tanks from entering the fray. On September 28, 1970, three days after the fighting ended, Nasser, who had attempted to bring the two sides together, suffered a fatal heart attack.

The following July, after additional clashes, Hussein expelled Palestinian guerrillas from the West Bank. They headed for Lebanon, where differences among the various Palestinian groups only heightened. Increasingly, however, terrorism was the weapon of choice, with the Black September group, linked to Fatah, murdering Wasfi Tell, the Jordanian prime minister, in Cairo in late 1971. The next summer witnessed the killing of 11 Israeli athletes at the Olympic Games in Munich. With the targeting of Israelis traveling abroad, retaliatory Israeli air strikes and military incursions were conducted in southern Lebanon. While rockets flew from Lebanon into northern Israel, Israeli agents singled out PLO officials to assassinate.

The PLO's establishment of bases in Lebanon helped to bring about a change in the Syrian government, with Hafiz al-Assad, a former supporter of Fatah, assuming the presidency in November 1970. Once in command, however, Assad attempted to control the PLO, fearing that Syria could be pulled into another confrontation with Israel. Assad also strove to improve relations with Egypt, Jordan and Saudia Arabia.

Egypt underwent alterations of its own following Nasser's untimely death at the age of fifty-two. His replacement, Anwar el-Sadat, sought to overcome his country's economic stagnation by discarding Nasser's preference for state control and garnering American financial support. Sadat proved more conciliatory regarding Israel, agreeing to an American proposal that would result in peace accords with Israel and the recognition of the Jewish state's right to exist with secure borders. Sadat additionally called for a resolution of the Palestinian refugee problem, demonstrating that he was willing to move beyond the position the PLO and other Arab leaders articulated. Israel, however, refused to accept the call to withdraw from the most recently occupied territories and demanded that direct negotiations be carried out. Henry Kissinger, the top foreign policy advisor to President Richard Nixon, reassured Israel that U.S. armaments would continue to be delivered; Israel accordingly adopted a hard-line position.

Sadat pressured the Soviet Union into delivering military hardware in February 1973. Sadat, as distressed as the Saudi leaders about Israeli control over Jerusalem, began warning American officials about the possibility of another Middle Eastern war. The Saudis also began considering using oil as an weapon to wound the United States, which was increasingly energy-dependent. In 1960, the Organization of Petroleum Exporting Countries (OPEC) had been established to acquire greater profits for oil-producing states. Two opposite bedfellows, the radical Muammar al-Qadhdhafi of Libya and the Shah of Iran, an American ally, had recently demanded a sharp increase in oil profits. By the early 1970s, King Feisal of Saudia Arabia sought a less dramatic bump in oil prices but linked such an increase to Middle Eastern power politics.

In the meantime, few Israeli leaders foresaw the possibility of another major military conflict with the Arab states unfolding anytime soon. American support, including the shipment of additional weapons, fed Israeli confidence. As elections approached in Israel in November 1973, the Labor Party and prime minister Golda Meir continued the policy of supporting the retention of more of the occupied territories. Two years earlier, Meir had declared that Israel would hold onto the Golan Heights, Sharm al-Shaykh and portions of the West Bank; moreover, the Sinai was to remain demilitarized after it was transferred back to Egypt. The Labor Party, condemned by Menachem Begin for failing to promise that more occupied lands would be retained, began allowing scores of settlements in the West Bank, the Golan Heights and northern Sinai.

The absorption of Arab lands angered Sadat, whose army joined with Syrian forces on October 6, 1923, a sacred day for both Jews and Muslims. This was Yom Kippur, the Jewish Day of Atonement, and the anniversary of the Prophet Muhammed's defeat of Arab foes at Badr. The Yom Kippur War lasted until October 22 and threatened to result in a nuclear confrontation involving the United States and the Soviet Union. The unexpected attack initially set Israel back on its heels, but the assault was rebuffed eventually; furthermore, Israeli forces threatened to achieve a massive victory over Syria and a defeat of Egyptian units along the Suez Canal. Israel took additional territory in the Golan Heights, while Israeli soldiers went across the canal, inflicted great damage on Egyptian

military hardware, and sought vainly to capture the Suez. Egyptian forces, on the other hand, held on to certain territory that Israel had claimed.

The Israeli situation had improved thanks to the infusion of American military support, which followed the shipping of large-scale Soviet aid to the Arab combatants. With U.S. backing, Israel took control of Mount Hermon and approached within twenty miles of Damascus. Nevertheless, the war shook Israel badly as a near-defeat had been warded off. Israel experienced some 2,800 fatalities, with another 8,500 injured, and a financial bill of $4 billion. The Arabs, who suffered yet another defeat at the hands of Israel, suffered 8,500 fatalities, with more than 19,500 wounded.

An Uneasy Peace

The latest hostilities produced important diplomatic, economic and political results. The long-sought increase in oil prices came about as an embargo was initiated when the Yom Kippur War neared an end. The impact on Western economies was grave, with the United States, for example, experiencing long gas lines, a loss of an estimated half million jobs and a significant reduction of the gross national product. Oil-starved European states and Japan attempted to convince Israel of the need to withdraw from the occupied lands.

Henry Kissinger, now the U.S. Secretary of State, ensured passage in the United Nations of Security Council Resolution 338. Besides calling for a cease-fire, the measure urged the implementation of all the provisions of Resolution 242 and that "negotiations start between concerned (parties)... aimed at establishing a just and durable peace in the Middle East." In the first half of 1974, Kissinger carved out two pacts through which the Israelis engaged in a withdrawal of territory in both the Suez and Golan Heights. Assad promised to prevent Palestinian guerrillas from striking at Israel from Syria.

The negotiations influenced Israeli politics, with Menachem Begin and General Ariel Sharon, who had led Israeli forces across the Suez Canal, forming a new right-of-center party, Likud. Prime Minister Meir, along with Minister of Defense Dayan, resigned in April 1974, having received great criticism for their nation's apparent state of unreadiness prior to the outbreak of the Yom Kippur War. The new head of state, Yitzhak Rabin, had previously served as chief-of-staff of the Israeli military and as his nation's ambassador to the United States. Shimon Peres became defense minister. In September 1975, Rabin reached another agreement with Egypt, withdrawing more Israeli forces and allowing Egypt passage to various oil fields in the Gulf of Suez.

But Israel's refusal to pull back from the West Bank strengthened the hand of the PLO, which in October 1974 had been proclaimed at the Rabat Arab summit "the sole legitimate representative of the Palestinian people." King Hussein now acknowledged his inability to negotiate for the West Bank. Palestinian groups remained divided regarding the means to bring about Palestine's liberation. In mid-1974, the PLO's position appeared to modify with calls for the establishment of "national authority" over the West Bank and Gaza. With some in the organization determined to prevent Syria and Israel from agreeing to Israeli disengagement, a number of terrorist strikes were carried out. In two of those incidents, several children died, resulting in a hardening of the Israeli stance concerning the Palestinians. Invited

to speak before the General Assembly of the United Nations, Yasser Arafat warned on November 13, 1974, that a settlement must emerge or the violence would continue.

The Palestinian riddle continued to beset Israel. Possession of territory on which more than a million Arabs existed presented the possibility that Jews could become an ethnic minority inside their own state. The democratic nature of the Jewish nation could be called into question if the rights of those inhabitants were abridged. Military control of the occupied lands resulted in soaring inflation rates. Some Israelis questioned the holding of another people as refugees, while others urged that the Palestinians be expelled from the occupied territories.

A series of changes unfolded in the Middle East. Despite the Labor Party's backing of new settlements, Begin and a Likud-led coalition swept into office in May 1977. Distrustful of the Arabs, Begin and his backers opposed the idea of swapping "land for peace." Furthermore, Begin supported the establishment of additional settlements, which enabled Jews to control a sizable portion of the occupied land and approximately 90 percent of the precious water reserve in the area. The PLO National Council declared its readiness to form an "independent national state," suggesting that the Palestinians were more willing than before to engage in diplomatic discussions.

Egypt and Israel, goaded by the United States, which was now led by President Jimmy Carter, were about to undertake such diplomacy. Sadat, who subscribed to an "Egypt first" approach, accepted an invitation to speak before the Israeli Knesset. On November 19, 1977, he stated forthrightly, "I declare to the whole world that we accept to live with you in permanent peace based on justice." After extended negotiations from late 1977 through September 1978, the Camp David accords were devised. Signed by Sadat, Begin and Carter on September 17, the agreements affirmed that a peaceful resolution centered around the upholding of UN resolutions 242 and 338. The purpose of those resolutions was "to achieve peace and good neighborly relations. They recognize that, for peace to endure, it must involve all those who have been most deeply affected by the conflict." Thus, it was agreed that "Egypt, Israel, Jordan, and the representatives of the Palestinian people should participate in negotiations on the resolution of the Palestinian problem in all its aspects." Additionally, a promised withdrawal of Israeli forces from the West Bank and Gaza was to occur provided that "a self-governing authority has been freely elected by the inhabitants of these areas." Israel also offered to withdraw from the Sinai during the next three years, while Israeli ships were to be allowed passage through the Suez Canal.

Following the accords, the United States delivered a profusion of aid to both Israel and Egypt. The PLO, Syria and Iraq sharply criticized the agreements and Sadat. Even moderate Arab states such as Jordan and Saudia Arabia refused to accept the pact. Nevertheless, negotiations continued, resulting in a peace treaty between Israel and Egypt that was signed at the White House on March 26, 1979. Egypt continued to suffer rebuke at the hands of its fellow Arab states, with only Oman and Sudan maintaining diplomatic ties; furthermore, the Arab League and the Islamic Conference kicked Egypt out.

Lebanon and the Intifada

In 1979, the already complex Middle Eastern world became still more so as an-
other series of important events unfolded. In January, as his hold on power disintegrated, the shah of Iran departed from his country, enabling the long-exiled Ayatollah Khomeini to return home to create an Islamic republic. Militants took control of the American Embassy in Tehran and began holding hostages. That December, Soviet forces began a bitterly contested occupation of Afghanistan. The following September, predominantly Sunni Iraq attacked Shi'ite Iran, whose fundamentalist regime threatened to induce revolts by Shi'ites throughout the region; the Shi'ites considered the Muslim caliph Ali and his descendants to be Muhammad's true successors.

The series of developments in the Middle East, coupled with economic woes in the United States, enabled the new, conservative administration of Ronald Reagan to take power in January 1981. At that point, after 444 days, the Iranian government finally released the American hostages in Tehran. However, that year proved another troubling one in the region. On October 6, a Muslim extremist assassinated the besieged Anwar al-Sadat, but Sadat's successor Hosni Mubarak continued to support the Camp David accords. In Lebanon, the Druze—who considered the Ismaili caliph al-Hakin to be the embodiment of God—the Syrian Socialist Nationalist Party, communists, and a host of unhappy Muslims formed the Lebanese National Movement. They engaged, through the mid-1970s, in civil war with the Maronite militia and the Lebanese government. The Lebanese army basically disintegrated. In early 1976, Syrian forces prevented a radical regime from emerging in Lebanon. A new militia group, the Christian Lebanese Forces, sprang up, greatly influenced by the Phalange, a Maronite party that Pierre Gemayel headed. Israel began funneling arms to Gemayel's fighters and to the South Lebanon

Army, another Christian militia group situated in southern Lebanon.

As PLO assaults against Israel escalated, a large-scale Israeli incursion into Lebanon took place in early 1978. The Israeli troops withdrew after three months, but established a security zone. Additionally, UN forces went to southern Lebanon. The PLO, nevertheless, still controlled a good amount of territory and conducted rocket assaults against the Jewish state. Another organization, Islamic Jihad, called for resistance to Israeli occupation; the Iranian revolution in 1979 served as another spur to anti-Israeli actions.

Israel, in turn, envisioned a means to lessen the PLO threat, while Bashir Gemayel, Pierre's younger son, sought to expel the Palestinians from his country. In early June 1982, after an assassination attempt against the Israeli ambassador to England, Israel invaded Lebanon. Aerial and land assaults inflicted considerable casualties, including many civilian ones. Israeli soldiers approached Beruit, while destroying a number of Syrian surface-to-air missiles and fighter planes. Within days, Syrian leader Assad agreed to a cease-fire. The siege of Beruit failed to expel the PLO. On August 14, Israeli forces moved into West Beruit, leading to the imminent departure of PLO fighters. American, French and Italian peacekeepers moved into the region to fill the breach, but soon departed.

Tragedies continued to unfold. Within weeks after his election as Lebanese president, Bashir Gemayel was murdered on September 14. Israeli units returned to West Beirut, thereby violating a truce agreement. Some 200 hundred Christian Phalangists, allowed by the Israelis to enter the Sabra and Shatila refugee camps, massacred hundreds of Palestinians in mid-September. In the aftermath of these horrors, multinational troops

returned to Lebanon. U.S. Secretary of State George Schultz called for Israel to relinquish some of the occupied territory to bring about the peace envisioned in UN Resolution 242.

Despite the departure of the PLO, Lebanon continued to experience strife. Disdainful of the PLO and angered by the Israeli occupation, new groups, including the radical Shiite Hezbollah, emerged. Hezbollah, influenced by the Khomeini regime in Iran, determined to conduct a *jihad* or holy war against the Jewish nation and to establish an Islamic state in Lebanon. On April 18, 1983, the American Embassy in Beruit was assaulted, resulting in over 60 fatalities. In October, a suicide bombing led to the killing of 247 at the U.S. Marine barracks in the Lebanese capital. The following March saw the withdrawal of American forces from Lebanon, but car bombings and other terrorist actions again made headlines throughout the Middle East. The new Lebanese president Amil Gemayel sought to smooth over relations with Syria, which maintained forces in Lebanon. Increasingly, various Lebanese groups grabbed Western hostages, while the various militias warred with one another. Expelled from Syria, Yasser Arafat, along with many other PLO members, returned to Lebanon. But Arafat was soon compelled to leave Lebanon once again, ending up in Tunis. In June 1985, Israeli forces departed from Lebanon but remained in the Security Zone. Hundreds of Israeli soldiers perished in Lebanon, casualties of the occupations that produced condemnations worldwide and marked internal divisions within Israel, leading to the collapse of the Begin government. However, the even more hard-line Yitzhak Shamir, who had to contend with rising foreign indebtedness and a seemingly ever-increasing reliance on U.S. aid, replaced Begin as the Israeli prime minister. In Lebanon, ongoing battles resulted in the further destruction of Beruit.

Operating out of northern Africa, Arafat attempted to revitalize the PLO, which remained divided. In 1985, Jordan's King Hussein and Arafat together urged the establishment of a Palestinian state on the West Bank that would incorporate East Jerusalem. Jordan was to possess final authority over the territory, which Israeli soldiers were to leave. In return, Arafat appeared ready to recognize openly Israel's right to exist, but only after both the United States and the UN acknowledged him to be a legitimate actor in Middle Eastern diplomatic circles. The American government, however, continued to insist that Arafat directly affirm Resolution 242 before it would support dialogue with PLO representatives. Terrorist actions, whether opposed by Arafat or not, and Israeli retaliatory strikes stymied the peace initiatives. By February 1986, Hussein favored private consultations between Jordanian and Israeli officials.

Throughout that year and the next, violent incidents mounted in the West Bank and Gaza. Then on December 8, 1987, an Israeli truck smashed into Arab vehicles in Gaza, killing four Palestinians and injuring seven others. During the funeral processions that followed, demonstrations unfolded, indicating the depth of Palestinian anger and frustration regarding both the Israeli occupation and the Palestinian leadership. These largely spontaneous uprisings, which were referred to as the *Intifada*, fanned out to the West Bank. After several weeks, PLO leaders in Tunis sought to direct the situation, which involved a revolt of the poor and the young. Fully cognizant that events would be captured by the international press, the participants, refusing to resort to guns or knives, relied on demonstrations and stones. They also turned to strikes, an economic boycott and a refusal to pay taxes.

As the resistance continued, it received sustenance from Islamic organizations that called for resistance to Israeli authority. Among those groups was the Islamic Jihad. In February 1988, Hamas, the Islamic Resistance Movement, was formed. Hamas, like the PLO, sought the establishment of a Palestinian state; however, Hamas desired one rooted in fundamentalist Islamic religious beliefs. Moreover, it refused to accept the compromise that Arafat soon endorsed of a federation involving Palestine and Jordan.

In Algiers, on November 15, 1988, the Palestine National Council proclaimed "the establishment of the State of Palestine on our Palestinian territory with its capital Jerusalem." The Palestinian National Council also revealed its acceptance of UN resolutions 242 and 338, something that Hamas bitterly opposed. At a press conference in Geneva on December 14, Arafat affirmed the Palestinians' "right to freedom and national independence . . . and the right of all parties concerned in the Middle East conflict to exist in peace and security . . . including the state of Palestine, Israel and other neighbors." Then, Arafat declared, "As for terrorism, I renounced it yesterday in no uncertain terms, and yet, I repeat for the record. I repeat for the record that we totally and absolutely renounce all forms of terrorism, including individual, group and state terrorism." He concluded, "We want peace. We want peace. We are committed to peace. We are committed to peace. We want to live in our Palestinian state, and let live. Thank you."

Notwithstanding the altered PLO position, Israelis proved increasingly divided about how to respond to the *Intifada*. The death of more than 600 Palestinians and 43

Israelis distressed many. So did the wounding of tens of thousands of Palestinians, the arrest of between 35,000 and 40,000, the shutting down of schools and universities and the demolition of homes. Demonstrations sprang up in Israel, with the Peace Now movement urging an end to the military occupation. Supporters of the Likud party and religious extremists insisted that the occupied lands remain in Israeli hands.

King Hussein, on the other hand, renounced his claim to the West Bank. He declared, "We respect the wish of the PLO, the sole legitimate representative of the Palestinian people, to secede from us in an independent Palestinian state. We say this in all understanding." He continued, "Jordan is not Palestine; and the independent Palestine state will be established on the occupied Palestinian land after its liberation, God willing."

◆ —— ◆ —— ◆ —— ◆ —— ◆ —— ◆ —— ◆ —— ◆ —— ◆ —— ◆

On November 13, 1974, sporting a scraggly beard and a *Keffiyeh* headress, Mohammed Yasser Abdul-Ra'ouf Qudwa Al-Husseini—known to the world as Yasser Arafat—addressed the United Nations General Assembly; he was the first representative of a non-government entity to do so. The General Assembly was beginning a debate of "The Question of Palestine." Arafat readied to enter the Assembly chamber, while the Israeli Ambassador Tekoah moved to depart. The delegates delivered a standing ovation on sighting Arafat.

With a pistol prominently displayed on his hip, Arafat spoke of the Palestinians's dream of a Palestinian state. "When we speak of our common hopes for the Palestine of tomorrow," Arafat declared, "we include in our perspective all Jews now living in Palestine who choose to live with us there in peace and without discrimination." He referred to the PLO's desire to create national authority in lands in the West Bank and Gaza that Israel would abandon. Arafat then coupled idealism and pragmatism:

> Yes, I have the right to dream. We all have the right to dream . . . but as a practical man who is prepared to face the reality of Israel's existence, I recognize and accept that dreams do not always come true . . . and that is why we talk about our national authority—that is what we are prepared to settle for, a little homeland of our own, in order to have peace with Israel, until the day when the Israelis decide of their own free will to join with us in the creation of the Democratic State of our dreams.

Concluding his address, Arafat suggested that two choices were available: the establishment of a Palestinian state or heightened violence. He stated, "I have come bearing an olive branch and a freedom fighter's gun. Do not let the olive branch fall from my hand."

At that point, the audience again rose and applauded their guest; the American representatives were the only ones who failed to do so. As Arafat later reflected, "My speech required my listeners to think for themselves and to make a connection between certain ideas . . . but I said enough for people of goodwill, even Israelis of

Fig. 11-2   Yasir Arafat addressing the United Nations General Assembly, November 14, 1974. (Pearson Education, Corporate Digital Archive, Corbis)

goodwill, to understand that I was offering a very big compromise in the name of my Palestinian people." The subsequent UN Resolution 3236, issued on November 22, confirmed "that the Palestinian people is entitled to self-determination," as articulated in the United Nations' charter.

As the *Intifada* continued in the late 1980s, Yasser Arafat had struggled to retain control over the Palestinians, something that he had been forced to contend with for a considerable period of time. Although mystery surrounds his early years, Arafat was born in either Jerusalem or Cairo on August 24, 1929, to a prominent family that was steeped in anti-Zionist activities; his father was a successful merchant, while his mother was devoutly religious. After his mother died when he was only four years old, Arafat lived with an uncle in Jerusalem. As a teenager, he became concerned about the future of Palestine. While a student at Cairo University, he helped to run guns into Palestine in the midst of the 1948–1949 Arab–Israeli conflict. He later joined in a conspiracy to oust King Faisal, which resulted in his exile from Egypt. At Cairo University, where he received a degree in architectural engineering in 1956, Arafat was chosen president of the League of Palestinian Students. That same year, Arafat, along with Salah Khalaf, Khalik Al-Wazir, Mahmoud Abbas and Faruz Qaddumi, helped to found *al-Fatah*, a guerrilla organization Gamal Abdel Nasser influenced that called for opposing Israel through armed conflict; support came from wealthy Palestinians who were residing in the Emirate. Following service in the Egyptian army during the Suez conflict, Arafat resided in Kuwait, where he made his mark as an engineer and trained commandos. He remained actively involved with Fatah, which carried out a series of raids against Israel. The larger Arab states, which were associated with the Palestine Liberation Organization, generally ignored Arafat and his organization.

Following the Six Day War, however, Arafat's call for guerrilla action against Israel began to be heeded. In 1969, the *Fedayeen* were incorporated into the PLO and Arafat was elected chairman; shortly thereafter he was chosen to lead the Palestinian Revolution Forces. From this point forth, the PLO discarded its earlier Pan-Arabist approach and concentrated on the plight of the Palestinians. The PLO conducted raids against Israel. King Hussein, who feared that the PLO was endangering his rule, drove Arafat and his fighters out of Jordan in 1970. Terrorist actions intensified, with airliners highjacked, Israeli civilians assaulted and Israeli athletes murdered at the 1972 Olympic Games in Munich. In 1973, Arafat became the military commander of Palestinian-Arab guerrilla fighters.

The following year, the Arab League determined that the PLO was the "sole legitimate representative of the Palestinian people, in any Palestinian territory that is liberated." Throughout the rest of the decade, Arafat and the PLO were effectively based in Beruit. From there, the PLO orchestrated attacks on Israel, while providing social services to Palestinian refugees.

During the following decade, Arafat's position and that of the PLO became more problematic after the organization's expulsion from Beruit in 1982; this resulted from Israeli military action to stave off Palestinian attacks. Compounding Arafat's difficulties was growing opposition from more militant Palestinian groups. But Arafat's stature soared in late 1988, when he presented the Palestinian peace initiative before the UN General Assembly in Geneva. Accepting resolutions 242 and 338, Arafat declared that "the PLO will seek a comprehensive settlement among the parties concerned in the Arab-Israeli conflict, including the State of Palestine, Israel and other neighbors." Such an agreement, Arafat stated, should guarantee "equality and the balance of interests, especially our people's rights to live in freedom, national independence, and respect the right to exist in peace and security for all." Arafat continued, "I come to you in the name of my people, offering my hand so that we can make true peace, peace based on justice. I ask the people of Israel to come here under the sponsorship of the United Nations so that, together, we can forge that peace." The PLO chieftain concluded, "And here, I would address myself especially to the Israeli people in all their parties and forces, and especially to the advocates of democracy and peace among them. I say to them: 'Come let us make peace. Cast away fear and intimidation. Leave behind the spectre of the wars that have raged continuously for the past 40 years'."

On November 15, 1988, the Palestinian National Council, meeting in Algiers, called for the formation of "a provisional government for the State of Palestine;" in March, the PNC proclaimed Arafat "president of the state."

•———•———•———•———•———•———•———•———•———•

Suggested Readings

BICKERTON, IAN J. and CARLA L. KLAUSNER. *A Concise History of the Arab-Israeli Conflict.* (1998).

CLEVELAND, WILLIAM L. *A History of the Modern Middle East.* (1994).

FARSOUN, SAMIH K. with CHRISTINA E. ZACHARIA. *Palestine and the Palestinians.* (1997).

FIELD, MICHAEL. *Inside the Arab World.* (1995).

GILBERT, MARTIN. *Israel: A History.* (1998).

GOLDSCHMIDT, A., JR. *A Concise History of the Middle East.* (1991).

HART, ALAN. *Arafat: A Political Biography.* (1989).

HILTERMANN, JOOST R. *Behind the Intifada.* (1991).

HOURANI, ALBERT. *A History of the Arab Peoples.* (1991).

KURZMAN, DAN. *Ben-Gurion: Prophet of Fire.* (1983).

LAMB, DAVID. *The Arabs: Journeys beyond the Mirage.* (1988).

LEWIS, JON E., ed. *The Permanent Book of the 20th Century: Eye-Witness Accounts of the Moments that Shaped Our Century.* (1994).

MACKEY, SANDRA. *Passion and Politics: The Turbulent World of the Arabs.* (1992).

MARGALIT, AVISHAI. *Views in Review: Politics and Culture in the State of the Jews.* (1998).

MORRIS, BENNIE. *Righteous Victims: A History of the Zionist-Arab Conflict, 1881–2001.* (2001).

SEGEV, TOM. *1949: The First Israelis.* (1986).

———. *One Palestine, Complete: Jews and Arabs under the British Mandate.* (1999).

SHLAIM, AVI. *The Iron Wall: Israel and the Arab World.* (2000).

SMITH, CHARLES D. *Palestine and the Arab-Israeli Conflict.* (2001).

WALLACH, JANET and JOHN WALLACH. *Arafat: In the Eyes of the Beholder.* (1990).

CHAPTER 12

A Superpower in War and Peace: the United States since 1945

On April 12, 1945, citizens of the United States received the unhappy news that President Franklin Delano Roosevelt had died. FDR had recently begun a fourth term as president, having guided his country out of the worst depths of the Great Depression to impending success in World War II. Less than three months into FDR's fourth term, Harry S Truman was called into Eleanor Roosevelt's White House study. "Harry," the president's widow indicated, "the President is dead." Truman asked, "Is there anything I can do for you?" Mrs. Roosevelt responded, "Is there anything we can do for you? For you are the one in trouble now." On the evening of April 12, 1945, Truman took the oath of office. The following day, he spoke to the White House press corps: "Boys, if you pray, pray for me now. I don't know whether you fellows ever had a load of hay fall on you, but when they told me yesterday what had happened, I felt like the moon, the stars, and all the planets had fallen on me."

The sixty-year-old Truman was a distinctly different man from the patrician Roosevelt, who claimed as a distant cousin another president of the United States. Truman, by contrast, had experienced hard times in the American Midwest, both before and after service during World War I as an artillery captain on the battlefields of Vosges, Meuse-Argonne and Sommedieu. Returning to his home town of Independence, Missouri, Truman married Elizabeth "Bess" Virginia Wallace, his childhood sweetheart. Prior to the war, Truman had unsuccessfully invested in mining and oil operations. Later,

Fig. 12-1   U.S. President Harry S Truman, 1945. (Pearson Education, Corporate Digital Archive, Getty Images Inc.)

an attempt at running a clothing business in Kansas City collapsed in the midst of a postwar recession. A bankrupt Truman turned to politics, joining the Pendergast political machine, which dominated Missouri political affairs. After serving as a county judge, Truman, who had acquired a reputation for honesty, was elected to the U.S. Senate in 1934.

Senator Truman served on the Senate Interstate Commerce Committee, where he headed an investigation into railroad finances. Despite uncovering damaging information about friends in his home state, Truman continued the investigation, which resulted in the Transportation Act of 1940 that regulated the financing of railroad operations. Another government study that led to indictments of various members of the Pendergast machine failed to implicate Truman, who was reelected to the Senate in 1940. As the United States continued its mobilization efforts, Truman called for the upper chamber to investigate military spending. In 1941, the Senate Committee to Investigate the National Defense Committee, was established with Truman as chairman. The Truman Committee searched for waste and inefficiency, saving some $15 billion and speeding up war production.

In the summer of 1944, Democratic Party leaders decided to replace Roosevelt's running-mate Vice President Henry Wallace—whom they viewed as too liberal—with Truman. Without ever having been taken into Roosevelt's confidence, Truman took over the mantle of the presidency as the Allied armies continued their march to victory in Europe the following spring. Indeed, on May 7, 1945, Germany surrendered; the following day, which happened to be his birthday, Truman declared victory in Europe, V-E Day. In July, Truman participated in the Potsdam Conference, along with Great Britain's Prime Minister Winston Churchill and the Soviet Union's Premier Joseph Stalin. While in Germany, Truman learned that the Manhattan Project, involving the creation of an atomic bomb, had proven successful. On August 6 and 9, American pilots dropped single nuclear bombs over the Japanese cities of Hiroshima and Nagasaki, respectively. On September 2, Japan formally surrendered, thereby bringing humankind's most catastrophic war to an end.

In the period ahead, Truman had to battle both domestic foes and America's wartime ally, the Soviet Union. He encountered opposition from the Democratic Party's left-wing, headed by the new Secretary of Commerce Henry Wallace; its right-wing, spearheaded by segregationists who called themselves Dixiecrats; labor unions; and a reinvigorated Republican Party. The 1946 elections resulted in Republicans capturing Congress; Truman appeared headed for defeat in the 1948 presidential race. International tensions heightened too, as the Soviets formed Stalinist communist governments in Eastern Europe, while threatening Western commercial and security interests in the Middle East. Adopting an anti-communist stance of his own, Truman expanded the National Security State in America, while backing the Soviet Union's foes overseas. In a surprise victory, Truman won in an upset over the Republican presidential candidate, New York governor Thomas Dewey, in 1948. Truman also produced the Marshall Plan to rebuild war-torn Western Europe and the North Atlantic Treaty Organization, which created a military alliance between the United States, Canada and a number of Western European nations.

Truman's attempts to expand the American welfare state through a program he called the Fair Deal proved less fruitful. Nevertheless, he highlighted civil rights concerns, while setting up a permanent Fair Employments Practices Commission and calling for federal legislation to ban the poll tax and lynching. By 1949, concerns about communism overrode other issues for the Truman administration, with the Soviets acquiring the atomic bomb and Chinese communists, led by Mao Zedong, taking control of the Chinese mainland. The next year Wisconsin Senator Joseph McCarthy accused both the Roosevelt and Truman administrations of sheltering communists. That summer, the United States led a United Nations-sponsored military operation after the North Korean communists invaded the South. A constitutional crisis threatened when American commander General Douglas A. MacArthur challenged presidential control over military operations. Truman, however, stood firm and recalled the wartime hero. Truman's popularity reached low ebb, as charges of corruption and coddling communists appeared to ensure a Democratic Party defeat in the 1952 general elections.

Declining to run again, Truman retired to his hometown of Independence, Missouri, where a presidential library, which housed a modest office for the former chief executive, was soon constructed. Democratic Party leaders, particularly possible presidential candidates, repeatedly made pilgrimages to Truman's home. With the passage of time, Truman came to be seen as a man who decisively took stands. He had, while president, insisted that "the buck stops here;" and represented the Democratic Party's readiness to expand the welfare state while ensuring that the nation's security interests were protected. Well-remembered was Truman's admonition, "If you can't stand the heat, get out of the kitchen."

•———•———•———•———•

The United States and the Early Cold War

Even before the war ended, problems had cropped up in the Grand Alliance that held together capitalist America, imperialist England and communist Russia in an anti-fascist front. Two issues particularly stood out: the failure to establish early a second front in Europe to alleviate pressure on the Soviet Union and that nation's determination to have a buffer zone to its west. Despite Joseph Stalin's requests and the horrific losses the Soviet army and citizenry suffered in their fight against German forces, the D-Day invasion of Western Europe was postponed until June 6, 1944. Within a year, the Soviet Union had set up puppet governments in Poland, Rumania and Bulgaria. The new American president Harry S Truman and key advisors such as Ambassador to the Soviet Union Averill Harriman and Secretary of War Henry Stimson adopted more of a hard-line stance toward the communist state. Shortly after assuming the presidency, Truman informed Secretary of State James F. Byrnes, "We must stand up to the Russians at this point and not be easy with them." The discovery that the United States had devised an atomic bomb undoubtedly emboldened the new chief executive to view the Soviet Union with greater suspicion than his predecessor.

During the early postwar period, relations between the Soviet Union and its former wartime partners began to deteriorate. In February 1946, Stalin, who was determined to shield his nation from future invasions, questioned whether co-existence between capitalist and communists states was possible. On March 5, in a speech delivered in Fulton, Missouri, former British prime minister Winston Churchill declared that a new, dark shadow had fallen across the European continent. President Truman was sitting in the audience, listening with evident approval, as Churchill bemoaned the fact that "from Stettin in the Baltic to Trieste in the Adriatic, an Iron Curtain has descended."

Throughout 1946 and early 1947, developments in the Mediterranean region disturbed British and American policymakers. For a time, the Soviets refused to remove their troops from Iran, apparently threatening oil and security interests. While those forces were soon withdrawn, unrest unfolded in Turkey and Greece. A civil war in Greece pitted guerrilla forces, with backing from Joseph Tito's Communist regime in Yugoslavia, against the British-supported government that contained former fascist elements. Nearly bankrupted by two major wars in the past thirty years, Great Britain in February 1947 informed the United States that it could no longer police the area.

Truman, relying on the containment theory put forth by George F. Kennan of the State Department, called for $400 million in aid to the embattled Turkish and Greek governments. Kennan urged the United States to confront Soviet aggression where it occurred, employing "long-term, patient but firm and vigilant containment." Arthur Vandenberg, the Republican chairman of the Senate Foreign Relations Committee, advised the president to "scare the hell out of the American people." Truman spoke on March 12, 1947, about a "global struggle between freedom and totalitarianism." He insisted that "it must be the policy of the United States to support free peoples who are resisting attempted subjugation by armed minorities or by outside pressures." During the next 40 years, the Truman Doctrine, along with containment, served as the cornerstone of U.S. foreign policy. In the process, the United States, insisting on the need to prevent communist successes, backed a number of individuals, groups and nations that hardly strove "to support free peoples."

Determined to stave off communist advances, the United States moved to provide economic assistance to war-ravaged nations, especially in Western Europe and Japan, and to afford military protection. In a speech at Harvard University on June 5, 1947, Secretary of State George C. Marshall, one of the great American military heroes of World War II, outlined a program to revitalize Western Europe. Over the course of the next five years, the Marshall Plan provided some $13 billion in assistance, which enabled countries including England, France, West Germany and Italy to rebuild economically. In the process, American businesses benefited from market developments, which received a great deal of government assistance. A comparable effort to transform Japan occurred, initially guided by General Douglas MacArthur, who sought to demilitarize and democratize that vital Asian country.

In the United States, policymakers devised a national security state, based on twin assumptions that communism was a threat every bit as grave as fascism and that the Soviet Union was no better than Nazi Germany. The National Security Act of 1947 collapsed the Navy and War departments into the Department of Defense, which was established within two years, and set up the Air Force as a branch equal to other military units. The legislation also called for a National Security Council (NSC), which would advise the president on foreign policy matters, and a Central Intelligence Agency (CIA), to collect and analyze intelligence information and conduct covert operations outside the United States. In 1949, Congress created a peacetime draft. The following April, the government produced NSC-68, an examination of American foreign policy that called for a near quadrupling of military spending.

The communization of Eastern Europe heightened anti-Soviet sentiments in the United States; the surge of communism in Asia resulted in an increase in the military budget from $13 billion in 1949 to over $40 billion after war broke out in Korea. The communist takeover in Hungary in 1947, followed by a similar development in Czechoslovakia the next year, particularly angered Americans of Eastern European ancestry. Conservatives and liberals alike feared the emergence of another totalitarian aggressor state. Tensions heightened in 1948 as the Soviets cut off access to Berlin, which resulted in a near year-long airlift, and rose even more the following year, as the Soviets broke the American nuclear monopoly and the Chinese communists under Mao Zedong took control of the mainland. In June 1950 Kim Il Sung's North Korean forces invaded across the 38th parallel, a move soon met by an American-sponsored United Nations' military expedition designed to prevent the fall of South Korea. Over the course of the next three years, a bloody stalemate ensued, prolonged by the participation of Chinese forces starting in late 1950 after American troops guided by MacArthur approached the Chinese border near the Yalu River. MacArthur's evident desire to bring China, and possibly Russia, into the war, led to his removal by President Truman, thus averting a constitutional crisis regarding civilian control of the U.S. military. In 1953, President Dwight David Eisenhower, fulfilling a campaign promise, helped to bring about an end to the war, after first threatening the use of nuclear weapons. Some 39,000 Americans lost their lives in the conflict, which resulted in over two million Korean deaths.

To a certain extent, the Eisenhower administration, led by the former World War II Allied commander and Secretary of State John Foster Dulles, maintained Truman's containment policy. That led to the United States' continued backing of the French, who were battling communist-led insurgents in Indochina. Ho Chi Minh and his Viet Minh forces, spearheaded by General Nguyen Giap, decisively concluded the French Indochina War (1946–1954) by surrounding French soldiers at Dien Bien Phu. The United States then helped to establish an anti-communist regime in the south under the Catholic nationalist Ngo Dinh Diem. Reunification elections, promised at the 1954 Geneva Accords that officially ended the war, never took place because of opposition by both Diem and the United States. In his memoirs, Eisenhower later acknowledged that had the elections been held, Ho Chi Minh would have garnered over 80 percent of the popular vote. The United States proceeded to engage in an experiment in nation-building in the south. There, the United States backed a brutal anti-communist campaign carried out by Diem and his brother

Ngo Dinh Nhu, who controlled a number of para-military and security forces.

Eisenhower and Dulles, like their immediate predecessors, sought to stave off communist advances. In the process, they often viewed nationalist elements in other lands as suspect. Consequently, they turned to the CIA—whose director was Allen Dulles, the Secretary of State's brother—which deposed governments in both Iran and Guatemala. In Iran, the nationalist regime of Premier Mohammed Mossadeq appeared to threaten British and American oil interests. In Guatemala, the democratically elected government of Jacobo Arbenz Guzman called for the takeover of 400,000 acres of land held by the United Fruit Company, a U.S.-based company. The CIA triggered discontent that resulted in the return of the Shah Reza Pahlavi to the Iranian throne and the crushing of the Guatemalan democracy by a military coup. Brutal regimes followed, which relied on secret police and para-military operations. Fearing that anti-Western forces might take control of Lebanon, Eisenhower sent 14,000 Marines into the Middle Eastern nation to establish a pro-Western government. Following Fidel Castro's march into Havana in January 1959, the United States soon adopted a trade embargo against the new regime, which quickly proved to be highly nationalistic and sympathetic to Marxism. Within a short while, the Eisenhower administration began plotting Castro's ouster.

At the same time, the United States adopted a more cautious attitude toward Eastern Europe, a region within the Soviet Union's sphere of influence. The American government supported Yugoslavia's Communist leader Joseph Tito's 1948 breakaway from Soviet dominance. It did little, however, as Stalin orchestrated additional purges, some anti-Semitic in nature, in the early postwar period. His death in 1953, nevertheless, heightened the determination by many in Eastern Europe to demand greater political freedom and economic prosperity. Riots broke out in East Berlin in 1953, but communist authorities quickly quelled the disturbances. Nikita Khrushchev, who won the power struggle to succeed Stalin, initially demonstrated a more flexible attitude regarding Soviet hegemony, which Eisenhower welcomed. Secretary of State Dulles blustered about massive retaliation through nuclear weapons, including possible deployment of the new hydrogen bomb (that the Americans produced in 1952 and the Soviets duplicated the following year) if the Russians misbehaved. But somewhat better relations emerged, with Eisenhower and Khrushchev meeting in Geneva in 1955. Early the next year, at the Soviet Communist Party's Twentieth Conference, Khruschev, who had recently indicated that different paths to socialism were possible, denounced Stalinist terrors. Restless elements in Poland and Hungary, in particular, took heart. In October, the new Hungarian premier Irme Nagy, who was seeking to humanize communism, encountered Soviet tanks in the streets of Budapest. Although the American government through Radio Free Europe had exhorted students, workers and intellectuals to revolt, it stood aside as the Soviets crushed the Hungarian Revolution; in 1958, the Soviets executed Nagy, who had been taken to the USSR.

The Eisenhower administration, in an effort to keep government spending in check, resorted to stockpiling nuclear arms. Such weapons, Dulles declared, offered "more bang for a buck." Eisenhower slightly reduced the military budget of the United States, by spending less on conventional forces. In October 1957, however, an announcement that

the Soviet Union had launched *Sputnik* I troubled the administration and the American public. Discussion ensued that America's national security might be imperiled. In reality, a nuclear stalemate was unfolding, as both the United States and the Soviet Union stockpiled armaments. As concerns about nuclear fallout occurred, Eisenhower and Khrushchev, in 1958, agreed to withhold additional tests. The ban was lifted three years later, months after another summit was called off following the shooting down of an American U-2 spy plane over Soviet airspace.

The Red Scare

The Cold War dramatically affected domestic developments in the United States. Following the 1946 congressional elections, the Democratic Party lost control of Congress for the first time since 1932. The rhetoric of anti-communism, fueled by developments overseas, proved a valuable weapon for some politicians in those races, including Joseph McCarthy, a previously obscure judge from Wisconsin, and Richard Milhous Nixon, a naval veteran from Orange County, California. McCarthy defeated Robert F. La Follette Jr. to win a Senate seat, while Nixon, portraying Congressman Jerry Voorhis as favorably disposed toward communism, was elected to the U.S. House of Representatives.

On March 21, 1947, little more than a week following the announcement of the Truman Doctrine, the president crafted Executive Order 9835, which triggered a loyalty program. Federal employees considered security risks confronted the loss of their jobs and public humiliation. In June, Congress overrode Truman's veto of the Taft-Hartley Act, which banned the closed shop where only union members could be employed and required union officials to sign affidavits indicating that they were not communists. Late in the year, Attorney General Tom C. Clark produced a list of supposedly suspect organizations. Following Truman's lead, the House Committee on Un-American Activities undertook highly publicized hearings into the film industry. Some, who refused to name names in the manner Congress demanded, received contempt citations, criminal trials and prison sentences. Hollywood faced blacklists and fears of producing socially conscious films.

Truman's anti-communist stance, both at home and abroad, along with his calls for an extension of the New Deal and civil rights legislation, enabled him to win the 1948 presidential election. His efforts to produce a Fair Deal for Americans, which included public housing and other social legislation, generally proved unavailing as the domestic Cold War deepened. To his credit, Truman issued executive orders that tackled the issue of racial discrimination in the U.S. civil service and the military. The U.S. Supreme Court, which eventually featured four Truman appointees, including Chief Justice Fred Vinson, delivered a series of rulings that somewhat diminished legal segregation.

In the realm of civil liberties, however, those same appointees, along with the U.S. Congress and J. Edgar Hoover's Federal Bureau of Investigation, enabled the postwar red scare to flourish. In February 1950, anti-communism featured a new champion, Senator Joseph McCarthy, who began charging that the State Department harbored communists in its midst. That year, Congress passed the McCarran Internal Security Act, which allowed for the detention of supposed subversives in concentration camps, during a time of national emergency. The measure

also required communist front organizations to register with the Subversive Activities Board. In 1951, in the *Dennis* case, the Supreme Court sustained the 1940 Smith Act, which criminalized advocating "the propriety of overthrowing or destroying any government in the United States by force or violence." Relying on that statute, prosecutors had tried and convicted American Communist Party leaders. Justice Hugo Black, in an impassioned dissent, expressed hope that "in calmer times, when present pressures, passions, and fears subside, this or some later Court will restore the First Amendment liberties to the high preferred place where they belong in a free society." In 1952, the Immigration and Nationality Act established political litmus tests to determine whether individuals should be denied entry into the United States. Supposed communists and leftists of various stripes were routinely refused admission, while those who claimed to be escaping communist tyranny were welcomed with open arms; included in that group were any number of right-wing extremists, including Nazis and other fascists.

The Eisenhower era (1953–1961) witnessed both the intensifying and ultimate waning of the worst excesses of the red scare. In 1953, two accused atomic spies who had been convicted of espionage, Julius and Ethel Rosenberg, were executed. Historians later contended that while Julius was probably guilty of low-level espionage, the evidence against Ethel was far less compelling. Even though his party was now in control of the executive branch, Senator McCarthy continued brandishing wild charges of communist subversion. After McCarthy insisted that the U.S. military was itself saddled with communists, the televised Army-McCarthy hearings occurred in 1954. Finally, the demagogic McCarthy overstepped his bounds. In a telling moment, after a junior member of his law firm was attacked, Joseph Welch, the army counsel, cuttingly asked McCarthy, "Have you no sense of decency, sir, at long last?" Equally damaging was CBS newsman Edward R. Murrow's exposé of McCarthyism on his television program, *See It Now*.

The domestic Cold War nevertheless continued to affect the national landscape. Investigative committees, both at the federal and state level, the firing of suspect employees and the withdrawal of security clearances from an individual as renowned as former Atomic Energy Commission chairman J. Robert Oppenheimer, all demonstrated as much. But in 1957, the U.S. Supreme Court, now led by Chief Justice Earl Warren and including liberals Hugo Black, William Douglas and William Brennan, issued a series of rulings that sustained First Amendment rights. The Yates case saw Justice John Marshall Harlan, who, like Warren and Brennan, had been named to the court by Eisenhower, deliver a majority opinion overturning Smith Act convictions of a second level of Communist Party leaders.

The red scare had clearly shifted the national spectrum rightward and helped to usher in the Eisenhower presidency. Eisenhower became identified with Modern Republicanism, which combined a staunch anti-communist foreign policy with a general, albeit reluctant acceptance of the American welfare state. To the dismay of hard-liners in the Republican Party, Eisenhower refused to engage in a wholesale assault against the social programs Roosevelt and Truman had established. The immensely popular "Ike" actually expanded government operations regarding social security and unemployment compensation coverage; construction of 35,000 additional public housing units; establishment of the Department of Health, Education, and Welfare; and passage of the 1956 Interstate Highway Act. National defense, Eisenhower claimed, required the building of an interstate highway network.

Ferment in Eisenhower's America

The generally prosperous times, coupled with the confidence Eisenhower afforded the American public at the height of the Cold War, ensured his enormous popularity, which only began to wane somewhat at the close of his presidency. That occurred as the third recession of his presidency helped to bring about the defeat of the 1960 Republican Party presidential candidate, Vice President Richard Nixon. Nevertheless, the 1950s were associated with the postwar economic boom that enabled many Americans to acquire middle-class economic status; to attend institutions of higher learning, thanks to the G.I. Bill; and to move into new suburban homes situated outside increasingly dilapidated urban centers.

Still, dissenting voices once again were heard even in the midst of the general celebration of American life that characterized the Eisenhower era. The campaign to eradicate Jim Crow or segregation practices gathered steam, while confronting dangerous obstacles along the way. In late 1945, Branch Rickey, the general manager of the Brooklyn Dodgers, signed the Kansas City Monarchs' second baseman Jackie Robinson to a minor-league contract, enabling him to become the first black athlete in organized baseball in the 20th century. By 1947, Robinson starred on the Dodgers' pennant-winning squad, and within two years, he won the batting title and became the National League's Most Valuable Player. Other former Negro Leaguers entered the big leagues, including catcher Roy Campanella, pitcher Don Newcombe and outfielders Monte Irvin and Willie Mays. Professional football and basketball followed suit, but the breakdown of the color barrier in the sport long viewed as America's national pastime was most significant.

During the same period, the National Association for the Advancement of Colored People or NAACP maintained its legal challenge to the American form of apartheid, which had been buttressed by an 1896 ruling by the United States Supreme Court declar-

ing that "equal but separate facilities" were constitutional. Guided by attorney Thurgood Marshall, the NAACP won a series of court cases, culminating with the decision of *Brown v. Board of Education*, issued by the nation's highest judicial tribunal in 1954. Speaking for a unanimous court, Chief Justice Earl Warren declared that "in the field of public education the doctrine of separate but equal has no place." Many white Southerners, led by elected public officials, demonstrated their unwillingness to abide by the court's decision. The Ku Klux Klan experienced a revival and the South witnessed the emergence of White Citizen's Councils,

Map 12-1   Blacks attending segregated schools

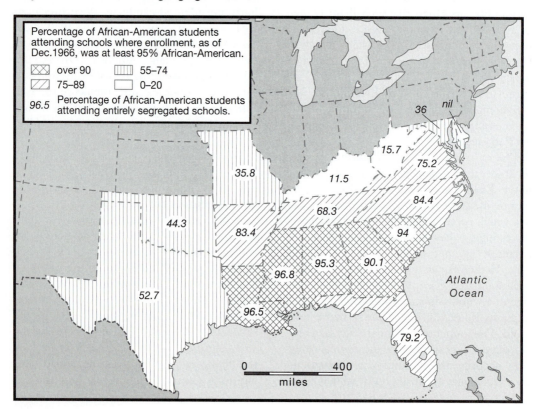

which also sought to uphold the Jim Crow system through economic pressure and legal maneuvering.

Determined to build on the promises of *Brown* and other federal court decisions, blacks in Montgomery, Alabama, conducted a year-long bus boycott to condemn segregation. They were led by a young black minister, Dr. Martin Luther King Jr., who was guided by his belief in non-violent direct action. King, in turn, drew inspiration from the nineteenth-century American writer Henry David Thoreau, the author of a classic essay on civil disobedience, and Mahatma Gandhi. In 1957, President Eisenhower federalized the Arkansas National Guard and sent paratroopers to Little Rock to uphold a federal court order requiring the desegregation of Central High School. The U.S. Congress passed the first civil rights legislation in over 80 years, thereby establishing a Commission of Civil Rights to investigate discriminatory practices, including infringements on the right to vote. On February 1, 1960, four college students deliberately violated segregation ordinances in Greensboro, North Carolina, by engaging in a "sit-in" at a Woolworth lunch counter. Sit-ins began to spread like wildfire across the South, while sympathy sit-ins were held in other parts of the nation. Civil rights activists created the Student Non-Violent Coordinating Committee (SNCC) to carry on the challenge to Jim Crow.

Others demonstrated their displeasure with the general conservatism, conformity and complacency of the Eisenhower era. A small but growing anti-nuclear movement condemned America's foreign policy that relied on weapons of mass destruction. In 1957, an anti-nuclear organization, SANE, was formed; "Ban the Bomb" demonstrations were carried out; and some protestors engaged in civil disobedience at nuclear sites or around nuclear-powered submarines. Cultural critics, such as the beats, whose most noteworthy representatives included a band of writers such as Allen Ginsberg, Jack Kerouac, William Burroughs and Gary Snyder, emerged too. The beats, many based in enclaves such as Greenwich Village, San Francisco's North Beach and Venice, California, condemned the conventional ways of middle-class Americans who lived in suburbia, favored the cult of domesticity, liked "Ike" and loyally toiled as organization men (or women). Young people, some attracted by the beats' call to go "on the road," were delighted by a new, energized popular music, rock 'n roll, whose greatest early practitioners included both whites like Elvis Presley and Jerry Lee Lewis and blacks such as Chuck Berry and Little Richard. Many Americans viewed with trepidation the bands of protestors and the anti-heroic cultural figures, such as film actors Marlon Brando and James Dean, who appealed to the young. Those same conservative sorts were equally displeased by the appearance of a new men's magazine, *Playboy*, first published by Hugh Hefner in 1953, which made light of the era's sexually restrictive norms.

America's Camelot

The early 1960s witnessed both heightened Cold War concerns and criticisms of U.S. foreign and domestic policies. Ironically, Dwight Eisenhower drew one of the most pointed perspectives in his farewell address, when the nation's greatest living general urged the American public "to guard against . . . the military-industrial complex." During his acclaimed inaugural address, John Fitzgerald Kennedy, the youngest man ever elected to the presidency, declared, "And so, my fellow Americans, ask not what your country can do for you, ask what you can do for your country." A number of young Americans in particular soon heeded Kennedy's call, with some choosing to join the newly created Peace Corps and others entering the beefed-up U.S. military. Through the Peace Corps, Americans volunteered to provide educational and technical aid to economically underdeveloped countries. Serving in Kennedy's favorite wing of the military, the Special Forces or Green Berets, some became proficient in the counterinsurgent techniques to be applied in many of the same Third World nations. Both vehicles were intended to lessen the appeal of communism throughout the globe.

As a committed Cold Warrior, Kennedy was determined to prevent communist advances and thus supported the CIA plan devised during the end of the Eisenhower administration to engineer an invasion of Cuba, now viewed as a Soviet satellite. When hostilities mounted between the American government and Fidel Castro's regime, the Cuban leader drew closer to the communist superpower and proclaimed Cuba a Marxist-Leninist state. In April 1961, Cuban exiles, with the backing of the Kennedy White House, sought to overthrow Castro. Instead, the Bay of Pigs expedition proved to be both a military and diplomatic disaster as the Cuban people failed to rise up against Castro and the exiles paid the price. Refusing to resort to airpower, Kennedy took full responsibility for the setback. That summer, a meeting in Vienna with Nikita Khrushchev went badly, with the young president coming away feeling somewhat bullied by the 67-year-old Soviet premier. A new crisis over Berlin threatened, with the Soviets building a wall that divided the East German sector from the rest of the city.

The most dangerous moments of the Cold War, which involved the Cuban missile crisis, occurred in October 1962. American reconnaissance planes uncovered the Soviet deployment of intermediate-range ballistic missiles in Cuba. With major American cities within range of such missiles, the Kennedy administration demanded their removal. Having resorted to a naval blockade, Kennedy's top advisers watched anxiously as Soviet ships approached. When those ships turned around, Secretary of State Dean Rusk was heard to say, "We're eyeball to eyeball and I think the other fellow just blinked." Eventually, Khrushchev agreed to withdraw the missiles, while the United States promised not to invade the island and to take out missiles it had housed in Turkey within six months.

Both emboldened and matured by the confrontation, President Kennedy, in a speech at American University on June 10, 1963, stated, "In the final analysis, our most basic common link is the fact that we all inhabit this planet. We all breathe the same air. We all cherish our children's future. And we are all mortal." Two months later, the United States, the Soviet Union and Great Britain signed a nuclear test-ban treaty pertaining to the atmosphere, seas and oceans. In addition, a hot line was set up allowing direct telephone communications between the two superpowers. At the same time, Kennedy continued to push for an increase in both military spending and nuclear arms stockpiling.

The president also intensified U.S. involvement in Southeast Asia. When Kennedy took office in January 1961, some 800 American advisers could be found in Vietnam. By the end of his presidency, over 16,000 American soldiers were in place in that war-torn land. Kennedy, like his predecessor, initially backed the regime of Ngo

Dinh Diem, an ardent anti-communist. But Diem's repressive ways and those of his brother Ngo Dinh Nhu helped to produce another guerrilla movement. Based in the South and guided by communists, the National Liberation Front grew in strength and threatened to topple the increasingly unpopular autocrat; Diem, like American officials, derisively called the guerrillas the Viet Cong. To the dismay of Washington, the Saigon government invaded the temples of protesting Buddhist priests. Even more troubling, seven of those clergymen, determined to call attention to their cause, burned themselves to death. Having received word that the U.S. government was not opposed to Diem's removal, South Vietnamese generals seized the president and his brother. JFK, who had recently declared that the war was the South Vietnam regime's to win, reportedly was stunned to learn that the pair had been murdered. Three weeks later, Kennedy was himself assassinated during a presidential motorcade in Dallas, Texas. Stories began to be spun about the Kennedy administration, likening it to King Arthur's Camelot.

Nevertheless, before his death, Kennedy encountered criticism on the domestic front from both the right and the left. Virulent right-wing forces, including members of the John Birch Society, denounced Kennedy and Earl Warren, the Chief Justice of the Supreme Court, as communists. On the left, the Students for a Democratic Society, founded in 1960, expressed disappointment with Kennedy's Cuban policy. A small number in the organization, like a few of their countrymen, demonstrated against U.S. involvement in Vietnam. The New Left, which had emerged out of the hibernation of the 1950s, also condemned the Kennedy administration's reluctance to support more forcefully the civil rights crusade. Building on the

momentum established by the sit-ins of 1960s, both black and white activists participated in Freedom Rides throughout the Deep South, in which they challenged segregation practices in interstate transportation. Many experienced arrests and beatings, and the Kennedy administration was forced to provide some legal protection.

Martin Luther King Jr. continued his nonviolent campaign to challenge Jim Crow, while young civil rights figures such as Bob Moses headed South to carry out voter registration drives in some of the region's most dangerous territories, such as rural Mississippi. After riots broke out in Birmingham in June 1963, Kennedy delivered an eloquent speech to the nation in which he asserted that the dilemma facing America was "as old as the scriptures and . . . as clear as the American Constitution." His administration now began to push for strong civil rights legislation, which bogged down in Congress. On August 28, 1963, the highlight of the nonviolent phase of the civil rights movement occurred when 200,000 participated in a March on Washington. The throng listened in rapt attention as King declared, "I have a dream that one day on the red hills of Georgia the sons of former slaves and the sons of former slaveowners will be able to sit down together at the table of brotherhood."

The Presidency of Lyndon Baines Johnson

During the first months after Kennedy's assassination, Lyndon Baines Johnson deftly guided the nation through a period of mourning. Using legendary legislative skill he acquired as Senate Majority Leader, Johnson pushed through a series of measures Kennedy had proposed that had stalled in Congress. Johnson added many more of his own. In the process, the most impressive package of reform bills since the New Deal became law. Many historians would argue in fact that Johnson's Great Society and War on Poverty packages actually surpassed those of his mentor FDR. Among the most significant accomplishments were the 1964 Civil Rights Act and the 1965 Voting Rights Act, which effectively ended *de jure* or legal segregation in the United States. The Civil Rights Act safeguarded black voting rights; broadened the powers of the Civil Rights Commission; outlawed discrimination based on race, religion or gender, in hiring or involving public accommodations; and cut off federal funding to state and local programs that were discriminatory. The Voting Rights Act prohibited the use of literacy tests to determine voter eligibility and authorized the Attorney General of the United States to assign federal registrars where patterns of discrimination existed.

Johnson's legislative program was truly expansive in nature. With the president declaring an "unconditional war on poverty" at the outset of his presidency, Congress passed the Economic Opportunity Act of 1964, which established the Office of Economic Opportunity to assist economically disadvantaged youth through educational and vocational training. The act also offered loans for small businesses and rural areas; created the Job Corps and VISTA, which sought to provide work experience of a socially conscious variety for young people; and authorized grants to local community organizations engaged in social action. A Model Cities program was set up and the departments of Housing and Urban Development and Transportation were created. Federal aid to education similarly mushroomed with the passage in 1965 of the Elementary and Secondary Education Act and the Higher Education Act. Medical

coverage expanded, with Medicare providing benefits for the elderly and Medicaid helping to take care of physicians' treatment of the indigent.

In his determination to create a Great Society, Johnson in 1965 also helped to spawn the National Endowment for the Humanities and the National Endowment for the Arts. In 1967, Congress, at Johnson's behest, created the Corporation for Public Broadcasting, which soon helped to fund programs such as *Sesame Street*. Encouraged by his wife Lady Bird, Johnson pushed for passage of the 1965 Highway Beautification Act.

Yet Johnson's expansion of the welfare state failed to ensure social harmony in the United States. Notwithstanding his administration's support for civil rights and anti-poverty legislation, American's inner cities continued to experience turmoil. From 1964 through 1968, the country endured race riots each summer. Police brutality, a lack of opportunities for many African-Americans, depressed conditions in the inner cities and rising expectations combined to produce a volatile mix. New civil rights figures sprang forth, challenging Dr. King's non-violent preachments and calling for Black Power. Influenced by the black Muslim Malcolm X, who was assassinated in early 1965, young activists including Stokely Carmichael and H. Rap Brown took over SNCC and guided it in new, more aggressive directions. Out west, two young college students, Huey Newton and Bobby Seale, founded the Black Panthers, a militant, revolutionary group.

Johnson's popularity, which resulted in a resounding victory in the 1964 presidential race against Republican nominee Senator Barry Goldwater, who was perceived as an extremist, began to wane. Social unrest in the United States, along with divisions concerning U.S. involvement in Vietnam, did not help. In 1965, Johnson initiated a systematic bombing campaign of both North and South Vietnam and introduced land forces. By the end of the year, 185,000 American troops were in Vietnam and opposition to the war mounted back home. An antiwar movement, which built on the Free Speech Movement that had unfolded at the University of California at Berkeley the previous year, condemned U.S. policy in Southeast Asia, arguing that it was both immoral and impractical. Elders such as A. J. Muste, the nation's leading pacifist; I. F. Stone, who published his iconoclastic newsletter out of his home in Washington, D.C.; and David Dellinger, who had been jailed as a conscientious objector during World War II, spearheaded the antiwar movement. So too did young activists from SDS and SNCC including Tom Hayden, Paul Potter and Julian Bond. Another organization emerged in 1966, the Resistance, headed by David Harris, which urged draft-eligible men to refuse to cooperate with the Selective Service System.

Anti-war demonstrations cropped up across the land, ranging from mass gatherings in major cities and on large university campuses to determined efforts of individual young men to say no to local draft boards. In 1965, efforts were undertaken to prevent the transporting of soldiers out of Oakland. The next year, Secretary of Defense Robert McNamara was unable to speak at Harvard because of protests. In 1967, Martin Luther King Jr. denounced the United States as "the greatest purveyor of violence" on the face of the earth and protestors undertook a March on the Pentagon. In January 1968, the Tet Offensive in South Vietnam dispelled notions that "light could be seen at the end of the tunnel": in other words, that the war was going better. The Democratic Party was torn apart with Senators Robert F. Kennedy and Eugene McCarthy running as anti-war candidates and Lyndon Johnson feeling compelled to withdraw from the presidential race. That spring, protestors seized buildings at Columbia University, while the university administration allowed police onto campus to restore order.

Violence seemed in the air, with both Martin Luther King Jr. and Robert Kennedy gunned down in the first half of 1968. Riots followed in the wake of King's murder in April, while unrest seemingly reigned in the midst of the Democratic Party's national convention in Chicago. Like the Black Panthers, some in SDS and SNCC now called for revolution, while others believed that altered consciousness should be sought. Many of the so-called hippies were characterized by their long hair, colorful clothing, willingness to dabble in drugs including psychedelics like LSD and rejection of conservative sexual ways. Hippies favored communal ways, with Be-Ins, pop festivals, co-ops and communes exemplifying their rejection of "the Establishment." Individuals including former Harvard psychology professor Timothy Leary, author Ken Kesey and preeminent folk artist Bob Dylan spread the gospel of the counterculture. By 1968, even pop music icons such as the Beatles were singing about "Revolution," while the Rolling Stones chortled about "Fighting in the Streets."

A Turn to the Right

Angered by the unrest that had appeared in the inner cities, on college campuses and in the parks and streets of Chicago, many Americans supported the calls for "law-and-order" demanded by third-party presidential candidate George Wallace. A strong supporter of segregation and a hawk on the Vietnam War, Wallace increasingly found that the

Republican Party nominee Richard Nixon preempted his positions. Running as "the new Nixon," the 1960 Republican candidate narrowly defeated Hubert Humphrey, Lyndon Johnson's Vice President, in the general election. During the campaign, Nixon promised to unveil a secret plan to end the war in Vietnam and to restore respect for America both at home and abroad; among his targets was the Warren Court.

In the end, Nixon did neither. Along with his top foreign policy adviser, Harvard University professor Henry Kissinger, Nixon planned to rely on the "madman theory." They sought to convince the North Vietnamese that Nixon was willing to deploy nuclear weapons in Southeast Asia if the communist leadership refused to stop backing the resistance in the South. But opposition at home prevented Nixon from even implying such a threat. The antiwar movement surged, ranging from the Weathermen faction that splintered from SDS and called for terrorism "to bring the war home," to the half-million marchers who appeared in Washington, D.C. in mid-November 1969 to demand a halt to U.S. operations in Vietnam. Nixon felt compelled to reduce the number of Americans deployed in the field, all the while seeking to extend the war in other ways. In the spring of 1970, American forces participated in an invasion of Cambodia, while the following year, a U.S.-backed incursion by South Vietnamese forces into Laos occurred; the air war involving those two countries likewise intensified as the U.S. pullback took place. Bitter protests in America unfolded alongside the Cambodia venture, which culminated with the killing of four college students at Kent State in Ohio and two more at Jackson State in Mississippi. Following the Kent State tragedies, campuses across the United States were rocked with protests, some resulting in

the burning of R.O.T.C. (Reserve Officer Training Corps) buildings.

Recognizing that the will to continue the fight had evaporated, Nixon and Kissinger sought "a decent interval" between the time when American troops would fully withdraw from Vietnam and the communists would prevail. Shortly following the heaviest bombing of the war, which was conducted in December 1972, peace accords were signed in Paris calling for the removal of the last 23,000 American troops. By contrast, the North Vietnamese forces were not required to head back across the 17th parallel dividing Vietnam.

Other key foreign policy endeavors of the Nixon administration proved equally problematic. The U.S. government worked hand-in-hand with multinational corporations such as IT&T to destabilize the democratically elected government of Chile's Salvador Allende, a Marxist. In a more positive vein, Kissinger, relying on shuttle diplomacy, had earlier helped to encourage détente between the United States, Russia and China, with Nixon visiting the great communist states in 1972. Events in the Middle East, which resulted in another Arab–Israeli clash in 1973, also saw Kissinger, now the U.S. Secretary of State, seek to placate the warring parties. However, the Middle Eastern cauldron led to an oil embargo that only further weakened the American economy.

The Nixon years (1969–1974) included some of the toughest economic times in the United States since the Great Depression. What economists had previously considered an impossibility had occurred: simultaneous high inflation and rising unemployment rates. Nixon, prior to the 1972 presidential election, had resorted to wage-and-price controls. Shortly following his landslide victory, Nixon removed those restraints and the economy spiralled downward into recession.

A rise in unemployment levels resulted in more government spending for social programs, something Nixon had campaigned against. The president, who had condemned the War on Poverty, had called for reducing the federal bureaucracy and returning responsibility for social programs to the states. At the same time, Nixon, influenced by adviser Daniel Patrick Moynihan, had proposed replacing Aid for Families with Dependent Children with a Family Assistance Program, which would amount to a negative income tax for poor Americans. The Democratic-led Congress refused to go along, although in 1972 it established another program, Supplementary Security Income, which afforded a guaranteed income for seniors, the blind and the disabled. Thanks to new consciousness regarding the ecosystem, environmental issues were discussed during Nixon's administration. The Environmental Protection Agency sought to restrain harmful corporate practices, while Congress created the Consumer Products Safety Commission and the Occupational Safety and Health Administration.

Coinciding with his efforts to usher in a New Federalism to strengthen government, Nixon sought to transform the federal judiciary. To that end, he strove to appoint law-and-order judges, particularly to the U.S. Supreme Court. With the retirement of Earl Warren, Nixon was able to select a conservative federal judge, Warren Burger, as chief justice. Thanks to three other resignations, the Burger Court came into existence and began to whittle away at some of the criminal due process rights called for by its successor. Yet in two areas at least, the Burger Court issued rulings that were deeply displeasing to conservatives. It declared that busing could be employed to bring about racial balance in public schools and, in *Roe v. Wade* (1973), affirmed that the right of privacy was "broad

enough to encompass a woman's decision whether or not to terminate her pregnancy." The author of that controversial decision was a Nixon appointee, Harry Blackmun.

While Nixon had run against government excesses, that was precisely what doomed his presidency, one that critics such as Arthur Schlesinger Jr. referred to as "imperial." Angered and frustrated by the antiwar movement, which had stymied his efforts to win the war in Vietnam, Nixon relied on government agencies and White House operatives to investigate those he considered his foes. An "enemies list" was concocted, while "dirty tricks" were resorted to by Internal Revenue Service agents, former intelligence operatives, Cuban exiles, and executive branch employees. They were used to intimidate individuals and groups, to disrupt their operations; to blackmail them and to break into various offices. In June 1972, five individuals tied to the Committee to Re-elect the President were caught attempting to burglarize the Democratic Party headquarters at the Watergate Apartments in Washington, D.C. Hoping to stave off a scandal, President Nixon ordered a cover-up. In May 1973, a White House aide, testifying before the Senate Watergate Committee, revealed that a taping system was present in the Oval Office. The Supreme Court in a unanimous ruling, *U.S. v. Nixon*, rejected claims of executive privilege regarding the tapes, leading to the president's resignation on August 8, 1974.

Economic Doldrums and Malaise

The Watergate scandal, coming on top of social discord exemplified by urban riots, anti-war protests and economic difficulties, fostered popular distrust of government. Nixon's hand-picked successor, Gerald R.

Ford, diligently strove to overcome that distrust. Ford, the former Minority Leader in the House, was selected as Vice President following the forced resignation of Spiro T. Agnew, Nixon's first Vice President, due to the discovery that Agnew had received kickbacks while a county official in Maryland. Ford confronted his own quandaries after ascending to the nation's highest office. Many were infuriated by his pardoning of Nixon "for all offenses against the United States which he ... has committed or may have committed or taken part in." Others were appalled by Ford's heavy reliance on the veto of such legislation as the Freedom of Information Act, which Congress ultimately overrode. With oil prices skyrocketing and wage-and-price controls lifted, inflation soared once again. When Ford emphasized his "Whip Inflation Now" program, unemployment jumped, along with the federal budget deficit.

Former California governor Ronald Reagan led conservative forces who were distressed about the turn of events, including the collapse of the South Vietnamese and Cambodia regimes, which opened the way for communist takeovers. Distrustful about détente and angered over talk about the United States' relinquishing control of the Panama Canal, Reagan ran in the 1976 Republican Party primaries against Ford. Although Ford barely managed to gain his party's nomination, he was weakened politically going into the general election against the Democratic nominee, Jimmy Carter.

Carter's presidency proved troubling, disappointing forces on both the right and left. The one-time governor of Georgia promised the American people, "I will never lie to you," but his moralistic bent often came across as merely sanctimonious. Carter did achieve certain accomplishments during his single term: he created the Department of Education, reconfigured the Department of Health, Education, and Welfare as the Department of Health and Human Services, brought about civil service reform that featured merit-pay, was responsible for environmental advances such as the preservation of over 100 million acres of the Alaskan wilderness and named a record number of women and minorities to public offices.

Notwithstanding such successes, however, Carter increasingly appeared befuddled by the job of reigning over the world's largest democracy. Like Ford, Carter confronted inflation, mounting energy costs and, ultimately, a recession. Both inflation and unemployment rose, while the budget deficit mounted. Ineptly, he sought to compel Americans to conserve energy and to emphasize domestic production. The economy suffered severe jolts in 1979 and 1980, as OPEC sharply raised prices. At the same time, profits for giant American-based oil companies increased sharply. By 1979, the foundering president bemoaned a national "malaise" that had seemingly enveloped America.

Guided by his own sense of moral rectitude, Carter called for the United States and other nations to respect human rights, yet he failed to apply such a standard consistently. "Fairness, not force," he asserted, "should lie at the heart of our dealings with the nations of the world." Working with Secretary of State Cyrus Vance, Carter pressured Chile, Argentina and South Africa, among other countries, to lighten their repressive ways.

Carter's administration also agreed to turn the canal over to the Panamanians by the end of the century, while retaining the right to ensure passage through it; helped to bring about the Camp David Accords that saw the Israeli and Egyptian heads of state agree to a peace treaty; and signed the SALT II accords with the Soviets. In 1978, he proclaimed that the Cold War had ended and urged his countrymen not to retain an unmitigated fear of communism. The following December, he formalized diplomatic relations with the People's Republic of China.

But as his presidential term neared its end, many Americans viewed both Carter's domestic and foreign policies unfavorably. The economy was again saddled with the triple crosses of raging inflation, escalating unemployment and surging budget deficits. Overseas, beginning in November 1979, Shiite followers of the Ayatollah Ruhollah Khomeini held 57 Americans hostage at the U.S. embassy in Teheran. For the duration of Carter's presidency, the media blared incessantly that "America was held hostage." An aborted U.S. rescue effort collapsed in the Iranian desert, resulting in eight American deaths and the resignation of Cyrus Vance, who had refused to back the operation. In the meantime, relations with the Soviets deteriorated, thanks to the USSR's invasion of Afghanistan in an effort to keep a Marxist regime in power. Carter increased defense spending and called for strengthening American intelligence agencies as well.

The Reagan Revolution

Challenged from within his party by Massachusetts Senator Edward M. Kennedy and outside it by Republican presidential nominee Ronald Reagan, Carter foundered and lost the general election in something of a landslide. Similar to the 1978 congressional elections, a number of leading liberals lost their seats in Congress, with the Republicans now controlling the U.S. Senate. Reagan's triumph and that of a number of right-wing candidates suggested that an ideological shift

had unfolded in the United States, or so many pundits claimed. A conservative tilt, in fact, had been developing for some time. Even in the midst of the 1960s, the zenith of postwar American liberalism, conservatives had been on the march, in their own fashion. In 1960, at the Sharon, New Jersey, estate of William Buckley, the editor of *The National Review*, conservatives had formed the Young Americans for Freedom. That same year, a number of leading conservatives urged Barry Goldwater to make a run for the presidency. While Goldwater was trounced in the 1964 presidential race, conservatives had moved to take control of the Republican Party. Reagan made a too-late bid for the nomination in 1968 and then barely lost out in an effort to unseat Ford in the 1976 Republican Party's presidential primaries.

All the while, conservative intellectuals such Buckley had been laying the groundwork for future political success. From the mid-seventies onward, neoconservatives including the likes of Irving Kristol and Norman Podhoretz, the editors of *The Public Interest* and *Commentary*, respectively, had helped to make conservativism intellectually respectable. Many were former liberals or radicals, who had become disillusioned by Soviet communism and were now infatuated with American capitalism. They strongly criticized welfare expenditures, while calling for a sizable increase in military spending. A growing number of social conservatives were similarly disturbed by what they perceived to be the weakening of family values, as sharp increases in drug usage, sexual promiscuity, abortions, divorces and unwed mothers demonstrated. Literally preaching the conservative gospel were televangelists, fundamentalist preachers such as Jerry Falwell and Pat Robertson who boasted their own television medium, the Christian Broadcasting Network. Groups like Falwell's Moral Majority, Phyllis Schafly's Eagle Forum and Terry Dolan's National Conservative Political Action Committee railed away at secular humanism, liberalism and the Democratic Party.

In addition to several congressional and gubernatorial candidates, the greatest beneficiary of the rise of the New Right was Ronald Reagan. Viewed as the Republican Party's equivalent of FDR, Reagan was generally depicted in the mainstream media as affable, well intentioned and true to conservative principles. Determinedly, the sixty-nine-year-old president, the oldest man ever elected to the nation's highest elective office, immediately strove to bring about a wholesale change in American governance. Two supposed enemies loomed large for him: government bureaucracy and the Soviet Union. After Reagan braved an assassination attempt that wounded him, Congress passed much of the legislative program of the former New Dealer, which, ironically whittled away at the welfare state. Substantial sums were sliced away from social programs, while a massive tax reduction, which largely benefited the wealthy, occurred. Similar to the trickle-down economics of conservative Republican administrations of the 1920s, Reagan's supply-side version, it was promised, would promote investment and savings. Coupled with large-scale increases in military spending, these policies drove the national deficit, which was already rising under Carter, to unprecedented levels. Unemployment did likewise, reaching 10 percent by 1982. Aided by decreasing oil prices, the economy rebounded by the following year, but budgetary deficits continued to appear.

In addition to redistributing income to the wealthiest of all Americans, the Reagan administration cheered conservatives in other ways. Funding for the Environmental Protection Agency was pared, to the delight of Secretary of the Interior James Watt, who urged that public lands out west be opened up for private exploration. The Securities and Exchange Commission adopted more of a hands-off approach to the stock market. In a similar vein, the Federal Communications Commission, the Federal Trade Commission, the Occupational Safety and Health Administration (OSHA), the Equal Employment Opportunity Commission and the antitrust division of the Department of Justice, along with other agencies, employed a laxer standard about regulations. Although Reagan appointed the first woman to the U.S. Supreme Court, Sandra Day O'Connor, she, like his other conservative selections for the federal judiciary, opposed the more protective rulings afforded criminal defendants, political dissidents and social pariahs by the Warren Court.

While seeking to weaken the welfare state, Reagan, along with Secretary of Defense Caspar Weinberger, welcomed massive increases in military spending. Little concern was paid to cost overruns, massive profits and the like. Reagan's backers were enthralled that the defense budget virtually doubled under his watch and were pleased by his call for a Strategic Defense Initiative—"Stars Wars program"—intended to provide a space-based shield against approaching missiles. The president was determined to strengthen the American military forces that he and other conservatives argued had been allowed to deteriorate since the Vietnam War. That conflict, they further contended, had produced "a Vietnam Syndrome," which supposedly made U.S. policymakers reluctant to fight. Such disinclination, Reagan believed, particularly made no sense, for the Soviet Union was "an evil empire . . . the focus of evil in the modern world." Reagan argued that the communist giant "underlies all the unrest that is going on. If they weren't engaged in this game of dominos, there wouldn't be any hot spots in the world."

Notwithstanding such rhetoric, however, relations between the United States and the Soviet Union actually began to improve by the end of Reagan's first term in office. Communist officials, he claimed, "reserve unto themselves the right to commit any crime, to lie, to cheat." Nevertheless, in 1985, the president met with the new Soviet premier, Mikhail Gorbachev, and, in a startling turn of events, the two eventually agreed to reduce their nations' nuclear stockpiles.

At the same time, the Reagan administration demonstrated a stark willingness to engage in military action, sometimes to disastrous ends. In 1982, Reagan sent a "peace-keeping force" of some 1,600 American marines into the midst of a long drawn-out civil war in Lebanon. A suicide mission by Islamic militants resulted in the bombing of a U.S. military barracks, which killed 241 American soldiers. Shortly thereafter, Reagan withdrew American troops from the troubled Middle Eastern state. In the meantime, the president, disturbed by the presence of a pro-Cuban government on the small island of Grenada, ordered the ouster of the regime, authorizing an invasion by 2,000 American soldiers.

Central America was a particular area of concern for the Reagan administration, which condemned the Sandinista regime in Nicaragua as communist-driven and dismissed left-wing guerrillas in El Salvador as communist agents. Consequently, Reagan backed the overthrow of the Sandinistas while lending support to government and private vigilante forces that battled El Salvadorean insurgents. Reagan's fixation on the possibility of communism surfacing in the region led to a new triangular trade involving the anti-Sandinista contras, Iranian arms merchants and U.S. government officials. As it became clear that congressional prohibitions against such activities had been circumvented, Reagan, in 1987, faced the possibility of a Watergate-like fate. With many in Washington, D.C., including congressional Democrats, not wishing to subject the nation to another such trauma, the Iran-Contra affair soon dissipated, leaving Reagan in a weaker position for the remainder of his presidency.

Nevertheless, Reagan retained the affection of many as his second term wound to a close. His Vice President George Bush swept to an easy electoral victory over the Democratic Party presidential nominee Michael Dukakis in 1988. During the campaign, Dukakis, the governor of Massachusetts, was portrayed as a "card-carrying member of the American Civil Liberties Union" who was soft on crime. At the same time, Bush called for the shaping of a "kinder, gentler nation." As he took office, the Cold War continued to dominate U.S. foreign policy.

In his first inaugural address on January 20, 1981, Ronald Reagan highlighted the themes that would dominate his administration. Referring to the economic woes confronting the United States, he insisted, "Government is not the solution to our problem." Indeed, he expressed his determination "to curb the size and influence of the Federal establishment and to demand recognition of the distinction between the powers granted to the Federal Government and those reserved to the States or to the people.

All of us need to be reminded that the Federal Government did not create the States; the States created the Federal Government." Later in his brief talk, Reagan delivered a warning to "the enemies of freedom, those who are potential adversaries," obviously referring to the Soviet Union and its allies. Such antagonists, he asserted,

> will be reminded that peace is the highest aspiration of the American people. We will negotiate for it, sacrifice for it; we will not surrender for it—now or ever. Our forbearance should never be misunderstood. Our reluctance for conflict should not be misjudged as a failure of will. When action is required to preserve our national security, we will act. We will maintain sufficient strength to prevail if need be, knowing that if we do so we have the best chance of never having to use that strength.

Reagan's focus on the need to get government "off the backs of the people" and to stand up to the Soviet Union in the era of a new Cold War resonated with many Americans. So too did his seemingly indomitable spirit, which many contrasted so markedly with the gloomy demeanor that had characterized the latter stages of his predecessor's administration. In an event that curiously proved fortuitous, Reagan, whose poll rating had been dropping as he sought to push through his legislative program, suffered an assassination attempt only months after taking office. On the way to the hospital, he was heard to say to his wife Nancy, "Honey, I forgot to duck." The news media reported the event, which seemed to capture Reagan's cheery optimism even in the face of adversity. A chastened Congress began to give way on many of his proposals and the Reagan era began in earnest.

His supporters credited the economic boom of the 1980s to Ronald Reagan, while simultaneously denying that the resulting costs were the byproduct of the Republican administration's policies. A stock market boom occurred until a panic unfolded in 1987; tax rates were reduced, particularly for the wealthy and for corporations. However, many less affluent Americans confronted a reduction of social services, as Reagan sought to curb or eliminate many programs Franklin Delano Roosevelt and Lyndon Baines Johnson had initiated. An ardent champion of conservative values, Reagan nevertheless failed to push hard for top items on the New Right's agenda, including prayer in the schools and a constitutional amendment banning abortion. Moreover, his determination to cut taxes and substantially increase military spending led to massive budgetary deficits. His first Director of the Budget, David Stockman, admitted that such a development was anticipated and would compel, or so Reagan hoped, a scaling down of the American welfare state.

Reagan's right-of-center agenda could scarcely have been predicted when he had championed the New Deal that helped to put his father to work in the midst of the Great Depression. Raised in Dixon, Illinois, some 100 miles west of Chicago, Reagan was imbued with traditional values. As a scholarship student, he attended Eureka College, associated with the Disciples of Christ, located near Peoria. After graduating in 1932, he found work as a radio sportscaster. Five years later, Reagan began a Hollywood film career that spanned more than 50 films, highlighted by starring roles in *Knute*

Fig. 12-2 President Ronald Reagan, February 8, 1984. (Pearson Education, Corporate Digital Archive, The White House Photo Office)

Rocke—All American (1940) and *King's Row* (1941). At the time a liberal Democrat, Reagan was elected six times as president of the Screen Actor's Guild.

His union position and the postwar atmosphere helped to reshape Reagan's political orientation. As the Cold War unfolded, both at home and abroad, Hollywood film actors, directors, screenwriters and producers began to face grillings regarding pro-communist sympathies, whether real or imagined. Reagan, by many accounts, readily attacked communists in his own industry, both by testifying before Congress and through providing information to the FBI.

In 1952, as his film career was winding down, Reagan married Nancy Davis, an actress from a deeply conservative Republican family. Two years later, Reagan began hosting a television program sponsored by General Electric and traveling around the country extolling the virtues of the free-enterprise system. At the 1964 Republican Party national convention, Reagan made an electrifying television address in support of the presidential candidacy of Arizona Senator Barry Goldwater. In 1966, riding the crest of a backlash against liberal governance, black militancy and student unrest, Reagan was easily elected governor of California. He made a brief aborted run at the GOP's presidential nomination in 1968, proving himself to be the darling of the Republican right.

While spouting conservative rhetoric condemning government excesses, other than in his dealings involving antiwar protests Reagan ruled in a fairly pragmatic manner, in part because the state legislature remained in Democratic hands. After winning a second term as governor, he pushed for a major revision of the state welfare system and used major budgetary surpluses to issue tax rebates. In 1976, Reagan again sought the Republican nomination for the president and came close to unseating the incumbent, Gerald Ford.

During the Carter administration, Reagan continued to be the favorite of both the New Right and neo-conservative intellectuals and think-tanks that insisted democratic excesses endangered the United States and its world standing. They, like Reagan, called for a curbing of social programs; a lowering of tax rates, particularly for the wealthy and corporations; and a rearming of America, which they believed must stand up more firmly to the Soviet Union. The passionate pronouncements delivered by such New Rightists and intellectuals appeared borne out by what the United States confronted as the 1970s ended: seemingly grave economic difficulties and a new Cold War.

The 1980 presidential campaign saw the Great Communicator—as Reagan was called by friends and many media-types alike—celebrate traditional values, the free market and a strong America. Reagan's administration featured a return to Cold War rhetoric, as he assailed the Soviet Union, which he referred to as "the Evil Empire." Sporting a clear, but arguably simplistic view of world affairs, Reagan determined to halt the tide of revolutionary movements in Central America and the Caribbean. Eventually, however, in an astonishing turn of events, Reagan and the new Soviet premier Mikhail Gorbachev held a series of summit meetings in which they promised to discard land-based intermediate and short-range nuclear missiles.

Reagan's final two years in office, despite the movement toward a new brand of détente with Gorbachev's Soviet Union, proved difficult. The Democrats had regained control of Congress during the 1986 congressional elections, Wall Street suffered extreme jitters in 1987 and the Iran-Contra scandal presented the possibility of the impeachment of the president. Not seeking to repeat the events of the previous decade, Congress allowed the hearings to end inconclusively. Reagan completed his term of office and headed for retirement back in California. He worked on his autobiography and prepared for the opening of the Ronald Reagan Presidential Library, which was being constructed in Simi Valley. Unbeknownst to all but those closest to him, the ex-president was suffering from the dreaded effects of Alzheimer's disease.

Suggested Readings

AMBROSE, STEPHEN E. *Rise to Globalism: American Foreign Policy since 1938.* (1996).

BLUM, JOHN MORTON. *Years of Discord: American Politics and Society, 1961–1974.* (1991).

BOYER, PAUL. *Promises to Keep: The United States since World War II.* (1995).

BROWNLEE, W. E. *Dynamics of Ascent: A History of the American Economy.* (1988).

CAUTE, DAVID. *The Great Fear: The Anti-Communist Purge under Truman and Eisenhower.* (1978).

CHAFE, WILLIAM H. *The Unfinished Journey: America since World War II.* (1991).

COTTRELL, ROBERT. *Izzy: A Biography of I. F. Stone.* (1992).

DIGGINS, JOHN PATRICK. *The Proud Decades: American War and Peace, 1941–1960.* (1988).

DUBOFSKY, MELVYN and ATHAN THEOHARIS. *Imperial Democracy: The United States since 1945.* (1988).

HAMBY, ALONZO L. *Liberalism and Its Challengers: F.D.R. to Bush.* (1991).

LAFEBER, WALTER, RICHARD POLENBERG, and NANCY WOLOCH. *The American Century: A History of the United States since the 1890s.* (1988).

NORTON, MARY BETH, *et al. A People and a Nation: A History of the United States.* (1999).

PATTERSON, JAMES T. *America in the Twentieth Century: A History.* (2000).

———. *Grand Expectations: The United States, 1945–1974.* (1996).

SCHALLER, MICHAEL, VIRGINIA SCHARFF, and ROBERT D. SCHULZINGER. *Coming of Age: America in the Twentieth Century.* (1998).

SITKOFF, HARVARD. *The Struggle for Black Equality, 1954–1992.* (1993).

WEISBROT, ROBERT. *Freedom Bound: A History of America's Civil Rights Movement.* (1990).

WHITFIELD, STEPHEN. *The Culture of the Cold War.* (1991).

CHAPTER 13

Latin America during the Cold War, 1945–1989

During a new dangerous phase of the Cold War, Ernesto Guevara de la Serna, born into a long line of Argentine aristocrats, became an icon for revolutionaries worldwide. Che, as Guevara was affectionately known, stood as a symbol of resistance to imperial or neocolonial rule throughout North America, Europe and the Third World. Not surprisingly then, his death in Bolivia at the hands of army forces produced an outpouring of grief in various circles and celebration in others, including government offices in the United States and in many parts of Latin America.

Disillusioned with events in Cuba, where he had helped to usher in Fidel Castro's regime, and disappointed by failed efforts to duplicate that success in the Congo, Guevara had sought to rekindle the revolutionary flame on his native continent. Like a Latin American version of Leon Trotsky, Guevara sought to create "two, three, many Vietnams" that would wound "the Colossus of the North." Instead, even the Communist Party of Bolivia failed to heed his admonitions, while the peasants turned the other way or supported the U.S.-backed Bolivian soldiers who hunted him down. His death, as the author Jorge C. Castandeda recognizes, allowed for Che's martyrdom. Indeed, a curious "Christlike image" remained, while Guevara "came to inhabit the social utopias and dreams of an entire generation through an almost mystical affinity with his era."

Born in Rosario, Argentina, of Spanish and Irish ancestry, on June 14, 1928, the strikingly handsome Guevara studied medicine at the University of Buenos Aires, receiving his degree in 1953. Present in Guatemala during the American-directed coup that overthrew the democratically elected government of Jacobo Arbenz, Guevara determined that armed insurrection was necessary to liberate the dispossessed.

Compelled to leave the Central American republic, Guevara ended up in Mexico City where he worked at a hospital. While there, Guevara encountered a young Cuban attorney, Fidel Castro, who had himself been exiled following the failed coup attempt to topple Fulgencio Batista's dictatorship. Within a year, Guevara joined

Fig. 13-1 Che Guevara, President of the National Bank of Cuba, speaking to students at the Punta Memorial on November 27, 1959, commemorating the execution of eight students from the University of Havana by Spanish armed forces in 1871. (Pearson Education, Corporate Digital Archive, AP/Wide World Photos)

Castro's guerrilla movement. At one point, Castro's forces dwindled to a band of two dozen but rebounded to enable Guevara, who had clearly displayed his courage and fortitude in battle, along with an iron-will regarding opponents of the revolutionary campaign, to serve as a military commander. Now viewing himself as a communist, Che was perhaps the most dogmatic of the guerrilla fighters in dealing with perceived foes.

Batista's departure from Havana on January 1, 1959, enabled a group of insurgents, led by Guevara and Camilio Cienfuegos, to sweep into the city; Castro soon called for a general strike to back the revolutionary drive. The new government held a series of trials involving Batista supporters that concluded with several hundred executions; Guevara presided over a number of the earliest trials that ended with death sentences meted out. Recalling the Guatemalan experience, Guevara insisted that the revolutionaries control the Cuban military. Bed-ridden with asthma, Guevara began drafting his book, *Guerrilla Warfare* (1961). Soon, the Cuban regime veered leftward, which was hardly displeasing to Guevara, who supported radical land reform. He envisioned the destruction of the *latifundios*—large landed estates—which would lessen the power of both the Cuban elite and American landholders. After initially heading the Institute of Agrarian Reform, Guevara directed the National Bank.

Che's closeness to Castro led *Time* magazine in August 1960 to proclaim him the "brain" of the Revolution. Guevara envisioned "the possibility of triumph of the popular masses in Latin America . . . in the path of guerrilla warfare, based upon a peasant army, an alliance between workers and peasants, the defeat of the army in a direct confrontation, the taking of cities from the countryside." In the face of increased hostility from the United States, Guevara urged closer ties to both Mao's China and the Soviet Union. Yet as early as 1961, he began to be disillusioned with the Soviets, a sentiment that intensified after the USSR backed down during the Cuban missile crisis.

For many who came of age during the 1960s, Che represented the purest type of freedom fighter. Like Mao, Guevara believed that a New Man, who had discarded antiquated or bourgeois ways, could be birthed in the midst of societal transformations. At the same time, Che insisted that "the true revolutionary is guided by a great feeling of love." Not surprisingly then, he reasoned that the "new person" could come to value moral incentives over material ones and strive to create a revolutionary state.

Along with other revolutionary leaders in Cuba, Guevara envisioned a "continental revolution" that would eradicate imperialism and social inequities. Challenging established Marxist theoreticians and the leaders of communist nations, Guevara championed the guerrilla *foco* theory. Even a small number of revolutionary cadre, he contended, could directly assault repressive government instruments, thereby demonstrating the vulnerability of the prevailing order. Communist parties throughout much of Latin America criticized Guevara's strategy; nevertheless, he had determined by 1963 that revolutions could succeed in most countries in Latin America, including democratic ones.

By the mid-sixties, Guevara headed for the Congo to help lead a new revolutionary struggle there. In 1966, he proclaimed that multiple revolutions should be spawned to challenge U.S. dominance. Guevara then traveled to Bolivia. The following year, CIA-backed army forces captured and executed him. Bolivian peasants had proved resistant to Guevara's entreaties, while the Communist Party had refused to back him. Guevara's death at the age of thirty-nine in the midst of a guerrilla campaign, no matter how faltering, only added to his legend.

Richard Gott, writing in the *Guardian,* reported on the death of the slain Argentine.

It was not just that he was a great guerrilla leader, he had been a friend of Presidents as well as revolutionaries. His voice had been heard and appreciated in inter-American councils as well as in the jungle. He was a doctor, an amateur economist, once Minister of Industries in revolutionary Cuba, and Fidel Castro's right-hand man. He may well go down in history as the greatest continental figure since Bolivar. Legends will be created around his name. He was a Marxist but impatient of the doctrinal struggle between the Russians and the Chinese. He was perhaps the last person who tried to find a middle way between the two and attempted to unite radical forces everywhere in a concerted campaign against the U.S. He is now dead, but it is difficult to feel that his ideas will die with him.

However, just over a generation following his death, fewer and fewer appeared to identify with Che's struggle to uplift the downtrodden or to adopt his ideological stance.

◆ —— ◆ —— ◆ —— ◆ —— ◆

Postwar Latin America

In the postwar era as during the Great Depression and World War II, Latin America was again influenced by global events, especially those pertaining to its powerful neighbor to the north. Thus, the Cold War that ensnared the United States also influenced, often tragically, the southern republics. In September 1947, the Rio Pact established a security alliance for 21 countries in the western hemisphere. In April 1948, the Organization of American States (OAS) ensured cooperation and consultation. The OAS's charter promised that member-states would not intervene in each other's internal affairs and would seek to foster peace and stability throughout the region. Through these avenues, the United States began to funnel military aid indirectly to Latin American states. By 1950, the U.S. government provided direct military assistance, long opposed by Congress. The outbreak of the Cold War was the determining factor as American policymakers worried about the possibility of left-wing governments and insurgencies in the hemisphere. That eventually resulted in greater

levels of military support, the training of Latin American armed forces by American advisers and moves by the CIA to prop up or destabilize various regimes.

In the early postwar period, some Latin American states undertook significant social, economic and political transformations. The people of the small Central American state of Costa Rica, the only one to retain a democratic system during the war, witnessed its government strive to overturn the 1948 national elections. The social democratic leader José Figueres Ferrer guided a civilian revolt that resulted in the abolition of the army and the nationalization of banks. While ushering in social welfare and educational reforms, Figueres also brought about universal suffrage. In Bolivia, Victor Paz Estenssoro, elected president in 1952, guided the nationalization of the tin mines, the expansion of the franchise to Indians and land reform.

While the Truman administration adopted a hands-off attitude regarding these social experiments, its successor considered another effort to be far more sinister. The result was the ouster of Guatemala's democratically elected president in 1954. In 1944, unrest had compelled the resignation of the dictator Jorge Ubico. After a short-lived military triumvirate, a group of young officers carried out the October Revolution. The next year, university professor Juan José Arévalo Bermejo, who envisioned the unfolding of "spiritual socialism," was elected president. Arévalo produced a new constitution, patterned after the 1917 Mexican document. With the new president's support, workers and peasants organized, industrial wages increased, agrarian reform began, social welfare was emphasized and a national literacy campaign was carried out.

Arévalo, at the same time, warded off more than a score of military coups but was able to turn over his office to the minister of defense, Colonel Jacobo Arbenz Guzmán, following the 1950 presidential election. Arbenz, who had participated in the October Revolution, sought to produce "a modern capitalist state" that was economically independent and would "raise the standard of living of the great mass of our people to the highest level." To that end, Arbenz desired to augment Guatemala's own private sector and to place controls over foreign investments. He highlighted infrastructural developments, along with Guatemala's first income tax, public works and oil exploration. Most significant, Arbenz pushed for and began to undertake land reform. Starting in mid-1952, that effort resulted in some 1.5 million acres of land being redistributed to approximately 100,000 peasant families; Arbenz himself had obtained a sizable dowry from his wife and now relinquished 1,700 acres.

Unfortunately for Arbenz, his land reform piqued the ire of both the United Fruit Company and the United States government. United Fruit possessed over 550,000 acres,

85 percent of which was uncultivated. The Guatemalan government tendered an offer of just over $600,000 in bonds for expropriating most of the United Front property. Already viewing Arévalo unfavorably, now the American government targeted him. In 1953, President Eisenhower approved a joint State Department–CIA plan to remove Arbenz from office. The American officials sought to replace him with Colonel Carlos Castillo Armas, who resided in Honduras because of his involvement in an earlier coup attempt.

Fearing American intervention, the Arbenz government moved to silence domestic opposition, acquiring small arms from the Soviet bloc. The CIA orchestrated an invasion led by Colonel Armas, while the Guatemalan military proved unwilling to arm workers and peasants. President Arbenz resigned, bringing an end to the reforms of the past 10 years. Land reform ended, with United Fruit reacquiring its expropriated land. A mutual Defense Assistance Pact with the United States followed in 1955.

The Eisenhower administration cautiously watched events in Cuba, where the United States had helped to maintain Fulgencio Batista y Zalvidar or his hand-picked puppets in power since 1934. The one exception had been the government of Dr. Ramón Grau San Martín, who won the 1944 elections against Batista's candidate. The one-time head of the short-lived revolutionary government of 1933, Grau did nothing to stifle rampant corruption and failed to undertake agrarian or economic reform. The charismatic Eddie Chibas, who battled government repression and corruption, lost an opportunity to compete fairly in the 1948 presidential campaign; then, in an obvious attempt to draw attention to national developments, Chibas committed suicide in the midst of a national radio broadcast in 1951. Prior to the next election, Batista, who had been voted in as president in 1940, again took over the reins of government, this time following a coup by junior army officers. New revolutionary figures arose, including a band headed by a young attorney, Fidel Castro, who led an assault on an army barracks in Santiago. Both Fidel and his brother Raul, who also participated in the attack of the garrison, received lengthy prison sentences; during his trial, Fidel proclaimed, "History will absolve me."

Batista issued a general amnesty, however, freeing the brothers after relatively short jail terms. Former Cuban president Carlos Prío Socorrás, future Venezuelan head of state Rómulo Betancourt and Argentinian Ernesto "Che" Guevara all befriended Castro, who arrived in Mexico in 1955. In 1956, Castro, along with 81 others, sailed for Cuba to undertake an insurgent campaign. The following February, Castro allowed Herbert Mathews of *The New York Times* to interview him; the veteran reporter's stories helped to publicize, in favorable terms, Castro's struggle against Batista. As civil war unfolded in Cuba, the United States placed an embargo on arms being shipped to the Batista regime. Batista's base of support crumbled as his increasingly repressive efforts to quash the rebellion only encouraged opposition to the regime. A last-ditch attempt to establish a new American-backed government failed. Meanwhile, Castro delivered a message to residents of Havana: "I shall be coming into Havana soon. Keep the peace until then. I am sending a company of Barbudos to administer Havana until I get there. They will preserve Havana—and you." On January 1 and 2, 1959, Guevara and Camilio Cienfuegos

guided rebel forces into Havana, while Castro arrived in the capital city on January 9.

Latin America's Big Four during the Early Cold War

U.S. policymakers helped orchestrate the overthrow of the Arbenz regime but had become increasingly disillusioned with Batista in Cuba. They similarly watched events unfold—and sometimes prodded them along—in the largest Latin American states: Brazil, Argentina, Chile and Mexico.

BRAZIL AND ECONOMIC GROWTH

The deposing of Getúlio Vargas by Brazilian military officers in 1945 led, the following year, to the passage of the constitution of the Second Republic that highlighted the importance of individual freedoms. New elections that December resulted in a triumph by General Eurico Dutra, who had been a strong champion of Vargas' *Estado Novo*. The communist candidate garnered 10 percent of the vote and the party soon appeared to be growing in strength in both Sao Paulo and Rio de Janeiro. Undoubtedly with support from the United States, Dutra moved to outlaw the Communist Party and to expel the organization's representatives in the Brazilian Congress in 1947. Labor repression similarly ensued while a wage freeze helped to ensure that workers' income plummeted. Dutra also pursued a laissez-faire economic policy, while encouraging foreign investment.

In 1950, Vargas made a successful political comeback, winning the presidential election with just under 50 percent of the vote in competition against two other candidates. Once again, Vargas adopted an economic program that possessed a highly nationalistic side. Although he encouraged foreign investment, Vargas relied on inadequate state financing to establish the oil corporation, *Petrobas*. A mixed public-private enterprise, *Petrobas* was intended to ensure state monopoly over a vital natural resource. But inflation ravaged the economy. The United States failed to provide economic assistance. Consequently, the government adopted austerity measures under Minister of Finance Oswaldo de Aranh. A wave of labor unrest resulted. Aranha clashed with the young Minister of Labor, João Goulart, who in February 1954 was removed from the cabinet. Within three months, Vargas appeared to side with Goulart in declaring that the minimum wage would be raised 100 percent. The attempted assassination of a newspaper critic by presidential bodyguards further crippled Vargas' public standing. Ordered by the armed forces to resign or face a coup, Vargas committed suicide on August 24.

Vargas' eventual successor was Juscelino Kubitschek, who ran with Goulart on his ticket; following their election, the victors warded off attempts by the military to deny them office. Beginning his presidency in January 1956, Kubitschek undertook an ambitious economic program that required greatly increased foreign investment, most of it from the United States. As the economic growth rate averaged 7 percent in the late 1950s, non-Brazilian entrepreneurs dominated the state's largest industries. A new capital, Brasilia, situated 600 miles northwest of Rio de Janeiro, was to be linked with the rest of the nation through a series of highways. As the national debt soared, however, the International Monetary Fund in 1959 demanded that Brazil implement austerity measures. Undoubtedly fearing the kind of public outcry that had doomed Vargas, Kubitschek instead increased the supply of *cruzeiro*, the Brazilian currency,

which led to a torrent of inflation, the worst of which the next administration had to confront.

ARGENTINA AND THE OUSTER OF PERÓN

Disorder also marked the immediate postwar period in nearby Argentina. Relying on his base of support among the working class, Juan Domingo Perón easily won the 1946 presidential election. His nationalistic condemnation of the U.S. State Department, which depicted him as a fascist sympathizer, helped Perón politically. The new president purged hostile military leaders, while increasing the salaries of officers overall and placing allies in command posts. But Perón's closest confidante was his former mistress Eva "Evita" Duarte, a beautiful and politically savvy young woman, who had become his second wife.

Perón's hyper-nationalism, buttressing his call for a "New Argentina," appealed to Argentines across the political spectrum, who had reason to be pleased as the immediate postwar period proved to be economically prosperous. Food exports to war-torn Europe and a large increase in the gross national product enabled Argentina to pay off its national debt by 1947. Nationalization of the central bank, the telephone company, the railways and the docks occurred. A government trade monopoly controlled the export trade. Welfare programs to aid urban workers began under the *Justicialist* banner, while Argentine industrialists received subsidies that enabled them to undersell foreign competitors.

This period witnessed the founding of Evita's Social Aid Foundation, which received support from unions, businesses and her husband's regime. Her popularity among the impoverished urban workers became nearly mythical, as her foundation offered assistance to schools, hospitals, the indigent

Fig. 13-2 Eva Perón with her husband, Argentine President Juan Perón, Buenos Aires, June 19, 1952. (Pearson Education, Corporate Digital Archive, AP/Wide World Photos)

and the infirm. Simultaneously, she helped to cement the alliance between Argentine unions and Peronism and enabled women to acquire the vote.

The appeal of Peronism proved considerable, but its architects steadily placed shackles on the political opposition, particularly as the economic situation deteriorated. By the end of the 1940s, the previously robust Argentine economy suffered from heightened foreign competition, reduced prices for exports, a trade deficit, inflation and a severe drought. Resorting to an austerity program, Perón tightened credit, cut government expenditures, froze wages and attempted to curb prices. He also began to welcome investments by multi-national corporations, in-

cluding Standard Oil, a giant company authorized to drill for oil in Patagonia.

Undoubtedly concerned about potential political unrest as the economic crisis unfolded, Perón clamped down on dissenters while seeking to maintain his grip on power. The Argentine Constitution, drafted in 1853, allowed for a single-term presidency only. The Peronists pushed for an amendment that enabled Perón to win a sweeping reelection bid in 1951. At the same time, the repression heightened, with the government expropriating *La Prensa*, a liberal newspaper that challenged many of Perón's policies. New laws were wielded against Ricardo Balbin of the Radical Party and non-compliant labor leaders.

All the while, propaganda helped to spread the gospel of Peronism and to push for the selection of Evita as the nation's vice-president. Military leaders, fearing that Evita might someday rule over them, refused to go along. Afflicted with cancer, Evita died in July 1952, leaving Perón without his most important adviser and political asset.

Other difficulties, which eventually proved insurmountable, soon confronted the crestfallen Argentine president. His efforts to curb wages, welcome foreign capital and deemphasize industrialization alienated key sectors of Argentine society. The heightening of Peronist rhetoric failed to overcome the increasingly conservative nature of the government's economic policy. Attacks on the Catholic Church as represented by the legalization of divorce and the placement of parochial schools under state control did not help matters. Massive religious processions followed. Then, in June 1955, an attempted military coup resulted in the bombing of the presidential palace and the killing of hundreds of Perón's followers. Enraged, the Peronists burned a series of cathedrals in Buenos Aires. The Vatican excommunicated Perón and his full cabinet. In September, the military struck again and Perón, who proved unwilling to arm the workers, headed into exile in Paraguay.

Peronism, however, was hardly finished, nor was the specter of Juan Perón. Eventually recognizing this fact, the Argentine military during the next few years sought to usher in "Peronism without Perón," but to no avail. At first, the military sought to quash Peronism altogether. *La Prensa* was handed back to the Gainza Paz family that had run it. Others whose property holdings had been expropriated saw them restored. Peronist unionists were singled out for persecution. But in June 1956, Anti-Peronist military men

conducted their own revolt, executing approximately 40 leaders, a practice that, as historians Thomas E. Skidmore and Peter H. Smith point out, the Peronists had not employed. Clashes again unfolded between Peronists and the government, but the military allowed a presidential election in 1958. With backing from the Peronists, Arturo Frondizi of the Radical Party took office.

CHILE AND THE RESURGENT LEFT

The early postwar period also ushered in changes in Chile, one of the few Latin American states with a relatively strong democratic tradition, albeit one that had not been uninterrupted. Attempts to maintain an alliance between Radicals and communists collapsed as the Cold War evolved. Strike activity throughout much of Chile in 1946 doomed another Popular Front-styled government that included three communists ministers under Gabriel Gonzales Videla of the Radical Party. Videla fired the communists while the police broke up a coal miner strike. The government declared a state of siege and conducted an assault against the Chilean left. In 1948, the Congress passed the Law for the Defense of Democracy that outlawed the Communist Party, compelling many members to go underground or to head into exile. The Socialist Party splintered, with the Socialist party of Chile supporting the anti-communist drive, while the Popular Socialist party condemned it.

In 1952, the former dictator Carlos Ibanez was elected president of Chile, defeating among other candidates, Senator Salvador Allende Gossens, who though supported by the Socialist Party and the outlawed communists, received only 6 percent of the vote. Professedly a nationalist, Ibanez faced sliding copper prices, trade deficits and rising inflation.

Compelled to turn to the International Monetary Fund, Ibanez initiated an austerity program that led to riots. Those in turn induced Ibanez to resort to repression, which further diminished his popularity.

The Conservative Party's Jorge Alessandri, whose father was the Radical Party icon Arturo Alessandri, won the 1958 election. The other candidates were the Radical Luis Bossay, the Christian Democrat Eduardo Frei and Allende, who lost by less than 34,000 votes. Chile's left-wing parties, including the reunited Socialist Party and the Communist Party, had established the *Frente de Accion Popular* (FRAP) or Popular Action Front, while Frei represented a new organization that reached out to Catholics and white-collar workers, while professing to avoid the extremes of both capitalism and socialism. The repeal of the Law for the Defense of Democracy, which the left referred to as the "Accursed Law," enabled Allende to garner 28.9 percent of the vote. That placed him just behind Alessandri's 31.6 percent and considerably ahead of Frei's 20.7 percent mark. Allende's lack of appeal to women voters cost him the election.

MEXICO AND ONE-PARTY RULE

In contrast to Chile, Mexico remained virtually a one-party state, as it turned to industrialization and economic growth in an effort to eradicate persistent poverty. Spearheading the task was Miguel Alemán, selected by the governing Mexican party—which changed its name to Partido Revolucionario Institucional (PRI) in 1946—to run the country. Alemán, the lone civilian head of state since the Mexican Revolution, featured economic development including the expansion of the infrastructure. The government also resorted to trade barriers, allowed domestic production to increase and encouraged foreign investment. Economic growth, including agriculture, temporarily alleviated a trade imbalance. Agri-business concerns could now hold large amounts of land, thanks to an amending of Article 27 of the Mexican Constitution. Also aiding the economy was a surge in tourism, which Alemán encouraged through the building of roads, hotels and resorts. One cost involved the massive corruption associated with construction projects. Moreover, Alemán's own family reaped financial benefits from the development of Acapulco as a favorite tourist spot and from the establishment of a potent communications network.

Under Alemán, both industrial and agricultural production experienced considerable growth, until inflation and a trade deficit riddled the Mexican economy. Charges of widespread corruption also confronted the PRI leaders who had to select a new figure to replace Alemán. They turned to Adolfo Ruiz Cortines, the former governor of Veracruz and a cabinet official, who lived up to his campaign promise to rid the national government of corruption. Under Ruiz Cortines, Mexico adopted a conservative economic policy, striving for reduced inflation. The devalued *peso* spurred tourism. Like Alemán, Ruiz Cortines reduced land redistribution, thereby enabling private estates to grow in size and compelling many to accept near-slave wages or abandon rural areas altogether.

The Impact of the Cuban Revolution

IN CUBA

By the end of the 1950s, the Cold War again dramatically influenced the course of developments in Latin America. The most striking example involved the growing clash between the United States and the new

Cuban government that Fidel Castro headed. Some historians have claimed that Castro long hated the United States. One indication is a letter Castro wrote in mid-1958 to a fellow guerrilla that declared, "The Americans are going to pay dearly for what they are doing. When this war is over, I'll start a much longer and bigger war of my own: the war I'm going to fight against them. I realize that will be my true destiny." At a minimum, Castro appeared determined to conduct an anti-imperialist revolution.

Castro also moved quickly to cement his hold on Cuban society. His government suppressed critical press tribunals, violated the long-standing autonomy of the University of Havana, controlled labor unions and shackled both professional organizations and private groups. In addition, the Castro regime conducted trials of former Batista supporters or officials. In the first half of 1959 alone, an estimated 550 *Batistianos* were executed, which produced an outcry in the United States. Later that year, Major Huberto Matos, one of the revolution's top military figures, began a lengthy jail sentence after criticizing the government's apparent drift toward communism. Numerous middle- and upper-class Cubans, many of them professionals or business operators, headed for Miami, where they hoped that an anti-Castro base could be constructed to help overthrow Castro.

The pace of the revolution quickened. On January 6, 1959, the new government suspended political parties; within a week, Castro officially recognized the *Partido Socialista Popular*. Raul Castro and Che Guevara proceeded to appoint PSP members to top military and government posts. In March, the Castro government took over the American-owned telephone company and ordered the U.S.-controlled electric power company to cut rates. In April, Castro postponed elections, declaring, "Revolution first, elections later!" He also dismissed all criticisms as counter-revolutionary. On May 17, the Agrarian Reform Law mandated the expropriation of estates larger than 1,000 acres, called for those properties to be handed out to individuals and cooperatives and denied foreigners the right to own farmland in Cuba. It quickly became evident that the Cuban government had no intention of compensating property-holders for confiscated land.

Thanks to these developments and the increasingly anti-American rhetoric Castro employed, relations with the United States deteriorated. In February 1960, Cuba reached an agreement with the Soviet Union to sell five million tons of Cuban sugar during the next five years. The USSR promised to provide Cuba a $100 million credit line to obtain Soviet technology. Soon, trade agreements were devised with Poland and China, while Czech arms began arriving. In July, Khrushchev blurted out that "the Soviet military can support the Cuban people with rocket weapons." Another source of contention involved the operations of Texaco, Standard Oil and Royal Dutch Shell. After those major oil companies, encouraged by the U.S. State Department, refused to process crude oil purchased at low cost from the Soviets, Castro took over the refineries. President Eisenhower in turn terminated the Cuban sugar quota and, in October, banned American exports to the island. More expropriations followed, involving Sears, Roebuck, Coca-Cola and large American nickel deposits.

The Cuban government also set out to transform the lives of the citizenry, with particular focus on the peasants. Cuba's illiteracy rate fell 25 percent by the end of 1960 and effectively disappeared later. Efforts were undertaken to improve medical care and provide housing and other basic benefits for all. Prices were frozen and large wage increases declared. More properties were acquired as additional middle-class and wealthy Cubans fled the island, leaving behind homes, offices and farms. The government also mobilized the people by creating an enormous militia that included a half million people by the close of 1960.

Still, discontent intensified, both in Cuba and on the U.S. mainland. Charges were flung out that Castro was molding a totalitarian communist state. The Eisenhower administration began plotting Castro's ouster as early as March 1960. The president authorized the CIA to train Cuban exiles, establishing a training camp in Guatemala by the summer. On January 3, 1961, Eisenhower's government broke off diplomatic relations with Cuba. Determined to avoid direct American involvement, newly elected President John F. Kennedy allowed the invasion to proceed. In mid-April, the infamous Bay of Pigs fiasco followed, in which Castro's army routed exile forces.

The failed endeavor strengthened Castro's hand in reconstructing Cuban society. It also convinced the Soviets to place intermediate-range missiles in Cuba. The Cuban tie to the Soviet Union strengthened shortly after the Bay of Pigs when Castro proclaimed the revolution "socialist." In December, he deemed it "Marxist-Leninist."

In October 1962, an American spy plane discovered the Soviet missiles that had been placed in Cuba, an act Nikita Khrushchev called a defensive move. Kennedy disagreed and a near nuclear confrontation ensued, aborted only after the Soviets refused to challenge an American naval blockade. Khrush-

chev, without consulting Castro, agreed to remove the missiles in return for a secret U.S. promise not to invade the island and to remove missiles in Turkey.

While the Cuban missile crisis passed, the revolutionary experiment in the Caribbean continued to trouble American policymakers and to influence the course of developments throughout Latin America. Concerns about the possibly contagious nature of the Cuban revolution led the Kennedy administration to support the Alliance for Progress. Established in August 1961, the program—to which the United States pledged as much as $20 billion over a ten-year period—sought to ensure "the maintenance of democratic government" in the region. To that end, the United States hoped to support social reform and economic growth. Among the national leaders obtaining American support were Brazil's Jañio Quadros, Argentina's Arturo Frondizi, Chile's Eduardo Frei, Peru's Fernando Belaúnde Terry and Venezuela's Rómulo Betancourt. Colombia, under both Albert Lleras Camargo and Carlos Lleras Restrepo, also adopted a reformist tact.

However, the aims of the Alliance for Progress were seldom accomplished. Rather, both the United States and Latin American elites often opted for military solutions to the economic dislocations and unrest that cropped up throughout the southern part of the Western Hemisphere.

IN BRAZIL

Quadros took office in early 1961, promising to wield a "new broom" to end pervasive corruption, to carve out an "independent foreign policy" less hostile to the communist bloc and to safeguard Brazilian economic interests. Austerity measures failed to rein in inflation, however, and only seven months into his presidency, Quadros dramatically resigned, claiming that foreign pressures had stymied his reform efforts.

Replacing Quadros was the populist Joaõ Goulart, whom the Brazilian military and right-wing parties viewed with disdain. The possibility of civil war loomed large, but military officers worked out a compromise that allowed for Goulart's inauguration under a new parliamentary system intended to curb his power. Nevertheless, revolutionary ferment, piqued by the Cuban experiment, could be witnessed on university campuses, in labor unions and among the peasants. Goulart sought foreign investments but adopted a nationalistic policy regarding trade and diplomatic dealings. His unwillingness to support the American-sponsored placement of sanctions on Cuba infuriated the Brazilian right. Goulart managed to achieve a few notable victories, including the establishment of *Electrobas*, a state-run enterprise handling electrical power. He also insisted on the passage of a law that compelled the registration of foreign capital and forbade profit remittances greater than 10 percent of invested capital. With the government industries compelled to increase the money supply, inflation shot upward, resulting in the cruzeiro's collapse, strikes and food riots and the greater radicalization of many workers and peasants. Relying on Celso Furtado, a young economist, Goulart attempted to transform the Brazilian economy. The president sought to usher in land and tax reforms and to increase social welfare spending.

Thanks to a landslide vote on January 1, 1963, Goulart regained the full range of presidential powers, but a number of problems still beset his government. Inflation and trade imbalances led to demands by the International Monetary Fund and the Kennedy administration for an austerity program. A short-lived attempt to curb prices produced considerable social unrest throughout the political spectrum. Abandoning the deflationary approach, Goulart sought to garner greater support by appealing to radical leftists. Peasants in the depressed, barren northeast flocked to join Peasant Leagues and rural unions, troubling large landowners. Media reports that the president was a communist dupe who should be overthrown by the military, something urged on by various state governors, barraged the middle class. Goulart alienated the right still further in March 1964 when he nationalized the oil industry and took control of a series of large estates. He followed those moves by seeking the vote for soldiers and the legalization of the Communist Party.

The new American administration of Lyndon Baines Johnson supported Goulart's removal. U.S. Ambassador Lincoln Gordon and military attaché General Vernon Walters consulted regularly with discontented elements; the American government promised to recognize a new government quickly, while preparing to help arm the rebels and to send U.S. troops if the need arose. A bloodless coup followed on March 31, and the next day Goulart departed for Uruguay as attempts to bring about a general strike failed.

While many Brazilians, hearkening back to their nation's history, undoubtedly anticipated that the military rule would be short-lived, such an expectation was not borne out. Instead, the military, wielding an iron grip, dominated Brazilian politics for over two decades. The military, along with other elements of the Brazilian elite, had been particularly disturbed by Goulart's attempts to create a mass base among workers and peasants as radical ideals became more popular. Replacing Goulart as the nation's president was General Humberto de Alencar Castello Branco, whose planning minister Roberto de Oliveira Campos sought out foreign investments, sharply reduced internal credit and froze wages. Hundreds of Brazilian companies went under, while foreign companies increasingly dominated industrial development. Dissent was quashed, thousands had their political rights suspended, thousands of federal workers were laid off and hundreds of military officers, viewed as too nationalistic, were fired or compelled to retire. Seeking to curry favor with the United States, Brazil severed diplomatic dealings with Cuba and backed American military action in the Dominican Republic and Vietnam.

IN ARGENTINA

In Argentina, the military also came to hold power by the mid-1960s. The prior government of Arturo Frondizi, confronting demands for stabilization programs from the International Monetary Fund and resulting sharp criticisms from the Peronists, generally proved ineffective. The income of industrial workers plummeted, leading to general strikes throughout 1959. Austerity programs also angered small businessmen, while farmers failed to increase production as expected. Eventually, economic growth was attained and the inflation rate plunged downward. However, Frondizi's political base of support was weak, as his policies enraged both laborers and nationalist leftists. When the Peronists, whose party had been legalized, outpolled its competitors in the March 1962 elections, the military annulled the results and removed Frondizi from the presidency.

Following elections in mid-1963, Dr. Arturo Illia, who had garnered only 27 percent of the vote, became head of the Argentine state. The next two years witnessed sizable economic growth, but a beef shortage angered consumers and hurt the trade balance. While unions benefited from early wage increases, those controlled by the Peronists conducted a number of strikes, some of which resulted in workplace takeovers. The March 1965 elections saw the Peronists win a plurality of the votes, which induced Juan Perón, who was exiled in Spain, to attempt to bring his often-warring followers together. As inflation and government deficits mounted and Illia failed to quash either the Peronists or the left, the military tossed Illia out of office in June 1966.

As in the case of their Brazilian counterparts, it soon appeared that the Argentine military was determined to retain power. Wielding the club of repression, General Juan Onganía called for "the Argentine Revolution." He closed Congress, kicked government foes out of the universities and targeted organized labor for suppression. Onganía also initiated yet one more austerity program, which required a two-year wage freeze. Finance minister Adalberto Krieger Vasena strove to increase agricultural production, curb inflation, maintain foreign trade and expand the Argentine infrastructure.

IN CHILE

For a time, Chile avoided the military solutions that both Argentina and Brazil adopted. Jorge Alessandri, a narrow winner of the 1958 presidential election over Salvador Allende, the candidate of the Popular Action Front (FRAP), managed to reduce the inflation rate sharply. However, low copper prices produced a trade imbalance. Like other Chilean leaders of his era, Alessandri adopted a nationalist approach regarding economic development, although one that failed to please the left, which insisted on a takeover of the copper industry. Undoubtedly because of the threat the Cuban Revolution posed, the challenge from the Chilean left, and the establishment of the Alliance for Progress, Alessandri supported a law that allowed for taking over large, underused estates; the left attacked this measure too as woefully inadequate. Despite public works programs, Alessandri proved incapable of slowing the movement of poor peasants to urban slums, particularly in Santiago. In the end, Alessandri relied on monetarism (which calls for regulating the economy through controlling the money supply), seeking to use fiscal policy to favor investment by both Chilean entrepreneurs and foreign companies.

Courted by the United States and assisted in the 1964 presidential election by right-wing parties who feared a possible victory by Allende, the Christian Democratic Party became the governing party under Eduardo Frei. With 56 percent of the ballots, Frei easily prevailed over Allende, who managed 39 percent of the vote. Promising a "Revolution in Liberty" and receiving considerable funds from the CIA, Frei condemned FRAP as seeking to carve out "another Cuba" in Latin America. U.S. Senate hearings later revealed that American operatives helped orchestrate a "campaign of terror" against the left. Allende's rhetoric probably aided Frei too, for the FRAP candidate had urged a wholesale transformation of Chilean society. Frei, on the other hand, sought to carve out a middle way toward a more humane society that steered clear of both laissez-faire capitalism and communism. At the same time, to the delight of the American government, Frei's

rhetoric was decidedly anti-communist. There was a progressive thrust to the Christian Democratic Program, which favored communitarianism, heightened government involvement and income redistribution, along with land and tax reforms. Frei called for Chile to buy out majority control of the copper industry.

Frei's actual reform efforts proved mixed at best while alienating both the left and the right. Land reform benefited only about a fourth of the 100,000 peasants who had been promised such assistance. Yet even that program angered resistant landowners. The government purchased a majority share of only one copper company, but Americans still controlled the largest companies at the end of Frei's term. Moreover, copper production had not increased sufficiently. Another government program, Popular Promotion, which sought to organize some of the urban poor through creation of neighborhood councils and mothers' centers, did not produce the base of political support that the Christian Democrats anticipated.

At the midpoint of Frei's six-year term, the Christian Democrats were obviously divided among themselves. Some, including the president, favored only moderate reform within a capitalist framework. Others wanted reforms, particularly involving land redistribution, to be speeded up. A third branch, comprised of more established party leaders, also desired greater change. By 1970, Frei's presidency had witnessed a rise in expectations among workers, peasants and slum dwellers, who sought state action to improve their condition. Frei's unwillingness or inability to satisfy their needs made them a potentially volatile lot in Chilean politics. Moreover, the economy was merely bumping along, with inflation taking off once again, thereby diminishing living standards. Election results indicated growing displeasure with the Christian Democrats, whose majority hold on the Chamber of Deputies ended in 1969.

IN MEXICO

By contrast, the fiscal conservatism that early postwar Mexican governments adopted maintained a degree of both economic and social stability, at least until near the end of the 1960s. With inflation kept in check and the Cuban Revolution in full swing, President Adolfo López Mateos, previously the secretary of labor, shifted leftward to curb labor unrest and to enable the PRI to reaffirm its revolutionary roots. Mateos broke a major railroad strike in 1959, arresting union leaders, including Demetrio Vallejo, who remained behind bars for years. At the same time, the new government turned to profit-sharing and provided opposition parties seats in congress if a certain number of votes were attained in a national election. Land reform involving 30 million hectares was achieved, almost matching the record of Lázaro Cárdenas. Cinematic and electrical companies were nationalized, rural schools constructed, and diplomatic relations maintained with Cuba. In the end, Mexico was the lone Latin American state to do so.

A rightward shift followed Gustavo Díaz Ordaz's accession to the presidency in 1964, a move undertaken in part to ward off an emerging threat from both a right-wing party, PAN (Partido de Ación Nacional), and a left-wing one, PPS (Partido Popular Socialista); the two smaller parties had recently captured seats in Congress. However, election results in Baja California Norte were discarded after PAN candidates triumphed in two cities. More striking, the federal government acted severely when unrest threatened to cast a shadow on the 1968 summer Olympics that

were held in Mexico City. By August, with the games approaching, students had conducted a strike at the national university. In sending military troops onto the campus, Díaz Ordaz violated the long-standing tradition allowing the university to serve as a sanctuary. Additional protests on October 2 at Tlatelolco's Plaza de las Tres Culturas in Mexico City resulted in hundreds of fatalities. Hundreds more were arrested following the street clashes. Thus, the Mexican government, under Díaz Ordaz, had also reached for the gun to silence domestic opposition.

Other Latin American Revolutions

The readiness of government forces throughout Latin America to resort to repression to quash dissent, particularly that emanating from the left, was readily apparent as the 1960s wound to a close. The threat posed by the Cuban Revolution, both as a model and in the form of guerrillas tied to Fidel Castro, appeared all too real to the U.S. government and to right-of-center elements in the region. Castro, like his longtime comrade-in-arms Che Guevara, believed in the revolutionary possibilities of a New Man shaped in the struggle to create an egalitarian society. Guevara had departed from the Cuban government in 1963, heading for the Congo before ending up in Bolivia. There, the promises of the 1952 revolution had been quashed, particularly following a military coup in 1964. Failing to appeal to the Andean Indians, Guevara also received little support from Bolivian communists. To the delight of both American officials and the Latin American right, Bolivian government forces captured and executed Guevara in October 1967. Guevara had called for the fomenting of "two, three, many Vietnams" to challenge U.S. hegemony in the western hemisphere.

American-trained counterinsurgents had captured and subsequently murdered the man who symbolized guerrilla unrest.

The earlier successful taking of power by revolutionaries in Cuba continued, nevertheless, to influence the Latin American left. In Peru, leftists appealed to Indian peasants but encountered military repression. In October 1968, the Peruvian military ousted the civilian president; to the surprise of many, including Castro, a "Revolutionary Government of the Armed Forces" of Peru came into existence. Headed by General Juan Velasco Alvarado, the new government condemned the "unjust social and economic order" that placed "national wealth solely within the reach of the privileged, while the majority suffer the consequences of a marginalization injurious to human dignity." Alvarado's regime nationalized oil interests, various media companies, the U.S.-owned Marcona Mining and Cerrode Pasco, along with ITT's Peruvian branch and that of Chase Manhattan Bank; ushered in major land reform; and supported workers' involvement in running and acquiring property interests in the businesses they toiled for. The government created cooperative farms, demanded by peasants. Velasco consciously sought support from the peasants, slum dwellers and industrial workers, all of whom the government attempted to organize.

Nevertheless, many labor unions and peasants did not take kindly to the government's "revolution from above" approach. In general, the Peruvian elite viewed with fear the expropriations of various companies and the government takeover of large estates. Many were put off by the repressive practices of the regime, which silenced critics. At the same time, Alvarado did not resort to the brutal ways an increasing number of Latin American states adopted in the 1960s and 1970s.

Saddled with soaring oil prices, Peru confronted the economic difficulties that afflicted countries worldwide in the early 1970s. Trade imbalances resulted as the price of Peruvian exports dropped. The earnings of urban workers plummeted. Resulting labor unrest, characterized by hundreds of strikes annually, demonstrated growing discontent with the Alvardo government.

In 1975, General Francisco Morales Bermúdez, who presided over the reining in of the Peruvian revolution, replaced a physically infirm Velasco. His regime implemented austerity programs, fostered foreign investment and sharply curtailed spending for state enterprises. Strikes and riots proliferated, resulting in a government crackdown. The incomplete agrarian program ended in 1976. Morales Bermúdez acceded to the IMF's demand for new austerity measures, causing workers to protest vehemently. Once again, government repression silenced its critics. At the same time, the generals, by 1978, prepared to restore civilian control of the government.

Military Takeovers and the PRI

BRAZIL AND URBAN GUERRILLA WARFARE

As the Peruvian revolution emerged and later withered, still more heavy-handed methods of suppressing dissent were adopted in many of the leading Latin American countries. In Brazil, where the military had taken power in 1964, a series of electoral defeats had resulted in the dissolving of political parties and the curbing of popular elections. In 1967, Marshal Artur da Costa e Silva became president and temporarily eased the government's repressive grip. In response, workers, intellectuals, students, nationalists and some clergy, led by Archbishop Helder Câmara, called for sweeping reforms. When Congress and the Supreme Court challenged military demands concerning student protest leaders and a deputy critical of governmental operations, a "coup within a coup" occurred in late 1968. Hardliners within the military prevailed and moved to shut down Congress, institute censorship, toss aside the constitution and grant Costa e Silva dictatorial powers. Increasingly, both military police and death squads aligned with the government resorted to unprecedented torture. Targets included intellectuals, students, workers and church leaders. Additionally, a major purge occurred at the University of Sao Paulo and within the Foreign Ministry, while several state and federal legislators lost their elected seats.

In this same period, urban guerrilla warfare cropped up in Brazil, as it did in other parts of Latin America. Banks and armories were hit, while known practitioners of torture were singled out for assassination. On September 4, 1969, left-wing guerrillas kidnapped U.S. Ambassador C. Burke Elbrick, subsequently obtaining the release of 15 political prisoners and the issuance of a revolutionary manifesto. However, in November, the charismatic Carlos Marighella, a guerrilla leader, died in a shootout with death squad members. Increasingly, the combination of torture and paramilitary operations ground down the guerrilla movement, which badly weakened by 1973.

Guerrilla activity had proven less successful that it might have been due to an upturn in the economy. Talk abounded of the Brazilian "economic miracle" that featured remarkable growth rates, a quadrupling of exports, considerable foreign capital and the abandonment of the nation's long-standing reliance on coffee. An industrial revolution benefited the expanding middle class, along with skilled workers. At the same time, the economic bounty was unevenly distributed, with the already wide gap between the wealthiest and poorest of Brazilians only deepening. People of color, especially blacks and mulattos, remained disproportionately situated at the bottom of the socioeconomic ladder.

By the mid-1970s, the luster of the supposed economic miracle began to fade. Wages remained too low for many to cover basic necessities, health care was abominable and most families lacked both tap water and sanitary facilities. The north and northeast remained impoverished regions, with almost all government projects directed at the southeast. At the end of the decade, inflation approached triple digits and a severe balance of payments deficit unfolded. Unemployment increased and workers, who received support from Cardinal Arns, conducted strikes that swept through São Paulo. By 1982, Brazil was unable to cover interest payments on its nearly $90 billion national debt, the world's largest. A number of wealthy Brazilians transferred funds out of the country, while corruption worsened.

Election results in 1974 and 1976 had demonstrated widespread discontent with the military regime. The Catholic Church adopted a progressive stance concerning political repression and social injustice. Some church leaders, such as Archbishop Helder Câmara, defiantly condemned capitalism and foreign domination of the Brazilian economy. The new president, General Ernesto Geisel, strove to bring about an *"abertura,"* an opening or a movement toward a less repressive order. By 1979, print censorship was discarded, although the government maintained shackles on both radio and television. It declared labor unions and strikes illegal.

The military governments also somewhat paradoxically began to adopt a more nationalistic foreign policy. Its leaders were stung by criticisms regarding human rights delivered by the U.S. administration of Jimmy Carter, the halt to American arms shipments and the unwillingness of the United States to sell nuclear reactors. Consequently, Brazil began trading with the Marxist states of Angola, Mozambique and the Soviet Union, along with Arab nations. To the displeasure of the United States, Brazil maintained cordial relations with the left-wing Sandinista government in Nicaragua.

Economic conditions, however, continued to worsen, further reducing the Brazilian government's base of support. The 1982 elections saw the Party of the Brazilian Democratic Movement edge out the government-backed *Partido Democratico Social*. While the PDS captured a majority in the electoral college, party dissidents in 1985 backed the candidacy of Tancredo Neves, the former prime minister under João Goulart. Neves died prior to being sworn into office, enabling the more conservative José Sarney to become president of Brazil. The economic situation failed to improve under Sarney, resulting in his growing unpopularity. In late 1988, the National Congress drafted a new democratic constitution that rebuked the military regime. Concerned about the left-wing shift of voters in that year's municipal elections, members of the Brazilian elite turned to Fernando Collor de Mello, a charismatic populist who condemned corruption, inefficiency and bureaucracy and promised free-market policies. In 1989, Collor was elected in a campaign against Luis Inacio Lula da Silva, a militant labor leader.

ARGENTINA AND "THE DIRTY WAR"

Long-time military control and repression, starting in the mid-1960s, also characterized developments in Argentina. General Juan Carlos Onganía's finance minister Adalberto Krieger Vaseña sought foreign investments, allowed for industrial denationalization and devalued the *peso*, a crippling blow to many domestic companies. Furthermore, wages were frozen as prices continued to rise, although inflation had slowed by the end of the decade. Talk of an Argentine economic miracle took hold as industrial investments increased, while labor activism appeared dormant.

In the spring of 1969, however, political unrest broke out. Students and industrial workers in Cordoba, where the automotive industry was based, exploded in rage following reductions in educational spending and employment. Riots swept through the city streets and a general strike threatened to take place, leading the local military commander to order his troops to fire on demonstrators, killing scores. Protest flowed forth in various sectors of Argentina, as renewed militancy on the part of Peronist-controlled labor unions indicated.

The weakened Onganía regime lasted a mere year longer, beset by a splintered military and a rising tide of political violence. Responding to the repression the government meted out, which included torture and executions, the revolutionary left responded in kind. The left targeted businessmen, such as those associated with multinational corporations. The *Monteneros* guerrillas, derived from the Peronist ranks and influenced by a former priest Juan García Elorrio, resorted to attacks on police headquarters, political assassinations and robberies. In March 1970, *Montoneros* terrorists grabbed General Pedro Aramburu, the former hard-line head of state who had helped to depose Perón a decade and a half earlier. Shortly following the discovery of Aramburu's corpse, Onganía was himself ousted. A *Montonero* manifesto, appearing in 1971, indicated the organization had come to believe that "everyone has a place and function in this contest... all forms of struggle from insurrectional acts such as the *cordobazo* to bank assaults are part of a combined strategy aimed at developing the *revolutionary war.*"

After the short-lived presidency of General Roberto M. Levingston, whose repressive thrust only induced the left into heightened acts of terrorism and who faced mounting inflation, the Argentine military turned to General Alejandro Lanusse. The new government encountered a still more perilous economic situation as both budget deficits and inflation soared, along with intensified terrorism. Only the now seventy-seven-year-old Juan Perón, Lanusse determined, could right the deteriorating situation. In the meantime, a conservative Peronist, Héctor Cámpora, was easily elected president of Argentina. Shortly following Perón's return, Cámpora resigned, allowing the aging party leader to run and win another presidential election; his wife Isabel Martínez de Perón was chosen as vice-president. A "Social Contract" was shaped that allowed for a freeze on wages and prices. With the freeze in place for a year, the economy rebounded, thanks to favorable markets for beef and grain; inflation lessened while real wages increased. Perón nationalized banks and various industries, while favoring native companies and consumers. But massive oil price increases soon reignited inflation. All the while, the Peronist movement fragmented.

The *Montoneros* continued their terrorist campaign, even assassinating José Rucci, the head of the Peronist CGT, a labor confederation. Backed by the military and trade unions, Perón attacked the *Montoneros*. The Argentine Anti-Communist Alliance—or Triple A—established by José López Rega and police commissioner Alberto Villar began a terrorist reign of its own, thereby strengthening the government's ability to deal with guerrillas. Perón evidently refused López Rega's request to employ death squads, but the Triple A was set up nevertheless. Abductions and killings followed, while the revolutionary left continued to rely on kidnappings.

The death of Perón in July 1974 accelerated the already rightward thrust of his government, now headed by his widow Isabel. Greatly influenced by Minister of Social Welfare López Rega, Isabel moved against the left and first denied massive wage increases obtained by labor unions, before reasserting labor settlements following bitter strikes. In November 1974, she seemingly discarded any restraints on the army, while proclaiming a state of emergency. The "dirty war" followed, which culminated in the crushing of the revolutionary left. In the process, some 10,000–30,000 individuals "disappeared;" unidentified paramilitary forces tortured many of these *desaparecidos* in secret detention centers before murdering them. Engaging in its own terrorist campaign, the government, in the name of national security, relied on right-wing death squads, along with its security forces, to stem the revolutionary tide.

In September 1975, military leaders, operating at the behest of General Jorge Rafael Videla, determined to overthrow the government of Isabel Perón, which was beset by both high inflation and rampant political violence. The Argentine military commanders, led by General Ramón J. Camps, sought to devise a "final solution" to eradicate the revolutionary left. The writer Jacobo Timerman later revealed that anti-Semitism and pro-Nazi sentiments abounded among the top military brass. Camps, for example, was heard to say, "With Hitler I coincide on several points. For example, my humanist concern to save humankind and to struggle against the permanent Communist campaign full of lies." To avoid moral suicide of the sort that was purportedly besetting the West, Camps insisted that "whoever participates in the war against subversion with the will to win must 'cover himself with mud'." In characteristic fashion, General Ibérico Saint-Jean asserted, "First we will kill all the subversives; then we will kill their collaborators; then their sympathizers; then . . . those who remain indifferent; and finally we will kill the timid!"

Having ousted Isabel in March 1976, the military held power for the next eight years. By 1980, the dirty war had succeeded in virtually silencing the Argentine left. However, the economy failed to improve noticeably. Iinflation hovered around 150 percent, real wages sank, a trade imbalance deepened and the national debt continued to rise, surpassing $35 billion by 1981. The new government of General Leopoldo Fortunato Galtieri had to confront marches in Buenos Aires by mothers of the *desaparecidos* and the furor caused by the imprisonment and subsequent torture of the journalist Timerman. To distract attention from economic woes and growing international condemnations, Galtieri moved to take over the Malvinas (or Falkland) Islands, occupied by Britain since 1833, situated in the South Atlantic. A British expeditionary force retook the islands within three months, compelling the surrender of 10,000 Argentine soldiers and delivering a shattering blow to the military regime. While Galtieri resigned, his successors promised general elections that would restore civilian authority. In December 1983, Raul Alfonsín of the Radical Party was elected president of Argentina.

Promising to heal his tormented land, Alfonsín had to confront two major problems: a sick economy and demands for trials of military officials involved in "the dirty war." Saddled with a now $45 billion foreign debt and interest payments that ensnared the majority of export earnings, Alfonsín adopted an austerity program that the International Monetary Fund demanded. At first, inflation continued to surge, nearing 600 percent in 1984 and hitting 1,200 percent by mid-1985. Wage and price controls, the replacement of the *peso* with the *austral* and curtailed government spending enabled inflation to drop to 25 percent. On the other hand, the foreign debt kept rising, albeit more slowly than before; unemployment was the highest in a generation. As the economy by 1989 suffered from reignited inflation of 12,000 percent and food riots swept across the land, a state of emergency was proclaimed. That year's presidential election witnessed the triumph of Carlos Sául Menem, who was backed by Peronist unions but favored market solutions for his nation's economic ills.

CHILE AND THE OVERTHROW OF *UNIDAD POPULAR*

Like their Argentine and Brazilian brethren, the Chilean military took over the reins of government. This was more startling still as Chile, notwithstanding exceptions along the way, possessed the longest tradition of democratic governance in Latin America. That tradition, however, was sorely tested as Salvador Allende won the presidential election in his fifth attempt. In a hotly contested three-man race in 1970, Allende captured 36.2 percent of the vote, barely prevailing over the 34.9 percent garnered by former president Jorge Allessandri of the conservative National Party and the 27.8 percent amassed by the Christian Democratic Party's Radomiro Tomic. Strikingly, Tomic, who was the leader of his organization's left wing, presented a platform similar to Allende, who was the candidate of the *Unidad Popular* or Popular Unity, which brought together the Socialist, Communist and Radical parties.

Allende had promised during the campaign that his government would strive to "change the constitution by constitutional means." At the same time, he hoped to draw support from workers, peasants, slum dwellers, the middle class and intellectuals, for his program to usher in the "Chilean road to socialism." As no candidate had received a majority of the popular vote, however, the Chilean Congress had to choose between the top two vote-getters to determine the nation's next president; traditionally, the Congress selected the candidate with the most votes in the general election. Because of Allende's avowed Marxism, intrigue swirled around that determination. Tomic declared his support for Allende, although the Christian Democratic Party as a whole appeared more reluctant to back him; eventually, that party did so once Allende promised to abide by democratic principles.

The right was still less favorably disposed, with many wealthy Chileans transferring funds out of the country and some right-wing military officers, in league with the CIA, determining to kidnap General René Schneider, the head of the armed forces and a firm supporter of constitutional practices. When Schneider resisted, he was gunned down. The shocking murder of Schneider perhaps ensured Allende's ascendancy to power, as the leading conspirators were singled out, arrested and ultimately convicted. Nevertheless, a far right group, *Patria & Libertad* (Fatherland and Liberty), which had sought to keep Allende out of office, immediately plotted his ouster. Opposition to Allende remained fierce and included the U.S. government and multinational corporations. Henry Kissinger, the top foreign advisor to President Richard M. Nixon, purportedly indicated that the election for Allende should not be allowed to stand. American policymakers feared another Marxist beachhead in the Western hemisphere.

The agenda of Popular Unity was indeed profoundly radical. The Allende government sought to curb the power of both the Chilean economic elite and foreign mining operations, banks and other multinational enterprises. As historian Edward Williamson has indicated, "people's power" was to be encouraged, centered around a single-house legislature and a series of people's councils established throughout Chile. The government planned to rely on centralized planning to attack inflation and to foster economic growth. At the outset, it began to redistribute income and to increase significantly consumption by middle- and working-class sectors.

An economic boom unfolded, along with inflation that approached 200 percent by late 1972. Production bottlenecks and shortages of consumer products, some deliberately induced by opponents of the government, occurred. Black marketeering abounded. Angered by government policies, including those involving nationalization of various properties, many members of the economic elite struck back through boycotts, depositing the funds outside Chile, production cuts and the reduction of the labor force. Nevertheless, the copper companies, banks and various subsidiaries of corporations such as the IT & T were nationalized. Infuriated by purportedly inadequate compensation for such holdings, the Nixon administration undertook an unannounced economic boycott against Chile. Funds from international agencies became more difficult to attain, the balance of payments worsened and Chilean foreign trade shrank.

Popular Unity's determination to usher in land reform also proved profoundly controversial. In little over a year, the government had surpassed the redistribution efforts of the Frei regime; by mid-1972, almost nine million hectares of land had been expropriated. Nevertheless, illegal seizures of land increased. The disruptions in the agrarian sector proved costly as production sharply diminished, despite considerable support from the government in the form of subsidies and credits.

Alongside the economic ailments, political tensions continued to rise. The distrust of the Allende government that many Christian Democrats felt only deepened after left-wing guerrillas murdered Edmundo Pérez Zujovic, a party leader, in June 1971. Several members of the Christian Democratic Party who comprised its Third Group, the *terceristas*, on the other hand, lined up with the Popular Unity coalition, proclaiming themselves the Christian Left. However, as the economy foundered, middle-class opposition heightened. Thousands of women, wielding pots and pans, took to the streets in protest. Professionals, students and businessmen, worried that the government might nationalize small and moderate-sized commercial enterprises, conducted other demonstrations. In the countryside, landowners hired armed men to hold off agrarian radicals. And as later revealed in hearings before a U.S. Senate subcommittee, President Nixon and Kissinger encouraged the CIA to expend $8 million to "destabilize" the Chilean economy. In late 1972, a truck drivers' strike that the CIA backed threatened to bring the economy to a halt; it ended only due to the combined efforts of labor unions and peasant leagues. An employers' strike in October terminated after Allende pledged support for "non-monopolistic" holdings.

In addition, Allende felt compelled to add military men to his cabinet to ensure the holding of congressional elections in March 1973. While Popular Unity increased its vote total to 44 percent, it still garnered only a minority of seats in Congress; moreover, that total was a drop from the nearly 50 percent Popular Unity had collected in municipal elections 18 months earlier. The opposition now intensified its operations, engaging in damaging strikes, backing terrorist action and urging the Chilean armed forces to overthrow the president. General Carlos Prats, who had succeeded Schneider as head of the army, put down one coup on June 29. Workers called for a takeover of factories and the passing out of arms to Allende's supporters. Allende refused to do so, while continuing to look to the military to maintain the peace. Increasingly, paramilitary forces stockpiled weapons as the armed forces took control of many areas. In a pair of disastrous portents, General Augusto Pinochet replaced Pratt, who resigned.

On September 11, in the midst of the army and the air force assault on the presidential palace, Allende declared, "I will not resign . . . I will pay with my life for the loyalty of the people." Evidently, before noon that day, he committed suicide or was murdered. Salvador Allende's attempt to usher in a democratic brand of socialism had come to a disastrous end. In the period ahead, as minimal resistance confronted the armed forces, the severity of that calamity became clearer. Determined to crush Allende's base of support, the military carried out mass arrests and imprisonments, relied on torture and murdered several thousand Chileans, along with a number of foreigners. One American professor from Catholic University in Santiago remembered being told in the midst of a ride to National Stadium where many dissidents were rounded up, "Goddamm foreigners. Came down here to kill Chileans. Well, we're going to kill you. You'll see." Colonel Walter Rauff, a Nazi involved with the horrors at Auschwitz, headed the *Direccion de Intelligencia Nacional* (DINA), which provided secret police forces for the junta. Assassinations were conducted in Europe and the United States, while concentration camps were established in Chile. In September 1976, Chile's former ambassador to the United States, Orlando Letelier, died when a car bomb exploded in Washington, D.C.

General Pinochet rolled back many of the progressive economic reforms carried out by both the Popular Unity and the Christian Democratic governments. Heavily influenced by the free market doctrine propounded by Milton Friedman at the University of Chicago, government economists— the so-called "Chicago boys"—resorted to "shock treatment" in the form of slashed public spending, privatized state enterprises, a devalued *peso* and reduced imports. The free-market dominated economy initially plunged downward, along with wages, while unemployment soared to 20 percent. Relying on exports, foreign capital and economy speculation, the economy rebounded in 1977, growing by some 8 percent a year by the end of the decade as inflation subsided. But as the economy slid again in 1980, the government nationalized the banks. Nevertheless, unemployment increased to over 30 percent, wages dropped yet again and production fell off markedly. Beginning in 1982, the Chilean economy experienced its worst depression ever. In the meantime, Chile's foreign debt mounted, while interest payments consumed almost half of the export earnings.

The social repercussions of the Pinochet economic policies were profoundly significant. The upper class, and to some extent the middle class, benefited, while the impact on workers was crushing. By 1983, mass opposition developed to the economic program and to the repression that characterized the Pinochet government. That year, Allende's Socialist Party, the Christian Democrats and other disgruntled organizations established the Democratic Alliance. By mid-July, Pinochet announced a state of siege, which was soon followed by an announcement that 11 political parties had agreed to a pact urging "transition to full democracy." Increasingly, even right-wing parties began to withdraw support from the Chilean dictator. In 1986, Pinochet, riding in his motorcade, barely escaped assassination at the hands of Communist Party agents. Subsequently, political opponents once again were rounded up. Furthermore, the economy, influenced by finance minister Hernan Buchi, began to recover, with public spending curtailed and diversified markets established.

In 1988, Pinochet declared amnesty for various political prisoners and exiles and allowed a plebiscite on whether he should remain in office for eight additional years. Chileans voted 54.6–43 percent against Pinochet's extended term. In December 1989, national elections resulted in victory for Patricio Aylwin, who was backed by the Democratic Accord of 17 parties, including the Christian Democrats and the Socialists.

MEXICO AND THE PRI STRANGLEHOLD

By the early seventies, Mexico encountered guerrilla insurgencies, but avoided the turn to military coups that the other great Latin American states experienced. The Mexican military comprised a key component of the government and effectively crushed the guerrilla movement. Angered by

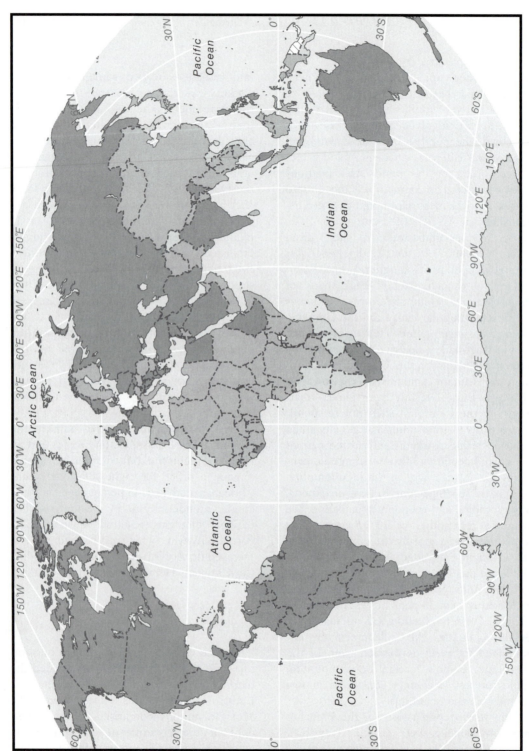

Map 13-1 World of the UN and the Cold War

the 1968 massacre in Mexico City, student leftists, like many throughout Latin America, remained enamored with the Cuban revolutionaries. Equally important, intellectuals such as Carlos Fuentes wrote about the government's betrayal of the ideals of the Mexican Revolution. The poet Octavio Paz resigned his appointment as ambassador to India and termed the PRI a "philanthropic ogre." A right-wing party, the Christian Democratic *Partido de Accion Nacional* (PAN), began drawing support from businessmen and industrials who supported free-market principles.

In 1970, the PRI chose Luis Echeverría, who had served as secretary of the interior when the massacre unfolded at Tlatelolco, as the next Mexican chief-of-state. He released many imprisoned dissidents and cultivated a liberal image in other ways too. Echeverría condemned colonialism, corruption and maldistribution of wealth, while championing a nationalistic foreign policy. The government greeted Salvador Allende, welcomed Chilean exiles following the coup and supported Cuba's peaceful involvement in hemisphere affairs. Echeverría increased public spending on food subsidies, education programs, housing construction and health services. But he encountered considerable resistance from the middle class and from conservative businessmen, who pulled investment funds, thereby precipitating an economic recession. Echeverría continued to attack colonialism and multinational companies, but allowed for intensified foreign dominance of Mexican industry. All the while, the country's foreign debt mushroomed. Echeverría ordered a sharp devaluation of the *peso*, and inflationary pressures proved crushing for workers and peasants. Until the very end of Echeverría's term, promised agrarian reform did not occur, with six million peasants remained landless. Only days before his presidency ended,

Echeverría, possibly in an effort to garner appointment as secretary-general of the United Nations, redistributed fertile farmland in Sonora to peasants. This plan failed, however, to appease the left, while enraging the right.

The International Monetary Fund saddled Echeverría's successor, José López Portillo, with an austerity program; Mexican wages dropped, while unemployment rose. However, the discovery of enormous oil reserves, amounting to perhaps 200 billion barrels, promised to improve markedly Mexico's economic situation. Unfortunately, the expected financial windfall resulted in bloated development projects, with state entities like the oil corporation *Pemex* amassing staggering debts. Moreover, a sizable increase in the Mexican population required increased social welfare spending. The impact of the world recession of the early 1980s was considerable, with inflation in Mexico hitting the 100 percent mark in 1982. At that same point, Mexico announced it was suspending interest payments on its $95.5 billion foreign debt. Wealthy Mexicans transferred billions of dollars to U.S. banks. The U.S. government, acting with the IMF and large banks, devised a loan program enabling Mexico to pay the interest on its foreign debt. Nevertheless, the economy continued to slide, compelling López Portillo to nationalize all Mexican banks and to establish stringent exchange controls.

The next president, Miguel de la Madrid Hurtado, consequently had to accept another IMF austerity plan that resulted in the removal of price controls and subsidies, lower tariff rates, wage decreases and reduced living standards as a sharper recession took hold. Despite these moves, Mexico's foreign debt surpassed the $100 billion mark by 1986. The number of bankruptcies of businesses continued to climb, along with unemployment and inflation. A severe earthquake on September 19, 1985, which resulted in 20,000 deaths and a transformed Mexico City, compounded the problems confronting the federal government. Madrid's government resorted to a policy of economic liberalization, which resulted in privatizing state companies and reducing public spending. Nevertheless, inflation contained to rise, surpassing 140 percent by 1988. The 1988 presidential campaign, in which the PRI candidate Carlos Salinas de Gortari had to contend with a challenge from former senator Cuauhtémoc Cárdenas, the son of the legendary president, witnessed mounting discontent. While political observers claimed that Cárdenas actually swept to victory, Salinas became president of Mexico. Calling for electoral reform, Salinas acknowledged PAN's gubernatorial triumph in Baja California in 1989. The president also planned to continue selling off most of the rest of Mexico's state-owned enterprises, including mines, mills, hotels and the national insurance company.

Guerrilla Warfare

By the mid-1970s, then, the largest Latin American nations had to contend with massive corruption, devastating inflation and repression, which led, except in Mexico, to military rule. By the close of the following decade, the generals had been compelled to relinquish power in both Brazil and Argentina. Even Pinochet's rule in Chile neared an end. During this same period, the same forces that led to those military takeovers had resulted in similar developments in countries such as Uruguay and El Salvador; in Nicaragua, by contrast, discontent with a repressive regime actually produced a new revolutionary government.

URUGUAY AND THE *TUPAMOS*

Thanks to the establishment of social welfare programs under José Batlle y Ordóñez in the 1920s, Uruguay, characterized by its generally homogenous population with Spanish or Italian roots, had come to be known as the "Switzerland of South America." Through the mid-1960s, Uruguay, the smallest South American republic, boasted a large middle-class, fine educational and medical systems and democratic politics. However, a sharp economic decline in the last part of that decade ushered in strident political sectarianism, with labor unions radicalized and the emergence of the *Tupamaro* guerrillas. Disillusioned with the Socialist Party, the *Tupamaros* initially effected a Robin Hood-like persona. The assassination and subsequent murder in 1970 of Daniel Mitrione, who worked for the U.S. Agency for International Development and operated out of police headquarters in Montevideo, dispelled such an image. As the police continued to rely on torture in dealing with dissidents, warfare between the government and the *Tupamaros* intensified. In 1972, government officials undertook an internal war, suspending individual liberties. The following June, President Juan María Bordaberry Avocena shut down Parliament, censored the press and unleashed the military and police forces to quash government opponents in unions, the university, the press and the general intelligensia. Arrests, tortures and killings surged.

The Uruguayan economy fared little better. Inflation reached 83 percent by 1979, with anti-inflationary measures resulting in a reduced gross national product rate and a significant increase in both unemployment and the foreign debt. The government budget shifted decidedly, with education expenditures dropping from 21 percent of spending in the early 1960s to 13.5 percent by 1981, as "security" expenditures shot up from 14 percent to over 40 percent. An estimated 10 percent of Uruguayans, including many professionals, academics, artists and other intellectuals, left the country.

The election in 1983 of Rául Alfonsín as president of Argentina, coupled with the move of many exiles to Buenos Aires and the sinking economy, put increasing pressure on the Uruguayan military to loosen its grip. The following year, the military dictatorship in Uruguay, having just encountered a general strike in Montevideo, ended.

NICARAGUA AND THE SANDINISTAS

The guerrilla movement in Uruguay clearly failed, while a series of rebel efforts in Guatemala ended disastrously. Military control in Guatemala that followed the overthrow of Jacobo Arbenz included brutal counterinsurgency campaigns that took some 200,000 lives. By contrast, the guerrilla efforts in Nicaragua and El Salvador proved far more potent. In 1956, the long-time dictator of Nicaragua, Anastasio Somoza García, was assassinated. Replacing him was his son, Luis Somoza Debayle, who served until 1963 and then controlled puppet regimes until his death in 1967. That year saw the election of Anastasio Somoza García Jr. who directed the country until 1979. The 45 year reign of the Somozas witnessed the amassing of a great family fortune; the National Guard, always run by a member of the Somoza family, safeguarded the finances of the economic elite. Massive exploitation of workers and peasants

ensued, with the maldistribution of wealth among the worst in Latin America.

Beginning in the 1950s, Pedro Joaquín Chamorro, who published *La Prensa* and whose parents' families were among the most powerful of the Nicaraguan upper class, spearheaded a series of aborted revolts. Then in 1961, Carlos Fonseca Amador, Silvio Mayorga and Tomás Borge established the Sandinista Front for National Liberation (FSLN), which called for guerrilla warfare. By the late 1960s, a number of young Nicaraguan priests endorsed Liberation Theology that called for the church to challenge political, social and economic oppression. The Somoza regime's theft of international assistance following the catastrophic earthquake in 1972 that killed 10,000 and leveled much of the capital of Managua further fueled anger. Subsequently, wages of urban workers fell, while unemployment neared 30 percent by 1979.

Throughout much of that period, a state of siege was in effect after several dignitaries, including the mayor of Managua, the Nicaraguan foreign minister and the U.S. ambassador, were kidnapped. Eventually, the guerrillas exchanged those hostages for 18 Sandinista prisoners, including the future Nicaraguan president Daniel Ortega Saavedra, $5 million, publication of an FSLN manifesto and safe transit to Cuba. During the period of martial law, the government struck at the FSLN, murdering many of its leaders, including Fonseca. The National Guard conducted a reign of terror against suspected FSLN supporters, killing hundreds of peasants.

U.S. President Jimmy Carter's human rights campaign pressured Somoza to relax controls somewhat, which enabled the Sandinistas to operate more freely. The murder in 1978 of Pedro Joaquín Chamorro, at the behest of Somoza or his supporters, led to a general strike and unfavorable publicity for the government. Hostilities heightened, notwithstanding the reimposition of martial law in 1978. In July of the following year, Somoza fled into exile as the FSLN approached Managua. The war cost 50,000 lives and some $1.3 billion. The foreign debt now stood at $1.6 billion. The struggle left tens of thousands homeless, while decimating numerous industries and businesses. On the other hand, the power of the National Guard had been broken, while a new force emerged that was "explicitly sandinist—that is, revolutionary and popularly oriented." Additionally, mass organizations that had supported the revolution appeared.

The initial revolutionary cabinet included both Marxists and Catholic priests, while a five-person executive committee featured Sandinistas, wealthy businessman Alfonso Robelo Callejas and Violeta Barrios de Chamorro, widow of the slain newspaper editor. The new government acted quickly to implement a revolutionary program. It redistributed some six million acres of land to indigent peasants and rural workers and nationalized properties held by the Somoza clan. The Sandinistas promised to support a mixed economic approach, to encourage private investment and to allow for political pluralism. The government instituted major literacy and health care programs.

All the while, opposition to the Sandinistas emerged, centered among business operators, the middle class and the United States government under Ronald Reagan. Some members of the economic elite departed from Nicaragua, taking with them vital capital and skills. Most of the leaders of the Catholic Church also were critical of the Sandinistas, as were Violeta Chamorro—who, like Robelo, resigned from the executive committee in April 1980—and various members of her influential family. Opposition developed too along the Atlantic coastal region, where many Indians viewed the Sandinistas programs as certain to subvert indigenous culture.

The inauguration of Reagan as the U.S. president resulted in hostile relations between the greatest hemispheric power and the Nicaraguan government. Trade between the two nations virtually disappeared, while the Reagan administration provided support for the contras or "counterrevolutionaries" who sought to remove the Sandinistas from positions of prominence in Nicaragua. Reagan, to the chagrin of many, proclaimed the contras "freedom fighters." A number of former National Guardsmen were involved in the campaign, but so too were many business figures, and several younger recruits, along with discontented Indians. Believing that the Sandinistas had betrayed their revolutionary ideals, Edén Pastora for a time led his own band of contras out of a base in Costa Rica.

The European democracies provided little support for the U.S.-sponsored campaign to destabilize the Sandinista government. Moreover, the World Court in 1984 attacked CIA operations involving the mining of Nicaraguan harbors. Two years later, the World Court ruled that the U.S. backing of the contras violated international law and required reparation payments. It was soon discovered that the Reagan administration, working in conjunction with Iranian middlemen and various Middle Eastern governments, had helped to funnel money to the contras, notwithstanding U.S. congressional mandates prohibiting such support.

The contra campaign proved devastating to the Sandinistas, with 30,000 lives lost and the Nicaraguan economy severely weakened. Over half the national budget involved defense expenditures, while a labor shortage ensured, thanks to the large number of Nicaraguans participating in military operations.

The severity of the war eventually cost the Sandinistas considerable support from the Nicaraguan populace, which had overwhelmingly supported the revolutionary party in the 1984 elections. A peace agreement was concocted in 1989, with the contra camps disbanded, amnesty and desired repatriation provided and national and municipal elections slated for February 1990.

EL SALVADOR AND CIVIL DISORDER

Guerrilla warfare also swept through neighboring El Salvador from the 1960s onward. In 1944, discontented junior officers in the Salvadoran military overthrew dictator Maximiliano Hernández Martínez. Liberals, conservatives and reform-minded military officials headed a succession of governments until 1961. At that point, the sympathetic attitude displayed toward the Cuban Revolution resulted in a coup that Colonel Julio Adalberto Rivera headed. While seeking to replicate the one-party dominance that characterized Mexico, Rivera nevertheless permitted opposition parties, including the Christian Democratic Party, the social democratic *Movimiento Nacional Revolucionario* and the Communist Party-affiliated *Union Democratica Nacionalista.*

Throughout the 1960s and 1970s, economic conditions, heightened by land monopoly, monocultural practices, sharp population increases and low wages, worsened. Border disputes, economic clashes and the presence of approximately 300,000 Salvado-

ran refugees culmininated in the so-called Soccer War of 1969 with Honduras that left thousands dead and at least 100,000 homeless in El Salvador. By the early 1970s, unemployment stood at 20 percent, unemployment was double that, inflation shot up to 60 percent and the number of landless peasants had increased nearly four-fold in the past quarter-century to over 40 percent.

Fueled by economic discontent, voters in 1972 apparently elected José Napoleon Duarte, former mayor of San Salvador, president. The military refused to allow Duarte to take office, declared Colonel Arturo Armando Molina the victor and arrested and tortured Duarte, before sending him into exile in Venezuela. Shortly thereafter, civil disorder heightened. Left-wing guerrillas, who had cropped up in 1970, continued to kidnap wealthy Salvadorans. Right-wing paramilitary units, including the *Organizacion Democratica Nacionalista* (ORDEN), targeted supposed subversives in villages, with many murdered and others kidnapped, never to be seen again. Another fradulent election in 1977 resulted in the election of General Carlos Humberto Romero and seemingly demonstrated that a peaceful road to change was futile.

Left-wing mobilization intensified, with increased guerrilla action, including the assassination of despised figures associated with the repression, and labor and peasant organizing. The right, fueled by ORDEN's death squads or heightened action by various security forces, escalated its tactics too.

In October 1979, reformist junior officers conducted a coup that ousted Romero. A military-civilian government, which included moderate leftists, was established. The government promised that ORDEN would be disbanded, human rights respected and agrarian reform carried out. However, security forces actually escalated their repression and the leftists resigned from the junta. Although Duarte became president in November 1980, the military and security forces controlled government operations. At the same time, ORDEN continued its assault against supposed subversives. The death squads, headed by the likes of Roberto D'Aubuissón—who was referred to by former U.S. Ambassador Robert White as a "pathological killer"—targeted peasants, union leaders, left-wing opponents of the government and even representatives of the Catholic Church. D'Aubussón, for his part, was the runner-up in the 1982 presidential election that Duarte won with 35.3 percent of the vote.

Throughout the 1980s, a bloody civil war raged throughout El Salvador. In April 1980, the left comprised a coalition, the *Frente Democratico Revolucionario* (FDR). The following year, the left established a "political commission" led by the social democrat Gui-

llermo Ungo, one of the former civilian members of the junta that replaced Romero. But much of the attention centered on the *Frente Farabundo Marti de Liberacion Nacional* (FMLN), which brought together five guerrilla groups that began to strike out in early 1981. Fearful that the left might prevail, the Reagan administration provided $2.7 billion in military and economic assistance to the El Salvadoran government. Counterinsurgent and bombing campaigns caused considerable damage through the countryside, while the war-ravaged economy suffered mightily.

Elections in 1988, boycotted by the FMLN, resulted in a victory for the right-wing Nationalist Republic Alliance (ARENA), which D'Aubuissón headed. Its candidate, Alfredo Cristiani, insisted that he was ready to negotiate with the rebels but the repression continued. As the decade ended, the level of violence had only escalated, as evidenced by an attempted offensive by the FMLN in San Salvador and the government bombing of working-class districts.

◆ ——— ◆ ——— ◆ ——— ◆ ——— ◆ ——— ◆ ——— ◆ ——— ◆ ——— ◆

As the Cold War continued, the people of Latin America endured a volatile political climate; heavy-handed practices by military juntas, death squads and revolutionary forces alike; and oppressive social and economic conditions. Repeatedly, governments were toppled, with the superpowers—especially the United States—playing a major role in such developments. Violence became the norm in many nations, as revolutionary and counterrevolutionary fighters battled in both the countryside and urban centers. Living standards plummeted in many instances, making life still more desperate for the millions already mired in poverty. Disaffected members of the Latin America elite, found on landed estates, in the military and throughout the church, joined with well-educated professionals and university students to support reform and sometimes radical movements. However uneasily at times, those well-bred sorts linked up too with peasants and urban working-class activists, determined to transform their social, economic and political orders.

Many of those compatriots remained nameless outside their own communities, but a few acquired folk hero-like status. One such individual was María Teresa Tula, a working-class housewife in El Salvador who helped to found *CO-MADRES*, a group of mothers and relatives seeking information about relatives who had been taken away by government or paramilitary forces, never to be seen again. On May 6, 1986, Tula suffered the fate endured by so many who attempted to challenge the repressive ways of governments in Latin America. Pregnant, she was abducted, tortured, raped and then released. Shortly thereafter, she was kidnapped yet again, accused of terrorism and tortured repeatedly. Sent to prison, she linked up with an organization comprised of political prisoners. While there, she participated in marches and hunger strikes. On August 20, 1986, President José Napoleon Duarte proclaimed his intention to free her. More than a month passed before a representative from the Red Cross told Tula that she was to go to Duarte's residence. That fall, she moved from house to house, attempting to remain outside the clutches of the police.

Born on April 23, 1951, Tula was raised by her mother and grandmother in dire economic straits. She grew up in Izalco, a small town located approximately 35 miles from San Salvador. When her mother moved to Santa Ana, Tula remained with her brother and grandmother, an illiterate Indian woman who adhered to the Catholic faith. The scantily educated and unmarried Tula became pregnant at the age of 15, subsequently delivering a girl. She later had five more children with another man, a labor organizer named José Rafael Canales Guevara.

With Rafael working as a blacksmith and Tula laundering clothes, the family struggled to get by. The children's needs were attended to, with Rafael declaring, "I'm not going to be like other men. They always say that they come first. Serve me first and then everyone else. In this house, the children should come first." A sugar mill strike in 1978 made times even tougher and altered the then apolitical Tula's life. The workers in her husband's cane-cutting factory—owned by one of El Salvador's wealthiest families—endured low wages and dangerous working conditions that resulted in numerous injuries. The company provide neither health coverage nor vacations, not even for Christmas or New Year's. The strikers demanded an eight-hour day, improved safety conditions and bus service into Izalco to prevent them from being robbed after receipt of their meager pay. Members of the National Guard poured into the sugar mill, arresting 22 of the strikers, including Rafael. All were tortured and then convicted of terrorist acts. Having visiting Rafael in prison, Tula departed "with a great sadness, but with a new vision of reality."

While at the jail, Tula first encountered a group of women who, she was informed, were searching for relatives who had "disappeared." One woman, whose son had been accused of terrorism, told her about an organization, *CO-MADRES*, which sought information about "disappeared children." The women gathered each week in San Jose de la Montana, Archbishop Oscar Romero's seminary. At a dinner, Tula met Romero, who appeared pleased when told that she was a new member of *CO-MADRES*. Promising to assist the group's efforts, Romero declared, "Hope is the basis of bounty, of love, and of humanity." A group from *CO-MADRES* conducted a sit-in at the United Nations office in San Salvador to help publicize the plight of the disappeared and their families. Next, the women occupied Catholic churches and the Red Cross building and then conducted a hunger strike. In July 1978, shortly after Rafael had been removed to a prison in San Vicente, Tula traveled to Costa Rica to attend the World Council of Peace as a representative of *CO-MADRES*.

On her return from Costa Rica, Tula learned that her husband had been released from jail. Tula soon had to contend with Rafael's desire that she remain home to care for him and their children and her own determination to assist her *CO-MADRES'* compatriots. Then, in 1979 and 1980, the political situation in El Salvador became more charged. Salvadoreans witnessed the abduction of the secretary of the SLES (Electrical Workers Union of Sonsonate), and two young men. A *coup d'etat* temporarily ushered in the Revolutionary Government. A massacre of demonstrators occurred near the Church of the Rosario, located in central San Salvador. Protesting workers were killed, students "disappeared" and members of *CO-MADRES* became still more politically engaged.

Increasingly, Archbishop Oscar Romero—who often met with the Mothers' Committee—condemned the escalating repression, which included the killing of several priests. The Catholic Church in Latin America was gradually affected by the tumultuous events of the Cold War era. As the period opened, the church remained what it had long been in Latin America: a conservative, even reactionary entity whose leaders joined with large landholders and military forces atop the social, economic and political hierarchy. The Second Vatican Council, carried out under Pope John XXIII in 1963, however, ushered in a new, more liberal atmosphere within the ranks of the church. A theology of liberation evolved, which argued that the priesthood should work to uplift the poor and the persecuted; some proponents asserted that revolutionary violence was itself justified. By the middle of the decade, radical priests such as Camilo Torres had discarded their clerical robes and joined Guevara-styled insurrectionary efforts. An upper-class Colombian, the scholarly Torres was murdered while battling against counterinsurgents in early 1966.

Held in Medellin, Colombia, the 1968 Conference of Latin American Bishops, which declared that the Church featured an "option for the poor," encouraged grass-roots missionary work among the downtrodden. As military regimes and right-wing death squads produced massive human rights violations, more churchmen began to protest vehemently. For his part, Romero came to determine that "the case for insurrection" could emerge "when all recourses to peaceful means have been exhausted." During his sermons, which could be heard on radios throughout El Salvador, Romero condemned the government's violations of human rights and called for social justice. Speaking on February 2, 1980, Romero declared, "When all peaceful means have been exhausted, the church considers insurrection moral and justified." The following month, he exhorted soldiers not to fire on unarmed civilians. The very next day, on March 24, while conducting mass in a church in San Salvador, Archbishop Romero became another victim of the politics of assassination. On being informed of the killing, a shocked Maria

Teresa Tula cried out, "This can't be. Oh, my God. Please don't let it be so. It can't be so!" Tula recalled Romero telling the mothers that he would be killed but that they should persevere: "I have faith in you. I know that you will go on with your work and that you will find your children. You will find the disappeared."

Less than three months later, men with machine guns came to Tula's home, supposedly to investigate a robbery. They handcuffed Rafael and took him away. Two days later, a friend informed Tula, now pregnant once more, that Rafael's death had been reported in the local newspaper. Rafael was referred to as a "member of a terrorist cell." He had received a .38-calibre bullet in his head. That same year the *CO-MADRES'* headquarters was bombed. The office of the Human Rights Commission, located in the same building, was also targeted. The number of mutilated corpses—some victims raped and decapitated—increased.

CO-MADRES continued to operate, providing food relief to families of individuals who had disappeared. In both 1981 and 1982, a state of siege existed. Starting in 1982, members of *CO-MADRES* began to be arrested. One woman was picked up, beaten, raped repeatedly and then burned. Another woman warned Tula that she was being sought out by the police. Fearing for her life, Tula left with her family for Mexico in 1983. There, she worked in a *CO-MADRES'* office in Mexico City. Back in El Salvador, *CO-MADRES* agitated more publicly than before, protesting at the U.S. embassy and conducting sit-ins in churches. In mid-1984, on receiving word that her mother had died, Tula returned to El Salvador and her *CO-MADRES'* work there. Tula and three other women were selected to pick up the Robert F. Kennedy Human Rights Award that *CO-MADRES* was to receive in the United States. The U.S. State Department, declaring that these were "four terrorist women," refused to grant them visas.

The international nature of *CO-MADRES'* operations continued to widen. In early 1985, Tula and two other members traveled to Europe, spending a week in Geneva with the head of the Human Rights Commission. After three months in Europe, where they spoke with individuals as prominent as West German Chancellor Willy Brandt, the women returned home. Back in El Salvador, they discovered that the government was now imprisoning political prisoners, rather than executing them. *CO-MADRES* began agitating for prisoners' rights. On her return to El Salvador, Tula endured kidnappings, torture and rape.

In January 1987, Tula left for Mexico. Asked by scores of members of Congress, including Massachusetts Senator Edward M. Kennedy, to come to the United States, Tula sought a visa. Her request was denied, she was informed, because "You are a communist and a terrorist." In February, she passed illegally across the Mexican border into Arizona. After a brief stay in Los Angeles, Tula went to New York City and determined to seek political asylum. She also became involved in *CO-MADRES'* enterprises in the United States that involved publicizing the phenomenon of those who had been "disappeared." Tula ignored an order by Immigration and Naturalization Services that she leave the United States by June 1988. She began speaking in communities across the country about her own experiences and those of many Salvadoreans. She determined "to keep moving forward and fighting for social change."

• —— • —— • —— • —— • —— • —— • —— • —— • —— •

Suggested Readings

BALFOUR, SEBASTIAN. *Castro.* (1995).

BURNS, E. BRADFORD. *A History of Brazil.* (1993).

CARR, BARRY and STEVE ELLNER, ed. *The Latin American Left: From the Fall of Allende to Perestroika.* (1993).

CASTANEDA, JORGE G. *Utopia Unarmed: The Latin American Left after the Cold War.* (1993).

COATSWORTH, JOHN H. *Central America and the United States.* (1994).

DEFRONZO, JAMES. *Revolutions & Revolutionary Movements.* (1996).

DONGHI, TULIO HALPERIN. *The Contemporary History of Latin America.* (1993).

DUNKERLEY, JAMES. *The Long War: Dictatorship and Revolution in El Salvador.* (1982).

GLEIJESES, PIERO. *Shattered Hope: The Guatemalan Revolution and the United States, 1944–1954.* (1991).

KEEN, BENJAMIN and KEITH HAYNES. *A History of Latin America: Independence to the Present.* (2000).

LAFEBER, WALTER. *Inevitable Revolutions: The United States in Central America.* (1993).

LOVEMAN, BRIAN. *Chile: The Legacy of Hispanic Capitalism.* (1988).

MEYER, MICHAEL C. and WILLIAM L. SHERMAN. *The Course of Mexican History.* (1999).

PEREZ, LOUIS A. *Cuba: Between Reform and Revolution.* (1988).

ROCK, DAVID. *Argentina, 1516–1987.* (1987).

SKIDMORE, THOMAS E. *The Politics of Military Rule in Brazil, 1964–1985.* (1988).

SKIDMORE, THOMAS E. and PETER H. SMITH. *Modern Latin America.* (1997).

SPALDING, ROSE J. *Capitalists and Revolution in Nicaragua: Opposition and Accommodation 1979–1993.* (1994).

WEAVER, F. S. *Inside the Volcano: The History and Political Economy of Central America.* (1994).

WILLIAMSON, EDWIN. *The Penguin History of Latin America.* (1992).

WOODWARD, RALPH LEE, JR. *Central America: A Nation Divided.* (1999).

PART THREE

The World Order in Transition, 1989–Present

Overview

The collapse of the Soviet empire in Eastern Europe and the ensuing breakup of the USSR had enormous impact on world affairs. With its longtime foe seemingly bested, the United States underwent the greatest period of sustained economic growth in the nation's history. At the same time, the world's lone superpower experienced the deepening of income gaps between the haves and the have-nots and challenges to U.S. hegemony around the world. Former Soviet states struggled as privatization and efforts to democratize political orders proved disruptive, incomplete and costly.

It became increasingly clear that the end of a bipolar world had resulted in new unsettling and dangerous developments. Ethnic, religious and ideological hostilities produced terrible bloodletting in southern Europe, the Middle East, Africa, Asia and Latin America. The arms race failed to slacken and Scud missiles hurtled toward Israel during the 1991 Gulf War. More nations than ever before held nuclear weapons and some, such as Pakistan and India, remained largely hostile to one another. Employing techniques acquired from American or Soviet allies, terrorist groups scattered across the globe threatened to wreak havoc on cities and nation-states.

The attainment of security in the new, globally linked world of the 1990s proved elusive at best. Yet technological advances, including many linked to the computer age, held out the promise that some of humankind's ancient ills—famine, plague and ignorance—might be overcome. The world's peoples, thanks to the internet, air travel and television, appeared more bound together than ever before. Nevertheless, mass poverty, tremendous gaps between wealthy and poorer nations and epidemic diseases remained while new threats, such as bio-terrorism, loomed larger. Thus, both great potentialities and considerable dangers of a global cast surfaced as the new millennium opened.

CHAPTER 14

The End of the Soviet Empire, 1989–1991

Mikhail Sergeyevich Gorbachev had been honored as *Time* magazine's "Man of the Year" for 1987; now, the publication's January 1, 1990, issue proclaimed him as "Man of the Decade" for the 1980s. In 1988, *Time* had suggested that Gorbachev "could be the most dangerous adversary the U.S. and its allies have faced in decades—or the most constructive." Two years later, Lance Morrow, in an essay exploring *Time*'s "Man of the Decade," heralded the "hallucinatory" end of the Cold War and the transformation of communist states in the Soviet sphere. Its chief architect, Morrow suggested, was the Soviet "magician" who had carried out "a bloodless revolution, without the murderous, conspiratorial associations that the word has carried in the past." As for Gorbachev himself, Morrow proclaimed him "simultaneously the communist Pope and the Soviet Martin Luther, the apparatchik as Magellan and McLuhan." At the same time, Morrow delivered a warning that "the world has acquired simultaneously more freedom and more danger. . . . The potential for violence, and even for the disintegration of the Soviet order, is enormous."

In 1989, the final great empire did indeed begin to come apart, as the Soviet Union started to relinquish its hold on Eastern Europe. The following year, the USSR itself began to dissolve. Gorbachev, declining, in effect, to be the last czar, had adopted a twin-fold policy of *perestroika* and *glasnost* after becoming general secretary of Communist Party in 1985. He attempted to restructure the Soviet economy in order to lighten the deadening hand of bureaucracy; after being elected president of the USSR in 1989, he also sought to open up Soviet society in the political and cultural realms, to remove the vestiges of Leninist-Stalinist terrors. His efforts eventually endeared Gorbachev to the international community; after *Time* magazine's salute he became the recipient of the coveted Nobel Peace Prize in 1990. At the close of the following year, however, Gorbachev, by now a terribly unpopular figure in his homeland, was compelled to resign from his post.

Mikhail Gorbachev's parents were peasants who resided in the village of Privol'noye, located in the agrarian district of Stavropol in southwestern Russia. Born in 1931, the young Gorbachev saw his native community endure the collectivization campaign of the early 1930s, the Stalinist horrors of that decade (which affected his own family) and German occupation during World War II. A first-rate student, Gorbachev entered the Communist Youth League in 1946. While attending law school at Moscow State University, he married Raisa Titarenko, a philosophy student, in 1951; the following year, Gorbachev joined the Communist Party of the Soviet Union. In 1956, the young lawyer was named first secretary of the Communist Youth League for Stavropol, heading the collective farms. Quickly moving up in the party ranks, Gorbachev became a top party official in Stavropol. Boasting a recommendation from party General Secretary Leonid Brezhnev, Gorbachev in April 1970 was selected first secretary of the CPSU committee in Stavropol, a distinct honor for a relatively young party official. The next year, he was placed on the party's Central Committee.

Gorbachev soon possessed the support of both Mikhail Suslov, a top CPSU figure, and Yuri Andropov, head of the KGB. In late 1978, Gorbachev left for Moscow to become Central Committee secretary in charge of agriculture, an area where he long had sought to usher in reforms that would improve productivity and working conditions. The following year, he became a nonvoting member of the Politburo; in October 1980, he acquired the right to vote on the Communist Party's central committee. Increasingly, Gorbachev possessed greater authority regarding the party position on economics and ideology.

The old guard Soviet leadership soon began to pass from the scene, beginning with the death of Leonid Brezhnev in November 1982. His successor was Gorbachev's mentor Andropov, who lasted little more than a year in office before dying. The next premier, Konstantin Chernyenko, presided over the Soviet state only until March 1985. His death resulted in Gorbachev's appointment by the party hierarchy as general secretary. Attacking corruption and ineptitude, Gorbachev placed young allies in strategic government posts and began his campaign of economic reform. In 1986, Gorbachev initiated his programs of *perestroika,* calling for the dramatic rebuilding of Soviet society, and *glasnost*, urging greater openness. By the following January, Gorbachev's agenda included support for *demokratizatsiia* or the democratizing of the Soviet state. In 1987, the Central Committee advocated gradual movement toward a market economy. The next year, the committee supported the establishment of small private businesses and cooperatives.

In September 1988, Gorbachev was selected as chairman of the Supreme Soviet and began working to revise the constitution. At his urging, a Congress of People's Deputies, comprised of elected representatives, became the USSR's top legislative body. The Congress elected a new Supreme Soviet that chose Gorbachev as chairman in May 1989. The 15 republics that made up the USSR held additional elections in 1990; those elections weakened the hold of the CPSU. That same year, the Congress of People's Deputies, doing Gorbachev's bidding, removed the CPSU's political monopoly, enabling non-communist parties to thrive. Gorbachev, who was elected president of the Soviet state by the Congress, continued his campaigns of *perestroika, glasnost* and *demokratizatsiia*. The Soviet leader helped to usher in religious toleration, greater artistic and journalistic freedom and fewer restrictions on travel.

He also maintained his efforts to transform the Soviet Union's dealing with other nations. A series of summit meetings held with American presidents Ronald Reagan and George H. W. Bush effectively culminated with the end of the Cold War. In 1987, a decision was reached to eliminate land-based intermediate and short-range nuclear missiles. In 1991, the Strategic Arms Reduction Treaty was inked, calling for significant reductions in the number of nuclear arms held by both the United States

Fig. 14-1   Soviet leader Mikhail Gorbachev (on the left) with French premier Francois Mitterand, Rambouillet Castle, 1990. (Corbis/Bettmann)

and the communist state. Gorbachev also acted to pull out Soviet troops from Afghanistan, to improve relations with Israel and even to back the United States-guided campaign in early 1991 to attack Iraq following Saddam Hussein's invasion of Kuwait.

In perhaps the most astonishing turn of events, Gorbachev acceded to the tumult that was unfolding in Eastern Europe, allowing for the dismantling of communist regimes. In a reverse application of the old domino theory, communist governments, starting in 1989, began to crumble. The East German state fell apart, as symbolically represented by the tearing down of the Berlin Wall. In 1990, Gorbachev acceded to the reunification of Germany, something Soviet leaders previously had fervently opposed. Additionally, Soviet troops departed from Germany, Poland, Hungary and Czechoslovakia.

Notwithstanding the remarkable developments unfolding in Eastern Europe, Gorbachev remained determinedly opposed to the breakup of the Soviet Union. Gorbachev ordered Soviet military forces to rein in secessionist nationalists in Lithuania and other constituent republics. Repeatedly, however, the republics formed new governments that demanded independence. The Baltic states, Estonia, Latvia and Lithuania, and, most significantly, the Russian republic, whose parliament was led, beginning in May 1990, by Boris Yeltsin, a staunch critic of President Gorbachev, posed challenges. The potential dissolution of the Soviet Union clearly was disquieting not only to hard-line Communist Party officials but to Gorbachev himself.

◆ ——— ◆ ——— ◆ ——— ◆ ——— ◆

From Stalin to Khrushchev

For nearly half a century, following the end of World War II, the Soviet Union's status as a mighty power appeared unquestioned. The close of that calamitous conflict left the United States as the most potent nation on the face of the earth. Its only rival was the then badly battered USSR, which had suffered the violation of 1,000 square miles of its territory, the destruction of an estimated 1,700 towns and 17,000 villages, and the loss of 20–30 million of its inhabitants. Stalin's determination to downplay communist ideology proved invaluable, enabling Russians to rally around the flag in support of the motherland. The doggedness of the Red Army finally allowed for German forces on the eastern front to be pushed back. For over two years leading up to the surrender of Ger-

many in the spring of 1945, Russian soldiers helped to liberate large portions of Eastern Europe from German control. Gradually in some places, more rapidly elsewhere, Russian commissars and pro-Soviet communists throughout the region began to take over political, security and military apparatuses. Only Yugoslavia, which largely had been liberated by Partisan fighters headed by Joseph Tito, managed to avoid the placement of Soviet divisions; that, of course, enabled Tito, unlike other nationalist communists, to establish his own path to the "socialist" state during Stalin's reign. Albania, under its own strongman Enver Hoxha, did depart from the Soviet sphere eight years after Stalin's death in 1953.

The Cold War, which had followed on the heels of the communization of large parts of Eastern Europe and resulting angry British and American denunciations, had character-ized U.S.–Soviet relations throughout the final years of Stalin's reign. Charged rhetoric flew back and forth across the Atlantic, as both sides strove to construct spheres of in-fluence. Initially, the Soviets concentrated on the countries to their immediate west, but the USSR's breaking of the atomic monopoly in 1949 and Mao Zedong's takeover in China that same year transformed international af-fairs. Historians now contend that Stalin probably knew of North Korean leader Kim Il Sung's readiness to cross the 38th parallel in an effort to reunify Korea, a decision that resulted in a deadening stalemate for the United States.

The outbreak of worker riots in East Ger-many, Bulgaria and Czechoslovakia and addi-tional signs of unrest in the Soviet bloc soon followed Stalin's passing in early 1953. Nikita Khrushchev eventually won the struggle for power in the USSR and began talking about the availability of different paths to social-ism. A cultural thaw of sorts began to unfold, with somewhat greater intellectual freedom allowed. In Znamia, Il'ia Ehrenburg, winner of the Stalin Prize, wrote, "A writer cannot correct his heroes' lives in the way a sub-editor corrects proofs."

Then in February 1956, during a late-night speech before the Twentieth Party Congress, Khrushchev, himself a longtime Stalinist, denounced "the cult of the person-ality and its consequences" that long had flourished in the Soviet state. Khrushchev spoke of the thousands of party leaders who were caught up in the Moscow Trials of the 1930s, the blunders Stalin made that pro-duced such horrifically high casualty figures during World War II and the wholesale de-portations of entire groups of people that epitomized the reign of the self-professed "Man of Steel."

However, as the rehabilitation of count-less individuals occurred and others were being released from the GULAG concentra-tion camps, signs of new ferment unfolded in Eastern Europe. A drive to liberalize contin-ued in Poland through Wladyslaw Gomulka's "national communism," while a more radical movement was afoot in Hungary. Industrial workers, students and intellectuals agitated for greater change, which the Hungarian Communist Party under the new premier, Imre Nagy, seemed disposed to grant. Most troubling of all to members of the Soviet Politburo was the announcement that Hun-gary desired to become a neutral state in the Cold War fight. Soviet tanks rolled into Bu-dapest, street fighting resulted in thousands of deaths, and the Hungarian Revolution col-lapsed. Nagy himself eventually was taken to the Soviet Union, where he was executed on June 16, 1958.

Although Khrushchev's commitment to de-Stalinization thus proved incomplete, some-what more liberal policies continued to unfold in various Eastern Europe states, particularly Poland and, eventually, Czechoslovakia. Eco-nomic changes seemingly went hand-in-hand with political reform in various portions of the Soviet sphere. For a time, Khrushchev's efforts to reinvigorate the Soviet economy and spur technological advances appeared to be suc-ceeding. The Soviet national economy grew at a rapid rate during the 1950s, with advances in both the agricultural and industrial sectors. The Soviet launching of the Sputnik satellite in October 1957 suggested that the USSR was indeed capable of competing with the world's foremost power in a less bellicose fashion. Im-proved economic conditions and augmented social services also allowed for an improved standard of living for many Soviet citizens.

While the Twenty-First Party Congress focused on economic matters, the following one that gathered in 1961 saw Khrushchev attack Stalin more directly, blaming him, in effect, for the 1934 murder of Sergei Kirov; the assassination of the Leningrad party chief had helped to trigger the massive purge trials of the depression decade. Stalin's mummified corpse, which had been placed next to Lenin's in the Masoleum, was now moved to an unmarked grave, alongside the Kremlin wall. The Twenty-First Party Congress also predicted that the USSR would become the dominant economic power by the end of the decade; communism, moreover, it was foreseen, would be ushered in by 1980. To help ensure such developments, the further "democratization" of the Communist Party was encouraged. One statement urged "the active participation of all citizens in the administration of the state, in the management of economic and cultural development, in the improvement of the government apparatus, and in supervision over its activity."

Such moves, coupled with international events, however, planted the seeds for Khrushchev's political demise. From the mid-fifties onward, the new Soviet leader had, on the one hand, seemingly sought to carve out less hostile relations with his nation's sharpest competitor. At the same time, Khrushchev aggressively professed support for wars of national liberation. In November 1958, he demanded the reunification of Berlin under communist hands within six months. Worried about the exodus of two million of its citizens, including many professionals, Khrushchev applauded as forces of the German Democratic Republic in 1961 began constructing a barbed-wired barrier dividing East and West Berlin. The Berlin Wall was designed to stem the flow of refugees to the west and became a lasting symbol of the Cold War. The following year, Khrushchev was compelled to back down during the Cuban missile crisis. The discovery of Soviet missiles on the Caribbean island resulted in an American quarantine and the apparent dismantling of the weapons.

Other developments weakened Khrushchev's position within the top hierarchy of the Soviet Communist Party. Many blamed him for the Sino–Soviet rift, pointing to de-Stalinization, Khrushchev's professed belief in the possibility of different paths to socialism and his unwillingness to help China obtain the atomic bomb. The granting of massive amounts of foreign aid to countries such as India and Egypt proved increasingly unpopular in a time of growing food shortages and a faltering economy. Khrushchev was not helped by his inconsistent stance regarding greater cultural freedom, which included the condemnation of Boris Pasternak, the Nobel-Prize-winning author of *Doctor Zhivago*, and an anti-religious campaign that proved crippling for the Russian Orthodox Church. At the same time, the maddeningly inconsistent Soviet premier allowed for the publication in *Pravda* of Yevgenii A. Yevtushenko's controversial poem, "Stalin's Heirs," which urged "double or treble the guard at his grave lest his spirit escape;" Khrushchev similarly allowed for the release of Alexander Isaevich Solzhenistsyn's *A Day in the Life of Ivan Denisovitch*, which highlighted the Soviet GULAG or forced labor camps.

The state of the Soviet economy also proved troubling, for it sputtered markedly following the successes of the previous decade. Afflicted with inefficiency, waste and outmoded equipment, the economy experienced considerable amounts of unemployment, inflation and a growing black market. High defense expenditures, the deadening hand of bureaucracy and low labor productivity did not help. Even agricultural production, despite considerable increases, failed to keep up with increased demand. A severe drought in 1963 necessitated the importing of 12 million tons of grain. Khrushchev's preference for massive collective farms proved disastrous as well, with peasants continuing to lavish greater attention on their private plots.

Discontent emerged as the government raised prices for meat and butter in mid-1962; at this same point, laborers at the locomotive construction works in Novocherskassk experienced sharp wage cuts. Several thousand workers went out on strike and, for a time, successfully battled with the police and army troops sent into the area. When massive disorders unfolded, troops fired on rioters; some 24 died and another 39 were wounded.

The Novocherskassk affair remained isolated, although it served as a foreshadowing of things to come. More troubling for Khrushchev was the mounting opposition to his efforts to contest the power of both local party functionaries and Moscow *apparatchiki* (members of communist government organizations). While striving for decentralization, Khrushchev's reform effort resulted in massive corruption and fraudulent accounts of government practices.

As concerns about both domestic and foreign affairs mounted, a campaign to oust Khrushchev began to unfold. On October 14, 1964, the Central Committee, which condemned Khrushchev's impetuous and at times boorish behavior, voted unanimously to remove him from power. Granted a pension, Khrushchev remained in Moscow, where he began devising his memoirs. To his credit, Khrushchev had terminated Stalinist terrors, reined in the security police and released millions from labor camps. At the same time, party control arguably intensified under his reign; certainly, he never considered dismantling the communist system to which he had devoted his life. Later, Khrushchev indicated that he should have done more. He wrote, "My leadership was sometimes more administrative than creative. I was too concerned with restricting or prohibiting. I admit my responsibility for the years I was in power, but today I am opposed to this form of government. I would have opened all the doors and windows if I could."

Bureaucratic Communism and Dissidence

Old Guard Communist Party members now resumed control of the Soviet government. The fifty-eight-year-old Leonid Ilyich Brezhnev, named General Secretary of the Communist Party, declared that party officials would retain their posts for life, unless they committed blatant misdeeds. The former Minister of Light Industry, Alexei Kosygin, who became Chairman of the Council of Ministers or Premier of the Soviet state, was placed in charge of industrial production. Reform of the national economy was called for, Kosygin recognized, with growth rates reduced to 4–5 percent per year and poor-quality goods produced by Soviet manufacturers. Kosygin promised more consumer goods and light industry, while Brezhnev favored greater investments and more scientific agricultural methods. The new Soviet leaders also increased military spending. Heavy industry, which required long-term capital investment, was slighted. Regional economic councils that Khrushchev established were dismantled, as recentralization of authority took place.

For a time, as had been the case under Khrushchev, both the national economy and the lot of average Soviet citizens appeared to improve; surges in both oil and gold prices in the 1970s proved helpful. During the 1966–1970 period, for example, national income rose 5.9 percent, while the Gross National Product increased 5 percent; this was aided by a 7.6 percent growth in investment capital. Agriculture production was augmented by 21 percent. From 1967 to 1977, real wages increased by half, while prices rose only about 1 percent annually. Industrial workers continued to be paid better than peasants, while members of the scientific and technical intelligentsia received even higher wages; at the same time, under Brezhnev, those income differentials lessened. Indeed, certain skilled laborers, such as coal miners, could obtain wages considerably greater than professionals. The best paid could purchase dachas, summer houses with gardens situated in the countryside. The government provided annual vacations of 12–15 days along the coastal regions, increased the minimum wage and expanded social welfare programs. It also constructed millions of high-rise apartments in metropolitan areas, as Soviet families acquired durable consumer products. Urban areas attracted more and more young people, drawn by educational opportunities and magnified cultural possibilities.

The apparent good times, however, shielded grievous and eventually fatal flaws in the Soviet economy. True, administrative decrees mounted, with over 200,000 in force by the end of the 1970s. Yet bureaucratic edicts did little to further economic growth, often proving stifling by contrast. Inefficiencies and bottlenecks characterized the Soviets' "command economy," with its guaranteed market and established prices. Troubling too were lower rates of labor growth in an economy still dependent on manual work. Additionally, labor was maldistributed in industrial areas and in regions such as Central Asia. Turnover rates were quite high, reaching 25–30 percent, while laborers proved increasingly restive, as a series of strikes broke out. Rates of alcoholism, long a problem in Russian society, soared.

Not surprisingly, then, national income began foundering in the 1970s, reaching the level of only 2.1 percent in the first half of the following decade. The Soviet GNP dropped to 4 percent from 1970 to 1978, and plunged to 2 percent thereafter. The growth in investment capital fell to 3.4 percent from 1976 to 1980. The rate of increase of agricultural production declined during the 1970s, then fell to a mere 6 percent from 1981 to 1985; in this same period, farming on private plots proved remarkably productive. The rise in income levels was noteworthy, yet failed to demonstrate fully how many Soviet workers lived: they confronted unemployment, industrial accidents and sharp price bumps. For many, salaries were hardly the most important consideration; instead, the availability of bonuses, access to government-run shops and subsidized stores shaped living standards. Additionally, bribes often padded salaries and the Brezhnev years witnessed a surge in graft and corruption. Indeed, as the state economy foundered, the black market thrived. One scholar has suggested that as many as 20 million people worked in this underground economy that the vast bulk of citizens partook of.

Inefficiency and bureaucratic demands appeared ever-present. Consumer goods were often difficult to obtain. To obtain scarce goods required connections and, often, payments on the side. Party officials, ironically the leaders of a "communist" state, made the greatest use of privileges and perquisites to obtain the items or services they sought. These ranged from basic foodstuffs to consumer products to medical care. In the fashion of the "New Ruling Class" that the Yugoslav dissident Milovan Djilas denounced, Communist Party higher-ups acquired large, rent-free apartments, boasted fine dachas in the countryside and traveled extensively abroad.

As Stalinist-styled repression continued to lessen during the Brezhnev years (1964–1982), dissident movements began to emerge. Russian nationalists, supporting a return to hard-line policies, now voiced their opinions. So did non-Russian nationalists in the Ukraine, the Crimea, the Caucasus and the Baltic states. Unrest was present in the Muslim republics in Central Asia. More attention, however, initially was paid to religious dissenters and to those who favored socialism of a humane cast. Various Christian groups, including Baptists, Catholics and Jehovah's Witnesses, desired to practice their faith. Jews sought to leave the Soviet Union for Israel. Critics opposed the Soviet Union's invasion of Afghanistan in 1979 and particularly the bloody and inconclusive stalemate that followed.

Initially, social democratic intellectuals, including the physicist Andrei Sakharov and the historian Roy Medvedev, who urged a melding of socialism and democracy, received the greatest attention. Instrumental in the Soviets' development of the hydrogen bomb, Sakharov began, by the early 1960s, to protest openly against his own nation's atmospheric testing of nuclear weapons. He helped to lay the groundwork for the 1963 Nuclear Test-Ban Treaty. Through *Progress, Coexistence and Intellectual Freedom*, published abroad in 1968 and calling for democraticization of Soviet society, Sakharov became an internationally known human rights advocate. The following year, he joined with 14 other activists—they called themselves an "Action Group for the Defence of Human Rights"—in drafting a letter to the United Nations that referred to abuses in the Soviet Union.

During the 1970s, the dissident movement continued to prove increasingly more political than its predecessor, which had been characterized by literary *samizdat*, secret publications distributed in spite of government censorship. It also was considerably broader in scope, purportedly involving hundreds of thousands of adherents. Thanks to Sakharov and other leading dissenters who established the Moscow Human Rights Committee in late 1970, this movement was far better organized. The committee soon sought to afford legal advice to victims of Soviet repression. The dissidents continued their struggle, notwithstanding increased pressure by the KGB against supposed oppositionists. Sakharov's involvement in the human rights campaign led to his receipt of the 1975 Nobel Peace Prize.

Other repression of dissent characterized this period; the seeming greater potency of this movement resulted in an attempted government crackdown. Condemning the "hostile activities of Solzhenitsyn and Sakharov," among others, Yuri Andropov, head of the KGB, urged that the writer be placed on trial and the physicist be quarantined in Novosibirsk. Human rights activist Sergei Kovalev was charged with "especially dangerous crimes against the state" and given a lengthy prison sentence. Capital sentences, although far less frequently resorted to than under Stalin or even Khrushchev, were still issued. Political offenders generally were sent off first to prison camps and then into exile. Corporal punishment of prisoners lessened, but beatings and killings still occurred; anger over mistreatment had resulted in a series of hunger strikes in the Dubroviag in 1969.

Prisoners of conscience frequently were shipped off to rural areas and then stripped of Soviet citizenship. Among the most noteworthy of those political prisoners were the writers A. A. Amalrik, Josef Brodsky, Andrei D. Siniavsky, Vladimir E. Maksimov and Solzhenitsyn. Stripped of his citizenship, Solzhenitsyn was forced to leave the Soviet Union, while the KGB continued to target Sakharov. Eventually, the Politburo, which initially had declined to single out Sakharov due to his immense prestige, exiled him in 1980 to Gorky.

Different fates confronted other dissenters. Continuing a Stalinist practice of housing political prisoners in mental wards, the KGB relied on the diagnoses of supposed medical experts to warehouse those it considered dangerous to the state. The KGB operated some 11 "special psychiatric hospitals," where individuals were exposed to dangerous patients, unwanted drug treatment and general abuse. By 1977, the World Psychiatric Association blasted these developments, resulting in the Soviet Union's withdrawal from the organization.

Soviet Foreign Policy and Postwar Eastern Europe

The Soviet Union during Leonid Brezhnev's eighteen-year reign also confronted issues beyond the domestic front. Most significant, his tenure, until the last few years, witnessed movement toward détente and generally improved relationships with the United States. In 1972, Soviet and American leaders signed the Strategic Arms Limitations Treaty (SALT I), the Anti-Ballistic Missile Treaty (ABM) and the Basic Principles agreement. SALT I placed caps on the number of missile launchers available to the two

superpowers. With the Soviets unwilling to allow on-site inspections, however, the United States needed spy satellites to verify compliance with the treaty. The ABM Treaty, predicated on the theory of Mutual Assured Destruction that the great powers recognized nuclear war would result in shared devastation, sought to prevent either side from building fail-safe missile defense systems. The Basic Principles document called for exchanges involving trade, the environment, culture and technology.

The Soviet leadership's support for détente was linked to the continued clash with China; in the midst of the Cultural Revolution, Soviet and Chinese troops clashed along the border near the Amur River. That backing also was ensured, ironically enough, because the Soviet Union had achieved general nuclear parity with the United States by the end of the 1960s.

Later during the Brezhnev era, the Soviet Union seemingly proved less concerned about the response of the great Western power to its foreign escapades. Those included the expansion of Soviet operations in Africa, especially Yemen, Angola and Mozambique, and the entrance of Soviet troops into Afghanistan in late 1979. That latter development soiled relationships with the United States, with President Jimmy Carter moving to embargo certain trade with the Soviet Union and refusing to allow American athletes to compete in the 1980 Olympics held in Moscow. Tensions and rhetoric between the two sides escalated further when Ronald Reagan first occupied the White House; Reagan denounced the existence of what he termed "the Evil Empire" and insisted that the peoples under Soviet control yearned for their freedom.

It was clear by the early 1980s that many who resided in the Soviet bloc were indeed restless. The Politburo in Moscow remained determined to retain both the Warsaw Pact and the growing presence of Soviet forces in Afghanistan. There, as in both Czechoslovakia and Poland, the Politburo made decisions during the Breshnev era that sullied the image of socialism, even within the Soviet sphere. The thaw that Khrushchev ushered in had been offset by the crushing of the Hungarian Revolution in 1956. While a lightening of a repressive grip occurred for a time, in several Eastern European states, including Romania, Czechoslovakia and Poland, the threat of another Soviet invasion remained ever-constant.

From the end of World War II until February 1948, a rebirth of Czech democracy had occurred. In 1945, the Communist Party, in open elections, received nearly 40 percent of the vote, the largest total tabulated by any political organization. At the beginning of 1948, 27 percent fewer Czechs voted for the party. Shortly thereafter, a coup occurred, with communists taking control of the police and the military. Czech communism now proved highly dogmatic, arguably the most Stalinist throughout the region, surpassing even Albania's. The hard-line party leaders appeared immune to the Khrushchev revelations of 1956, with Antonin Novotny likening de-Stalinization with "weakness and yielding to the forces of reaction." Pressured by Khrushchev, Novotny in late 1962 finally agreed to reexamine purge trials of the immediate postwar era, including those with an anti-Semitic twist. Led by Alexander Dubcek of the Slovak Central Committee, a campaign was undertaken, which Novotny bitterly opposed, to rectify "distortions of socialist legacy" that had afflicted Czechoslovakia since the 1948 takeover. An attempted coup by Novotny failed in late 1967, enabling Dubcek to be selected as party first secretary.

The forty-six-year-old Dubcek had resided in the Soviet Union for 16 years altogether, most recently from 1955 to 1958 as a student at the Soviet Higher Party School in Moscow; earlier, he had dwelled in the USSR during the traumatic period of 1925 to 1938. Attempting to walk a fine line, Dubcek envisioned considerable reform within the existing communist system. Nevertheless, he spoke of the need for "socialism with a human face." With censorship lifted, public debate began to flourish, beginning in 1967, in the midst of the so-called "Prague Spring." Moves were undertaken to honor victims of communist repression. Among the most eloquent spokespersons calling for additional change was the playwright Vaclav Havel. In plays such as *The Garden Party* and *The Memorandum*, Havel had condemned totalitarianism.

Worried about the possibly contagious nature of the Czech experiment, Soviet leaders feared that anti-communist elements were influencing the Dubcek government. In late June, the Warsaw Pact undertook a large-scale military exercise on Czech soil; this included the first Soviet troops in Czechoslovakia since 1945. After Ludvik Vaculik produced a manifesto, "Two Thousands Words," on June 27, those forces failed to withdraw. The document roundly condemned the Communist Party's political monopoly and called for greater reform. Leonid I. Brezhnev soon insisted that "we cannot remain indifferent to the fate of socialism in another country." Condemnations of the Prague Spring poured forth from other Warsaw Pact states, except Romania. At the same time, his fellow reformers warned Dubcek not to slacken the pace of change.

New proposals to lessen the Communist Party's stranglehold on power further convinced the Soviets of the need for action. On August 20 and 21, troops from the Warsaw Pact rolled into Czechoslovakia. The Czechs responded with nonviolent civil disobedience, but the Prague Spring was effectively over. Dubcek was removed as party first secretary on April 17, 1969; the Czech reformer did manage to avoid the fate of Imre Nagy. The Soviets justified the *putsch*, claiming that the Brezhnev Doctrine allowed for such action whenever counterrevolution or the loss of party control was threatened.

The march into Czechoslovakia shattered more illusions. Vanished for many was any hope that an authentic socialist society could be constructed in the Soviet sphere. The latest developments there jolted the communist parties in Western Europe, which had been seeking to present more democratic faces. Quashed was any sense that the existing Soviet political hierarchy would allow for fundamental change. Yet repeated calls for protection of human rights demonstrated that Soviet wishes to turn the clock back proved only somewhat successful. Individuals such as Havel remained determined to continue the struggle to liberate their homeland. In an essay, "The Power of the Powerless," Havel insisted that lies sustained totalitarian states. An individual, consequently, must feel compelled to condemn such a regime. In the process, Havel wrote, "he rejects the ritual and breaks the rules of the game. He discovers once more his suppressed identity and dignity. He gives his freedom a concrete significance. His revolt is an attempt to *live within the truth*."

Poland's Wladyslaw Gomulka was among those discredited by their participation in the ousting of Alexander Dubcek's government.

Once viewed as something of a reformer himself, Gomulka had been ill-disposed toward "revisionism" virtually since he had replaced a Stalinist as chief of state in 1956. In the midst of student demonstrations in 1968, a slogan could be heard, "*Polska czeka na swego Dubczeka*": "Poland was awaiting a Dubcek of its own." Popular unrest mounted by December 1970, with workers in the Baltic port cities of Gdansk, Gdynia and Szczecin conducting strikes after the announcement of increased food prices. The increasingly discredited Gomulka was removed from power, purportedly the first occasion since World War II when a European leader had been ousted because of worker unrest.

The new party boss, Edward Gierek, rescinded the government action, but new demonstrations occurred in June 1976 when he increased basic food prices. In an important turn of events, workers and intellectuals, following an attempted government crackdown, responded by forming the Workers' Defense Committee, KOR (*Komitet Obrony Robotnikow*). Intended to afford legal counsel for persecuted workers and to publicize government actions, KOR called for democratic socialism, Polish nationalism and civil liberties. In 1978, workers from the shipyards established a Committee on Free Trade Unions for the Baltic Coast; one of those involved was the electrician Lech Walesa. He and many other Poles were heartened that October when Cardinal Karol Wojtyla, the archbishop of Krakow, was annointed Pope John Paul II. The following June, the new pope paid a nine-day visit to his homeland. Massive crowds turned out to greet the first Polish head of the Roman Catholic Church.

By 1980, the Communist Party in Poland was foundering badly. Little helping matters were the government's perceived failings: its incompetence, repressiveness and lack of popular support. In July, after the regime sought to boost food prices, whose cost had been kept down because of massive government subsidies, strikes spread throughout the nation. Once again, the coastal area at Gdansk drew considerable attention, as Walesa led 16,000 workers, who refused to return to work at the Lenin Shipyards. During negotiations with a government delegation, the workers insisted on "acceptance of Free Trade Unions independent of both the Party and the employers." The strikers named their organization Solidarity.

At the end of August, Walesa and government representatives signed a historic agreement. Price increases were scaled back and wages raised, but most important of all was the recognition afforded the workers' right to establish independent trade unions and to strike. No such independent labor movement had previously existed in a communist state. In addition, the government promised to allow the broadcasting of Sunday masses on state radio, to release political prisoners, to address economic ailments and to improve social services.

Over the course of the next sixteen months, approximately three-quarters of the nation's workforce joined Solidarity or an agrarian-based confederation. By contrast, the Communist Party increasingly appeared weakened, with hundreds of thousands of resignations submitted. The Kremlin dismissed a gathering of Solidarity representatives in September 1981 as amounting to an "anti-socialist and anti-Soviet orgy." The following month, General Wojciech Jaruzelski, the prime minister and defense minister, became head of the Communist Party. In mid-December, Jaruzelski proclaimed martial law, establishing the Military Council of National Salvation. Solidarity was banned and its leader arrested.

While Jaruzelski had possibly acted to stave off a Soviet invasion, which also might have been precluded by the earlier move into Afghanistan, his moves further discredited the Polish Communist Party. Many Poles now refused to consider the possibility of "socialism with a human face." Although weakened, Solidarity, for its part, remained in existence underground. In the middle of the decade, Jaruzelski lifted martial law, freed many political prisoners, and relaxed censorship. Hardliners within the party wanted more repressive action, as the assassination in October 1984 of Father Jerzy Popicluszko, a strong foe of the military government, evidenced. With the economy continuing to founder, an uneasy political climate remained in Poland.

The Reign of Mikhail Gorbachev

The quandaries in both Czechoslovakia and Poland eventually were resolved, at least to a considerable extent, by events in the Soviet Union. There too an economic crisis was mounting, while various groups appeared increasingly restive. The Brezhnev era closed on November 10, 1982, with the death of the Soviet head of state. Over the course of the next two-and-a-half years, first ex-KGB boss Yurii Andropov and then the *apparatchik* Konstantin Chernyenko served as leader of the Communist Party. Andropov sought to tackle the problems of widespread corruption and widespread alcohol abuse; furthermore, he removed countless functionaries in an effort to reenergize the Soviet nation. His death within 15 months after assuming office led to an even shorter reign by Chernyenko, whose appointment disturbed reformers.

They proved more content, at least for a time, when Mikhail Gorbachev became General Secretary on March 11, 1985. Gorbachev had been selected for a variety of reasons, including the fact that, in contrast to his predecessors, he was not a member of the Soviet gerontocracy. His intelligence, charm and ambition served him well too, as did the fact that he had been a loyal party official for three decades. Gorbachev and his top advisers recognized, above all else, that the stagnant nature of the Soviet economy had to be overcome. Andropov had begun a reexamination of Soviet economic policies, selecting two members of the Secretariat, Gorbachev and Nikolai Ryzhkov, to devise recommendations for reform. Recent worker unrest in Eastern Europe and the Soviet Union, the sociologist Tatiana Zaslavskaya had warned, indicated that alienation was becoming more widespread. There was hardly a dearth of reform proposals once Gorbachev became head of the Soviet Union, but he had to contend with the many party figures who remained strongly resistant to change.

Gorbachev moved quickly to replace a series of older party functionaries with younger, reform-minded individuals. Gorbachev's allies included Eduard Shevardnadze, who took over for Andrei Gromyko as Minister of Foreign Affairs, and Aleksandr Yakovlev, who became the new Soviet leader's top adviser and believed in the need for "new thinking" to take hold. Boris Yeltsin became party boss in Moscow, wielding a mandate to eradicate the corruption that had abounded in the capital.

Gorbachev sought to revitalize Soviet socialism. As he indicated, "If we learn to work better, be more honest and decent, then we shall create a truly socialist way of life." It soon became apparent that Gorbachev believed fundamental changes were necessary to sustain the socialist state. To effect such an end, along with economic reconstruction and reform, *perestroika*, Gorbachev called for openness, *glasnost;* and democratization, *demokratizatsiia*. He also reasoned that a thaw in Cold War relations must come about.

While many scholars contend that Gorbachev hardly envisioned the introduction of western-style democracy, he had recognized, even before coming to power, that sweeping changes were needed. Required was a diminution of the influence of the "command-administrative" bureaucracy that stunted economic growth. Also demanded was a larger commitment to democratization and greater involvement by workers in economic affairs. Scientific and technical progress was needed, along with improved living standards for the Soviet citizenry. In a fashion startlingly similar to the Yugoslav dissident Milovan Djilas, Gorbachev, in speaking before the Twenty-Seventh Congress of the Communist Party, acknowledged the existence of something akin to a new ruling class; Gorbachev repeatedly affirmed his determination that social justice be aspired to.

As the economy failed to respond adequately to early efforts at *perestroika*, Gorbachev became more firmly committed to political reform. Open debate, he came to determine, was required to challenge bureaucratic arteriosclerosis. Consequently, considerable measures of *glasnost* characterized his handling of political dissidents. After an extended period of exile in Gorky, Sakharov was released in 1986; within two years, he was permitted to travel overseas. Invitations were sent to the cinematographer A. A. Tarkovsky and the theatrical director Yurii P. Liubimov to return from exile. While Tarkovsky died before he was able to do so, his work became readily available in the Soviet Union. Also shown now was Tengiz Abuladze's *Repentance*, a sharp look at Stalinism.

Press censorship was lightened, while writings of the Stalinist era such as Anatolii Rybakov's *Children of the Arbat,* which had been banned for two decades, were now released. Novels by Pasternak, Zamiatin, George Orwell and Vladimir Nabokov also became available.

Some of the authentic history of the Soviet Union was unveiled. In early 1988, Gorbachev asserted that "there must be no forgotten names or blank spots" in examining past events. In what would have been considered an astonishing turn of events just a short while before, a rehabilitation or reevaluation occurred of figures like Nikolai Bukharin, Solzhenitsyn and Leon Trotsky. An excavation at Kuropaty produced the remains of approximately 30,000 victims of Stalinist horrors. Eventually, even the work of Lenin and Marx was called into question.

Perhaps not surprisingly, then, opposition voices began to be allowed within the party, a phenomenon soon repeated across much of the Soviet landscape. In mid-1988, Gorbachev orchestrated a party conference that urged "free dialogue, criticism, self-criticism and self-control." That gathering also saw Gorbachev attempt to reduce the party Secretariat while calling for an executive-oriented president to lead the Soviet state. In late November 1988, the Supreme Soviet voluntarily gave way to a new organization, the Congress of People's Deputies (CPD). During elections held the following March, several members of the Central Committee were defeated, while Sakharov, Roy Medvedev and Boris Yeltsin were elected. A clash ensued between Gorbachev and Yeltsin, with the latter nevertheless winning a spot on the Supreme Soviet; there, Yeltsin condemned party privileges and Gorbachev's policies. In March 1990, other party officials lost in a series of elections.

For a time, Gorbachev was able to hold on to power and, indeed, seemingly solidify his position. He was first elected head of state by the CPD, which later named him executive President, with considerably strengthened powers. He was authorized to appoint the Council of Ministers, to head the Defence Council and to negotiate with foreign states. Gorbachev signed decrees issued by the Supreme Soviet and received considerable authority to tackle economic problems and the issue of law and order. Eventually, a National Security Council, which featured military, police and KGB representatives, replaced the Presidential Council that Gorbachev selected.

Notwithstanding such institutional changes, economic and political difficulties abounded. The economy was stagnant through 1989, while budgetary deficits reached dangerous levels. Unemployment proved plentiful in various parts of Central Asia and the Caucasus. Shortages became more evident and rationing became commonplace. By 1990, it was apparent that Prime Minister Nikolai Ryzhkov's attempt to nurture a mixed economy had not succeeded. Eventually, Gorbachev and Yeltsin together sought to speed up the process of privatization. But as the economy plunged more precipitously, Gorbachev shifted course once again, in the face of opposition from party conservatives.

Gorbachev's own vacillations hardly helped matters. As late as December 1989, he referred to the Communist Party as a "consolidating and uniting force." However, various members of the Supreme Soviet, including Sakharov and Yeltsin, called for an opposition party. Gorbachev spurred the Central Committee to break the monopolistic hold of the Politburo. The amended Soviet constitution declared that the party only helped to run the country and acknowledged that it "does not lay claim to full governmental authority." Such moves pleased neither party conservatives nor reformers such as Yeltsin. To Gorbachev's dismay, the Communist Party of the Russian Federation met in mid-1990. The conservative Egor Ligachev insisted that Gorbachev relinquish his post as General Secretary.

Nevertheless, at the Twenty-Eighth Party Congress, Gorbachev was reelected as General Secretary. Gorbachev asked for support from "democratic, progressive forces dedicated to carrying through the democratization of society." His supporters also indicated that market forces would be emphasized more fully. No matter, Yeltsin and a number of prominent figures submitted their resignations from the Communist Party.

In the meantime, other problems mounted. Many Soviets were unhappy over both the explosion of a nuclear reactor in Chernobyl, located in the Ukraine, and the lack of information initially presented about the incident. A temperance campaign continued to develop, but its moderate successes were hardly matched by improvements in the economic arena, as had been anticipated. The emergence of *glasnost* resulted in a flood of new publications and films, which delivered critical analyses, in lesser or greater fashion, about the communist system. Longstanding fears of reprisals for voicing such perspectives began to lessen dramatically. On the other hand, stories began to be released indicating that crime, drug use and prostitution all were surging.

Diplomatic Breakthroughs

Increasingly, questions were raised about Gorbachev's foreign policy. True, the Soviet leader's determination to terminate the second Cold War helped to shape his reputation within the international community and among scholars. However, his efforts to reshape the Soviet Union began to be duplicated throughout Eastern Europe. Within a very short while, that led to the disintegration of the Soviet bloc, which in turn helped to bring about the collapse of the Soviet state.

In the end, like Khrushchev, another Soviet leader who attempted to reform the system, Gorbachev acquired lasting popularity abroad that he was unable to retain at home. Recognizing the weakened nature of the Soviet economy, Gorbachev determined that military spending must be reduced. That required something akin to détente with the United States, the Soviet Union's foremost adversary. It also demanded that the Communist power reduce its involvement in various conflicts outside Eastern Europe.

Relations between the Soviet Union and the United States underwent a dramatic transformation during the Gorbachev era. Gorbachev met with U.S. President Ronald Reagan for a summit in Geneva in November 1985. The two leaders issued a declaration calling for the halving of their nations' nuclear armaments. A stalemate ensued at the second summit held in Reykjavik the following October, with the Soviets expressing grave concerns about Reagan's proposed Strategic Defense Initiative. However, a third gathering in Washington in December 1987 resulted in a breakthrough: an agreement to eliminate intermediate-range and short-range nuclear missiles. For the first time, the two superpowers accepted on-site monitoring of nuclear facilities. In May and June of 1988, Gorbachev and Reagan met once again, this time in Moscow. There, they signed the Intermediate Range Nuclear

Treaty. In 1990 and 1991, Reagan's successor George Bush and Gorbachev signed additional arms control agreements, the Conventional Forces in Europe Treaty, which reduced conventional forces in Europe, and the START Treaty, which sharply curbed strategic arms. Then, in an astonishing turn of events, Gorbachev's government was part of an American-orchestrated coalition that attacked Iraq following Saddam Hussein's invasion of Kuwait.

In additional efforts to curb Cold War tensions and to stem economic hemorrhaging, Gorbachev opted for more conciliatory policies regarding other nations; he insisted that the peace dividend could be used to bolster economic development and living standards inside the Soviet Union. In 1988, Gorbachev declared that the USSR would remove its troops from Afghanistan within a year. The war, termed a "bleeding wound" by Gorbachev, took over 13,000 Soviet lives and concluded with little more than a stalemate. Gorbachev strove to improve economic relations with China and called for the removal of 200,000 Soviet troops from Asia. In September 1990, the Soviet Union, despite strong protest from North Korea, established diplomatic ties with South Korea. The USSR encouraged trade with South Korea, which envisioned making investments in the Soviet Union.

Eastern European Revolutions

Along with the withering of the latest version of the Cold War, Gorbachev's foreign policy, coupled with the example set by *perestroika* and *glasnost* at home, produced the greatest changes in Eastern Europe. Starting in 1987, Gorbachev began urging Eastern European leaders to undertake reform in their own countries. Speaking in Prague, the Soviet leader called for the Czechs to follow the Soviet lead: "Today a reliable yardstick of the seriousness of a ruling communist party is not only its attitude toward its own experience but its attitude toward the experience of friends." Beginning that year, Czechoslovakia, Poland, Hungary and Bulgaria initiated economic reforms. The German Democratic Republic and Romania, on the other hand, appeared intransigently opposed to the calls for reform. Gorbachev favored both transformed relations with the West and economic reform. Consequently, he applauded as several Eastern European states joined the International Monetary Fund and adopted the General Agreement on Tariffs and Trade (GATT), which sought to break down commercial barriers between nations.

In a seemingly striking rejection of the Brezhnev Doctrine, Gorbachev also insisted that nations had the right to self-determination. As he indicated, "The entire system of political relations between the socialist countries can and should be built unswervingly on a foundation of equality and mutual responsibility. No one has the right to claim a special position in the socialist world. The independence of each party, its responsibility to its people, the right to resolve questions of the country's development in a sovereign way—for us these are indisputable principles."

The stage was set for dramatic changes in the Eastern bloc. Eastern European leaders remained resistant, however, perhaps due to their own Stalinist heritage. Nevertheless, they began to fall like dominoes. In the spring of 1988, Hungary's Janos Kadar gave way to Karoly Grosz, who was termed the "Hungarian Gorbachev." Under Kadar, Hungary in the late 1960s had adopted a liberal economic program, referred to as "goulash communism." However, by the 1980s Hungary's economy was stagnant, like the Soviet Union's. Only months after Grosz came to power, larger transformations threatened to take hold in Hungary. In February 1989, the Communist Party allowed the reburial of Imre Nagy. The party also affirmed that the Hungarian Revolution of 1956 had been "a popular uprising against an oligarchy that was humiliating the nation." Disavowing the need for a party monopoly, Hungarian reformers ushered in a multi-party system. In May, the Hungarians moved to break apart the Iron Curtain that was perched on the border, dividing Hungary from the West. A few months later, an agreement was carved out to allow for opposition parties and the holding of free elections the following year. In October, the parliament declared that "the Hungarian Republic is an independent, democratic state based on the rule of law, in which the values of bourgeois democracy and democratic socialism are equally recognized." The Communist Party disbanded, renaming itself the Hungarian Socialist Party.

In 1988, a new wave of labor unrest reignited the Polish Solidarity movement headed by Lech Walesa. An inflationary rate of 60 percent, a $40 billion hard currency debt and worker demands for wage increases produced a series of protests and strikes. Negotiations were carried out between the Polish government of General Jaruzelski and Walesa, which ultimately led to the relegalization of Solidarity and movement toward political pluralism. An agreement was arrived at to hold parliamentary elections in which 35 percent of the lower house (Sejm) and all of the seats in the upper chamber would be contested. Walesa exulted, "This is the beginning of democracy and a free Poland." Those elections, held in June 1989, enabled the opposition to take all the contested Sejm seats and 99 of 100 Senate spots. By August,

Jaruzelski allowed Solidarity leader Tadeusz Mazowiecki, an attorney and editor, to become head of a coalition government. This was the first time that a non-Communist-headed government had been allowed in the Soviet bloc.

Events in Hungary and Poland affected the German Democratic Republic, one of the final Stalinist strongholds. In 1989, a number of East German tourists began pouring from Hungary into Austria, on their way to West Germany. Despite protests from the GDR government, which criticized the absence of "fraternal socialist solidarity," the Hungarian borders were opened up altogether by early September. The issue of the refugees perplexed the East German regime, which first allowed passage into the West and then attempted to halt it. Protests, along with sharp condemnations of communism, cropped up in several cities. In the midst of the turmoil, Gorbachev visited East Berlin in October to help commemorate the German Democratic Republic's fortieth anniversary. Cheered by protestors, Gorbachev appeared to give support to those who were calling for the ouster of Erich Honecker, the head of the East German Communist Party. By mid-October, 100,000 demonstrators gathered in the streets of Leipzig, an obvious repudiation of Honecker. Only days later, Honecker stepped down as Egon Krenz, a younger member of the East German politburo, took over.

Krenz attempted reforms, including the lightening of travel restrictions and the granting of amnesty to political prisoners. Nevertheless, protests continued to unfold, with hundreds of thousands of demonstrators appearing in both Leipzig and East Berlin. On November 9, Krenz tossed aside all restraints on travel and opened up the Berlin Wall. The impact of the collapse of the wall was profound, with opposition forces gaining confi-

Fig. 14-2   East German soldiers examining a hole in the Berlin Wall, following a demonstration at the Brandenburg Gate in Berlin, November 11, 1989. (Pearson Education, Corporate Digital Archive, AP/Wide World Photos)

dence and party stalwarts appearing increasingly dispirited. Subsequently, Gregor Gysi replaced Krenz as head-of-state and brought about the transformation of the East German Communist Party, which now proclaimed itself to be socialist. Free elections were promised but momentum built for the reunification of East and West Germany. That union occurred on October 3, 1990.

Bulgaria, long a hard-line Stalinist state, experienced its own revolution. Seventy-eight-year-old Todor Zhivkov had ruled Bulgaria since 1954 and had even attempted to join the Union of Soviet Socialist Republics in 1977. Beginning in the mid-1980s, how-

ever, Zhivkov sought to bring about a socialist "regenerative process." In reality, that effort largely involved the attempted assimilation or expulsion of Turks. By the summer of 1989, approximately 300,000 Turks had left Bulgaria. Condemned in the international press and confronting a surging opposition group, Eco-Glasnost, Zhivkov resigned as president on November 10. His replacement, fifty-three-year-old Petar Mladenov, goaded by a series of opposition groups, which formed the Union of Democratic Forces, strove to usher in a "gentle revolution." Following a demonstration by 50,000 on December 10, Mladenov promised to end the monopoly long held by the Communist Party and to hold free elections. Continued demonstrations indicated that many demanded quicker and more sweeping changes.

Pressured by the Soviet Union, the hardline regime of Gustav Husak in Czechoslovakia had initiated some reforms. In 1987, Milos Jakes took over as party leader. Jakes ushered in an experiment in economic decentralization, replacing Husak, who retained his post as president of Czechoslovakia. A degree of political liberalization also took hold, with the publication of previously banned works, including those of Franz Kafka. Again following Moscow's lead, the Czech government in December 1988 stopped blocking broadcasts from Radio Free Europe. Now allowed to resurface, Alexander Dubcek conducted a series of interviews with Western reporters.

The slackening of the repressive yoke in Czechoslovakia, as elsewhere in Eastern Europe during this period, aroused demands for greater reforms. Underground publications flourished, along with independent associations, while large-scale demonstrations cropped up. A top figure in the human rights organization, Charter 77, declared, "Gorbachev has opened up a new climate here. He is destroying the old atmosphere of fear." A prison sentence meted out in early 1989 to Vaclav Havel, a Charter 77 leader, produced great outcry and international condemnation. The government felt compelled to parole him. The regime backfired once again in November when the police roughed up a number of demonstrators in central Prague. Havel and other activists formed the Civic Forum, which spearheaded protests and called for both Jakes and Husak to resign.

The demonstrations in Prague became ever larger, further weakening the government's position. In Wenceslas Square on November 24, a crowd of 350,000 applauded Havel and Dubcek; the Communist Party leaders resigned en masse. As a general strike unfolded, the regime promised to shape a coalition government, hold the first democratic elections in Czechoslovakia in over four decades and lift travel barriers to the West. On December 29, Dubcek was selected President of the Federal Assembly, while Havel was elected to head the Czech Republic. Along with Havel, who exulted in the fact that the transformation had come swiftly, many Czechs cheered the triumph of the "velvet revolution." The Civic Forum and Public Against Violence in Slovakia crushed the communists at the polls the following June.

Yet another revolution broke out in Romania, which Nicolae Ceausescu had ruled with a red fist since 1965. Cultivating Romanian nationalism, Ceausescu had adopted an independent stance in foreign affairs, declining to participate in the 1968 smashing of the Prague Spring. He also had refused to allow Warsaw Pact games to be conducted on Romanian soil or to back the Soviets in their confrontation with Mao's China. Relations with the Soviet Union worsened following Romania's refusal to accept *perestroika*. At the same time, Ceausescu remained a staunch Stalinist determined to quash any potential dissent; no group similar to Czechoslovakia's Charter 77 emerged to contest his one-man rule. Indeed, a cult of Ceausescu continued to evolve, with the Romanian strongman referred to as the "genius of the Carpathians" and "the shepherd and savior of the nation; its most beloved son."

However, by December 1989, Ceausescu was the last of the Stalinist leaders still in power in Eastern Europe. Ceausescu's downfall came quickly and ended violently. On December 15, members of Ceausescu's secret police, the Securitate, attempted to arrest Laszlo Tokes, a Protestant cleric, who had condemned the repression suffered by two million ethnic Hungarians. A clash ensued in the town of Timisoara, followed by a large protest gathering two days later. When Securitate forces killed several hundred demonstrators, the resulting outrage caused the revolt to spread. Ceausescu blamed hooligans and "fascist reactionary groups" for the unrest. An inebriated Ceausescu then delivered a public address at the Palace Square in Bucharest; protestors began to cry out, "Ceausescu is a dictator." Military officials ignored his attempts to declare martial law, while many army units began battling the Securitate. Ceausescu and his wife Elena were captured while seeking to escape by helicopter. On December 25, a military court, after accusing the Ceausescus of genocide, issued death sentences, which were carried out on the spot.

A provisional government, headed by the newly formed National Salvation Front, took power. It was comprised of reform communists and opponents of Ceausescu, including Ion Iliescu, earlier a member of the Communist Party Central Committee. The new government called for ushering in democracy and democratic elections in 1990. Gorbachev's government responded with a declaration that "the will of the Romanian people" had been served. However, questions remained about the new government's commitment to reform. The May 1990 elections demonstrated that such concerns were not misplaced. Fraud and intimidation characterized the elections, while Iliescu called in coal miners and former Securitate forces to beat students who had been holding sit-ins at Bucharest's University and to harass opposition parties and newspapers. Still, an independent Students' Union appeared, along with critical print journalism.

The Disintegration of the USSR

The revolutions in Eastern Europe, which developments in the Soviet Union influenced, in turn helped to bring about the demise of that superpower. This involved a series of events that Gorbachev clearly had not foreseen or desired, as evidenced by a pronouncement he delivered after the Twenty-Seventh Party Congress in February 1986: "The national question, a legacy of the past, has been successfully solved in the Soviet Union." Gorbachev himself soon indicated that "Soviet patriotism" would enable the USSR to "further strengthen the Union and Brotherhood of free peoples in a free country." By February 1988, however, Gorbachev was forced to admit that the "nationalities question" was "the most fundamental, vital (one) . . . of our society."

The revolutions that were triggered in 1989 stoked the fires of nationalism in the USSR, which saw five republics issue declarations of independence or sovereignty by early 1990. In June, the Russian Parliamentary and its president Boris Yeltsin declared that the Russian Federation was a sovereign state. By the close of the summer, 13 of the 15 republics in the USSR had proclaimed their independence. Gorbachev had encouraged the discarding of Stalinist regimes in Eastern Europe and had refused to send in Soviet tanks when Eastern bloc countries began to break away from communism. He sought, however, to draw the line when it came to his own nation; this involved, Gorbachev asserted, "a last stand" to hold together "a multinational nation." That effort proved, ultimately, to be unsuccessful and resulted in his loss of power.

By 1989, the forces of nationalism had grown in strength in several Soviet republics. Early in the year in Moldavia, a separatist movement appeared. That state had been swallowed up by the Soviet Union after the signing of the infamous Nazi–Soviet Pact of August 1939 that led to the rape of Eastern Europe. Once Ceausescu fell, Moldavians no longer proved reluctant to insist on the need to link up with the new Romania. Already simmering unrest in the Trans-Caucasusian republics of Armenia, Azerbaidzhan and Georgia similarly threatened to ignite. Mass demonstrations supporting independence appeared by February 1989. The killing of female protestors in Tbilisi in April fueled the fires of Georgian nationalism.

Ferment brewed in the Baltic republics of Estonia, Latvia and Lithuania. Sovereign nations during the interwar years, those states had been taken over by the Soviet Union in 1940. Now, nationalists called for "re-sovereignisation," which Gorbachev opposed, fearing that other republics would follow their lead. Top opposition forces, including the Lithuanian Sajudis and the Estonian and Latvian popular fronts that sought market developments and multiparty systems, declined to talk about wholesale independence. Sensing that new relationships had to be carved out, the Supreme Soviet in July afforded economic autonomy to the Baltic states.

The next month, however, on the fiftieth anniversary of the Nazi–Soviet Pact, massive demonstrations took place in Estonia, Latvia and Lithuania. Viewed as a collective "Freedom Chain," the ring of protests linked Tallinn, Riga and Vilnius, the Baltic capitals. As if to ward off the possibility of Soviet intervention, Popular Front leaders insisted, "The time when military force can solve everything has long since passed. Tanks are not only an immoral argument, they are no longer omnipotent. The main thing is that such a turn of events could once and for all put the Soviet Union back into the ranks of the most backward of totalitarian states." *Pravda* decried the nationalism that could threaten the Soviet Union's hold on the constituent republics. The Soviet Politburo demanded that party leaders in the Baltic states curb "extremism and separatism."

The demands for decolonization quickened in late 1989 and 1990. Tensions were in no way lessened by the acknowledgment of the Supreme Soviet regarding the illegitimacy of the 1939 pact. In December 1989, the Lithuanian Communist Party proclaimed its independence from the CPSU. As a crisis loomed, the Lithuanian Supreme Soviet agreed to allow for a multi-party system. In January 1990, Gorbachev met with Lithuanian party leaders but failed to stem the separatist movement. The next month, the CPSU, proclaiming the need for *demokratizatsia*, allowed for non-communist parties to appear in the Soviet Union.

Such a move hardly diminished the demands within the various republics for autonomy. The massacre of over 150 Azeri nationalists in Baku in January 1990 and similar events further aggravated matters. Elections in March produced substantial majorities for secessionists in the Baltic states and Moldavia. Lithuania, Estonia and Latvia declared their independence from the Soviet Union. An unhappy Gorbachev deemed the proclamations illegal, while Soviet forces remained stationed in the Baltics. Clashes involving Soviet troops occurred in Lithuania and Latvia, which led to Boris Yeltsin's condemnation of Gorbachev and an appeal for UN sanctions.

In the spring of 1991, the Baltic states resoundingly voted for independence.

Russian autonomy had been proclaimed the previous May. The Russian Congress had declared that its laws superseded Soviet ones, while Yeltsin indicated that a multiparty government would be established. A draft of the Russian constitution failed to refer to socialism or the USSR. By early 1991, moves were afoot to elect a president of the Russian Federation. In June, Yeltsin captured 57 percent of the votes; his support was strongest in the cities, but weaker in the countryside where the communists remained influential.

In July 1990, nationalists, spearheaded by the Popular Front movement Rukh, proclaimed Ukranian independence. Communists had linked up with nationalists. In March 1991, a referendum saw 80 percent of

Map 14-1   Contemporary Russia

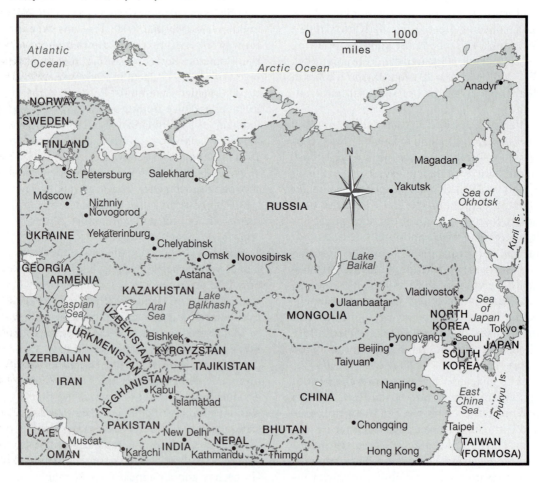

the Ukranians back a call for a "union of soviet sovereign states based on the declaration of sovereignty."

Greater turbulence took hold in the Caucasus, with ethnic rivalries, particularly those involving Armenians, proliferating. Hostilities in Nagorno-Karabakh in Azerbaijan led to a mass exodus by Armenians to Armenia and by Azeris to Azerbaijan. When the Soviet Union in January 1990 returned control of Nagorno-Karabakh to Azerbaijan, a massacre of Armenians ensued. Soviet troops, sent in to stem the unrest, killed or wounded hundreds in Baku. Leaders in Azerbaijan threatened to secede from the USSR, while Nagorno-Karabakh and the nearby Shaumian *oblast* (an administrative territorial division in the USSR) proclaimed themselves to be free of Azeri control.

After Levon Ter-Petrosian triumphed in the presidential election in August 1990, his Armenian government considered the possibility of breaking away from the Soviet Union. Armed militias appeared to battle Soviet forces. Both Armenians and Azeris claimed that the Soviets were backing the other side.

A nationalist movement, centered around opposition to massive hydroelectric development, also cropped up in Georgia by late 1988. Early the following year, demonstrators were heard calling for Georgian independence. The Tbilisi tragedy in April proved more catalytic still, with a Georgian commission insisting that a "planned mass massacre" had occurred. Elections in October 1990 led to a victory by the Round Table-Free Georgia Alliance, which Zviad Gamsakhurdia guided, resulting in a loss of power by the Communist Party. Yet Georgia too was rent by divisions, with the autonomous republic of Abkhazia, which contained about one-sixth of the population of Georgia, calling for secession and a place as a republic inside the Russian Federation. In addition, South Ossetia declared itself a republic in September 1990, resulting in a clash with Georgians. Russian President Yeltsin and Gamsakhurdia worked together to reestablish order. In a referendum in late March 1991, 99 percent of the voters demanded Georgian independence.

The 1991 Coup and Boris Yeltsin

The disintegration of the Soviet Union spelled the political demise of Mikhail Gorbachev. Heightened unrest in Eastern Europe and the Soviet republics, coupled with a deteriorating economic and political situation in the Soviet Union, made Gorbachev's hold on power tenuous by 1991. Events in Eastern Europe distressed party conservatives and the military. Ethnic conflicts continued to intensify, along with demands for independence. The CPSU itself was divided between conservatives, reformers and radicals.

Increasingly, various elements in the CPSU, the military, the police and the KGB, who soon proclaimed themselves the State Committee for the State of Emergency, determined that a coup was demanded; former Foreign Minister Shevardnadze had warned Gorbachev back in December 1990 that such a development was possible. Hard-liners were distressed about the impending signing of the new Union Treaty that would have transferred authority to the republics. On August 18, 1991, coup leaders demanded that Gorbachev resign but he refused. The next day, tanks rolled into Moscow but inexplicably reformers including Yeltsin, Russian Republic Prime Minister Aleksandr Rtskoi, Supreme Soviet Chairman Ruslan Khasbulatov and Leningrad mayor Anatoly Sobchak were not arrested. Moreover, little force was directed against demonstrators who gathered at the White House, which housed the Russian republican government. Demanding Gorbachev's return as president, Yeltsin called for a general strike and claimed sovereignty for the Russian Federation. By August 21, the coup attempt had collapsed.

While Gorbachev was temporarily returned to power, his reign and the continued existence of the Soviet Union became shakier still. A month after the August coup, Latvia, Lithuania and Estonia asserted their formal independence. In November, Yeltsin banned the Communist Party in Russia. On December 1, Ukraine, through a referendum, overwhelmingly asserted its independence, while a week later, Russia, Ukraine and Belorussia, in their "Minsk Declaration, declared that the Commonwealth of Independent States had replaced Gorbachev's regime. Eleven republics signed the manifesto, but Estonia, Latvia, Lithuania and Georgia proved unwilling to do so. On December 31, 1991, Gorbachev, in the face of the demise of the once-mighty Soviet empire, resigned. After nearly three-quarters of a century, the effort to create a communist state had disintegrated.

◆ —— ◆ —— ◆ —— ◆ —— ◆ —— ◆ —— ◆ —— ◆ —— ◆ —— ◆

David Remnick of the *New York Times* referred to it as "the most stunning display of dissatisfaction with Communist Party rule since the founding of the Soviet state." Dozens of party regulars were routed in elections to the Congress of People's Deputies of the USSR held in March 1989; the unopposed party chief in Leningrad was among those who were denied seats in the new congress. During the open campaigning, Boris Yeltsin, a former member of the Politburo who had fallen out of favor with Party leaders, including his one-time mentor Mikhail Gorbachev, captured the imagination of many Soviet citizens. Yeltsin called for far more than Gorbachev had intended: "It is time to open the question of the multiparty system to wider discussion." The elections were the first in the history of the Soviet Union where candidates had been allowed to compete in parliamentary elections.

Yeltsin, who had run afoul of both conservatives and Premier Gorbachev and been ousted from the Politburo, captured 89 percent of the vote in a Moscow district. The victorious Yeltsin declared, "The *apparat* wouldn't give me my rehabilitation, but the people did." In the same vein, historian Roy Medvedev, who was himself involved in a runoff for a legislative seat, asserted, "The *apparat* is surely weaker today, and it is all a very sobering day for the Communist Party and for {Soviet President} Mikhail Gorbachev." As for Yeltsin, strikes and public outcries were threatened if he were not placed on the Supreme Soviet; the seat was granted to him. Significantly, Yeltsin had triumphed by running as an ardent reformer, who condemned party corruption and the privileges of the new ruling class that Djilas had vilified. Not all were happy about the turn of events, as some viewed Yeltsin as a demagogue, while others worried about his purported autocratic makeup. Others were more pleased, including members of the

Fig. 14-3 Russian President Boris Yeltsin. (Pearson Education, Corporate Digital Archive, AP/World Photos)

grassroots *neformal'nye* (informal) movement who had reached out to Yeltsin before the election. In the period ahead, Yeltsin became even more of a thorn in the side of the Communist Party, eventually challenging Gorbachev's hold on power.

Gorbachev's departure left the gregarious and hard-drinking Yeltsin as the most powerful political figure in the former Soviet Union. Yeltsin was born in 1931 in Butko, a village located in Sverdlovsk in the Ural Mountains region. His family, comprised of relatively well-off peasant farmers, suffered through Stalin's collectivization campaign during the 1930s. Raised in Butko and the industrial town of Berezniki, Yeltsin watched as his father Ignaty, who had been accused of sabotaging state property, was compelled to toil at a labor camp for three years. Not surprisingly, the Yeltsins were impoverished throughout World War II. In 1955, Yeltsin graduated as a construction engineer from the Urals Polytechnic Institute. For the next 13 years, he worked in the construction industry, which enabled him to support his wife Naina and their two daughters.

In 1961, Yeltsin became a member of the CPSU; seven years later, he was placed on the party's *oblast* committee, becoming its secretary in 1975. The following November, General Secretary Brezhnev named Yeltsin the first secretary of the Sverdlovsk District Central Committee. By 1981, Yeltsin was sitting on the CPSU's Central Committee. Following Gorbachev's ascension to power in 1985, Yeltsin was appointed secretary of the Central Committee for construction. In November, he was chosen first secretary of the Moscow City Party Committee. Within three months, Yeltsin was a nonvoting member of the Politburo. Viewed as a liberal reformer, Yeltsin cultivated relationships with newly formed grassroots political organizations. He had developed a reputation for battling both party perquisites and corruption.

By 1987, the increasingly popular Yeltsin was clashing with Gorbachev; Yeltsin considered *perestroika* to be moving too slowly, while his dismissal of "half measures" angered Gorbachev. Removed from both his Moscow post and the Politburo, an ailing Yeltsin was compelled to acknowledge his "errors" in criticizing the central government. Making skillful use of the media, Yeltsin staged a political comeback in 1989, as frustration mounted regarding the pace of Gorbachev's economic and political reforms. In early 1989, Yeltsin, with nearly 90 percent of the vote, was picked to represent Moscow in the Congress of People Deputies. In the congress, Yeltsin aligned himself with radical reformers such as Sakharov. In March 1990, Yeltsin won a seat in the deputies' congress of the Russian Soviet Federated Socialist Republic. In late May, he narrowly was elected congress chairman.

Yeltsin next moved to sever his relationship with the CPSU, which he recognized was becoming increasingly unpopular. Resigning his membership, Yeltsin demanded that economic and social reforms be speeded up; going a step further, he claimed that Gorbachev and conservative forces inside the CPSU were preventing needed reforms from taking place. Increasingly, Yeltsin steered the Russian republic toward a breakaway from the Soviet Union. In March 1991, a referendum provided for the direct election of a Russian president. On June 1991, Yeltsin routed five other candidates, as he garnered almost 60 percent of the vote. This provided Yeltsin with an aura of legitimacy matched by no other figure, including Gorbachev, inside the USSR.

Continuing to position himself deftly and exuding great personal courage, Yeltsin helped to thwart the August Coup by communist hard-liners. Yeltsin's stature soared following an incident when he got on top of a T-72 tank, derided the perpetrators of the coup and urged the Russian populace to resist the attempted takeover. Gorbachev, by contrast, appeared indecisive and incapable of responding firmly to the Emergency Committee that had spearheaded the coup. As a power vacuum ensued, Yeltsin's reputation only continued to grow. Wielding his power and stature as the democratically elected president of the Russian Republic, Yeltsin issued decrees that augmented his control and stymied Gorbachev's efforts to rebound. On December 8, Yeltsin joined with the heads of the republics of Ukraine and Belarus to proclaim the death of the Soviet Union. In its stead, they created the Commonwealth of Independent States. The USSR effectively had come to an end, with the Russian Republic the most powerful state to emerge from its ashes. Yeltsin was the leader of that newly independent republic, which possessed a vast array of nuclear arms and retained a seat in the United Nations.

◆ —— ◆ —— ◆ —— ◆ —— ◆ —— ◆ —— ◆ —— ◆ —— ◆ —— ◆

Suggested Readings

BANAC, IVO, Ed. *Eastern Europe in Revolution.* (1992).

BROWN, ARCHIE. *The Gorbachev Factor.* (1995).

COLEMAN, FRED. *The Decline and Fall of the Soviet Empire: Forty Years that Shook the World, from Stalin to Yeltsin.* (1996).

FOWKES, BEN. *The Post-Communist Era: Change and Continuity in Eastern Europe.* (1999).

FREEZE, GEOFFREY L., Ed. *Russia: A History.* (1997).

GARTHOFF, RAYMOND L. *The Great Transition: American-Soviet Relations and the End of the Cold War.* (1994).

GORBACHEV, MIKHAIL. *Memoirs.* (1996).

GRACHEV, ANDREI. *Final Days: The Inside Story of the Collapse of the Soviet Union.* (1995).

KEEP, JOHN. *Last of the Empires: A History of the Soviet Union 1945–1991.* (1995).

MARLOCK, JACK F., JR. *Autopsy of an Empire: The American Ambassador's Account of the Collapse of the Soviet Union.* (1995).

MASON, DAVID S. *Revolution in East-Central Europe: The Rise and Fall of Communism and the Cold War.* (1992).

NOVE, ALEX. *An Economic History of the USSR.* (1992).

PEARSON, RAYMOND. *The Rise and Fall of the Soviet Empire.* (1998).

REMNICK, DAVID. *Lenin's Tomb: The Last Days of the Soviet Empire.* (1993).

ROBERTS, J. M. *A History of Europe.* (1997).

ROTHSCHILD, JOSEPH. *Return to Diversity: A Political History of East Central Europe Since World War II.* (1993).

STOKES, GAIL. *The Walls Came Tumbling Down: The Collapse of Communism in Eastern Europe.* (1994).

SUNY, RONALD GREGOR. *The Revenge of the Past: Nationalism, Revolution, and the Collapse of the Soviet Union.* (1993).

TOMPSON, WILLIAM J. *Khrushchev: A Political Life.* (1995).

YELTSIN, BORIS. *Against the Grain: An Autobiography.* (1990).

ZIEGLER, CHARLES E. *The History of Russia.* (1999).

CHAPTER 15

The Search for a New World Order: New Issues and Challenges, 1989–Present

The Kenyan Wangari Wuta Maathai co-founded the Green Belt Movement on World Environmental Day, June 5, 1977. Concerned about the issue of "economic degradation" and the disfranchisement of the masses, Maathai "realized that to break the cycle, one has to start with a positive step." The creation of the Green Belt Movement was intended to do precisely that. As Maathai explained, "It is a movement to empower people, to raise their consciousness, to give them hope, to give them a feeling that they can do something for themselves that does not require much money, does not require much technology or information. The power to change their environment is within them and within their own capacities." To begin, the original participants—all women—in the Green Belt Movement planted seven trees. A decade-and-a-half later, over 10 million trees had been planted.

The movement, as Maathai saw it, would also help to empower women in Kenya, who averaged eight children. At the time, they lacked firewood, fruits to prevent their children from being afflicted with malnutrition and clean drinking water untainted by pesticides and herbicides. In contrast to their earlier experiences, these women declared that "their families are now weak, cannot resist diseases, and that their bodies are impoverished because of an environment that is degraded."

"Poverty and need have a very close relationship with a degraded environment," Maathai observed. "It's a vicious cycle." Writing in *The Green Belt Movement,* she indicated, "Land is one of the most important resources of Kenya and all of Africa. Its fertile topsoil ought to be considered a valuable resource—especially since it is so difficult to create. . . . Losing topsoil should be compared to losing territories to an invading enemy."

Born in Nyeri, Kenya, in 1940, Maathai traveled away from her native Kenyan lands to study biological sciences in the United States on a scholarship. After acquiring both a bachelor's and a master's degree, Maathai returned home to continue her studies at the University of Nairobi, where she obtained a doctorate. The university's first

Fig. 15-1   Wangari Maathai, Kenyan environmentalist and women's rights advocate. (Corbis/Bettmann)

female senior lecturer, she eventually became an associate professor and then Chair of the Department of Veterinary Anatomy. Her husband was a member of the Kenyan Parliament, and the two had three children. In the midst of her husband's initial campaign, Maathai reached out to the poor. "I decided to create jobs for them—cleaning their constituency, planting trees and shrubs, cleaning homes of the richer people in the communities, and getting paid for most services." Her marriage disintegrated, resulting in a contested divorce. Seeking a seat of her own in Parliament, Maathai was denied the opportunity to run; still more tellingly, she was dismissed from her university post.

Increasingly, Maathai devoted her energies to the operations of the National Council of Women of Kenya. Operating through the Council, Maathai determined to plant trees to safeguard the environment, increase rural development and improve women's standing in Kenyan society. Several hundred tree nurseries, supported by 2,000–3,000 women, appeared by the early 1980s. Approximately 2,000 public green belts were devised; more than 500,000 children participated in the projects, while thousands of farmers planted woodlots of their own. By 1986, the Green Belt Movement had spread throughout many other African countries, including Tanzania, Ethiopia and Zimbabwe. Maathai explained her program:

> Suppressed, poverty-stricken, and hungry people do not plan their families, and they are not concerned with environmental conservation, even though they are the first victims of environmental degradation. They do not take their destiny into their own hands. . . . Africans have survived for millions of years. Isn't it ironic that this 'primitive,' technologically backward group survived all these years, only to be threatened after they were discovered by 'civilized' groups? There must be some old wisdom which needs rediscovering. . . . Africans need to go back to their roots with a new awareness and confidence and rediscover our old wisdom. We need to draw from our past experience and build on it. But we can only do this if we have the courage to rediscover ourselves and to liberate our minds from centuries of indoctrination.

By the end of the 1980s, Maathai's crusade made her both revered and controversial inside her native Kenya. She had been granted the Right Livelihood Award, referred to as the "alternative Nobel Prize;" the Better World Society Award; the United Nations' Environmental Program Global 500 prize for protecting the environment; the Windstar Award for her environmental activism; and the Africa Award. However, in 1989, she challenged Kenyan President Daniel arap Moi's call for the construction of a sixty-story skyscraper in the center of Nairobi's most expansive park. Security forces grilled Maathi, members of Parliament denounced her and the government-controlled press discussed her sexual history. The government removed the Green Belt Movement from its headquarters, while President Moi declared that Maathai and other activists "have insects in their heads."

While Moi aborted the government's plan for the Nairobi skyscraper, repression in Kenya escalated. He banned opposition parties and journals. Some dissidents became political prisoners. Pressure from the World Bank compelled Moi to announce in late 1991 that an opposition party, Forum for the Restoration of Democracy (FORD), would be allowed. Maathai soon became involved in a campaign orchestrated by mothers of political prisoners who sought to garner attention for the treatment of their children. When government forces attacked a tent holding hunger strikers, they beat Maathai senseless. Government officials urged that Maathai's genitals be mutilated so that she would act "like women should."

After receiving word of an impending military coup that Moi planned, FORD leaders, including Maathai, denounced the government in a public press conference in 1993. Following a siege that lasted three days, 150 policemen stormed into Maathai's house and arrested her. As she recalled, "I felt as a rabbit must feel when the dogs catch up with it." Maathai was accused of "spreading malicious rumors." Although suffering from arthritis and heart disease, Maathai was denied medical treatment and thrown into a cold, barren cell. Eventually, the charges against her were dismissed.

In September 1995, Maathai delivered an address at the behest of the Commission of Global Governance. The Commission had recently released a report, *Our Global Neighbourhood,* reinforcing the interconnectedness of the world's peoples. The report, Maathai noted, called "for putting women at the centre of global governance. It emphasizes that gender sensitivity must be introduced into the conceptual, decisionmaking, and operational stages of all multilateral and government agencies." Maathai discussed the issues all of humankind confronted: "the globalization of the economy; increasing impoverishment and marginalization of millions of people, especially women; militarization and the growing trade in small arms and land mines; fear and the culture of violence which is exemplified by racism, xenophobia; and rising ethnic nationalism; and the degradation of the environment due to population pressure, overconsumption, and pollution." Maathai spoke of the need for "peoples' movements" to remain vital and involved in the quest to ensure "respect for basic human rights, justice, equality and equity, nonviolence, caring, and integrity." Five years later, Maathai was referring to the need to both continue and expand the horizons of the Green Belt Movement. As for herself, Maathai declared, " I see myself moving to new areas all the time being the peacemaker."

◆ —— ◆ —— ◆ —— ◆ —— ◆

Approaching the Millennium

As the final decade of the twentieth century unfolded, a disintegration of the old bipolar dualities of the Cold War took place. A new millennium appeared unlikely to usher in peace, justice and security for the world's burgeoning population of over six billion inhabitants, however. Instead, ancient antipathies were revisited, and some of a most recent vintage were kindled, as sophisticated technologies threatened planetary survival. Still, such developments hardly went unchallenged as groups and individuals such as Wangari Wuta Maathai ushered in new relationships between people, economic processes and the eco-system. New scientific and technological findings also afforded the means to diminish chasms of a national, regional and ethnic variety.

Nevertheless, reputable scientists pointed to the likelihood of global warming, the so-called greenhouse effect and the depletion of the ozone layer, an unintended by-product of chlorofluorocarbons. They also noted that AIDS, which had infected over 34 million people worldwide by 1999, was a veritable new plague, while new strains of tuberculosis and diphtheria emerged. Others dismissed such talk as amounting to fear-mongering and hysteria. The same kind of clash surrounded the purported impact of globalization of the economy, which some welcomed as a means to elevate living standards and to eradicate the last remnants of state-directed economic orders. Not all agreed, with critics pointing to the destruction of the rain forests and indigenous populations in Brazilian jungles and other previously isolated spots.

Chroniclers of the era will record that the proponents of fundamentalism and particularism continued to do battle with the advocates of a more universalist approach. Longstanding empires and nation-states crumbled, with simmering hatreds sometimes violently erupting in their wake, producing millions of casualties and recalling the horrors of the darkest days of the 20th century. The same kind of confrontation occurred outside the political or national realm; self-appointed shepherds of the world's fragile ecosystem skirmished with their nations' political representatives and corporate leaders from massive multinational enterprises over apportioning resources and protecting the very environment that all depended on.

With the collapse of the Soviet Union and communist states in Eastern Europe, many analysts contended that such conflicts would be determined by market developments now certain to prevail. Yet the impact of market-shock tactics from the 1960s onward hardly justified the celebration of laissez-faire economic practices that had led to the creation of welfare states earlier in the century. The evident hope of some, in economically advanced countries such as the United States, that conservative economic policies would now have free rein, hardly appeared justified. Social-welfare proponents and even backers of a democratic brand of socialism continued to garner support throughout the globe, and, by the end of the 1990s, were acting as heads of state or leading opposition elements on virtually every continent. Advocates of government programs pointed to the widening, not the lessening, of chasms that separated the rich and the poor, even in more affluent nations.

All seemed to agree on one point: technology in the form of nuclear weapons and other weapons of mass destruction endangered the very existence of the world's population. Nuclear proliferation, long feared, indeed had come about, with an untold number of nation-states, including some unstable ones, possessing such devices. Global militarization threatened regional, even world peace and prevented vital resources from being used for more productive purposes. Some saw additional dangers originating from technology in other, more subtle manners. Mass communications spread across the planet Earth, thanks to videocameras, personal computers, internet access, and around-the-clock news coverage flowing from sources such as the Cable News Network (CNN).

Still, that very occurrence both frightened some and emboldened others in their belief that national, regional and ethnic boundaries might soon be surmounted. There was some supposition that dictatorships could not survive the news coverage and mass communications link-ups that allowed for seemingly instantaneous transmission of information. Yet while dictators and dictatorships were toppled throughout the 1990s, some held on and others emerged. Indeed, the question remained whether a golden media age would occur or whether Orwellian employment of mass media could allow for manipulating national audiences, even in democratic states. The Gulf War in 1991 suggested all kinds of possibilities, but demonstrated that this latest media war hardly prevented wholesale devastation or government-crafted stories later proven to be fabricated. At the same time, the response to repeated images of slaughtered and suffering populations suggested that viewers could prove little troubled by such horrors. On the other hand, the response to assassinations of public figures indicated that many remained moved by the kinds of violent acts that befell Yitzhak Rabin and Rajiv Gandhi.

Media coverage at least offered the chance that a concern for human rights, so often horrifically violated over the course of the 20th century, would remain at the forefront of national and international concerns. At the very least, globally based communication devices ensured that a transnational quality had been added to the mix, so to speak. Someone, somewhere, was likely to hear of human rights abuses, although it remained unknown to what effect.

The issue of human rights stood at the forefront of international considerations during the 1990s. For many, the shielding of human rights had become vitally necessary in the wake of the terrors of World War I, the aggressive militarism of the 1930s and the horrors of World War II; all had demonstrated the full dimensions of man's inhumanity to his fellow man. The opening up of Hitler's

death camps offered a particularly striking warning of the depths to which individuals, groups and entire societies could sink. On December 5, 1948, the General Assembly of the United Nations adopted a Declaration of Human Rights. Fundamental liberties and human rights, the document proclaimed, were required, regardless of whether race, gender, ethnicity or religion was involved. The Eastern bloc countries, led by the Soviet Union, along with Saudia Arabia and South Africa, refused to support the resolution. In ensuing decades, additional measures, such as a condemnation of genocide in 1951 and an attack on apartheid a quarter-century later, were forthcoming from the international community.

Throughout the Cold War, both East and West leveled accusations of human rights violations. Communist regimes charged that right-wing states and forces, particularly in Third World lands, abridged elementary rights, while Western governments blasted various Politburos for justifying abuses where Marxist-Leninist ideals held sway. Concerns about human rights hardly lessened following the collapse of communist governments in Eastern Europe, the disintegration of the Soviet Union and the turn to market economies by China and Vietnam. Even with the spread of political democracy by the close of the century, many continued pointing to human rights abuses around the globe.

Western Europe in the Late Cold War Era and Beyond

The end of the Cold War greatly influenced the course of events on the European continent, where it had begun nearly a half-

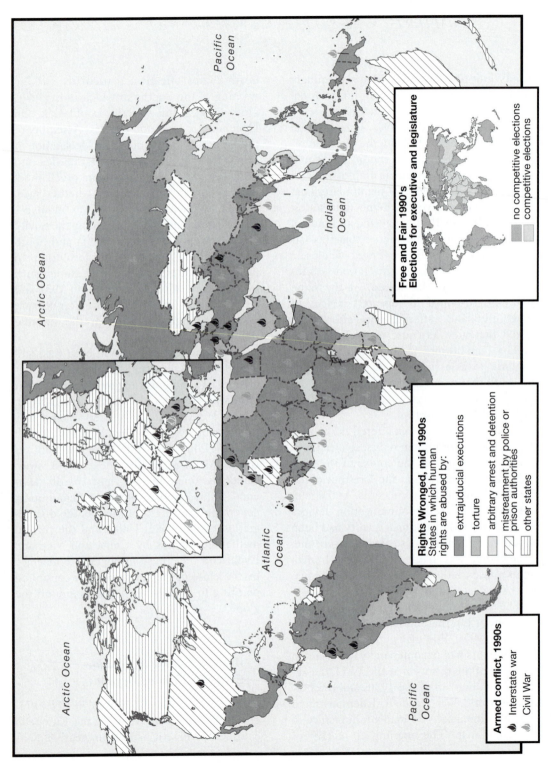

Rights Wronged, mid 1990s
States in which human rights are abused by:

- extrajudicial executions
- torture
- arbitrary arrest and detention
- mistreatment by police or prison authorities
- other states

Armed conflict, 1990s

- Interstate war
- Civil War

Free and Fair 1990's
Elections for executive and legislature

- no competitive elections
- competitive elections

Arctic Ocean

Pacific Ocean

Indian Ocean

Atlantic Ocean

Arctic Ocean

Pacific Ocean

Map 15-1 Human Rights

century earlier. Ironically, its passing resulted in the greatest amount of bloodletting in Europe since the close of World War II. On a less catastrophic front, talk abounded about welfare state excesses and the need for free market policies. As the 1990s neared an end, however, electoral results hardly demonstrated universal support for conservative solutions or the demise of either liberal solutions or the democratic left.

In Great Britain, Margaret Thatcher had served longer than any other British prime minister during the 20th century, in office from 1979–1990. Her heightened criticisms of the European Community, haughty manner and imposition of a poll tax led to a challenge from within the Conservative Party. Fearing that electoral defeat loomed ahead, Thatcher resigned, to be replaced by then little-known John Major. The new prime minister appeared friendlier to Europe, abolished the poll tax and supported the Citizens' Charter that safeguarded individual rights. At the same time, he continued Thatcher's privatization campaign. A surprise victor in the 1992 general election, Major faced dissension within his own party's ranks, largely regarding the possibility of European financial and political union. Major triumphed once again in 1995, aided by an improving economy and the beginning of peace talks involving Northern Ireland. Nevertheless, a mere two years later, Tony Blair and the Labor Party routed Major and the Conservative Party, thanks to financial and sexual scandals.

Forty-three-year-old Blair, the youngest British prime minister of the 20th century, had pushed for Labor's abandonment of Clause Four, which called for sweeping nationalization of economic sectors. "The Blair project" also involved attempts to lessen his party's identification with organized labor

and public projects, to reach out to business operators and the middle class and to avoid the use of the word "socialism" in public pronouncements. At the same time, Blair desired to strengthen educational standards in British schools, to improve the national health and social security systems and to help produce more representative governments for Scotland, Wales and London. Blair's stepped-up involvement regarding a peace accord in Northern Ireland led to the Good Friday Agreement of April 1998, which called for a return to home rule, establishment of a legislative assembly and protection of minority rights. Dissidents associated with the Irish Republican Army, seeking to sabotage the accord, continued to engage in terrorist acts. Blair also improved relationships with Europe and formed a close alliance with the American president Bill Clinton.

In France, Francois Maurice Marie Mitterand achieved the lengthiest tenure of any president in the nation's history, serving from 1981 to 1995. Mitterand joined in the American-led alliance against Saddam Hussein during the Gulf War and backed the North Atlantic Treaty Organization. While concerned about German reunification, he favored improved relations between France and Germany. A strong proponent of European unity, Mitterand supported the Maastricht Treaty in 1992 and helped to ensure its passage in a French referendum. The treaty, initially agreed to in 1991, called for a single European market, along with complete economic and monetary union, by the end of the decade. All nationals from participating nations, other than those from the United Kingdom, were accorded citizenship in the European Union. Various labor practices and social benefits were also agreed to. Political setbacks, marked by a center-right coalition prevailing in the 1993 legislative elections, and financial scandals marred the last half of Mitterand's second term in office.

Former prime minister Jacques Chirac, long-time mayor of Paris and head of the Conservative Party, succeeded Mitterand in office. Beginning in the summer of 1995, Islamic fundamentalists displeased with France's backing of the Algerian government purportedly carried out a wave of terrorist strikes in France. Other controversies unfolded over sharp welfare cuts and France's conducting of nuclear tests in the south Pacific and a series of public protests followed. Chirac called for new national elections that resulted in the selection of Lionel Jospin, the Socialist Party's unsuccessful candidate for the presidency in 1995, as prime minister.

German Chancellor Helmut Kohl was a stronger backer of the Euro, a single currency for European states, which was supposed to help ensure a more united Europe. Another long-running head of state, Kohl served as chancellor of West Germany from 1982 to 1990 and as chancellor of Germany from 1990 to 1998. The role he played in bringing about reunification on August 23, 1990, of West Germany and East Germany, two bastions of the Cold War era, magnified Kohl's stature. In 1994, the last Russian, British and French troops departed from German soil. As the decade unfolded, however, Germany paid a heavy economic price for reunification, experiencing a good deal of discontent. Kohl's popularity suffered from austerity programs he initiated in preparation for his country's adoption of the Euro. As Germany experienced its highest levels of unemployment since the Great Depression, Kohl lost the 1998 national elections to the Social Democratic Party candidate, Gerhard Schröder.

Kohl's reputation further plummeted as allegations of financial improprieties followed his term in office.

A New Order in Eastern Europe and Russia

While Germany undertook reunification, other European countries experienced fragmentation after the Cold War ended. One of the heroes of the cultural and political resistance against communist oppression, Czechoslovakia's Vaclav Havel, proved unable to prevent the breakup of his nation-state. Under Havel, Czechoslovakia, like Poland and Hungary, sought to join the EC but also attempted to avoid the pain engendered by market developments. Havel also confronted the issue of nationality that afflicted both Slovaks and Czechs. His failure to do so successfully led to his resignation as president of Czechoslovakia. At the end of 1992, an agreement was made to split the nation into the Czech Republic, which was soon headed by Havel, and Slovakia. Rapid privatization unfolded in the Czech Republic, resulting in a cooling down of the economy; Slovakia featured a less developed economy.

Democratic practices initially appeared to prevail in several other former communist states. In 1990, a noncommunist government emerged in Hungary, while in Poland, Lech Walesa was elected president. Hungarian nationalism temporily threatened relationship with Slovakia, Serbia and Romania, all of which possessed large numbers of ethnic Hungarians. By 1993, however, it appeared that moderates were prevailing. Worsening inflation and unemployment resulted in Walesa's defeat in the 1995 elections. Al-

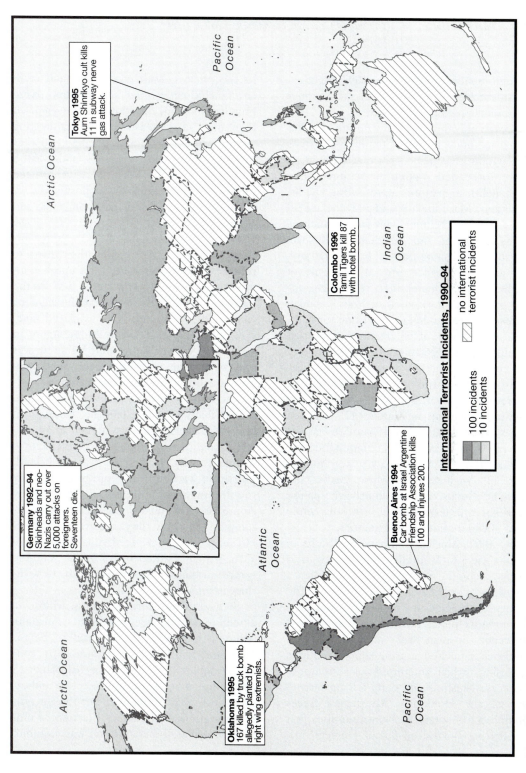

Tokyo 1995
Aum Shinrikyo cult kills
11 in subway nerve
gas attack.

Colombo 1996
Tamil Tigers kill 87
with hotel bomb.

Germany 1992–94
Skinheads and neo-
Nazis carry out over
5,000 attacks on
foreigners.
Seventeen die.

Buenos Aires 1994
Car bomb at Israel Argentine
Friendship Association kills
100 and injures 200.

Oklahoma 1995
167 killed by truck bomb
allegedly planted by
right wing extremists.

Arctic Ocean

Pacific
Ocean

Indian
Ocean

Atlantic
Ocean

Arctic Ocean

Pacific
Ocean

International Terrorist Incidents, 1990–94

no international
terrorist incidents

100 incidents
10 incidents

Map 15-2 Armed Conflict

though Solidarity won the 1997 election, President Aleksander Kwasniewski, a former communist, prevailed in 2000.

Less happy developments unfolded in Yugoslavia, following the Communist Party's declaration in January 1990 that its hold on power had ended. A political vacuum ensued that political parties representing Serbs, Croatians, Macedonians and Sloveneians all sought to fill. National minorities, such as Serbs in Croatia and Albanians in Kosovo, began to claim autonomy. The federal government in Belgrade proved incapable of dealing with the increasingly restless regions and groups, while figures such as Slobodan Milosevic acted to heighten ethnic tensions. Milosevic spoke of a greater Serbia that would include Serbian minorities in some of the new states that had emerged in the wake of Yugoslavia's disintegration. Serbia desired to reestablish control over Kosovo, while fighting broke out in March 1991 between Serbs and Croats. That June, Croatia and Slovenia asserted their independence; Bosnia-Herzegovina, with its mixed population of Muslims, Orthodox Serbs and Catholic Croats, did so shortly thereafter. Moslems and Serbs battled in Bosnia, while fears of wider ethnic clashes mounted.

By 1992, Moslems, Croats and Serbs in Bosnia vied for supremacy in villages and towns, including Sarajevo, which endured a lengthy siege that was televised around the globe. All three groups proceeded to slaughter minority populations in their spheres of influence. Bosnian Serbs under Milosevic's guidance launched a campaign of "ethnic cleansing," which amounted to an attempt to eradicate Muslims and conjured up memories of the Holocaust. Milosevic's forces promised to liberate Serbian minorities that dwelled in Croatia and Bosnia-Herzegovina.

In the process, both combatants and civilians, including women and children, were brutalized. Concentration camps housed thousands of increasingly skeletal-looking victims. Tens of thousands died, another three million became refugees, and a half a million fled to the West. Massive refugee camps sprang up in Croatia, Bosnia-Herzegovina, Serbia, Montenegro, Slovenia and Macedonia.

While a few European states, notably Germany, responded by opening their doors to refugees, the response of the European community as a whole was meager at best. As the massacre of Muslims in Bosnia-Herzegovina continued, the United Nations placed sanctions on Serbia and its ally Montenegro. In 1994, NATO troops prepared for air strikes against Bosnian Serbs; those air raids, however, proved largely ineffective. Acting in solidarity, European countries and the United States finally moved to halt the atrocities. In late 1995, a cease-fire was agreed to and international peacekeeping units were sent to maintain order. Under the Dayton Accord, purported war criminals were to be tried by the International Tribunal at The Hague. Approximately 60,000 NATO troops attempted to uphold the peace accord. Milosevic subsequently targeted Albanians in Kosovo, which resulted in a NATO bombing campaign that compelled the Serbs to withdraw in mid-1999.

In a surprising turn of events, Milosevic agreed to hold presidential elections in 2000. Milosevic's toughest foe proved to be his long-time critic, Vojislav Kostunica, a constitutional lawyer backed by a coalition of 15 opposition parties. By all objective indicators, Kostunica triumphed, but the government-controlled Federal Election Commission declared that a run-off was required.

Hundreds of thousands of demonstrators began congregating in Belgrade, demanding Milosevic's resignation. A general strike followed, while the police refused to fire on protestors in Kolubara. Eventually, even the state newspaper and television station declared support for Kostunica. On October 6, Milsosevic relinquished power, leaving Kostunica with the task of holding together diverse political groups, preventing Montenegro from seceding and dealing with Albanians in Kosovo who remained under international control.

Similar disarray characterized the former Soviet Union. Russia remained the most potent force in the newly formed Commonwealth of Independent States. It was headed throughout most of the decade by Boris Yeltsin, a former Communist and one-time Gorbachev ally, who had helped to bring about Gorbachev's fall from power. Beginning in January 1992, Yeltsin initiated an economic program that sought to unleash the free market and remove state control. As he did so, Russia confronted inflation, increasing unemployment, sharp drops in wage and national income levels and rampant crime. Yeltsin also had to placate the 21 non-Russian republics, where some 27,000,000 Russians dwelled, and the 20 autonomous Russian republics inside the Russian federation, 18 of which signed a treaty in 1992.

The following year, a new constitution, narrowly approved by a less than fully enfranchised electorate, was devised. Critics denounced Yeltsin's heavy-handed treatment of foes of the constitution as undemocratic, similar to his earlier disbanding of the Russian Communist Party. Such actions, coupled with the failure to bring about economic recovery, produced increased opposition to his rule. Opponents included former communists, right-wingers, nationalists and reformers displeased with Yeltsin's antics and his failure to deliver on his promises. Like Gorbachev, ironically enough, Yeltsin retained considerable support from Western leaders, particularly German Chancellor Kohl.

Beginning in December 1994, Yeltsin contended with an insurrection in the Russian republic of Chechnya. Within a year, Russian troops killed thousands of civilians in Chechnya, Russian planes and tanks pummeled the capital city of Grosny and the Chechens began taking hostages.

While the communists did well in parliamentary elections in December 1995, Yeltsin defeated his communist foe in the presidential election in July 1996. In a stunning development the following month, Chechen rebels retook Grosny. A peace agreement enabled the last Russian troops to depart from Chechnya in January 1997.

Yeltsin's international reputation continued to soar, although the Russian economy tottered toward bankruptcy. In May 1997, he agreed to improve relations with NATO and refused to oppose the entrance of former Warsaw Pact nations into the military alliance. On a less happy note, Russia defaulted on its foreign debt in August 1998. The next year, Russian military units were attempting to quash Islamic fighters in Dagestan, a struggle that moved into Chechnya. Apparently overwhelmed, an ailing Yeltsin resigned from the Russian presidency on December 31, 1999. Under his replacement Vladimir Putin, Russian forces again took control of Grosny. In March 2000, Putin won the presidential election.

As the new century opened, Russia, although the greatest force in the Commonwealth of Independent States, was hardly the power that the Soviet Union of the Cold War era had been. Economically troubled, facing a variety of deep-seated social problems, including pervasive crime, widespread alcoholism, unemployment, inflation and prostitution, Russia also no longer boasted the military might its predecessor had. While the Soviet Union at one point had five million soldiers under arms, the Russian military now contained only slightly more than one million. Draft evasion and desertions soared, while ships and planes lacked fuel and basic maintenance. Fears continued to take hold, as they had since the collapse of the USSR, that nuclear weapons might fall into the hands of terrorists or unstable states.

The Only Superpower

With the dissolving of the Soviet Union, by the early 1990s the United States stood as the lone superpower. George H. W. Bush, the first president of the decade, headed a cabinet most noted for its foreign policy enterprises, including a military assault into Panama that resulted in the capture and arrest of President Manuel Noriega, accused of spearheading drug-running operations. In early 1991, Bush, a World War II-torpedo-bomber pilot, helped to piece together a coalition that brought together the United States, the Soviet Union, Israel and several Middle Eastern states to attack Iraq's Saddam Hussein. The Iraqi strongman had recently invaded oil-rich Kuwait, sparking fears of another oil embargo. The United States was equally concerned that Hussein was stockpiling chemical agents that might be directed against Israel. In a lightening-fast war, Hussein was pushed out of Kuwait while his own country was pummeled, but he held onto power.

Bush's seeming inattention to domestic concerns, as exemplified by the economic downturn that the United States experienced during his tenure, helped make him a one-term president and brought about the election in 1992 of Arkansas governor Bill Clinton, who had deliberately avoided military service during the Vietnam War. Only the second Democratic Party candidate elected to the presidency since 1964, Clinton proved to be a dynamic and at times charismatic political figure. Tall and charming, Clinton promised to be a "New Democrat," less enamored with expansive government operations and the welfare state. After an early failed effort to bring about universal health coverage, which his wife Hillary guided, Clinton battled with Congress, particularly when it was dominated by the likes of the controversial Republican Speaker of the House Newt Gingrich. Selecting the most diverse cabinet in American history, Clinton supported the removal of various welfare protections in place since the mid-1930s, backed free trade policies that organized labor disliked and sent U.S. troops into Haiti, Somalia and the former Yugoslavia in efforts to restore order. During his second term, Clinton endured impeachment proceedings following a sexual scandal that came close to felling him. Clinton's approval ratings remained high notwithstanding sharp-edged attacks from the Republican Party and the national media alike, thanks in large part to a booming economy that saw some 22 million new jobs created under his watch. The stock market, greatly aided by telecommunications, personal computers and other industries associated with advanced technology, flourished. The United States, experiencing heady times, appeared at least to some to be as preeminent as it had threatened to become when World War II ended.

At the same time, the United States hardly proved immune to the scourge of terrorism that had so long afflicted many other nations. In 1993, radical Islamic fundamentalists bombed the World Trade Center in New York City, resulting in several fatalities. Two years later, right-wing extremists set off a truck bomb outside the headquarters of a federal building in Oklahoma City; 169 died as a consequence. Then, on September 11, 2001, both the World Trade Center and the Pentagon were targeted, with terrorists turning commercial airliners into fuel-filled guided missiles. The mammoth twin towers that made up the World Trade Center collapsed, resulting in the loss of nearly 3000 lives. Once again, Islamic extremists were blamed, with most attention directed at a wealthy Saudi Arabian exile, Osama bin Laden, who had become the leading financial backer of the hard-line fundamentalist Taliban regime in Afghanistan. There, bin Laden operated a series of terrorist camps, headed by his al Qaeda network, which vilified Western society altogether.

Democracy, Development and Human Rights in Latin America

As it had throughout much of the Cold War era, Latin America continued to experience great strife. The end of the 1980s witnessed the waning of the kinds of military regimes that had flourished since Fidel Castro came to power in Cuba. However, the region remained afflicted with severe maldistribution of wealth and unsteady economic development. Brazilian president Fernando Collor de Mello's monetarist policies proved disastrous, as inflation approached 1,600 percent in 1991. Charges of corruption resulted in his impeachment by the Chamber of Deputies and Mello's resignation in 1992. Under his successor, Itamar Franco, inflation actually worsened, nearing 2,500 percent in 1993. Finance Minister Fernando Henrique Cardoso, an early academic proponent of the dependency theory, shaped a new anti-inflation program that proved more successful. It enabled Cardoso, once viewed as a left-wing senator, to receive the backing of conservative forces when he successfully ran for the presidency in 1994. Cardoso's government was compelled to undertake more austerity programs.

Economic pressures similarly dominated Argentine politics. The 1980s had concluded with prices soaring and per capita income having dropped 25 percent during the decade. The Peronist candidate, Carlos Sául Menem, had captured the 1989 presidential election. Menem took office six months ahead of schedule after the resignation of Raul Alfonsin, who had proclaimed a state of siege due to deteriorating economic circumstances. With the country confronting an annual inflation rate of 1,800 percent, Menem adopted a stringent economic program that resulted in a lifting of price controls, the cutting of export and import taxes and the encouragement of foreign trade. Menem also effectively allowed for the confiscation of middle-class savings. As inflation plummeted, the government conducted an ambitious program to privatize government-owned companies, including those controlling the national telephone system and the national airlines. Economics minister Domino Carvallo oversaw greater privatization. Inflation virtually disappeared and annual economic growth approached six percent, resulting in talk of an Argentine "economic miracle." Unfortunately, unemployment rates nearly doubled, triggering labor unrest. Menem faced other dilemmas, including the military's demands for pardons pertaining to the "dirty war." His applauding of the military's role in that affair produced a public outcry from human rights proponents. In late October 1999, Fernando de la Rúa, the mayor of Buenos Aires, was elected president of Argentina.

Human rights considerations, along with economic concerns, were at the forefront of national debate in Chile throughout the 1990s. Many Chileans demanded a reconsideration of the recently retired Pinochet regime and the coup that had enabled the general to take power. The Christian Democrat Patricio Aylwin, who promised to rekindle his country's democracy, examine human rights abuses and improve the plight of the poor, had won the 1989 presidential election. At the same time, Aylwin planned to continue building on the supposed economic successes of the Pinochet era, through the encouragement of exports, foreign investment and the privatization of the economy. The same coalition backed the *Concertacion*, which had enabled Aylwin to take power. Eduardo Frei, whose father had preceded Salvador Allende as Chile's president, won the 1993 presidential election.

A seemingly strong economic order strengthened Chilean democratic practices, which enabled Ricardo Lagos to win the 2000 presidential race; Lagos thus became the second socialist to be elected president of Chile. A 62-year-old attorney and economist, Lagos promised to seek a consensus from the Chilean people. One member of Parliament, Isabel Allende, the daughter of the former president, was heard to say, "I can't help feeling greatly moved. This is a great democratic moment which brings back memories of when my father became president in November 1970." Lagos confronted various obstacles in his attempt to revitalize Chilean democracy, including the role played by the military and other supporters of former dictator Pinochet, who had been arrested in London in October 1998 and charged by a Spanish judge with having committed crimes against humanity. After Pinochet left England, many critics of his regime and opponents of the coup that toppled Allende demanded that the general be forced to face Chilean justice. That issue, which promised to reopen the wounds caused by the deaths of over 3,000 who had been murdered or "disappeared" during Chile's darkest days, produced enormous controversies.

In Mexico, the ruling Partido Revolucionario Institucional (PRI) confronted human rights dilemmas of its own. President Salinas de Gortari, who had won the disputed 1988 election, also contended with accusations that the government had intimidated and even murdered allies of opposition leader Cuauhtémoc Cárdenas. In 1990, a leading human rights proponent was killed, while some 60 followers of Cárdenas were murdered or "disappeared." All the while, Salinas sought to transform the Mexican economy through the promotion of trade and the privatization of various industries, including the telephone company and the recently nationalized banks. Inflation slowed somewhat, while the nation's gross domestic product increased a bit. Salinas' policy of economic liberalization was highlighted by the North American Free Trade Agreement or NAFTA, which discarded trade barriers such as duties and tariffs pertaining to various products, for a fifteen-year period. The Mexican, American and Canadian governments had accepted NAFTA in August 1992; the following year, additional provisions relating to labor and the environment were also adopted.

Unrest unfolded as NAFTA became effective on January 1, 1994. That very day, a mysterious, charismatic figure, Subcommandante Marcos, headed guerrilla forces that emerged in the economically depressed state of Chiapas. Proclaimed the Zapatista National Liberation Army, the guerrillas demanded deep-seated reforms that the government was unwilling or unable to concede. Declaring that "zones of rebellion" had been carved out, the Zapatistas undertook land seizures and ousted PRI officials. Various members of the PRI and the right-wing opposition party, *Partido de Accion Nacional* (PAN), and foreign business operators called for military action. However, a military drive proved unsuccessful, while resulting in massive protests in Mexico City. The PRI had

suffered another blow a short time after the Chiapas movement began, when Luis Donaldo Colosio, selected to succeed Salinas as Mexican president, was assassinated. Consequently, the new PRI candidate and eventual head-of-state was Ernesto Zedillo Ponce de Léon, a forty-two-year-old economist with a Ph.D. from Yale University. Economic woes immediately afflicted the new administration, which felt compelled to devalue the peso. The United States crafted a massive economic package that prevented Mexico from defaulting on its foreign debt.

Mexico's financial difficulties, which included a surge in poverty ranks and foreign indebtedness, spilled over into the political

Fig. 15-2 Parade of the Zapatista National Liberation Army in Chiapas, April 11, 1994, commemorating the 75th anniversary of the assassination of Emiliano Zapata and the outbreak of guerrilla insurgency in Chiapas, Mexico. (Pearson Education, Corporate Digital Archive, Corbis)

arena. After Salinas criticized Zedillo's economic policies, the new president effectively exiled his predecessor and charged Salinas' older brother with corruption. Another top PRI official was assassinated in September 1994, while talk was heard about a possible military takeover. PAN won the governorship of Jalisco in southwestern Mexico. Powerful drug cartels, transporting cocaine from Colombia, raised the level of violence, which included the murder of a Roman Catholic cardinal.

Throughout this period, Mexican citizens experienced a phenomenon that the nation had endured since the 1988 election: militarization of their society. In the 1990s alone, the Mexican government sent troops into Tabasco, Chiapas, Guerro, Oaxaca, Hidalgo, Baja California and Chihuahua, among other locales, either to stave off unrest or to quash social movements. At the same time, more paramilitary operations unfolded. Such developments helped to further discredit the PRI, resulting in the election of Vicente Fox Quesada, a businessman, rancher and member of PAN, as president of Mexico. Thus, the PRI's seventy-one-year-old hold on power, the longest by any political organization during the past century, ended.

In other parts of Latin America, the dissipation of the Cold War appeared to have considerable impact; at the same time, very sharp maldistribution of income, land and power aggravated long-standing tensions, continuing to shape government policies and producing grave resentment. A newer concern, the stranglehold that drug cartels were acquiring entire countries, took hold at the same time. On December 20, 1989, military troops from the United States stormed into Panama, seeking the arrest of General Manual Antonio Noriega, who headed his country's Defense Forces and who allegedly ran a drug ring. Noriega surrendered on January 3, 1990, to be herded off for trial and incarceration in the United States. In 1989 and 1990, drug traffickers purportedly murdered three leading presidential candidates in Colombia. In the mid-1990s, a drug cartel reputedly backed President Ernesto Samper Pizano. Violence wracked his country throughout the decade, and charges of human rights abuses abounded. President Alberto Fujimori, who began his first term as a guerrilla campaign was waged by the Shining Path (*Sendero Luminoso*) by shutting down the national assembly, suspending various parts of the constitution and censoring the press, governed Peru during most of the 1990s. As the Shining Path continued its guerrilla activity, the government's repressive antiterrorist campaign produced widespread criticism.

Earlier hot spots, Nicaragua and El Salvador, began to move away from the Cold War-heightened conflicts that had enveloped those countries during the 1980s. In an election in February 1990, Violeta Barrios de Chamorro, the wife of the martyred newspaper publisher, upset President Daniel Ortega, a Sandinista leader. As warfare ended in Nicaragua, the civil conflict in El Salvador also wound to a close. On January 16, 1992, the government and leftist rebels signed peace accords; the war had taken 75,000 lives. Military and political reforms were called for, but the National Assembly in March 1993 called for a wholesale amnesty program. Both Nicaragua and El Salvador experienced impoverished economies, badly damaged infrastructures and high levels of unemployment.

The Middle East Tinderbox

In one sense, the dissolving of the Cold War also greatly influenced the course of events in the Middle East; in another fashion, the evaporation of tensions East and West hardly affected developments in the ancient holy lands. On August 2, 1990, Iraq, led by President Saddam Hussein, attacked the tiny, oil-rich nation of Kuwait. Four days later, the United Nations placed an embargo on all trade with Iraq, which responded by proclaiming Kuwait an Iraqi province. An international coalition led by the United States and including Great Britain, France, Russia, Saudia Arabia, Syria and Egypt, among others initiated massive air and missile strikes against Iraq on January 16, 1991. Iraq fired off Scud missiles against Saudia Arabia and Israel. Starting on February 23, ground troops retook Kuwait; meeting little resistance, the allied forces prevailed within four days, capturing 175,000 soldiers, and inflicting some 65,000 casualties. To bring a halt to the Gulf War, Iraq promised to destroy its stockpiles of chemical and biological weapons and to allow United Nations' inspections.

The end of the war failed to dislodge Hussein's hold on power. As revolts against Hussein's reign unfolded, Iraqi troops attacked Kurdish rebels. Thousands of Kurdish refugees ended up in camps in Iran and Turkey. Throughout the remainder of the decade, disputes regarding the treatment of the Kurds, the inspection of weapons sites and Hussein's despotic rule produced international outcries; at times, Hussein's antics also resulted in new strikes by the United States and Great Britian.

The Gulf War had temporarily produced a strange alliance that included the United States, Great Britain, Saudia Arabia and Israel, among other nations. Underneath the surface, however, tensions continued to brew between the Jewish state and its Arab neighbors. Once again, the issue of the Palestinian refugees was at the center of the controversy

that resulted in the spilling of more blood. As the 1990s opened and the *infitada* continued, Israeli police killed 20 Palestinians near the Temple Mount. Nevertheless, the victory by Yitzhak Rabin of the Labor Party in the June 1992 Israeli national elections led to significant diplomatic breakthroughs regarding the Palestinians. In September 1993, the PLO acknowledged the state of Israel's right to exist while the Israelis accepted the PLO as the representative body of the Palestinians. Furthermore, Palestinians were afforded limited self-rule in the West Bank and Gaza. The following year, Israel and Jordan signed a document declaring an end to the fighting between the two states; Shimon Peres declared that the agreement "crossed a gulf of forty-six years of hatred and war."

Extremists on both sides sought to prevent more amicable relations between Israel and the Arabs countries. On February 25, 1994, a Jewish gunman in Hebron murdered more than a score of Arabs who were worshipping at a mosque. On October 19, a Muslim suicide bomber rammed into a bus near Tel Aviv, killing 22 Israelis. The following July, just as Israeli and Palestinian negotiators neared agreement regarding the removal of Israeli forces from several Palestinian cities along the West Bank, another suicide bomber tore into a bus in Tel Aviv, murdering five Israelis. In September, Rabin and Yasser Arafat signed another agreement, Oslo II, which extended Palestinian self-rule in the West Bank. Arafat, Rabin asserted, should help to "prevent terrorism from triumphing over peace." If not, Rabin declared, "we will fight it by ourselves." Back in Israel, critics villified Rabin for dealing with Arafat, with some calling the prime minister "Traitor" and "Murderer." Leah Rabin, the wife of the Israeli leader, was informed on one occasion of the fate that purportedly would befall her husband: "After the next election, you and your husband will hang from your heels in the town square like Mussolini and his mistress."

On November 4, the seventy-three-year-old Rabin spoke at a large peace rally in Tel Aviv. Rabin eloquently affirmed, "This is a course which is fraught with difficulties and pain. For Israel there is no path without pain. But the path of peace is preferable to the path of war." But to ensure safety for the families of the Israeli soldiers, Rabin continued, "I want this government to continue to exhaust every opening, every possibility, to promote and achieve a comprehensive peace. Even with Syria, it will be possible to make peace." As Rabin headed for his car, he was shot in the back by a twenty-seven-year-old law student, an Israeli Jew who insisted, "I acted alone on God's orders and I have no regrets."

Rabin's successor, Shimon Peres, faced additional suicide bombings and rocket attacks. Although Israel struck at purported guerrilla camps in Lebanon, the May 1996 national elections returned the Likud Party, now headed by Benjamin Netanyahu, to power. In October 1998, a new agreement, accepted by Netanyahu and Arafat, resulted in the Palestinians controlling additional territory on the West Bank. Violating the spirit of the accord, Netanyahu allowed for the construction of a new Jewish settlement on the outskirts of east Jerusalem; Arafat, for his part, had failed to rein in the suicide bombers, many of whom were associated with Hamas or the Islamic Jihad. The unwillingness to adhere to the promises of the latest accord helped to bring about Netanyaha's defeat at the hands of Eliud Barak, the most decorated soldier in Israeli history, in the May 1999 general election. The following May, the last Israeli troops departed from Lebanon. Negotiations between Barak and Arafat stalled, however, soon to be followed in the fall of 2000 by the most serious outbreak of violence in Israel in many years.

Terrorism and fundamentalism afflicted other Middle Eastern states, including Egypt and Iran. Both Naguib Mahfoub, the 1988 Nobel Prize winner for literature, and President Hoani Murabak, were the victims of assassination attempts involving Islamic fundamentalists. In Iran, Islamic hard-liners repeatedly battled with more moderate, reformist-minded elements. President Mohammed Khatami headed a moderate regime that was condemned by extremists, some of whom saw fit to murder proponents of free speech. The writers Mohammed Jahed Poyhandeh and Mohammed Mokhtari were two of their victims.

Darkness and Light in Africa

Throughout the decade of the 1990s, the African continent experienced triumph and tragedy, stunning advances and shattering setbacks. No single figure appeared more luminous than Nelson Mandela and no nation underwent such dramatic political transformations as South Africa, the home country of the 1992 Nobel Peace Prize winner (an honor shared with F. W. de Klerk, another South African). In 1990, President de Klerk, who also lifted prohibitions against the African National Congress (ANC), the Pan-Africanist Congress (PAC) and the South African Communist Party (SACP), released the seventy-one-year-old Mandela, who had spent 27 years as a political prisoner. Mandela immediately undertook a campaign to put international pressure on South Africa to end its long-standing policy of apartheid. De Klerk removed various discriminatory barriers confronting blacks in the social sphere, before eradicating the legal edifice of *apartheid.* Unfortunately, thousands died in clashes between supporters of the ANC and the Inkatha Freedom Party, which Chief Buthelezi and Zulu warriors led and which favored a less conciliatory approach toward whites. In 1993, all racial groups finally got the vote, which enfranchised 28 million blacks by the following year. That year, Mandela was easily elected as his nation's president.

As head-of-state Mandela acquired even greater stature as a figure of international repute and as one determined to bring about national reconciliation. In 1995, Mandela established the Truth and Reconciliation Commission, led by Archbishop Desmond Tutu, the 1984 Nobel Peace Prize laureate, to chart human rights abuses that had occurred under apartheid. In an astonishing turn of events, televised proceedings captured victims and torturers facing one another. Policemen confessed to having murdered Steve Biko, the martyred proponent of "black consciousness," in 1977. On February 25, 1999, speaking before the South African parliament, Mandela referred to the work of the Truth and Reconciliation Commission:

> As we reached out across the divisions of centuries to establish democracy, we need now to work together in all our diversity, including the diversity of our experience and recollection of our history, to overcome the divisions themselves and eradicate their consequences.
> Reconciliation is central to that vision which moved millions of men and women to risk all, including their lives, in the struggle against apartheid and white domination. It is inseparable from the achievement of a non-racial, democratic and united nation affording common citizenship, rights and obligations to each

and every person, and respecting the rich diversity of our people. Such were the wounds and the polarization caused by apartheid and the conflict which it generated, such was our yearning for peace, and such the balance of forces in our settlement, that reconciliation demanded a uniquely South African instrument to help us to start dealing with our past.

The African National Congress swept to victory in the 1999 general election, enabling Thabo Mbeki to succeed Mandela as president.

Notwithstanding its impressive accomplishments, South Africa continued to be afflicted with large economic and social ailments, particularly rampant crime and pervasive poverty. Other African states appeared, if anything, to be even more troubled, confronting epidemic diseases such as malaria and AIDS, mass starvation, drought, flooding, political turmoil and tribal warfare. After a failed effort to quell civil war in Somalia in the early 1990s, Western nations largely dismissed the possibility of military intervention. Certain UN-sponsored efforts at mediation succeeded, as in Namibia, Mozambique and Angola. However, in many other instances such attempts proved futile. Bloody civil conflagrations continued, despite pressure from the West, in Liberia, Rwanda and Burundi. The results proved catastrophic, with the Hutus in Rwanda slaughtering more than two million Tutsis. As the decade neared an end, civil wars continued in Sudan and Somalia. Nigeria, which in 1999 acquired its first civilian government in 15 years, still confronted strife in northern sectors after the imposition of Islamic fundamentalist codes. In Zimbabwe, ruled since 1980 by Robert Mugabe, a land redistribution plan spurred on by the government resulted in violent attacks against white farmers.

Africa possessed over 800 million inhabitants as the new century arrived. It also suffered from the highest rate of HIV/AIDS infection in the world. An estimate 24,500,000 people were so afflicted, comprising 71 percent of the world's total. Due to political and economic strife, more refugees could be found in Africa than on any other continent as of 1999: over 3,100,000, with more than 400,000 in both Guinea and Tanzania; more than 300,000 in the Sudan; over 200,000 in Kenya, Ethiopia, the Congo-Kinshasa and Zambia; and more than 100,000 in Uganda and Cote d'Ivoire. The greatest number of those refugees had fled from Sierra Leone, Sudan, Angola, Eritrea, Burundi, the Congo-Kinshasa and the Western Sahara.

Economic Development and Political Transformation in Asia

In South Asia, India, Japan and China remained powerful states, although the so-called Asian Tigers, Hong Kong and a number of smaller nations, including South Korea, Singapore and Taiwan, became more competitive economically. India, like so many nations in the areas once referred to as the Third World, experienced sectarian battles. The assassination on May 21, 1991, of former Prime Minister Rajiv Gandhi, in the midst of another campaign for his nation's highest electoral office, proved politically unsettling. Indian representative government became somewhat more tenuous, as leaders of the new Hindu-nationalist Bharatiya Janata Party played on anti-Muslim sentiment to garner public support. In December 1992, riots broke out across India following

the destruction of a 16th-century Muslim mosque in Ayodhya. The following spring saw terrorism take hold in Bombay, long an amicable setting for Muslims and Hindus, and in Calcutta.

The presence of corrupt political figures, many associated with the long-governing Congress Party, only compounded India's difficulties. As its population surpassed one billion by the end of the decade, India remained afflicted with government bureaucracy and sharp income gaps separating the affluent and the poor. In a noteworthy turn of events, an "untouchable," K. R. Narayanan, became president of India in July 1997. Parliamentary elections in February swept the Hindu Atai Bihari Vajpayee into the prime minister's office.

Japan also endured economic and political woes during the decade of the 1990s. Beginning in 1990, the mighty Japanese economy began to quake, while a series of scandals involving the ruling Liberal Democratic Party (LDP) unfolded. As stories were unveiled that renowned securities companies had fixed stock prices, the Japanese Stock Exchange experienced a nosedive. Prime minister Toshiki Kaifu was respected for his honesty but little preferred by top figures in the LDP, who replaced him with Kiichi Miyazawa, who had been associated with the earlier political-corporate scandal involving Recruit. In 1992, Miyazawa was in office when the even greater Sagawa scandal was unveiled. Approximately one hundred political figures, most members of the LDP, were implicated; among those were a pair of cabinet ministers.

A jostling for political power unfolded, which culminated in June 1994 when Tomiichi Murayama became Japan's first socialist premier since the early Cold War era. The American military presence on Okinawa began to be scaled back following the rape of a twelve-year-old girl by three U.S. soldiers there. By the fall of 1996, the LDP was back in control, led by Prime Minister Ryutaro Hashimoto, who called for "administrative" bureaucratic reforms; few actually were forthcoming. Notwithstanding a sharp recession that further weakened the Japanese economy, the LDP remained in power as the decade ended.

In contrast to the Japanese economy, China's grew steadily during the 1990s. This economic progress occurred despite the repression of the student-based movement of the previous decade for which China had been castigated. The Chinese sought to improve diplomatic relations with Western nations, even supporting the condemnation by the UN Security Council that followed the Iraqi invasion of Kuwait in 1990. At the same time, Chinese Communist Party leaders were determined to avoid the fate of their ideological brethren in Eastern Europe and the former Soviet Union. Thus, dissidents were harshly dealt with, suffering trials, capital sentences, incarceration or exile. All the while, the Communist Party worked strenuously to improve living standards, particularly in major cities such as Beijing; nevertheless, 850 million of China's 1.2 billion people still resided in rural areas. To that end, the 14th Communist Party Congress declared its support for Deng Xiaoping's support of market developments, all the while retaining a political stranglehold on power. The market approach proved unsettling for many, with millions of peasants compelled to seek a new way of life in teeming cities. Unemployment beset the countryside, where numerous protests and riots continued to break out. China's relations with Taiwan remained strained, hardly improved by the great Asian nation's meddling in Taiwanese politics and

its threats to deploy military force against the island. On an equally ominous note, China continued to rely on military force to silence dissidents in Buddhist Tibet, while ethnic and religious minorities appeared increasingly restless in areas such as Xinjiang.

In 1997, a series of epochal events unfolded that greatly affected China. One was the death of long-time leader Deng. The other was Great Britian's handing over of Hong Kong, one of the Asian Tigers, to China, as mandated in an 1898 agreement. In September, President Jiang Zemin, Deng's handpicked successor, visited the United States, the first Chinese government leader to do since the 1989 massacre in Tiananmen Square. Zemin made no promises to safeguard human rights in China, but he declared a willingness to work more diligently to prevent the spread of nuclear devices. President Clinton of the United States paid an official state visit to China in mid-1998. The following year, China and the United States agreed to a comprehensive trade package, while on September 19, 2000, the U.S. Congress supported the normalization of trade relations.

Southeast Asia at the Close of the Century

In the 1990s, a transfer of power occurred in Vietnam involving old-line revolutionaries—part of the same type of aging ruling group that had afflicted other communist regimes—and somewhat younger reformers. For many Vietnamese, the Communist Party came to be viewed as all but irrelevant; they were displeased with the party's conservatism, incompetence and corruption. The party also offended Buddhist monks, who wanted to establish their own church outside the control of the Communist Party. Social concerns mounted, pertaining to, for example, the presence of an estimated 50,000 prostitutes and 30,000 drug users in Ho Chi Minh City alone. Human rights abuses, as exemplified by lengthy incarcerations meted out to the educator Doan Viet Hoat, referred to as Vietnam's Sakharov, continued.

Efforts to improve the economy proceeded apace, with 1990 targeted as the Year of the Tourist. Hotels were built and airline traffic to Ho Chi Minh City increased. By 1992, the economy had improved, as evidenced by augmented rice production and curtailed inflation. The level of exports and imports jumped markedly, as trade with Japan, Singapore and other ASEAN (Association of Southeast Asian Nations) states surpassed the now-absent dealings with the former Soviet Union. The American-sponsored embargo was still crippling, but the economy continued to progress.

During the mid-1990s, Vietnam's relations with the international community also improved. In 1993, the International Monetary Fund no longer refused to consider requests from Vietnam. The next year, the United States ended its trade embargo and the following year moved to normalize relations; surprisingly, the Clinton administration received little criticism for backing better relations with Vietnam. Also in 1995, Vietnam joined ASEAN; a Vietnamese official termed this "an eloquent testimony to the ever growing trends of regionalization and globalization in the increasingly interdependent world."

Although still led by increasingly geriatric CP officials, Vietnam began encouraging Western investments and worked to produce a mixed economy. Increasingly, Vietnam was considered a "new economic frontier," propelled onward by "its disciplined workforce,

cheap labor and materials, and zealous goal" to enter the global economic marketplace. In 1994 and 1995, Vietnam experienced 9.5 percent annual growth rates, the highest in the world, while inflation remained below 10 percent.

Consequently, economic woes that unfolded in 1997 were unanticipated. The economic growth rate dropped to 8.5 percent, foreign investments waned by one-third, and tourism dropped sharply. Bureaucracy and corruption abounded. Vietnam remained saddled with an antiquated banking system. The economy continued to founder, as outside investment plummeted. Per capita income in 1999 topped out at $1,850, while 37 percent of the population existed below the poverty line. Unemployment stood at 25 percent as late as 1995. Vietnam owed other nations billions; the largest creditors were Russia, Iraq and Iran. In short, Vietnam remained an extremely poor, densely populated nation, still suffering from prolonged warfare, a paucity of external support and a highly inefficient, centralized economy. On July 13, 2000, Vietnam and the United States agreed to a comprehensive trade package.

Cambodia and Laos, both desperately poor with per capita incomes of only a few hundred dollars, also remained troubled lands that lacked the political stability of Vietnam. Two large shadows continued to loom over Cambodia: Norodom Sihanouk and the Khmer Rouge. With Hun Sen remaining the head-of-state for twenty years, supporters of Sihanouk, the Khmer Rouge and the Khmer People's National Liberation Front, an anticommunist faction, led resistance forces. Beginning in 1991, the United Nations became directly involved in efforts to devise a cease-fire and conduct elections for a National Assembly. The Khmer Rouge refused to participate, but the elections were conducted, with forces tied to Hun Sen and Prince Ranarrid garnering the largest number of legislative seats. With Hun Sen threatening a new civil war, a decision was made to name him and Prince Ranarridh co-prime ministers; Sihanouk returned to the throne but cancer treatments compelled him to leave Cambodia. Both Hun Sen and Prince Ranarridh sought the support of dissident Khmer Rouge leaders, including Ieng Sary. After granting Sary amnesty, Hun Sen pulled off a coup, supposedly backed by the drug kingpen Theng Bunma on July 6, 1997; the government imprisoned many supporters of Prince Ranarridh and assassinated others. Foreign investments and international aid dried up, to be restored after another election was held in 1998.

In the midst of the coup, the infamous Pol Pot had been taken before a "people's tribunal" in northern Cambodia, and placed under house arrest. Unrepentant to the end, Pol Pot declared that the Vietnamese had murdered Cambodians. As efforts to bring him before an international tribunal proved unavailing, Pol Pot died in April 1998.

Vestiges of early civil conflagrations and the Vietnam War also continued to haunt Laos. The communist Lao People's Revolutionary Party, long headed by Kaysone Phomvihan, had governed since 1975. Along with other former Pathet Lao, Kaysone presided over the Laotian state until his death in 1992. As early as 1979, Kaysone had discarded hard-line policies and begun instituting "new thinking" reforms. Beginning in the mid-1980s, Kaysone had initiated reforms designed to decentralize economic practices and usher in expanded political participation. In reality, nothing akin to democracy unfolded, with no opposition parties

allowed. The hill tribes, particularly the Hmong, continued to battle with the central government.

The Laotian economy, now lacking Soviet assistance and suffering from hyper-inflation, a dearth of infrastructural developments, heavy-handed bureaucracy, droughts and floods, continued to founder, like Cambodia's. One particularly severe ecological problem involved deforestation that resulted from the sale of timber to Thailand. By 1990, forest land had diminished from 70 percent of the land mass at the end of the 19th century to less than half that amount. Again, similar to Cambodia, Laos held an untold number of land mines, which produced hundreds of casualties annually.

Other nations in Southeast Asia experienced upheavals during the last decade of the 20th century. Although Suharto was elected to a seventh consecutive presidential term in Indonesia in March 1998, economic difficulties, coupled with widespread charges of corruption, led to violent protests and his resignation that May. Indonesia also endured escalating religious strife between Christians and Moslems, along with independence demands by Timorese. In the face of considerable bloodletting, the United Nations sent international peacekeepers to Indonesia in late 1999.

Political intrigue continued to afflict the Philippines, as government forces battled against Muslim separatists. An autonomous Muslim region was carved out on Mindanao, but the sectarian strife continued. The American military presence, which also induced protests, ended, as the Subic Bay Naval Station was turned over to the Filipinos.

The "little dragons" of Southeast Asia, particularly South Korea, Taiwan, Hong Kong and Singapore, continued to experience economic growth. Literacy rates were quite high, while the educational systems served as models for the region. However, in these states, as in Myanmar, Thailand and Malaysia, governing elites demonstrated a readiness to resort to repression to silence dissent. In Myanmar, Aung San Suu Kyi continued to suffer house arrest; on her release in the middle of the decade, restrictions were placed on her political activities. Thailand endured a military coup, heavy-handed government practices, a sharp economic downturn and a terrible AIDS epidemic. Malaysia underwent a steep recession of its own, political chaos and turmoil at the highest levels of government.

◆ — ◆ — ◆ — ◆ — ◆ — ◆ — ◆ — ◆ — ◆ — ◆ — ◆

The Vietnamese dissident, Doan Viet Hoat, residing in the United States as the 21st century began, indicated,

> My dream for the future is a dream of Vietnam. Our country has a long history of people who fought against aggression and injustice. Our highest calling is love of country, as has been demonstrated by many Vietnamese patriots in the past. I, too, have been moved by the love of my country and also by the greatness of my country's future and the world's future. I believe in a very bright future for Vietnam and for the whole region of Southeast Asia. . . . And I always believe that truth, justice, and compassion will prevail, no matter how strong the dictators are, no matter how bad the situation might be.

Hoat's own history was far too typical of many in nations across the globe, whether in the once-characterized underdeveloped countries or more advanced industrialized states. He was a prisoner of conscience who suffered long punishment at the hands of a government that sought, however unsuccessfully, to break him. His indomitable spirit, however, enabled him to endure two decades of imprisonment under often terribly stark conditions.

Hoat was born December 24, 1942, in Ha Dong in northern Vietnam. He emigrated with his parents to the south following the signing of the 1954 Geneva Accords that left the communists in control of the territory north of the 17th parallel. In 1963, Hoat participated in the student demonstrations that unfolded as Buddhist priests battled with the government forces of the U.S.-backed regime of Ngo Diem Diem. Due to his political activism, Ho was compelled to leave his country during the 1960s; in the United States, he earned a doctorate in education at Florida State University. After his return to Vietnam in 1976, Hoat, who had become vice president of Van Hanh University in Saigon, was jailed because of his "ties" to the United States, and remained imprisoned for a dozen years. Despite never receiving a trial, Hoat was placed in a re-education camp at the Chi Hoa Prison. Upon his release from incarceration, Hoat served as Professor of English at the University of Agriculture and Forestry in Ho Chi Minh City.

Fig. 15-3 Professor Doan Viet Hoat, a leading Vietnamese dissident, following his arrival at the Los Angeles airport on September 3, 1998. Viet Hoat had endured approximately 20 years of imprisonment due to his determined support of democracy and human rights. (AP Photo/Kevork Djansezian)

In 1990, Doan Viet Hoat, founded a publication, "Freedom Forum," which called for "peaceful change from a monopoly of power to shared power." Imprisoned once again, Hoat was detained for an additional 28 months and then charged with "founding a reactionary organization." Sentenced to 15 years in jail, to be followed by five years of house arrest, Hoat cried out:

Our fatherland is undergoing a very important transitional period. Communism is dying but the future of our country is still obscure. Through a few improvements on the surface are noticeable . . . the country within has been gravely damaged, materially as well as psychologically. Education, literature, medicine have all become bankrupt. . . . The gap between the rich and the poor is as conspicuous as it has ever been, and is still increasingly rapidly. Smuggling and corruption have dominated over our country as a way of life. . . . Only a true democracy can reconstruct the trust and the responsible thinking of the people, therefore democracy is the sole surviving road of the country.

Hoat continued,

There are important periods in the history of all countries in the world which require bravery and consciousness on the part of everybody, foremost the intellectuals. We are presently in that period. Our land has been build with the bones, blood, sweat, and tears of our forefathers, left for their offspring to build and savor together. We cannot allow any group to appropriate this country for their possession. . . . Throughout our history of more than 4000 years, countless heroes and martyrs had committed their lives to protect the land and the sovereignty of our people. Our matter at present is democratization. . . . Human virtues will conquer brutality. No oppression can conquer the legitimate aspirations of a population of 72 million people.

Writing from prison in November 1992, Hoat urged Communist Party leaders to "release all political prisoners," to usher in political freedom and to hold "free and fair elections." Hoat continued to be shuffled off to a series of prisons, including the Thanh Cam Labor Camp located next to the Laotian border. His wife, the former Tran Thi Thuc, and their three sons, had begun residing in Minneapolis, Minnesota; Mrs. Hoat helped to keep international attention focused on her husband's plight. In 1998, the World Association of Newspapers (WAN) awarded him the Golden Pen of Freedom, which was delivered annually to those considered to have worked diligently to sustain journalistic freedom. In announcing the award, the organization's board of directors saluted the "extraordinary commitment and courage shown by Mr. Doan in the fight for freedom of expression in Vietnam." Hoat, WAN proclaimed, "has made an immense personal sacrifice for his principles, spending 19 of the past 21 years in prison for his declarations and writing in favour of democracy. . . . To return with such courage to the struggle for freedom of the press after suffering so many years in detention is an outstanding demonstration of courage which humbles us all." The organization urged Hoat's release. On September 1, 1998, Hoat, after agreeing to head into exile yet again, was allowed to go to the United States.

In a later interview, Hoat related the lesson he desired his oppressors to learn.

I felt that if I kept silent in jail, then the dictators had won. And I wanted to send a message to the people who wanted to fight for freedom that the dictators could not win by putting us in jail. I wanted to prove that you cannot, by force, silence someone who doesn't agree with you. That's why the prisoners, both political and criminal, tried to circulate my writings. Without their help I could not have sent my messages out. We united to continue our fight for freedom and democracy, even from within the prison walls.

◆ —— ◆ —— ◆ —— ◆ —— ◆ —— ◆ —— ◆ —— ◆ —— ◆ —— ◆ —— ◆

Suggested Readings

COLE, LEONARD A. *The Eleventh Plague: The Politics of Biological and Chemical Warfare.* (1996).

CUOMO, KERRY KENNEDY. *Speak Truth to Power: Human Rights Defenders Who Are Changing Our World.* (2000).

DORRAJ, MANOCHEHR, Ed. *The Changing Political Economy of the Third World.* (1995).

EKINS, PAUL. *A New World Order: Grassroots Movements for Global Change.* (1992).

FREEZE, GILBERT, Ed. *Russia: A History.* (1997).

FUKUYAMA, FRANCIS. *The End of History and the Last Man.* (1992).

GIDDENS, ANTHONY. *Runaway World: How Globalization is Reshaping Our Lives.* (2000).

GILBERT, MARTIN. *A History of the Twentieth Century: Volume Three 1952–1999.* (1999).

GRENVILLE, J. A. S. *A History of the World in the Twentieth Century.* (2000).

HARRISON, PAUL. *Inside the Third World.* (1993).

———. *The Third Revolution: Environment, Population, and a Sustainable World.* (1992).

HOBSBAWM, ERIC. *The Age of Extremes.* (1994).

HOWEVER, MICHAEL and WILLIAM ROGER LOUIS, Eds. *The Oxford History of the Twentieth Century.* (1998).

HUNTINGTON, SAMUEL P. *The Clash of Civilizations and the Remaking of World Order.* (1996).

JUERGENSMEYER, MARK. *The New Cold War? Religious Nationalism Confronts the Secular State.* (1993).

KEEN, BENJAMIN. *A History of Latin America.* (1996).

KENNEDY, PAUL. *Preparing for the Twenty-First Century.* (1993).

NEHER, CLARK D. *Southeast Asia in the New International Era.* (1999).

ROBERTS, J. M. *A History of Europe.* (1997).

SILBER, LAURA and ALLAN LITTLE. *Yugoslavia: Death of a Nation.* (1997).

SKIDMORE, THOMAS E. and PETER H. SMITH. *Modern Latin America.* (1997).

WALLACE, AUBREY. *Eco-Heroes: Twelve Tales of Environmental Victory.* (1993).

YERGIN, DANIEL. *The Commanding Heights: The Battle between Government and the Marketplace that is Remaking the Modern World.* (1998).

Index

Abdication Crisis, 188
Abdul-Hamid II, Sultan, 29, 63
Abyssinia, 62
Acerbo Law, 181
Adenauer, Konrad, 282
Afghanistan, 42, 485, 486, 492
Africa, 4, 522–24
    agriculture in, 361, 367, 369, 379
    anticolonial struggles in, 137–41
    Belgium in, 140, 357, 358, 373, 374
    blacks in, 359, 375–78
    boundariees of states in, 360
    challenges in independent, 378–82
    civil war in, 363
    climate of, 359
    coups d'etat in, 361–62, 372
    culture of, 381
    decolonization of, 381
    economy in, 361, 379
    first generation of leadership in, 361
    French in, 38, 266, 357, 358, 363
    Great Britain in, 137–40, 219
    Holocaust in, 36
    illiteracy in, 361, 379
    imperial expansion in, 32–36
    independence in, 355
    Italy in, 35, 139
    Marxism in, 138
    military strongmen in, 351, 362
    nationalist movement in, 358, 363
    natural resources in, 359, 364, 371
    population of, 361, 379
    Portugal in, 35, 140, 357, 358
    prelude to independence in, 356–64
    pre-World War I colonial rivalries in,
        61–62
    problems in post-independence,
        351
    raw materials in, 356
    refugees in, 524
    Socialism in, 361, 368–70, 379
    Soviet operations in, 485
    Spain in, 35
    tribal divisions in, 359, 371
    white rule in, 375–78
    in World War I, 72
    World War II fighting in, 356
African-Americans. See also Blacks.
    in post-World War I U.S., 99
    in wartime, 110
Africanization, 367

African National Congress, 140, 377, 382,
        384
    banning of, 385
Africanness, 363, 376
African Socialism, 361, 368–70
Afrika Korps, 222
Afrikaners, 140
Agent Orange, 341
Agrarian Reform Law, 450
Agricultural Adjustment Act, 106
Agriculture, 11, 269
    African, 361, 367, 369, 379
    collectivized, 288
    European demand for, 45
    in Soviet Union, 192, 193
Aguinaldo, Emilio, 47–51
AIDS, 381, 479
Air bases, U.S., 242
Air control, 136
Air force, 219, 234–35
    Allied, 234
    Italian, 221
    Japanese, 228
    in World War I, 73
Airplane, 104
Albania, 64, 293, 479
Alessandri, Arturo, 117
Aleutian Islands, 241
Alessandri, Jorge, 449, 453, 454
Alexandria Protocol, 393
Alfonsin, Raul, 460
Alfonso XIII, King, 199
Algeria, 35, 266, 279, 280, 358, 399
All-African People's Conference, 357
Allende, Salvador, 122–24, 449, 460, 461,
        462
Alliance for Progress, 451
Allied offensives
    in south Pacific, 229
    superior supply of, 244
    in western France, 238–40
Allied Powers, 66
All-India Muslim League, 38
Allon, Yigual, 403
American Civil Liberties Union (ACLU),
        96, 97, 98
American First Committee, 109
American Lend-Lease aid, 230
American Liberty League, 106
American Revolution, 43
Amin, Idi, 351–55, 362

Amritsar Massacre, 143, 298, 299
Andropov, Yuri, 289, 477, 484, 488
Anglo-American Committee of Inquiry, 393
Anglo-French offensive, 69
Anglo-German Naval Treaty, 202
Anglo-Persian Oil Company, 137
Anglo-Russian Accord, 61
Angola, 266, 358, 363
Annihilation Campaigns, 152
Anschluss, 204
Anti-Ballistic Missile Treaty, 485
Anticolonial nationalists, 333
Anticolonial struggles in Middle East and
        Africa, 131–41
Anti-Comintern Pact, 202
Anti-communism, 421–23
Anti-German sentiment
    in France, 29–30
    in United States, 79, 80, 81
Anti-immigrationists, 100
Anti-Japanese sentiment, 157
Anti-monopoly Law, 316
Anti-nuclear movement, 209, 425
Anti-Semitism, 20, 26, 136, 167, 198
Antiwar activities, suppression of, 74
Antiwar movement, 200, 429, 430
ANZAC troops, 127
Apartheid, 140, 376, 377, 378, 523
    opposition to, 382–86
Appeasement, policy of, 204
April Theses, 76
Aquino, Corazon, 330
Arab cause, 392–93
Arab-Israeli War, 388, 395
Arab kingdom, 391
Arab lands, absorption of, 406
Arab League, 388
Arab Liberation Army, 395
Arab Revolt, 134
Arabs
    in Palestine, 391
    religious minorities among, 134
    response to Israel, 396–401
Arab states, 398
Arafat, Yasser, 402, 404, 407, 409, 410,
        411–14, 521, 522
Arbenz, Jacobo, 444
Arendt, Hannah, 272
Arévalo, Juan Jose, 444
Argentina, 114–16, 446–48, 453, 458–60
    economy in, 447, 460, 517

Argentine Anti-Communist Alliance, 459
Armenian Massacres, 71
Armistice, World War I, 81–82
Arrow Cross, 199
Arsenal of Democracy, 231
ARVN, 340, 344
Arusha Declaration, 369
Asia, 4, 524–25
    challenges to colonial rule in, 141–47
    in imperial age, 36–43
Assassination
    Japanese, 155
    of Mexican political leaders, 119
Atlantic Charter, 220, 245, 356
Atomic bomb, 209, 313. *See also* Nuclear
    weapons.
Atrocities, Nazi, 247
Atlee, Clement, 275, 393
August Coup, 502
Aung San Suu Kyi, 331
Auschwitz, 233, 246
Austerity measures, in Britain, 294
Austin, Warren, 394
Australia, 36
    in World War I, 71
Austria, 26, 30, 263, 286
    German absorption of, 204
    post-World War I, 87
    pre-World War I alliances of, 59
Austro-Hungarian Empire, 81
    breakup of, 86
    industry in, 11
    minorities in, 19
    in second half of nineteenth century, 26
    and start of World War I, 63–65, 69, 70
Austro-Italian front, 71
Automobile, 10, 100, 104, 173
    ownership of, 271
Auxiliary Labor Bill, 73
Aviation, 11, 173
Aviation fuel, U.S. sale of, 158
Aylwin, Patricio, 518
Azerbaijan, 499

Baby boom, 271
Baden, Max von, 82
Badoglio, Pietro, 238, 283
Balance of power, European, 29–31
Baldwin, Roger Nash, 95–96, 316
Baldwin, Stanley, 175, 188
Balewa, Abubakar, 371
Balfour Declaration, 88, 135, 391
Balkan League, 64
Balkan policy, 222
Balkan wars, 62–64, 71–72
Baltic republics, 497
Bangladesh, 304
Bantu Education Act, 377
Bao Dai, 333, 334
Barak, Eliud, 522
Basic Principles agreement, 485
Batista y Zalvidar, Fulgencio, 444, 445
Battle of the Atlantic, 220, 234
Battle of Britain, 219, 220

Battle of the Bulge, 239
Battle of the Coral Sea, 228
Battle of Leyte Gulf, 242
Battle of Manila, 242
Battle of Midway, 228, 229
Battle of Omdurman, 32
Battle of the Philippine Sea, 241
Battle of Savo Island, 229
Bay of Pigs, 451
Beckett, Samuel, 273
Beer Hall Putsch, 168
Begin, Menachem, 393, 394, 395, 398, 403,
    407
Beijing, 312
Beirut, American embassy in, 409
Belgian Congo, 36
Belgium, 29, 68, 75, 191, 218, 266, 275, 286
    in Africa, 140, 357, 358, 373, 374
Belorussia, 500
Benes, Eduard, 290
Ben-Gurion, David, 209, 387–90, 391, 394,
    395, 398, 401, 402
Benin, 362
Bentham, Jeremy, 18
Benz, Karl, 10
Bergson, Henri, 16
Beria, Lavrentia, 287
Berlin, 264
Berlin Airlift, 261
Berlin Blockade, 261
Berlin Crisis of 1961, 282
Berlin Olympics, 203
Berlin Wall, 481, 493
Bhindranwale, Sant Jarnail Singh, 305
Bhutto, Zulfikar Ali, 304
Biafran War, 371, 372
Biko, Steve, 378, 523
bin Laden, Osama, 517
Bipolar world order, 246, 256
Birth control, 101
Bismarck, Otto von, 25, 29, 30, 59
Bismarckian system, 30
    unraveling of, 59–60
Biyogo, Macias Nguema, 362
Black, Hugo, 422
Black Hand, 64
Black Panthers, 428
Blacks, 104. *See also* African-Americans.
    in Africa, 359, 375–78
    in U.S. during World War II, 231
Black September group, 405
Black Ships, 39
Blackshirts, 180, 181
Blair, Tony, 511
Blitzkrieg, 216, 218
Blum, Leon, 190, 191
Boers, 35, 140
Boer War, 8, 35, 60
Bohemia, 26
Bohlen, Charles, 51
Bokasso, Jean-Bedel, 362
Bolivia, 442, 443, 455
Boll, Heinrich, 273
Bolshevik Revolution, 56, 57, 184–85

Bolsheviks, 56–57, 76–77
Bonus Army, 105
Boris, King, 199
Bormann, Martin, 249
Borneo, 41, 331
Bosnia, 30
Botha, P.W., 378, 386
Boulanger Affair, 24
Boxer Rebellion, 39
Brandt, Willy, 281
Brazil, 44, 112–14, 445–46, 451–53,
    456–58, 517
Brazza, Savofgnan de, 34
Brecht, Bertolt, 178
Brest-Litovsk, Peace of, 77
Bretton Woods Conference, 269
Brezhnev, Leonid, 289, 477, 482, 486
Brezhnev Doctrine, 264
Britain. *See* Great Britain.
British Colonial Office, 357
British East India Company, 36
British Malaya, 145
British North America Act, 45
British Union of Fascists, 188
Brittain, Vera, 90–93
Brotherhood of Sleeping Car Porters, 101,
    110
Brown Revolution, 195–99
Brown v. Board of Education, 424
Brussels Pact, 263
Bryan, William Jennings, 79
B-29 bomber, 243
Buddhists, 340
Bulgaria, 29, 30, 63, 64, 71, 82, 88, 199,
    237, 291, 293, 480, 492, 494
Bundesrat, 25
Burma, 37, 145, 265, 331
Burundi, 363
Bus boycott, 425
Bush, George, 435, 492, 516
Busing, 431

Caliphate, 132
Callaghan, James, 277
Calles, Plutarco Elias, 119, 120
Calles Law, 120
Camacho, Manuel Avila, 121
Cambodia, 41, 335, 337, 338, 343, 344, 346,
    526–27
Campaign for the Defiance of Unjust
    Laws, 384
Camp David accords, 408, 432
Campora, Hector, 459
Camps, Ramon J., 459, 460
Camus, Albert, 272
    and Communism, 291
Canada, 43, 45
Cape to Cairo vision, 35
Cardenas, Cuauhtemoc, 518
Cardenas, Lazaro, 120, 121
Cardoso, Fernando Henrique, 517
Carol II, King, 199
Carranza, Venustiano, 118
Cartel deo Gauches, 176

Cash and carry provision, 217
Castro, Fidel, 420, 426, 440–41, 442, 445, 450, 451, 455
Catholic church, 17
  in Argentina, 448
  in Brazil, 457
  and communism, 291
  in France, 24
  in Germany, 25, 197
  and Holocaust, 274
  in Italy, 182
  in Latin America, 472
Catholics, militant, 119
Caudillos, 44
Ceausescu, Nicolae, 293, 495, 496
Central African Republic, 362
Central America, 435
  between world wars, 111–12
Central Powers, 66
Ceylon, 145, 265
Chad, 359, 363
Chamberlain, Houston Steward, 15
Chamberlain, Joseph, 8, 30
Chamberlain, Neville, 188, 204, 205
Chamorro, Pedro Joaquin, 467
Chang Tsang-chang, 150
Chechnya, 515
Cheka, 77, 79
Chemical industries, 10
Chen Duxiu, 150
Chernyenko, Konstantin, 289, 477, 488
Chiang Kai-sheck, 151, 152, 156, 157, 304
Chibas, Eddie, 444–45
Chile, 116–18, 448–49, 453–55, 460–63, 518
Chilean Popular Front, 118
Chilean Socialist Party, 123
China, 4, 8, 232, 240, 535
  between world wars, 147–53
  Britain in, 38
  collectivization of land in, 308
  communism in, 308–10
  and India, 303, 309–10
  Japan in, 147, 149, 157
  Marxism in, 148, 150, 151
  nationalist movement in, 151
  opening of, 310–12
  People's Republic of, 305–12
  rift with Soviet Union, 288, 485
  spread of bourgeois culture in, 310
  student demonstrations in, 312, 321, 324
  United States in, 38–39
  and Vietnam, 342, 347
  war with Japan, 40, 147, 149, 157
China-Burma-India Theater, 240
Chinese Communist Party, 150, 151, 152, 153
Chirac, Jacques, 281, 512
Christian Democracy, 275
Christian Democratic Union, 282, 284
Christian Democrats, 454
Christmas bombings, 344

Churchill, Winston, 58, 71, 144, 182, 211–14, 217, 219, 220, 234, 261, 267, 275, 357, 418
Church-state relations, 182
Chu The, 152
CIA, 419, 420, 462
  in Latin America, 444
Cities
  rise of, 12
  wartime obliteration of, 259
Civilian Conservation Corps, 106
Civil Liberties Directive, 315
Civil rights, 417, 427
Civil Rights Act, 428
Civil rights movement, 110
Civil War, U.S., 40
Clemenceau, George, 75, 83, 85
Cold War, 254, 274, 418–21, 443, 479
  in Brazil, 445
  end of, 478
  Europe and, 261–63
  and Japan, 316
  and Vietnam, 339
  western Europe in late, 509–12
Collectivization of land, 192, 193, 288
  in China, 308
Collor de Mello, Fernando, 458
Colonial representatives, African, 358
Colonial rivalries, pre-World War I, 61–62
CO-MADRES, 471–73
Comfort women, 320
Comintern, 79
Commission of Civil Rights, 425
Committee to Defend America by Aiding the Allies, 109
Committee to Re-elect the President, 431
Commonwealth status, 265
Communications, mass, 508–09
Communism
  in Brazil, 445
  in Cambodia, 343, 344
  Catholic church and, 291
  in China, 308–10
  end of, 478
  in Eastern Europe, 419
  impact of, 1
  in north Vietnam, 336, 346
  outlawed in Chile, 448
  start of, 3
Communist Manifesto, 20, 148
Communist Party, 113, 116, 184, 488
  bureaucratization of in USSR, 482–85
  Chinese, 150, 151, 152, 153
  democratization of Soviet, 481
  French, 189
  Italian, 284
  in Poland, 487–88
Communist party auxiliaries, 193
Communists
  and ACLU, 98
  in Germany, 195
Concentration camps, 246–48
Concordancia, 115

Conference for Progressive Political Action, 100
Congo, 62, 266, 358, 373, 442. *See also* Zaire
Congo Free State, 34
Congolese National Movement, 373
Congress of Berlin, 30, 63
Congress of Europe, 267
Congress of Industrial Organizations, 107
Congress of Oppressed Nationalities, 86
Congress of People's Deputies, 477, 490
Congress of Racial Equality, 110
Conscientious objectors, 74
Conscript armies, 59
Conscription, in U.S., 109
Conservatism, 18–19
Conservative Party, in Great Britain, 275–77
Conservatives
  in Germany, 25
  in Great Britain, 23
  in post-World War I U.S., 100
  U.S., 433
Constituent Assembly, 113
Consumerism, new, 270
Containment theory, 418, 420
Continental revolution, 442
Contragate, 435, 438
Contras, U.S. support for, 468
Conventional Forces in Europe Treaty, 492
Convention People's Party, 364, 365
Coolidge, Calvin, 99, 100, 174
Corporation for Public Broadcasting, 428
Corporatism, 181
Costa e Silva, Artur, 456–57
Costa Rica, 443
Council for Mutual Economic Assistance (COMECON), 263
Coups d'etat
  in Africa, 361–62, 372
  in Ghana, 366
Court-packing plan, 107
Crawling Order, 298
Craxi, Bettino, 284
Creole class, 44
Crimean War, 29
Criminal syndicalism acts, 99
Crispi, Francesco, 28
Cristeros, 119, 120
Croatia, 26, 514
Croix de Feu, 190
Cuba, 363, 420, 426, 444, 445, 449–51
  and Spanish-American War, 40
Cuban Missile Crisis, 289, 426, 451, 481
Cuban Revolution, 449–55
Cult of domesticity, 98
Cult of Lenin, 57
Cultural despair, 170–72
Cultural exchange, 271
Cultural Revolution, 310, 311, 323
Czechoslovakia, 86, 87, 199, 204, 262, 290, 292, 480, 486, 487, 492, 495, 512
  invasion of, 206
Czechs, 19, 26, 233

Dachau, 246
Dadaism, 171
Daladier, Edouard, 205, 206
Dalai Lama, 303
Darwin, Charles, 14–15
Darwinism, social, 15, 31
D'Aubuisson, 470
Dawes Plan, 176, 186
Dayan, Moshe, 398, 403
Dayton Accord, 514
D-Day, 239
Debs, Eugene V., 95
Declaration of Humanity, 314
Declaration of Lima, 109
Declaration of Panama, 109
Decolonization, 265, 279
    of Africa, 381
Deconstructionism, 273
Defense of the Realm Act, 73
Defiance Compaign, 377
de Gasperi, Alcide, 284
de Gaulle, Charles, 254–56, 278, 280, 358
de Klerk, F.W., 386, 522
de Lattre de Tossigny, Jean, 334
Democracy, 148
    in Nigeria, 370–73
    and socialism in India, 303
Democracy Wall, 312
Democratization of politics, 13
    in Great Britain, 21
Demokratizatsia, 477, 478, 489
De-Nazification, 262
Deng Xiaophing, 311, 321–24
Denmark, 29, 191, 218, 275, 286
Department of Defense, 419
Depression
    in Germany, 195
    post-war European, 185–87, 188
deRivera, Miguel Primo, 199
Derrida, Jacques, 273
Desai, Morarji, 305
Desaparecidos, 459, 460, 471
Desegregation, 425
d'Estaing, Valery, 281
De-Stalinization, 288, 480
Détente, 264, 485
Dialectical materialism, 20
Diaz Ordaz, Gustavo, 455
Dictatorship
    European, 192–200
    in Ghana, 365
    in Latin America, 44
Diem, Ngo Dinh, 336, 337, 339, 340, 420, 427
Dirty war, 459, 460
Disarmament, 172
Displaced persons, 257
Doctors' Plot, 287
Documentation Center, 248
Dollfuss, Engelbert, 199
Doolittle, James, 228
Doumer, Paul, 332
Dreadnought, HMS, 60
Dreyfus, Captain Alfred, 24

Dreyfus Affair, 24, 255, 390
Drug cartels, 520
Drugs, discovery of new, 32
Dual Alliance, 30, 59
Dual Monarchy, 26
Duarte, Jose Napoleon, 469, 470, 471
Dubcek, Alexander, 292, 293, 486, 487, 495
Dulles, Allen, 420
Dulles, John Foster, 420
Duma, 27
Dunkirk, 218
Dutch East Indies, 266, 330
Dutra, Eurico, 445
Dyer, Reginald, 143, 298
Dzhugashvili, Joseph. See Stalin.

Eastern Bloc, 286–93
Eastern Europe, 420–21, 512–16
    communism in, 419
    during World War II, 232–33
    lack of industrial development in, 11
    purges in, 290–91
    revolutions in, 492–96
    Soviet occupation of, 257
    and USSR, 479, 485–88
Eastern Question, 62–64
East Indies, 146
Ebert, Frederick, 177
Echeverria, Luis, 465
Economic miracle, 268
Economic Opportunity Act of 1964, 428
Economic reforms, in Ghana, 366
Economic relationships
    global, 12
    government authority over in World
        War I, 73
Economy
    African, 361, 379
    agricultural, 269
    in Argentina, 447, 460, 517
    bad U.S., 430, 431–33
    in Brazil, 446, 452, 457, 458
    in Chile, 454, 461, 462, 463
    of Egypt, 401
    in El Salvador, 469
    free trade policies, 508
    German, 197–98
    in Ghana, 365
    Japanese, 318, 319–20
    in Kenya, 367
    in Mexico, 449
    national in U.S., 46
    reform of Soviet, 482–83, 489, 490
    rise of global, 11
    Southeast Asia, 525–28
    in Tanzania, 370
    Uganda, 354
    in Uruguay, 466–67
    Vietnamese, 347
    wartime, 109
    Zaire, 375
Eden, Anthony, 276
Edge Act, 111

Education, 13, 14
Edward VIII, 188
Edwardian Age, 16
Egypt, 138–39, 396–98, 400, 404, 405, 407
    Britain in, 34, 36
    economy of, 401
Eichmann, Adolf, 249
Einstein, Albert, 17, 206–10, 301
Eisenhower, Dwight, 246, 318, 374, 421, 422, 423, 444, 450, 451
Eisenhower Doctrine, 400, 420
Eisenhower era, 423–25
Electrification, 173
Eliot, T.S., 101, 170
El Salvador, 112, 469–70, 520
Emergency Committee of Atomic
    Scientists, 209
Emigration, 12
Emperor cult, 159
Empire
    end of European, 264–68
    in Indochina, 330–32
    post-World War I, 88–90
Enabling Act, 196
Enemies list, 431
Engels, Friedrich, 20, 58
Enola Gay, 244
Entebbe hijacking, 354
Entente Cordiale, 61
Entertainment, in post-World War I U.S.,
    102–04
Environmental issues, 431
Environmental Protection Agency, 431
Equatorial Guinea, 362
Eritrea, 35, 62
Eshkol, Levi, 402
Espionage Act, 81
Estenssoro, Victor Paz, 443
Estonia, 217, 497
Ethiopia, 201–02, 359, 363
Europe
    and Cold War, 261–64
    democratic post-war, 187–92
    dictatorships in, 192–200
    end of empire of, 264–68
    golden age of western, 268–74
    government in postwar, 274–75
    need for united, 267
    in 1920s, 172–74
    post-war depression in, 185–87
    postwar Eastern, 290–93
    post-World War II, 256, 257–61
    and prelude to independence in Africa,
        356–64
    quest for united, 264–68
    reconstruction of, 269
    redefining post-World War II, 264–68
    western, 509–12
    in World War II, 233–40
European Coal and Steel Community, 267
European Community, 267
European Defense Community, 268
European Economic Community, 267
European Economic Miracle, 257

European empires, 9
European Market, 511
European Movement, 267
European powers, 3
  political structures of, 21–28
  post-World War I reshaping of, 86–88
Evolution, theory of biological, 14–15
Executive Order 9835, 421
Existentialism, 272
Expressionsim, 18, 171
Extraterritoriality, 38

Fabian socialism, 23
Fair Deal, 417
Fair Deal for Americans, 422
Fair Employment Practices Commission,
  110
Fair Labor Standards and Practices Act,
  107
Faisal, Prince, 391
Falange, 200
Falkenhayn, Erich von, 68
Falklands War, 277, 294, 295, 460
Families, wartime shattering of, 259
Familyhood, 369
Famine, in Russia, 184, 193
Farmers, 104
  collectivized in China, 308
  in India, 304
  Japanese, 154
  U.S., 46
Fascism, 275
  challenge to European order by,
    200–203
  in France, 190
  in Italy, 179–84
Fatah, 402, 404, 405, 413
February Revolution, 53, 56, 75
Federal judiciary, 431
Federation of Malaysia, 331
Feisal, King, 406
Feminist movement, modern, 273
Feng Yu-hsiang, 150
Fermi, Enrico, 207
Ferrer, Jose Figueres, 443
Fifth Point, 88
Final Solution, 233, 389, 392
Finland, 191, 262
  Winter War in, 217
First Amendment freedoms, 92, 423
First Indochina War, 279, 333
Fists of Righteous Harmony, 39
Fitzgerald, F. Scott, 102
Five-Power Treaty, 172
Five-Year Plans, 192, 193
  in China, 308
Flame-throwers, 68
Florida, 43
Flying Tigers, 158
Foch, Ferdinand, 90
Ford, Gerald, 432
Ford, Henry, 100, 103, 104
Foreign markets, European loss of, 186
Foster, William, 106

Four Modernizations, 312, 323
Fourteen Points, 83, 86
Fox, Vicente, 520
France, 21, 24, 174, 186, 511–12
  in Africa, 36, 266
  in Algeria, 399
  allied offensives in, 238–40
  and Arab world, 400
  anti-German sentiment in, 29–30
  and Cambodia, 335
  collaborationist, 232, 275
  collapse of, 219
  and colonial possessions of, 265
  colonies in Africa, 357, 358, 363
  communist party in, 189
  declaration of war, 218
  end of Third Republic, 188–91
  and *Entente Cordiale*, 61
  failure to act against Germany, 216
  fascism in, 190
  German attempts to isolate, 59
  industrial growth in, 11
  in Middle East, 134, 137–39
  and Morocco, 62
  in North America, 43
  postwar, 277–81
  post-World War I, 88, 176
  pre-World War II, 200, 202, 204
  prior to 1900, 23
  reprisals against collaborators, 260
  rule in Indochina, 332
  socialism in, 279
  in Southeast Asia, 41, 146
  and start of Schlieffen Plan, 65
  in World War I, 75, 82
Franco, Francisco, 108, 203, 285
Franco-Russian Alliance, 60
Franz Ferdinand, assassination of, 58, 64
Franz Joseph, emperor, 26, 81
Freedom Charter, 377
Freedom righters, 442
Freedom Rides, 427
Free French of the Interior, 256
Free Khmer movement, 335
Free Republicans (Turkey), 133
Frei, Eduardo, 454
French Community, 358
French-Indochina War, 329, 420
French-Israeli ties, 399
French National Committee, 256
French resistance, 254
Frente de Accion Popular, 449
Frente Democratico Revolucionario, 470
Freud, Sigmund, 17, 182
Frondizi, Arturo, 453
Fuhrerprinzip, 167, 195
Futurism, 171

Gaddafi, Muammar, 363
Galicia, 26
Gallipoli, 71, 126, 212
Galtieri, Leopoldo Fortunato, 460
Gandhi, Indira, 304, 307
Gandhi, Mohandas, 141, 142, 144, 304, 305

Gandhi, Rajiv, 305, 507, 524
Gang of Four, 311
Geisal, Ernesto, 457
Geneva Accords of 1954, 329, 334
Georgia, 499
German Democratic Republic, 263, 291
German Expressionism, 171
German Federal Republic, 263
German Labor Front, 196
German Protestant Church, 274
Germany, 174, 245, 512
  aid to Marxists by, 53–54
  alliances with other countries, 30
  and Brazil, 114
  Catholic church in, 25, 197
  center party in, 25
  communists in, 195
  declaration of waron U.S., 224
  demilitarization of post-World War I, 85
  democracy in West, 281–83
  depression in, 195
  displaced people from, 257
  disrupted production in, 234–35
  East, 290, 292, 480, 493
  economy in, 197–98
  future of post-World War II, 262
  imperial, 25–26
  industrial output of, 230
  industrial production in, 11
  inflation in postwar, 177, 178
  Italian alliance with, 30
  naval power of, 60–61
  occupation, 232
  in the Pacific, 41
  place in the sun for, 61–62
  post-World War I, 85
  preparedness for war, 229
  pre-World War I alliances of, 59, 65
  pre-World War I tensions with Britain,
    61–60
  Protestant church in, 197
  recovery in, 267
  refugees in, 493
  and reparations, 83, 85
  Russian peace with, 56
  sentiments against, 29–30, 79, 80, 81
  under Hitler, 195–99
  unification of, 29
  wartime shortages in, 75
  Weimar Republic, 176–79
  in World War I, 71–73, 79–82
Gestapo, 197
Ghana (Gold Coast), 357, 359, 361, 362,
  364–66
Giap, Vo Nguyen, 333, 334, 336, 342, 420
Gierek, Edward, 487
Giolitti, Giovanni, 28
Glasnost, 476, 478, 489
Gleichschaltung, 196
Global warming, 508
Gobineau, Joseph de, 15
Goebbels, Joseph, 196, 230, 237
Goering, Herman, 260
Gold Coast, 35

Gomulka, Wladyslaw, 292, 480, 487
Good Friday Agreement, 511
Gorbachev, Mikhail, 289, 435, 476–79, 488–91, 493, 496, 497, 499–502
Gorman, Margaret, 101
Gortari, Salinas, 518
Goulash Communism, 292
Goulart, Joao, 452
Gowon, Yakubu, 371, 372
Grass, Gunter, 273
Grau, Ramon, 444
Great Britain, 186, 511
  in Afghanistan, 42
  in Africa, 137–40
  and Arab world, 400
  in Asia, 36–38
  attack in Africa, 219
  in China, 38
  Conservative Party in, 275–77
  constitutional monarchy in, 21
  declaration of war, 218
  and decolonization, 265
  and EEC, 267
  in Egypt, 34, 36
  empire of, 130
  and Entente Cordiale, 61
  expanding middle class in, 18
  failure to act against Germany, 216
  and Idi Amin, 352–53
  in India, 37–38
  industrial production in, 11
  liberals in, 23
  in Middle East, 134–36, 391
  mobilization of, 230
  monarchy in, 21, 188
  national government in, 187, 188
  naval power of, 60
  in 1920s, 174–76
  in North America, 43
  postwar politics in, 275–77
  post-World War I, 83, 88, 89, 187–88
  pre-World War I tensions with Germany, 60–61, 65
  pre-World War II, 200, 202
  recovery in, 269
  Royal Navy of, 5, 60, 234
  socialism in, 275–77
  under Queen Victoria, 5–9
  women's rights in, 6–7, 93
  in World War I, 71–72, 73
Great Confrontation of the 1950s, 272
Great Depression, 104–06
Greater East Asia Co-Prosperity Sphere, 147, 157, 225, 313
Great Leap Forward, 309
Great Mutiny, 37
Great Proletarian Cultural Revolution, 310
Great Society, 428
Great Strike of 1926, 175
Great Terror, 194
Greece, 64, 199, 286, 418
  attack on, 221–22
Green Belt Movement, 504, 506

Green Gang, 306
Green Revolution, 269, 304
Grenada, 418
Grosz, Karoly, 492, 493
Group Areas Act, 377
Guam, 40, 227
Guatemala, 443, 444
Guerrilla foco theory, 442
Guerrilla warfare, 403, 457, 463, 466–70
Guevara, Che, 440–43, 455
Guinea, 358, 361
GULAG, 194
Gulf War, 521
Gunboat diplomacy, 47
Gysi, Gregor, 494

Habre, Hissane, 363
Haganah, 393, 394, 395
Hague Conference of 1899, 15
Haig, Douglas, 75
Hajj Amin al-Husseini, 391–92, 393
Hamas, 410
Harding, Warren G., 99, 100
Harlem Renaissance, 101
Hatayama Ichiro, 317
Havel, Vaclav, 487, 495, 512
Hawaii, 41
Hay, Secretary of State John, 39
Heart of Darkness, 36
Heath, Edward, 277
Heidegger, Martin, 272
Helsinki Conference, 264
Hemingway, Ernest, 101
Heng Samrin, 347
Herriott, Edouard, 176
Herzegovina, 30
Herzl, Theodor, 20, 390
Hess, Rudolf, 260
Hesse, Hermann, 170, 178
Hezbollah, 409
Himmler, Heinrich, 197, 232, 233
Hindenberg, Paul von, 69, 75, 178, 197
Hindu despotism, 144
Hindus, 38
  in India, 142, 305
Hindu Untouchables, 300
Hirohito, 154, 158–62, 314
Historical materialism, 20
Hitler, Adolf, 4, 85, 164–70, 177, 178, 182, 195–99, 202, 203, 215, 218, 222, 224, 235, 237, 240
Hitler Youth, 196
HIV, 381, 524
Hoat, Doan Viet, 528–30
Ho Chi Minh, 88, 141, 146, 326–30, 333, 336, 341, 342, 420
Holland, 218
Holocaust, 232–33, 274, 392
Holocaust revisionism, 249
Homelands, removal of black Africans to, 377
Homelessness, mass, 259
Honecker, Erick, 292, 493
Hong Kong, 38, 227, 265, 323, 330, 525

Hoover, Herbert, 100, 104, 187
Hoovervilles, 104
Horthy, Nicholas, 88, 199
Hostages
  American, 408, 433
  of guerrillas, 467
House Committee on Un-American Activities, 422
House, Edward, 86
Hoxha, Enver, 293, 479
Hua Guo Feng, 311, 323
Huerta, Victoriano, 118
Hughes, Charles Evan, 107, 172
Human rights, 509, 518
Humbert, King, 28
Humphrey, Hubert, 430
Hungarian Revolt, 292
Hungarian Revolution, 480
Hungary, 26, 86, 87, 199, 237, 291, 292, 480, 492, 493, 512–13
Hun Sen, 527
Husak, Gustav, 495
Hussein, King, 403, 404, 405, 407, 410, 411
Hussein, Saddam, 516, 521
Hussein Ibn Ali, 134
Hu Yaobang, 311, 312

Ibanez, Carlos, 117, 122, 448
Ibn Saud, 135
Ideologies, major, 18–21
Ikeda Hayato, 319
Iliescu, Ion, 496
Illia, Arturo, 453
Illiteracy
  in Africa, 361, 379
  in Cuba, 450
Immigration and Nationality Act, 422
Immorality Acts, 376
Incendiary bombs, 243
Independence
  in Nigeria, 371
  preparation of African colonies for, 357, 358
India, 131, 265, 298–301, 524
  Britain in, 37–38
  confrontation with China, 303, 309–10
  demand for independence, 301–303
  farmers in, 304
  Hindus in, 142, 305
  Muslims in, 142, 144, 305
  national movement in, 141–45
  religion in, 142, 305
  split with Pakistan, 302
India Act of 1919, 141
India Act of 1935, 145
Indian Councils Act, 38
Indian National Congress, 38, 143, 299
Indochina, 146, 265, 420
  bombing of, 344
  empire in, 330–32
Indochinese Communist Party, 328
Indonesia, 330, 331, 527
Indo-Pak War, 303

Industrial Conciliation Act, 377
Industrial Revolution, 10, 46
  in Japan, 40
  Second, 11, 45
Inflation, in post-war Germany, 177, 178
Intellectual universe, of 1900 Europe,
    14–18
Intermediate Range Nuclear Treaty,
    491–92
International Bank for Reconstruction and
    Development (World Bank), 269
International Brigades, 203
International Monetary Fund, 269
International monetary system, 187
International Working Men's Association,
    21
Internment, of Japanese, 98, 110, 231
Intifada, 408–11, 412
Iran, 136–37, 405, 408
Iran-Contra scandal, 435, 438
Iraq, 134, 398, 401, 521
Irgun, 393, 394, 395
Irish home rule, 19, 23
Irish Republican Army (IRA), 277
Irish Treaty, 175
Iron Ring, 26
Ironsi, General, 371
Irrationalism, 16
Islam
  Sarekat, 146
  in Turkey, 132, 133
  in Uganda, 353–54
Island-hopping campaign, 240–41
Israel, 400, 401, 409, 521
  establishment of, 387–88, 389, 395
  occupation of land by, 403, 404
  peace in, 407
  population of, 396
  prelude to war in, 394–95
  pro-western ally, 399
  state of, 390–96
  truce in, 395–96
Italian front, in World War I, 69–71
Italian Somaliland, 35, 62
Italy, 21
  in Africa, 35, 139
  alliance with Germany, 30
  collapse of Fascist, 238
  communist party in, 284
  Fascism in, 179–84
  industrial development in, 11
  late 19th century, 27–28
  Mussolini in, 169
  postwar, 283–86
  post-World War I, 84
  pre-World War I alliances of, 59, 62
  pre-World War II, 200–202, 206
  recovery in, 267
  reprisals against collaborators, 260
  shortages in, 230
  unification of, 29
  in World War II, 220–22
Ivory Coast, 358
Iwo Jima, 242

Jadid, Salah, 401
Jakes, Milos, 495
January Revolution, 117
Japan, 131, 186, 240–46, 312–21, 419,
    524–25
  aggression against China, 147, 149, 157
  army officers in, 155
  between world wars, 153–58
  Cold War and, 316
  defeat of, 243–46
  economy in, 318, 319–20
  farmers in, 154
  imperial ambitions of, 4
  and Indochina, 329
  Industrial Revolution in, 40
  in Manchuria, 155, 305, 306
  occupation by, 232
  occupation of, 313–17
  oil embargo of, 158
  opening of, 39–40
  pact with Germany, 202
  political and economic change in,
    317–18
  post-World War I, 89
  relations with United States, 318–21
  sentiments against, 157
  shortages in, 230
  stemming the advance of, 228–29
  triumphs of, 224–28
  United States and, 153, 157, 318–21
  war with China, 40
  war with Russia, 42
  in World War I, 72, 78
Japanese internment, 98, 110, 231
Japanese miracle, 312–13
Jaruzelski, Wojciech, 487, 493
Java, 41
Jewish homeland, 88
  support for, 135–36
Jewish National Fund, 390
Jews, 233, 259
  and anti-Semitism, 20, 26, 136, 167, 198
Jiang Quing, 311
Jiang Zemin, 312
Jihad, 409
Jim Crow practices, 101, 423
Jinnah, Muhammed Ali, 143, 144, 145, 302
John XXIII, Pope, 274
John Paul II, Pope, 487
Johnson, Lady Bird, 428
Johnson, Lyndon Baines, 341, 427–29, 452
Jones Act of 1916, 146
Jordan, 265, 398, 401
Jordan, David Starr, 58
Juan Carlos, 285
Justo, Agustin P., 115
Jutland, battle of, 72

Kadar, Janas, 292, 492
Kafka, Franz, 171
Kalahari Desert, 359
Kamikaze, 242
Kampuchea, 347
Kandinsky, Wassily, 171

Kapp, Wolfgang, 177
Kasavubu, Joseph, 373, 374
Kashmir, 303
Katango, 374
Katayma Tetsu, 316
Katipunan, 48
Kaysone Phomvihan, 527
Kellogg-Briand Pact, 173
Kemal, Mustafa, 88, 126–30, 131–34
Kennan, George, 418
Kennedy, John F., 264, 339, 340, 401,
    425–27, 429, 451
Kent State tragedy, 430
Kenya, 35, 139–40, 265, 361, 362, 366–68,
    504–07
Kenyan African Democratic Union
    (KADU), 367
Kenyan African National Union (KANU),
    367
Kenyatta, Jomo, 140, 361, 362, 363, 366,
    367
Kerensky, Alexander, 76
Keynes, John Maynard, 185, 186, 187,
    188
Khmer Revolutionary Party, 335
Khmer Rouge, 346, 347, 348, 526
Khomeini, Ayatollah, 408, 433
Khrushchev, Nikita, 264, 288, 289, 421,
    450, 480
Kikuyu Central Association, 140, 366
Killing Fields, 347
Killing Fields, The, 349
King, Martin Luther, 425, 427, 429
Kipling, Rudyard, 40, 49, 143
Kirov, Sergei, 194
Kishi Nobusuke, 316, 317, 318
Kissinger, Henry, 405, 406, 407, 430, 461
Kleptocracies, 363
Kogon, Eagen, 272
Kohl, Helmut, 283, 512
Komilov, Lavr, 76
Korea, 40, 419–20, 480
Korean War, 316
Kostunica, Vojislav, 513–15
Krenz, Egon, 493
Kruger Telegram incident, 60
Krystallnacht, 198
Kuan Yew, Lee, 332
Kubitschek, Juscelino, 446
Ku Klux Klan, 100, 424
Kulaks, 192
Kulturkampf, 25
Kun, Bela, 87
Kuomintang, 149, 151, 304, 308
Kursk, 237
Kuwait, 521

La belle epoque, 16
Labor clashes, in Japan, 318
Labor unions, in Mexico, 121
Labour party, 23, 175, 275–76
LaFollette, Robert, 100
Lagos, Ricardo, 518
laissez-faire, 18, 100

Land reform
  in Chile, 462
  in Guatemala, 444
Lanusse, Alejandro, 459
Lao Issarak, 335, 336
Laos, 41, 335, 336, 338, 340, 343, 346, 347, 526, 527
Lasting peace, 83
Lateran Pact, 182
Latin America, 44–45,
  between world wars, 111
  Catholic church in, 472
  postwar, 443–45, 517–19
Latvia, 217, 497
Laval, Pierre, 189, 260
Law, Andrew Boner, 175
Law of 10/59, 337
Lawrence, D. H., 171
Lawrence of Arabia, 72
League for the Independence of Vietnam, 329
League of Arab states, 393
League of Nations, 83, 86, 89, 99, 172, 200
Lebanese National Movement, 408
Lebanon, 134, 135, 265, 401, 408–11, 435
Lebensraum, 203
Le Bon, Gustave, 16
Lend-Lease Act, 220
Lenin, Vladimir Illyich, 53–57, 76, 77, 79, 184
Leo XIII, Pope, 17
Leopold II, King of the Belgians, 34, 36, 275
Lesotho, 360
Libya, 35, 139, 221, 363
Likud, 407, 411
Lindbergh, Charles, 103, 104
Linguistic differences
  in Africa, 359
  in Nigeria, 371
Li Peng, 312
Literary renaissance, 101
Lithuania, 217, 497
Livingstone, David, 34
Lloyd George, David, 58, 83, 84, 85, 174
Lodge, Henry Cabot, 58, 340
London Naval Treaty, 155
Long March, 153, 306
Lon Nol, 344, 345
Lopez Marcos, Adolfo, 455
Lopez Portillo, Jose, 465
Lost Generation, 101
Louisiana, 43
Loyalty program, 421
Luce, Henry, 45
Ludendorff, Erich, 57, 75
Ludendorff Offensive, 82
Ludlow Amendments, 109
Luftwaffe, 202, 215–16, 219
Lumumba, Patrice, 373, 374
Lusitania, sinking of, 73, 80
Luthuli, Albert, 377
Luxembourg, 286
Lysenko, Trofim, 287

Maathai, Wangari Wata, 504–07
Macabebes, 48
MacArthur, General, 48, 162, 241, 313, 314, 316, 420
MacDonald, Ramsay, 175, 187
MacDonald White Paper, 389
Macedonia, 64
Mach, Ernst, 17
Macmillan, Harold, 276, 357
Madero, Francisco, 118
Madman theory, 430
Maginot Line, 218
Magsaysay, Raymond, 330
Mahathir bin Mohamed, Datuk Seri, 332
Maintenance of Order Law, 133
Major, John, 277, 296, 511
Major War Criminals, 260
Malaya, 37, 331
Malaysia, 265, 330, 332, 528
Malcolm X, 428
Mali, 359
Manchuria
  Japan in, 155, 305, 306
  Soviets in, 307
Manchurian Incident, 155
Mandate Commission, 137
Mandate system, 89
Mandela, Nelson, 377, 382–86, 522–23
Mandela, Winnie, 385
Manhattan Project, 207, 232, 417
Manifest destiny, 147
Mann, Thomas, 178, 273
Manpower reserves during war, colonies as source of, 43
Mao Zedong, 152, 306, 308, 310
March on Rome, 180
Marcos, Ferdinand, 330
Marshall, George C., 308, 395, 419
Marshall Plan, 263, 267, 269, 417, 419
Marx, Karl, 20–21
Marxism, 20
  in Africa, 138
  in China, 148, 150, 151
  divided opinion on, 272–73, 275
Marxism-Leninism, 56
Masaryk, Thomas, 87, 199, 290
Mater et Magistra, 274
Mau Mau Emergency, 366
May Fourth Movement, 150
Mboya, Tom, 357
McCarran Internal Security Act, 422
McCarthy, Eugene, 429
McCarthy, Joseph, 417, 421, 422, 423
McKinley, William, 49
Medicaid, 428
Medicare, 428
Mediterranean, World War II in, 220–22
Mehmed VI, 129
Meiji Era, 153
Meiji Restoration, 39
Mein Kampf, 168
Meir, Golda, 404, 406
Mello, Fernando, 517
Mellon, Andrew, 100

Mendes-France, Pierre, 279
Menem, Carlos Saul, 517
Mengele, Josef, 251
Mensheviks, 56
Metaxas, Ioannis, 199
Mexico, 118–21
  economy in, 449
  oil in, 465
  in World War I, 80
Middle class, 13, 18
  conservatism in, 19
Middle East, 391, 520–22
  anticolonial struggles in, 131–37
  in World War I, 71–72
Midway Island, 40
Militarism, 59
Militarization, 520
Military aid
  U.S. to Latin America, 443
  to Zaire, 374
Military rule
  in Argentina, 453, 460
  in Brazil, 452
  in Chile, 460, 462
  and PRI, 456–66
Military strongmen, in Africa, 351, 362
Mill, John Stuart, 18
Milosevic, Slobodan, 514–15
Ministry of International Trade and Industry, 317
Minsk Declaration, 500
Missouri, 244
Mitterand, Francois, 281, 511
Mladenov, Petar, 494
Mobile armored units, 255
Mobutu, Joseph, 374, 375
Modernism, 18, 170–72, 178
Modern society, and total war, 229–32
Moi, Daniel arap, 360, 368, 506, 507
Moldavia, 497
Mollet, Guy, 279
Moltke, Helmut, 58
Monarchy, in Great Britain, 21, 188
Monetarism, 295
Montenegro, 63, 64
Monteneros guerrillas, 458, 459
Morales Bermudez, Francisco, 456
Moravia, 26
Morgenthau Plan, 262
Moroccan Crises of 1905 and 1911, 61, 62
Morocco, 35, 61, 62, 139, 358, 363
Moscow Human Rights Committee, 484
Moscow trials, 98
Mosley, Sir Oswald, 188
Motion pictures, 102, 173
Mountbatten, Louis, 302
Mozambique, 266, 358
Mubarak, Hosni, 408
Mugabe, Robert, 376
Muhammed, Murtala, 372
Munich Pact, 109, 206
Murrow, Edward R., 423
Muslim League, 145, 302

Muslims, 38, 514
  Arab, 134
  in India, 142, 144, 305
Mussolini, Benito, 169, 180, 181, 183, 200–202, 219, 221, 238
Myanmar, 331, 528
My Lai, 342

NAFTA, 518
Nagy, Imre, 292, 421, 480
Nakasone Yasuhiro, 320
Namibia, 359
Napalm, 341
Napoleonic Wars, 44
Nasser, Gamal Adbdul, 396, 398–99, 400, 401, 403, 405
National Association for the Advancement of Colored People (NAACP), 110, 424
National Bloc, 176
National Council of Women of Kenya, 506
National deficit, U.S., 434
National Endowment for the Arts, 428
National Endowment for the Humanities, 428
National extinction, 216
National Industrial Recovery Act, 106
Nationalism, 4, 26, 131–41, 148
  forces of in Soviet republics, 497
  post-World War I, 81–82
  and pre-World War I tensions, 58
Nationalist movement
  in Africa, 358, 363
  anticolonial, 333
  Chinese, 151
  in Indochina, 330
Nationalist Party, 376
Nationalities question, 496
National Labor Relations Act, 107
National Liberation Front, 337
National Origins Act, 153
National Police Reserve, 316
National Revolutionary Party, 120
National Security Act of 1947, 419
National Security Council, 419
National Security State in America, 417
National self-determination, 86, 88
National Socialist revolution, 197
Native Americans, 104
NATO, 261, 267, 268, 417
Naturalism, 18, 19–20
Natural resources, African, 361, 364, 371
Naval powers, 11
  expansion of Germany's, 60
  Great Britain's, 60
  Italy's, 221
  U.S., 220
  in World War I, 72–73
Naval war, 234–35
Navarre Plan, 334
Nazi party, 118, 164–70, 195–99
Nazi sympathizers, 376
Negritude, 363

Nehru, Jawaharlal, 143, 145, 300, 301, 302, 303
Neocolonialism, 45
Netanyahu, Benjamin, 522
Netherlands, 29, 191, 266, 275, 286
  and Dutch East Indies, 330
  in Southeast Asia, 41, 146
Neutrality Acts, 217
Neutrality laws, 108, 109
New Culture Movement, 150
New Deal, 106–08
New Guinea, 41, 229
New Imperialism, 8, 30–32
Ne Win, 330
New Life Movement, 152
New Negro, 101
New Right, rise of, 434
New Soviet Man, 193
New Zealand, 37, 71
Nhu, Madame, 340
Nhu, Ngo Dinh, 337, 420
Nicaragua, 111–12, 467–69, 520
Nicholas II, 27, 53, 65, 76
Niemueller, Martin, 274
Nietzsche, Friedrich, 16
Niger, 359
Nigeria, 35, 140, 363, 370–73, 523
Night of the Long Knives, 197
Nihilism, 27
Nineteenth Amendment, 101
Nixon, Richard, 311, 319, 343, 421, 429–31
Nkrumah, Kwame, 357, 361, 363, 364
NKVD, 287
Non-Aggression Pact, 206
Nonaligned nations, in Third World, 303
Non-Nuclear Proliferation Treaty, 289
Nonviolent civil disobedience, 299
Non-violent protest, 143
Noriega, Manual, 520
Norris, George, 100
North America, 43–44, 45–47
North Atlantic Treaty Organization (NATO), 263, 267, 268, 417
Northern Ireland, 276–77
Northwest Borneo, 331
Norway, 29, 191, 232, 275, 286
November Criminals, 85
Novotny, Antonin, 486
Nuclear weapons, 244, 417, 421
  campaign to abolish, 209, 425
Nuclear test ban treaty, 426
Nuremburg Laws of 1935, 198
Nuremberg Rally, 166
Nuremburg Tribunal, 260
Nyasaland, 375
Nye Committee, 108
Nyerere, Julius, 354, 361, 362, 363, 368

Obote, Milton, 350–52
Obregon, Alvaro, 118, 119, 120
Occupation
  during World War II, 232–33
  of Japan, 313–17
Occupation zones, 262

October Manifesto, 27
October Revolution, 444
Oil
  in Brazil, 446
  in Mexico, 465
  in Middle East, 135, 137
  U.S. in Cuba, 450
  as weapon against U.S., 410
Oil boycott, 277
Oil embargo, 406
  of India, 304
  of Japan, 158
Oil leases (Latin America), 119, 120, 121
Oil reserves, in Nigeria, 371, 372
Okinawa, 241–43
Old Bolsheviks, 194
Olympic Games
  Mexico City, 455
  Moscow, 485
  murder of Israelis at Munich, 405
  Tokyo, 317
Olympio, Sylvanus, 362
Ongania, Juan, 453, 458
OPEC, 270, 405
Operation Barbarossa, 222–24, 235
Operation Cartwheel, 241
Operation Dynamo, 219
Operation Overlord, 239
Operation Phoenix, 341
Operation Rolling Thunder, 341
Opium War, 38
Opposition party, and USSR, 490
Oregon, 44
Organizacion Democratica Nacionalista, 469, 470
Organization of African Unity, 363, 364
Organization of American States, 443
Organization of European Economic Cooperation, 267
Orlando, Vittorio, 84, 85
Ortiz, Roberto M., 115
Orwell, George, 188, 203, 271
Oslo II, 521
Ottoman Empire, 8, 29
  decline of, 63, 64, 129, 131

Pacem in Terris, 274
Pacific, World War II in, 224–33, 240–46
Pacifists, 74, 93, 109, 200
Pact of Steel, 206
Pakistan, 265, 301
  civil war in, 304
  and Kashmir, 303
  split with India, 302
Palestine, 88, 135, 136, 265, 404, 411–14, 521
  immigration to, 390–92
  partition of, 393–94
  prelude to war in, 394–95
Palestine Liberation Army, 402
Palestine Liberation Organization (PLO), 402, 403–05, 407, 409, 413, 521
Palestine National Council, 410

Palestinians, 396
  as refugees, 403
Palmer Raids, 96
Pan-African Conference, 138
Pan-Africanism, 138, 363, 379
Panama, 520
Panama Canal, 47
Pan-Arabism, 399
Pan-Germanism, 19
Pan-Islam, 379
Pankhurst, Emmeline, 23
Pan-Slavism, 19
Papen, Franz von, 196
Pareto, Vilfredo, 17
Paris Commune of 1871, 23
Paris Peace Accords, 344, 430
Paris Peace Conference, 82–86
Partido de Accion Nacional, 465
Partido Revolucionario Institucional, 449,
  465, 518
Partido Socialista Popular, 450
Passchendaele, 75
Pathet Lao, 336, 339, 346
Patriotic Front, 376
Patriotic murders, 15
Paulus, Friedrich, 237
Peace Conference in San Francisco, 316
Peace Corps, 426
Peace Now, 411
Peace Pledge Union, 93
Peace Preservation Law, 154
Pearl Harbor, 110, 158, 226
Peel Commission Report on Palestine,
  392
Penderecki, Kryszstof, 273
People's Liberation Army, 309
People's Party (Turkey), 132
Peres, Shimon, 399, 407, 521, 522
Perestroika, 476, 477, 478, 489
Perón, Evita, 446, 448
Perón, Juan, 15, 116, 446, 448, 459
Peronism, 447, 448, 453
Perry, Commodore Matthew, 39
Persian Empire, 42
Personality cult, 287
Peru, 456
Petain, Philippe, 219, 232, 252, 255, 260
Peters, Karl, 34
Petrobas, 446
Petroleum industry, 10–11
Phalange, 408
Phetsarath, Prince, 335, 336
Philippine Insurrection, 41, 49, 51
Philippines, 41, 47–51, 146, 227, 241–43,
  527
  independence of, 330, 357
Phoenix Program, 344
Phony War, 216–18
Pilsudski, Joseph, 8, 199
Pinochet, General, 463, 518
Pius XI, Pope, 182
Pius XII, Pope, 274
Planck, Max, 17
Poincare, Raymond, 176, 189

Poland, 199, 480, 487–88, 493, 512–13
  invasion of, 206
Poles, 19, 26
Politics
  democratization of, 13
  in postwar Europe, 274–75
Poland, 69, 86, 87, 259, 262, 290, 292
  Communist party in, 487–88
  World War II conquest of, 215–18
Political discontent, postwar, 279
Pol Pot, 338, 527
Pompidou, Georges, 281
Popular Front, 190, 191
Popular Movement of the Revolution, 374
Popular Registration Act, 376
Popular Republican Movement, 279
Population transfer, mass, 259
Populism, 27, 46
Portugal, 28–29, 199, 266, 285
  in Africa, 35, 140, 357, 358
  in Latin America, 44
Post-industrial age, 270
Postwar era, 256–57
Potsdam Conference, 261, 262, 417
Potsdam Declaration, 160, 243
Prague Spring, 293, 486, 487
Pran Dith, 348–50
Presidential cultism, 362, 374
Prestes, Luis Carlos, 113
Princip, Gavrilo, 64
Prison camps, 291
Profumo Scandal, 276
Progressivism, 46, 100
Prohibitionists, 100
Prohibition of Mixed Marriages Act, 376
Protestantism, 17
Prussia, 262
Public Works Administration, 106
Puerto Rico, 40
Purges
  in Eastern Europe, 290–91
  in Soviet Union, 287
Putin, Vladimir, 515
Pu-yi, 148, 149, 155

Qadhdhafi, Muammar, 405
Quadros, 451
Quezon, Manual, 146
Quisling, Vidkun, 232, 260

Rabin, Yitzhak, 403, 407, 521, 522
Race riots, 428
  during World War I, 81
  in post-World War I U.S., 99, 110
Racial discrimination, 422
Racial eugenics, 198
Racial hierarchy, under Dutch in
  Southeast Asia, 41
Racialism, 15, 31
Racial policies, Hitler's, 224
Racism, western toward Japan, 153
Radical ideology, rejection of, 275
Radical Socialism, 28
RAF, 219

Randolph, A. Philip, 101, 110
Rape of Nanking, 157
Rawlings, Jerry, 366
Raw materials
  from Africa, 356
  new sources of, 31, 45
Reagan, Ronald, 296, 408, 432, 433–38,
  468, 470, 485, 491
Rearmament program, Hitler's, 198
Reconstruction and recovery, 260
Reconstruction Finance Corporation, 105
Recruit Scandal, 321
Red Army, 78
Red Brigade, 284
Red Scare, 175, 421–23
Red Terror, 79
Refugees
  in Africa, 524
  in East Germany, 493
  Jews as, 135–36
  Palestinians as, 403
Reichstag, 25
Reinsurance Treaty, 30, 59
Reparations, 83, 85, 174, 177, 185, 186
  Japanese fund for, 320
Rerum Novarum, 17
Revolutionary Alliance, 148
Revolution of 1905, 56
Rexism, 191
Reynaud, Paul, 191, 255
Reza Shah Pahlavi, 137
Rhodes, Cecil, 8, 35
Rhodesia, 265, 359, 375–78
Rhodesian Front, 375
Riefenstahl, Leni, 166
Rights recovery movement, 151
Rio Pact, 443
Risk fleet, 60, 61
Robinson, Jackie, 423
Rockoff, Al, 348
Roe v. Wade, 431
Rohm, Ernst, 197
Romania, 237, 262, 293, 495
Romaro, Oscar, 472
Rome-Berlin Axis, 202
Roosevelt, Franklin Delano, 100, 157, 207,
  217, 220, 261, 357, 415
  and New Deal, 106–08
Roosevelt, Theodore, 46, 47, 49, 80
Roosevelt Corollary, 47
Roosevelt Court, 107
Rosenberg, Julius and Ethel, 422
Round Table Conference, 373
Rowlatt Acts, 143, 298
Royal Navy, British, 5, 60, 234
Ruiz Cortines, Adolfo, 449
Rumania, 29, 63, 71, 82, 199
Russia. See also USSR.
  alliance with Germany, 30
  expansionist ambitions of, 63
  imperial, 26–27
  peace with Germany, 56
  pre-World War I alliances of, 59, 65
  provisional government, 54, 76

refusal to bend to Germany, 224
as sovereign state, 496, 500, 502, 515, 516
under communism, 184–85
war with Japan, 42
in World War I, 75–79
Russian Front, 69–71
Russian Social Democratic Labor Party, 55
Russo-Japanese War, 40
Russo-Turkish War, 30, 63
Rwanda, 363, 523

SA (*Sturmabteilungen*), 195
Sacco, Nicola, 96
Sadat, Anwar, 405
Sahara Desert, 359
Sakharov, Andrei, 484, 489
Salan, Raoul, 334
Salazar, Antonio, 199, 285
Salgado, Plinio, 113
Salinas, Carlos, 466
Salt Acts, 299
Salt March of 1930, 144
Sandinista Front for National Liberation, 467, 468
Sandinistas, 435, 468
Sandino, Augusto Cesar, 111–12
Sanger, Margaret, 101
Sarney, Jose, 458
Sartre, Jean-Paul, 272
Sato Eisaku, 319
Satyagraha, 143, 299
Saudi Arabia, 135, 398, 405
Savang Vathana, 335
Schanberg, Sydney, 348
Scandinavia, 29
  importance of in World War II, 218
Scandinavian Way, 191
Schleicher, Kurt von, 196
Schlieffen, Count Alfred von, 62
Schlieffen Plan, 62, 65, 66
Schmidt, Helmut, 289
Schneider, Rene, 461
Schoenberg, Arnold, 171
Schumacher, Kurt, 282
Schuschnigg, Kurt, 199, 204
Scientific racialism, 31
Scientific research, during World War II, 231–32
Second Reich, 25
Security Council Resolution, 242, 404
Sedition Act, 81
Selassie, Haile, 202
Selective Service Act, 95
Selective Training and Service Act, 109
Self-Defence Forces, 316
Self-determination
  national, 86, 88
  USSR recognition of right to, 492
Senegal, 363
Senghor, Leopold, 363
Separation movements, 285
Serbia, 63, 64, 65, 71, 81, 514
Seven Years' War, 37, 43

Sexual revolution, 101
Shagari, Shehu, 372
Shamir, Yitzhak, 409
Shanghai Communique, 311
Sharpeville Massacre, 378
Sharrett, Moshe, 398
Shastri, Shri Lal Bahadur, 303
Shaw, George Bernard, 182, 193
Shining Path, 520
Showa Restoration, 154, 160
Show trials, 194
Shuqayri, Ahmad, 402
Siberian intervention, 78
Sierra Leone, 34
Sihanouk, Norodom, 335, 337, 338, 343, 344, 526
Sikhs, 140
Simon Weisenthal Center and Museum for Tolerance, 250
Singapore, 227, 265, 332
Singh, Vishwanath Pratap, 305
Sino-Japanese War, 156, 306
Sino-Soviet rift, 481
Sisavang Vong, 335
Sisulu, Walter, 377, 384
Sit-ins, 425
Six Day War, 389–90, 400–403
Slave trade, 32
Slavs, 19
Slovakia, 512
Smith, Ian, 375, 376
Smith Act, 422, 423
Social Aid Foundation, 446
Social conservatives, 433
Social contours, of western Europe, 270
Social Darwinism, 15, 31, 100, 167
Social Democratic Party, 21, 25, 177, 282
Socialism, 21, 148, 180
  African, 361, 368–70, 379
  Burmese way to, 331
  Chilean road to, 461
  and democracy in India, 303
  Fabian, 23
  in France, 279
  in Great Britain, 275–77
  radical, 28
Socialist realism, 287
Socialists, 74
Social Revolutionaries, 78
Social Security Act, 107
Social structure, reordering of, 12
Social trends, in 1920s, 173
Solidarity, 488, 493
Somalia, 360, 363, 523
Somoza, Anastasio, 112, 467, 468
Somoza, Luis, 467
Son Ngoc Thanh, 335
Soong Ching-ling, 308
Souphannouvong, 335, 336, 338, 347
South Africa, 35, 60, 140, 265, 359, 375–78, 522–23
South African National Congress, 140
South African Students Organization, 378

Southeast Asia, 145–47, 227, 279, 525–28
  colonization in, 41
  Dutch in, 41, 146
  economy in, 525–28
  Soviet-Iranian expansionism, 136
  U.S. involvement in, 426
Souvanna Phouma, 335, 336, 338, 346
Soviet economic model, 290
Soviet Union. *See* Russia, USSR.
Soweto uprising, 378, 385
Space race, 288
Spain, 28, 199
  in Africa, 35
  civil war in, 202, 203
  industrial development in, 11
  in Latin America, 44
  in North America, 43
  postwar, 285
Spanish-American War, 40, 46, 49
Spanish Republicans, 108
Speer, Albert, 230, 260
Spengler, Oswald, 170
Spirit of Lucarno, 178
Sports, 102–04
Spring Offensive, 344
SS (*Schutz Staffel*), 195, 197, 224
Stalin, Joseph, 169, 184, 185, 192–95, 206, 217, 222, 237, 261, 286, 287, 418
Stalingrad, 235–37
Stanley, Henry M., 34
Stavisky Affair, 189, 190
Stern Gang, 393, 394, 395
Stilwell Road, 401
Stock market collapse, 186
Stolypin, Peter, 27
Strategic Arms Limitation agreement, 289, 485
Strategic Arms Reduction Treaty, 478
Strategic Defense Initiative, 434
Stresemann, Gustav, 178
Stresa Front, 202
Student Non-Violent Coordinating Committee, 425
Suarez, Adolfo, 285
Submarine warfare, 72–73, 80, 220, 234
Sub-Saharan Africa, 139–41
Sudan, 359, 363
Suez Canal Zone, 399
Suez Crisis, 276
Suffrage
  broadened, 13
  universal male, 26
  women's, 23, 101, 173
Suharto, General, 331
Suicide bombings, 521–22
Sukarno, Kusno Sasro, 146, 331
Sultanate, abolition of Turkish, 129
Sumatra, 41
Sunday, Billy, 81
Sun Yat-sen, , 148, 149, 150, 305
Supplementary Security Income, 431
Supreme Court, U.S., 107
Suppression of Communism Act, 377, 385
Surrealism, 171

Suzuki Zenko, 319
Swain, Jon, 348
Swaziland, 360
Sweden, 29, 191, 286
Switzerland, 29, 191, 286
Sykes-Picot Agreement, 88, 134, 135
Syllabus of Errors, 17
Symbolism, 18
Syndicalism, 16
Syria, 88, 134, 135, 265, 394, 398, 401
Szilard, Leo, 207

Taaffe, Count Edward von, 26
Taft, William Howard, 46, 47
Taft-Hartley Act, 419
Taisho democracy, 153, 154, 159
Taiping Rebellion, 38
Taiwan, 308, 525
Takeshita, Noboru, 320
Tambo, Oliver, 377
Tanaka Kekuu, 319
Tanganyika African National Union
    (TANU), 368
Tanzania, 354, 361, 362, 368–70
Technological superiority, 31
    German, 215
Technologies, new, 10
Teheran Conference, 237, 240
Telephone, 173
Television, 271
Tennessee Valley Authority, 106
10-10 Revolution, 148
Tet Offensive, 342, 429
Texas, 44
Thailand, 330, 528
Thanarat, Sarit, 330
Thatcher, Margaret, 277, 278, 293–97
Thatcherite Revolution, 294
Theater of the absurd, 273
Thoc, Ngo Dinh, 340
Thomas, Norman, 106
Three Emperors' League, 30
Three Principles of the People, 148, 150
Thousand Year Reich speech, 166
Tiananmen Square, 312, 321, 324
Tibet, 303, 525
Tinsulanond, Prem, 330
Tito, Josip, 291, 479
Togo, 362
Tojo, 158
Tokyo Trials, 313
Tomic, Radomiro, 460–61
Torres, Camilo, 472
Totalitarianism, 179–85
Total war, 57, 229–32, 237
Toure, Sekou, 358, 361
Trade practices, Japanese, 320
Transformismo, 28
Treason Trial, 377, 385
Treaty of Lausanne, 130
Treaty of Nanking, 38
Treaty of Neuilly, 88
Treaty of Peace, Friendship and Cooperation
    with the Soviet Union, 304

Treaty of Portsmouth, 40
Treaty of Saint-Germaine, 86
Treaty of Sevres, 88, 129
Treaty of Trianon, 87
Treaty ports, 38
Treblinka, 233
Trialism, 64, 360
Tribal divisions, in Africa, 359, 371
Trickle-down economics, 100, 434
Tripartite Pact, 158, 221
Triple Alliance, 30, 59, 61
Triple Entente, 61, 65
Tripoli, 62
Tripolitanian War, 62, 129
Trotsky, Leon, 77, 185
Trotskyists, 109
Truman, Harry, 243, 316, 393, 415–18, 419,
    420
Truman Doctrine, 263, 419
Truth and Reconciliation Commission, 523
Tshombe, Moise, 373
Tula, Maria Teresa, 470–74
Tunisia, 35, 358
Tunku Abdul Rahman, 330
Tupamaro guerrillas, 466
Turkey, 62, 88, 127–30, 131–34, 286
    Ottoman, 29
Turks, explusion of from Bulgaria, 494
Turnip Winter, 75
Tutu, Desmond, 378, 523
Twenty-First Party Congress, 481
Twenty-One Conditions, 79
Twenty-One Demands, 149, 153
Two-power standard, 60
Tydings-MacDuffie Act, 146
Tz'u-his, Dowager Empress, 39, 148

Uganda, 351–55, 362, 370
Ujamaa, 369
Ukraine, 498
Ulbricht, Walter, 291, 292
Ulianov, Vladimir. *See* Lenin.
Ultranationalism, 155, 275
Umkhonto we Sizwe, 382, 385
Unified field theory, 209
Unified Issarak Front, 335
Unilateral Declaration of Independence,
    376
Union Act, 45
United Arab Republic, 401
United Fruit Company, 444
United Nations, 246, 404, 514
United Nations of Security Council
    Resolution 340, 406
United Nations Relief and Rehabilitation
    Administration, 259
UN Resolution 3236, 412
United States, 45–47, 408
    in Africa, 363
    backing in Vietnam, 333–34, 339–40
    bad economy in, 430, 431–33
    between the world wars, 98–104
    and Brazil, 114
    Camelot in, 425–27

    and Castro, 450
    in China, 38–39
    and Cold War, 418–21
    Cold War policy, 263
    conscription in, 109, 419
    culture of, 271
    deficits in, 436
    Democratic party in, 108
    farmers in, 46
    German declaration of war on, 224
    in Guatemala, 444
    industrial development in, 11
    involvement in Southeast Asia, 426
    and Israel, 399, 407
    and Japan, 153, 157
    and Kenya, 367
    in Latin America, 520
    military aid to Latin America, 443
    as military power, 231
    military spending by, 484
    as new superpower, 2
    and Nicaragua, 468
    as North American power, 44
    occupation of Japan, 153, 157
    oil and, 410, 450
    as only superpower, 516–17
    and OPEC oil, 406
    in the Pacific, 40–41
    and Palestine, 395
    in the Philippines, 49–51, 146
    pre-World War II, 108–11, 200, 217
    public opinion on World War II in, 220
    relations with Japan, 318–21
    relations with USSR, 491–92
    and Republic of Vietnam, 336
    rudiments of empire of, 9
    in Southeast Asia, 426
    as superpower, 246, 256
    and Vietnam, 526
    and war debt, 174, 186
    war in Vietnam, 340–43
    wartime economy of, 231
    wartime reshaping of society in, 231
    in World War I, 79–81
    and Zaire, 374
U.S. v. Nixon, 430
U.S. v. Roger Nash Baldwin, 95
Unity, African quest for, 363–64
Untermenschen, 216
Untouchables, 300
Universal Suffrage Act, 154
USSR, 2, 169, 184, 202, 233, 263. *See also*
    Russia.
    agriculture in, 192, 193
    aid to Arabs, 406
    in Africa, 363
    breakup of, 476, 496–99
    bureaucratization of Communist party
        in, 482–85
    clash with China, 150, 288, 485
    and Cold War, 418–21
    confrontation with India, 309–10
    consumer goods in, 483
    and Cuba, 450

cultural freedom in, 481
dissident movements in, 482
democratization of Communist party in, 481
and Eastern Bloc, 286–93
and Eastern Europe, 257, 479, 485–88
economy of, 481
and Egypt, 399
establishment of, 56
famine in, 184, 193
foreign policy of, 485–88
and Ghana, 365
industrial and military recovery of, 230
invasion of, 222–24
in Manchuria, 307
and Middle East, 405
offensive in Europe, 239–40
in Pacific, 226
pact with Germany, 206
political offenders in, 484
purges in, 287
reform of economy of, 482–83, 489, 490
relations with U.S., 490–92
religious dissenters in, 484
resurgence of, 235–38
Stalinist terror in, 192–95
as superpower, 246, 256, 261
territorial gains during World War II, 217
and Truman, 417
and Vietnam, 342
wartime devastation of, 258–59
and Zaire, 374
U Nu, 331
Uruguay, 466–67

Vandenberg, Arthur, 419
Vanzetti, Barolomeo, 96
Vargas, Gerulio, 112–13, 445–46
Vasconcelos, Jose, 119
Velasco Alvarado, Juan, 456
Verdun, 68, 69
Versailles Treaty, 83–86
Victor Emmanuel III, King, 180, 284
Victoria, Queen, 5–9
Videla, Gabriel Gonzeles, 448
Vietcong, 341
Vietminh, 333, 334, 336, 420
Vietnam, 41, 88, 265, 326–30, 426, 427, 429, 430, 525, 528–30
aid to, 342
and China, 342, 347
Cold War and, 339
communism in North, 336, 346
divided, 336–39
economy of, 347
neighboring states, 332–36
postwar, 346
reunifying, 337
U.S. backing in, 333–34, 339–43, 526
U.S. bombing campaign in, 341
Vietnamese nationals, 332
Vietnamization policy, 344
Vietnam War, 343–45

Villa, Francisco, 118
Vorster, John, 376
Voting Rights Act, 428

Wages and working conditions, improvement in, 270
Wagner Act, 107
Wake Island, 227
Waldheim, Kurt, 250
Walesa, Lech, 487, 493, 512
Wallace, George, 429
Wannsee Conference, 233
War, destructive power of modern, 258–61
War communism, 79
War correspondents, 348–50
War debt, 174, 186
War guilt clause, in Treaty of Versailles, 85
War Industries Board, 81
Warlords, 149–50
Warsaw Pact, 263
Washington Conference of 1921–1922, 153, 172
Watergate, 431
Weapon of mass destruction, 206, 508
Weapons technology, advances in, 32
Weimar Constitution, 177
Weimar Republic, 176–79
Weizmann, Chaim, 208, 391, 392
Welfare state, 108
Weltpolitik, 61
West Bank, 407
Western Front, 66–69
Westmoreland, William, 343
White Armies, 78
White man's burden, 49
Wiesenthal, Simon, 247–50
William I, German Emperor, 25
William II, German Emperor, 25, 59, 60, 82
Wilson, Harold, 276
Wilson, Woodrow, 46, 47, 58, 73, 79, 80, 81
and Versailles Treaty, 83–86
Winter War, 217
Women
in Germany, 198
in Great Depression, 104
in Italy, 182
new opportunities for in World War I, 74
postwar issues of, 273
in postwar Europe, 270
in post-World War I U.S., 99, 101
in society, 13–14
suffrage for, 23, 101, 173
in Turkey, 133
in U.S. during World War II, 231
in USSR, 193
in wartime, 110
Women's rights, in Britain, 6–7, 93
Women's Social and Political Union, 23
Workers' Defense Committee, 487
Working class, industrial, 12
World Court, 89, 468
World depression, 169
World Trade Center, 517

World War I, 3, 53–94
Africa in, 72
air power in, 73
ambiguity of borders after, 87
artillery in, 68
Australia in, 71
Austria and start of, 63–65, 69, 70
blockade of Britain in, 72
casualties in, 68, 69
Commonwealth troops in, 71
France in, 75, 82
Great Britain in, 71–72, 73
Hitler in, 168
Italian Front in, 69–71
Japan in, 72, 78
machine gun in, 68, 73
Mexico in, 80
mutinies in, 75
naval power in, 72–73
origins of, 57–64
poison gas in, 68
race riots during, 81
Russia in, 75–79
tanks in, 68
U.S. as mediator in, 79
World War II, 4. *See also* Battle of. . .
blacks in U.S. during, 231
and China, 306
Churchill in, 211–14
demographic impact of, 259
Eastern Europe during, 232–33
in Europe, 215–24, 233–40
fighting in Africa, 356
Germany in, 71–73, 79–82
importance of Scandinavia in, 218
Italy in, 220–22
in Mediterranean, 220–22
Occupation during, 232–33
in the Pacific, 224–33, 240–46
pre, 200, 203–06
scientific research during, 231–32
World Zionist Organization, 390
Wright brothers, 11
Wu Pei-fu, 150

Yalta Conference, 240, 261, 290
Yamamoto, Isoroku, 226
Yeltsin, Boris, 479, 489, 490, 496, 498, 499–503, 515
Yemen, 401
Yom Kippur War, 403–06
Yoshida Doctrine, 316
Yoshida Shigeru, 315, 316
Yoshihito, Emperor, 153
Young Turk Revolt, 128
Yrigoyen, Hipolito, 115
Yuan Shih-kai, 149
Yugoslavia, 87, 199, 222, 291, 479, 514

Zaibatsu, 154, 316
Zaire, 359, 360, 363, 373–75
Zambia, 375
Zapata, Emiliano, 118
Zapatista National Liberation Army, 519

Zedillo, Ernesto, 519–20
Zemin, Jiang, 525
Zeppelins, 73
Zhao Ziyang, 311, 312
Zhivkov, Todor, 293, 494

Zhou Enlai, 308, 311, 323
Zinoviev Letter, 175
Zimbabwe, 376, 523–24
Zimbabwe African National Union, 376
Zimmermann Telegram, 80

Zionist movement, 20, 88, 135, 208, 389
Zola, Emil, 24
Zulu Wars, 35
Zweig, Stefan, 16